"To Save the People from Themselves"

In this expansive history, Robert J. Steinfeld offers a thorough reinterpretation of the origins of American judicial review and the central role it quickly came to play in the American constitutional system. Beginning with Privy Council review of American colonial legislation, the book goes on to provide detailed descriptions of the character of the first American constitutions, showing that they drew heavily on traditional Anglo/American constitutional assumptions, which treated legislatures as the primary interpreters of constitutions. Steinfeld then expertly analyses the central role lawyers and judges played in transforming these assumptions, creating the practice and doctrine of American judicial review in a half dozen state cases during the 1780s. The book concludes by showing that the ideas formulated during those years shaped critical decisions taken by the Constitutional Convention of 1787, which turned the novel practice into a permanent, if still deeply controversial, feature of the American constitutional system.

Robert J. Steinfeld is Professor of Law Emeritus at the SUNY Buffalo School of Law. He has been a Visiting Scholar at the Charles Warren Center for Studies in American History at Harvard University, and at the Center for the Study of Law and Society at the University of California, Berkeley.

Cambridge Historical Studies in American Law and Society

Recognizing legal history's growing importance and influence, the goal of this series is to chart legal history's continuing development by publishing innovative scholarship across the discipline's broadening range of perspectives and subjects. It encourages empirically creative works that take legal history into unexplored subject areas, or that fundamentally revise our thinking about familiar topics; it also encourages methodologically innovative works that bring new disciplinary perspectives and techniques to the historical analysis of legal subjects.

Series Editor

Christopher Tomlins, *University of California, Berkeley*

Previously published in the series:

Robert J. Steinfeld, *"To Save the People from Themselves": The Emergence of American Judicial Review and the Transformation of Constitutions*

Lee B. Wilson, *Bonds of Empire: The English Origins of Slave Law in South Carolina and British Plantation America, 1660–1783*

Jordan T. Watkins, *Slavery and Sacred Texts: The Bible, the Constitution, and Historical Consciousness in Antebellum America*

Ashley T. Rubin, *The Deviant Prison: Philadelphia's Eastern State Penitentiary and the Origins of America's Modern Penal System, 1829–1913*

Nate Holdren, *Injury Impoverished: Workplace Accidents, Capitalism, and Law in the Progressive Era*

Catherine Wells, *Oliver Wendell Holmes: A Willing Servant to an Unknown God*

Michael F. Conlin, *The Constitutional Origins of the American Civil War*

Angela Fernandez, *Pierson v. Post, The Hunt for the Fox: Law and Professionalization in American Legal Culture*

Justin Desautels-Stein, *The Jurisprudence of Style: A Structuralist History of American Pragmatism and Liberal Legal Thought*

William Kuby, *Conjugal Misconduct: Defying Marriage Law in the Twentieth-Century United States*

Rebecca E. Zietlow, *The Forgotten Emancipator: James Mitchell Ashley and the Ideological Origins of Reconstruction*

Robert Daniel Rubin, *Judicial Review and American Conservatism: Christianity, Public Education, and the Federal Courts in the Reagan Era*

Matthew Crow, *Thomas Jefferson, Legal History, and the Art of Recollection*

Oren Bracha, *Owning Ideas: The Intellectual Origins of American Intellectual Property, 1790–1909*

Anne Twitty, *Before* Dred Scott*: Slavery and Legal Culture in the American Confluence, 1787–1857*

Leia Castañeda Anastacio, *The Foundations of the Modern Philippine State: Imperial Rule and the American Constitutional Tradition in the Philippine Islands, 1898–1935*

Robert Deal, *The Law of the Whale Hunt: Dispute Resolution, Property Law, and American Whalers, 1780–1880*

Sandra F. Vanburkleo, *Gender Remade: Citizenship, Suffrage, and Public Power in the New Northwest, 1879–1912*

Reuel Schiller, *Forging Rivals: Race, Class, Law, and the Collapse of Postwar Liberalism*

Ely Aaronson, *From Slave Abuse to Hate Crime: The Criminalization of Racial Violence in American History*

Stuart Chinn, *Recalibrating Reform: The Limits of Political Change*

Ajay K. Mehrotra, *Making the Modern American Fiscal State*

Yvonne Pitts, *Family, Law, and Inheritance in America: A Social and Legal History of Nineteenth-Century Kentucky*

David M. Rabban, *Law's History*

Kunal M. Parker, *Common Law, History, and Democracy in America, 1790–1900*

Steven Wilf, *Law's Imagined Republic*

James D. Schmidt, *Industrial Violence and the Legal Origins of Child Labor*

Rebecca M. McLennan, *The Crisis of Imprisonment: Protest, Politics, and the Making of the American Penal State, 1776–1941*

Tony A. Freyer, *Antitrust and Global Capitalism, 1930–2004*

Davison Douglas, *Jim Crow Moves North*

Andrew Wender Cohen, *The Racketeer's Progress*

Michael Willrich, City of Courts, *Socializing Justice in Progressive Era Chicago*

Barbara Young Welke, *Recasting American Liberty: Gender, Law and the Railroad Revolution, 1865–1920*

Michael Vorenberg, *Final Freedom: The Civil War, the Abolition of Slavery, and the Thirteenth Amendment*

Robert J. Steinfeld, *Coercion, Contract, and Free Labor in Nineteenth Century America*

David M. Rabban, *Free Speech in Its Forgotten Years*

Jenny Wahl, *The Bondsman's Burden: An Economic Analysis of the Common Law of Southern Slavery*

Michael Grossberg, *A Judgment for Solomon: The d'Hauteville Case and Legal Experience in the Antebellum South*

"To Save the People from Themselves"

The Emergence of American Judicial Review and the Transformation of Constitutions

ROBERT J. STEINFELD
State University of New York

CAMBRIDGE
UNIVERSITY PRESS

CAMBRIDGE
UNIVERSITY PRESS

University Printing House, Cambridge CB2 8BS, United Kingdom

One Liberty Plaza, 20th Floor, New York, NY 10006, USA

477 Williamstown Road, Port Melbourne, VIC 3207, Australia

314–321, 3rd Floor, Plot 3, Splendor Forum, Jasola District Centre, New Delhi – 110025, India

103 Penang Road, #05–06/07, Visioncrest Commercial, Singapore 238467

Cambridge University Press is part of the University of Cambridge.

It furthers the University's mission by disseminating knowledge in the pursuit of education, learning, and research at the highest international levels of excellence.

www.cambridge.org
Information on this title: www.cambridge.org/9781108839235
DOI: 10.1017/9781108989619

First published 2021

A catalogue record for this publication is available from the British Library.

Library of Congress Cataloging-in-Publication Data
NAMES: Steinfeld, Robert J., author.
TITLE: "To save the people from themselves" : the emergence of American judicial review and the transformation of constitutions / Robert J. Steinfeld, State University of New York, Buffalo.
DESCRIPTION: Cambridge, United Kingdom ; New York, NY : Cambridge University Press, 2021. | Series: Cambridge historical studies in American law and society | Includes index.
IDENTIFIERS: LCCN 2021012655 (print) | LCCN 2021012656 (ebook) | ISBN 9781108839235 (hardback) | ISBN 9781108989619 (ebook)
SUBJECTS: LCSH: Judicial review – United States – History – 18th century.
CLASSIFICATION: LCC KF4575 .S74 2021 (print) | LCC KF4575 (ebook) | DDC 347.73/12–dc23
LC record available at https://lccn.loc.gov/2021012655
LC ebook record available at https://lccn.loc.gov/2021012656

ISBN 978-1-108-83923-5 Hardback

For Jennifer and
Noah and Ezra

Contents

Acknowledgments

This book has been a long time in the making. I began it after the election of 2000 with a simple question. How had the United States Supreme Court managed to acquire the power to end a presidential election in favor of one of the candidates? That question continues to be of great importance today, twenty years later following the presidential election of 2020. I knew enough about American judicial review at the time to understand that its origins were a bit murky. For the most part, American constitutions had not expressly authorized the practice. I set about trying to figure out precisely how that astonishing power had come into existence. The subject of course had been addressed before many, many times. A huge library of work devoted to the "origins of judicial review" already existed. But somehow this enormous body of scholarship had not laid the question to rest. Historians kept returning to it, it seemed, because no account had proven entirely satisfactory. This book is my effort to provide a clearer answer to the questions of how precisely American judicial review had originally been brought into being, and how, within a short period of time, it had managed to become a defining feature of the American constitutional system.

I'd like to begin by giving especial thanks to Fred Konefsky for his indefatigable help and encouragement through many, many years of work. He has read and commented upon more drafts than I care to remember. The work would not be the same without his sharp-eyed commentary. When I first became interested in the subject, he and I put together materials for a constitutional history seminar devoted to judicial review, which we taught for many years at the SUNY Buffalo Law School, enriching immeasurably my (and hopefully our students') understanding of the field. I spent the academic year 2003–4 as a Fellow at the Warren Center at Harvard University. By the end of the year, I had produced an early draft of parts of the book. When I presented these at a Center seminar, the late Pauline Maier's critical response sent me hurrying back to the drawing board to dig deeper. Her reaction served to shape fundamentally the kind of finely detailed historical reconstructions this book now offers. I've also benefitted from the insights of participants in seminars at the Center for Law and Society at University of California, Berkeley, where I was a visiting scholar, and the University of Toronto Legal History Workshop. My former colleague Markus Dubber encouraged my early efforts, publishing a summary account of the book's argument a number of years ago. My colleague Matt Steilen read several chapters and offered detailed observations, which helped to clarify my thinking on a number of important issues. Stanley Engerman read an earlier version of the entire manuscript and sensibly urged me to elaborate political contexts more fully. Ted White read a later version of the manuscript, and his comments helped me to make the book considerably clearer and tighter. Barry Sullivan read a recent version of the Introduction and offered helpful remarks about the differential treatment "vertical" and "horizontal" review received at the Federal Convention. Dianne Avery helped to figure out how best to shorten and tighten an earlier version of the manuscript. My wife Jennifer Bayles offered close textual appraisals of several chapters, greatly improving their readability. I'd also like to thank the two anonymous reviewers for Cambridge University Press whose suggestions certainly strengthened the book.

At the SUNY Buffalo Law School, former dean Nils Olsen made it possible for me to enjoy several research semesters to complete work on individual chapters. My former student Joseph Belluck and his wife Laura Aswad generously provided financial support for the work, allowing me to take the time to carefully assess the enormous literature on the subject. Roger and Karen Jones kindly provided summer financial support.

I'd also like to thank Marcia Zubrow and John Mondo, librarians at Buffalo, whose grasp of the sources and unhesitating willingness to help with the project made the research journey a pleasure. Finally, I wish to thank my faculty assistant Debbie Nasisi for cheerfully and efficiently producing the next version of the manuscript, whenever I had finished tinkering with it. Without the support of these people and others, this book might never have seen the light of day. Remaining errors, of course, are mine alone.

Introduction

Most historians trace the immediate origins of American judicial review to a series of half a dozen cases that arose in half a dozen states during the 1780s. In these cases, lawyers began to argue that such and such a state statute was unconstitutional and that the judges should not consider it law in reaching their decisions. In several of these cases, the judges agreed and proceeded to take what a number of contemporaries regarded as the unprecedented step of "dispensing with"[1] the challenged act. Many historians believe that before these cases arose, no established tradition in the Anglo/American constitutional world authorized judges to "do away" with the duly enacted laws of their own legislatures.[2] By the mid-eighteenth century, it was largely taken for granted that English judges did not possess the authority to disregard acts of Parliament in deciding cases, and the same held true for American judges with respect to the laws their own legislatures had passed, although that proposition was occasionally tested, as Chapter 1 will make clear. After Independence, not a single one of the written constitutions the states adopted expressly

[1] The term "judicial review" was not used during the eighteenth century. Edward Corwin seems to have coined the expression at the beginning of the twentieth century, see Mary S. Bilder, "Idea or Practice: A Brief Historiography of Judicial Review" (2008) 20 *The Journal of Policy History* 6, 16. The phrases "dispense with laws" and "do away with laws" were commonly used during the early period to describe the judges' actions.

[2] This type of review is often referred to as "horizontal," in that it involves review of the laws a legislature has passed by one of the nonlegislative branches in the same government, and is normally contrasted to "vertical" review, which involves review by agents of a "superior" government of the laws a subordinate jurisdiction has passed. An example of "vertical" review is to be found in British Privy Council review of the laws of American colonial governments. The significance of the distinction is discussed below.

authorized judges to review and set aside the statutes their legislatures had passed.

How then were American judges able to acquire such an "alarming"[3] power? The answer to that question has not been all that obvious. The early cases themselves failed to provide clear-cut answers. They arose in a number of different states, more or less haphazardly (it seemed), and had little apparent connection to one another. And they posed other problems for historians. Most states had not yet begun to publish official court reports, and a number of the early cases had to be reconstructed from more or less fragmentary manuscript materials or from accounts published years, even decades, later. As a result, over the last century and more, historians have repeatedly returned to the question, producing an enormous body of scholarly literature, too large to cite here, in an effort to develop some clear, comprehensive picture of how precisely American judicial review came into being. The subject has continued to engage historians largely because none of the resulting accounts seems to have proven entirely satisfactory; none has managed to produce a consensus among historians about how the emergence and development of early American judicial review should properly be understood. One recent article has described this state of affairs as "Judicial Review's Uncertain Origins."[4]

Over the last several decades, historians have continued to seek a clearer picture of the practice's initial development. During that time, they have produced an additional large body of scholarship that describes the early history of American judicial review in great detail. This literature shows that the 1780s and 1790s were crucial decades in judicial review's formation and dissemination. For all that this work has added to our knowledge of the practice in the early period, however, it does not appear to have provided a definitive resolution of the larger problem.

The two major books that have been published on the subject since 2000 have both, in their different ways, attempted to produce

[3] Ironically, this is the word used by one of the leading early proponents of judicial review, James Iredell, to characterize the novel practice in 1787 (see letter from James Iredell to Richard Spaight, August 26, 1787) in Griffith McRee (ed.), *Life and Correspondence of James Iredell* (1857, repr. New York, Peter Smith, 1949), II, 176. In a similar vein, another early supporter of judicial review, Gouverneur Morris, referred to the new practice as "dangerous" but nevertheless "necessary" in 1785, see Jared Sparks (ed.), *The Life and Times of Gouverneur Morris, with Selections from His Correspondence and Miscellaneous Papers* (Boston, Gray Bowen, 1832), III, 438.

[4] Thomas Bettge, "Marbury in the Vanishing Cabinet: Evaluating Originalism in the Light of Judicial Review's Uncertain Origins" (2018) 55 *Willamette Law Review* 1.

comprehensive historical accounts aimed at generating agreement among historians about how precisely to understand the emergence of early American judicial review. The problem has turned out to be that while both books represent major contributions to the field, they contradict one another almost completely on the larger questions.

The People Themselves by Larry Kramer[5] was published in 2004. Kramer depicts American judicial review as an entirely novel practice, so much so that when the judges began to engage in it in the 1780s, it was, he argues, as a form of revolutionary judicial civil disobedience waged on behalf of the people, rather than as a claim that the formal authority of judges included that power. By the 1790s, the status of judicial review had changed, according to Kramer, thanks largely to the efforts of the Federalists, but he does not present nearly enough detail to allow us to understand precisely how this process occurred. There is much to learn from Kramer's book, and much to admire, but it does not offer, at the end of the day, an account of the early period that makes the initial emergence and dissemination of the practice fully comprehensible.

Philip Hamburger's *Law and Judicial Duty*,[6] the second major book to be published on the subject in recent decades, is a consummate, comprehensive work of historical research. But his larger thesis completely contradicts central aspects of Kramer's. Hamburger argues that far from being a novel and deeply controversial practice, American judicial review arose relatively unproblematically from the simple duty under which judges had long held office, to decide cases according to the laws of the land. There is simply too much evidence from the period, however, that American judicial review was in fact a novel and deeply controversial practice for Hamburger's core contention to be persuasive. In particular, Hamburger fails to credit precisely how deep were the disagreements in the period over precisely what counted as a "law of the land" that judges were obligated to take into account in making their decisions.

This book has the immodest ambition of providing a detailed account of the emergence of early American judicial review that yields a clearer picture of how precisely it was brought into being in the 1780s and how, by the early 1790s, it had managed to achieve wide acceptance in the American constitutional system. It approaches this subject, however, by

[5] Larry D. Kramer, *The People Themselves: Popular Constitutionalism and Judicial Review* (Oxford, Oxford University Press, 2004).

[6] Philip Hamburger, *Law and Judicial Duty* (Cambridge, Mass., Harvard University Press, 2008).

beginning with an earlier period. The book first, in Chapter 1, offers a description of the constitutional arrangements under which American colonial governments operated and then, in Chapters 2 and 3, proceeds to describe the constitutional design of American governments immediately following Independence in the 1770s, under the first written constitutions. By beginning in this way, the book aims to show that before the 1780s, Americans inhabited a constitutional universe structured by a fundamentally different set of premises than the one that would subsequently emerge beginning in the 1780s, a set of premises that were unfavorable to the development of a practice of "horizontal" judicial review. The book approaches the subject by widening the lens beyond judicial review itself to examine more broadly the kinds of institutional checks that were placed on the lawmaking power of legislatures in the earlier systems. And rather than restrict itself to ideas abstractly considered, the book seeks to explore what the concrete operation of those kinds of checks reveals about the constitutional assumptions upon which they were based and the profoundly different shape they gave to this earlier constitutional order. The constitutional arrangements in American colonial governments, to be certain, differed substantially from those that replaced them following Independence. But for all their differences, they shared a core constitutional logic that was deeply incompatible with the type of judicial review that emerged in the American states during the 1780s. In both earlier systems, the question of constitutionality was viewed largely as a matter for legislatures to decide, an integral aspect of their duty to promote the wellbeing of the polity as they went about enacting the laws. Courts simply had nothing to do with these kinds of judgments.

By developing a detailed account of this earlier constitutional design, the first three chapters seek to pinpoint the ways in which the premises underlying the emerging practice of American judicial review were both novel and controversial. And having done this, subsequent chapters seek to develop a richer understanding of precisely what changes had to take place in constitutional assumptions to make the early practice of judicial review not only viable but, for many, self-evidently legitimate. The balance of the book is devoted to describing how a new constitutional order was brought into being, and how it managed to gain broad acceptance, supplanting (but by no means eliminating) the older constitutional thinking. Judicial review was made possible, the book argues, by changing basic views about constitutions and constitutional obligations. In this period constitutions began to be seen as a form of ordinary (higher) law. This development transformed constitutional logic almost completely and opened the way for lawyers to argue that judges were entitled to expound constitutions on the same terms as they expounded any other law. In developing this story, each of the Chapters 4 thru 9 gives a detailed account of one of the early constitutional cases that arose during the 1780s. The final chapter, Chapter 10, describes the critical role the Federal Convention of 1787 played in bringing judicial review into the new constitutional design, and in promoting the constitutional logic that underlay it. Thanks in significant part to the decisions taken at the Federal Convention, the book argues in conclusion, by the early 1790s, the recently developed practice and doctrine of judicial review was being rapidly disseminated, and had become a permanent, if still deeply controversial, feature of the American constitutional order.

I

Chapter 1 begins by describing how legislatures and legislation were treated in American colonial governments. In the vast majority of these governments, governors and upper houses of the legislature were appointed, rather than popularly elected, and they possessed absolute vetoes over bills emerging from the popularly elected lower houses. All American colonial governments operated under one version or another of the imperial constitutional restriction that the laws they made should not be contrary or repugnant to the laws of England but "as near as may be, agreeable [to English law], considering the nature and constitution of the place and people there."[7]

One function of the vetoes governors and appointed upper houses wielded was to enforce this constitutional restriction, through a kind of "horizontal" review. The chapter seeks to highlight how fundamentally different this form of constitutional review was from the judicial review to which we are accustomed. It was a type of review deployed in the course of lawmaking, as an aspect of the decision whether to enact a bill into law, or to repeal or amend a law already made. The initial judgment that a proposed or existing law satisfied constitutional standards was typically made (most often implicitly) by the popularly elected lower house of the legislature. It was then reviewed by the appointed upper house and the governor, both of which had to assent before a bill became law. In this

[7] On these restrictions see Mary S. Bilder, *The Transatlantic Constitution: Colonial Legal Culture and the Empire* (Cambridge, Mass., Harvard University Press, 2004), 41.

way, determinations of constitutionality were viewed as an integral aspect of lawmaking.

These judgments about constitutionality, moreover, were made as part of the wider political obligation under which legislatures operated to make laws that did not harm but promoted the welfare of the polity. In fulfilling this duty, legislatures were bound to consider, for example, whether a proposed law represented wise policy, and whether it promoted the public good. The judgment about constitutionality, rather than being an entirely separate "legal" inquiry, was primarily considered to be one type of decision about the good of the polity that legislatures were obligated to make as they went about enacting or changing laws. And as a result, the quality of this kind of judgment was somewhat different from modern judgments about constitutionality. It involved a more fluid, open textured legislative determination that the proposed law would preserve the fundamental principles of the constitution, and reflected a view of constitutional restrictions as imposing a form of "political" duty on legislatures.

Within the empire, of course, American governments were considered "limited and dependent jurisdictions," whose laws should not be contrary or repugnant to the laws of the "superior" British government. Most (but not all) American colonies were required to transmit their laws to England for additional "vertical" review by the Board of Trade and Privy Council; the second section of Chapter 1 takes up this subject. Historians have been interested in Privy Council review for a long time, often because they viewed it as foretelling the development of American judicial review. This part of the chapter seeks to show, however, that in the overwhelming majority of cases, the "vertical" review to which American laws were subjected was more nearly akin to the "legislative" review they had undergone in the colony itself. In other words, in most cases, the Board of Trade and Privy Council reviewed American laws sitting in their capacity as a higher legislative body with the power to reconsider and reverse the decisions American legislatures had made to enact a law in the first place.

In deciding whether to reverse an American legislature's decision, the Privy Council considered a variety of factors that were understood to enter into legislative determinations more generally. These included, for example, considerations of whether the statute conflicted with the commercial policies of the empire. But the Council also commonly undertook to review the question whether the statute satisfied the constitutional standard that the act not be repugnant to the laws of England. In doing so they deployed an analysis that also involved a number of policy determinations.[8] If after this mixed (constitutional and nonconstitutional) "legislative" review, the Council determined that the statute did not promote the welfare of the empire or that it violated constitutional standards, most commonly they would order the law to be "disallowed." This enforcement mechanism was employed in the vast majority of cases in which the Council intervened, and it reveals a good deal about the assumptions underlying most Privy Council reviews. "Disallowance" repealed a statute going forward. If a colonial legislature had reconvened to reconsider and reverse its original determination that a statute satisfied constitutional standards, and then proceeded to repeal that statute, it would operate (in law) in the same way as did a Privy Council "disallowance."

That in the overwhelming majority of cases, the Privy Council repealed a colonial statute rather than declaring it void *ab initio* is also significant for what it tells us about the implicit view of constitutional restrictions that it reflects. Up until the Privy Council handed down its order of disallowance, a statute continued to possess the full force of law. In other words, not only was the determination of constitutionality viewed as a legislative matter primarily, but an adverse constitutional determination by the Council was not viewed as a decision that the colonial legislature lacked the constitutional power to confer the force of law on an act in the first place. That result reinforces the view that rather than being understood as a kind of rigid, disabling legal limitation, with a right and wrong answer, constitutional restraints were understood to impose more open-ended political duties over which there could be differing legislative judgments. It was the superiority of the Council's "legislative" authority that gave it the power to reverse the colonial legislature's determination of constitutionality and to repeal the statute.

The brief account here emphasizes the predominant role "vertical" "legislative" review played in the career of American colonial governments, with its "repeal" remedy (in the overwhelming majority of cases) for constitutional violations. But the subject of Privy Council review is considerably more complex than this short summary can convey. For one, the Council, did, on several occasions, declare colonial statutes to be void *ab initio* upon "vertical" "legislative" review. And this irregularity, among others, is examined more fully in Chapter 1.

[8] Bilder, Transatlantic Constitution, 40–42.

The chapter also addresses the role "vertical" judicial review played in the imperial system, but it shows how relatively uncommon and unimportant in the larger scheme such review was. The Privy Council did sit as the principal court of appeal for the empire. And in this capacity, they reviewed numerous decisions from colonial courts. But of the large number of cases they heard on appeal, the constitutionality of a statute was only challenged before them in a small handful of cases, and the Council, while sitting in its judicial capacity, only acted to declare a colonial statute void *ab initio* in a single instance. But because Privy Council practice was radically under-theorized, historians have even disagreed about whether that single instance represented an exercise of judicial or legislative power, as the discussion in Chapter 1 will make clear.

On the overwhelming majority of occasions, constitutional review of colonial legislation took the form of "vertical" "legislative" review, and led to the repeal of offending statutes, reflecting the quite distinctive constitutional logic of the British system. But Chapter 1 also shows that "vertical" judicial review of the laws and bylaws of dependent jurisdictions was a well-established British constitutional practice, and though it only played a vanishingly small role in the review of American colonial legislatures, it would serve as inspiration for one specific form of the American judicial review that appeared in the 1780s, the "vertical" judicial review of state laws established by the Federal Constitution of 1787. And that subject is taken up in Chapter 6 and more substantially in Chapter 10. There was no similarly established practice of "horizontal" judicial review in the British system, and when that form of review began to appear in the American states during the 1780s, it arrived as a controversial novelty.

The final section of Chapter 1 takes up the subject of "horizontal" judicial review, showing that serious efforts to establish the practice in one colony, South Carolina, ultimately foundered because it was judged to be deeply incompatible with the basic premises of the British constitutional system. This section describes the attempts that were made in South Carolina over a period of decades to have courts of the colony dispense with statutes that had been enacted by their own legislature, on the ground that the laws violated the repugnance restriction of the imperial system. One early South Carolina Chief Justice did in fact find that ordinary colonial courts possessed this authority, holding that constitutional obligations actually operated as a limitation on the legislature's power to confer the force of law on acts that conflicted with the constitutional prohibition. But that opinion seems to have represented a distinctly minority view. And ultimately, in the middle of the eighteenth century, two different Chief Justices of South Carolina laid these efforts definitively to rest, rejecting the idea that a colonial court could possibly possess the authority to overturn an act duly passed by the legislature of that colony. Their reasoning is especially revealing of the standard British constitutional assumptions upon which they relied.

The justices gave three main reasons for their opinions. First, they held that determinations of constitutionality and unconstitutionality were properly the province of the legislature alone, rendered by that body as part of the lawmaking process. If a colonial judge were to refuse to apply a duly enacted provincial law on the ground that it was unconstitutional, he would be improperly engaging in a legislative act, unmaking an existing law, and courts simply did not possess that kind of legislative authority. Second, allowing a court of the colony to overturn the decision of the legislature of that colony would establish the court as a superior authority sitting in judgment of the legislature's determinations, an outcome that was deeply inconsistent with fundamental British assumptions about the proper role of legislatures (and courts) in government. Legislatures were widely seen as supreme within government because they acted as the representatives of (and with the authority of) the entire nation (or of "the people"). Placing judges above legislatures would overturn the entire constitution. Third, the legitimate role of judges was to decide cases according to the laws of the land, but this duty was interpreted to mean that the judicial obligation was to apply existing common and statute law as it then stood, in the same way English judges were ordinarily expected to do. Judges possessed no authority to pick and choose between duly enacted laws, to decide to enforce some and turn their back on others. Doing so would not only represent a violation of their duty to decide cases according to the laws of the land but would also represent an attack, the Chief Justices made clear, on the rule of law itself. The central contention of Philip Hamburger's book, that the judicial duty to decide cases according to the laws of the land led straightforwardly to acceptance of judicial review, runs into the problem that that duty was often being interpreted in a quite different way even during the 1780s.

The authority to reverse the colonial legislature's judgment about the constitutionality of a law, and to repeal that law, was exercised by a superior legislative authority alone, the monarch and his privy council. These South Carolina judicial opinions reveal precisely why the earlier constitutional system did not provide fertile ground for the development of "horizontal" judicial review, and in part explain why this form of judicial review was so controversial when it was later introduced in the American states. But the analysis contained in these opinions also points toward the changes in constitutional assumptions that would have to take place for "horizontal" judicial review to become a viable practice.

Chapter 2 moves the story forward to consider the treatment of legislatures and legislation, and the nature of constitutional restraints, under the first written American constitutions. Most obviously, these constitutions swept away the entire apparatus of imperial review. But they went further; they established genuinely republican governments. The actual details, state by state, are complicated and examined in greater detail in the chapter itself, but in the majority of states both houses of the legislature were now to be popularly elected, and the popularly elected legislature itself (in most cases) would choose the governor. Perhaps even more significantly, governors, with only a few exceptions, were stripped of any power to veto bills, which upon passage by the two houses of the legislature became law. In this way, Americans self-consciously decided not to impose any institutional check on their legislatures. They did so, it seems, not only because they believed that in their now fully independent states the constitutional position of legislatures should resemble that of the two houses of Parliament, which had achieved independence from the royal veto (de facto) by the early eighteenth century, but also because many Americans had long detested the layers of review to which the laws issuing from their colonial assemblies had been subjected and were now in a position to eliminate them. In effect, this institutional design carried over from the British constitutional tradition the assumption that legislatures in sovereign states were supreme within governments and were the proper bodies to make determinations about constitutionality as part of their duty to promote the welfare of the polity as they went about enacting the laws. And at least within government, those judgments were to be final.

At the same time, many Americans on both ends of the political spectrum were (often for quite different reasons) deeply suspicious of governmental power, including even that of their own legislative representatives. Breaking with British tradition, or at least drawing on subordinate strands in that tradition, several constitutions included clauses that indicated, but mainly in hortatory language expressed in passive constructions, that rights included in constitutions ought not to be done away with, or in a few cases that constitutions themselves should not be altered, abolished or infringed. These clauses (and their language) are examined in detail in the chapter itself. In only two states, Pennsylvania and New York, did constitutions create any institution to enforce these restraints, and even in those states, the constitutions explicitly conferred on the legislature the final word about the constitutionality of laws. In both states, the question of constitutionality was itself treated as a matter to be disposed of in the course of lawmaking. But these clauses did produce a distinctive undertone in the early American constitutional tradition, evoking the idea that the power of government and of their own representatives should somehow be subject to constitutional limitations, and created genuine destabilizing tensions between institutional design and ideological aspiration within the early tradition. These issues are examined in Chapter 3.

In sum, for all the ways they departed from the dominant British tradition, the first American constitutions continued to treat constitutional restraints primarily as establishing a set of fundamental principles and norms, which imposed a form of political duty on legislatures, and were enforceable, in the vast majority of these constitutions, *only* through political processes. There was not the slightest suggestion, direct or indirect, in any of them that the judiciary should have the power to review the laws. The constitutional duties imposed on legislatures were understood to run directly to the people, and the people themselves were the ones to enforce them. It is no coincidence that except in a single case, every American constitution of the period required that elections for the lower house of the legislature be annual. In a number of states, the entire legislature was elected every year. Inscribed implicitly in these constitutions was the view that frequent elections, together with other forms of popular political action, were the principal means by which the duties constitutions imposed on legislatures were to be enforced. In this way, the people were also to be the final interpreters of constitutions, in a quite direct sense. If the people concluded that the legislature had not lived up to their constitutional obligations in the laws they had passed, then the people could remove them from office at the next election, and replace them with men who would abide by the people's view of what their constitution demanded. On the other hand, if the people concluded that the laws the legislature had passed did not overstep constitutional bounds, that would be an end of it.

The absence of any other check on legislatures, however, and the greatly expanded role of elections and of the people in these new constitutional arrangements made certain groups of Americans uneasy. If the people were to play such a central role in the new constitutional design, it was critical that they be virtuous and capable. One of the principal struggles that broke out in the congresses and conventions responsible for drafting the early constitutions, consequently, was over how far down the social and economic hierarchy the right to vote should extend. Many prominent political leaders fought in these drafting bodies to retain, or even increase, existing property-owning requirements to vote and to hold public office. Formed in the British mold, America was still a deeply hierarchical society, and traditional fears about the capacities of common people to participate wisely in the running of government often drove these efforts. But in a Revolution that was based in part on the idea that there should be no taxation without representation, many men who paid taxes, but owned little or no property, felt themselves to have a legitimate claim to the vote, and a formidable movement emerged to expand the suffrage to taxpayers. The outcome of these struggles in the different states produced a complex picture, which is examined in detail in Chapter 2. But in general, they led to a greater or lesser expansion of the suffrage in all the states, a result which left those who were apprehensive about the large role the common people played in the new constitutional order with a lingering sense of uneasiness.

Chapter 3 turns to consider the early conservative response to this situation by examining the New York Constitution of 1777. It was adopted by a convention led and controlled by a group of prominent conservative upper-class New Yorkers. This group not only succeeded in preserving property-owning requirements to vote for members of both houses of the legislature in the new constitution, they also brought back for the first time in any permanent constitution of the period, a modified gubernatorial veto, in the form of a Council of Revision. A detailed account of its creation appears in Chapter 3. The New York Constitution charged this Council, composed of the governor and the high court judges of the state, with the duty to review all bills passed by the legislature to determine whether they were "inconsistent with *the spirit of this constitution*, or with *the public good*"[9] (emphasis added), and if the Council found that they were and objected, the bill did not become law, unless a 2/3 majority of both houses passed it again over the Council's objections.

The creation of this council represented a substantial departure from almost every other early constitution in that it established a robust

[9] Section III of the New York Constitution of 1777 in Francis Thorpe (ed.), *The Federal and State Constitutions, Colonial Charters, and Other Organic Laws of the States, Territories and Colonies* (Washington, D.C., Government Printing Office, 1909, Reprint Buffalo, N.Y., William S. Hein, 1993), V, 2628.

institutional process for review of legislation, and imposed a substantial check on the legislature, one that explicitly extended to enforcing the "spirit of the constitution." And it did so in order to address the problem of laws that "may be hastily and unadvisedly passed"[10] by that popularly elected body.

At the same time, it seems clear that this conservative effort to create a meaningful check on the legislature did not break with the early constitutional system's core premises. For one, the Council's constitutional review was to take place as part of the lawmaking process, as was traditional. Also traditional was that constitutional review was to be lumped together with review of a range of other political considerations that bore on the welfare of the polity. In addition to conducting a review for constitutionality, the Council was charged with determining whether proposed laws were consistent "with the public good." Both kinds of review represented different aspects of the broad political duty under which legislatures operated to promote the good of the nation by passing laws that preserved the principles of the constitution, and enacted advantageous policies. But perhaps most important, Council "legislative" review continued to leave the final word about the constitutionality of the laws with the legislature, if now only after legislators had reached a broad consensus (2/3) that a proposed law did not conflict with the spirit of the constitution.

Extant Council of Revision opinions, however, also reveal that its members were drawing on a more amorphous current circulating in early American constitutionalism, which held that constitutions did in fact limit the actual power of legislatures to enact laws in some nebulous sense that went beyond political duty. A later section of Chapter 3 examines Council of Revision opinions more closely to discuss the tensions that attitude created. These internal strains left the early constitutional tradition vulnerable to disruption.

In sum, the first three chapters, attempt to flesh out the logic of a system in which constitutions were mainly understood to impose "political" (rather than "legal") duties that were owed directly to the people. Under this system, legislatures, as the people's representatives, were viewed as possessing the authority to determine, in the final resort during the lawmaking process, whether a proposed law complied with the "spirit" of a constitution. These legislative judgments were subject to revision only by the people themselves through forms of political action aimed at

[10] Ibid.

persuading or compelling legislatures to repeal a law the people viewed as violating their constitution. Until such a statute had been repealed, however, it continued to enjoy the full force of law.

This earlier constitutional tradition helped to bring into being a particular version of republican government, one in which "the people" (and their elected representatives) played a greater, more direct role in determinations of constitutionality and unconstitutionality. And this tradition posed serious difficulties for the very idea of judicial review.

Not everyone, however, was happy with republics organized in this way, as the discussion in Chapters 2 and 3 make clear. Many prominent conservatives were left uneasy by the thought that these republics tended to give the oft-times tumultuous people nearly unlimited power to make, through their legislatures, just any law by which they might wish to govern themselves.

II

Part II of this book begins with Chapter 4 and takes up the subject of the emergence of American judicial review itself. Each of the Chapters 4 thru 9 is given over to an extended account of one of the half dozen cases that arose in the 1780s and were responsible for launching judicial review in the American constitutional system. Among other things, these reconstructions follow the lawyers (and judges) as they worked to create a powerful counter constitutional logic to justify the new practice. By approaching the subject of the first appearance of judicial review from the vantage point of an earlier constitutional tradition, the book hopes to denaturalize the set of presuppositions that underlie the constitution of judicial review in order to make the steps in its construction clearer.

A case-by-case account, however, yields a narrative that is far from linear and that does not move neatly from point to point. The larger story emerges bit by bit as critical issues arise, are debated, and disposed of in each state. At times, the book revisits an issue that arose first in one state and then independently in another. This is a complicated story, which is distinctive, if not unique, in each state. But a case-by-case reconstruction is the one certain way to convey an accurate sense of precisely how the practice and doctrine actually emerged and progressed during the early period. Perhaps, the character of this disorderly process also helps to explain why it has proved so difficult for historians to arrive at a clear and comprehensive consensus about the practice's early development.

It is possible nevertheless to assemble from the accounts of these individual cases a more orderly story, although that risks distorting and simplifying the original one. Perhaps, the place to begin is with the first written constitutions themselves. It is important to emphasize, as Chapters 2 and 3 do, that the first constitutions were primarily understood in the traditional British way, as imposing a set of political duties. Larry Kramer has shown that they were considered to be a form of higher fundamental political law, an early modern species of law that unlike ordinary law was not normally taken to be cognizable by courts.[11]

But almost from the beginning, the adoption of these constitutions began to move conceptions about them in a new direction. It was not so much that they had been committed to writing, as that they had been drafted, debated, revised, and adopted by representative bodies chosen by the people. These procedures bore a striking resemblance to ordinary legislative processes that resulted in the enactment of laws. Indeed, several of the first constitutions were drafted and approved by representative bodies that later reconvened as legislatures. A few second-generation constitutions made the evolution in constitutional thinking clearer by explicitly stating that these constitutions were part of the laws of the land.[12] A sense that these constitutions might represent a form of ordinary (higher) law, consequently, began by the 1780s to enter mainstream constitutional thinking.

By that time, Thomas Jefferson had certainly begun to see the Virginia Constitution as law in this way, as the discussion of his views in connection with the Virginia Case of the Prisoners in Chapter 5 makes evident. This notion represented an important conceptual precondition on the road to making the argument for judicial review viable, but in itself was far from sufficient. As Jefferson understood, in the British tradition one legislature lacked the power to bind succeeding legislatures. Later legislatures remained free to amend or repeal the enactments of earlier ones. This reasoning led him to conclude that the Virginia legislature possessed the power to alter at will the Virginia Constitution, as that constitution had originally been adopted by a legislative body. For those like Jefferson who shared an increasingly urgent desire to place constitutions beyond the power of legislatures to alter, this was a large problem.

11 See in general, Kramer, The People Themselves, 24.

12 See in particular, Massachusetts Constitution of 1780, in Thorpe (ed.), Federal and State Constitutions, III, 1911, and New Hampshire Constitution of 1784, in Thorpe (ed.), Constitutions, IV, 2470.

But by the time Jefferson was writing, constitutional developments in parts of New England pointed toward a conceptual solution, which Jefferson also realized and embraced. In Massachusetts and New Hampshire, popular demands had led to the development of novel procedures for adopting constitutions. Constitutions must be drafted by stand-alone conventions, whose members were to be chosen by a broad electorate representing the entire people and were to dissolve once their work was complete. The results of their efforts, moreover, could not be put into effect until the people had voted a second time to ratify them. In this way, the idea that constitutions represented not only a form of ordinary law but a form of ordinary law that had been directly enacted by the people received institutional life. The New Hampshire Constitution of 1784 was adopted using the new procedures, and its text stated expressly that it was the work, not of the representatives of the people as its 1776 constitution had, but of the people themselves.[13] One critical implication of these developments was that since legislatures were not the authors of this type of law, they could not possibly possess the power to change it, only the original authors, the people themselves, enjoyed that power.

Other developing constitutional ideas began to find their way into the texts of some constitutions. The view that governments exercised all their powers as a direct delegation from the people, for one.[14] A few second-generation constitutions also began to include a clause that for the first time expressly and clearly deprived legislatures of the power to enact any law that was "repugnant or contrary to this constitution."[15] And these ideas could readily be read into earlier constitutions that did not explicitly contain them.

On the other hand, no constitution, even those adopted during the first half of the 1780s, established any regular institutional mechanism[16] to enforce their terms, beyond the overridable gubernatorial veto that the

[13] Compare the language in New Hampshire's 1776 constitution, in Thorpe (ed.), Constitutions, IV, 2451, with that in its 1784 constitution, in Thorpe (ed.), Constitutions, IV, 2458.

[14] See, for example, Section I of Declaration of Rights in North Carolina Constitution of 1776, in Thorpe (ed.), Constitutions, V, 2787, and New Hampshire Constitution of 1784, in Thorpe (ed.), Constitutions, IV, 2458.

[15] See Massachusetts Constitution of 1780, in Thorpe (ed.), Constitutions, III, 1894, and New Hampshire Constitution of 1784, in Thorpe (ed.), Constitutions, IV, 2458.

[16] The Massachusetts Constitution of 1780 called for a new convention to be called in 1795 to "correct" possible constitutional violations that had arisen in the interim, in Thorpe (ed.), Constitutions, III, 1911.

Massachusetts constitution of 1780 put into place. As a result, whatever the texts may have said, these restrictions must still be understood as imposing political duties on legislatures, in so far as they could only be enforced in the traditional way through frequent elections or other forms of political action.

But it is against the background of these wider changes in constitutional ideas, institutions, and text that lawyers began to make the case for judicial review. It is important to understand that there were still important conceptual and practical obstacles to overcome for this argument to be successful. Perhaps, the most significant remained that for many, it continued to make a kind of intuitive sense that the interpretation of the people's constitution should be left in the final resort (at least within government) to the people's own representatives, as they went about making laws for the polity. And the duty of courts was to enforce those duly enacted laws until legislatures had been persuaded or pressured into changing their decision and acted to repeal the offending law. This view, moreover, resonated deeply with broader sentiments about how simple republican governments should properly operate.

The long revolutionary war, in which Americans at times fought against one another, and which generated, as a result, bitter, divisive feelings in the country, was followed by a severe economic downturn after the war ended. For many of those who had felt anxiety about unchecked popularly elected legislatures, the policies legislatures sometimes adopted in response to this state of affairs only heightened distrust, not only of legislatures, but of the character and capacities of ordinary people who had chosen these bodies, and whose bidding they were presumed, more often than not, to be doing. Each of the chapters describes in some detail the political situation out of which the constitutional cases in each state developed. Every single case of the original half dozen down to 1787 arose either as a consequence of legislation that had been enacted to address an issue connected to Loyalists or to an issue that grew out of the severe economic slump.

The cases themselves fall into two broad categories: those that developed while the war was still being fought and those that developed following the signing of the peace. The first two cases, which arose during the war, convey a palpably different sense than the four later ones. The two early cases present themselves, in their different ways, as tentative forays onto the terrain of judicial review. In the first, the New Jersey case of *Holmes* v. *Walton*, it appears that the court ventured to reject a state statute, but, only at the conclusion of a long process in which it worked hand in glove with the legislature to pass a "corrected" version of the statute before it acted to "do away with" the original. In the second, the Virginia *Case of the Prisoners*, the lawyers who argued the case engaged in a thorough, highly sophisticated debate, pro and con, over the question whether judges possessed the power to nullify a statute as unconstitutional. The Attorney General of Virginia at the time, Edmund Randolph, presented an argument showing that courts did not possess such a power. On the other side, St. George Tucker presented a fully developed argument demonstrating that judges did in fact possess the power of judicial review. The court, however, seeing no pressing need to resolve the "great constitutional question" at that moment, decided to leave the question of whether it actually possessed the authority to nullify a statute undecided.

Following the signing of the peace, the tone of the cases changed and the question of judicial review became more immediate and pressing. Many Americans turned their energies to calling collaborators to account for their behavior during the war, fellow countrymen who had taken up arms with the British or who had merely failed to join the Patriot side. Legislatures often seemed inclined to cooperate with popular anti-Loyalist sentiments, passing a variety of punitive measures directed at the Loyalist "minority." The peace itself also led, for a number of reasons, to a painful, extended economic depression, and a fair number of legislatures responded to popular pressures by passing laws to relieve debtors, which seemed to invade traditional common law property or process rights. A number of legislatures issued paper money in response to the crisis, measures fervently opposed by larger merchants and other hard money creditors. These kinds of legislative actions set off a wider reaction among mainly conservative men, who now began to question more pointedly and more persistently the wisdom of permitting legislatures, who were subject to frequent popular elections, to continue to enjoy the unfettered power to enact into law just any measure the people might momentarily desire, however unconstitutional it might appear to be.

The lawyers who first began to take up the cause of judicial review did so from a variety of motives. Their immediate object, of course, was to win cases for clients, by preventing a particular law from being put into effect in a particular suit or prosecution. But many prominent lawyers of the period were inclined mainly to accept clients whose positions aligned with their own political beliefs. The lawyers themselves often considered the statutes they were challenging to be unjust, and/or unconstitutional, and to have been enacted in response to intemperate popular passions. A significant number of the lawyers who argued these cases were also leading political figures and hoped to achieve something more lasting, to bring into being unilaterally through the courts, an institution that could operate as a check not only on legislatures but on the people themselves, to whom the structure of existing republics had made legislatures unduly responsive. The words of leading early advocates for judicial review, Alexander Hamilton, James Iredell, James Varnum, and William Plumer, are unmistakable in this ambition.

It was under these circumstances that lawyers began to take hold of the new constitutional ideas to fashion a tight legal argument justifying the practice of judicial review. The primitive inspiration for challenging statutes as unconstitutional and void, of course, was not new. Americans had been using words like these for decades, particularly in the run up to the Revolution, when they regularly challenged the constitutionality of Parliament's acts, insisting that they were not binding upon Americans and that, consequently, Americans were justified in resisting them. But if the rudimentary inspiration for the later challenges can be found in these words, they do not explain in themselves what the lawyers were actually contending for in these cases. They, and the judges who responded favorably to their arguments, were arguing for a radical reinterpretation of the traditional words. The lawyers were not asking judges to engage in revolutionary acts of resistance against the governments in which they themselves served as officials; they were asking them to use their formal power as judges to "dispense with" (treat as not law) state statutes, whenever the judges found them to be unconstitutional. And they began to develop a powerful legal logic to support their case.

Constitutions were not only, or even primarily, foundational political documents, the lawyers insisted, drawing upon recent developments in constitutional culture; they were one of the laws of the land, in fact the most fundamental law. A few constitutions had even begun to say so explicitly. As part of the laws of the land, judges could now claim more persuasively that they possessed jurisdiction to take these foundational texts into account, together with other laws, in reaching their decisions in cases. Indeed, their oaths of office, it began to be argued, actually obligated them to do so. There was only this difference: constitutions were laws that had been directly enacted by the people and were thus superior to the ordinary laws that emerged from legislatures. Legislatures, moreover, had never been delegated the authority to alter the terms of these constitutions. A statute that conflicted with a constitution, consequently, must be beyond the power of a legislature to enact.

But two crucial steps remained to complete the argument for judicial review. What was it, precisely, about judges, of all government officials, that gave them authority not only to decide that a duly enacted law of the state was in conflict with a constitution but to then also treat that statute, in the course of their official duties, as not possessing the force of law? Parties who had brought suits, after all, were relying on state statutes to define their legal rights and duties. The crucial authority of judges, the lawyers argued in response, was that of expounding, or interpreting the laws, all the laws, including the constitution. The assertion that judges possessed the authority to interpret the laws was, in itself, uncontroversial. And now that constitutions had begun to be viewed more often as law proper, the argument that judges had jurisdiction also to interpret this form of law seemed increasingly persuasive.

The final step in this argument is especially important, but in taking it, the lawyers, ironically, moved to invoke the authority of Blackstone, champion of Parliamentary supremacy, to support their position. In his Commentaries, Blackstone had laid down a series of "rules to be observed with regard to the construction of statutes,"[17] and these included rules governing situations in which a judge confronted conflicting laws as he went about determining which law decided a case. Blackstone made clear that in these situations, judges had the authority, following widely accepted rules of construction, to treat one of the laws as abrogated. So, for example, Blackstone wrote, when a later statute and an earlier statute were found to be irreconcilably in conflict, judges, not unreasonably, were to apply the later statute and to treat the earlier one as having been repealed.[18]

The analogy to situations in which a judge confronted conflicts between the law of the constitution and the ordinary laws of the legislature apparently seemed obvious to lawyers, as St. George Tucker, James Iredell and Alexander Hamilton all relied on it in making their arguments for judicial review.[19] By invoking the authority of Blackstone, moreover,

[17] William Blackstone, *Commentaries on the Laws of England* (Chicago, University of Chicago Press, 1979, reprint of 1765 ed.), Book I, Section 3, 87.

[18] Ibid., 89. In a recent article, Ian Bartrum, "The People's Court: The Intellectual Origins of American Judicial Power" (2020–2021) 125 *Dickinson Law Review* 283, at 328 points out that Blackstone's position on Parliamentary supremacy actually stood in some tension with the broad interpretive discretion he was willing to see judges wield. The matter of equitable interpretation in Blackstone is discussed further in Chapter 6 in connection with the case of *Rutgers* v. *Waddington*.

[19] St. George Tucker, Argument in the *Case of the Prisoners*, in Charles F. Hobson (ed.), *St. George Tucker's Law Reports and Selected Paper, 1782–1825* (Chapel Hill, N.C.,

the lawyers may well have hoped to clothe their otherwise novel and controversial arguments in the garb of traditional doctrine.[20] And a clear rule of construction seemed readily to hand. Constitutions were superior to the ordinary law legislatures produced, and when a judge construed the two to be irreconcilably in conflict, he should have the power to treat the statute as abrogated, as not having the force of law. The argument transformed judicial review into an exercise of ordinary judicial interpretive authority. The question whether it was appropriate to treat constitutions simply as another species of law appropriate for ordinary courts to expound, given the weighty political consequences that often turned on these constructions, was discussed less frequently.

Crucially, the new practice answered the increasingly felt need for establishing a sanctuary in the courts from the unfettered majoritarian politics of the early republics, especially for individual (and "minority") rights. The new practice, however, also had a serious political downside, to which traditionalists pointed in their criticisms. It left decisions about what the laws of the land were to be, at the end of the day, to a small number of men who held offices that were least accountable to the people in republican governments. But this drawback was precisely one of the practice's main appeals for those who harbored deep distrust of the capacities and motivations of the (common) people.

The argument for judicial review relied on a straightforward, powerful logic that quickly succeeded in persuading many lawyers and judges, and held great attraction for a range of political leaders. The case for judicial review, rested, in large measure, on commonly held, and mainly uncontroversial common law assumptions about the legitimate authority of judges. The lawyers in effect had developed a judicial account of judicial review, one that, among other things, cut the ground out from under the assertion that the practice constituted an illicit judicial exercise of legislative power.

While the logic of the argument for judicial review relied on the idea that judges were enforcing the people's will embodied in their constitutions, numerous statements from its principal creators establish pretty

University of North Carolina Press, 2013), III, 1742; McRee (ed.), Life and Correspondence of James Iredell ("To the Public," August 1786), II, 148, and (letter from Iredell to Richard Spaight, August 26, 1787), II, 173; Alexander Hamilton, #78 Federalist, in Clinton Rossiter (ed.), *The Federalist Papers* (New York, Penguin, c. 1961, Mentor Book, 1999), 436.

20 James Duane also invoked Blackstone to help him justify his decision in *Rutgers v. Waddington*; for details see Chapter 6 below.

clearly that these men were motivated primarily by a determination to see the sovereign people bound to the terms of their own constitutions as the judges interpreted those "legal" texts, and in this way to see significant limitations placed on their power to enact (through their legislatures) just any laws they might find desirable. Larry Kramer's depiction of judges as revolutionaries acting on behalf of the people during the 1780s mistakes the formal logic of the argument for judicial review for the openly expressed motives that mainly drove its creation and does not withstand a close examination of the political contexts out of which it grew. Two decades after the initial appearance of judicial review, Gouverneur Morris trenchantly observed that the practice had been created to "save the people from themselves."[21] As Edmund Morgan taught us to see decades ago, "the very exaltation of popular power [could] furnish a means of directing and controlling it."[22]

The simple, elegant argument for judicial review had far-reaching constitutional consequences. The separation of powers clauses found in a number of early state constitutions began increasingly to be understood as limiting each branch to a single functional power, legislatures to making laws, judges to interpreting and applying those laws to individual cases, and the executive to executing the laws according to the judges' decisions. This way of thinking undercut the previously held "natural presumption"[23] that legislatures, as the people's representatives, were the proper bodies to interpret constitutions as they went about deliberating upon whether to enact a bill into law. It might be appropriate for legislatures to provide explications of their own statutes, but as they were not the "authors" of constitutions, their claim to be proper expositors of those instruments was now greatly weakened. It seemed increasingly obvious that the new "natural presumption" should be that judges, whose job and expertise lay in interpreting the laws, should ordinarily be the expositors of constitutions.

Courts also began to use their newly assumed authority to call into question certain powers popular assemblies had traditionally exercised. Up to this time, legislatures, in a number of states, had continued to act as

21 From a speech Gouverneur Morris delivered in the United States Senate in early January 1802, arguing against repeal of the Second Judiciary Act, *The Debates and Proceedings of the Congress of the United States, Seventh Congress, 1st Session* (Washington, Printed and Published by Gales and Seaton, 1851), 41 ("Judiciary System").

22 Edmund Morgan, *Inventing the People: The Rise of Popular Sovereignty in England and America* (New York, Norton, 1988), 152.

23 This phrase is Hamilton's used in #78 Federalist, Rossiter (ed.), Federalist Papers, 435.

legal tribunals or as courts of final resort, even where a constitution had not explicitly conferred that power on them. Increasingly, courts held legislative resolutions of private disputes, or legislative reversals of court decisions, to be unconstitutional retrospective laws, or unconstitutional exercises of judicial power in violation of separation of powers clauses, or unconstitutional infringements of the right to trial by jury, and refused to enforce the results of these legislative adjudications. The consequence of the simple, elegant argument for judicial review was to set a constitutional revolution in motion.

The reconstruction of these early cases also helps to clarify other matters. Some historians have made much of the fact that there appears to have been little public debate about judicial review during the early years. But this contention neglects that a kind of public debate did occur at the time, when legislatures in four of the six cases moved to sanction judges for engaging in the practice. A careful reading of the resulting legislative debates and resolutions reveals that legislatures were often acting on principle to defend the terms of the traditional constitution (as well as their own authority under it) against a new constitutional order the (lawyers) and judges were seeking to bring into being.

These debates pitted traditional constitutional understandings against the new ideas that underlay the case for judicial review and reveal a traditional constitutionalism struggling to retain its authority. On the level of ideas, the chapters depict these repeated encounters as a (coherent) confrontation between competing constitutional visions played out between legislatures and courts, in which opposing visions of republican government were at stake. But there were also institutional consequences riding on the outcome of these ideological conflicts. Would legislatures, subject only to review by the people themselves, continue to determine the scope of their own constitutional powers to enact law on behalf of the people, or would the unelected judges, who, in a number of states, enjoyed tenure during good behavior, become ultimate deciders (within government) of the scope not only of their own judicial powers, but at the end of the day, of the power of the people to make, through their legislatures, the laws by which they wished to govern themselves?

The accounts of these encounters show that many legislators of the period did not view the judges' actions as we might. They saw them from the perspective of the constitutional tradition that still dominated American political culture, and as such many of them were certain that by "dispensing with laws," judges were unquestionably committing a wrong, usurping the legitimate constitutional authority of the legislature, and should be removed from office for doing so. From a modern perspective these legislative assaults on the judiciary are often seen as radical attacks on judicial independence and on the rule of law itself. But from the vantage point of the traditional constitution, legislators more often thought of themselves as defenders of the rule of law against judges who were threatening to undermine it. By "dispensing with laws," judges were making rights fixed by public statutes insecure, as their enforceability would now depend upon the uncertain outcome of litigation. Nor could the judges point to any provision in a constitution which entitled them simply to pick and choose between the existing laws they saw fit to enforce and those they decided not to. No government official was entitled to ignore a duly enacted law of the state as they went about executing their duties simply because, in their opinion it violated the constitution. Down that path lay anarchy.[24] Why should judges be different? In North Carolina, a grand jury moved to present criminally one lawyer who had advocated judicial review, accusing him of urging the judges "in open court" to disobey the express commands of a state statute. A number of pamphleteers pointed out that by "dispensing with laws" judges were violating their sacred duty to decide cases (only) according to the duly enacted laws of the land.

In mounting these assaults on the judiciary, legislators were also of the view that the judges were illicitly and unilaterally moving vastly to expand their own powers, in among other ways by assuming the legislative power to repeal existing laws, and in doing so were impermissibly placing themselves above the people's representatives. This was a set of weighty traditional objections to the practice that had also been raised decades earlier. In the *Case of the Prisoners*, Chancellor Edmund Pendleton was still willing to point out that since judicial nullification of duly enacted laws appeared to represent an exercise of legislative power, judicial review might well constitute a violation of the Virginia Constitution's separation of powers clause.

This contest over ideas between legislatures and courts, however, is only part of the story these chapters tell. As there was no ultimate judge to declare a winner in this ideological struggle, and as no efforts were made

[24] This book does not undertake to examine the question of refusals by the executive to enforce the laws based on the executive's views about the constitutionality of a statute, which has recently given rise to an extensive literature, see, for example, Matthew Steilen, "Judicial Review and Non-enforcement at the Founding" (2014) 17 *University of Pennsylvania Journal of Constitutional Law*, 479–568.

to amend constitutions expressly to authorize judges to engage in the practice, the chapters also seek to explain precisely how the doctrine and practice of judicial review managed to secure a foothold in several states over a relatively short period. They analyze this problem from the perspective of the traditional understanding that changes in basic law can sometimes be achieved through principled acts (supported by the force of ideas) that are steadfastly maintained over time in the face of opposition.[25]

In pursuit of a clearer understanding of precisely how this process worked in the case of the emergence of judicial review, the chapters use the repeated clashes between legislatures and courts as case studies to assess the strategic positions of each branch in relation to the other. If courts steadfastly (and uniformly) refused to enforce a law, were legislatures in any position to ensure that the law would, nevertheless, remain in effect, or would the law effectively become unenforceable, a dead letter? If the latter, then the judges would have succeeded unilaterally in turning the idea of judicial nullification into an institutional reality. Would legislatures, which viewed the new practice as an unconstitutional usurpation of their authority, be in any position to put a stop to its development? Using the early cases as studies, these chapters come to the conclusion that for a variety of reasons, legislatures were normally in a poor position to prevent judges from giving institutional life to judicial review through their acts, the legitimacy of which were supported by the spread of the new constitutional logic.

Of singular importance for assessing the trajectory of this process were the attempts made by groups of legislators in every one of the post-war cases to remove judges from office for engaging in the practice. In every single instance, these attempts failed to muster the votes to do so, leaving judges, for the most part, in a position simply to assert and reassert in their decisions that they legitimately possessed the power to dispense with laws and to act on those assertions.[26] Those who supported the judges in these removal debates succeeded in reframing the issue as one of judicial

[25] See John Phillip Reid, *Constitutional History of the American Revolution* (Madison, Wisc., University of Wisconsin Press, Abr. Ed., 1995); and Kramer, The People Themselves.

[26] Legislatures, of course, possessed other powers they might employ to cow judges into abandoning the practice, or to reverse the consequences of particular decisions. In a number of states, and in the Federal system, legislatures could, for example, simply repeal the statute creating a particular court, dissolving that court, and eliminating the jobs of the judges who sat on it, see John Phillip Reid, *Legislating the Courts: Judicial Dependence in Early National New Hampshire* (DeKalb, Northern Illinois. University Press, 2009). The chapters discuss these and other possible legislative responses to acts of

independence; judges should not be punished even for their erroneous judicial opinions, so long as they had been rendered without corruption. Ironically, these legislative failures also helped to bolster the legitimacy of the new practice, as they were often construed as legislative acceptance of, or acquiescence in the new practice. All together this series of early legislative failures contributed to reshaping constitutional culture by leaving behind crucial precedents (and a powerful rationale) that militated against the likelihood that in the future, legislatures would be inclined on a consistent basis to attempt to remove judges from office simply for engaging in judicial review.

By the time the Federal Convention met, state legislatures had shown repeatedly that they were unable to muster the votes to remove judges from office for engaging in judicial review and in several of these states were unable to put a stop to its development.[27] Legislatures were, in effect, losing the argument over legislative supremacy on the ground.[28]

Although by 1787, judicial review had successfully taken root in only a small handful of states, these states served as a critical proving ground for the practice. The judicial decisions there produced precedents to which advocates could point in arguing for its extension. But above all, the events in the states had led to the development of an easy to grasp, powerful logic for judicial review. By the time the Federal Convention met, that logic was almost fully developed. Lawyers (and judges) were its natural carriers and disseminators. In most states, the community of the bar (and bench) was small and face to face. Lawyers regularly encountered one another in the courts, or in the legislatures where many of them served, or in the Confederation Congresses, which brought leading lawyers from across the country into contact with one another. The majority of the early cases also provoked political crises, which served to acquaint a broader public with the new practice. And the arguments lawyers made in these cases were widely reported not only in local and regional newspapers but often also in out of state papers.

III

Part III of this book consists of a single, final Chapter 10, devoted to the Federal Convention. Delegates to the Convention, even from states in

judicial review, but conclude that none were employed consistently and persistently enough to put a stop to the rapidly developing practice.

[27] New York and Rhode Island were exceptions but were only able to delay the adoption of judicial review for several more decades, see Chapters 6 and 8 for details.

[28] Judicial review, of course, also suffered serious setbacks, which are described in Chapter 10.

which there had not yet been a constitutional challenge to a statute, showed pretty clearly, in their remarks about judicial review, that they grasped (and in the majority of cases accepted) its simple, powerful logic. Their invariably succinct comments indicated that most of them thought it to be self-evident that judges possessed the power of judicial review as an attribute of their authority to expound the laws, a description that mirrored the logic lawyers, like James Iredell, had utilized in the states.

One of the main reasons the Federal Convention had been called into existence in the first place was that leading political figures in the country had come to the conclusion that if republican government was to be preserved, the existing constitutional system had to be modified, especially to establish some type of check on state legislatures. Since it quickly became apparent that a federal legislature was also to be created, some kind of check on that body would also be necessary. James Madison, who was mainly responsible for drafting the Virginia Plan, which framed many of the early discussions at the Convention, included proposals for both kinds of checks. Under the Virginia Plan, the new national legislature would be given an absolute veto over state laws, and a Federal Council of Revision would be created to wield a conditional veto over Congressional acts. Both of Madison's proposals drew on the older Anglo/American constitutional tradition. Both kinds of checks would be exercised in the traditional way as part of the lawmaking process. National legislative review of state laws bore a distinct family resemblance to the "vertical" "legislative" review in which the Privy Council had engaged. And the Council of Revision imagined judges playing the kind of "legislative" role in evaluating constitutionality that they did in New York.

The debates over these proposals, as a result, were also implicitly debates over whether the constitution would be understood and treated in the traditional way, as a foundational political-legal document, or in the new way, as a primarily legal text. The defeat of both of Madison's proposals at the Convention marked a decisive setback for traditional constitutionalism. Rejecting Madison's suggestions, the Convention adopted judicial review as the principal means to enforce the new constitution against state legislatures. They also rejected Madison's Council of Revision, refusing to permit judges to participate in the veto over Congressional legislation as part of the lawmaking process, with the expectation, the book argues, that judges would engage in judicial review of legislation (including by implication Congressional legislation) as part of their normal judicial duties. And the Convention proceeded to write this "legalistic view of the constitution"[29] into the texts of the Supremacy and Judicial Power clauses.

These decisions represented the pivotal moment when judicial review became a permanent, defining feature of the American constitutional system. Under the Supremacy Clause, state judges were explicitly obligated to engage in judicial review, whenever they were confronted with an irreconcilable conflict between Federal and state law. Crucially, this clause also made the Constitution the (supreme) "law" of the land. But the Convention went further. It expanded the Federal judicial power so that it expressly extended to all "Cases arising under this Constitution." There could, thereafter, be no question that Federal judges had jurisdiction to treat the Constitution as the supreme law in the cases that came before them. Although the new Constitution refrained from explicitly saying that Federal judges possessed the authority to engage in the judicial review of acts of Congress, it expressly included all the premises that were necessary to make that argument. By writing "the legalistic view of the constitution" into the text, the Convention secured the conceptual foundations of judicial review for the future. At the same time, these decisions represented a significant defeat for traditional constitutionalism. After the Constitution had been ratified, and a Federal judiciary had been created, it was unlikely that the clock could ever be turned back again to a time before judges enjoyed such a power, despite the stiff opposition judicial review continued to encounter for many decades to come.

The Convention and its aftermath, however, were also crucial in a second respect. In mounting a defense of the new constitution, Alexander Hamilton generated and published a full-dress theoretical justification for judicial review. In his Federalist essays on the judiciary, the ever fertile genius of Hamilton distilled a synthetic, general theory of judicial review out of the arguments and ideas circulating in the legal community, in the states, and at the Convention, which encompassed both "vertical" review, in which judges would hold that "inferior" state laws must give way before the "superior" law of the Federal government, and "horizontal" review, in which judges would hold that the acts of their own legislatures must give way before the "supreme" law in their constitutions. Hamilton's essays elaborated a unified logic upon which the practice would thereafter primarily rely, as it came to be more widely disseminated, and as it withstood repeated assaults on its legitimacy.

[29] This is Edward Corwin's term, see Edward Corwin, "Marbury v. Madison and the Doctrine of Judicial Review" (1914) 12 *Michigan Law Review* 538, 565.

The Constitution itself had made judicial review a key feature of the Federal system. Once a Federal judiciary had been established, these judges were in a position to declare state laws unconstitutional with relative political impunity. The bar and bench, where the logic of the new practice was well established, were able to carry the doctrine to more and more states. And state judges, in turn thereafter, were able to look to the Federal example, and to other states, for further inspiration. By the early 1790s, judicial review had established ideological and institutional roots that were deep and strong enough to resist every effort to extirpate the new practice.

Down to the Federal Convention, there had been roughly half a dozen cases in which lawyers had challenged statutes as unconstitutional, and in at least four of them, judges had responded favorably.[30] But during the decade or so following the Convention, the number of judicial review cases in Federal and state courts multiplied more than fivefold.[31] And the practice spread steadily in the states, even in the face of substantial opposition. It was during these years that judicial review became a permanent, defining feature of the American constitutional system, a result in no small measure of the conservative constitutional counterrevolution the Federal Convention had succeeded in carrying out.

[30] *Rutgers* v. *Waddington* has not been included in this number. James Duane, who wrote the Mayor's Court opinion in the case, purported not to be engaging in judicial review; for more details, see Chapter 6.

[31] See William Michael Treanor, "Judicial Review Before Marbury" (2005) 58 *Stanford Law Review* 455, 457–58.

PART ONE

LEGISLATURES AND LEGISLATION UNDER THE FIRST AMERICAN CONSTITUTIONS

1

The Largely "Legislative" Character of the ("Horizontal" and "Vertical") Constitutional Checks Placed on Colonial Legislatures

1.1 THE STRUCTURE OF COLONIAL GOVERNMENTS

American colonial governments, which were established over the course of the seventeenth and early eighteenth centuries, took, as is well known, one of three basic forms. They were organized either as royal, proprietary, or corporate colonies. By the middle of the eighteenth century, the majority of colonies (eight of the thirteen) had been taken under the direct rule of the British Monarch. Three colonies remained proprietorships, Maryland, Pennsylvania, and Delaware, which "until the Revolution ... had [a separate legislature but] the same governor as Pennsylvania."[1] Only two, Connecticut and Rhode Island, retained their status as corporate colonies.

Two features of the eleven royal and proprietary governments, under which most Americans then lived, are of particular importance for this book. The first being that in both types of governments popular elections were limited to the selection of members of a single house of the legislature, the lower house.[2] Decisions about who would serve as governor of the colony and who would sit as a member of the upper house of the legislature (the Council) lay not with the inhabitants of the colony but with the governor and monarch or the proprietor.[3] Both governors and councillors received their appointments from and served at the pleasure of

1 Richard Hofstadter, William Miller and Daniel Aaron, *The American Republic: Volume One to 1865* (Englewood Cliffs New Jersey, Prentice Hall, Inc., c. 1959), 57.

2 Pennsylvania and Delaware had unicameral legislatures, which were popularly elected, see Jackson Turner Main, *The Upper House in Revolutionary America, 1763–1788* (Madison, Wisc., The University of Wisconsin Press, 1967), 96.

3 Except in Massachusetts where members of the upper house of the legislature were selected by the lower house and by outgoing members of the upper house, subject to the governor's veto, ibid., 68.

the king or the proprietor.[4] Although the subject is complicated,[5] councillors were often chosen from among a colony's elites, with an eye toward securing support for the colonial government from the colony's leading persons and as a counterweight to the lower houses, which were sometimes referred to as the "democratical" part of these governments.[6] In royal colonies, governors were instructed to nominate men to the Council who were "of good life, well affected to our government, of good estates and abilities, and not necessitous people."[7] In these colonies, the crown also appointed the judges, who like governors and members of the Council ordinarily served at pleasure. In this world, governors, legislatures, and judges all exercised a mix of capacities, judicial, legislative, and executive. Modern separation of powers ideas and practices were still at a formative stage. And so, in royal colonies, governors together with the upper house of the legislature normally sat as provincial courts of final resort in civil matters, often called Courts of Error.

The second noteworthy feature of royal and proprietary governments was that bills passed by the popularly elected legislative representatives of the people of the colony were subject, in colonies with bicameral legislatures, to a double "veto" wielded first typically by the unelected Council and then by the governor. Both governors and Councils exercised their "vetoes" as part of their role in lawmaking. Like the English monarch, governors were considered to be a third branch of the legislature, and the express assent of all three branches was required in order to confer the force of law on a bill.[8]

It was not coincidental that these "horizontal" constitutional constraints on popular assemblies were incorporated into the lawmaking

4 "[I]n practice," according to Jackson Turner Main, "[councillors] usually enjoyed tenure for life," ibid., 4.

5 Ibid., 3–4.

6 See Daniel Hulsebosch, *Constituting Empire: New York and the Transformation of Constitutionalism in the Atlantic World, 1664–1830* (Chapel Hill, N.C., The University of North Carolina Press, 2005), 72.

7 Leonard Labaree, *Royal Government in America: A Study of the British Colonial System before 1783* (New Haven, Ct., Yale University Press, 1930), 136.

8 When Joseph H. Smith, a delegate to New York's Provincial Constitutional Convention, which was drafting the state's first constitution, proposed to give New York State's new governor "a negative upon all laws passed by the Senate and Assembly," he thought it necessary to add "the Governor ... as a third branch of the Legislature." *Journals of the Provincial Congress, Provincial Convention, Committee of Safety and Council of Safety of the State of New York, 1775–1776–1777* (Albany, N.Y., Printed by Thurlow Weed, Printer to the State, 1842), I, 834. In many colonies, governors were also vested with judicial authority, sitting as Chancellor or as a member of the Court of Errors.

process. It was commonly understood that legislatures operated under the duty to deliberate upon and determine that proposed laws both promoted, or at least would not be detrimental to, the welfare of the polity (including the wider empire) and did not violate constitutional restrictions. Definitive judgments about constitutionality, in the eighteenth-century Anglo-American system, were to be made by legislatures (explicitly or implicitly) during the lawmaking process. In the case of colonial legislatures, these determinations were subject to further "vertical" review and reversal by the King's Privy Council, acting (almost always) in its "legislative" capacity. The imperial review process is described in greater detail later in the chapter.

For all the considerable differences among them, these American governments took their basic form from that of the British. The monarch was of course an unelected hereditary ruler who served as a third branch of the legislature;[9] the British Parliament consisted of two houses, of which only the lower house was popularly elected. The upper house of the British legislature, the hereditary House of Lords, also sat as the court of final resort in the realm. American governments were often thought to imperfectly mirror this "mixed" constitution of Britain, which combined elements of monarchical, aristocratic, and democratic government, maintaining a balance that was commonly viewed as keeping in check the natural evils that had long been associated with each type of government alone.[10]

In a number of colonies, over the course of the eighteenth century, constitutional clashes broke out between governors and the popularly elected lower legislative houses. Less often, the lower houses engaged in struggles with the colony's upper house, the Council.[11] But in more colonies, the most sustained and intense conflicts were those that erupted with governors. Many Americans viewed these battles between their legislatures and governors as a reprise of the long constitutional struggle that had taken place in England between Parliament and the English kings. English and American Whigs believed that in this long battle Parliament had steadfastly opposed the evils of excessive executive

[9] In his *Lectures on Law* delivered in 1790–1, James Wilson noted that in Britain, "the legislature consists of three branches, the king, the lords and the commons." Robert G. McCloskey (ed.), *The Works of James Wilson* (Cambridge, Mass., Harvard University Press, 1967), I, 312.

[10] Gordon Wood, *The Creation of the American Republic, 1776–1787* (Chapel Hill, N.C., The University of North Carolina Press, 1969), 18–20.

[11] Main, The Upper House in Revolutionary America, 5.

power and defended the liberties of the people. At a fundamental level, mid-eighteenth-century Anglo-American constitutional politics was still framed as a conflict between magistrates (monarchs or governors), on one side, and the people's (legislative) representatives, on the other. Not only did the gubernatorial "veto" in royal and proprietary colonies create a frustrating practical situation in which, at times, the people of the colony were prevented from enacting through their representatives the laws by which they wished to govern themselves. The continued existence of the "veto" was also understood to be of wider constitutional significance. Parliament had emerged from its battles with the English monarch having placed firm limits on the crown's power. After 1707 no British monarch ever refused assent to a bill that had been passed by the houses of Parliament. Increasingly, over the course of the eighteenth century, the two houses of Parliament came to be viewed as a sovereign legislature, essentially unchecked by the monarch. But colonial governors continued to wield an absolute "veto" over bills coming out of their legislatures. Over the decades leading up to the Revolution, many Americans developed a deep antipathy toward what they viewed as the excesses of gubernatorial power, and a strong desire to reduce it, among other ways, by eliminating the gubernatorial "veto."

For imperial officials and some Americans these clashes between governors and lower legislative houses were sometimes viewed as disordering the fine balance in these governments. Often, they attributed the problem to the dogged pursuit of greater power by popular assemblies. In a number of colonies, governors and Councils were effective in restraining the power of lower legislative houses.[12] But in other colonies, lower houses aggressively sought to expand their authority and often succeeded. Governors depended on the lower houses for payment of their salaries and expenses, and these bodies used this leverage to rein in their chief magistrates. As a result, in a number of colonies, governors, at times, felt compelled to give their assent to objectionable but especially popular bills that came to them from the legislature. In 1744–5, Cadwallader Colden, then an adviser to New York's royal governor George Clinton, wrote in a report prepared for Clinton that the actions of New York's lower house, the Assembly, placed at risk the "proper Balance between the Monarchical Aristocraticall & Democratical forms of Government."[13] Governor Clinton was "without force, without

[12] See ibid., for an excellent colony by colony description of the social composition and various political postures of the colonial Councils.

[13] Colden, "Observations on the Balance of Power in Government," [1744–45], *NYHS Coll.* (1935), 251, 253, quoted in Hulsebosch, Constituting Empire, 72.

money (which he can only obtain of an Assembly), without Friends or any Natural Interest."[14] Daniel Hulsebosch has written of this situation that

> [m]ost troubling, Colden believed, was the absence of the aristocratic element. The Council, on which he served for fifty years, was too weak to help counter the popular forces associated with the Assembly. He lamented the mistreatment of the councilors and other faithful crown servants, and he sought ways to insulate them from provincial harassment.[15]

If the actual power of governors was often less than their formal power, and if unelected Councils did not always operate to counterbalance lower houses as imperial officials hoped they would, still, when Americans had the opportunity to newly fashion their governments following Independence, the changes they made reflected their antagonism toward these features of their colonial regimes. In their new constitutions, they greatly reduced the powers of their governors. In most states, governors were stripped entirely of the authority to "veto" laws enacted by the houses of the legislature, in two states they were granted a limited "veto" that could be reversed by a super-majority vote of the legislature.[16] These new republican frames of government represented, for the time, sweeping change. The democratic principle of popular election was extended in nearly every state to the upper house of the legislature.[17] Legislatures could now more truly be considered the representatives of the people than at any time. But as a result of their colonial experiences, and their basic constitutional assumptions, the distrust of governors continued to run deep, and in the first years following Independence, most of the new constitutions did not even accord governors the dignity of popular election. They were reduced to being creatures of the legislature, appointed to their office by a vote of that body, in what

[14] Ibid. [15] Ibid.

[16] South Carolina retained a gubernatorial "veto" in its temporary 1776 constitution, which was eliminated just two years later in its constitution of 1778. Of the original permanent constitutions adopted down to 1780, only New York (1777) and Massachusetts (1780) gave "vetoes" of any kind to bodies outside the two houses of the legislature, and in both states these "vetoes" were reversible by a supermajority vote of the legislature. Chapter 2 discusses these provisions in greater detail.

[17] Under the first constitutions of Massachusetts, New Hampshire and South Carolina, members of the upper house were not popular elected but chosen by the popularly elected lower house. This arrangement was changed to popular election of the upper house within a few years, South Carolina (1778), Massachusetts (1780) and New Hampshire (1784).

can perhaps be seen as the ultimate triumph (for the moment) of popular assemblies in their long struggles with governors.[18]

These changes created significantly more democratic constitutions in which legislatures were given the plenary power to make laws on behalf of the people, unchecked by another branch of government. Under these first constitutions, American legislatures would be both considerably more democratic and substantially less constrained than they had been. A system replete with "vetoes" over legislation would be replaced by one in which, in many cases, there were none. In one respect, these developments were even more radical than the emergence of Parliamentary sovereignty in Britain, for in Britain, the hereditary House of Lords still stood as a bulwark against the popularly elected House of Commons.[19]

The first state constitutions brought governments in the rest of the country into broad conformity with the type of government the two corporate colonies, Connecticut and Rhode Island, had long enjoyed. In these colonies, both houses of the legislature had been popularly elected, as had the governor, from whom the power to "veto" laws had been withheld.[20] Following Independence, legislatures in Connecticut and Rhode Island, evidently satisfied with their existing frames of government, simply readopted their colonial charters.

Even during the early years following Independence, however, some Americans found these developments to be more than a little disquieting. Many conservative Whigs believed that they unhinged the fine balance of government by giving excessive power to the popular element. When these men thought about what could be done, they looked back to the example of their colonial constitutions for ideas about how to impose checks upon the largely unfettered power the first state constitutions had conferred on popularly elected legislatures. As attitudes toward these popularly elected legislatures grew less favorable during the early 1780s, more Americans

[18] Except in the two corporate colonies, and in Pennsylvania and New York, where the chief executives were popularly elected.

[19] To be certain, most members of the British lower house during this period were only "common" in so far as they were not generally members of the nobility. The overwhelming majority were large landowners drawn from the gentry sitting just below the landed aristocracy. The Commons was elected under a highly restrictive suffrage that gave perhaps only 20 percent of English men the right to vote for members of Parliament.

[20] In Connecticut, the governor also sat as a member of the upper house of the legislature where he was entitled to break ties by casting an additional vote when necessary, see Zephaniah Swift, *A System of the Laws of the State of Connecticut: In Six Books* (Windham, Ct., 1795, repr. Arno Press, 1972) I, 59–63.

began to look more approvingly on such efforts. Chapter 2 takes up the story of the first constitutions in greater detail.

If the distaste most Americans initially seem to have felt toward "vetoes" over the enactments of their legislatures can be traced in part to the role colonial governors had played in their governments, undoubtedly these sentiments also found their source in the further imperial review to which colonial laws had been subjected. But as with the "vetoes" of governors, from the beginning, some Americans saw in these imperial review procedures a prudential check that might serve to rein in the passions to which popularly elected legislatures seemed at times prone, and that they hoped might be re-established in their new governments in some acceptably modified domestic form.

1.2 PRIVY COUNCIL "LEGISLATIVE" REVIEW OF COLONIAL STATUTES

The broad contours of the system under which the legislative enactments of the American colonies came to be reviewed by the King-in-Council emerged over the course of the last quarter of the seventeenth century and the first decades of the eighteenth. Colonies were considered to be part of the king's demesnes, "his possessions, which, through indulgence of a fiction, he was deemed to hold by right of conquest .... [T]he whole apparatus of imperial administration was set up and elaborated on this premise."[21] In the charters of proprietary and corporate colonies, and in provisions in the governors' commissions in royal colonies, the king conveyed the authority to make laws. Most of these charter and commission grants contained one version or another of the restriction that colony laws must not be "contrary [or] repugnant" to the laws of England but should be "as near as may be, agreeable" to the laws of the realm "considering the nature and constitution of the place and people there."[22] These formulas left considerable room for colonial legislatures and the Privy Council to engage in broad, flexible evaluations directed at determining whether, because of the distinctive social and economic conditions in a colony, the welfare of that colony and the welfare of the

[21] Julius Goebel, Jr., *History of the Supreme Court of the United States I: Antecedents and Beginnings to 1801* (New York, Macmillan, 1971), 36.

[22] From the Rhode Island Charter of 1663, quoted in Mary S. Bilder, *The Transatlantic Constitution: Colonial Legal Culture and the Empire* (Cambridge, Mass., Harvard University Press, 2004), 41; see also Goebel, Antecedents and Beginnings, 3.

empire would be served by allowing a divergence from English law.[23] These kinds of considerations were integral to many Privy Council decisions about whether a statute actually violated the constitutional "repugnance" restriction.[24]

It took a number of years to settle the question whether the king's assent was required *before* a colony bill could become law, but in 1677, "[t]he Crown relinquished the claim to the formula 'Be it enacted by the King's Most Excellent Majesty by and with the consent of the General Assembly' and permitted the prevalent colonial 'Be it enacted by the Governor, Council and assembly.' The plantation enactment thus was not to be the act of the King [and consequently] in English eyes stood on no more stately footing than the act of any inferior jurisdiction in England."[25] Thereafter, in practice (even if the theory remained somewhat ambiguous) colonial bills gained the force of law when passed by the legislature and assented to by the governor of the colony. Confirmation by the king was not a necessary step in the lawmaking process. The king's Privy Council review, consequently, primarily involved the question of whether colonial laws should remain in force.

In a number of charters, the king had explicitly required colonies to transmit their statutes to his Privy Council for "approbation or disallowance."[26] In royal colonies this requirement was included in the governors' commissions. By the middle of the eighteenth century, all the colonies, except Connecticut and Rhode Island, were obliged to send copies of their statutes to England for review.[27] Statutes also came to the Council as the result of petitions for review brought by interested parties.[28] After its establishment in 1696, the Board of

[23] On the "interpretive flexibility of early written constitutionalism," see Mary S. Bilder, "Charter Constitutionalism: The Myth of Edward Coke and the Virginia Charter" (2016) 94 *North Carolina Law Review* 1545, 1590.

[24] Bilder, Transatlantic Constitution, 40–46; and Elmer Beecher Russell, *The Review of American Colonial Legislation by the King in Council* (New York, Columbia University, 1915), 139.

[25] Goebel, Antecedents and Beginnings, 66.

[26] Bilder, Transatlantic Constitution, 54–57; Goebel, Antecedents and Beginnings, 65–66; for a number of years there remained ambiguity about whether the king's "approbation" in his Privy Council served to pass a colony act into law or merely to confirm it. "In any event, so many acts, even in royal provinces, were operative as law without the royal pleasure ever being signified that we must conclude that whatever the theory, the Crown was practically not an indispensable party," 68.

[27] Bilder, Transatlantic Constitution, 56–57; Russell, Review of American Colonial Legislation, 20–22, 31–34, 36–37, 97–103.

[28] Russell, Review of American Colonial Legislation, 50–51.

Trade, upon which was placed the responsibility to advise the Council, performed the initial evaluation of statutes and issued a recommendation as to what the statute's fate should be. To arrive at these opinions the Board conducted extensive deliberations, which involved procuring the advice of the Board's counsel, or law officers of the Crown, and holding hearings at which colony agents and other parties presented their arguments about the validity, benefits or dangers of a statute.[29]

In cases in which individuals or groups of petitioners sought to have the Council disallow a statute (or declare it null and void *ab initio*), hearings became increasingly "formal and elaborate, each side being represented not only by an agent, but also by a solicitor. Thus, to cite one example among many, when in 1725 the Board considered several acts of New York regarding the Indian trade, the hearings extended over several days and the agent for the province and a solicitor for the merchants each addressed their lordships at considerable length."[30] Recommendations of the Board were sent to the Lords Committee of the Privy Council, where an additional round of hearings might be held. In one case in which the Board had advised a disallowance of statutes, a party petitioned the Lords Committee to reconsider this recommendation and instead to declare the acts null and void in their original creation. In urging the Lords Committee to propose this course of action to the Council itself, the British Attorney General Pratt made a number of arguments, which were answered in turn by those of Alexander Wedderburn, speaking for the colony.[31] "[O]nly after a report from [the Lords Committee] to the Council itself and a vote there would [an] Order in Council issue."[32]

These Council deliberations were distinctively "legislative" in that they revisited a broad range of issues, which typically included considerations both of constitutionality and of policy.

> Board ... committee reports and orders in council ... show that under normal conditions each individual law was scrutinized not only for violations of the instructions ... but also with a view to its probable expediency for the colony

[29] Goebel, Antecedents and Beginnings, 66–67.

[30] Russell, Review of American Colonial Legislation, 51.

[31] An account of this case is presented in Joseph H. Smith, *Appeals to the Privy Council from the American Plantations* (New York, Columbia University Press, 1950), 612–14; the report of the arguments made before the Committee is derived from Lord Hardwicke's notes, ibid., 613 fn. 465.

[32] Goebel, Antecedents and Beginnings, 67.

and the Empire, possible injury to other colonies, and unseemly infringements upon rights to private property or individual liberty.[33]

If the vote in the Council went against an act, as a result of "legislative" review, the Council normally ordered the statute to be "disallowed." The formula contained in the governors' commissions indicates that upon disallowance a statute would "*thenceforward* cease determine and become utterly void."[34] Disallowance, in other words, operated as a repeal of the statute, rendering it void going forward but leaving intact rights that had attached under it while it had been in effect.[35] In a small number of cases, however, the Privy Council went further, issuing an Order in Council that declared a statue null and void *ab initio*, that is of absolutely no legal effect from the beginning. Coming after some interval of time in which the act had been in operation "[a] declaration of nullity was something close to catastrophic, for everything that might have been done under it was rendered nugatory."[36] Though the Board of Trade repeatedly recommended declarations of nullity, because of the serious consequences and the persuasive arguments colony agents often made, the Council only followed this advice in a handful of cases.[37]

As the king had reserved only the power to "*disallow*" acts in certain colonial charters and in the royal governors' commissions, the basis of the Council's authority to render *declarations of nullity* in its legislative proceedings was somewhat unclear, as was much else about Privy Council practice. Goebel speculates that the Council's authority may have been based either on the principle that there were "few restraints upon the King's power in his demesnes" or on a statute passed by the King-in-Parliament in 1696 declaring colonial acts to be null and void if they were repugnant to certain English laws, which the Council later interpreted very broadly as giving it the authority to nullify all acts repugnant "to the known laws and statutes of the Kingdom."[38] At times, because of the confusing, internally contradictory verbal formulas the Council sometimes used,[39] it was difficult even to say

33 Russell, Review of American Colonial Legislation, 109.

34 Goebel, Antecedents and Beginnings, 68.

35 Goebel comments that "[n]o wonder that the Crown strove to require suspending clauses . . . .," ibid.

36 Ibid., 69. 37 Ibid., 71.

38 Ibid., 69–71; and Smith, Appeals to the Privy Council, 523–32. Smith argues that the Council's power to nullify statutes in "legislative" proceedings derived solely from the 1696 Parliamentary statute, as broadly construed by the Council.

39 Goebel notes the ambiguous and internally contradictory formulas the Council sometimes used, Antecedents and Beginnings, 68–71 ("Even so, the formula is on its face

whether they had disallowed an act or declared it null and void. Joseph Smith, who studied the Council's work exhaustively, devoted a number of pages in his monumental history to an attempt to clarify whether, in several cases, the Council, had disallowed an act or had declared it null and void from its inception.[40] In the case of a 1706 Order in Council, for example, he concluded that "[a]s to whether this is a disallowance or a declaration of nullity, there is support for either view."[41] Smith made clear that eighteenth century contemporaries were as apt to be confused by the formulas the Council sometimes used as modern historians. He noted that in 1767 both of the ambiguous cases he has just discussed were regarded as declarations of nullity.[42]

In other respects, as well, the basis of Council action was often obscure. A number of lawyers were of the view that since the king had not explicitly required Connecticut and Rhode Island to submit their statutes for "approbation or disallowance" in his charters to them, the Council had no authority to review their laws "legislatively."[43] Yet under pressure from the British government both colonies had in fact submitted copies of their statutes to the Council on a number of occasions,[44] and the Council had in fact disallowed both a Connecticut law and a Rhode Island law upon "legislative" review earlier in the century.[45] Joseph Smith observed that Council practice was poorly theorized and discussions about it were often "clouded by confused conceptions."[46]

Privy Council "legislative" review had a significant impact on the conduct of American provincial governments. Some "8,563 acts [were] submitted [to the Board of Trade] by the continental colonies[,] 469 or 5.5% were disallowed or declared null and void by orders in council."[47]

ambiguous since it could stand as well for a declaration of nullity," 69; "where the formula used was highly ambiguous," 71).

40 Smith, Appeals to the Privy Council, 534–36.

41 Ibid., 534–35; after a long discussion, he decided that another Order issued in 1718 must have been a disallowance, ibid., 536.

42 Ibid., 535, 536. 43 Ibid., 549, 652.

44 Russell, Review of American Colonial Legislation, 103 and 103 fn. 1 ("But to the recurrent insistence of the government that they send home complete copies of their acts, [even Connecticut and Rhode Island] yielded a somewhat dilatory compliance.") ("Collections of Connecticut laws were transmitted in 1699, 1706, 1710, 1740 and 1752; of Rhode Island in 1699, 1700, 1710"); see also Bilder, Transatlantic Constitution, 58–59.

45 Smith, Appeals to the Privy Council, 549 fn. 121; Russell, Review of American Colonial Legislation, 103; and Goebel, Antecedents and Beginnings, 78.

46 Smith, Appeals to the Privy Council, 523.

47 Russell, Review of American Colonial Legislation, 221. Forrest McDonald reports the same numbers, *States' Rights and the Union, Imperium in Imperio, 1776–1876* (Lawrence, Kans., University of Kansas Press, 2000), 2. Russell goes on to say that

Perhaps as troubling, from the perspective of frustrated colonists, numerous colonial laws had been passed containing suspension clauses pending Privy Council approval and these and other statutes that had been submitted to the Board of Trade were simply not acted upon but were left in imperial limbo. It was Privy Council "legislative" review that Americans singled out to denounce in the Declaration of Independence.

There were certain subjects upon which American colonial legislatures repeatedly enacted laws that the Privy Council repeatedly intervened to disallow. One of these involved the jurisdiction of justices of the peace.[48] In England, JPs possessed the authority to hear cases that involved no more than forty shillings, £2. Reflecting, evidently, the desire of their constituents in many colonies for local, informal and inexpensive justice, colonial legislatures time and again passed statutes to increase the jurisdictional limit of the cases justices of the peace were authorized to hear. Justices' courts were local and often conducted by men with little or no legal training. Cases were ordinarily heard without observing common law formalities, and often without juries or lawyers. But these courts offered colonists, community based, inexpensive and speedy justice, of which they could avail themselves without having to travel great distances and without having to pay lawyers' fees.

In quite a few cases, the Privy Council reacted to these attempts to expand the scope of summary justice by disallowing a statute. In recommending that the Privy Council disallow a 1769 New Jersey statute that attempted to raise the jurisdictional limit of justices' courts to £10, the Board of Trade, for example, engaged in a not untypical judgment, which combined a repugnant to the laws of England analysis with a determination that the change would be damaging to the well-being of the colonial polity. The Board submitted that this type of law

> serves too often to favour the establishment of much petty Tyranny in men altogether unfit to be intrusted with such power, and that these Reasons have weighed so far with the Legislature of Great Britain, that this kind of Jurisdiction

"[b]y colonies the percentages of laws disallowed are: New Hampshire, 7.2 per cent.; Massachusetts, 2.8 per cent.; New York, 3.4 per cent.; New Jersey, 4.5 per cent.; Pennsylvania, 15.5 per cent.; Virginia, 4.3 per cent.; North Carolina, 8.8 per cent.; South Carolina, 4.9 per cent.; and Georgia, 9.4 per cent.," although he also concedes that "[n]umerous discrepancies preclude perfect exactitude, and the figures are only approximately correct," 221 and 221 fn. 2.

48 On summary justice see Russell, Review of Colonial Legislation, 165–67.

has been always given with caution, sometimes with reluctance, and never hitherto ... extended beyond the Sum of forty Shillings Sterling.[49]

Exercising its "legislative" judgment in constitutional matters, however, the Privy Council was, at times, prepared to allow some colonies to diverge from English law, based on its assessment of their local circumstances. New York, for example, was permitted to raise the jurisdictional limit on cases that mayors, justices of the peace and recorders could hear to £5 in local money. And the Council also allowed New Jersey to raise the jurisdictional threshold in its summary process courts to £5.[50] But should the Privy Council judge that a province had attempted to raise the jurisdictional amount too much or too quickly, it usually intervened to disallow it. When New York sought again to raise its limit, this time to £10, that act was disallowed.[51] "In like manner, New Jersey enjoyed for some years a five-pound limit, and attempted in vain to raise the amount to ten pounds."[52]

Privy Council dealings with these colonial laws are noteworthy because as it turns out, during the 1770s and 1780s a number of state legislatures took up where their colonial predecessors had left off, passing statutes to raise the jurisdictional limits of summary process courts. Only now the evaluation of the constitutionality of these statutes was (mainly) handled as a judicial, rather than as a legislative matter.[53] Of the roughly half dozen early American "judicial review" cases that arose down to 1787, two at least involved state courts declaring such statutes unconstitutional.[54]

This course of events looks very much like a continuation of the struggle between colonial legislatures and the Privy Council. The New Jersey case of *Holmes* v. *Walton*, decided in 1780, appears to be the first

[49] James Munro (ed.), *Acts of the Privy Council of England, Colonial Series* (London, His Majesty's Stationery Office, 1912), V, 310 (June 7, 1771).

[50] Russell, Review of Colonial Legislation, 165 fn. 1. [51] Ibid., 165–66.

[52] Ibid., 166 fn. 1.

[53] In 1782, New York's Council of Revision did deliberate upon one such case in the traditional way, as part of the lawmaking process, see Alfred B. Street, *The Council of Revision of the State of New York; and Its Vetoes* (Albany, N.Y., William Gould, Publisher, 1859), 241–42 ("An act to empower justices of the peace, mayors, recorders and aldermen to try causes to the value of ten Pounds").

[54] In particular, see *Holmes* v. *Walton* (N.J., 1780), and the New Hampshire £10 Act cases (1786–87). But several other of these early American "judicial review" cases also involved constitutional challenges to statutes that eliminated recourse to jury trials in other types of judicial proceeding, see *Trevett* v. *Weeden* (R.I., 1786) and *Bayard* v. *Singleton* (N.C., 1787). These cases are discussed in greater detail in later Chapters 8 and 9.

clear case in which an American court declared a state statute null and void on grounds that it was unconstitutional. The case involved a New Jersey act that had given justices of the peace authority to adjudicate disputes summarily in which personal property of great value was at stake. The statute did give parties the option to have the matter heard by a six-man jury before a single justice if more than £2 (40 shillings) was in controversy. The summary process the statute provided was nearly identical to that in a provincial New Jersey act that the Privy Council had disallowed in 1771, on the ground that it had sought to authorize the use of that process in the adjudication of disputes up to £10.[55] Whatever the judges in *Holmes* v. *Walton* may have thought about the grounds of their authority,[56] from a functional perspective, they were assuming a role that had been played (primarily) "legislatively" by the Privy Council under the previous government. Now, however, they were acting under a state constitution from which any express authority to "review" and "veto" the enactments of the state legislature were entirely absent.

1.3 PRIVY COUNCIL "JUDICIAL" REVIEW OF COLONIAL STATUTES

Although the Privy Council had lost its domestic judicial authority during the upheavals of the reign of Charles I,[57] it retained the authority to hear appeals from British colonies, and became, for all intents and purposes, the court of final resort for the empire. Litigants aggrieved by a decision of colonial courts, could if they met certain monetary and other requirements, appeal to the Privy Council, which sitting in its judicial capacity would decide whether to reverse or uphold the colonial court's judgment. It was not unusual at this time for a governmental body like the Council to exercise what we would today describe as both "legislative" and "judicial" powers. The House of Lords, after all, operated as both the upper house of the British legislature and the highest court in the land. In many

[55] Munro (ed.), Acts of the Privy Council of England, Colonial Series, V, 309–11 (June 7, 1771). The Privy Council also repeatedly intervened in its capacity as a "superior" legislature to disallow colonial paper currency laws, debtor relief legislation, legislation governing property rights, and acts vesting legislatures with authority to settle matters that "do constitutionally belong to courts of justice alone," Russell, Review of Colonial Legislation, 120–33, 152–56, quote at 191. These issues would also come to play a significant role in post-revolutionary American constitutional politics and law.

[56] The written record in the case is fragmentary; *Holmes* v. *Walton* is discussed in greater detail in Chapter 4.

[57] Goebel, Antecedents and Beginnings, 37; and Smith, Appeals to the Privy Council, 3.

American colonies, governors and the upper houses of colonial legislatures wielded both kinds of power as well.

After threshold legal issues were disposed of, appeals at the Privy Council were heard on their merits before the Lords Committee.[58] The Committee did not sit to hear appeals during defined terms as courts normally did but was scheduled for hearings by the Lord President of the Council, and hearings could be held during any month of the year.[59] Typically, two English barristers would appear for appellants and two for respondents. Each lawyer would ordinarily be entitled to make his main argument and to offer a rebuttal following opposing counsel's argument. At hearings, objections to the admissibility of evidence would be entertained and after discussion the Committee would rule on these. Oral arguments were usually devoted in part to the presentation of English precedents.[60]

Sitting in its judicial capacity, the Privy Council had heard appeals from colonial courts for quite a number of decades before, in February 1727/28 in the Connecticut case of *Winthrop* v. *Lechmere*, for the first and only time, the Council held a colonial statute null and void *ab initio* sitting in its judicial capacity.[61] In several other cases appellants asked the Council to strike down statutes, but in all of these, after considering the possibility, the Council decided against doing so.[62] *Winthrop* v. *Lechmere* introduced into Privy Council practice a new "judicial" procedure for controlling colonial legislation.[63]

It is commonly supposed that the basis of Privy Council action in *Winthrop* v. *Lechmere* was clear. Although Connecticut's charter contained no requirement that the colony submit its statutes to the Board of Trade and Council for approval or disallowance, it did contain the restriction on the legislature's lawmaking power that statutes must not be repugnant or contrary to the laws of England. When one of the parties in the case challenged the validity of Connecticut's partible inheritance statute, the Council undertook to determine whether the statute was valid in order to decide the controversy between the parties, which turned on the question whether the rule of partible inheritance was in effect at the time in Connecticut. In this case, the Council found the Connecticut partible inheritance statute to be repugnant to the English law of

[58] On the Council's appellate procedure see Goebel, Antecedents and Beginnings, 43–45.

[59] Smith, Appeals to the Privy Council, 289. [60] Ibid., 293–95. [61] Ibid., 537.

[62] Ibid., 562–77; Goebel, Antecedents and Beginnings, 76–79.

[63] Goebel, Antecedents and Beginnings, 76.

primogeniture and hence invalid. The adjudication, as adjudications generally do, necessarily involved a retroactive judgment about the state of the law at the time the controversy arose. Hence, if the Order in Council were to adjudge the statute invalid in order to decide the case, it would have to apply that decision retroactively by declaring it to have been void *ab initio*, i.e., without legal force from its inception, as it in fact did.

There were certainly clear differences in the way statutes reached the Privy Council in "legislative" as opposed to "judicial" proceedings, and key differences in the posture in which the Council examined statutes under the two types of proceedings. In "legislative" review, statutes reached the Council mainly as a result of having been submitted by a colony for "approval or disallowance." But statutes could also reach the Council, in this kind of proceeding, as a result of petitions from individuals or groups, who wished to see a colony statute they opposed, disallowed or nullified. And while, in "legislative" proceedings, the Council held hearings in which proponents and opponents of a statute made constitutional and policy arguments, they arrived at their opinion of the statute outside the context of a full-blown factual controversy. In "judicial" review, statutes came before the Council on appeal from the decision of a colonial court, and as part of a factual controversy that the parties had developed during a colonial adjudication.

For all their differences, however, there were certain inescapable similarities between Council "legislative" and "judicial" proceedings. As in the case of "legislative" review, hearings on appeal before the Lords Committee led not to a decision but to a report to the Council itself, "a mere tender of advice to the crown."[64] And after the full Council considered and voted upon the Lords Committee's report, their decision was embodied in an Order in Council, the same instrument employed to effectuate their decisions in "legislative" reviews. "There can be no doubt from the nature of the proceedings," Smith avers, "that we have to do with the exercise of a judicial function .... [But while] the judicial quality of conciliar proceedings is conceded ... we venture to suppose that no common lawyer would have called the Order in Council a judgment, even if emitted in a common law cause."[65] He acknowledges that the Council was "a body where because of the confusion of functions the range of policy making was broader than would have been tolerable

[64] Smith, Appeals to the Privy Council, 314–17.

[65] Ibid., 316. He believes that it more closely resembled a decree in chancery as an expression of the king's "pleasure in peremptory form."

in an agency confined to the settlement of issues presented solely by litigation."[66]

With only a single exception, every (constitutional) "repugnance" determination the Council made occurred in the course of a "legislative" review of colonial statutes. "In point of sheer bulk the process of legislative review completely overshadowed the Council's judicial business; moreover, the Board of Trade in 1760 termed conciliar judicial power of 'less importance and inferior dignity' to the legislative."[67] Because Orders in Council disallowing (repealing) colonial statutes (or in a few cases declaring them null and void) upon "legislative" review had been issued for decades before the sole order of nullity in the appeal in *Winthrop* v. *Lechmere* was handed down, and because "legislative" Orders in Council continued to be issued in great numbers thereafter, Americans who were not intimately acquainted with Privy Council practice often seemed to assume that the decision in the Connecticut intestacy case was actually a "legislative" rather than a "judicial" determination, which involved a disallowance rather than a decree of nullity.[68]

Connecticut Governor Talcott upon learning of the Privy Council decision in *Winthrop* v. *Lechmere*, for example, drafted an address to the King asking for reconsideration. His text reveals that he did not comprehend precisely what the Council had done and how. "'Youre Excelent Majesty in Counsill was pleased to declare that the law ... should be vacated, and that it was thereby *Repealled* and made Void .... [T]is humbly prayd it may not now be *disallowed*" after being in effect for so many decades[69] (emphasis added). In 1740, an agent for Connecticut, Francis Wilks, seems to have been equally confused. Wilks wrote Governor Talcott of the Council's decision that if Lechmere had argued the case properly "that law wou'd never have been *repealed*"[70] (emphasis added).

[66] Ibid., 655. [67] Ibid., 524 fn. 2. [68] Ibid., 577, 626.

[69] Talcott, 5 *Connecticut Historical Society Collection* (1896), 419, 420 quoted in Dudley Odell McGovney, "The British Origin of Judicial Review of Legislation" (1944) 93 *University of Pennsylvania Law Review* 1, at 17 fn. 40.

[70] McGovney, "British Origin of Judicial Review," 17 fn. 40, quoting a letter from Wilks, 5 *Connecticut Historical Society Collection* (1896), 330. There are other examples as well. "Despite his successful handling of the appeal in *Philips* v. *Savage*, it is startling to find [the distinguished solicitor Ferdinand John] Paris failing in his advice [in another case] to make any distinction between the ordinary disallowance of an act and a judicial declaration of voidness *ab initio* upon appeal," Smith, Appeals to the Privy Council, 572. A number of modern historians have seemed similarly confused, see Smith, Appeals to the Privy Council, 524 fn. 2. Although Julius Goebel thought absurd the idea that the order in *Winthrop* v. *Lechmere* could ever be taken to have been decided "legislatively" (Antecedents and Beginnings, 79) that is precisely what the distinguished scholar Edward

To be certain, a number of lawyers understood the differences between the two types of proceedings and began to make arguments in an effort to sharpen the distinction, perhaps going beyond what actual Privy Council practice would admit of. In a 1759 case, petitioners sought to have the Council declare a Virginia statute null and void *ab initio* upon "legislative" review. Alexander Wedderburn, arguing for the colony before the Lords Committee, maintained that "a declaration of nullity was not possible in the present proceeding. It was contended that the crown was here acting in a legislative capacity; that a declaration of nullity in such proceeding would bind nobody. The question of nullity was not to be tried in a summary way; but in a judicial proceeding in a court of appeals."[71] But Attorney General Pratt forcefully rejected that position. He "replied that surely the present body had as high authority to declare the act void as any court of judicature. The [Lords] Committee was reminded that it sat as a council of state to advise the King in *lawmaking*"[72] (emphasis added).

Although Smith contends that over time the Council increasingly was of the view that judicial proceedings were preferable if a statute was to be nullified, he notes that there was still "substantial opinion that an act could be declared null and void *ab initio* without judicial proceedings."[73]

S. Corwin seems to have believed. "[T]he Privy Council viewed its action in annulling the Connecticut [statute in the case of *Winthrop* v. *Lechmere*] as legislative rather than judicial . . . ." Edward S. Corwin, "The Establishment of Judicial Review, I" (1910) 9 *Michigan Law Review* 102, 103; see also Francis Fane, *Reports on the Laws of Connecticut* (Charles M. Andrews, ed., New Haven, Ct., Acorn Club, 1915), 18 (Fane reported that the Connecticut statute had been "disallowed by the Privy Council").

71 Smith, Appeals to the Privy Council, 613; see also 612 and 614 for an elaboration of this argument by James Abercromby, an agent for Virginia. Abercromby argued that even if the statute was repugnant "it did not ly within their Lordships Jurisdiction to declare it *ab initio* void, all that they could do was, if they saw good Cause, to represent it to his Majesty as *voidable*, nor could the King from the manner in which Mr. Camm had pursued his Remedy [by legislative review], go further than to *repeal* the Law . . . " (612) He went on to add that "the Grand Point in Argument was whether this Case, coming by way of Petition to the King in Council, in their Legislative or Ministerial Capacity could authorize their Lordships to determine in the first Instance what was, or what was not, Law. We argued that this could not be done otherwise than by a Judicial Appeal to their Lordships, and that then and not till then their Lordships sitting in Judgment as Judges, . . . could in the Kings Name, as Judges declare what was Law . . . ." (614) William Samuel Johnson, a Connecticut agent, made a similar argument in correspondence with the Earl of Hillsborough, who was then Secretary of State for the American Department, see Smith, Appeals to the Privy Council, 652.

72 Ibid., 613–14.

73 Ibid., 634–35. Goebel notes that "[t]he bias in favor of judicial proceedings if a question of voiding an act *ab initio* was posed may be laid to the indurated common law tradition that issues of such moment should be settled in true adversarial proceedings," Antecedents and Beginnings, 72.

In fact, the Council nullified statutes upon "legislative" review at least five times, but only once sitting in its judicial capacity.[74] Indeed, four of these five "legislative" declarations of nullity took place after 1761.[75] And Goebel points to an interesting aspect of the last three of these "legislative" declarations of nullity. He notes that in all three cases the Council used the term "*adjudge* and declare ... the said act to be void," employing the language of judgment to conclude a "legislative" review.[76] This is either an attempt by the Council "to cloak their action with the semblance of a judgment" as Goebel suggests,[77] or, just as likely, reflects the view that in both kinds of proceedings the King-in-Council was thought in fact to be delivering "judgments" upon what the law should be.

Philip Hamburger has recently reminded us that

> [i]n fact, all acts of Parliament ... were [considered] "judgments" of the court of Parliament .... In the early seventeenth century, Henry Finch explained: "The Parliament is a Court ... having an absolute power in all causes," whether "to make Lawes, to adjudge matters in Law, to trie causes of life and death," or "to reverse errors in the Kings Bench," and "*all their Decrees are as Judgments*."[78] (emphasis added)

"As many scholars have argued," Alison LaCroix notes, "the parsing of distinctions between such modern notions as judicial and legislative review and applying them retrospectively to seventeenth-and eighteenth-century legal proceedings is fraught with peril. Anglo-American jurists of the period did not recognize a firm distinction between adjudication and legislation .... Th[is] ambiguity endured in the American colonies. Consequently, to expect the legal forms of the period to conform neatly to modern taxonomies is to court anachronism."[79] The same can plausibly be said of the King-in-Council during the eighteenth century. Indeed, that the Council did upon "legislative" review occasionally declare statutes null and void *ab initio*, i.e., retroactively, served only to confuse further the distinction between its "judicial" and "legislative" capacities when it came to the review of statutes.

[74] Goebel, Antecedents and Beginnings, 70–72. [75] Ibid., 71–72. [76] Ibid., 71–72.

[77] Ibid., 72.

[78] Philip Hamburger, *Law and Judicial Duty* (Cambridge, Mass., Harvard University Press, 2008), 242.

[79] Alison LaCroix, *Ideological Origins of American Federalism* (Cambridge, Mass., Harvard University Press, 2010), 141; for a similar account of the lack of a clear binary distinction, see Paul D. Halliday, *Habeas Corpus: From England to Empire* (Cambridge, Mass., Harvard University Press, 2010), 20–21.

When the Council "disallowed" a colonial statute on the ground that it was "repugnant to the laws of England" following "legislative" review, it is clear enough that the Council was not rendering a "judgment" about the power of the colonial legislature to enact the law in the first place. The "disallowance" repealed the law prospectively, as the colonial legislature itself might have done if it had been persuaded of the statute's constitutional defects. Before the Privy Council intervened to repeal it, however, the statute would have possessed the full force of law. The Privy Council's act reflected the superior "legislative" authority of the Council, which empowered it to reconsider and reverse the "legislative" judgment of the "inferior" colonial assembly.[80] In the many proceedings that resulted in disallowance (repeal), the constitutional "repugnance" restriction would implicitly have been understood to be a "legislative/political" constraint on colonial legislatures, not a legal limitation on their powers.

Serious ambiguities about the nature of Privy Council review would naturally arise, however, when consideration was given to the cases in which the Council, upon "legislative" review, declared colonial statutes to be null and void, *ab initio*. Did this kind of decision represent a repugnancy judgment of an entirely different character, not a "legislative" judgment that a colonial statute should not have been enacted and was now being repealed retroactively, but a judgment in the nature of what may be termed a legal-judicial decision that a statute had never been law in the first place because by virtue of being repugnant to the laws of England was *ultra vires* under the terms of a charter or a governor's commission? What distinguished these two possible characterizations of Privy Council action in cases of retroactive voiding was that in the first the Council might well have been seen as acting to repeal an existing law retroactively, a "legislative" act. But in the second account, it might be viewed as simply declaring (finding) what the law was, arguably a "judicial" act. Were colonial statutes that were repugnant to the laws of England *ipso facto* void in themselves or only voidable by his Majesty?[81] Certainly, in the cases in which the Council voided colonial acts *ab initio* upon "legislative" review, it is not surprising that some plausibly seemed to think that the Council's determination was not essentially different from the repugnancy determination in which it normally engaged in other cases of "legislative" review. It merely involved a "legislative judgment"

[80] For numerous instances in which this happened see Russell, Review of American Colonial Legislation, 147–50.

[81] See Smith, Appeals to the Privy Council, 578.

that an existing law, being voidable, should be repealed, only in these cases retroactively.[82]

Inevitably, a similar ambiguity arose in connection with the Council's judgment in *Winthrop* v. *Lechmere* when the Council was sitting in a "judicial" capacity. Was its repugnancy determination in this case of an entirely different character than those in which it engaged when sitting "legislatively"? Some knowledgeable lawyers certainly seem to have believed that the Council's repugnance judgment in *Winthrop* v. *Lechmere* must have been in the nature of a legal-judicial judgment that the statute in question was simply not, and had never been, law, in that under its charter the Connecticut legislature had lacked the power to enact it. But other contemporaries seem to have been of the view that the judgments in all these cases of retroactive voiding were not essentially different from the judgments the Council normally delivered when they disallowed statutes upon "legislative" review. They were judgments that a legislative decision to enact a statute should be reversed, and that the existing law should be repealed retroactively. Privy Council practice, radically under theorized as it was, provided uncertain clarification of the issue, and perhaps no sharp distinction was in fact as yet commonly drawn between these two possibilities, because nothing of practical consequence turned on the distinction.[83] "As with so many other aspects of British constitutionalism," John Phillip Reid observes, "[perhaps] it was a question not only better left unanswered, but better left unasked."[84] When several colonial courts, however, began to claim the power to render judgments declaring statutes to be null and void, the question began to take on practical significance. Were such judgments properly "judicial" or were they "legislative" judgments that courts had absolutely no business engaging in?

[82] In the eighteenth century, legislatures did on occasion repeal laws retroactively. In 1704, for example, the Maryland legislature passed a statute that repealed an earlier 1699 one on the same subject, stating in the repealing clause of the 1704 act "That all acts of assembly [on the subject] made before [with certain exceptions] should be *null and void.*" In 1784, the Maryland General Court interpreted this language to mean that no rights could be claimed under the 1699 act because the legislature in effect had retroactively declared it to be null and void from its inception. See *Helms's Lessee* v. *Howard*, 2 Har. & McH. 57 (Md., 1784), 98. I wish to thank my colleague Matt Steilen for this reference.

[83] The Chief Justice of South Carolina, Benjamin Whitaker, sought clarification from the Board of Trade on precisely this issue early in 1743, apparently to no avail. The Board "appear to have done nothing to enlighten the chief justice" on the question, see Smith, Appeals to the Privy Council, 577–78.

[84] John Phillip Reid, *Constitutional History of the American Revolution: The Authority to Legislate* (Madison, Wisc., University of Wisconsin Press, 1991), 94.

These ambiguities about the nature of review of legislation persisted in America after Independence and became a factor both in bringing the American practice of judicial review into being and in efforts to halt its development by calling into question its lawfulness as an unauthorized exercise of the lawmaking power by judges.

Julius Goebel, Jr. and Joseph Smith agree that the origins of Privy Council "judicial review" can be traced back to domestic English judicial policies.

> The judicial doctrine that local law must conform to the common law was developed by the courts with reference to so-called local customs as well as by-laws, and represents a phase of their effort to reduce the law of the realm to uniformity .... The applicability of these conceptions to the plantations was facilitated by the circumstance that the corporate form had been employed in the case of early settlements .... Since the patents to proprietors in various particulars, including the limitation upon legislation, were substantially identical [to those imposed on domestic corporations], the extension of these precedents was no great *tour de force*, especially since the courts had executed with regard to private franchises identical rules respecting by-laws made at a court leet.[85]

This judicial doctrine rested on the idea that the king's courts exercised a supervisory enforcement authority over "inferior jurisdictions,"[86] both those within England and those abroad, to ensure that the acts of those jurisdictions conformed to the laws England. The doctrine and practice of English "judicial review" relied heavily on the idea that a superior jurisdiction (and its courts) enjoyed the authority to nullify the nonconforming laws enacted by the limited and dependent jurisdictions that were subordinate to it.

What English judges never did do, despite the dictum in *Bonham's Case* and in a few other opinions, was to declare an act of Parliament *null and void* upon judicial review.[87] Common law tradition had long barred English judges from doing so.[88]

Parliament, of course, did not exercise its lawmaking authority as a limited, dependent, "inferior" body and, under traditional English constitutional principles, had the common law courts assumed the power to nullify its acts, they would necessarily have been claiming an authority "superior" to Parliament's, a result that practically no

[85] Smith, Appeals to the Privy Council, 525–26; Professor Mary Bilder has filled in the picture of just how well established this English judicial doctrine was, see "The Corporate Origins of Judicial Review" (2006) 116 *Yale Law Journal*, 101.

[86] The term is Smith's, Appeals to the Privy Council, 527. [87] Ibid., 570–71.

[88] Hamburger, Law and Judicial Duty, 237.

one considered to be constitutionally acceptable, as it would have given judges, rather than Parliament, the final word on the making of the laws.[89] Another way of putting the matter is to say that while the English had a rich tradition of "vertical," "legislative" and "judicial" review, they did not possess a settled practice or doctrine of what may be called "horizontal judicial review." But it was precisely this type of constitutionally controversial "judicial review" that American state court judges and lawyers began to bring into being during the 1780s.

In one colony, however, ordinary "judicial" courts attempted, intermittently over many years, to call into question the validity of the colony's legislative enactments. Eventually, these efforts to establish judicial review by the ordinary courts in a colonial government failed. But the debate that grew out of their attempts reveals a good deal not only about the underlying ideas upon which judges could draw, even at that time, to justify such a practice, but also about the dominant assumptions of English constitutionalism that worked against this form of judicial review. To a remarkable extent, this earlier ideological and political contest would be played out again during the 1780s, with the opposite result.

1.4 THE COLONIAL DETERMINATION THAT ORDINARY JUDICIAL COURTS LACK THE AUTHORITY TO REVIEW THE ENACTMENTS OF THEIR LEGISLATURES

Historians have discovered only an occasional instance here and there in which an American colonial court refused to enforce or attempted to nullify a colonial statute, and no firm conclusions can be drawn from these isolated incidents. But in South Carolina, historians have uncovered evidence of an intermittent, decades-long conflict between the legislature and the courts over the proper constitutional relationship between the two. Beginning with an incident in 1693 under the proprietary government, South Carolina judges appear to have begun to question, from time to time, the validity of legislative acts; the legislature, especially the lower Commons House, responded forcefully to these challenges, in each instance by asserting its preeminence in the colonial government, arguing that ordinary courts simply did not possess the authority they were

[89] William Blackstone, *Commentaries on the Laws of England* (Chicago, University of Chicago Press, 1979, reprint of 1765 ed.), Book I, Section 3, 91.

attempting to claim. This was a battle of constitutional ideas as well as a political struggle, where the legislature seems to have relied on prevailing English constitutional ideas about the proper relationship between Parliament and the courts to vindicate its position by analogy.

Although the two opposing constitutional positions were not fully developed in this series of confrontations, in the end, two South Carolina Chief Justices repudiated the ideas that other lawyers and judges had advanced to justify review of legislation by ordinary courts, and recognized the legislature's preeminent authority to deliver judgments about the constitutionality of laws within the colony's government. This form of judicial review by ordinary courts of the colony, a controversial new practice, was not likely to become an established feature of these governments without the broad and steadfast support of the bench and bar. The rejection by two Chief Justices of the colony of the principal ideas upon which it rested marked its death knell in South Carolina. Thereafter, more traditional British constitutional ideas would be taken definitively to govern the relationship between courts and the legislature in South Carolina's colonial government. In the process, an alternative set of ideas that would have given judges of ordinary colonial courts authority to declare statutes null and void was rejected.

The constitutional confrontations between South Carolina's legislature and courts, of course, involved more than internecine struggles between branches of the colonial government; they were overlaid by an imperial dimension, clashes between the colonial legislature and the proprietors of the colony in one instance, and – after 1721 when South Carolina became a royal colony – between the popularly elected lower house of the legislature and the monarch's appointee, the Chief Justice of the colony. Although the larger context was somewhat different, there are striking similarities between the conflicts in colonial South Carolina and those that would arise during the 1780s between state legislatures and courts, when the latter began to claim the authority to judge the validity of state statutes. A number of the key arguments and ideas found in the South Carolina controversies reappeared in these subsequent conflicts. Only the outcome then would be different; in the 1780s the judges and the ideas that justified their actions would prevail, and in the process supplant traditional Anglo-American conceptions about the proper relationship between legislatures and courts with a set of ideas that marked a constitutional revolution. But that was not the result in eighteenth-century colonial South Carolina, where traditional constitutional ideas continued, in the end, to govern that relationship. A particular understanding of the specific character of the written constitutional limitations that had been imposed on colonial legislatures, one that broadly resonated with the dominant British view of the nature of the constitutional constraints that operated on Parliament, played a pivotal role in this outcome.

In 1693, the General Assembly of the colony, in a statement of its grievances addressed to the proprietors, complained of "Inferior Courts takeing upon them to try adjudge & Determine the power of assembly for ye Validity of Acts made by them or of such matters and things as are acted by or Relateing to ye House of Commons all which we humbly Conceive is only inquireable into and Determinable by ye Next Succeeding General Assembly."[90]

It is evident from this brief entry that the colony's General Assembly believed the proprietors' courts had overstepped their bounds by judging the validity of the Assembly's acts, which, they asserted, were matters proper only for the Assembly itself to consider and decide upon. One interpretation of the brief text is that the Assembly was styling itself a court "superior" to all others in the colony, and, as such, "Inferior Courts" had no authority to question its judgments. This would not have been an absurd claim at the time: not only was Parliament viewed as a high court, but colonial legislatures of the time sometimes operated as courts of final resort.[91] Nothing more, however, is known about this incident.

But a number of decades later, in August 1724, the General Court of South Carolina, sitting in Charlestown, apparently ignored an Assembly statute in ruling on a motion in a case.[92] It is not known why it took more than two years for the legislature to respond, but in December 1726 the Commons House of the General Assembly voted "that the opinion of the Generall Court in Charles Town of the 22nd of August One thousand

[90] Edward McCrady, *History of South Carolina under the Proprietary Government, 1670–1719* (New York, The Macmillan Co., 1897), 242.

[91] See, for example, Scott Douglas Gerber, *A Distinct Judicial Power: The Origins of an Independent Judiciary, 1606–1787* (Oxford, Oxford University Press, 2011), 50 ("The general Assembly [of Virginia] served until 1682/3 as the highest court in the colony.... The assembly ceased serving as a judicial body in 1682/3 [as the result of an] order of the crown."); 71 (Plymouth Colony); 76 (Massachusetts Bay Colony); Swift, A System of the Laws of Connecticut I, 93 (the general assembly of Connecticut served as the court of final resort in that colony and state until 1784 when it was replaced by a court consisting of the governor and the upper house of the legislature); see also Smith, Appeals to the Privy Council, 637–51; Wood, Creation of the American Republic, 154–56.

[92] McGovney, British Origin of Judicial Review, 48–49.

Seven hundred & twenty four was *contrary & repugnant* to a clause in an Act of the Generall Assembly of this Province"[93] (emphasis added). The Chief Justice of the colony, who sat on the General Court, was also a member of the Commons, and submitted to that chamber a representation, also signed by two assistant judges, justifying their action. Upon reading this representation a committee of the Commons reported that the judges had taken "several Positions of a dangerous Tendency to this Province, as first the whole Government is arraigned for passing Laws as 'tis suggested contrary to the Kings Instructions and Repugnant to the Laws of England. Secondly, the Judges Suggest they have a power of *dispensing with all such Laws at pleasure* & that they are Sole Judges & Interpreters of our Laws which *your Committee are of opinion is assuming a power Superior to that of this house & equal with that of the whole Legislative body united.*"[94] (emphasis added).

The Commons committee appears to have been suggesting that the judges were claiming a power to unmake or repeal laws that would in effect equal the authority of the whole legislature together, and since no single chamber acting alone could repeal a law, the court would, in effect, possess power "superior" to that of either legislative chamber. At the same time, the committee implied that in taking such action, the judges were improperly exercising the lawmaking power.

The judges for their part seem to have been attempting to create a practice of judicial review on the basis of the written constitutional limitations that had been imposed on South Carolina legislatures. Both the original Carolina charter and later, the royal governor's commission, contained versions of the requirement that the colony's laws must not be repugnant or contrary to the laws of England. The judges seem to have taken the position that a colony statute passed contrary to these provisions would be *ultra vires*, beyond the granted power of the legislature to enact, and hence void, i.e., not law at all. But the judges could not have taken this position unless they also thought that the authority to engage in repugnancy determinations was not the legislature's and the King's alone, that the duty of ordinary colonial judges to "interpret the law" extended to consideration of the terms of the king's charter and his commission to his governor, and authorized them to make determinations as to whether an ordinary law passed by their own legislature was or was not repugnant to the terms of these foundational political-legal documents.

[93] Ibid., 10. [94] Ibid., 10–11.

The Commons' view, not surprisingly, was quite different. Their resolution denounced the court's action as "contrary & repugnant to a clause in an Act of the Generall Assembly of this Province."[95] The use of this language suggests that the Commons wished to make the point that the relevant standard of repugnancy with which the courts of the colony should be concerned was the one established by the colony's own laws, since the judges were bound to apply these as written. This is all that has been found about this incident, but it is hardly the end of the larger story.

Following a decade-long transition to royal government during the 1720s, the crown authorized South Carolina's governor to commission Robert Wright the Chief Justice of the colony. What followed were years of conflict between the Chief Justice and the legislature. During the early 1730s the Commons House of the Assembly committed several men into their custody for wrongs they were alleged to have committed. The men sued out a writ of *habeas corpus*, which Chief Justice Wright granted. "On the 7th of April, 1733, the House [in response] passed a series of resolutions, in which they declared that it was the undeniable privilege of the Commons' House of Assembly to commit into [their] custody any such persons as they might judge to deserve to be so committed."[96] McCrady writes of this incident, "Chief Justice Wright stands alone at that time ... in resisting the power of a legislature in such a case. The theory of such [legislative] power rests on the theory of the omnipotence of Parliament and on the theory that either House sits as a court."[97] For his pains, the Commons voted to withhold Wright's salary.[98]

Sometime following Wright's appointment as Chief Justice, the legislature passed an act empowering the governor to appoint two or more Assistant Judges to sit with him in deciding cases.[99] These were invariably laymen and they had the numbers under the statute to outvote the Chief Justice in any ruling.[100] Wright complained of this act to the Board of Trade in 1733,[101] saying that under it the governor had appointed persons that "are intirely ignorant of the Laws and [can] over rule the Petitioner in

[95] Ibid., 10.

[96] Edward McCrady, *History of South Carolina under the Royal Government, 1719–1776* (New York, The Macmillan Co., 1899), 152.

[97] Ibid., 162. [98] Ibid., 159.

[99] James Munro (ed.), *Acts of the Privy Council of England, Colonial Series*, III (1720–45) (London, His Majesty's Stationery Office, 1910), 411. The original of these acts to empower the governor to appoint assistant judges was apparently enacted in the 1720s, see McCrady, History of South Carolina under the Royal Government, 7–8, 461.

[100] Ibid., at 8. [101] Ibid., at 460–61.

all Judicial Acts."[102] In March 1736, the Privy Council "repealed" this act along with others that had "allowed the Governor to appoint ... [such] Assistant Judges."[103] Either because the Council's decision had not yet reached South Carolina by May 1736 or because the legislature had already passed a new act empowering the governor to appoint assistant judges, when Chief Justice Wright called into question the validity of a South Carolina statute, in the course of deciding to grant a motion in arrest of judgment in a case in May of the same year, the Assistant Judges were still sitting, and intervened to call Wright's view of the matter into question.

Wright's is the fullest opinion by a colonial judge that has been found asserting the view that American colonial courts possessed the power to judge the validity of their colony's statutes. The case involved a colonial inhabitant convicted of counterfeiting under an act of the Assembly that imposed the death penalty for the crime. Under English law, first time offenders in these kinds of cases were entitled to relief from the death penalty. Defendant's lawyers moved in arrest of judgment that the colony's statute conflicted with English law.[104] Chief Justice Wright took the position that the motion should be granted. He opined that under the British constitution, subjects were bound by "no laws but those of our own making, that is by the King, Lords and Commons in Parliament assembled."[105] As the prisoner was a British subject he was entitled to the protection of these laws. "Far be it from me," Wright said,

> to impeach or question the Validity of any Law of this Province, or the Authority by which it is made; but by my Commission I am required and sworn to judge between the King and his People, according to the Laws and Statutes of *Great Britain* and the Laws of the Province, [and] therefore must inquire by what Authority they are made, and whether this Law be agre[e]able to the Laws of *Great Britain*, or can operate to supersede any Law of *Britain*.[106]

Wright was therefore "of Opinion that this Act exceeds *the Power* granted by the King's Commission, and is repugnant to the Laws of *Britain* [and] ... by the King's instructions ought not to operate to affect the Lives, Liberties, Estates and Properties of the People."[107]

[102] Munro (ed.,) Acts of the Privy Council, Colonial Series, III, 411.
[103] Ibid., 412. "Repealed" is the language the Council used.
[104] Hamburger, Law and Judicial Duty, 266.
[105] Quoted in ibid., 266 (based on reports in the *South Carolina Gazette* of May 1–8, 1736).
[106] Ibid., 267. [107] Ibid.

One of the lay Assistant Judges, Thomas Lamboll, dissented strongly from Wright's opinion. It was his view that the colony law was not repugnant to English law at all, in that the proper standard for evaluating colony statutes under the language of the charter was whether laws had been made "as near as conveniently may be" to English law, and this statute satisfied that standard. He then proceeded to turn on its head Wright's point about being governed by laws made by one's own representatives, arguing that among the rights and privileges Englishmen possessed "in their Mother Country, and retain'd and brought over with them hither ... [was] that of giving their Consent by the legal Representatives to such good and wholesome Laws for the Government of the whole Community."[108] Lamboll was of the opinion that, as Englishmen, the inhabitants of the colony were entitled to be governed by laws made by their own representatives in their own legislatures. Decades later, after the imperial apparatus had been swept away by the Revolution, the principle that the people were entitled to govern themselves by laws made by their representatives was again asserted as a reason for rejecting the claims state judges were beginning to make that they possessed the power to set aside such laws. Following Lamboll's dissent, proceedings were adjourned until a "*fuller Bench*" could be assembled "*to decide the Cause by a Majority.*"[109] The record ends there; nothing further is known about the outcome of the disputed ruling.

Chief Justice Wright died in 1739 in a yellow fever outbreak, and after a brief interim term served by one of the lay judges, Benjamin Whitaker was appointed and apparently confirmed in 1742 as Chief Justice of the colony.[110] In September 1742, at the beginning of the new legislative session, Whitaker was also chosen Speaker of the Commons. On the one hand, Whitaker would seem to have been aligned with the Commons. On the other, he confronted the problem that following the king's repeal of the laws providing for assistant judges, the General Assembly had enacted new ones authorizing these judges to continue to play the role they had under the old statutes. Whitaker did not like the idea of being outvoted by lay judges any more than Wright had, but also must have understood that so long as the Assistant Judges continued to sit on the court, there would be no possibility of declaring those statutes void. Soon after his election as Speaker of the Commons, he appears to have decided to pursue a political strategy to address the problem. He wrote a memorial to the Lieutenant

[108] Ibid. [109] Ibid., 268.

[110] McCrady, History of South Carolina under the Royal Government, 180, 464.

Governor in which he attempted to undermine the power of the Assistant Judges by pointing out that the new laws could not possibly be interpreted to reenact "part of an Act, [which] the King had repealed."[111]

While relying on the king's disallowance to call into question the legitimacy of the new statutes, he simultaneously disclaimed any authority in his own court to declare acts of the legislature void. The king had the sole power of "judging" the colony's statutes; colonial judges had to apply the laws of the colony as written, until the king intervened to make his "judgment" known.[112] Whitaker wrote,

> in the Plantations in America which are dependent Governments and are only impowered to make Laws, under certain Conditions, Limitations and Restrictions, the Judges ... are bound to Observe the laws that are pass'd by the General Assembly till they are repealed by the King. [F]or though such Laws ... may be repugnant to Ye Laws of England, yet it is conceived Such Laws are not Ipso facto void in themselves, but only voidable by his Majesty's *disallowance or repeal,* who tis humbly Apprehended *has reserved to himself the sole power of Judging* of Such Contriety, or repugnancy.[113] (emphasis added)

There were important ideas beneath the surface of Whitaker's statement. With only a few exceptions, when the Privy Council found a colonial statute to be repugnant to the laws of England, it concluded its proceedings by disallowing the statute. In these cases, a duly enacted colonial statute continued to possess the force of law in a colony until the king intervened to repeal it. Many Americans understood this to be the normal mode of proceeding in the Privy Council and as such seem to have drawn a number of inferences from it. First, the written constitutional constraint of repugnancy was not a limitation on the power of colonial legislatures to make binding law in the first instance. Duly enacted colonial laws enjoyed the force of law from their signing, pending the king's subsequent judgment of repugnance. They were not void in themselves for want of power in the legislature but were voidable by the king later. There is the further implication that the king's authority over colonial laws involved a "legislative judgment," i.e., the monarch "repealed" offending legislation. It was simple enough to see that as judges did not possess

111 Hamburger, Law and Judicial Duty, 269–70.

112 The account in the above paragraph is derived largely from Hamburger's, ibid., 269–70.

113 "Memorial of Benjamin Whitaker, Esqr. To the Honble William Bull Esqr Lieut Govr" (September 16, 1742), quoted in Hamburger, Law and Judicial Duty, 270. A year later Whitaker appears to have thought that it remained an open question whether colonial statutes should be considered void if repugnant to English law or merely voidable at the election of the king, ibid.; see also Smith, Appeals to the Privy Council, 577–78.

"legislative" authority, they certainly did not have the power to repeal or void laws.[114]

But there is a second thread running through Whitaker's statement. Whether an actual statute was or was not repugnant to the laws of England depended upon an act of interpretation. Even when a statute looked as though it might be repugnant to the laws of England, it did not automatically follow that the law was void and without effect. Someone with the definitive authority to say so would have to make that determination. It would invite chaos if simply anyone could declare a law to be void and without effect when they thought it to be repugnant to the laws of England. Did an ordinary court possess the interpretive authority to make the determination that would be necessary to void the statute? Whitaker answered no, the king had reserved to himself alone the sole authority to "judge" whether a colonial statute was or was not repugnant to the laws of England. These ideas remained somewhat undeveloped in Whitaker's memorial, waiting for a later Chief Justice of South Carolina, James Michie, to elaborate, in an opinion that represents the fullest expression of the view, offered by a colonial judge, that ordinary courts were entirely without authority to declare colony statutes null and void.

In January of 1760, Chief Justice Michie handed down, in the case of *Williams, Administrator de bonis non* v. *Executors of Watson*, an opinion rejecting the arguments of counsel that the court had power to declare a provincial law of South Carolina void as repugnant to the laws of England. Colonial assemblies, Michie said, were certainly obligated to conform their enactments to English law as closely as local circumstances permitted.[115]

> But in their deviations they and they *alone* in the first and his Majesty in his Privy Council in the last instance were the *judges* … whatever dissonance it [the provincial act at issue] may have to the laws and customs of England or how repugnant soever it may be to them, it is apprehended that this court can give no relief. *For if this court has a power of judging whether the laws which the General Assembly made are void or not, they have a power superior to the General Assembly.* But this is a power which I conceive this court has not. *Judges in England are the proper expositors of Acts of Parliament when they are made, but I don't remember that they ever questioned the power of making laws.*

[114] It is possible that Whitaker was not aware that the Council had voided a colonial statute sitting in its judicial capacity, or perhaps as was true of others, that he viewed the Council's actions under either procedure as a type of "legislative judgment" made by the king upon colonial laws.

[115] Smith, Appeals to the Privy Council, 591.

> *The plantations are limited and dependant governments.* They have power to make laws, and the King has reserved to himself and his Privy Council a *right of judging those laws* and till the King thinks fit to *repeal* them *they continue their full force and obligation. This power of repealing* the King has reserved to himself and to himself alone, with the advice of his Privy Council. *But if the courts of America had a power to adjudge them void it would anticipate the King's judgment* and would be two powers of *repealing*, which is inconsistent with the nature of our constitution; *this would be for the courts jus dare [to make the law] and not dicere [to say what the law is]*. It is easy to see the consequence of those arguments. *For if this court has a power to adjudge our laws to be void, they have a power to dispense with them. [A]nd everything will be left to precarious and arbitrary will and pleasure.*[116] (emphasis added)

Michie drew on a number of widely held British constitutional understandings to support his opinion rejecting judicial review. The first was simply that "judgments" about the constitutionality of a bill were properly the colonial legislature's "alone in the first and his Majesty in his Privy Council in the last instance" to make. In England, he noted, judges were rightfully "expositors" of the law, but they never "questioned the power of making laws." Once a bill had been passed by the assembly and signed by the governor, it possessed the force of law, regardless of whether some might think that it conflicted with constitutional restrictions. Nullifying such an act, consequently, involved making a change to existing law. And only the legislature possessed the authority to do that. If judges were to assume that kind of power, Michie wrote, "*this would be for the courts jus dare [to make the law] and not dicere [to say what the law is]*"[117] (emphasis added).

To understand why judgments about the constitutionality of a law were commonly viewed as uniquely an aspect of the lawmaking power, it is necessary to understand something more about certain basic English views about the distinction between judicial and legislative functions. Parliament, of course, was understood to be a body that possessed both legislative and judicial capacities. In its bill proceedings these two kinds of functions were often deeply confused as Parliament would commonly pass legislation to settle private disputes, a judicial function, but would often

[116] Quoted in ibid., from the MS Journal So. Car. Court Common Pleas, 1754–63, 237. Note Michie's consistent use of the term "judge" and "judgment" to describe the king's "legislative" decision to repeal or declare void a colony statute.

[117] Ibid.; the distinction *jus dicere/jus dare* had apparently been introduced into English legal discourse by Francis Bacon during the early seventeenth century to distinguish between the proper and improper functions of courts, see Hamburger, Law and Judicial Duty, 224–25.

do so not by invoking an established legal rule to decide the controversy, but by enacting a new rule, seemingly a legislative function.

The upheavals of the seventeenth century began to force some to develop a sharper distinction between Parliament's functions. When a bill of attainder charging the Earl of Strafford with treason was introduced in the Commons during 1641, it set off a debate that produced some clarifications. Lord Digby argued that the evidence in the case did not support a charge of treason under existing laws but acknowledged that the Commons had the power to enact a new law defining the kind of conduct in which Strafford had engaged as treason. Digby, however, went on to condemn the idea that such a law should be applied retroactively to Strafford's conduct. "God keep me from giving Judgment of Death," he said, "upon a Law made *a posteriori*."[118] It was in this connection that Digby drew a distinction between the way Parliament should properly exercise its judicial as opposed to its legislative powers.

> There is in Parliament a double Power of Life and Death by Bill, *a Judicial Power, and a Legislative*; the measure of the one, is what's *legally just*, of the other, *what is Prudentially and Politickly fit for the good and preservation of the whole.*[119] (emphasis added)

The judicial power was devoted to delivering justice under existing law. The essence of Parliament's legislative power was to make new, general laws for the nation. Parliament possessed wide discretion in exercising this legislative power, but that discretion was to be guided by "prudence" and a "political" consideration for "the good and preservation of the whole." By "Politickly fit" Digby seems to have meant something like fitting for the broad polity. The discretion exercised in making laws (for the nation) should necessarily be guided by judgments about these larger considerations. As the representatives of the nation (or the people), Parliament, in its legislative capacity, was properly the body to make such judgments as it went about deciding whether to enact a bill into law or to repeal an

[118] I draw upon my colleague Matt Steilen's account of the Strafford case in this paragraph. The quotation, drawn from John Rushworth's 1680 account of *The Tryal of Thomas Earl of Strafford*, 52, appears in Matthew Steilen, "Bills of Attainder" (2016) 53 *Houston Law Review* 767, 814.

[119] Rushworth, The Tryal of Strafford, 53 quoted in Steilen, "Bills of Attainder," 814; in the same period, Matthew Hale drew a distinction between the two capacities of Parliament that seemed to rely on a roughly similar notion: "The supreme jurisdiction of parliament acts either *deliberative* where it makes laws or *Judicative* when it gives judgment." Mattthew Hale, *The Prerogatives of the King*, 181 (D.E.C. Yale, London, Selden Society, 1976), quoted in Hamburger, Law and Judicial Duty, 239 fn. 4.

existing one. In the British constitutional tradition, John Phillip Reid observes, the legislature, as it proceeded to enact statutes, was commonly thought to be subject to "the duty to protect society or 'the general good' or 'the good and happiness of the people', [and as one aspect of that duty] to 'preserve the constitution,' which meant making no laws '*inconsistent* with the *fundamental* Principles of just Government."[120] The determination that a colonial statute was "politickly fit" and not repugnant to the laws of England, was, as Michie put it, to be "judged" only by the colonial legislature in the first instance, and the king in council in the last. Courts did not possess the authority to make law. They operated under the duty to deliver justice under existing laws, as the judges interpreted the requirements those imposed.

The characterization of judicial review as an illegitimate exercise of legislative power, appeared, as already noted, in earlier South Carolina clashes between judges and the legislature, and would reappear during the 1780s as one of the principal reasons urged for rejecting the new judicial practice, one of those persisting criticisms that would continue to plague the legitimacy of American judicial review.

The second basic reason Michie offered for finding that ordinary courts did not possess the authority to review and nullify legislative enactments grew out of the idea of review itself. Review was (is) considered to be an inherently hierarchal practice. Only a body with "superior" authority can legitimately reconsider and reverse the decisions of another authority. Only "higher" courts, for example, review and reverse the decisions of "lower" ones. Michie noted that English judges never questioned the power of Parliament to make law, and implied that the same applied to the relationship between colonial legislatures and their courts. While it was legitimate for the Privy Council, a "superior" legislative body, to review and repeal or void the laws of an "inferior" jurisdiction coming under its authority, it was improper for the courts of a jurisdiction to do so, not only because (1) they should not be exercising legislative power, but (2) also because the authority they possessed was inferior to – but at any rate certainly not superior to – that possessed by the legislature in that government. To allow courts to call into question the validity of acts of the legislature would necessarily be to place them above legislatures as a "superior" supervising authority, a constitutional position courts certainly did not, and were not entitled to, occupy.

[120] John Phillip Reid, Constitutional History of the American Revolution: The Authority to Legislate, 95.

Michie disclaimed any authority in his court to declare colonial acts void, saying that "if this court has a power of judging whether the laws which the General Assembly made are void or not, they have a power superior to the General Assembly."[121] This was certainly not an idiosyncratic view. Just a few years later, Blackstone would write that if judges possessed the power to reject a statute enacted by Parliament that would be to "set the judicial power above that of the legislature, which would be subversive of all government."[122] Like the criticism that judicial review involved the improper exercise of legislative authority by courts, the objection that it placed judges over legislatures, had also appeared earlier in the century in South Carolina, and would reappear in the post-Independence clashes that developed during the 1780s between state legislatures and courts, another one of those intractable issues about the legitimacy of this form of judicial review that could not easily be resolved.

Americans of that later generation, however, sometimes addressed this problem not by denying that the grant to one party of the authority to review and reverse the decisions of another necessarily involved making that party constitutionally "superior" to the other but by completely reframing the description of the pertinent hierarchy. Judicial review, Alexander Hamilton acknowledged, involved the exercise of a superior authority over an inferior one, but it did not, he went on to argue, place courts above legislatures. As they went about their task, he said, judges were only acting on behalf of the higher authority of the people declared in their constitutions, and as such, their actions represented a legitimate exercise of the superior authority of the people over the inferior authority of their legislatures.[123] Judicial review, both Blackstone and his American audience recognized, necessarily involved the exercise of "vertical" authority. Hamilton's re-characterization served to acknowledge that reality, while brilliantly reformulating it as a constitutionally legitimate form of review that properly placed the people over their legislatures.

Chief Justice Michie offered a third crucial reason for holding that courts did not possess the authority to void duly enacted statutes of

[121] Quoted in Smith, Appeals to the Privy Council, 591.

[122] Blackstone, Commentaries, Book I, Section 3, 91; in a separate place in the Commentaries, Blackstone also observed that "[b]y the sovereign power ... is meant the making of laws; for wherever that power resides, all others must conform to, and be directed by it.... [A]ll the other powers of the state must obey the legislative power in the execution of their several functions, or else the constitution is at an end," 49.

[123] No. 78 Federalist, in Clinton Rossiter (ed.), *The Federalist Papers* (New York, Mentor, 1999), 435.

the colony. He believed that such power in the courts would undermine the rule of law itself, creating chaos. That courts, which had not explicitly been granted this power could nevertheless claim it, raised the specter of widespread disobedience of the law. Could just anyone decide that a statute was repugnant to the laws of England and no longer need be obeyed. If judges, Michie observed, have the power to declare the colony's laws void, they "have a power [simply] to dispense with [laws] .... [and] everything will be left to precarious and arbitrary will and pleasure."

The repudiation by two Chief Justices of the colony of a number of the basic ideas upon which Chief Justice Wright had earlier relied, fatally undermined the case for review of legislation by ordinary courts. For now, more traditional Anglo/American constitutional understandings about the proper relationship between courts and legislatures prevailed, and the efforts to establish this form of judicial review in colonial South Carolina failed to bear fruit.

Not everyone accepted views like Michie's and Whitaker's, of course, either in the colonies or in England.[124] The very fact that an earlier Chief Justice had thought to argue for the practice and that, in the very case in which Michie delivered his opinion, counsel for the defendant had been asking the court to nullify a statute, testifies to the potential viability of the opposing ideas. James Abercromby, a "British-born barrister, who prior to 1743 had served nearly thirteen years as Attorney and Advocate General of South Carolina and had acted since 1749 as colonial agent for North Carolina," tried in 1752 to interest the British ministry in his proposal for a Parliamentary statute that would have overturned views like Whitaker's and Michie's by explicitly authorizing colonial courts to "judge" the repugnancy of colonial statutes, but the ministry seems to have ignored his efforts.[125] Abercromby, of course, must have believed that without such a statute the case for review of legislation by ordinary courts would founder, as it in fact did.

But the basic ideas that underlay the judges' claims to a power of judicial review did not disappear. As Chief Justice Wright had made apparent, the case for this form of judicial review began with a different opinion about the status of laws that were in conflict with the terms of charters and governors' commissions. Statutes adopted in contravention of such limitations simply did not possess the force of law; colonial legislatures lacked the power to enact them. Such laws were void, not

[124] Smith, Appeals to the Privy Council, 592. [125] Ibid., 578–82.

voidable. Underneath it all, this represented a different view of the nature of the restrictions under which colonial legislatures operated. Repugnancy was a limitation upon the power of colonial legislatures to make law in the first place. A very similar underlying dispute about the precise nature of the constraints written constitutions imposed on state legislatures would continue to separate supporters and opponents of judicial review during the 1780s. These highly technical disagreements about the exact nature of constitutional constraints were beneath it all fundamental disputes about the constitutional terms and conditions under which these governments would operate.

If constitutional restrictions limited the power of legislatures to enact law in the first place, it might well be appropriate for judges, who were charged with determining what the law was as they went about deciding cases, to say that a statute in conflict with a charter or governor's commission was not law, and did not bind the court or the litigants before it. To arrive at this conclusion, of course, ordinary judges would have to interpret the terms of a statute and the provisions of a charter or a governor's commission, and it would still be a question whether they possessed the authority to deliver authoritative interpretations of these foundational "political-legal" documents. But it would be entirely plausible to characterize their determinations as "judicial," not "legislative," in that they would not be viewed as altering existing law but as finding that a statute had not been law in the first place.

There were other isolated incidents in which colonial judges declared provincial statutes not to be binding law, or in which, during the run up to Independence, they declared an act of Parliament void,[126] but these did not grow into a movement that might have made judicial review a regular feature of colonial governments. Not only were prevailing constitutional ideas of the period unfavorable to this development, but so also was the broader political situation.

The notion that colonial courts could enforce the imperial repugnancy standard by overturning the enactments of provincial legislatures would not likely have held a great deal of appeal for many American political leaders. Nor would the British have accepted the idea that a colonial court could possibly possess the power to declare an act of Parliament void. In any case, the enactments of American legislatures were already subject to several layers of review and an additional one would not only seem unnecessary but might actually lead to the overturning of established

[126] Hamburger, Law and Judicial Duty, 272–80.

constitutional hierarchies, as Michie implied. Suppose the king had decided to confirm a colony law; was it conceivable that the decision of a colonial court declaring a statute void could possibly preempt the king's judgment?

Drawing upon one strand in existing British constitutional ideas, an elementary case for judicial review by ordinary courts could be (and had been) made out, but it conflicted with other more fundamental constitutional values, and for that reason, among others, failed to persuade crucial members of the South Carolina bench. Without a firm commitment to these ideas by the judges, no movement for judicial review was likely to succeed. As important, the practice did not generate the wider political support that would have been necessary to make it a regular feature of American colonial governments.

When the case for this form of judicial review began to be made again in the 1780s, the Privy Council, of course, had been eliminated from American life (and gubernatorial vetoes had been eliminated or restricted), but advocates for the novel practice still had to contend with several of the dominant premises of British constitutionalism that had contributed to its earlier defeat in South Carolina, and to which many Americans continued to adhere. Promoters of judicial review found that a good place to start was with the idea that the written constitutions, which Americans had adopted upon declaring Independence, were in themselves a form of ordinary law and operated to deprive legislatures of the power to make binding any act that was in conflict with these instruments. From there, it was possible to begin to build a persuasive case for "horizontal" judicial review.

Of decisive importance this time around was that the political and constitutional climate had been transformed by the Revolution and its aftermath. Unlike most of their colonial predecessors, which had operated under layers of review, the first written constitutions, by conscious design, left the new state legislatures almost entirely unchecked. By the 1780s, more Americans had grown disenchanted with the resulting state of affairs. These new conditions drew an impressive group of elite American lawyers (and judges) into a largely spontaneous movement devoted to formulating convincing rationales for a practice of judicial review, which they believed to be essential to check the excesses of legislatures. The arguments and ideas, which emerged from their fertile legal imaginations, now circulated in a much more favorable political and constitutional environment, one that made it possible for this new thinking to supplant to a considerable extent the fundamental assumptions that formed the bedrock of traditional Anglo/American constitutionalism– producing a constitutional revolution.

2

The Traditional Nature of the First Written Constitutions and the Role of Legislatures as Their Primary Expounders

The framers of the first state constitutions established a system in which the representatives of the people, embodied in their legislatures, were to be supreme within governments. With only two partial exceptions, the early constitutions imposed no formal check on the power of legislatures to make law. But these representative bodies were not, for the most part, regarded as sovereign. Rather, most Americans believed that the sovereign people themselves would supervise the conduct of their representatives.[1] Constitutional restrictions would be enforced against legislatures "politically" through a variety of forms of popular action, but most especially by means of the frequent (annual) elections almost all the first constitutions required for their lower houses. Legislatures would be held to constitutional standards as popular opinion interpreted those. Under this system, the people would be entirely free to enact (through their legislatures) the laws by which they wished to govern themselves. Whenever they came to believe that their legislators had overstepped constitutional bounds in passing a particular statute, they possessed the plenary power to replace them with representatives who would more faithfully adhere to constitutional standards, and repeal offending legislation.

The introduction of judicial review and the reasoning that justified it, during the 1780s, a seemingly small matter, had the outsize consequence of transforming the foundations of this early American constitutional

[1] For the most comprehensive description of this system, see Larry Kramer, *The People Themselves: Popular Constitutionalism and Judicial Review* (Oxford, Oxford University Press, 2004).

system. Increasingly thereafter, written constitutions would come to be viewed and treated as imposing judicially enforceable "legal" limitations on the power of legislatures to make law. For many political leaders at the time, judicially enforced constitutional limitations had the benefit not only of placing a formal restriction on the power of legislatures to make law but in that way also of placing a crucial constraint on the power of the sovereign people to put into place just any law they might wish. Several of the principal early theorists of judicial review made explicit how important they considered it to be that the people be bound by the terms of their own constitutions (as the judges expounded those).

This chapter and the next describe the American constitutional system of the 1770s in greater detail, attempting to convey a fuller sense of what precisely it meant to have written constitutions that imposed "political" rather than "legal" obligations on legislatures and to drive home the point that this system had been consciously chosen by Americans in their first constitutional conventions. But the chapter also describes the internal tensions dogging this constitutional regime and the external "political" pressures that provided the impetus to alter it.

Chapter 3 moves the story forward by examining the New York constitution of 1777, which introduced important changes into the constitutional system. The lack of a meaningful institutional check on popularly elected legislatures led conservative leaders in New York to create a Council of Revision. This response, however, the chapter argues, did not overturn the early system's core premises, in that it continued to treat constitutional limitations as a matter to be assessed in the course of lawmaking, and to be determined, in the final resort (at least within government) by the legislature. In the 1780s, James Madison and, more ambiguously, Thomas Jefferson urged their own and other states to adopt Councils of Revision, in some cases as an alternative to judicial review, in order to reform the existing constitutional system without superseding the core principle that determinations of constitutionality were properly a matter for the legislative representatives of the people and the people themselves. It is possible that if they had prevailed in their efforts, a reformed system of written constitutions understood as a form of "political/legal" compact might have endured. But at the Federal Convention a different path was chosen, as Chapter 10 makes clear.

Most state constitutions did not establish a Council of Revision, and even in New York, leading conservatives thought that it did not go far enough to solve the problems of legislative and popular excesses. The internal inconsistencies in this first American constitutional system placed one strand of Anglo-American thinking about the nature of constitutional limitations in tension with the institutional realities of the new governments and pointed toward the emergence of the transformative practice of judicial review as a different kind of response to the system's perceived problems. In the political climate of the 1780s, many leading lawyers embraced and promoted the new practice.

This chapter and the next focus on the constitutional system of the 1770s, but they also lay the groundwork for understanding the emergence of judicial review in the 1780s, which the succeeding chapters take up in detail.

2.1 "REVIEW" OF LEGISLATION REJECTED

Upon their declaration of independence, the American colonies transformed themselves from limited and dependent governments into sovereign states. Their legislatures would henceforth enjoy the same authority to make law that the British Parliament possessed. Unlike the British, however, many Americans viewed their own legislatures as subject to the direct and active supervision of "the people," an understanding implemented and reinforced by the requirement, adopted in most of the first state constitutions, that elections to lower houses be annual. "[A]ll the states except South Carolina provided for the yearly election of their houses of representatives a radical departure from their previous experience for all except the New England charter colonies and Pennsylvania."[2] At the same time, most Americans had come to see the traditional practices of review, by which the work of the people's representatives in legislatures was reassessed and subject to rejection by a body other than the people themselves, as fundamentally incompatible with the nature of their independent, self-governing republics. Their colonial experiences had certainly left them with deep feelings of antipathy toward Privy Council review, but those experiences had also led most to develop an equally deep distaste for the "vetoes" governors had wielded in most colonies.

In the bill of particulars drawn up against the King and presented in the Declaration of Independence, the offenses that are mentioned first all involve review of colonial laws:

[2] Gordon Wood, *The Creation of the American Republic, 1776–1787* (Chapel Hill, N.C., The University of North Carolina Press, 1969), 166–67.

He has refused his Assent to Laws, the most wholesome and necessary for the public good.

He has forbidden his Governors to pass Laws of immediate and pressing importance, unless suspended in their operation till his Assent should be obtained; and when so suspended, he has utterly neglected to attend to them.

He has refused to pass other Laws for the accommodation of large districts of people, unless those people would relinquish the right of Representation in the Legislature, a right inestimable to them and formidable to tyrants only.[3]

In his autobiography, Thomas Jefferson wrote that upon leaving Congress in 1776 after it had adopted the Declaration of Independence, he returned home with a determination to completely revise Virginia's code of law. "[N]ow that we had no negatives of Councils, Governors & Kings to restrain us from doing right, [our code of laws] should be corrected, in all its parts, with a single eye to reason & the good of those for whose government it was framed."[4]

It is not surprising that in their first constitutions, Americans largely eliminated the "negatives" to which their legislative assemblies had previously been subject. Under these new constitutions, governors were deprived of many of the powers their colonial predecessors had enjoyed.[5] Indeed, in most states, governors were to be appointed by legislatures themselves. "The Americans' emasculation of their governors," Gordon Wood has written, "lay at the heart of their constitutional reforms of 1776."[6] Of the constitutions adopted in 1776, only one, South Carolina's temporary constitution, gave the executive (styled president and commander-in-chief in that document) an absolute veto over bills passed by the legislature. This constitution was replaced just two years later with a permanent constitution that deprived the governor of all power to review and veto legislation, bringing South Carolina into line with every other state except New York, up to that time.[7] Even leaders

3 Declaration of Independence, adopted July 4, 1776.

4 Thomas Jefferson, *The Autobiography of Thomas Jefferson, 1743–1790* (1821) (Philadelphia, Pa., University of Pennsylvania Press, 2005), 66–67.

5 For a detailed description of this constitutional "Restructuring of Power," see Wood, Creation of the American Republic, 127–61.

6 Ibid., 149.

7 For South Carolina, see Francis Thorpe (ed.), *The Federal and State Constitutions, Colonial Charters, and Other Organic Laws of the States, Territories and Colonies* (Washington, D.C., Government Printing Office, 1909, Reprint Buffalo, N.Y., William

who did not place complete faith in popular government, and who pressed for constitutional frameworks that would check the powers of popular assemblies through a variety of expedients, drew back at resurrecting the authority to veto legislation that colonial governors had enjoyed. William Hooper of North Carolina, for example,

> worried much about popular power. The people had good intentions, he acknowledged, but they often fell "short in the means made use of to obtain them." "A Warmth of Zeal" induced them to make errors .... Nevertheless, Hooper opposed a gubernatorial veto. In a long letter to the provincial congress [of North Carolina] offering recommendations for the new constitution, he confessed that he "once thought it would be wise to adopt a double check as in the British Constitution." But now he worried about "the Abuses which power in the hand of an Individual is liable to, & the unreasonableness that an individual should abrogate at pleasure the acts of the Representatives of the people, refined by a second body" [i.e., an upper house of the legislature].[8]

Americans objected to the restoration of a gubernatorial veto on other grounds as well, one important one being that a veto would violate the increasingly important principle of separation of powers.[9] A similar separation of powers complaint would be raised in the near future about judicial review. At a time before modern conventions had been settled about what precisely constituted a violation of separation of powers principles, it was perfectly reasonable to believe that giving the executive a veto over the laws would violate that principle.[10] In Virginia, which was one of four states that would go on to mandate a separation of powers in its constitution, "Democraticus" insisted that governors should not have

S. Hein, 1993), VI, 3244 (S.C.,1776), and Thorpe, Constitutions, VI, 3248 (S.C., 1778); for New York see Thorpe, Constitutions, V, 2628–29 (New York, 1777). The New York Constitution of 1777 gave a qualified veto to a Council of Revision upon which the governor sat. The Council is discussed in greater detail below. In a few states, the governor was given a casting vote as a member of the Council, the upper house of the legislature. See Marc Kruman, *Between Authority and Liberty: State Constitution Making in Revolutionary America* (Chapel Hill, N.C., University of North Carolina Press, 1997), 124. The Massachusetts constitution of 1780 also conferred a qualified veto, which the governor alone exercised, Thorpe, Constitutions, III 1893–94 (Mass., 1780). But except for New York and Massachusetts no other permanent state constitution of the period gave any sort of legislative veto to a governor or a governor sitting with a council.

8 Kruman, Between Authority and Liberty, 124 (quoting in part Hooper letter to North Carolina congress, October 1776); see also Wood, Creation of American Republic, 141.

9 Kruman, Between Authority and Liberty, 123.

10 Mary S. Bilder, "Expounding the Law" (2010) 78 *George Washington Law Review* 1129, 1139–40; James T. Barry, III, "The Council of Revision and the Limits of Judicial Power" (1989) 56 *University of Chicago Law Review* 235, 252–55.

a negative upon the laws as "it is a solecism in politick[s] to invest the different power of legislation and the execution of the laws in the same hands."[11] In Maryland, citizens of Anne Arundel County argued "that the persons appointed to hold the executive power, [should] have no share or negative in the legislature."[12]

John Adams was one of a small number of leaders in 1776 to support the retention of a gubernatorial veto, but even Adams did so waveringly and believed that little harm would result if the governor were instead given only a casting vote in the upper house of the legislature, as was the practice in Connecticut. But if a traditional gubernatorial veto were granted, he thought, it would pose little danger so long as governors were subject to annual election. At the same time, he believed that governors should certainly be stripped of their traditional "prerogative" powers. In a letter to William Hooper containing his "Thoughts on Government," Adams gave his advice on the shape the governor's office should take under a new North Carolina constitution.

> [T]here should be a third Branch [of the legislature as was traditional] which for the Sake of preserving old Style and Titles, you may call a Governor whom I would invest with a Negative upon the other Branches of the Legislature and also with the whole Executive Power, after divesting it of most of those Badges of Domination call'd Prerogatives. I know that giving the Executive Power a Negative upon the Legislative, is liable to Objections, but it seems to be attended with more Advantages than Dangers, especially if you make this Office elective annually, and more especially if you establish a Rotation by which no Man shall be Governor for more than three years .... However, if you like it better, give him only a casting Voice in Council [i.e., in the upper house of the legislature].[13]

In a letter to Francis Dana written a few months after the pamphlet version of "Thoughts on Government" had appeared, Adams qualified his recommendation further. He said that he did not believe the traditional gubernatorial veto would ever be accepted by the people of Massachusetts and did not favor its reestablishment there in any case. He thought,

[11] Quoted in Wood, Creation of American Republic, 153; and in Kruman, Between Authority and Liberty, 123.

[12] Kruman, 123.

[13] Robert J. Taylor (ed.), *Papers of John Adams* (Cambridge, Mass., Belknap Press of the Harvard University Press, 1979), IV, 76. Three versions of Adams' 1776 "Thoughts on Government" are extant; the final one was printed as a pamphlet in April 1776. Though the wording on the subject of governors differs somewhat from version to version, Adams presented essentially the same ideas about governors in all of them. These versions of "Thoughts on Government" appear in Taylor (ed.), Papers of John Adams, IV, 73–92.

however, that it might be suitable for Southern colonies, which, in his view, inclined toward less popular governments.[14] He wrote:

> Let the first Executive Magistrate be the Head of the Council board, and no more. Our People will never Submit to more, and I am not clear that it is best they should . . . The Thoughts on Government were calculated for Southern Latitudes, not northern.[15]

To drive home the point that governors should not interfere with the laws as the legislature made them, the Maryland, North Carolina, and Virginia constitutions of 1776, the Massachusetts constitution of 1780, and the New Hampshire Constitution of 1784 added clauses, borrowed from the English Bill of Rights of 1689, declaring "That all power of suspending laws, or the execution of laws, by any authority, without consent of the representatives of the people, is injurious to their rights, and ought not to be exercised."[16]

The weight of opinion in these years was set firmly against giving governors any role in lawmaking. None of the permanent state constitutions adopted in 1776 granted governors a veto over the enactments of legislatures.

While governors had possessed a "veto" over legislation in most colonies, there was no tradition of ordinary judges exercising an authority to overturn the enactments of colonial legislatures. Indeed, norms of judicial independence were weak and overshadowed by older practices that aimed to keep judges from becoming totally independent. It was widely assumed that if judges were reliably to deliver justice, they must in some measure be kept accountable for their decisions.[17]

American colonial legislatures had certainly struggled with the British monarch to make the tenure of colonial judges more secure, but they had done so less in order to promote the pure independence of judges than to free them from dependency upon the crown. Most colonial judges had been appointed to serve at the pleasure of the king. On numerous occasions legislatures had pressed to have judges appointed to serve during good behavior (as they did in England under the Act of Settlement), a step

[14] Ibid., IV, 182 (letter to James Warren, May 12, 1776, "In New England the 'Thoughts on Government' will be disdained, because they are not popular enough. In the Southern Colonies, they will be despised and dissected, because too popular.")

[15] Ibid., IV, 466 (letter to Francis Dana August 16, 1776).

[16] Thorpe, Constitutions, III, 1687 (Md., 1776); Thorpe, Constitutions, V, 2787 (N.C., 1776); Thorpe, Constitutions, VII, 3813 (Va., 1776); Thorpe, Constitutions, III, 1892 (Mass., 1780); Thorpe, Constitutions, IV, 2457 (N.H., 1784).

[17] Gerber, A Distinct Judicial Power, 45 (Virginia).

that would have made them less dependent on the monarch.[18] But throughout the colonial period, it was also true that the lower houses of legislatures set and paid the judges' salaries, and there was little support in legislatures for giving up this power. Just as colonial legislatures had agitated on occasion to confer good behavior tenure on judges in order to emancipate them from the king's influence, the king on several occasions had attempted to arrange to have judges' salaries fixed or paid from some independent source of revenue so that they would be less dependent upon colonial legislatures.[19] Only weak support seems to have existed in either camp, however, for making judges independent of both legislatures and kings.[20]

Following the Revolution, more Americans seem to have wished to see judges made genuinely independent, holding their offices during good behavior with "fixed and adequate salaries,"[21] but the weight of opinion at most state constitutional conventions seems to have been against granting judges that kind of independence from legislatures, and from the people. In 5 of the 13 original states (New Jersey, Pennsylvania, Rhode Island, Connecticut and Georgia), judges were appointed to serve not during good behavior but for a prescribed number of years, after which they might be reappointed by the legislature.[22] In 5 more (Delaware,

[18] On these struggles, see Joseph H. Smith, "An Independent Judiciary: The Colonial Background" (1976) 124 *University of Pennsylvania Law Review* 1104.

[19] Gerber, A Distinct Judicial Power, 84; Smith, "Independent Judiciary," 1143–51 (Townsend Act).

[20] On several occasions, colonial legislatures did show themselves willing to vote fixed salaries for judges in exchange for good behavior tenure, see Smith, "An Independent Judiciary," 1120 (Pa.), 1141 (South Carolina), and 1152 (Benjamin Franklin's suggested terms of reconciliation with Britain).

[21] Gerber, A Distinct Judicial Power, 60 (quoting Virginia Constitution of 1776).

[22] Wood, Creation of the American Republic, 161 fn. 65. Even in some states that ultimately adopted good behavior tenure, there seems to have been broad popular support for limiting judges to a prescribed term, see Gerber, A Distinct Judicial Power, 89 fn. 78 (sentiment in Massachusetts for having judges serve only for a prescribed term) and 113 fn. 101. ("Some members of the 1781 (NH) constitutional convention wanted to limit judges to five year terms, rather than permit them to serve for life during good behavior"); see also Martha Andes Ziskind, "Judicial Tenure in the American Constitution: English and American Precedents" (1969) 1969 *Supreme Court Review* 135, 146 (returns from Massachusetts towns with respect to the proposed Massachusetts Constitution of 1778, "Tenure during good behavior was unacceptable to a number of towns. Sutton criticized the vagueness of the term 'good behavior' . . . . New Salem preferred direct election of justices by the people for a fixed term. Boothbay thought one-year terms were more democratic as did Shelburne. Lenox, located in the radical western part of the state, objected to tenure during good behavior because judges were made independent both of the legislature and of the people.")

Maryland, Massachusetts, New Hampshire and South Carolina), constitutions made judges removable upon address of the legislature,[23] provisions almost certainly derived from the English Act of Settlement. Although no English judge had actually been subjected to removal upon address up to that time, and the permissible grounds and the procedural requirements for doing so had never been worked out, many Americans believed that the standard exposed judges to the possibility of removal from office without any sort of trial and for arbitrary or political reasons.[24] In only 3 of the original 13 states (Virginia, New York and North Carolina) did constitutions grant judges tenure during good

[23] See Gerber, A Distinct Judicial Power, 89–90, 114; and Ziskind, "Judicial Tenure in the American Constitution," 139–43.

[24] See, for example, remarks of Gouverneur Morris and James Wilson at the Federal Convention of 1787 in Max Farrand (ed.), *The Records of the Federal Convention of 1787* (New Haven, Ct., Yale University Press, 1966), II, 428–29. "See also James E. Pfander, "Removing Federal Judges" 74 (2007) *University of Chicago Law Review* 1227, 1243, and Ziskind, "Judicial Tenure in the American Constitution," 150–51 for accounts of the debate over removal upon address at the Federal Convention. For a penetrating discussion of the precise meaning of and the ambiguous requirements for removal upon address under the Act of Settlement, see C. H. McIlwain, "The Tenure of English Judges" (1913) 7 *American Political Science Review* 217. McIlwain was of the view that the removal upon address provision of the act was intended to constrain the king, not to authorize Parliamentary removal of judges. Under the clause, McIlwain believed, the king could not remove a judge unless Parliament requested him to do so, but Parliament's address merely authorized removal, it did not require the king to do so. In an attempt, apparently, to clarify the standard for removal upon address and to raise the threshold a bit, the Delaware constitution of 1792 provided that "The chancellor and the judges of the supreme court shall hold their offices during good behavior; but, *for any reasonable cause* which shall *not* be *a sufficient ground for an impeachment*, the governor *may, in his discretion*, remove any of them, *on the address of two-thirds of all the members* of each branch of the legislature" in Thorpe, Constitutions, I, 575 (emphasis added). In addition to this Delaware clause, several other early state constitutional provisions governing removal upon address can be read to support McIlwain's main point. "Judges ought to hold commissions during good behavior ... and *may* be removed by the Governor, upon address of the General Assembly ...." Section XXX, Declaration of Rights, Maryland Constitution of 1776 in Thorpe, Constitutions, III, 1689 (emphasis added). Judges "shall hold their offices during good behavior ... provided, nevertheless, the governor, with consent of the council, *may* remove them upon the address of both houses of the legislature." Ch. III, Art. I, Massachusetts Constitution of 1780 in Thorpe, Constitutions, III, 1905 (emphasis added); *but compare* the South Carolina constitution of 1778, Section XXVII, Judges serve "during good behavior, but *shall* be removed on address of the senate and house of representatives" in Thorpe, Constitutions, VI, 3254 (emphasis added), and the similar provision in Art. 23 of the original Delaware constitution of 1776. "[A]ll officers *shall* be removed ... upon the address of the general assembly," Thorpe, Constitutions, I, 566 (emphasis added).

behavior without a provision also subjecting them to removal upon address. This state of affairs led Gordon Wood to conclude that

> most of the early constitution-makers had little sense that judicial independence meant independence from the people .... These constitutional provisions giving control of the courts and judicial tenure to the legislatures actually represented the culmination of what the colonial assemblies had been struggling for in their eighteenth-century contests with the Crown.[25]

It should come as little surprise, therefore, that there is complete silence in the record of the proceedings and debates of the state constitutional conventions of this period on the subject of judicial review, and not the slightest hint in the resulting constitutions themselves that their framers even imagined the possibility that judges would exercise a power to set aside acts of the legislature.

By design, the frames of government in the overwhelming majority of early constitutions contained no check upon legislation that would be wielded by another branch of the government, entrusting the final, unappealable judgment about what the laws would be to legislatures alone, subject only to review by the people themselves at frequent elections or otherwise.

2.2 THE NATURE OF WRITTEN CONSTITUTIONS IN THE FIRST REPUBLICAN GOVERNMENTS

Starting early in 1776, even before Independence had been formally declared, the American colonies began to create new governments by drafting and adopting written constitutions. These instruments were not easily defined. Americans did not have completely settled views about what precisely they entailed. Since one of the principal tasks of these documents was to establish the institutional frames for new governments, they were sometimes viewed as analogous to the charters under which a number of colonies had been set up. Indeed, Connecticut and Rhode Island, satisfied with the frames of government their colonial charters had established, simply moved to readopt these charters as their constitutions. But written constitutions were certainly viewed by most Americans as involving a good deal more. Beginning with Virginia, a number of early constitutions appended a declaration of rights or provided for certain fundamental rights in the body of the constitution itself. A rich stew of

[25] Wood, Creation of the American Republic, 161.

constitutional ideas circulated in America during this period, some drawn from prevailing English constitutional traditions, others set up in opposition to these, still others drawn from a variety of sources, which influenced the drafting and the understanding of the political significance of these documents. They were after all, in their guise as written constitutions for fully sovereign states, new in the Anglo/American world. From the perspective of modern American constitutionalism, there is a certain strangeness about them; they are artifacts of a constitutional world that has passed away. To understand their character, even imperfectly, it is perhaps best to begin by considering basic features of the English constitutional tradition, which they simultaneously drew upon and reacted against.

The word "constitution" had several different meanings during the seventeenth and eighteenth centuries; one of these equated constitutions with "fundamental law."[26] As fundamental law, the English constitution consisted of basic principles that were derived from a variety of sources, certain common law doctrines, natural law, certain documents like Magna Carta, a number of legal and political treatises, and Parliamentary statutes like the English Bill of Rights of 1689, and the Act of Settlement. These together constituted a fundamental law that imposed, in principle, limits on the sovereign power in the state.

There are several aspects of this tradition that are especially important for the inquiry here. The English constitution, though drawn from written sources as well as unwritten ones, was understood to be a form of customary law, not unlike the common law. The distinction between interpretation and revision in systems of customary law was not sharply drawn. Like the common law, which, it was often said, was "simultaneously immutable and evolving, unchanging yet always different,"[27] fundamental law was understood to evolve organically through a process that involved the application, by means of interpretation and explication, of fixed abstract principles to new situations. Except in unusual circumstances, it would have been something of an oxymoron to speak of Parliament violating the constitution, as it was through Parliament's statutes that this highest court in the realm was commonly viewed as elucidating what the constitution meant. Today, it would only be under similar extraordinary circumstances that it might be said of a decision of the Supreme Court of the United States that it violated the constitution, as the court itself explains the meaning of the constitution. At the same time,

[26] Kramer, The People Themselves, 9–10. [27] Ibid., 14.

English constitutionalism still carried the idea that Parliamentary power was subject in some sense to limitations contained in this fundamental law.

On those occasions when an act of Parliament was widely viewed as violating basic principles of the constitution, the polity itself would be called into action. Opponents of the act would denounce it in pamphlets, petition Parliament for its repeal, demonstrate against it in the streets, perhaps resist its implementation, mount electoral campaigns designed to change Parliament's membership, all with the object of prevailing upon Parliament to change its mind and repeal the offending act. Until Parliament had repealed that act, however, it continued to be viewed by most, including British judges, as binding law, which one disobeyed at one's own risk. The dominant British view of the relationship of Parliament to the constitution during the eighteenth century was that only Parliament had the authority to void a law, by reversing its earlier judgment and repealing it. In this sense, constitutional constraints upon Parliament were understood by most Englishmen to impose moral or political duties, rather than "strictly legal limitation[s] on parliament's legislative capacity."[28] The long constitutional controversy provoked by Parliament's repeal in 1716 of the 1694 Triennial Act, substituting a septennial act in its place, illustrates how these constitutional understandings operated, but also the tensions within them.

Since the revolutions of the seventeenth century, many Englishmen had viewed the frequency of Parliamentary elections as of critical constitutional significance. More than a decade after the Triennial Act was repealed, the constitutional crisis had not abated. Viscount Bolingbroke wrote that "frequent elections to parliament were an 'ancient and fundamental rule of our constitution', in order that 'the people should have frequent opportunities of calling their representatives to account, as it were, for the discharge of the trust committed to them.'"[29] But "Bolingbroke did not pretend that the Septennial Act was impossible or invalid."[30] His constitutional objections were raised as part of

[28] J. W. Gough, *Fundamental Law in English Constitutional History* (Oxford, Oxford at the Clarendon Press, 1971), 184–85.

[29] Ibid., 185, quoting Viscount Bolingbroke's *Dissertation on Parties* (1733); see also Isaac Kramnick, *Bolingbroke and His Circle: The Politics of Nostalgia in the Age of Walpole* (Cambridge, Mass., Harvard University Press, 1968), 127, 130, 251; and John Trenchard, *Cato's Letters*, Nos. 60, 61 (1721).

[30] Gough, Fundamental Law, 185.

a parliamentary campaign to repeal the Septennial Act and to replace it with a new Triennial Act.[31]

Even so, some eighteenth-century Englishmen believed that their constitution did, under certain circumstances, impose actual limits on Parliament's legal capacity to legislate. During the original debates over the passage of the Septennial Act, several members of Parliament had argued that the proposed bill, which extended Parliament's term from three years to seven years, violated the constitution and even if enacted would "not obtain the force of a law," but would be "void of itself."[32] One member reasoned that "the power of the legislature was derived from the electors. 'You have no legislative capacity,' he told his fellow-members, 'but what you derive from them. You were chosen under the Triennial Act, and could only be chosen for three years. Our trust therefore', he inferred, 'is a triennial trust; and if we endeavor to continue it beyond its legal duration, from that instant we cease to be trustees of the people, and are our own electors; from that instant we act by an assumed power and erect a new constitution.'"[33]

The difficulty for this position was that so long as there was no other authority within government that held the power to say that a statute in conflict with the constitution did not possess the force of law, or that wielded the power to deny such a statute the binding force of law, the view of some that such statutes were void had to remain an abstract proposition. It might almost be said that unless this view could find an institutional home in some part of the government other than the legislature, such laws would continue to bind in every practical sense. So long as Parliament itself possessed the final, un-appealable power to say that a bill was to have the binding force of law, constitutional constraints could in practice only impose "political" or "moral" duties. In effect, only a council, or a governor, or a court, possessing the authority to and/or the power formally to deny an enactment the force of law, could effectively turn constitutional precepts into limitations on Parliament's legal capacity to enact legislation.[34]

[31] See Kramnick, Bolingbroke and His Circle, 29.

[32] Gough, Fundamental Law, 181–83.

[33] Ibid., 181 (quoting the remarks of Mr. Shippen).

[34] For a similar view, see Edward S. Corwin, "Establishment of Judicial Review, I" (1910) 9 *Michigan Law Review* 102, 110. The English monarch, of course still formally enjoyed the authority to refuse his/her assent to bills, thereby preventing them from becoming law, but after 1707 no monarch ever did.

Here is how Henry Goodricke understood the matter during the final quarter of the eighteenth century.

> [The supremacy of Parliament means] nothing more,– than that it is *absolutely supreme* in command; that there is no *civil* or *legal* power in the state *superior* to it, and that its acts can not be controlled or annulled by any other *authority*. This does not preclude in the least its being limited, as to the extent of its power, either by laws of Nature, or by rules and principles of the Constitution.[35]

These tensions in eighteenth-century British constitutional thought gave rise to at least two different principal accounts of Parliament's position in the constitutional system. "Although Whigs," Philip Hamburger notes, "being usually a majority, were apt to agree with Blackstone about Parliament's absolute power, other more radical Whigs continued to insist that there were constitutional limitations on Parliament, even if enforceable only outside the courts."[36]

The ultimate remedy in this eighteenth-century Anglo/American constitutional tradition was one enforced by the polity as a whole, the people's right of revolution. During 1688–89, Parliament, convening itself as a convention (in the absence of the king), and acting as the representatives of the people, had replaced one monarch with another. John Locke, among others, took these events to have established the people's right to replace the existing form of government in extraordinary circumstances, when rulers committed serious violations of fundamental law. But this remedy for constitutional violations was squarely in line with, if more extreme than, the other "political" remedies for constitutional violations available to the people: frequent elections, petitions to the government, pamphletting, civil disobedience, rioting, and ultimately revolution. Until Parliament changed its mind, however, or the government was replaced, duly enacted statutes continued to possess the binding force of law.

"Fundamental law" [in this tradition], Sylvia Snowiss observes, "contemplated unresolved controversy over contending legitimate interpretations, and unlike ordinary law did not need authoritative resolution of this controversy in order to maintain its efficacy. In the absence of authoritative determination of fundamental law's meaning, challenged

[35] Henry Goodricke, *Observations on Dr. Price's Theory and Principles of Civil Liberty and Government* (York, 1776), 43–44, quoted in John Phillip Reid, *Constitutional History of the American Revolution: The Authority to Legislate* (Madison, Wisc., University of Wisconsin Press, 1991), 83.

[36] Philip Hamburger, *Law and Judicial Duty* (Cambridge, Mass., Harvard University Press, 2009), 252.

governmental action stood, debate continued, and constitutional principles retained all their vitality."[37]

When American constitutions were committed to writing, a sharper distinction between interpretation and amendment, between explication and violation, began to take shape, but the older assumption that legislatures might properly expound constitutions through their statutes continued to hold significant sway over how America's first framers conceived of the relationship between legislatures and the new constitutions. Written constitutions may have weakened older ways of thinking, but they did not render them obsolete.

One reason Parliament could play the role it did in interpreting and explicating the constitution in the English tradition was that it was viewed as embodying the nation itself. J.W. Gough observes that "there was no question yet of distinguishing between the people and Parliament. Parliament was just assumed to represent and so to be equivalent to the people themselves."[38] Similarly, Philip Hamburger writes, "Parliament was the court in which the entire realm was presumed to be present to declare or alter their custom, including what came to be considered England's constitution."[39] This was a deeply rooted, taken-for-granted assumption that shaped the way many Americans understood their own legislatures in the early years following Independence; legislatures were *the* representatives of the people and were presumed to express the people's will definitively. There was as yet little sense that "the people" might have more than a single will, embodied in their governments in different ways.

Nor would the written constitutional constraints that had been contained in their foundational colonial documents necessarily have led Americans to a different conclusion. The earlier South Carolina conflict over judicial review had ended with the triumph of the view that written constitutional constraints did not operate as limitations on the power of legislatures to make law in the first instance. And this view resonated with dominant Anglo-American understandings about the nature of the constraint the English constitution imposed on Parliament. Under political pressure, Parliament could certainly be induced to repeal a statute that the nation considered unconstitutional, but until it had done so, the statute continued to possess the force of law.

[37] Sylvia Snowiss, *Judicial Review and the Law of the Constitution* (New Haven, Ct., Yale University Press, 1990), 6.

[38] Gough, Fundamental Law, 87 fn. 2.

[39] Hamburger, Law and Judicial Duty, 238.

Nevertheless, the colonial debate, like certain English constitutional debates about the character of Parliament's power, revealed the existence of another, different view about the nature of constitutional limitations. This view was subordinated to the first almost everywhere in practice, but it held that legislatures simply lacked the power to confer the force of law on an act that conflicted with a constitution; such statutes were widely termed "void." And while the expression "void" was not always used in the modern way to indicate that an objectionable statute had automatically lost the force of law,[40] the term could certainly be read to imply that. Constitutions would then have to be understood as imposing what might be termed "legal" limitations on the capacity of legislatures to make law.

The story of the drafting and adoption of the first American state constitutions is enormously complicated. States followed a number of different procedures in forming new governments. But it is possible to acknowledge this irreducible variety while pointing to some general patterns. Constitution making, it seems to have been widely agreed, was certainly distinct from ordinary lawmaking. It involved the solemn and momentous process of forming new governments. For this serious task, representatives in many states sought the sanction of new elections, in which the people would explicitly authorize their representatives to draft a constitution. In most cases, these elections were to fill seats in the revolutionary provincial congresses that had been administering governments, exercising legislative, executive, and in some cases judicial powers, after imperial officials had withdrawn from the country.

In most cases, these elections were designed not to create a new representative body for the purpose of performing this solemn task but to renew the popular sanction of an existing one and to give explicit authority to undertake the new task of drafting a constitution. New York's provincial congress recited, for example, that "whereas doubts have arisen whether this congress are invested with sufficient power and authority to deliberate and determine on so important a subject as the necessity of erecting and constituting a new form of government ... and whereas it appertains of right solely to the people of this colony to determine the said doubts,"[41] the congress established an electoral process to ascertain the people's will on the subject. After holding the election and

[40] See, for example, Edmund Randolph's use of the term "void" in his argument in the Virginia *Case of the Prisoners* discussed at length in Chapter 5.

[41] Quoted from the preamble to New York's 1777 constitution in Thorpe, ed., Constitutions, V, 2625.

receiving its answer from the people, New York's provincial congress proceeded to convene itself as a convention during the times it debated a new constitution, reconvening at other times as a congress or committee of safety to perform legislative and executive tasks. And it made certain to recite in the resulting constitution the grounds of its authority to form a new government. "And whereas the good people of the said colony, in pursuance of the said [election] resolution, and reposing special trust and confidence in the members of this convention, have appointed, authorized, and empowered them for the purposes, and in the manner, and with the powers in and by the said resolve specified, declared, and mentioned."[42] And this was not untypical.

In two states, however, Virginia and South Carolina, special elections were not held.[43] Some years later as constitutional thinking evolved, this omission became a subject of some controversy, at least in Virginia. In the early 1780s, Thomas Jefferson questioned whether the Virginia revolutionary congress had possessed the requisite sanction from the people to form a new government, and believing that it had not, argued that the existing Virginia constitution enjoyed no greater authority than an ordinary statute, which could be changed at will by any succeeding legislature.[44] In those two states and in New Hampshire, congresses or conventions transformed themselves into the lower house of the legislature once constitutions had been adopted.[45]

These procedures did not by and large provoke a great outcry at the time because of the taken-for-granted assumption about the nature of these bodies, an assumption that was characteristic of the English constitutional tradition. In most people's eyes, revolutionary congresses were *the* representatives of the people, and they remained the people's representatives whether they were making laws or ordinances, in one of their capacities, or undertaking the distinct and more serious task of writing constitutions, in a separate capacity. For the same reason it was not immediately seen as an outrage when the representatives of the people transformed themselves into the lower house of a legislature once a constitution had been adopted. What was crucial was not so much the particular task that the representative body performed, but that it had received its sanction at a recent election, where the will of the people could be ascertained.

[42] Ibid. [43] Kruman, Between Authority and Liberty, 20.

[44] Thomas Jefferson, *Notes on the State of Virginia* (Boston, Lilly and Wait, 1832, "written in the year 1781, and somewhat corrected and enlarged in the winter of 1782"), Chapter 13 "Constitution," Note 5, 125–34.

[45] Kruman, Between Authority and Liberty, 22.

A formal process for amending constitutions was an innovation that was introduced in a number of the first written constitutions.[46] For the same reason that there had been no widespread criticism of the procedures employed to draft and adopt many constitutions (outside of New England), framers of the first constitutions in a number of states felt little compunction about giving legislatures the authority to amend constitutions by using procedures that were distinct from those provided for the enactment of laws, and which called, in some cases, for ascertaining the will of the people anew at an election, in others for a supermajority vote of the legislature. Maryland's 1776 constitution, for example, provided "[t]hat this Form of Government, and the Declaration of Rights, and no part thereof, shall be altered, changed, or abolished unless a bill so to alter, change or abolish the same shall pass the General Assembly, and be published at least three months before a new election, and shall be confirmed by the General Assembly, after a new election of Delegates, in the first session after such new election ...."[47] In a similar vein, South Carolina's 1778 constitution provided "[t]hat no part of this constitution shall be altered without notice being previously given of ninety days, nor shall any part of the same be changed without the consent of a[n absolute] majority of the members of the senate and house of representatives."[48] Delaware's 1776 constitution prohibited any "violation" of a number of its provisions. As for others, they could be "altered, changed, or diminished with ... the consent of five parts in seven of the Assembly, and seven members of the legislative council."[49]

In New Jersey, the 1776 constitution prohibited the "repeal," "annulment" or "alteration" of certain sections[50] and did not explicitly provide for an amendment procedure. But the New Jersey legislature seems to have assumed that it was free to amend other sections of the constitution, as it subsequently did by statute.[51] This view would have been in keeping with English constitutional traditions, reflecting the assumption that as the representatives of the people, legislatures possessed the authority to

[46] Not surprisingly, because a formal procedure for amending constitutions was a departure from British tradition, three early state constitutions, New York's (1777), North Carolina's (1776) and Virginia's (1776), failed to provide expressly for amendments at all, ibid., 55, as did New Jersey's 1776 constitution.

[47] Thorpe (ed.), Constitutions, III, 1701 (Md. 1776).

[48] Ibid., VI, 3257 (S.C., 1778).

[49] Ibid., I, 568 (Del. 1776).

[50] Ibid., V, 2598 (N.J., 1776). The language of the document explicitly prohibited the "repeal" of the right to trial by jury.

[51] Kruman, Between Authority and Liberty, 56.

interpret (explain or modify) a constitution. John Adams, for example, wrote in his influential 1776 proposals in "Thoughts on Government" that "[t]he Legislature . . . will have Power to make any alterations [in the constitution] from Time to Time, to Supply Defects which experience may point out."[52]

Even in the early days following Independence, however, some believed that since legislatures derived their very being and authority from constitutions, a separate representative body, a stand-alone constitutional convention, should be chosen by the people to draft these foundational instruments, and some thought that it was also necessary for the people themselves subsequently to express their approval by ratifying this work.[53] But these opinions did not immediately become widespread (outside of New England), as traditional assumptions about the proper relationship between constitutions and the ordinary representatives of the people remained a powerful influence on the way Americans conceived of their constitutional system.

It is apparent, at the same time that framers in a number of states meant to depart from or reject certain aspects of English tradition. In Delaware, the constitution provided that certain crucial sections "ought [n]ever to be violated on any pretence whatever,"[54] in New Jersey that "the inestimable right of trial by jury shall remain confirmed as a part of the law of this Colony, without repeal, forever."[55] The North Carolina instrument went further, declaring that the Declaration of Rights was part of the constitution and "ought never to be violated on any pretence whatsoever."[56] The language the framers used in these efforts to effect a departure from English tradition, however, often came out of that same tradition. The words and sentence structure in most declarations of rights from this period often reflect language in the English Bill of Rights of 1689 and are not well suited for their apparent task. Injunctions were mainly framed in passive constructions, using the words "ought" or "should," reflecting the character of these English constitutional provisions as statements of fundamental "political" norms.[57] The use of the word "ought" or even

[52] Taylor (ed.,), Papers of John Adams, IV, 77, 84, 90 ("Thoughts on Government," several versions).

[53] Kruman, Between Authority and Liberty, 29, 31.

[54] Thorpe (ed.), Constitutions, I, 568 (Dela. 1776).

[55] Ibid., V, 2598 (Section XXII, N.J., 1776). [56] Ibid., V, 2794 (N.C., 1776).

[57] A typical provision of the English Bill of Rights of 1689 states "That excessive bail ought not to be required, nor excessive fine imposed, nor cruel and unusual punishments inflicted" (http://avalon.law.yale.edu/17th_century/england.asp).

the less common "shall" in the passive constructions used in the Delaware, New Jersey and North Carolina constitutions (as well as in many provisions in most of the other first constitutions) failed to identify the actors against whom they were aimed and the specific types of violations they wished to foreclose.[58] Like the English provisions they resembled, the precatory language used to declare these rights suggest that they were not meant to impose fully "legal" limitations on their governments, including their legislatures. But it is not only the language in which these restrictions were cast that points toward this conclusion, it is also that the documents created no institutional mechanism within governments for declaring that acts in conflict with a constitution would be void and without the force of law.

Pennsylvania's constitution went further than most, specifically identifying the legislature as the body against which some of its injunctions were aimed. The legislature shall have all "powers necessary for the legislature of a free state or commonwealth: But they shall have no power to add to, alter, abolish, or infringe any part of this constitution."[59] These various early constitutional efforts to restrict the power of legislatures to alter or infringe constitutions reflected a growing sense that even the representatives of the people could not be completely trusted with unlimited power over fundamental rights and liberties. And they reflected the beginnings of a process in which the representatives of the people assembled in legislatures would no longer be seen to be trustworthy enough to serve as the sole explicators of constitutions within government. A wall was beginning to be erected separating constitutions from legislatures, attempting to place the former beyond the power of the latter to alter or elucidate, implicitly reflecting a growing sense that the will of the people might not be fully embodied in the acts of their legislatures.

But these constitutional provisions attempted to impose restrictions using language that looks strange to modern eyes. The words the early framers chose to express the idea that they were imposing limitations on the power of legislatures reveal that they were still working from squarely within the English constitutional tradition, in which Parliament in fact possessed and exercised the power to alter the fundamental law by statute.

58 The term "shall" was used considerably more frequently in these instruments when the frame of government itself was being defined, see Donald S. Lutz, *Popular Consent and Popular Control: Whig Political Theory in the Early State Constitutions* (Baton Rouge, La., Louisiana State University Press, 1980), 65.

59 Thorpe (ed.), Constitutions, V, 3084 (Pa. 1776).

In some states, like Pennsylvania, framers felt it to be crucial to state explicitly that they were rejecting certain of the core assumptions of this tradition. Today, a statute in conflict with a constitution is not ordinarily thought to represent an attempt to amend or alter the fundamental law. Alteration of constitutions is instinctively thought to be the result of an entirely separate process often involving constitutional conventions and popular ratification. Today, one simply says that a statute conflicts with a constitution, taking for granted the very different constitutional statuses of the two kinds of law and the very different institutional processes and actors responsible for making each. It is certainly arguable that the words in these early constitutional clauses were intended to extend to statutes that did not attempt formally to "alter" or "amend" a constitution but that conflicted with it. Any such statute does in a sense alter the constitution, but there are much clearer more direct ways of expressing this idea. And not only were Americans familiar with these from their colonial experience, they utilized them, in other contexts, in several of the first constitutions.

The language in the Pennsylvania constitution and in other constitutions of the period simultaneously assumed a closer affinity between statutes and constitutional provisions than is common today and moved in the direction of making the two independent of one another, placing constitutions beyond the power of a simple statute to alter.[60] But taking for granted that a statute could "alter" a constitution also had the effect of making written constitutions seem more like statutes, a regular form of law, albeit a higher form, rather than a form of fundamental "political law," existing in an altogether different sphere.

[60] Section XXIII of New Jersey's 1776 constitution requires that legislators take an oath "not [to] assent to any law, vote, or proceeding" that would "annul, repeal, or alter" several sections of the constitution. Besides the ambiguity that this provision may have been aimed primarily at formal legislative "amendments" of constitutions, it enforces its restriction by imposing an obligation on legislators, for violations of which the most obvious remedy would seem to be impeachment, rather than the voiding of the legislation itself. If the provision was also meant to operate as a restriction on the power of legislators to make law, this certainly could have been done more clearly and directly. This kind of approach to constitutional enforcement also appears in some other constitutions of the period, see, for example, North Carolina Constitution of 1776, Art. XXIII, which, however, seemed to be directed only at persons in the executive and judicial branches. "[T]he Governor, and other officers, offending against the State, by violating any part of this Constitution ... may be prosecuted, on the impeachment of the General Assembly, or presentment of the Grand Jury of any court of supreme jurisdiction in this State," in Thorpe (ed.), Constitutions, V, 2792.

The use of this elliptical language in these constitutional provisions, however, is also revealing of the framers' intentions. The drafters of these first constitutions knew how to talk more clearly about conflicts between statutes and constitutions that actually deprived a statute of the force of law. A section of New Jersey's 1776 constitution, for example, provided "[t]hat the common law of England, as well as so much of the statute law, as have been heretofore practiced in this Colony, shall still remain in force, until they shall be altered by a future law of the Legislature; such parts only excepted, as are *repugnant* to the rights and privileges contained in this Charter ... "[61] (emphasis added). Another section similarly provided "That all the laws of this Province [contained in a definitive collection of provincial statutes] shall be and remain in full force until altered by the Legislature of this Colony (such only excepted, as are incompatible with this Charter) ...."[62] When it came to protecting the right to trial by jury, apparently from the new state legislature, on the other hand, the constitution did not use language of "repugnance" or "incompatibility." Instead, it seems to have attempted to protect the right by limiting the new legislature's otherwise plenary power to alter existing provincial law.[63] From a modern perspective, this seems like an odd, indirect way to go about trying to secure a single constitutional right against legislative action. By their express terms, these early "repugnance" clauses were limited to preexisting provincial laws and placed no similar restriction on the laws their new legislatures were about to begin enacting.[64] The New York constitution of 1777 demonstrates that framers there also knew how to use the language of repugnance to deprive preexisting provincial law of its obligation. The constitution contained a provision "abrogating and rejecting" "all ... parts of the ... common law ... " that "are *repugnant to this constitution*"[65] (emphasis added). It also, however, contained

[61] Thorpe (ed.), Constitutions, V, 2598 (Section XXII, N.J. Const. of 1776).

[62] Ibid., 2598 (Section XXI, N.J. Const. of 1776).

[63] Ibid., V, 2598 (Section XXII, N.J. Const. of 1776) ("[T]he inestimable right of trial by jury shall remain confirmed as a part of the law of this Colony, without repeal, forever.")

[64] The "repugnance" clauses in some later constitutions, however, were noticeably different, containing an express limitation on the power of the new state legislature to make law, see, for example, the text of the Massachusetts constitution of 1780. The constitution gave the Massachusetts legislature plenary power to legislate "so as the same be *not repugnant to this constitution* ... ." (Art. IV, Mass. Const. of 1780), in ibid., III, 1894 (emphasis added). And the nearly identical provision in the New Hampshire Constitution of 1784 in ibid., IV, 2458). Neither constitution, however, created any institutional mechanism, other than a conditional gubernatorial veto, to enforce this limitation.

[65] Ibid., V, 2635–36 (Section XXV, N.Y. Const. of 1777).

a quite clear and forceful provision prohibiting the legislature from enacting bills of attainder (once the war had ended).[66]

But when it came to declaring flatly that the new legislature of the state had not been granted the power to make laws that conflicted with the constitution, only Georgia's constitution (of the first generation of state constitutions) came close to stating this limitation on legislative power unambiguously. "The house of assembly shall have power to make such laws and regulations as may be conducive to the good order and well-being of the state; provided such laws and regulations be not repugnant to the true intent and meaning of any rule or regulation contained in this constitution."[67] In this case, however, as in the case of every other early state constitution (except for Pennsylvania's, New York's and Vermont's) and like the English constitution itself, the Georgia constitution failed to create any institution in government that would have the authority actually to declare that such acts did not possess the force of law.

The strongest desire to impose limitations on legislatures seems to have arisen among Americans at opposite ends of the political spectrum, among the most radical and the most conservative framers, but for very different reasons. Radical Whigs feared and distrusted the exercise of all governmental power that might violate the liberties and rights of the people, whether wielded by executives or legislatures, and the most radical constitutions of the period, Pennsylvania's, Vermont's and Georgia's, reflect this suspicion, in their attempts to impose limits on the power to legislate. Many conservative Whigs distrusted legislative power for another reason; too often it reflected the ill-considered and sometimes dangerous views of the mass of the common people. From this other end of the political spectrum, New York's constitution reflected conservative desires to place limits on the power of popular assemblies to make law.

It is only in these most radical and conservative constitutions of the period (Pennsylvania, Vermont and New York) that attempts were made to introduce an explicit institutional mechanism to enforce constitutional limitations on legislative power. In Pennsylvania (and Vermont), the mechanism was entirely novel. Every seven years the people were to elect a Council of Censors "whose duty it shall be to enquire whether the constitution has been preserved inviolate in every part; and whether the legislative and executive branches of government have performed their

[66] Ibid., V, 2637 ("[N]o acts of attainder *shall* be passed by the legislature of this state . . . ." Section XLI, N.Y. Const. 1777) (emphasis added).

[67] Ibid., II, 779 (Art. VII of the Georgia Constitution of 1777).

duty as guardians of the people, or assumed to themselves, or exercised other or greater powers than they are intitled to by the constitution . . . ."[68] The constitution gave this council "power to send for persons, papers, and records; they shall have authority to pass public censures, [and] to order impeachments . . . ."[69] But crucially, when it came to creating an institution that might enforce these constitutional limitations against the legislature and the legislation that emerged from it, the constitution did not depart far from British tradition. The Council of Censor's authority was to be merely advisory, "to *recommend* to the legislature *the repealing* [of] such laws *as appear to them* [,the Council,] to have been enacted contrary to the *principles* of the constitution"[70] (emphasis added). The clause took for granted that even when it "appear[ed] to the Council" that a law might be "contrary to the *principles* of the constitution" the statute nevertheless continued to possess the full force of law until the legislature had been persuaded to repeal it. Whatever language there is in the Pennsylvania constitution that appears to withhold power from the legislature to do certain acts, at the end of the day the document drew back from actually creating any institutional mechanism to enforce it.

The New York constitution took a different tack, as befitted the conservative document it was. It brought back, in modified form, a version of the gubernatorial veto, only now wielded by a Council of Revision, on which the governor sat.[71] This provision was also one of the few in early constitutions that focused clearly on the issue of laws passed by the legislature that might conflict with the constitution. It framed the problem this way.

> [W]hereas laws *inconsistent* with the *spirit of this constitution*, or with *the public good*, may be hastily and unadvisedly passed ... all bills which have passed the senate and assembly shall *before they become laws*, be presented to the said council for their revisal and consideration; and if, upon such revision and consideration, it should *appear improper* to the said council, or a majority of them, *that the said bill should become a law of this State*, that they return the same, together with their *objections* thereto in writing [to the house of the legislature in which the

[68] Ibid., V, 3091 (Sect. 47 of the Pennsylvania Const. of 1776). The "Council of Censors [was] modeled loosely on Greek and Roman institutions recently praised by Montesquieu and Rousseau," David E. Kyvig, *Explicit & Authentic Acts: Amending the U.S. Constitution, 1776–1995* (Lawrence, Kans., University Press of Kansas, 1996), 31.

[69] Thorpe, Constitutions, V, 3091.

[70] Ibid., V, 3092; for the identical "recommending repeal" clause in the Vermont Constitution of 1777, see ibid., VI, 3761.

[71] The New York Constitution of 1777 and its Council of Revision is discussed in greater detail below.

bill originated for their reconsideration.] But if, after such reconsideration, *two-thirds* [of both houses] shall, notwithstanding the said *objections*, agree to pass the same *it* ... *shall be a law*.[72] (emphasis added)

On a number of occasions following the adoption of the 1777 constitution, the Council of Revision actually did "object to [a] bill as being inconsistent with the spirit of the constitution of this State" and afterwards, "[n]otwithstanding the objections, the Legislature passed the bill ... into a law."[73] As in the Pennsylvania constitution (and every other constitution of the period) the final, un-appealable power to confer the force of law on a bill, despite constitutional objections, lay with the legislature. In New York, however, if this legislative judgment was to prevail over constitutional objections, it had to overcome the hurdle of a super-majority vote. It must, in other words, be based upon a broad consensus among legislators that the bill was constitutionally proper. But if that broader consensus were present among legislators (2/3 of both houses), their judgment (and power) over the matter would be final.

It is important to focus closely on the language in which these clauses were expressed. In Pennsylvania, laws should not be enacted that "*appear to the Council of Censors*" to be "contrary to the *principles* of the constitution." In New York, they should not "*appear improper*" to the Council of Revision by being "inconsistent with the *spirit* of this constitution." Under the Georgia constitution, laws should not be repugnant to the "*true intent and meani*ng of any rule or regulation contained in this constitution."[74] The language in these clauses suggests that early framers considered broad and flexible interpretation to be the essence of the constitutional inquiry, in keeping with the broad discretion legislatures enjoyed to make new laws guided by a double duty to promote "the public good" and to preserve "the spirit of the constitution," as the New York constitution now explicitly required. It was not the text of the constitution

[72] The New York Constitution of 1777, Section III, in Thorpe (ed.), Constitutions, V, 2628–29. It should be noted that the current federal constitution of Canada has a similar "notwithstanding" clause (Section 33 of the *Canadian Charter of Rights and Freedoms*).

[73] Council Veto of a bill entitled "an act to prevent the exportation of flour, meal and grain out of this State," February 20, 1778, in Alfred B. Street, *The Council of Revision of the State of New York and Its Vetoes* (Albany, N.Y., William Gould Publisher, 1859), 203, quote taken from pages 203 and 208; for another instance in which the Council found a bill to be inconsistent with the spirit of the constitution and the legislature notwithstanding the Council's objections went on to pass the bill into law, see Street, Council of Revision, 212–13.

[74] Thorpe (ed.), Constitutions, II, 779 (Art. VII of the Georgia Constitution of 1777).

(the letter of the law) these provisions pointed to,[75] but the "principles" of the constitution, or the "spirit" of the constitution, or its "true intent and meaning." Under the New York constitution the Council of Revision would say that a law found to be "inconsistent with the spirit of this constitution" "appeared improper" to them and would present their "objections" to it to the legislature.

What a constitution, whose principles were set down in abstract terms, demanded in any particular instance might not be all that obvious. Many early framers appear to have believed that like Parliament, the legislatures of their newly sovereign states, as the representatives of the people, should be the ones with the authority to determine what the principles or spirit of the constitution demanded in any particular situation and that their interpretive judgment on these matters should be final within government. That these kinds of determinations about what was fitting for the broad polity, as to both utility and constitutionality, might be the peculiar province of the people's representatives makes a kind of sense that modern constitutional understandings often fail to appreciate.

The view that legislatures should be entitled to a broad and flexible interpretive discretion under constitutions as they went about their lawmaking task does not seem to have been limited to the framers of the New York, Pennsylvania and Georgia constitutions. In 1782, Edmund Randolph, then Attorney General of Virginia and a member of the convention that framed Virginia's constitution, argued to the Virginia Court of Appeals in the *Case of the Prisoners* that courts should interpret constitutions and statutes very differently. In the case of constitutions, he wrote, "the liberality, necessary to catch its spirit, must be adopted."[76]

In the two constitutions of the period that perhaps reflect the deepest distrust of legislative power, New York's and Pennsylvania's, the framers were prepared to go no further in restricting the capacity of legislatures to make law. At the end of the day, for all their apparent desire to place limits on the power of legislatures, these framers were still working within a traditional set of British constitutional presuppositions; in a sense, it was because they continued to assume that legislatures should possess the

[75] On "letter" vs. "spirit" as interpretive approaches to determining intent, see Hamburger, Law and Judicial Duty, 54, 300.

[76] Quoted from Randolph's "Rough Draft of Arguments in Respondent v. Lamb" (*the Case of the Prisoners*) in William Michael Treanor, "The Case of the Prisoners and the Origins of Judicial Review" (1994) 143 *University of Pennsylvania Law Review* 491, 508.

final, un-appealable authority to give a bill the force of law, that constitutional constraints could only operate as a form of moral or political duty.

All of this seems to point to the conclusion that Americans of the period felt deeply ambivalent about imposing firm restrictions on their legislatures. On the one hand, many Americans seem to have been hesitant to allow legislatures to wield the kind of unchecked power that Parliament did. On the other hand, no constitutional convention of the period permitted the re-introduction of any of the traditional checks on legislatures, such as the absolute gubernatorial veto that had been previously used to limit the power of popular assemblies to make law, or created a new one with the express authority to deny the force of law to a legislative enactment that might be in conflict with a constitution.

This ambivalence reflected a deeper one. The English constitutional tradition had taught Americans that only legislatures in limited and dependent governments operated under express constitutional restrictions on their right to make law. The "repugnant to the laws of England" language in their colonial charters and governors' commissions was an attribute of colonial dependency. No such explicit limitation was imposed on Parliament as the legislature of a fully sovereign state. Now that their own governments were no longer "limited and dependent," most Americans seem to have believed that imposing hard restrictions on the power to make law would deprive their legislatures of the dignity to which they were entitled. Many Americans had also not forgotten that such restrictions could readily be used to impose limits on the power of the people themselves to make, through their legislatures, the laws by which they wished to be governed.

2.3 ANNUAL ELECTIONS

The idea that "annual elections" were critical to the preservation of the liberties of the people went back to the English Revolution of the mid-seventeenth century.[77] In the eighteenth century, it became a central pillar of Anglo/American constitutional thought. During the controversy over the Septennial Act, even the Tory Bolingbroke spoke of its fundamental importance in the English constitution.[78] He proceeded to point out how

[77] Edmund Morgan, *Inventing the People: The Rise of Popular Sovereignty in England and America* (New York, W. W. Norton & Co., c. 1988), 68, 79, 159.

[78] See Gough, Fundamental Law, quoting Bolingbroke's *Dissertation on Parties* (1733), 185; see also Kramnick, Bolingbroke and His Circle, 127, 130, 251.

following the Glorious Revolution of 1688 "patriots ... who remembered long parliaments, who still felt the smart of them ... struggled hard for annual, and obtained with much difficulty, at the end of five or six years, triennial parliaments ... ."[79] The framers of the first American constitutions achieved what these British "patriots" could not; they inscribed into nearly every one of their early constitutions the requirement that lower houses be elected annually.

In the heady years immediately following Independence, at a time when the people were playing an active and direct role in political affairs, this venerable constitutional tradition supplied an obvious answer to the problem of how legislatures were to be controlled, without the need to consider further checks on their legislative capacity. The people themselves, acting at annual elections, would enforce their own constitutional compacts. They would regularly review the work of their legislatures at frequent elections, and if it was their sense that legislators had exceeded their authority, they would turn them out of office, replacing them with men who would repeal offending statutes and adhere more faithfully to the people's understanding of what the principles or spirit of their constitutions demanded.[80] At this moment, the radical proposition first laid down during the English Revolution of the mid-seventeenth century began to serve as a concrete answer to the question of how legislatures were to be kept within constitutional bounds. "[F]or my own Part," John Adams wrote in 1776, "I think [elections] ought to be annual, for there is not in all science a Maxim more infallible than this 'Where Annual Elections End, there Slavery begins.'"[81]

"Rather than prohibit the exercise of specific powers," Jack Rakove has written, "the early constitutions expected political mechanisms to keep lawmakers accountable."

[79] Quoted in Gough, Fundamental Law, 185.

[80] The view that the people would act at elections to interpret and enforce their constitutions was, under the circumstances, a moderate view. A more radical view held that the people were not limited to the single annual occasion of an election to enforce their constitutional understandings, but possessed the authority to do so throughout the year by means of popular action. See Barbara Clark Smith, *The Freedoms We Lost: Consent and Resistance in Revolutionary America* (New York, The New Press, 2010), 17–46; and Christian G. Fritz, *American Sovereigns: The People and America's Constitutional Tradition Before the Civil War* (New York, Cambridge University Press, 2008), 97–100, 126.

[81] See John Adams, "Thoughts on Government," in Taylor (ed.), Papers of John Adams, IV, 80, 90.

If a legislature violated its trust, the proper remedies lay with the citizenry, who could petition or instruct their representatives, or eject errant law makers through the device of annual elections, which orthodox republicans regarded as a sufficient protection for all popular rights. "While all kinds of governmental power reverts [sic] annually to the people, there can be little danger of their liberty," observed "Demophilus," one of the more radical writers of 1776. "Because no maxim was ever more true than that, WHERE ANNUAL ELECTION ENDS, SLAVERY BEGINS."[82]

It is possible to see these views at work in a number of early constitutions. The Maryland Declaration of Rights of 1776, for example, stated "[t]hat the right in the people to participate in the Legislature is the best security of liberty, and the foundation of all free government; for this purpose, elections ought to be free and frequent . . . ."[83] Similar views found their way into the 1776 North Carolina Declaration of Rights. "That, for the redress of grievances, and for amending and strengthening the laws, elections ought to be often held."[84] The Pennsylvania Declaration of Rights contained a more elaborate presentation of the same principle. "That those who are employed in the legislative and executive business of the state, may be restrained from oppression, the people have a right, at such periods as they may think proper, to reduce their public officers to a private station, and supply the vacancies by certain and regular elections."[85] And in a separate article went on to admonish the people "that a frequent recurrence to fundamental principles, and a firm adherence to justice, moderation, temperance, industry and frugality are absolutely necessary to preserve the blessings of liberty and keep a government free: The people ought therefore to pay particular attention to these points in the choice of officers and representatives, and have a right to exact a due and constant regard to them, from their legislatures and magistrates, in the making and executing such laws as are necessary for the good government of the state."[86]

The conventional wisdom held that the only significant danger facing frequent elections as a method for enforcing constitutional limitations was that legislatures might vote to postpone or suspend them. The provision in the New Jersey constitution requiring legislators to swear an oath not to

[82] Jack N. Rakove, *Original Meanings, Politics and Ideas in the Making of the Constitution* (New York, Vintage, 1996), 304.

[83] Thorpe, Constitutions, III, 1687 (Art. V, Maryland Declaration of Rights, 1776).

[84] Ibid., V, 2788 (Art. XX, North Carolina Declaration of Rights, 1776).

[85] Ibid., V, 3083 (Art. VI, Pennsylvania Declaration of Rights, 1776).

[86] Ibid., V, 3083–84 (Art. XIV, Pennsylvania Declaration of Rights, 1776).

alter the system of annual elections was specifically directed at this problem.[87] English constitutional history provided an object lesson in the dangers posed when legislatures took it upon themselves to delay or suspend elections.[88] During the English Revolution of the mid-seventeenth century, the Long Parliament had continued itself in power from 1640, the year in which it was elected, until 1648.[89] This act of Parliamentary usurpation was one of those momentous events in English constitutional history that had been etched into collective memory, and had contributed to molding basic political attitudes among educated Americans.[90] Even more recently, in 1716, Parliament had voted to extend the time between its elections from three to seven years, setting off a long, bitter constitutional controversy over the importance of frequent elections for maintaining the liberties of the English people.[91]

But aside from this danger, and so long as the power to alter the frequency of constitutionally prescribed elections was withheld from legislatures, many Americans expected this system to face few difficulties in protecting their rights and liberties against legislative encroachment. In 1776, this view of constitutions and of how legislatures might be kept within their constraints appears to have been widespread. Even a number of fairly conservative men seem to have been forced to conclude that it was the only viable approach. Samuel Johnston, for example, in an April 1776 letter to his brother-in-law James Iredell, explained that "[w]e have not yet been able to agree on a Constitution."

> We have a meeting on it every evening, but can conclude nothing – the great difficulty in our way is how to establish a check on the representatives of the people, to prevent their assuming more power than would be consistent with the liberties of the people – such as increasing the time of their duration, and such like. Many projects have been proposed, too tedious for a letter to communicate .... After all, it appears to me, that there can be no check on the representatives of the

87 New Jersey Constitution of 1776 (Section XXIII), in Thorpe (ed.), Constitutions, V, 2598.

88 Kruman, Between Authority and Liberty, 84.

89 By many accounts, the Long Parliament lasted until 1660, when a new king was installed on the English throne.

90 It was one of the reasons John Adams gave for opposing unicameral legislatures. "A Single Assembly will become ambitious, and after Some Time will vote itself perpetual. This was found in the Case of the long Parliament [which had abolished during its long tenure both the monarchy and the House of Lords]: but more remarkably in the Case of Holland whose Assembly first voted that they should hold their Seats for seven Years, then for Life-and after some Time, that they would fill up Vacancies as they should happen without applying to their Constituents at all," Taylor (ed.), Papers of John Adams IV, 81 ("Thoughts on Government").

91 Kramnick, Bolingbroke and His Circle, 127, 130, 251; Trenchard, Cato's Letters, Nos. 60, 61 (1721); see also, Gough, Fundamental Law, 181–85.

people in a Democracy, but the people themselves; and, in order that the check may be the more efficient, I would have annual elections.[92]

This view of elections as providing the principal means for enforcing constitutional constraints against legislatures was closely tied to the traditional view that constitutions imposed "moral" or "political" duties on legislators rather than fully legal ones. In 1788, criticizing the proposed new Federal Constitution, "Brutus," writing in New York, argued in favor of the superiority of a version of the traditional constitution. "Had the construction of the constitution been left with the legislature," he wrote,

> they would have explained it at their peril; if they exceed their powers, or sought to find, in the spirit of the constitution, more than was expressed in the letter, the people from whom they derived their power could remove them, and do themselves right; and indeed I can see no other remedy that the people can have against their rulers for encroachments of this nature. A constitution is a compact of a people with their rulers; if the rulers break the compact, the people have a right and ought to remove them and do themselves justice; but in order to enable them to do this with the greater facility, those whom the people choose at stated periods, should have the power in the last resort to determine the sense of the compact; if they determine contrary to the understanding of the people, an appeal will lie to the people at the period when the rulers are to be elected, and they will have it in their power to remedy the evil . . . .[93]

By the time Brutus was writing, advocates of judicial review had made considerable headway in undermining this way of thinking about constitutions, a development that moved several supporters of traditional constitutionalism to defend that tradition by articulating, perhaps more clearly than before, its often unspoken premises. Just as Brutus had done in his 1788 attacks on the proposed Federal Constitution, Zephaniah Swift, in his 1795 treatise on Connecticut law, provided a cogent summary of the tradition's core assumptions.

> The legislature have the sole power of making laws . . . . [I]f they pass laws which are unconstitutional, they are responsible to the people – who may in the course of elections dismiss them from office, and appoint such persons as will repeal such unconstitutional acts. On this power of the people over the legislature, depends their security against all encroachments . . . .[94]

[92] Griffith J. McRee (ed.), *Life and Correspondence of James Iredell* (1857, repr. New York, Peter Smith, 1949), I, 276–77 (Letter from Samuel Johnston, April 20, 1776).

[93] "Brutus," XV (March 20, 1788) in Ralph Ketcham (ed.), *The Anti-Federalist Papers and the Constitutional Convention Debates* (New York, Signet Classics, 2003, c. 1986), 309.

[94] Zephaniah Swift, *A System of the Laws of the State of Connecticut: In Six Books* (Windham, Ct., 1795, repr. Arno Press, 1972), I, 53; Swift was articulating these views as part of his critique of judicial review, see 51–54.

Swift went on to say that

> [t]he constitution of the state of Connecticut is unalterable by the legislature in every respect that is necessary to its preservation, and at the same time permits the legislature to make alterations, wherever improvements can be introduced. It is unalterable in these respects, that it cannot be changed from a representative republic; that the people cannot be deprived of the rights of an annual election of one branch of the legislature, and of a semi-annual election of the other; that the number of representatives cannot be lessened; that the legislative power cannot be exercised, but in the two branches; that two assemblies must be holden annually. While these principles are adhered to, there is not the remotest danger that the government will verge to tyranny.[95]

Above all, perhaps, this approach to constitutional constraints befitted the dignity to which legislatures of fully sovereign states were entitled; it placed the enforcement of the fundamental political obligations of legislatures in the hands of the sovereign people where it might properly be said to belong. This system rested on a view of constitutional constraints quite different from the modern American one. It was a view of constitutions as fluid, open-textured, political instruments, and it bound the people and their legislatures only in ways resembling those in which the English constitution bound Parliament.

Life under this constitutional system, however, did not unfold exactly as hoped. It is by now a familiar story that the actions of legislatures began increasingly over the next decade to alienate elements both of the common people and of elites, and both groups contributed to rethinking the original system's basic premises. But where ordinary people, being the majority, often placed greater faith in the electoral process for correcting abuses, conservative elites were more likely to focus on the ways legislative abuses reflected the ill-considered, intemperate, and sometimes dangerous views of the mass of the people, who had elected legislatures and who, more often than not, they faithfully served. Over the next decade, it would be conservative men primarily, drawn from the ranks of lawyers and judges, who would play the greater role in devising a new check on legislatures in the form of judicial review, and in waging the political and cultural struggles

95 Swift, A System of the Laws of Connecticut I, 62. John Phillip Reid describes a similar list of what were regarded as the unalterable features of the British constitution, see Reid, Constitutional History of American Revolution: The Authority to Legislate, 95 ("Parliament could not vote itself perpetual, vest the king with its delegated power of legislation, change the mode of representation even by eliminating the rotten boroughs, alter the right to trial by jury, give the nation a different religion, or repeal Magna Carta.")

that would be necessary to have it accepted as an integral feature of a new American constitutional system. Basic constitutional assumptions would be recast to create a system that did not rely so wholly upon popular elections to enforce constitutional constraints, in large measure because of a growing sense, particularly among elites, that if the new republics were to survive, the terms of constitutions must bind even the people themselves, so that their otherwise plenary power to enact, through legislatures, just any law they might wish was not without limits. Popular elections could not possibly provide the basis for such a constitutional check.

The reaction of elites to the behavior of legislatures was shaped in considerable part by a set of traditional attitudes they often held about the mass of ordinary people, an integral feature of the British and American political culture of the time. To understand this aspect of the growing feeling that it was essential to establish some form of restraint on the people themselves, it is necessary to understand something more about the constitutional politics of the 1770s.

2.4 STRIVING TO PRESERVE THE TRADITIONAL POLITY: PROPERTY REQUIREMENTS TO VOTE, HOLD PUBLIC OFFICE, AND SERVE IN THE "UPPER" HOUSE OF THE LEGISLATURE

In the minds of many, the very viability of this constitutional system, which relied so heavily on popular elections, depended crucially on the character and capacities of the people who would be responsible for electing legislatures and supervising them. And on that question, a major contradiction ran through American thinking. On the one hand, nearly all Americans celebrated "the People" as the foundation of society and the fount of all government. This was a bedrock principle of Whigs of all political hues. On the other hand, many wealthy, educated Americans harbored grave doubts and fears about the capacity for government of the actual mass of ordinary people. Speaking at the Federal Convention in 1787, Alexander Hamilton captured perfectly this double-sided state of mind. "The voice of the people," he observed,

> has been said to be the voice of God: and however generally this maxim has been quoted and believed, it is not true in fact. The people are turbulent and changing; they seldom judge or determine right.[96]

[96] Farrand, Records of the Federal Convention, II, 299 (Yates Report of Hamilton's speech); these appear to have been views Hamilton had long held. In 1775, he had written to John Jay that the mass of men "have not sufficient stock of reason and knowledge to guide them ... [and when] the unthinking populace [become] loosened from their attachment to

Men of Hamilton's class still had one foot in a hierarchical universe, which understood society to be organized by ranks and conditions and believed that the ranks to which most ordinary people belonged ill fit them for the deep and important business of devising and running governments. Reacting to the radical constitution that had been framed in Pennsylvania in 1776 when "mostly honest well-meaning Country men"[97] from obscure backgrounds had taken control of the constitutional convention, opponents of the constitution questioned the fitness for the task of those who had brought the document into being. They wrote that in making this constitution

> "many men of excellent characters" had been turned out by "upstarts," who were "totally unacquainted with the principles of government." Too many ignorant persons, it seemed, were meddling in business that was over their heads, "deviating from that line of conduct allotted to every one, and undertaking things beyond their reach," and unsettling the social order by advising the people to avoid electing gentlemen of the learned professions.[98]

These attitudes were common among men of higher social rank, who, when pressed, were prepared to say, at least in private, that the "common people" were subject to fits of passion, prone to cupidity and susceptible to the blandishments of demagogues; their rule, if unchecked, would inevitably lead to anarchy.[99]

These views came increasingly into conflict not only with the popular rhetoric of the Revolution but with a new set of political realities. As the revolutionary process unfolded, ordinary Americans assumed the reins of government in many locales, helping to form and serve on extra-legal revolutionary committees that sprang up throughout the country to administer the affairs of government after imperial officials had fled or been driven out.[100] Ordinary Americans began to wield political authority, for the first time in many cases, and in the process became crucial to the

ancient establishments and courses, they seem to grow giddy and apt more or less to run into anarchy," quoted in Kruman, Between Authority and Liberty, 134.

97 Robert L. Brunhouse, *The Counter-Revolution in Pennsylvania, 1776–1790* (Harrisburg, Pa., Pennsylvania Historical Commission, 1942), 12–17; cf. Terry Bouton, *Taming Democracy: "The People," the Founders, and the Troubled Ending of the American Revolution* (New York, Oxford University Press, 2007), 52–53.

98 Quoted in Wood, Creation of the American Republic, 233.

99 Smith, The Freedoms We Lost, 114–15, 128–29. See also Wood, Creation of the American Republic, 205, 213; and Taylor (ed.), Papers of John Adams, IV, 208–11 (John Adams letter to James Sullivan, May 1776).

100 See in general, T. H. Breen, *American Insurgents, American Patriots: The Revolution of the People* (New York, Hill and Wang, 2010); and Smith, The Freedoms We lost.

success of the Revolution. Yeomen farmers, small and middling merchants, manufacturers and mechanics became the backbone of a new political class that began to press for a larger role in their governments.

There had been significant obstacles to their participation in provincial governments. Property-owning requirements to vote and to hold public office had excluded many of them.[101] And these formal restrictions were supported by powerful social norms of deference in many provinces.[102] Their betters, in any case, were commonly viewed as fully representing them, in that they shared fundamental interests in common. Now, these barriers were beginning to be challenged, often producing a distinct uneasiness among members of the landed and commercial gentry and the professional classes.

The young New York aristocrat, Gouverneur Morris, oozed contempt mixed with disquiet as he took in, on May 19, 1774, the spectacle of lowly New York City mechanics vying with the City's elite, at a mass outdoor meeting, for election to an extra-legal committee that was going to formulate the city's response to the Coercive Acts. He wrote of the event that

> [t]he mob begins to think and to reason. Poor reptiles! It is with them a vernal morning, they are struggling to cast off their winter's slough, they bask in the sunshine, and ere noon they will bite, depend on it. The gentry begin to fear this . . . . I see, and I see it with fear and trembling, that if the disputes with Britain continue, we shall be under the worst of all possible dominions. We shall be under the domination of a riotous mob.[103]

In North Carolina, James Iredell had a similar reaction to the popular celebrations that erupted when his brother-in-law, Samuel Johnston, was defeated at the October 1776 election to choose representatives for the North Carolina Congress that was about to restart the process of drafting a constitution. Iredell penned a bitter, sarcastic screed he entitled "Creed of a Rioter" that mocked the views he attributed to the demonstrators.

101 On provincial suffrage and office holding requirements, see Robert J. Dinkin, *Voting in Provincial America: A Study of Election in the Thirteen Colonies, 1689–1776* (Wesport, Ct., Greenwood Press, 1977), especially Chapters 2 and 3.

102 "But the [colonial] voters themselves seem to have adhered, in practice at least, to the traditional view [of the limited capacities of the common people], for when the people were asked to choose their representatives they seldom elected common farmers and artisans. Instead they put their trust in men of the upper class," Jackson Turner Main, "Government by the People: The American Revolution and the Democratization of the Legislatures" (1966) *The William and Mary Quarterly* XXIII, 392–93.

103 (Gouverneur Morris to John Penn, May 20, 1774), quoted in Jared Sparks (ed.), *The Life and Times of Gouverneur Morris, With Selections from His Correspondence and Miscellaneous Papers* (Boston, Gray Bowen, 1832), I, 23–26.

"Lastly, I am of opinion that our affairs would prosper much better, if gentlemen who read and consider too deeply for us, were totally banished from all public business, and if those who neither read nor think at all ... were intrusted with the management of our present arduous concerns."[104]

One of the great virtues of the British constitution, which many Americans continued to admire, was that it was thought to combine elements of monarchical, aristocratic and democratic government, maintaining a balance that drew on the virtues of each type of government, but that simultaneously kept in check the evils that had long been associated with each alone.[105] Most American provincial governments had conformed, even if imperfectly, to this idea: a powerful governor, an appointed "aristocratic" "upper" legislative house and a popularly elected "lower" house representing the people. In these governments, the popular element had been checked, in principle, both by the governor and by the "upper" house of the legislature. Privy Council review of legislation provided an ultimate safeguard. It should be emphasized that even within the so-called democratic part of these governments, the role of the actual people was restricted by property requirements to vote and to hold public office that reflected the view that men of no or little means were not properly part of the political nation at all.[106]

Given that Privy Council review had now been eliminated and that in framing new governments a broad consensus had emerged that governors should not possess, as previously, an absolute veto over legislation, men who had limited confidence in the people came to see that it was critically important to retain other features of the earlier governments that had served to check and balance the popular element. In 1776, a political furor erupted over the decision by the Pennsylvania constitutional convention to adopt a unicameral legislature. The controversy over that decision produced a literature that brought out the importance many attributed to the check on "lower" houses that an "upper" house could provide. In the event, all of the states that had had bicameral legislatures previously, except Georgia, made what appear to have been relatively uncontroversial decisions at their conventions to retain them. Where sharp disagreements did develop in nearly every state was over the question of whether traditional property-owning qualifications to vote and to run for office should

104 McRee (ed.), Iredell, I, 335–36.

105 Wood, Creation of the American Republic, 18–20.

106 For estimates of the percentage of adult white males entitled to vote in each province, see Dinkin, Voting in Provincial America, especially Chapters 2 and 3.

also be retained and at what levels, and whether those requirements should be set higher for "upper" houses, so that their membership might continue to be drawn from the upper reaches of society, which might in turn allow these bodies to continue to operate as a check on popular "lower" houses – in the face of radically changed circumstances.

As the first governments were being framed, contributors to newspapers and numerous delegates to state congresses and conventions called for the reduction or elimination of property-owning requirements to vote and to hold public office. In most states, a good deal of support existed for expanding the suffrage to all adult men who paid taxes. Certainly, the intimate connection between taxation and representation that the Revolution posited pointed strongly in this direction. In the face of these challenges to traditional political exclusions, men who harbored significant doubts about unchecked popular rule resisted, mounting campaigns to fight the reduction or elimination of these restrictions. Their opposition to greater popular participation was galvanized by a set of traditional ideas about the infirmities of men who owned no or little property. In 1774, James Iredell invoked these views to explain his opposition to a greatly broadened suffrage.

> Some think every man ought to have an individual vote for a representative. If every man was a good one, and had a tolerable understanding, this rule would be proper: but when poverty leads to temptation, and folly is ever capable of deceit, there must be some restriction as to the right of voting: otherwise the lowest and most ignorant of mankind must associate in this important business with those who it is to be presumed, from their property and other circumstances, are free from influence, and have some knowledge of the great consequence of their trust.[107]

In a well-known letter to James Sullivan in May 1776 John Adams repeated similar ideas as he presented the case for retaining gender, age, but especially property-owning requirements, for the vote. He concluded by saying,

> [d]epend upon it, sir, it is dangerous to open So fruitfull a Source of Controversy and Altercation, as would be opened by attempting to alter the Qualifications of Voters. There will be no end of it. New Claims will arise. Women will demand a Vote. Lads from 12 to 21 will think their Rights not enough attended to, and every Man, who has not a Farthing, will demand an equal Voice with any other in all Acts of State. *It tends to confound and destroy all Distinctions, and prostrate all Ranks, to one common Levell.*[108]

[107] McRee (ed.), Iredell, I, 210 ("To the Inhabitants of Great Britain," 1774).
[108] Taylor (ed.), Papers of John Adams, IV, 208–12, quote from 211–12 (John Adams to James Sullivan, May 1776).

Others offered additional reasons for continuing these exclusions. The conservative New Yorker, William Smith, wrote, in reaction to a draft proposal for a New York constitution that would have expanded the suffrage and office holding to all taxpayers and allowed them to vote annually by secret ballot, that

> [i]t is dangerous to Society to admit Persons with very small Property to participate in your Councils. The richest Member of the Community under a Government annually elective and that too by Ballot is put upon the same Term with one who has scarce a Farthing to lose. What Security from such a Legislature against an agrarian law and all sorts of Rapine and Plunder! If every individual Legislator is not opulent, yet certainly they ought in general to be above the Temptations of Indigence. The Poor being the Majority ought not to refuse a Security to others against the Spoil of their Property. They lose Nothing by being obliged to elect Men of Substance attached to the Territory.[109]

Property requirements to stand as candidates for legislative and gubernatorial office relied on similar ideas, and on the idea that the ownership of substantial property conferred, or at least helped to provide some confidence, that its owners possessed the qualities of mind and character to offer disinterested and wise public service. Members of the "upper" house of the legislature, William Hooper of North Carolina wrote in 1776, should be "selected for the Wisdom, remarkable Integrity, or that Weight which arises from property and gives Independence and Impartiality to the human mind."[110]

In New York, numerous pamphlets, newspaper columns and several detailed reconstructions of the deliberations of the New York constitutional convention make it possible to present a somewhat more detailed account of how these battles over political exclusion unfolded.[111] Largely because in New York three men, whose views ranged from conservative to

109 Quoted in Bernard Mason, *The Road to Independence: The Revolutionary Movement in New York, 1773–1777* (Lexington, Ky., University of Kentucky Press, 1966), 235 fn. 75. There were some grounds for this fear. The Pennsylvania convention had gone so far as to circulate a preliminary draft of a Pennsylvania Declaration of Rights that contained an article stating "'that an enormous Proportion of Property vested in a few Individuals is dangerous to the Rights, and destructive of the Common Happiness of Mankind,' and therefore should be discouraged by the laws of the state." See Wood, Creation of the American Republic, 89; and Bouton, Taming Democracy, 52–53 for discussions of this Pennsylvania initiative.

110 Quoted in Wood, Creation of the American Republic, 217; and Kruman, Between Authority and Liberty, 135.

111 See especially, Charles Z. Lincoln, *Constitutional History of New York, from the Beginning of the Colonial Period to the Year 1905* (Rochester, N.Y., Lawyers Cooperative, 1906), I, 490–558; and Mason, Road to Independence, 213–53.

extremely conservative, John Jay, Robert R. Livingston, and Gouverneur Morris, dominated the proceedings of the convention,[112] the defense of traditional exclusions was in the end more successful than in some other states.

By June 1776, the revolutionary atmosphere in New York City was palpable. The City's artisans and mechanics claimed an "inalienable right" to ratify any constitution that the Provincial Congress might draft. If that document should fail to be submitted to the people for ratification they warned, it "would cast them into 'absolute slavery' and would destroy the Provincial Congress's 'lawful power' over them."[113] As the Fourth New York Provincial Congress convened in July 1776 and quickly converted itself into a convention for the purpose of drafting a new constitution, the newspapers published a range of views as to the form the new frame of government should take. "Spartanus" called for a unicameral assembly exercising both executive and legislative power.[114] An "Independent Whig" wrote that the governor and house should be chosen annually by ballot, and that the governor and Council should have no power to suspend the laws.[115] As the convention was about to open, John Jay wrote to Edward Rutledge of the uncertainty of the moment. "We have a government, you know, to form; and God only knows what it will resemble. Our politicians, like some guests at a feast, are perplexed and undetermined which dish to prefer."[116]

In August 1776 a drafting committee of 13 men was chosen. Among them sat a solid core of conservative delegates: John Jay, Gouverneur Morris, Robert R. Livingston, and William Duer.[117] James Duane, another conservative, was added to the committee later.[118] The main objective of the conservative group seems at first simply to have been to slow down the drafting process, until passions had cooled a little, so that they might find a more favorable moment to introduce a somewhat more conservative frame of government.[119] It was not until the following March that the committee finally brought a draft constitution to the floor of the convention. By this time there were also a number of other

[112] Lincoln, Constitutional History, I, 496.

[113] Mason, Road to Independence, 156–57. The New York Constitution adopted by the convention in 1777 was not submitted to the people for ratification, the idea having faded after the British invaded New York City.

[114] Ibid., 232. [115] Ibid., 233, see also 234.

[116] (Jay to Rutledge, July 6, 1776) quoted in ibid., 214 fn. 1. [117] Ibid., 217 fn. 10.

[118] Ibid., 216–17; and Lincoln, Constitutional History of New York, I, 490–91.

[119] Mason, Road to Independence, 219.

non-committee drafts circulating among representatives. One radical plan called for extending the suffrage to taxpayers and denying any veto power to the executive; a conservative plan called for restricting office holding in the upper house to those who owned land worth £10,000, and granting them tenure "during good behavior."[120] The latter plan "provoked a direct rejoinder [in which it was proposed that] all taxpayers [be enfranchised] and [all be] permit[ted] to be candidates for any office."[121]

The New York drafting committee presented to the convention a constitutional plan that featured a legislature consisting of two houses, an upper house initially called the Council (changed to the Senate in a later committee draft), and a lower house called the Assembly.[122] The committee proposed a taxpaying qualification for Assembly voters. Indeed, over the course of its deliberations the committee had made the proposed taxpaying qualification less restrictive.[123] Under the circumstances, lowering suffrage requirements to this extent must have seemed politically expedient. The state contained a large Loyalist population, and at times came close to descending into outright civil war. By the end of August, the British army occupied New York City. Winning over the lesser sort to the revolutionary cause, or at least not alienating them, must have been a factor influencing the committee's thinking.

Nevertheless, on March 14, 1777, when the committee draft came to the floor of the convention for debate, Robert R. Livingston moved, in a motion seconded by Gouverneur Morris, that the requirement be added that voters for the Assembly who did not own a freehold must not only have paid taxes but also have "rented a tenement."[124] The convention voted to adopt this requirement. Six days later when the convention took up the question of the Assembly franchise again, there were a series of interventions that produced in the end a much more restrictive franchise. Mr. Tredwell moved that the "rented tenement" should be of "the yearly value of 40s" and the convention voted in favor.[125] Nearly at the same time, Gouverneur Morris moved that the simple freehold requirement,

120 Ibid., 234–37. 121 Ibid., 236.

122 Lincoln, Constitutional History of New York, I, 501.

123 An early committee draft required voters to pay "both public and County Taxes … within the said year" A later draft required only the payment of "public or County Taxes … at least one year before the day of such election," quoted in ibid., 514.

124 *Journals of the Provincial Congress, Provincial Convention, Committee of Safety and Council of Safety of the state of New York, 1775–1776–1777* (Albany, New York, T. Weed Printer to the State, 1842), I, 836.

125 Ibid., I, 867

which had served as an alternative basis for qualifying under the committee draft, be amended to require that freeholders "[own] a freehold of the value of twenty pounds"[126] and the convention also adopted this amendment. These amendments appear to have been aimed primarily at disfranchising New York City artisans, many of whom neither owned freeholds nor rented tenements of the required value.[127]

Perhaps concluding that under the circumstances Gouverneur Morris and Robert Livingston had pushed the matter a bit far, John Jay offered a proposal designed to mollify artisans but at the same time to prevent further growth in their political power. Jay proposed that artisans and mechanics, who had gained the freedom of Albany and New York City on or before October 1775 (but not thereafter), should be permitted to vote.[128] And the convention also adopted his amendment. Despite the tenuous political and military situation in New York (perhaps because of it) the conservative members of the convention succeeded in establishing a franchise for the lower house that was considerably more restrictive than the taxpaying qualification the drafting committee had initially proposed. Over the course of deliberations, they had moved the convention halfway back to the £40 free hold requirement that provincial voters had previously had to meet. It has been estimated that while the percentage of eligible voters for the Assembly increased somewhat under this suffrage requirement, in 1790 "just 58 percent of adult white males and 70.7 percent of the heads of families" were entitled to vote for that body. In New York City "only about 60 percent of the adult men could ... legally qualify."[129]

The drafting committee viewed the voting requirement for the upper house quite differently. From the beginning the committee set the property requirement for Senate voters much higher.[130] In an early draft, the section of the constitution devoted to the upper house began by saying "that the Burthen of supporting and defending this State does at all times rest principally on the freeholders and therefore that they of right ought to have an ascendancy in the Legislature."[131] This statement bears a striking

[126] Ibid. [127] Mason, Road to Independence, 241.

[128] Journals of the Provincial Congress of New York, I, 867.

[129] Robert Dinkin, *Voting in Revolutionary America: A Study of Elections in the Original Thirteen States, 1776–1789* (Greenwood Press, Westport, Ct., 1982), 38, citing the statistics compiled by Alfred F. Young, *The Democratic-Republicans of New York: The Origins, 1763–1797* (Chapel Hill, N.C., University of North Carolina Press, 1967), chap. 4 and appendix.

[130] Mason, Road to Independence, 238.

[131] These words were subsequently stricken from the document, Lincoln, Constitutional History, I, 516.

resemblance to one that John Jay was fond of repeating during this period: "those who own the country ought to govern it."[132] The committee initially proposed a £40 freehold requirement for Senate voters, apparently adopting the provincial requirement for voters for the lower house. But after additional deliberations, it decided to more than double the property requirement for these voters to "one hundred pounds over and above all Debts and Incumbrances."[133] There seems to have been only weak opposition in the convention to the high property-owning requirement for Senate voters. Robert Harper, a radical delegate from New York City, moved to strike out the words "possessed of freeholds of the value of one hundred pounds, over and above all debts and incumbrances" but the negative vote on his motion was apparently not even close enough to record.[134] The same £100 freehold requirement was to apply to voters for governor. It has been estimated that by 1790 "only about 33 percent of all electors in New York could vote for senators and governor."[135] In the same year, only 10% of "male residents of New York city possessed enough property to vote for governor."[136]

Unlike the Assembly, moreover, which was to be elected annually, Senators were to serve a four-year term, a tenure that insulated them somewhat even from their wealthier electorate.[137] The longer tenure together with a suffrage restricted to more substantial property owners presumably reflected a view that the "upper" house of the legislature should be elected by and drawn from men who occupied higher positions in society than those who were to elect and serve in the "lower" house.

When the committee presented its draft of the constitution to the convention, the document also contained clauses requiring elections for Assembly and Senate to be conducted using secret ballots. In New York, colonial electors had been required to offer their votes for candidates by

132 Allan Nevins, *The American States During and After the Revolution, 1775–1789* (New York, A. M. Kelley, 1969), 164 (quoting William Jay's "Jay," I, 70); see also William Howard Adams, *Gouverneur Morris: An Independent Life* (New Haven, Ct., Yale University Press, 2003), 44; Sparks (ed.), Life and Times of Gouverneur Morris, I, 24; and George Dangerfield, *Chancellor Robert R. Livingston of New York, 1746–1813* (New York, 1960), 60.

133 Lincoln, Constitutional History, I, 516. 134 *Journals*, I, 843.

135 Chilton Williamson, *American Suffrage: From Property to Democracy, 1760–1860* (Princeton, N.J., Princeton University Press, 1960), 111. Dinkin, Voting in Revolutionary America, 38 gives similar figures ("[J]ust 28.9 percent of the men could select members of the upper house").

136 Nevins, The American States During and After the Revolution, 164.

137 Kruman, Between Authority and Liberty, 140–41; Wood, Creation of the American Republic, 213.

voice in the presence of their neighbors. Under this system of *viva voce* voting, of course, it was possible for the great landowners of the Hudson valley to supervise the voting of their tenants, and for the wealthy in general to influence the voting of those who were economically dependent upon them. The secret ballot would have made possible greater political independence for those among the economically vulnerable who would be entitled to vote. When this proposal was presented to the convention, Gouverneur Morris moved to delete the secret ballot provisions, and the convention voted in favor.[138] As elsewhere in the convention proceedings, John Jay intervened to moderate Gouverneur Morris's proposals, in this case by putting forward a clause to introduce secret ballots in Assembly and Senate elections following the end of the war, and the convention adopted his proposal. But in the interim, *viva voce* voting was retained for Assembly and Senate elections. Given that the Assembly franchise was being expanded somewhat to include smaller freeholders, and some leaseholders and artisans, conservative Whigs like Morris might have hoped that retaining *viva voce* voting would make it possible for the old provincial elite to hold on to a good deal of its political power in a government now based largely on popular elections.[139]

A secret ballot provision for gubernatorial elections that was tucked away in another section of the constitution somehow survived convention debates. And this oversight seems to have led to a minor political revolution in New York when, in the first gubernatorial election held under the new constitution, George Clinton, favored by small free holders, soldiers and some tenants was elected the first governor of the State.[140] One member of New York's provincial "aristocracy," Philip Schuyler, who had run against Clinton, commented in a letter to John Jay that Clinton's "family and connections do not entitle him to so distinguished a predominance" but that his fine personal character reconciled Schuyler to his election.[141]

The New York constitution of 1777 produced one of the two or three most restrictive suffrages in the thirteen states.[142] But while it may have

[138] Lincoln, Constitutional History of New York, I, 512–13; Adams, Gouverneur Morris, 86. The irony of Morris's position is that men of his class often justified the refusal to allow men of little property to vote by saying that they lacked the independence necessary to carry out this important duty.

[139] Adams, Gouverneur Morris, 86.

[140] John P. Kaminski, *George Clinton: Yeoman Politician of the New Republic* (Madison, Wisc., University of Wisconsin Press, 1993), 24–25.

[141] Ibid., 25 (quoting Schuyler to John Jay, July 14, 1777).

[142] Dinkin, Voting in Revolutionary America, 39.

excluded from political participation many of the "lowest and most ignorant," it had not been set nearly high enough to stop, let alone reverse, ongoing political changes; every year more and more of the middling sort were being elected to seats in the Assembly.[143] Even the restrictive Senate suffrage yielded mixed results. In rural areas, many farmers owned enough land to vote for senator and governor,[144] and the new constitution had allotted a greater number of seats to rural constituencies. Some decades ago, the historian Jackson Turner Main examined in great detail the social composition of legislatures following the adoption of the first constitutions, and concluded that in New York, the suffrage requirement for the lower house did not prevent it from being dominated by men drawn overwhelmingly from the middling sort. He also found that while the differential suffrage for the two houses made some difference in the social composition of their respective memberships, the Senate suffrage fell far short of restoring the dominance the wealthy had previously enjoyed. "[T]he counties west of the Hudson and north of Westchester," Main wrote,

> now chose a majority of both houses. As a result of these developments, the balance of power shifted northward from New York City and downward socially and economically. After 1776, not over 40 percent of the senators and only one-sixth of the representatives were wealthy. Three out of four councilors [colonial upper house] had been merchants, but now only one in four senators and one in seven assemblymen were in commerce. Farmers, almost excluded from the colonial legislature, now comprised one-third of the senators and actually outnumbered men of the upper class in the Assembly. The family background of the legislators was radically different from the prewar era. Descendants of prominent old families were powerful in the upper house; but even here they held only between a fourth and a third of the seats, while in the lower house they were a nearly ineffectual minority.[145]

He went on to say that while the higher suffrage requirement for the Senate made some difference in its political orientation, elite control of that body was often successfully contested.

> The Senate, like the state generally, was divided into two major parties, the allies and the adversaries of Governor Clinton. The Clintonians derived their strength primarily from the upstate farmers. Scores of votes in both houses, revealing a consistency unusual for legislatures of that period, show the Clinton group

[143] Main, "Government by the People," 399–400.

[144] Jackson Turner Main, *The Upper House in Revolutionary America* (Madison, Wisc., University Wisconsin Press, 1967), 134.

[145] Ibid., 135.

supporting pro-debtor laws, opposing a strong central government, and advocating bills favorable to its rural constituencies. In the lower house the popular party was almost always successful, but in the Senate, which contained a far larger proportion of the wealthy elite, the two sides were quite evenly matched.[146]

As in New York, in nearly every state, there were those who wished to replace property-owning requirements to vote with a tax-paying requirement. And in nearly every state, there were those who opposed them, seeking to continue to restrict political participation to men who owned at least moderate amounts of property, by maintaining traditional suffrage and office holding requirements. In North Carolina, an extended struggle took place over the tax-paying qualification that in the end yielded a compromise that, like New York, set lower and higher property-owning requirements for voters for the two houses.

> Instructions to several representatives to the provincial congress at Hillsborough (August, 1775), calling for lower suffrage levels, were not favorably acted upon. Proposals to abolish the freehold requirement at the congress in Halifax (April 1776) also met with rejection. In each case, conservatives succeeded in holding back attempts at reform, but then their support began to weaken. Finally, some months later, state leaders worked out a compromise for the new constitution by creating two levels of eligibility .... While only fifty-acre free holders could elect persons to the senate, taxpaying freemen could vote for members of the [house]. Since taxation was by poll, all adult males except "sons living under their paternal roof, apprentices, slaves and indentured servants" were enfranchised for house elections.[147]

But if the movement to enfranchise taxpayers as voters for the lower house succeeded in the end in North Carolina, it did not prevent the convention from also voting to require candidates for office in that house to own a freehold of at least 100 acres. Voters for the Senate, under the new constitution, were required to own a 50-acre freehold, but to stand as a candidate for that body, it was necessary to own a freehold of at least 300 acres. Gubernatorial candidates were required to own freeholds of no less than 1,000 acres.[148]

These battles over the extent of the political participation of the people were repeated in most states. Demands for suffrage reform also arose in

[146] Ibid., 137.

[147] Dinkin, Voting in Revolutionary America, 32, citing Elisha P. Douglass, *Rebel and Democrats: the Struggle for Equal Political Rights and Majority Rule During the American Revolution* (Chapel Hill, N.C., University of North Carolina Press, 1955), chap. 8; and Williamson, American Suffrage, 105–6.

[148] Thorpe (ed.), Constitutions, V, 2790–91 (North Carolina Constitution of 1776).

Maryland, New Hampshire, and New Jersey.[149] In Massachusetts, an effort to establish a taxpaying qualification for voters for the lower house was incorporated into the proposed constitution of 1778, but was ultimately defeated when the constitution of 1780 imposed the requirement that voters own at least £60 of real or personal property.[150] The 1780 constitution imposed the same requirement for Senate voters.[151] But to run for office in the lower house, candidates were required to own a freehold of the value of £100 or personal property of the value of £200. Senators were required to own a freehold of the value of £300 or personal property of the value of £600. Candidates for governor had to own a freehold of the value of £1000.[152]

The contests between those who pressed to reduce or eliminate property-owning requirements to vote and to run for office, and those who strove to maintain these requirements played themselves out in state conventions in a wide variety of ways.[153] In a few states, Delaware, New Jersey and Georgia, property-owning requirements to vote were retained, but set at such a low level that practically no one was excluded. Yet two of these three states, New Jersey and Georgia, imposed substantial property-owning requirements to hold public office. In New Jersey candidates for the legislative council (the upper house) were required to own 1000 Pounds proclamation money, and candidates for the lower house 500 Pounds. In Georgia, it was necessary for candidates for the unicameral legislature to own 250 acres of land.[154] Maryland not only required voters for both houses to own a freehold of fifty acres or thirty pounds current money but also required office holders to own progressively greater amounts of property, five hundred pounds current money for House of Delegates, one thousand pounds current money for Senate, five

149 Willi Paul Adams, *The First American Constitutions: Republican Ideology and the Making of the State Constitutions in the Revolutionary Era* (Chapel Hill, N.C., The University of North Carolina Press, 1973), 199–200, 205, 206; and Dinkin, Voting in Revolutionary America, 33–34.

150 Thorpe (ed.), Constitutions, III,1898 (Mass. Const. of 1780); see Adams, First American Constitutions, 200–3; and Dinkin, Voting in Revolutionary America, 34–35 for discussions of the debates over the taxpaying requirement in Massachusetts.

151 Thorpe (ed.), Constitutions, III, 1896 (Mass. Const. of 1780).

152 Ibid., III, 1897, 1898, 1900.

153 For excellent accounts of these debates, see Kruman, Between Authority and Liberty, 87–109; and Williamson, American Suffrage, 92–137.

154 Thorpe (ed.), Constitutions, V, 2595 (New Jersey, 1776); II, 779 (Georgia 1777, 250 acres of land).

thousand pounds current money to be eligible to serve as Governor.[155] South Carolina adopted a tax-paying qualification of sorts for voters[156] but imposed a high property-owning qualification to hold a seat in the Senate (two thousand pounds currency).[157]

These results present a complicated, messy picture, yet a few things seem clear. Of the state constitutions adopted between 1776 and 1780, only two, those of New Hampshire and Pennsylvania, completely eliminated traditional restrictions on political participation, ending property-owning requirements both for voting and office holding.[158] All the rest conditioned the full participation of the people in their governments on the ownership of greater or lesser amounts of property. By 1784, seven of the eleven states with bicameral legislatures (Massachusetts, New York, New Jersey, Maryland, North Carolina, South Carolina and New Hampshire) imposed higher property-owning requirements to vote for or to hold office in the upper house than the lower house. These requirements make apparent that in many early conventions the inclination existed to try to exclude entirely from the political nation "the lowest and most ignorant," and beyond that to try to maintain in government a social hierarchy that reflected the organization of society at large, requiring office holders or voters to own progressively greater amounts of property to serve in or to vote for lower houses, upper houses, and governors. For conservative members of these conventions, the hope seems to have been that in these ways the worst impulses of the mass of the people could be kept in check in the new governments.

Despite the considerable energies expended at the state conventions to restrict the growth of the political nation, over the following years it would become apparent that the practical results of these efforts would not produce the outcomes for which conservative Whigs might have hoped.

> [I]n the thirteen states as a whole, the electorate, as a result of the changes in property qualifications, probably expanded from a range of 50 to 80 percent [of

[155] Ibid., III, 1691–96.

[156] Ibid., VI, 3252 ("tax in a sum equal to the tax on fifty acres of land").

[157] Ibid., VI, 3249–52 (S.C., 1778).

[158] Vermont, an independent republic at the time, also eliminated these requirements in its 1777 constitution. See in general Alexander Keyssar, *The Right to Vote: The Contested History of Democracy in the United States* (New York, Basic Books, 2000), Appendix, Table A.1; Williamson, American Suffrage, 92–116; New Hampshire re-imposed property-owning requirements to hold public office in 1784 (Senate, freehold estate of the value of 200 pounds) (governorship estate of the value of 500 pounds), Thorpe (ed.), Constitutions, IV, 2460, 2463 (New Hampshire Constitution of 1784).

adult males] in the late provincial period to about 60 to 90 percent by the close of the Revolutionary era. This actually represents more than a 10 percent rise, as many states were now near the upper rather than the lower end of the span.[159]

Because, among other reasons, those pressing to retain traditional political exclusions were confronted in many states with the need to mobilize patriots of all classes for war, in the end they struck a variety of compromises with the rising tide of democratic sentiment. As a result, the property restrictions that were retained were set too low to prevent a flood of new men from entering state legislatures over the following years, definitively changing their social character.[160] Nor, would the social composition and political orientation of upper houses prove to be, after a few years of experience under the new constitutions, all that different from that of lower houses.[161] Any hope conservative leaders might have had that these restrictions on political participation could inoculate legislatures against the influence of the often ill-considered views of ordinary Americans was surely disappointed by these developments.

Many men of higher social rank felt the problem of popular sovereignty particularly acutely at this historical moment because of a profound clash of world views that ran not only through the Revolution but through their own thinking. On the one hand, as revolutionaries they were of necessity Whigs of one political stripe or another, and Whig political philosophy had, since the seventeenth century, been based on the idea that society and government emerged from agreements of the people, and that all legitimate governmental authority was exercised with their consent. This Lockean world was composed, at bottom, of rights bearing individuals, not of stratified hierarchies. But the actual social, economic and political world these men inhabited and which shaped many of their basic attitudes was organized differently, it was a traditional world still ordered in many ways according to hierarchical principles. In this world, most ordinary men occupied roles that neither fit them for, nor entitled them to govern; they were properly subjects rather than rulers. Until this moment, it had been possible to hold comfortably in one mind both these views because popular sovereignty had remained, for the most part, an abstraction. Now that the Revolution threatened to make it more of a reality, these men initially strove to try to construct forms of government in which the people

159 Dinkin, Voting in Revolutionary America, 39.
160 Main, "Government by the People," 397–407.
161 Main, Upper House in Revolutionary America, 202–15.

would be celebrated, but in which their crudest sentiments, it was hoped, could be sifted, refined, filtered, distilled or at least checked through an electoral process that restricted participation to voters and office holders who owned at least moderate amounts of property.

John Adams' well-known letter to James Sullivan written in 1776 provides a perfect example of the dilemma such men faced and the typical response it provoked: principle must be tempered by harsh reality. Adams wrote,

> [i]t is certain in Theory, that the only moral Foundation of Government is the Consent of the People. But to what an Extent Shall We carry this Principle? Shall We Say, that every Individual of the Community, old and young, male and female, as well as rich and poor, must consent, expressly to every Act of Legislation? .... [W]hy exclude Women [from the vote]? You will Say, because their Delicacy renders them unfit for Practice and Experience, in the great Business of Life, and the hardy Enterprizes of War, as well as the arduous Cares of the State .... And Children have not Judgment or Will of their own. True. But will not these Reasons apply to others? Is it not equally true, that Men in general in every Society, who are wholly destitute of Property, are also too little acquainted with public Affairs to form a Right Judgment, and too dependent upon other Men to have a Will of their own? If this is a Fact, if you give to every Man, who has no Property, a Vote, will you not make a fine encouraging Provision for Corruption by your fundamental Law? Such is the Frailty of the human Heart, that very few Men, who have no Property, have any Judgment of their own.[162]

For many men of higher standing, the results produced by the first conventions failed satisfactorily to address what they increasingly believed to be the pressing problem of establishing some form of check on the power of the mass of the people to enact just any law they might desire. In a constitutional system in which the people themselves served as the primary constraint on legislatures, this was increasingly seen as a critical deficiency that threatened the very existence of the new republics. In such a climate, many of these men were naturally drawn to ideas and initiatives that promised to address this omission. But the ground for the favorable reception of such ideas had already been laid by broader political currents. The texts of a number of early constitutions, placing those instruments beyond the "power" of legislatures to alter, point toward a more widespread, if somewhat amorphous, desire to confer on constitutions an

[162] Taylor (ed.), Papers of John Adams, IV, 208–10 (Letter to James Sullivan, May 26, 1776); see also *The Works of John Adams, Second President of the United States* (Boston, Ma., Little Brown & Co., 1854), IX, 375–78.

existence independent of legislatures, at least in part, and to delineate some form of limitation on their powers. In the event, these ideas were swamped in practice in the early constitutions by the more traditional idea that the representatives of the people, gathered in legislatures, possessed the plenary authority to make law on their behalf.

3

Restoring "Legislative" Review of the Laws: The New York Constitution of 1777

An "upper house" established as a check on a "lower" one, with members enjoying a longer tenure in office, and elected under more restrictive property-owning requirements, was not without precedent among the constitutions adopted in 1776. Entirely absent from the permanent frames of government adopted until that time, however, was any authority vested in a body outside the legislature to review and prevent its bills from becoming law. There had been some discussion in a number of states of restoring to governors a veto over legislative enactments, but none of the congresses and conventions, save that establishing South Carolina's temporary constitution of 1776, had decided to do so.

In New York, however, where conservative members dominated the convention, an initiative to establish a significant external check on legislative power succeeded. On March 13, 1777, Joseph Smith, a delegate from Orange County, moved that "the Governor [should] have a negative upon all laws passed by the Senate and Assembly."[1] In Provincial New York, the royal Governor had participated in the lawmaking power as a third branch of the legislature; his assent was required before a bill could become law. Adhering to this tradition, Smith also moved to make the governor a branch of the legislature. Gouverneur Morris intervened to speak up in favor of the idea of granting the governor an absolute veto over bills, but wanted to be certain that Smith's motion would not give the governor power to "originate or amend any law, but simply to

[1] *Journals of the Provincial Congress, etc., Provincial Convention, Committee of Safety and Council of Safety of the State of New York, 1775–1776–1777* (Albany, New York, T. Weed Printer to the State, 1842), I, 834.

give his assent or dissent thereto."[2] The next day the convention voted in favor of giving the governor an absolute veto over legislation, but did not designate the office a third branch of the legislature.[3] Robert R. Livingston, James Duane, and Morris all voted in favor of the provision.[4] This vote, conferring an absolute veto on the governor, would have placed the chief magistrate in a position flatly to prevent a bill from becoming law.

The constitution proposed by the drafting committee had called for the governor to be elected by an at large state-wide vote (rather than by the legislature as was typical of early state constitutions),[5] but only by voters who could meet fairly high property-owning requirements. The committee had also proposed that the Governor should serve a four-year term, rather than stand for election annually.[6] While an absolute veto would have given him a formidable role in the making of the laws, it could not have been expected to operate in quite the same way that the colonial governor's veto had. Unlike colonial governors who had been appointed by and were accountable to the Crown, the new governors of New York were to be elected by "the people." Still, perhaps because New York's governor was to be elected by an at large state wide vote, by electors who owned significant amounts of property, and was to serve for a three-year term, it could be hoped that he might just be capable of exercising the kind of independence that would render such a veto an effective brake on both legislative and popular excesses.

John Jay was absent from the convention the day it approved the absolute gubernatorial veto, but a week later, having returned, was apparently unhappy with the development. He intervened to rein in his more zealous colleagues, as he also did on the questions of the Assembly franchise and the secret ballot. On March 20 he gave notice that he would move the next day for a reconsideration of the veto provision.[7] After holding discussions with Morris and Livingston,[8] on April 1, Jay and Livingston moved to have the governor's veto stricken and to substitute

[2] Ibid., I, 834. [3] Ibid., I, 836.

[4] Ibid., I, 836; see also Bernard Mason, *The Road to Independence: The Revolutionary Movement in New York, 1773–1777* (Lexington, Ky., University of Kentucky Press, 1966), 243 fn. 92.

[5] Gordon Wood, *The Creation of the American Republic, 1776–1787* (Chapel Hill, N.C., University of North Carolina Press, 1969), 139.

[6] The Convention ultimately reduced the governor's term to three years.

[7] Journals of Provincial Congress of New York, I, 843.

[8] Mason, Road to Independence, 243 fn. 92.

for it "a check upon every bill" in the form of "a Council to revise all bills about to be passed into laws by the Legislature."[9] Their proposal was adopted by the convention the next day.

The Council of Revision was to be composed of the Governor, the Chancellor and the justices of the supreme court, and was to exercise a qualified rather than an absolute veto over bills passed by the legislature. There is little direct evidence indicating where the idea for a Council of Revision came from, or why it seemed more expedient than an absolute gubernatorial veto, but it is possible to suggest plausible answers to both questions. Under the circumstances, a qualified veto exercised by a council would have been considered significantly more politically palatable than an absolute veto exercised by a single individual over the entire body of the representatives of the people.

In his exhaustively thorough *Constitutional History of New York*, Charles Lincoln pointed out that in early drafts of the constitution, the framers had proposed to have the state's high court judges sit in the Senate to advise [but not vote] upon legislation, and suggested that "the principle of [that proposal] was practically adopted in the provision for a Council of Revision."[10] In the Council of Revision, the judges would certainly be giving their advice about the constitutionality of legislation, but now the force of their advice would be bolstered by a qualified veto.

Jay and Livingston viewed the Council as an instrument for "checking" bills that had been "hastily and unadvisedly passed" by preventing them from becoming law until the Council had had the opportunity to present to the legislature in writing its objections and suggested revisions. The Council did introduce into the constitutional structure of an American government for the first time since Independence, a form of outside review of legislation, supported by a veto wielded (in part) by judges who held their offices during good behavior.[11] But it did not overturn the bedrock premises of traditional constitutionalism. Under the constitutional provision creating the Council, the legislature retained the final, un-appealable

[9] Journals of Provincial Congress of New York, I, 860.

[10] Charles Z. Lincoln, *The Constitutional History of New York, From the Beginning of the Colonial Period to the Year 1905, Showing the Origin, Development, and Judicial Construction of the Constitution* (Rochester, N.Y., The Lawyers Cooperative Publishing Co., 1906, repr. Buffalo, N.Y., William S. Hein & Co., Inc., 1994), I, 537.

[11] New York Constitution of 1777, Article XXIV, Francis Thorpe (ed.), *The Federal and State Constitutions, Colonial Charters, and Other Organic Laws of the States, Territories and Colonies* (Washington, D.C., Government Printing Office, 1909, Reprint Buffalo, N.Y., William S. Hein, 1993), V, 2634; the 1777 constitution, however, did require judges to retire at age 60, and under it the legislature continued to set judges' salaries.

power to confer the force of law on its acts, if now at times, only following a super-majority vote.

Several of the Council of Revision's features are especially revealing of the assumptions the framers brought to the question of constitutions and constitutionality. The constitutional clause creating the Council charged the legislature (and the Council) not only with considering whether bills were "inconsistent [with the constitution's] spirit" but simultaneously with evaluating whether they were inconsistent with "the public good." The critical clause read "whereas laws inconsistent with *the spirit of this constitution, or with the public good,* may be hastily and unadvisedly passed," etc. (emphasis added). Yoking together judgments about constitutionality with those about whether a bill served the public good, suggests that the framers took for granted not only that determinations of constitutionality were peculiarly "legislative," but that they were "legislative" in much the same way that legislative determinations that a bill would promote the public good were. Both kinds of judgments about new general rules for society flowed from the legislature's discretion to make law guided by a broad duty to determine that those laws would promote the good of the polity, but also that they would preserve the "principles" of the constitution. Unconstitutionality was understood to be one type of "political/legislative" objection to a bill.

The subsequent history of the Council of Revision in New York confirms that the framers of the 1777 constitution were working with a quite different set of constitutional assumptions than those that would emerge over the following decades, as judicial review became more and more firmly established as the "normal" mode for determining constitutionality in the American system. By1821, when New York convened a convention to amend the 1777 constitution, the Council of Revision appeared to most delegates to be a completely antiquated institution, one that simply no longer made sense, and the convention proceeded to vote it out of existence.

Debates at the convention reveal that the delegates were moved to take this step by two basic ideas that expose how completely the development of judicial review (together with separation of powers doctrine) had transformed constitutional understandings.[12] The great weight of opinion among the delegates was that the judges (who sat on the Council of

[12] The account in this paragraph and the next are derived largely from Jeff Roedel, "Stoking the Doctrinal Furnace: Judicial Review and the New York Council of Revision" (1988) 69 *New York History*, 279–83. For a similar account, see also James T. Barry III, "The

Revision) should no longer be permitted to play that kind of role in law-making, as it represented a clear violation of separation of powers.[13] Additionally, it was now felt to be improper for judges as independent, disinterested dispensers of justice to be so deeply implicated in partisan "political" matters. At the same time, quite a few delegates applauded the recently developed practice of judicial review in which judges evaluated the constitutionality of laws, as they went about adjudicating cases in their "normal" role as judges.

By 1821, the formal veto exercised "legislatively" by the Council of Revision had come to be viewed as a "political" instrumentality that should be wielded by an elected "political" actor, the governor, while the question of the constitutionality of laws had come to be seen as a distinctively "judicial" matter, a question primarily of "law."[14] Over the period since the New York constitution had first been framed in 1777, determinations of "constitutionality," on the one hand, and of the "public good" on the other, had come to be pulled apart in prevailing thought. The latter now was primarily taken to belong to the realm of "legislative/political" discretion, while the former now seemed more naturally to belong to a realm outside of ordinary "legislative politics," instinctively part of the realm of "constitutional law," administered by judges and lawyers. By 1821, the constitutionality of laws was regarded, in most instances, as a "legal" rather than a "political" question, to be determined by judges, who would exercise a narrower judicial discretion to expound "legal" rules and principles set out in constitutions.

By the time New York finally got around to eliminating the Council of Revision in 1821, however, this new constitutional framework had been developing and spreading for more than three decades, and was well established. As long before as 1787, the Federal Convention had considered and, following an extended debate, rejected the idea of creating a Council of Revision for the new federal government, on nearly identical grounds to those which moved New Yorkers belatedly to eliminate their Council of Revision several decades later.[15] Between 1777, when the New York constitution was written, and 1787, when the Federal Convention met, the constitutional world was transformed by a struggle over judicial review, which the next chapters describe in greater detail.

Council of Revision and the Limits of Judicial Power" (1989) 56 *University of Chicago Law Review* 235, 245–48.

[13] Ibid. [14] Ibid.

[15] The debate at the Federal Convention is described in detail in Chapter 10.

3.1 THE "TRADITIONAL" POSITION OF JUDGES UNDER THE NEW YORK CONSTITUTION OF 1777 AND THE STATUS OF JUDICIAL REVIEW

In creating a Council of Revision, the conservative drafters of New York's constitution had revived a form of *legislative review*, "notionally related to that earlier performed by the English Board of Trade in conjunction with the Privy Council,"[16] but the arrangements they established for the judicial power, which also drew on New York's colonial inheritance, strongly suggest that they had not even imagined the possibility that the judiciary would soon begin to play a significant independent role in checking legislative power.

Apparently acting upon a desire to conserve as much of the former system of government as possible and to impose checks upon power wielded by all branches of the government, including the judiciary, the framers of New York's 1777 constitution structured the judicial power in such a way that final appellate jurisdiction within the state would lie with the members of the upper house of the legislature (the Senate) together with the state's high court judges. The highest court in provincial New York had been composed of the Governor and Council sitting as a "Court of Errors," hearing cases brought up by writ of error from the supreme court, and more controversially, appeals from decrees in equity.[17] The provincial Council, of course, had also served as the upper house of the legislature. In a clause adopted by the convention without debate, the drafters of the 1777 constitution authorized the legislature to institute a court for "the correction of errors," which, like its colonial predecessor, would sit as the state's highest court.[18] Modeled on the provincial "Court of Errors," the new "Court for the Correction of Errors" would hear cases brought up by writ of error from judgments of the supreme court, and on appeal from the Chancellor's decrees in equity.[19] Like its colonial predecessor, the members of the upper house of the legislature (the Senate) would sit as judges on this court, outnumbering the Chancellor and the judges of the supreme court, who, under the

[16] Julius Goebel Jr., *The Law Practice of Alexander Hamilton: Documents and Commentary* (Columbia University Press, New York, 1964), I, 286.

[17] Joseph H. Smith, *Appeals to the Privy Council from the American Plantations* (New York, Columbia University Press, 1950), 239, 409, 638 n. 578 (discussing role of Courts of Error).

[18] Thorpe (ed.), Constitutions, V, 2635 (New York Constitution of 1777, Section XXXII).

[19] Ibid.

new constitution, would replace the governor on this highest state court.[20] The New York framers proposed to establish this court, they wrote in an early draft of the constitution, in order "that the subject may be secured . . . against the errors and mistakes of those who shall be entrusted with the dispensation of justice . . . ."[21]

In colonial New York, members of the upper house, the Council, had been nominated by the governor, and appointed by the crown. Under the new constitution, the upper legislative house, the Senate, would be popularly elected, even if under a restrictive suffrage. As a result, a majority of the members who would sit on the court of final appeal in the state, a court that would correct the errors of the supreme court, and hear appeals from the Chancellor, would consist of the popularly elected members of one house of the legislature. Although under the New York constitution of 1777, the high court judges of the state would hold their offices during good behavior, their decisions would neither be treated as final when they sat in their legislative capacity as members of the Council of Revision, nor, more significantly, when they sat in their judicial capacity as Chancellor or as members of the supreme court.

Why Gouverneur Morris, John Jay, Robert R. Livingston and James Duane, who would all shortly become devoted advocates of judicial review, agreed to vest in one house of the popularly elected legislature the power to overturn on appeal any judicial decision rendered by the state's high court judges, conferring on that legislative body, a "veto," in effect, over decisions and doctrine emerging from those courts, is a question worth asking. In 1777, these conservative Whigs seem still to have inhabited a pre-judicial review universe.[22] In their experience, courts

[20] The New York upper house, the Senate, consisted of 24 members. Section XI, N.Y. Const. of 1777, Thorpe (ed.), Constitutions, V, 2631. 5 judges, including the chief justice, sat on the New York supreme court during these years, the Chancellor made a sixth. But in cases in which a decision of the N.Y. supreme court was brought up to the Court for the Correction of Errors for review, "the judges of [the supreme court] shall assign the reasons of such their judgment, but shall not have a voice for its affirmance or reversal." The same applied to the Chancellor in appeals from decrees in equity. Section XXXII, N.Y. Const. of 1777, Thorpe (ed.), Constitutions, V, 2635.

[21] Lincoln, Constitutional History of New York, I, 538 (preamble to later § 32 in early draft of 1777 Constitution, omitted in later drafts).

[22] Edward S. Corwin made a similar point about constitutional developments in New Jersey. The first arguably genuine case of judicial review, *Holmes* v. *Walton*, was brought in New Jersey in 1779 but not decided by that state's supreme court until 1780. Corwin writes, "[i]t is interesting to note . . . that the idea of judicial review had not occurred to those who drafted the New Jersey Constitution three years before [in 1776], the fact that they relied for the preservation of this . . . most fundamental provision of the constitution upon the good faith of

of final appeal had not been composed of ordinary judges sitting in ordinary courts.[23] Within provincial New York the court of final appeal in civil matters had consisted of the Governor and the Council. Appeals from this court were taken to the court of appeal for the empire, the Privy Council, itself no ordinary court of law. Within England, the House of Lords sat as the court of final appeal. "[T]he tribunal of final resort in the realm was in essence a court no more than was the Privy Council. The antic hand of history had left the House of Lords the 'last great stage of appeal,' where the ultimate correction of errors occurred; thus the capstone of the system of judicature for the realm, as for the dominions, was in each instance a body where the votes of laymen predominated . . . ."[24]

For these deeply conservative men, re-establishing a Court for the Correction of Errors may have represented part of a program to retain as much of the traditional system of government as seemed possible under the radically changed circumstances they now confronted. Whatever their motives may have been, at that moment, they appear to have failed completely to anticipate the development of judicial review.

In 1777 when the framers of New York's constitution sought to impose an "external" check upon the legislature, what they thought to do was to revive the gubernatorial veto and a Privy Council like process of *legislative review*. They seem not yet to have even imagined a practice of *judicial review* that might operate as a further check upon legislative power. If anything, they appear to have resolved to impose a *legislative check on the judiciary*. Under the new constitution, consequently, the people's representatives would possess the power to override Council of Revision objections, leaving the legislature with the final say (within government) as to

the legislature, it being required by the final section of the constitution that every member of that body should take an oath not to assent to any law, vote, or proceeding, to repeal or annul 'that part of the twenty-second section respecting the trial by jury.'" Edward S. Corwin, "Establishment of Judicial Review I" (1910) 9 *Michigan Law Review* 102, 111. Beyond that, as in New York, New Jersey's 1776 constitution did not make the supreme court, which delivered the judgment in *Holmes* v. *Walton*, the court of final resort in the state. By Section IX of the constitution, the supreme court's judgments were subject to correction by the Court of Appeals, comprised, as it had also been in the colony, of the "Governor and Council" (the upper house of the legislature); see Thorpe (ed.), Constitutions, V, 2596 (NJ Const. of 1776, Section IX).

[23] The conservative nature of the structuring of the judicial power in four states, New York, New Jersey, Delaware, and Connecticut is made clearer by the provisions contained in many of the first state constitutions to "stri[p] their new governors and privy councils of their former judicial role by setting up separate courts of appeal and chancery," Wood, Creation of the American Republic, 160.

[24] Smith, Appeals to the Privy Council, 655.

whether a law was or was not consistent with the spirit of the constitution, and the authority, lodged in the upper house of the legislature sitting on the Court for the Correction of Errors, to reverse any judgment and correct any doctrine issuing from the judges that might threaten the legislature's constitutional position.

The emergence of judicial review in the 1780s transformed this constitutional landscape. From being a reassuring reminder of the continuity of tradition, courts of final appeal constructed in this way (New Jersey, Connecticut and Delaware[25] had similar courts) began to be viewed by some as an obstacle to the successful implementation of a judicial restraint on legislative power, and by others as a means of defending the traditional constitutional authority of legislatures. In Federalist #81, Alexander Hamilton roundly criticized the idea of "vesting the ultimate power of judging in a part of the legislative body."[26]

> From a body which had even a partial agency in passing bad laws we could rarely expect a disposition to temper and moderate them in the application. The same spirit which had operated in making them should be too apt to operate in interpreting them: still less could it be expected that men who had infringed the Constitution in the character of legislators would be disposed to repair the breach in the character of judges.[27]

At the opposite end of the political spectrum, when a lower court in New York refused to enforce part of a controversial statute in its decision in the case of *Rutgers* v. *Waddington* in 1784, the New York legislature responded by doing what it had neglected to do for the first seven years of the constitution's life. Within a few weeks it drafted and enacted legislation finally setting up the Court for the Correction of Errors,[28] which the

[25] For New Jersey, see Thorpe (ed.), Constitutions, V, 2596 (NJ Const. of 1776, Section IX); for Delaware, see ibid., I, 565 (DE Const. of 1776, Art. 17); for Connecticut, see Zephaniah Swift, *A System of the Laws of the State of Connecticut: In Six Books* (Windham, Ct., 1795, repr. Arno Press, 1972), I, 93.

[26] #81 Federalist, Clinton Rossiter (ed.), *The Federalist Papers* (New York, Mentor Books, 1999), 451.

[27] Ibid., #81Federalist, 451–52. Hamilton appears to have written Federalist #81 as a response to a critique of the proposed Federal Constitution published by "Brutus" (No. XV) on March 20, 1788, in which Brutus condemned the judicial arrangements in the new constitution for failing to provide just such a court of final appeal in which the judges' "errors may be corrected … ." in Ralph Ketcham (ed.), *The Anti-Federalist Papers and the Constitutional Convention Debates* (New York, Signet Classic, 2003, c. 1986), 305, 307–8.

[28] *Journal of the Assembly of New York, Oct.-Nov. 1784* (Early American Imprints, First Series; no. 18649), 34 (November 2, 1784), and 37, 50, 59, 60, 67, 70; and *Laws of New York, Eighth Session* (1784), Chap. XI, 21.

constitution of 1777 had authorized. In this way, the legislature seems to have hoped to preserve its constitutional prerogatives against a budding judicial insurgency. By the time the New York legislature got around to instituting the Court for the Correction of Errors in 1784, courts of final appeal constructed in this way had begun to become part of the struggle between legislatures and judges over the developing practice of judicial review.

3.2 THE REJECTION OF EXPRESS ABSOLUTE VETOES OVER LEGISLATION

The most conservative men at the New York convention, however, had not gotten all that they had initially wanted. In the end, they had failed to convince the convention to adopt an absolute gubernatorial veto. And even though, in a concession to prevailing constitutional norms, they had compromised by agreeing to confer only a qualified veto on the Council of Revision, over the years, they came to believe that they had not been mistaken in their original assessment. Often enough, they continued to argue, the Council's veto had failed to prevent the New York legislature from enacting unjust, destructive and unconstitutional laws at the urging of an aroused populace. A closer examination of the Council's record, however, indicates that the veto had been far from a complete failure. On the one hand, of the 169 bills the Council returned to the legislature with objections over its 44-year history, only 51 bills, about 30%, were repassed over the Council's objections.[29] On the other hand, among the 51, the legislature overrode the Council's veto in a number of politically charged instances that dealt with the treatment of Loyalists, one of the subjects, along with debtor/creditor relations, that stirred deep passions during the decade following Independence. The legislature, for example, overrode the Council's veto of a bill that stripped Loyalists of the right to vote and to hold political office in March 1778.[30] In 1780, it overrode the Council's veto of "An act for the immediate sale of part of the forfeited estates [of Loyalists]."[31] And in 1784, it did so again, overriding the Council's veto of a bill making penal "the voluntarily remaining with the fleets and armies of the King of Great Britain" during the war for Independence.[32] For all that, the Council also enjoyed a number of

[29] Alfred B. Street, The Council of Revision of the State of New York, and Its Vetoes (Albany, William Gould Publisher, 1859), 7.
[30] Ibid., 208–10. [31] Ibid., 229–31. [32] Ibid., 254–55.

notable successes. Council vetoes were sustained in a number of cases in which popular anti-Loyalist legislation had been at stake.[33]

But looking back on this mixed record in 1787, the Council's failures loomed larger than its successes in the eyes of Gouverneur Morris and Alexander Hamilton. At the Federal Convention they argued in favor of the need for a ¾ supermajority vote of Congress to override a proposed Presidential veto, opposing a motion to re-adopt a 2/3 requirement. Gouverneur Morris asserted that[34]

> [t]he example of N. York shows that 2/3 is not sufficient to answer the purpose. Mr. Hamilton added his testimony to the fact that 2/3 in N. York had been ineffectual either where a popular object or a legislative faction operated; of which he mentioned some instances.[35]

Requiring a ¾ vote to override would have made the Presidential veto into an instrument more nearly approximating the absolute veto which Gouverneur Morris had sought from the beginning in New York, and in favor of which Morris and Hamilton had argued at the Federal Convention.[36] But the Federal Convention voted, in the end, to re-adopt a 2/3 requirement to override Presidential vetoes.

In doing so, it was following a well-established constitutional norm. No constitutional convention in this period, state or federal, ever conferred on the executive (or the judiciary) an express absolute veto over legislation. We have seen that the New York Convention refused, in the end, to adopt such a veto. That was not the only instance. In his draft of the 1780 Massachusetts Constitution, John Adams proposed giving the

[33] Ibid., 219–26 ("An act for forfeitures and confiscations [of Loyalist estates] . . . "); 233–34 ("An act for the amendment of the law directing the sales of forfeited land"); 246–49 ("An Act declaratory of the alienism of the persons therein described"), and ("An act to amend an act relative to debts due to persons within the enemy's lines").

[34] The Convention had originally adopted a 2/3 requirement to override executive vetoes, but in later deliberations had increased it to ¾. At the time Hamilton and Morris intervened the Convention was reconsidering the decision to establish the ¾ requirement, and ultimately did reject that requirement in favor of a 2/3 vote to override. In earlier debates both Hamilton and Morris had advocated that the executive be given an absolute veto over Congressional legislation rather than a suspensive veto, and James Wilson had joined with them in making this argument, Max Farrand (ed.), *The Records of the Federal Convention of 1787* (New Haven, Ct., Yale University Press, 1966), I, 98, 100, 103, 105–7, 292–93, 300–1, II, 200.

[35] Farrand, Records of the Federal Convention, II, 585.

[36] See speeches by Hamilton and Morris advocating absolute vetoes to be exercised by the executive, Farrand, Records of the Federal Convention, I, 98, 103, 105–7, 292–93, 300–1, II, 200.

Massachusetts governor such a veto.[37] When Adams's draft reached the floor of the Massachusetts convention, however, his veto plan was voted down.[38] As in New York, the Massachusetts convention gravitated instead toward "some mode to be established by the constitution for the revision of laws by the Governor and Council."[39] There were others in Massachusetts besides Adams, who wished to see the governor exercise an absolute veto over legislation, and they suggested a compromise. They moved that "the Governor of this Commonwealth [shall] have a negative upon all the laws, except those which shall be made and passed for the military defence of the state, and that he [shall] have a revision on those . . . ."[40] But this motion was also defeated. Instead, the convention adopted a plan to give the governor the same type of qualified veto, overridable by a 2/3 vote of the legislature, that the Council of Revision enjoyed in New York.[41]

The proposal to give a governor an absolute veto over legislation was defeated in Massachusetts as it had been in New York in favor of placing a check on the legislature without, however, depriving that body of the final say on the laws. The weight of political opinion on this question remained remarkably stable even as anxieties about the excesses of popular government intensified during the 1780s. Whenever an express absolute veto over legislation was proposed at the Federal Convention, and several different types of absolute vetoes were proposed on more than one occasion,[42] just as in New York and Massachusetts, the Convention refused to adopt them. Faced with this reality, men like Gouverneur Morris, James Wilson and Alexander Hamilton, all of whom had advocated the adoption of an absolute (executive) veto, would naturally have been drawn to the emerging practice of judicial review, which held out the promise of erecting a kind of absolute judicial veto over the laws. Nor

[37] "The Report of a Constitution or Form of Government for the Commonwealth of Massachusetts," in *The Works of John Adams* (Boston, Ma., Little, Brown & Co., 1851) IV, 231

[38] *Journal of the Convention for Framing a Constitution of Government for the State of Massachusetts Bay: from the commencement of their first session, September 1, 1779, to the close of their last session, June 16, 1780* (Boston, Dutton and Wentworth, Printers to the State,1832), 126.

[39] Ibid., 127. [40] Ibid., 132.

[41] See Article II of the Massachusetts Constitution of 1780, in Thorpe (ed.), Constitutions, III, 1893–94.

[42] Farrand, Records of the Federal Convention (proposed absolute veto in the executive I, 98, 103, 105–7, 292–93, 300–1, II, 200); (Va. Plan vesting absolute veto over state laws in Congress I, 47).

were these men likely to have missed the point that this substantial check on legislatures had been developing without the need for a vote from any popularly elected constitutional convention.

3.3 EXPOSING THE DEEP TENSIONS WITHIN THE EARLY CONSTITUTIONAL SYSTEM: NEW YORK COUNCIL OF REVISION OPINIONS

New York's Council of Revision had come into existence in 1777 as an alternative to an absolute gubernatorial veto. By the 1780s, experience with the Council of Revision had reinforced the views of some that it had proved inadequate as a check on legislatures and that a more robust constraint was necessary. But by this time, others began to view the Council of Revision as a possible alternative to the veto that judges had begun to wield in the emerging practice of judicial review. James Madison in particular held distinctly ambivalent views about the new practice of judicial review. While he saw the need, in varying degrees, for a robust check on popularly elected legislatures, he seems to have been inclined to take a more traditional view of the nature of constitutions, as essentially "political," subject to conflicting interpretations that affected the broad polity that were best resolved by the legislative representatives of the people, or by the people themselves. He also seems to have had an instinctive preference for a check on legislatures that would be created explicitly through the process of constitution making, rather than one that would arise by implication through judicial interpretation.[43] Chapter 10 discusses in greater detail various proposals Madison (and to a lesser extent Jefferson) advanced during the 1780s to establish Councils of Revision, in several instances explicitly as an alternative to judicial review. Madison, more clearly and consistently than Jefferson, seemed reluctant completely to abandon the principle of legislative finality in decisions about the constitutionality of the laws. The defeat of Madison's proposal for a Council of Revision at the Federal Convention marked an important moment in the ascent of judicial review in the constitutional firmament.

[43] Edward S. Corwin, "Progress of Constitutional Theory" (1925) 30 *The American Historical Review* 511, 521. ("[W]hile the executive veto and judicial review have a common explanation in the political necessity which they were devised to meet, the manner in which they were respectively articulated to the American Constitutional system was widely and for us most significantly divergent.") ("[Judicial review] was introduced solely by the processes of interpretation and without the slightest textual alteration being made in the constitutions involved.")

But if, on the one hand, Councils of Revision began to be offered as an alternative to judicial review, on the other hand, the creators of the original Council had expressly conferred on the judges of the New York supreme court and New York's Chancellor the authority and duty to deliver their formal opinions on the question whether a (proposed) statute was inconsistent with the (spirit of the) constitution. In the course of performing this task, the New York Council of Revision produced a substantial body of written opinion, often drafted by one of the judges, that provides a rich and rare source for understanding somewhat more about the assumptions these judges brought to the task of evaluating constitutionality.

Chapter 2 of this book made clear that conflicting British views about the precise constitutional status of Parliament had carried over to America. On the one hand, many believed that both Parliament and the first American state legislatures wielded supreme power within their governments unchecked by any authority other than the people themselves. Legislatures elected by the people were sometimes said to possess, during their designated terms, "every power of the people, except that of opposition."[44] On the other hand, a number of the first American constitutions had explicitly stated that they were depriving legislatures of the power to alter, amend or change them, in whole or in part. Americans, however, had balked at establishing any institutional mechanism to enforce these constitutional limitations. New York's Constitution came closest, but in the end it, like all the others, entrusted the final decision on the constitutionality of laws to the legislature itself (subject to later review by the people). As a result, whether legislatures were thought on the one hand to be absolutely supreme within governments, or whether on the other, they were thought to exercise only limited powers under constitutions came, as a practical matter, to the same thing. Whatever the theory, in practice legislatures continued to have the unchecked power to confer the force of law on their bills, subject only to the power of the people to remove them from office and to have the offending law repealed. This institutional reality, however, would continue to exist in some tension with the idea that legislatures were created under constitutions and

[44] See, for example, Edmund Randolph's statement of this principle (subsequently lined through) in his manuscript argument in *the Case of the Prisoners*, at 3. Randolph's manuscript is preserved in the James Madison papers held at the Library of Congress, 91 James Madison Papers, Manuscript Division, Library of Congress, Washington, D.C., and online at www.loc.gov/item/mjm021836/.

possessed only the powers (including the power to make law) that those instruments had delegated to them.

In one sense, it is hard to understand how the judges who first sat on New York's Council of Revision could possibly have subscribed to the second view of constitutions, given the constitutional framework which they themselves had helped to create and under which they now served. As members of New York's constitutional convention, Robert R. Livingston and John Jay had been responsible for bringing forward the original proposal to establish a Council of Revision; now the two men sat on that Council as judicial members, Jay as Chief Justice of the New York supreme court, and Livingston as Chancellor of the state. Despite this history, both men at times employed language in their Council of Revision opinions that indicated they viewed the New York constitution as imposing actual limits on the "power" of the legislature to confer the force of law on a bill. In suggesting this, they must have thought it was possible in principle to separate the question of the basic nature of a constitution from the question of who possessed the final power to interpret the instrument, and to think that the constitution's essential character, as a limitation on the power of legislatures, was not changed by the fact that the New York constitution had explicitly conferred on the legislature the final authority to determine its own powers to make law under it.[45]

The Council of Revision issued fifty-eight vetoes before 1787. Of these, twenty-one included objections based on violations of the constitution.[46] In February 1778, the council vetoed a bill on the ground, among others, that it was "inconsistent with the spirit of the Constitution of this State." The proposed bill purported to "confirm" and "continue" resolutions that had been adopted by the Council of Safety. The Council of Revision was of the opinion that once the new constitution had been adopted, temporary expedients like the Council of Safety ceased to exist and that the legislature did not possess the power to revive them or to confirm their earlier resolutions as binding on the people of the state. In objecting to the bill, John Jay, reported for the Council that it was their

[45] Many contemporaries understood quite well that an intimate connection existed between the nature of a constitution and where the final power to interpret it lay, see John Phillip Reid, "Another Origin of Judicial Review: The Constitutional Crisis of 1776 and the Need for a Dernier Judge" (1989) 64 *New York University Law Review* 963.

[46] Roedel, "Stoking the Doctrinal Furnace," 270.

> *opinion* that all Conventions and Councils of Safety had ceased and could not thereafter be instituted or appointed consistent with the Constitution of this State; and that *the people did not give or delegate to their representatives* in Senate or Assembly, *any power or authority*, at their discretion, to revive the Government by Conventions or Councils of Safety, or in any other manner to dispense with or suspend the government established by the Constitution . . . .[47] (emphasis added)

In its bill, the Council continued, the legislature "recognizes and speaks of this Council of Safety as if it had been a body constitutionally instituted and known to the law of the land; it speaks of their resolution as *laying an embargo* which it was expedient to *continue*, thereby intimating that the said resolution *was obligatory on the people, when, in fact, it was not obligatory, nor were they in the least bound to obey or regard it*"[48] (emphasis added). "[N]either the mode of the [Council of Safety's] institution nor the edicts they made, ought, *in the opinion of this Council*, to be held up by the *Legislature as constitutional or obligatory*, especially as the Constitution does expressly 'Ordain, determine and declare, that no authority shall, on any pretense whatever, be exercised over the people or members of this State, but such as shall be derived from and granted by them'"[49] (emphasis added).

Several aspects of the Council's language stand out. On the one hand, the Council refers to its "objections" as "opinions." Certainly, the use of this term is susceptible to more than one reading, but in this context, it seems to suggest that the Council considers interpretation to be crucial to the enterprise of determining constitutionality, and is quietly acknowledging that its interpretation may have to give way to the legislature's contrary interpretation, which under the constitution, would then be binding on everyone. On the other hand, the Council also uses language that indicates that the constitution contains limitations that deprive the legislature of "the power" to do certain things. And where a governmental body lacks constitutional authority, its edicts will not be binding on the people, will not be obligatory. And even though in this instance, the Council of Revision is referring specifically to the enactments of the Council of Safety, it indirectly implicates the power of the legislature to make binding law, in that the legislature has apparently attempted, unsuccessfully in the Council's opinion, to give its formal sanction to these Council of Safety edicts. "*Notwithstanding [the Council's] objections*,"

[47] Street, The Council of Revision and Its Vetoes, 204 (reproducing the Council veto and objections of February 20, 1778, "reported by the Chief Justice").
[48] Quoted ibid., 205. [49] Quoted ibid., 204.

however, "the Legislature *passed the bill*, with a slight verbal amendment, *into a law*"[50] (emphasis added).

Just a month later the Council vetoed "*An act to regulate elections within this State*" again highlighting both aspects of the Council's thinking. In this bill, the legislature had attempted to deprive certain categories of Loyalists of the vote. In its objections, the Council as reported by Jay, wrote that

> the Constitution of this State hath expressly ordained 'that every elector, before he is admitted to vote, shall, if required by the returning officer, or either of the inspectors, take an oath or (if of the people called Quakers) an affirmation of allegiance to the State,' from whence, in the *opinion* of this Council, it clearly follows that every elector who will take such oath, has a *constitutional right* to be admitted to such vote, and therefore that the Legislature have *no power to deprive* him thereof . . . . (emphasis added)

Once again, despite the Council's objections, the legislature's contrary interpretation of its powers prevailed, and it also passed this bill into law.[51]

The same day, the Council vetoed another bill, "*An act for raising moneys ... etc.*" The bill attempted to shift from "the people" to the county supervisors the authority to select property tax assessors. The Council was of the opinion that this provision violated the clause in the constitution that read, "assessors and all other officers *heretofore eligible by the people, shall always continue to be so eligible* in the manner directed by then present or future acts of the Legislature" (emphasis added). In its objections, again reported by Jay, the Council interpreted the provision to mean that "the Legislature may constitutionally direct the manner in which the people at large shall exercise this important right [to choose assessors], yet that *the Legislature hath no authority to divest them of it, and transfer it to the supervisors*"[52] (emphasis added).

In another veto delivered on March 30, 1778, and reported by Chancellor Livingston, the Council "object[ed] to the said bill becoming a law of the State, because *repugnant to the Constitution* therof."[53] On

[50] Quoted ibid., 208.

[51] Quoted ibid., 211–12 (Council Veto and Objections of March 25, 1778, reported by Chief Justice Jay).

[52] Quoted ibid., 213 (Council Veto and Objections of March 25, 1778, reported by Chief Justice Jay). Again, despite the Council's objections, the legislature also passed this bill into law, 213.

[53] Ibid., 214 (Council Veto, March 30, 1778). Once again despite Council objections the legislature also passed this bill into law.

November 5, 1778, the Council vetoed "*An act for raising a further sum by tax* ... " writing, as reported by Chief Justice Jay, that the Council objected to the proposed legislation "because *the Legislature are not authorized by the Constitution to delegate the right of determining*, at discretion, how much shall be levied on all or part of the people to any body of men whatever, much less to the assessors"[54] (emphasis added).

In yet another veto, the Council's language implied that if a statute had been in clear contravention of a clause in the constitution, it would not be "legal." Because this was not a clear-cut case, the Council wrote that "[i]f, however, the Legislature *could legally pass such [a] law*" and then went on to object to the law on other grounds [55] (emphasis added). In another veto delivered on October 21, 1779, and reported by Chancellor Livingston, the Council wrote that it objected to the bill

> [b]ecause the power vested in a single Justice of the Peace to determine cases to an unlimited amount upon his own knowledge, or upon the oath of a single witness, without a jury, is a *direct violation of that clause of the Constitution* which ordains "that trial by jury in all cases in which it hath heretofore been used in the Colony of New York, shall be established and remain inviolate forever;" and may be considered as a new court, not proceeding according to the course of the common law, which *the Constitution expressly prohibits the Legislature from instituting*.[56] (emphasis added)

After Jay retired as Chief Justice in October 1779, this kind of language showed up less frequently in Council vetoes. Perhaps, it should not come as a surprise, after all, that judges in New York would have been inclined to treat the constitution as imposing restrictions on the power of legislatures to make binding law. And from there it would seem to require only a short step to make out a rudimentary case for judicial review. Where a statute's terms clearly conflicted with provisions in a constitution, it would have seemed natural for judges, who held such a view of constitutions, to conclude that they had no obligation to enforce in their courts an act that was not in fact binding law. Indeed, as Philip Hamburger has so brilliantly shown, since judges served under a centuries old duty to decide cases according to the law of the land, some would have felt an obligation absolutely to refuse to enforce any statute

54 Ibid., 217 (Council Veto, November 5, 1778). In this case, "[t]he Assembly refused to pass the bill; consequently, it did not become a law," 219.

55 Ibid., 222 (Council Veto of March 14, 1779).

56 Ibid., 228 (Council Veto of October 21, 1779); "The Legislature refused to [re]pass the bill; consequently, it did not become a law." See also ibid., 234 (Council Veto of October 9, 1780).

that was unconstitutional as being beyond the power of a legislature to make, and hence "not obligatory, nor were they in the least bound to obey or regard it."[57] The very simplicity and obviousness of the elementary case for judicial review speaks for itself, but in certain ways it belies the difficulties the argument for judicial review actually confronted.

The example of New York itself illustrates one of the principal problems. Even if New York's constitution was thought to limit, in some theoretical sense, the "power" of the legislature to make law, that same constitution had conferred on the legislature the final interpretive authority, within government, to determine whether their legislative acts were in conflict with the constitution. The judges and the governor on the Council of Revision might have their own opinions about whether an act conflicted with the spirit of the constitution, and might "object" to proposed legislation on those grounds, but at the end of the day their interpretations, their opinions, had to give way, under the constitution, to the final interpretive authority of the legislature. Even sitting in their ordinary judicial capacity, the opinions and interpretations of New York's judges were subject to being overridden by members of the upper house of the legislature sitting on the Court for the Correction of Errors. As a consequence, merely saying that constitutions limited the power of legislatures to make binding law was far from sufficient to make out a case for judicial review- so long as legislatures were also generally understood to possess final interpretive authority (within governments) to judge whether their acts conflicted with the (spirit, principles, true intent and meaning) of a constitution– and with this interpretive authority the power in the final resort to confer the force of law on an enactment.

There were other serious obstacles on the road to judicial review as well. In New York, the judges on the Council of Revision had been given the explicit authority to provide their opinions about the constitutionality of proposed laws. But that was not the case in other states; in no other instance had the explicit authority to consider the constitutionality of laws been conferred on judges.[58] Consequently, a crucial question remained

[57] Quoted ibid., 205; see Philip Hamburger, *Law and Judicial Duty* (Cambridge, Mass., Harvard University Press, 2009).

[58] Most constitutions of the period, however, had also not explicitly granted legislatures the authority finally to determine the constitutionality of a law. Since most constitutions made no provision one way or the other for disagreements in interpreting them, as James Madison later pointed out, in the absence of any explicit provision, courts might well claim that their interpretive authority under a constitution was at least the equal of the legislature's.

whether constitutions were even cognizable by ordinary courts; did judges even possess the authority to consider them in the course of arriving at their decisions, or were they bound by their duty to decide cases according to the established statutory and common law of the land. At this time, constitutions were not commonly regarded as conventional law, but were often considered to be foundational political compacts (political law), standing above governments, and under which governments were formed. By contrast, ordinary laws were understood to be the product of governments themselves, having the force of law only under those governments.[59]

On the other hand, New York's experience seemed to point to the fact that judges were often thought to possess a certain kind of "legal" expertise that might make their opinions especially valuable in the process for determining whether a proposed statute was consistent or inconsistent with a constitution. That such expertise seemed particularly relevant in this way may also suggest that the traditional view of constitutions as a kind of "political law"[60] had already begun to shift subtly over to a view that they more nearly constituted a form of "superior conventional law." But then again, the governor of New York also served as a member of the Council of Revision.

There were a number of other serious questions about the authority of judges that required answers before a convincing case for judicial review could be fully made out. Judges might be entitled to their own opinions about the constitutionality of a statute, but could their judicial determinations based on those opinions actually deprive a statute of the force of law. As a practical matter, of course, their offices placed them in a position to block the execution of any statute they judged to be unconstitutional. And in this sense, they possessed the raw power effectively to nullify such statutes, to make them not law in fact, at least in their own courts. But could a judge's opinion that a statute was unconstitutional and void *legitimately* deprive that statute of the force of law? Was a judge's opinion different than the opinion of just any citizen or governmental official who might believe that a particular law was unconstitutional and void? Could a sheriff, a town clerk, or any citizen cherry pick among the duly enacted laws of the land they would agree to enforce or abide by, if they believed

[59] Sylvia Snowiss, *Judicial Review and the Law of the Constitution* (New Haven, Ct., Yale University Press, 1990), 2–6; and Larry Kramer, *The People Themselves: Popular Constitutionalism and Judicial Review* (Oxford, Oxford University Press, 2004), 24.

[60] Snowiss, Judicial Review, 2–6; and Kramer, The People Themselves, 24.

a statute to be unconstitutional? Down that path lay chaos and a serious undermining of the rule of law itself.

It would be one thing if judges were only thought to be engaging in a form of civil disobedience by resisting a statute they believed should not be binding, but which in fact continued to possess the force of law. If that was the case, judges might at the very least be subject to removal from office for failing to decide cases according to the law of the land. But judicial review was based on a contention that judges enjoyed the formal authority to declare that a statute did not enjoy the force of law, and at a minimum was not obligatory on the parties before the court. What characteristics of the judicial office made judges different from every other actor, giving them a "legal" authority to pronounce a statute void as unconstitutional, and in that way "legitimately" deprive it of the force of law? Although conceived of as a judgment that the offending statute had not been law in the first place, as a practical matter that was a legal fiction. The judicial act of declaring a statute unconstitutional would in fact operate to undo the original act of the legislature in conferring the force of law on its enactments.[61] Having received no explicit grant from any constitution, to what possible source could judges point to establish that they possessed the legitimate authority to unmake laws?

Implicit in their claims that they possessed such a power was the contention that their interpretive authority on questions of constitutionality did not have to give way to the interpretive authority of a legislature, that legislatures should no longer be viewed as possessing the final word on matters of constitutionality. The interpretive authority of courts, it was implicitly asserted, equaled, at the very least, that of legislatures. Quite a few Americans quickly came to the conclusion that judicial review in fact gave the opinions of courts in these matters greater weight than legislatures, in that courts now, in a specific but very real sense, exercised power in the final resort to reverse the legislature's decision to confer the force of law on a bill.

If the judges prevailed in their contention that they possessed the legitimate power to act in this way, it would also transform the nature

[61] An adjudication of unconstitutionality in one case might technically only bind the parties to that case, but it would also operate as precedent, and in practice would mean that any subsequent person bringing a case under the statute in that court would only be able to avail themselves of rights and duties arising under the statute, if they could meaningfully distinguish the earlier case from their own. Of course, Americans also often wrote and spoke, even at this time, as though an adjudication of unconstitutionality had the effect of nullifying a law more generally.

of the constraints imposed by written constitutions. These would now begin to operate in fact as "legal" limitations on the capacity of legislatures to make law, as legislatures would no longer be the final judge of their powers under the constitution to confer the force of law on a measure. As Edward Corwin saw a century ago, "[t]he fact of the matter is, that the establishment of judicial review [was the final step in giving] constitution[s] the character of law . . . ."[62]

The simple judicial act of refusing to enforce duly enacted statutes, underwritten by an increasingly persuasive argument that these were constitutionally legitimate acts within the office of judges, had profound effects on the constitutional system, completing the transformation of written constitutions into conventional law, and radically altering the position not only of legislatures but of the people themselves in the new constitutional order these acts and arguments brought into being. This was a constitutional revolution effected, to begin with, primarily by the bench and bar.

There were other consequences as well. From being viewed primarily as a legislative matter, determinations of the constitutionality of law would increasingly be viewed as the domain of judges and lawyers, whose skills and expertise lay precisely in interpreting the laws. To an important extent, the crucial constitutional authority of deciding what powers legislatures possessed under a constitution would now begin to shift from legislatures to judges. In the process, "the people" would be displaced from their central role as direct, active interpreters of constitutions. And their power to enact through their legislatures just any law they might desire would be curtailed. The judges' simple act of refusing to execute a duly enacted law of the land, together with the justifications that were offered for this conduct, had the outsize consequence of transforming the constitutional system.

Whether this constitutional revolution succeeded, however, would depend in the end on the outcome of several different struggles that developed during the 1780s; a political struggle that pit state legislatures against the courts, on the one hand, and on the other, a struggle over ideas. The outcome of the contests in these two arenas, needless to say, were intimately interconnected.

When judges first began to refuse to enforce duly enacted statutes during the 1780s, their actions provoked widespread hostility in state legislatures. To a crucial extent realpolitik would decide the outcome of

[62] Corwin, "The Establishment of Judicial Review I," 110.

this conflict. Would judges succeed in holding onto their offices after engaging in such acts, or would legislatures, believing such acts to be an unconstitutional usurpation of legislative power, remove any judge from office who acted in this way, at once discrediting the practice, in a very concrete way, and simultaneously discouraging other judges from even considering doing the same. The outcome of this struggle would depend, not to put too fine a point on the matter, on whether legislatures were prepared to test the full extent of their powers to impeach or otherwise remove from office any judge who did. The steady assertion of such powers might have served to vindicate the view that duly enacted statutes were obligatory as the law of the land, unconditionally, until the legislature repealed them, and might have left the practice of judicial review stillborn, as in colonial South Carolina. On the other hand, by failing to act assertively to prevent judges from engaging in this conduct, legislatures would tend to promote the view that judges did indeed possess the legitimate authority to "dispense with" duly enacted statutes. The judicial acts themselves, steadfastly maintained, would contribute to establishing the constitutional legitimacy of the new practice. And by failing to remove judges from office, legislatures might even be seen as acquiescing in or approving the new practice.

Beyond the willingness to exercise the full extent of their powers, however, the outcome of the battle over judicial review would be decided by a contest over ideas in the court of public opinion, or more precisely, the court of legal opinion. Lawyers in a number of states made rapid progress in developing a highly persuasive case for judicial review during the 1780s, elaborating a powerful logic for the practice based on a few simple, widely accepted propositions about the nature of constitutions and of judging in common law culture. As a result, in part, because their account of judicial review resonated so deeply with broader common law assumptions, it succeeded in convincing substantial numbers of elite lawyers and judges to accept, promote and engage in the new practice. There were other reasons, however, that these newly minted ideas received a sympathetic reception during the 1780s. The general constitutional climate favored their success.

With the winding down of the war, more Americans became convinced that the failure of the framers of most of the first constitutions to include checks against the excesses of popularly elected legislatures had produced a constitutional crisis, for which a practice like judicial review could serve as a remedy. For many conservatives, the behavior of state legislatures in these years confirmed that it was imperative that the people themselves be bound by the terms of their own constitutions if the new republics were to survive, a task judges were in a perfect position to perform. Other Americans criticized these ideas, however, arguing that judicial review would undermine practices that were essential for the continued healthy functioning of simple republican governments.

Ideas that in another environment might have remained marginal, without a great deal of political support, as they had in colonial South Carolina, were, under the circumstances, taken up and disseminated. But the fate of judicial review nevertheless remained somewhat tenuous for a number of years. Only a handful of courts in a handful of states had acted on these ideas down to 1787, and a number of the judges who did had been called before their legislatures to answer for their conduct. In the end, the practice of judicial nullification became an irreversible feature of the American constitutional landscape as a result of the decisions of the Federal Convention. After prolonged debates, the Convention decided to employ the developing practice as the principal means for enforcing the new constitution, and wrote that decision into the constitution. Two years later, Congress bolstered judicial review (and the position of the Federal Government) by inserting several crucial sections into the First Judiciary Act of 1789. The next chapters flesh out this story of the emergence and rapid, if contested, acceptance of American judicial review.

PART TWO

THE EMERGENCE OF AMERICAN JUDICIAL REVIEW: 1779–1787

1

THE EMERGENCE OF AMERICAN JUDICIAL REVIEW, 1779–1782

American Judicial Review emerged during the 1780s as the result of a series of court cases, and of the events that surrounded them. On the one hand, these cases do not appear to have arisen from a systematic, concerted litigation strategy; on the other, they all do seem to have grown, in different ways, out of a common constitutional culture, containing deep tensions, that was being placed under great stress by war, and internal conflict. Each of the cases involved a partly unique story, which, however, also contributed to the larger constitutional development. It is difficult to describe the emergence of judicial review in these years except by going back to re-tell, yet again,[1] the stories of these early cases. By placing these cases squarely against the background of the traditional constitutional order, which they were rapidly undermining, and by closely (re)-reading the extant primary sources, however, it is possible to garner significant new insights about this transformative constitutional development. Part Two of the book is divided into two sections. The first consists of Chapters 4 and 5 which deal with the two cases that arose while the Revolutionary war was still ongoing.[2] The second subsection, contained in the succeeding

[1] The number of articles and books that have described and discussed these cases are too numerous to cite.

[2] There is now pretty wide agreement among historians about the relatively short list of cases that introduced judicial review into the American constitutional system down to the Federal Convention: *Holmes* v. *Walton* (N.J., 1780), *Commonwealth v. Caton* (*The Case of the Prisoners*) (Va., 1782), *Rutgers* v. *Waddington* (N.Y., 1784), The Ten Pound Act Cases (N.H., 1786), *Trevett* v. *Weeden* (R.I., 1786), and *Bayard* v. *Singleton* (N.C., 1787); some historians add the *Symsbury Case* (Ct., 1785). But recent work has pretty convincingly removed the Josiah Philips case from the list, see Matthew Steilen, "The Josiah

four chapters, discuss cases down to 1787 that were brought after the war had ended. This division reflects the view that the two early cases (decided before the war had concluded) were distinctly transitional, and did not, in themselves, challenge the existing constitutional system nearly as straightforwardly as did the cases that arose following the signing of the peace, though they were often viewed later as having done so.

Philips Attainder, and the Institutional Structure of the American Revolution" (2017) 60 *Howard Law Journal* 413.

4

Supplementing Traditional Legislative "Revision" with Judicial Review: The New Jersey Case of *Holmes v. Walton*, 1779–1780[1]

The British Army invaded New York City during the late summer of 1776 and occupied it until the very end of the Revolutionary war in 1783. At various times, the British mounted armed forays into New Jersey just across the river. For the balance of the war, New Jersey remained on the front lines.

On October 8, 1778, the New Jersey legislature enacted a law to try to stop the rampant smuggling that had developed between "disaffected Subjects of this State" and those behind British lines. "An ACT to prevent the Subjects of this State from going into or coming out of, the Enemy's Lines, without Permissions or Passports . . . "[2] not only authorized regular military forces and militia to seize smuggled goods, but also gave that authority to "any Person or Persons whomsoever."[3] The statute directed that seized goods and the persons from whom they were confiscated be brought before a justice of the peace of the County who was directed to

[1] At least two sources, one old, one more recent, should be consulted for their comprehensive descriptions of this case, see Austin Scott, "Holmes vs. Walton: The New Jersey Precedent" (1899) 4 *The American Historical Review* 456–69; and Philip Hamburger, *Law and Judicial Duty* (Cambridge, Mass., Harvard University Press, 2008), 407–22.

[2] "An ACT to prevent the Subjects of this State from going into, or coming out of, the Enemy's Lines, without Permissions or Passports, and for other Purposes therein mentioned," *Acts of the General Assembly of the State of New Jersey* (October 8, 1778) (Trenton, Printed by Isaac Collins, 1778), Chap. XLV, 104; this act was amended in December 1778, see Peter Wilson, *Acts of the General Assembly of the State of New-Jersey*, Appendix VI (Trenton, N.J., Isaac Collins, Printer to the State, 1784), 11, "An Act to explain and amend an Act, intitled, An Act to Prevent the Subjects of this State from going into, or coming out of, etc." (December 11, 1778).

[3] Chap. XLV (October 8, 1778), Section 6, 105.

determine whether the smuggling allegations were true and if found to be so, the act decreed that "the Goods ... shall be forfeited to and for the Use of the Person or Persons who seized the same ...."[4]

Under the statute, either party could demand "a Jury" to try the matter, "and upon such Demand the said Justice is hereby required to grant the same, and to proceed in all other Respects as" under an earlier (Feb. 11, 1775) "Act, intitled, *An Act ... for the Trial of small Causes.*"[5] The 1775 small causes statute had defined the summary process a justice of the peace was to follow in cases involving actions of debt "and other Demands" up to "the real Value of *Six Pounds* ...."[6] If a case coming before the justice involved sums exceeding "*Forty Shillings*" (i.e., between 2 and 6 pounds), the 1775 small causes statute gave either party the option of demanding a jury trial and "upon such Demand, the said Justice is hereby required and commanded" to impanel a jury of six men to hear and decide the case.[7] Normally, cases involving sums greater than 6 pounds would not have been tried summarily by justices of the peace at all, but according to common law, which afforded the parties a range of procedural protections, including full juries of 12, that were not normally available in summary justice proceedings. By making the summary procedures defined by the 1775 small causes act an integral part of the 1778 smuggling act, however, many believed that that act required justices in smuggling cases only to seat juries of six, even when, as was common in such cases, the goods involved were of considerably greater value than 6 pounds.

The scope of summary justice (and of the right to trial by jury) had long been controversial in the American colonies, and it is necessary to understand something of this background to fully understand the issues in dispute in the case of *Holmes* v. *Walton*.

> In England, the jurisdiction of the common law courts in civil cases had long been for claims above forty shillings [2 pounds] which thus became the English division between claims that could not be denied a jury trial and claims that could be relegated to justices of the peace ... which proceeded without a jury .... The problem faced by many American colonies, including New Jersey, was how to adjust the right to a jury for inflation. Some colonies passed statutes that raised the jurisdictional barrier substantially above forty shillings and thus sent a broad swath of small claims to justices of the peace.[8]

[4] Ibid., Sect. 6, 106. [5] Ibid., Sect. 6, 106.

[6] "An ACT to erect and establish Courts in the several Counties in this Colony for the Trial of small Causes, and to repeal the former Act for that Purpose," *Laws of the Colony of New Jersey, XV Geo. III* (February 11, 1775), Chap. DCXXIII, Sect. 1, 469.

[7] Ibid., Sect. 4, 470. [8] Hamburger, Law and Judicial Duty, 410.

When the Privy Council came to review these American statutes, however, they sometimes disallowed them, in an effort to keep summary justice restricted to cases that did not involve large sums, because of what the Council (and common law judges) often considered to be the inherent shortcomings of such proceedings.[9] Local justices of the peace were often laymen, not well educated in the law; and commonly, proceedings were informal, conducted without regard to the more stringent evidentiary, testimonial and other procedural rules of the common law. In 1740, New Jersey enacted a small causes law that raised the jurisdictional threshold for summary justice from 40 shillings (2 pounds) to 5 pounds.[10] In an attempt apparently to accommodate the traditional common law obligation that required juries in disputes involving more than 40 shillings, the 1740 New Jersey statute added that in such cases, either party was entitled to demand a jury and the justice of the peace must then call a pared down jury of 6 to try the dispute. This requirement found its way into every subsequent New Jersey small causes act down to 1775. In 1760, New Jersey again raised the monetary threshold for summary justice to 6 pounds and apparently the Privy Council did not object.[11] But when in 1769, the colonial legislature sought to increase the jurisdictional threshold a third time to 10 pounds, the Privy Council balked, disallowing the statute.[12]

The Council cited a variety of objections that the Board of Trade had raised in its report recommending disallowance. In his memo for the Board, Mr. Jackson had questioned the character and qualifications of the personnel who administered summary justice and the integrity of the procedures they followed. But he did not raise in particular an objection to the size of the jury. Writing for the Board, Jackson submitted "That Summary ... Justice, under the specious pretext of facilitating the

[9] Several of these encounters with the Privy Council are discussed in Chapter 1.

[10] "An Act to erect and establish Courts, in the several Counties of this Province, for the Tryal of small Causes" (1740), *Laws of the Royal Colony of New Jersey II*, 520–24 (New Jersey Archives, 3rd series) (Trenton, New Jersey State Library, 1977), cited in Hamburger, Law and Judicial Duty, 410.

[11] "An Act to erect and establish Courts, in the several Counties of this Colony, for the Trial of small Causes" (1760), *Laws of the Royal Colony of New Jersey* IV, 28 (New Jersey Archives, 3rd series) (Trenton, New Jersey State Library, 1977), cited in Hamburger, Law and Judicial Duty, 411.

[12] "An Act to erect Courts, in the several Counties of this Colony, for the Trial of Causes of Ten Pounds, and under" (1769), *Laws of the Royal Colony of New Jersey IV*, 564 (New Jersey Archives, 3rd series) (Trenton, New Jersey State Library, 1977), cited in Hamburger, Law and Judicial Duty, 411.

Recovery of Debts necessarily encourages a litigious Spirit, and frequently the practice of perjury . . . . [moreover] that it serves too often to favour the establishment of much petty Tyranny in men altogether unfit to be intrusted with such power . . . " which is why in Great Britain it has not been "extended beyond the Sum of forty Shillings Sterling . . . ."[13]

Jackson continued in this vein for another page and a half, and while he did not criticize the use of small juries as such, he did not think that the option the state had established for a jury trial adequately protected parties from the defects of the proceedings. "[E]very plaintiff will naturally resort to a Justice [of the Peace], that is his Friend, Friendship often biases insensibly the honest man, but should he be dishonest there seems little Remedy in the power of demanding a Jury, [not because it would only consist of 6 persons but because] the Justice may order the Jury to be Summoned from any Town or precinct . . . .[14] Presumably, such jurors would be subject to the justice's undue influence as they would not have personal knowledge of the parties or the facts in the case. Jackson concluded by saying that since New Jersey had just recently (in 1760) raised the jurisdictional limit from 5 to 6 pounds, it was too dangerous to extend that experiment further so quickly.[15] Having been rebuffed in its efforts to raise the monetary threshold for summary justice to 10 pounds, in 1775 the New Jersey legislature enacted a small causes act that re-adopted the 1760 jurisdictional threshold of 6 pounds.

The case of *Holmes v. Walton* arose against this background. On May 22, 1779, Elisha Walton, a major in the militia, seized goods in the possession of John Holmes and Solomon Ketcham, claiming that they had been transported from within enemy lines.[16] He took the goods and the men to his house and two days later, on May 24, 1779, obtained from a local Monmouth County justice of the peace a trial by a jury of six, which produced a verdict and judgment in favor of Walton, and an order for the forfeiture of the seized goods.[17] The goods Walton confiscated, turn out to have been of great value, apparently worth upwards of £29,000,[18] and it

[13] James Munro (ed.), *Acts of the Privy Council of England: Colonial Series* (London, His Majesty's Stationary Office, 1912), V, 309–11 (Privy Council decision concerning a New Jersey act of November 1769 delivered June 7, 1771).

[14] Ibid., 310. [15] Ibid., 311.

[16] *Holmes* v. *Walton*: Chronology, http://njlegallib.rutgers.edu/hw/chronology.html and Scott, "Holmes v. Walton," 456, 457.

[17] *Holmes* v. *Walton*: Chronology http://njlegallib.rutgers.edu/hw/chronology.html and Scott, "Holmes v. Walton," 457; see also Hamburger, Law and Judicial Duty, 412–13.

[18] Scott, "Holmes v. Walton," 457, and April 25, 1781 Writ of Capias Corpus for debt of £29,428:13:41/2 in *Holmes* v. *Walton*: Chronology http://njlegallib.rutgers.edu/hw/chronology.html

is not surprising that the defendants Holmes and Ketcham immediately retained the services of the very accomplished lawyer William Willcocks[19] to defend their property. Even while the case was pending before the justice of the peace, Willcocks applied for and was granted a certiorari by Chief Justice Robert Morris, "returnable at the next session of the Supreme Court [to be held in September. In the m]eantime Morris resigned his seat on the bench and on the 10th of June David Brearly was appointed Chief Justice."[20] On September 9, 1779, the Supreme Court noted in its minutes that the record of the case had been received from the justice of peace and gave notice to the parties that the matter would be "argued on Thursday in the next Term [in November]."[21] In the meantime, the court expressed considerable unhappiness about how much the 1778 smuggling act had "extended the Jurisdiction of Justices of the Peace without any limitation of the value of the Property seised, which occasions the frequent prosecuting of Certioraries for removing the Plaints before the said Justices to the Supreme Court."[22]

At its next term, on November 11, 1779, the Supreme Court heard arguments in the case. These were conducted orally, and no record remains of them, except for two brief written memoranda that Willcocks submitted to the court outlining his positions. The first entitled "Reasons ... that the Judgment given by" the justice of the peace "ought to be reversed and annulled" set out eight arguments. Five of these presented claims that Walton's evidence did not support the judgment, and one that Walton had "treat[ed]" the jury "with strong Liquor ... before they gave their verdict."[23] Only the final two raised strictly legal or constitutional objections to the judgment, but in an extremely summary form, which make them difficult to interpret.

[19] Willcocks practiced law in New York City before the war, fleeing to New Jersey after the British invasion. He apparently returned to New York after the British departed, switching sides in effect, to serve as co-counsel for plaintiffs in the case of *Rutgers* v. *Waddington*, against Alexander Hamilton who served as co-counsel for defendants, see Julius Goebel Jr., *The Law Practice of Alexander Hamilton: Documents and Commentary* (New York, Columbia University Press, 1964), I, 301, and 301 fn. 58.

[20] Scott, "Holmes v. Walton," 457. As discussed in greater detail in a later chapter, David Brearly became a delegate to the Federal Convention in 1787, participating in the drafting of the New Jersey Plan, which was to have a significant impact on the future of judicial review.

[21] *Holmes* v. *Walton*: Entries in Minutes of N.J. Supreme Court, September 9, 1779, http://njlegallib.rutgers.edu/hw/Minutes.html#1779_09

[22] *Holmes* v. *Walton*: Entries in Minutes of N.J. Supreme Court, September 9, 1779, http://njlegallib.rutgers.edu/hw/Minutes.html#1779_09

[23] http://njlegallib.rutgers.edu/hw/Reasons_Nov_1779.html

7. Because the Jury sworn and who tried the above Cause, and on whose Verdict Judgment was entered, consisted of six men only, when by the Laws of the Land, it should have consisted of twelve men.
8. For that the said Justice gave Judgment for the said Elisha [Walton] against the said [defendants], when according to the Laws and Customs of the State of New Jersey, he should have given Judgment for the said [defendants] . . . .[24]

From this brief outline it is difficult to say with any degree of certainty what Willcocks' arguments may have been, except that the phrase "Laws of the Land" was commonly used to refer to fundamental law. Fundamental Law, he may have been arguing, required a jury of twelve. In a second filing, "Add'l Reasons," Willcocks fleshed out his legal and constitutional arguments in a little greater detail, making it possible to speculate somewhat more credibly about the arguments he may have brought before the court.

His first "additional" argument contended that "the said Justice had not Jurisdiction of the said cause in plaint but the same was *coram non judice*."[25] A good lawyer would have seen that the Small Causes act of 1775 had specified a jurisdictional threshold of £6. The 1778 smuggling act had not repealed the earlier act, nor had it explicitly increased its jurisdictional threshold. One could certainly read the two acts together to give justices of the peace jurisdiction in smuggling cases– up to the value of £6. Cases involving goods of greater value, as here, would be, it might be argued, beyond their statutory jurisdiction. This would appear to be a perfectly sound legal argument based on statutory interpretation. Of course, Willcocks might also have been arguing that since the 1778 smuggling act was unconstitutional and void (hence not law), justices of the peace could not possibly have jurisdiction over smuggling cases, under any circumstances. But from his writing, it is not possible to be certain.

Willcocks' second "additional" argument may also have been based on statutory interpretation rather than on constitutional considerations. "For that the Jury who tried the said plaint before the said Justice consisted of six men only contrary to law."[26] The 1778 act did not explicitly mention or require a pared down jury of six. It stated only that when

[24] http://njlegallib.rutgers.edu/hw/Reasons_Nov_1779.html
[25] http://njlegallib.rutgers.edu/hw/Additional_Reasons.html
[26] http://njlegallib.rutgers.edu/hw/Additional_Reasons.html

a party demanded "a Jury" the justice was "required to grant the same." Afterwards, the justice was to proceed in "all *other* Respects" as under the earlier small causes act.[27] It would have been perfectly legitimate for Willcocks to argue that the ambiguous text of the 1778 smuggling statute should be read as requiring justices of the peace to impanel full juries of twelve in cases where the value of the goods at issue exceeded £6. If so, by seating a jury of six, the justice in the case at bar would have acted "contrary to law" i.e., to the statute itself. It is also possible that Willcocks meant by "contrary to law," contrary to common law[28] or contrary to the law of the constitution, but he appears to have reserved his explicitly constitutional claims for his final two "additional reasons."

> For that the Jury who tried the said plaint before the said Justice consisted of six men only contrary to the constitution of New Jersey.[29]

Notice that Willcocks' argument did not directly assail the constitutionality of the 1778 smuggling acts. He objected to the calling of a jury of six as contrary to the constitution. In a sense, this might have been consistent with his prior point; if the 1778 acts (or the common law) were interpreted to require the calling of a jury of twelve, and if under the circumstances the constitution also did, then by calling a jury of six, the justice of the peace would not only have acted contrary to law, but contrary to the constitution, without a question having been directly raised about the validity of the 1778 acts. Perhaps this is what Willcocks was driving at in his final "additional reason." "For that the proceedings and trial in the said plaint in the Court below and the Judgment thereon given were had and given contrary to the Constitution, Practices and Laws of the Land."[30]

It is possible that Willcocks framed his arguments in this way because he did not want to embroil the case in a novel type of claim that the court might be reluctant to grant. After all, a good deal of money was apparently

27 "An ACT to prevent the Subjects of this State from going into, or coming out of, the Enemy's Lines, without Permissions or Passports, and for other Purposes therein mention," *Laws of the State of New Jersey* (October 8, 1778), Chap. XLV, Section 6, 106.

28 Where a jury trial was required at common law, it had to be a jury of twelve. English courts often reversed the judgments of inferior courts when they were based on trials by juries of six rather than twelve, see *Tredymmock* v. *Perryman*, 79 Eng. Rep. 826, Croke, *Reports* (7 Car. I), 259–60 ("A custom to try causes in an Inferior Court by six jurors instead of twelve is bad .... [A]ll the Court held, that such a custom is void, and against the common law ...."); see also Hamburger, Law and Judicial Duty, 410 fns. 26, 27.

29 http://njlegallib.rutgers.edu/hw/Additional_Reasons.html

30 http://njlegallib.rutgers.edu/hw/Additional_Reasons.html

at stake and perhaps the point was to try to get the judgment reversed as quickly and easily as possible. The statutory interpretations suggested in the previous paragraph, however, would probably not have been accepted by the court given what is known about the way the 1778 smuggling acts seem to have been commonly interpreted. If the justice of the peace was therefore found to have acted not contrary to the 1778 acts, but in conformity to them, then Willcocks' contention that "the proceedings and trial in the said plaint in the Court below and the Judgment thereon given were had and given contrary to the Constitution" would also have been an (indirect) claim that at the very least the jury provisions in the 1778 acts were also "contrary to the constitution."

There are reasons to think that something like this probably happened, because if the case could have been resolved through acts of statutory interpretation or by simply reversing the judgment below without adverting to the constitutionality of the jury provisions in the statutes, it is not likely that the court would have put off rendering a decision for almost a year, as it in fact did. Nor is it likely that the legislature would have immediately begun to take the kind of intense interest in the 1778 acts that it in fact also did.

The question does remain why Willcocks framed his written arguments as he did, directing his objections to the jurisdiction of the court, and to the constitutionality of the proceedings and trial by a jury of six, without ever explicitly calling into question the statutes under whose authority they had been conducted. Given the largely undeveloped character of his "Reasons," and only somewhat more developed quality of his "Additional Reasons," it may have been that Willcocks was working out his positions on the fly, and either was reluctant to place such a novel and potentially explosive claim directly before the court, or had not yet come to the point of clearly formulating his constitutional claim as a claim that a law of the state might be invalid. What is impossible to overlook is that Willcocks' arguments were consistently framed as attacks on the unconstitutional character of the practice of using juries of six, while omitting any mention of the constitutional status of the authorizing statutes on which they were based.

This case arose at a very early stage in the development of American judicial review, and it may be that more well-defined ideas about how precisely to formulate this kind of constitutional claim would be worked out only as a result of more experience. Recall that when the framers of the New Jersey Constitution, which had been adopted just a few years earlier in 1776, had thought about enforcing the constitution's terms, what they thought to do was to require an oath from legislators who would "solemnly declare" that they would "not assent to any law, vote or proceeding" that would violate specified sections of the constitution. The constitution was to be enforced, presumably, by holding legislators to their oaths, through impeachment or otherwise. The possibility that judges might treat duly enacted statutes that conflicted with the constitution as not law, had apparently, according to the great constitutional scholar Edward Corwin, not even occurred to the framers.[31]

No record survives of a Willcocks argument explaining precisely how trial by a jury of six (and its authorizing statute) violated the New Jersey constitution of 1776, and so here again, historians can only make informed guesses, in this case by attempting to reconstruct what such an argument might have looked like.

The New Jersey constitution of 1776 was among the early constitutions adopted even before the Declaration of Independence had been signed, and it drew heavily on traditional constitutional ideas. Where "We, *the people* of the State of New Jersey ... ordain[ed] and establish[ed]" the much later New Jersey constitution of 1844, it was by contrast "We, *the representatives* of the colony of New Jersey, having been elected by all the counties, in the freest manner, and in congress assembled, [who] have, after mature deliberation, agreed upon" the constitution of 1776.[32] The 1776 constitution specified that only certain sections should be unalterable, implying, given traditional constitutional understandings, that all the rest might be altered or amended by "the freely elected representatives of the colony" when they gathered later, not in congress, but as a legislature.[33]

Two sections of the constitution of 1776 are especially relevant for understanding Willcocks' possible claim. Both are structured as broad grants of authority to the legislature to change existing law, with a single specific limitation and another broader but ambiguous one.[34]

31 Edward S. Corwin, "Establishment of Judicial Review I" (1910) 9 *Michigan Law Review* 102,111.

32 New Jersey Constitutions of 1844 and 1776, in Francis Thorpe (ed.), *The Federal and State Constitutions, Colonial Charters, and Other Organic Laws of the States, Territories and Colonies* (Washington, D.C., Government Printing Office, 1909, Reprint Buffalo, N.Y., William S. Hein, 1993), V, 2599, 2595.

33 For a more detailed discussion of this point, see Chapter 2.

34 Other explicit limitations on altering or repealing other sections of the constitution were contained in the oath legislators were required to take.

XXI. That all the laws of this Province, contained in the edition lately published by Mr. Allison, shall be and remain in full force, until altered by the Legislature of this Colony (such only excepted, as are incompatible with this Charter) ....

XXII. That the common law of England, as well as so much of the statute law, as have been heretofore practiced in this Colony, shall still remain in force, until they shall be altered by a future law of the Legislature; such parts only excepted, as are repugnant to the rights and privileges contained in this Charter; and that *the inestimable right of trial by jury shall remain confirmed as a part of the law of this Colony, without repeal, forever.*[35] (emphasis added)

The 1775 small causes act was contained in Allison's compilation of New Jersey statutes, which the constitution declared to "be and remain in full force."[36] Together with the common law, the 1775 act defined the precise legal scope of the "inestimable right of trial by jury" in New Jersey, which the constitution appeared explicitly to prohibit the legislature from "repealing."[37] By enacting the 1778 smuggling statutes, the legislature had arguably violated that express constitutional prohibition, changing the law of the state to eliminate the pre-existing right to a jury of twelve in any case above the value of £6. And as the 1778 smuggling laws were consequently "repugnant to the rights and privileges contained in this Charter," they did not, it might be argued, "remain in full force," in the same way that provincial laws "incompatible with this Charter" did not. Such might have been Willcocks' contention.[38]

After hearing arguments in the case, the Supreme Court decided on November 11, 1779, that it wanted to give the matter further consideration before rendering a decision, and entered a *Curia advisare vult.*[39]

[35] This limitation was repeated in the oath legislators were to take "not to assent to any law, vote or proceeding ... that shall annul or repeal ... that part of the twenty-second section in said Charter, respecting the trial by jury ... " N.J. Const. of 1776, section XXIII, in Thorpe (ed.), Constitutions, V, 2598.

[36] Hamburger, Law and Judicial Duty, 411 fn. 30.

[37] The court was being asked, in effect, to do precisely the thing the Privy Council had done when it had disallowed New Jersey's attempt to increase the threshold for summary justice to £10, but on substantially different grounds.

[38] Of course, it is also possible to argue that even the 1775 small causes act was incompatible with the constitution in so far as it had increased the common law jurisdictional threshold for trials by juries of twelve, and in that way curtailed "the inestimable right of trial by jury." But there is no indication that the 1775 small causes law had been placed in dispute in this case.

[39] http://njlegallib.rutgers.edu/hw/Minutes.html#1779_11

Apparently, after thinking the matter over for a few more days, the court on November 15 decided that it needed still more time to "advise on the Arguments, had in this Cause, till next Term."[40] The court was certainly behaving as though Willcocks had presented it with a novel, important, and controversial claim.

At this point, the case took an interesting turn when the legislature began to involve itself. On November 12, 1779, just a day after the Supreme Court had heard arguments in the case and had reserved judgment on the matter, Jonathan Deare, a member of the Legislative Council (the upper house of the legislature), moved to introduce a bill seeking to "supplement" the 1778 smuggling act. The bill was read for the first time that day and a second reading was ordered.[41] So far as it is possible to reconstruct, the principal change Deare's bill sought to make to the earlier legislation was to require juries of twelve in smuggling cases.[42] Deare was almost certainly attempting to address the principal issue that had been raised the day before in arguments at the Supreme Court by moving to have the legislature "revise" the statute in light of the problem with jury size pointed out at the hearing. Whether he took this step believing the jury provisions in the 1778 Acts to be contrary to the constitution, or believing that they needed to be clarified, or believing that sound policy recommended the change, or for some other reason, is not known. It does seem probable, however, that Deare's bill sought to address the constitutional arguments Willcocks raised the day before at the hearing, and with which one of the judges may have indicated his agreement.

Given traditional understandings about the proper constitutional role of legislatures and courts, this development should not be surprising. In the course of judicial proceedings, a serious question had been raised about the constitutionality of summary justice proceedings that had been brought under a statute. It should now be up to the legislature to reconsider and revise that statute in light of the objections that had been brought to its attention. A similar understanding had certainly been responsible for producing New York's Council of Revision.[43] And

[40] http://njlegallib.rutgers.edu/hw/Minutes.html#1779_11

[41] "A Bill, intitled, A Supplement to the Act intitled, An Act to explain and amend an Act, intitled, An Act to prevent the Subjects of this State from going into, etc.," *Journal of the Proceedings of the Legislative Council of New Jersey* (1779), November 12, 1779, 14, https://archive.org/details/journalofproceed1779newj

[42] A copy of the bill does not survive, but one of the principal points of contention in later attempts made in the Assembly (the lower house) to amend the bill was that the bill required juries of twelve.

[43] See the extended discussion of New York's Council of Revision in Chapter 3.

comparable views appear to have been at work shaping the Advisory Opinions clause of the Massachusetts constitution of 1780.

It is noteworthy that the Council, rather than the Assembly, originated both this 1779 "Supplement" to the smuggling acts, and a bill the following year to further modify procedures in smuggling cases, passed in December 1780. By tradition, most bills originated in lower houses;[44] in Virginia, the upper house was prohibited from originating any bill.[45] In 7 states, upper houses could not initiate money bills.[46] As a result, the framers of New Jersey's 1776 constitution felt it necessary explicitly to confer on the Council legislative powers equal to those of the Assembly, except in the case of money bills.[47]

That the Council now took the lead in revising the jury provisions of the smuggling acts, two years running, may have been the result of its complicated position under the constitution of 1776. It should be recalled that the constitution had made the Council, sitting with the governor, the court of final resort in the state.[48] Far from being an obsolete relic of the colonial era, this court continued to play an active role in New Jersey's legal life. By 1784, it had to contend with so many cases that the legislature felt it necessary to establish separate terms for the court, outside legislative sessions.[49]

44 Jackson Turner Main, *The Upper House in Revolutionary America, 1763–1788* (Madison, Wisc., University of Wisconsin Press, 1967), 191 ("The senate's primary function [in the post-revolutionary period] was that of a revisory body").

45 Virginia Constitution of 1776 in Thorpe (ed.), Constitutions, VII, 3816 ("All laws shall originate in the House of Delegates, to be approved of or rejected by the Senate, or to be amended, with consent of the House of Delegates; except money-bills, which in no instance shall be altered by the Senate, but wholly approved or rejected").

46 Main, Upper House, 188.

47 Section VI, N.J. Const. of 1776, in Thorpe (ed.), Constitutions, V, 2596 ("[T]he Council shall also have power to prepare bills to pass into laws, and have other like powers as the Assembly, and in all respect be a free and independent branch of the Legislature of this Colony; save only, that they shall not prepare or *alter* any money bill – which shall be the privilege of the Assembly . . . .")

48 Section IX, N.J. Const. of 1776, in Thorpe (ed.), Constitutions, V, 2596 ("That the Governor and Council . . . be the Court of Appeals, in the last resort, in all causes of law, as heretofore . . . .")

49 "An ACT to regulate and fix the Terms for holding the Court of Appeals or Errors," *Acts of the Ninth General Assembly of the State of New Jersey* (Trenton, N.J., Isaac Collins, Printer to the State, 1784), Chap. LXXII (December 22, 1784), 142–43 ("Whereas by the ninth Section of the Constitution, the Governor and Council are constituted a Court of Appeals in the last Resort in all Causes of Law: And whereas the Number of Suits removed into that Court, renders it impracticable to hear and determine them finally during the Sittings of the Legislature, and makes it necessary, that Terms for holding the

As both a branch of the legislature and the court of final resort, members of the Council must have taken an especial interest in the question of the constitutionality of the jury provisions in the smuggling acts. It was entirely conceivable, for example, that the *Holmes v. Walton* litigation might one-day land on their desks, though this does not in fact seem to have happened. Acting in a legislative capacity, it may be that the Council took the lead in "revising" the 1778 acts partly because, as the state's highest court, they saw themselves as exercising a supervisory function to lay down proper procedures for lower courts to follow. In a sense, by seeking to amend the law, the Council might be understood to be rendering a legislative/judicial judgment that the jury provisions were at the very least in need of "revisal."

Deare's bill passed the Council on December 6, 1779, and was sent to the lower house, the Assembly, for their concurrence.[50] There, the twelve-person jury provision in Council bill encountered some resistance. On December 17, a motion was made to strip the twelve men requirement out of the bill. But the Assembly voted overwhelmingly 14–6 to reject the motion.[51] The next day Mr. Hornblower moved "to strike out the Words 'of twelve Men,' and to insert in their Stead, 'of six or twelve Men, at the Option of the Defendant.'"[52] But the Assembly also voted against this motion. It seems that after a brief struggle, the Assembly was on the whole favorably disposed to accept the idea of authorizing justices of the peace to call juries of twelve.

But while the Assembly rejected attempts to eliminate the twelve men standard from the Council bill, it voted to add a somewhat obscure proviso to the first section of the Council bill aimed, it seems, at negating any inference that the twelve men standard in the bill represented a legislative judgment that the jury provisions in the original acts were unconstitutional and void.

> Provided always, That Nothing herein contained shall be taken or construed to invalidate or make void any Trial or other Proceedings had by virtue of the said recited Acts, or either of them, because such Trial was had by a Jury of six Men

said Court should be fixed and established; Therefore ... there shall hereafter be two fixed Terms ... annually ....")

50 *Journal of the Proceedings of the Legislative Council of New Jersey* (1779), December 6, 1779, 26; https://archive.org/details/journalofproceed1779newj

51 *Votes and Proceedings of the General Assembly of the State of New Jersey* (December 17, 1779), 86, https://archive.org/stream/votesproceedings1779newj#page/86/mode/2up

52 Ibid. (December 18, 1779), 87, https://archive.org/stream/votesproceedings1779newj#page/86/mode/2up

only, if such Trial and other Proceedings have been in other Respects agreeable to Law, but the same shall be valid to all Intents and Purposes.[53]

The proviso sought to preserve, it seems, the validity of trials conducted under the original 1778 laws, like the proceedings at issue in *Holmes* v. *Walton* itself. But like so much other evidence in this case, the proviso is worded somewhat obscurely. Ordinarily, an amended law would take effect prospectively; there would be no danger of it being understood to invalidate proceedings held under an earlier, superseded law. The Assembly appears to have been trying to accomplish something more with this proviso. They seem to have been seeking to forestall the possibility that the amendments would be used as evidence of a legislative determination that proceedings held under the original statutes were invalid because contrary to the constitution. Accordingly, the proviso sought to place the legislature on record as expressly declaring that despite having adopted these amendments to the jury provisions, the legislature's view continued to be that those earlier proceedings were "valid to all Intents and Purposes." The very fact that the Assembly sought to add this proviso suggests that even at this early stage in the *Holmes* v. *Walton* litigation, the questions that had been raised about the constitutionality of the proceedings held pursuant to the 1778 smuggling acts, were serious enough to elicit this statement from the Assembly about the legislature's intent.

Just a week later, a December 24, 1779, letter from Governor William Livingston confirmed that the possibility the court might declare the proceedings in the justice's court invalid appeared real enough (one judge already seems to have indicated an inclination to do so) to have led Livingston to begin to think about how the legislature might address the consequences of such a judgment. Like the Council, Livingston's interest must have been more than casual in that he too sat as a judge on the court of final resort in the state. In particular, he seems to have been mulling over whether it would be possible for the legislature to preserve claims made under the original acts, if the proceedings conducted under them were declared to be invalid, and if the acts themselves (or parts of them), which had created those claims, were declared not to be law? The legislature, Livingston was sure, could easily amend the 1778 acts to correct their deficiencies, but he was less sanguine that they could apply the new law retroactively to the facts of cases that had arisen long before

[53] Ibid., 87–88, https://archive.org/stream/votesproceedings1779newj#page/86/mode/2up

the amended law would have been passed, without violating a fundamental principle of justice.

> The Cause between Walton & Holmes is of the greatest Moment; & I hope none of the Judges have given their opinions, as you have heard respecting one before they have been judicially called upon. I should be sorry that the supposed Event of the Controversy should give the Tories any Cause of Triumph; but the Judges you know are bound to determine according to Law in whose favour soever that may appear to be, let the Consequences be what they may; & tho' the Legislature may apply a Remedy, yet those ex post facto Laws have always been considered as unfriendly to Liberty.[54]

After the Assembly had completed its deliberations, it sent the amended bill back to the Council for their concurrence. But the Council balked at some of the changes the Assembly had proposed, and would not agree to them. In turn, the Assembly refused to eliminate several of the amendments it had inserted into the Council bill. For a moment the two chambers seemed to be at a deadlock. But an agreement seems to have been reached shortly thereafter to appoint committees to attempt to reconcile the two versions of the bill.[55] What came out of the reconciliation process was a modified Section One that no longer contained the Assembly proviso, but that did address what seemed to be the central Assembly uneasiness about the Council's bill.[56] The new Section One was approved by the Assembly and by the Council, and found its way into the final legislation, passed on December 25, 1779.[57] It read:

> And whereas Causes of considerable Value may, by Virtue of this or the before recited Acts, be prosecuted before a Justice of the Peace, where-in *it may be prudent* to have the Judgment of a greater Number than six Jurors, Be it therefore enacted by the Council and General Assembly of this State, and it is hereby enacted by the Authority of the Same, That in all Causes *hereafter* to be prosecuted before any Justice of the Peace, by Virtue of this or either of the said recited Acts, it shall and may be lawful for either of the Parties in such Suit to demand a Jury of twelve Men, which Jury such Justice is hereby *empowered* to grant . . .[58] (emphasis added)

54 Excerpt from Letter from New Jersey Governor William Livingston to Nathaniel Scudder, December 24, 1779, in *The Papers of William Livingston* 3: 279–80, http://njlegallib.rutgers.edu/hw/Livingston_letter.html

55 Votes and Proceedings of the General Assembly of the State of New Jersey (December 23, 1779), 96–98, https://archive.org/stream/votesproceedings1779newj#page/96/mode/2up

56 Ibid. (December 24, 1779) at 101–2, https://archive.org/stream/votesproceedings1779newj#page/100/mode/2up

57 Ibid. (December 25, 1779) at 106, https://archive.org/stream/votesproceedings1779newj#page/106/mode/2up

58 *Acts of the General Assembly of the State of New Jersey, At a SESSION begun at Trenton on the 26th Day of October, 1779* (Trenton, Printed by Isaac Collins, 1780), Chap. XXI, 48–49.

Use of the word "prudent" in this section is especially noteworthy. It appears to signal that the legislature was exercising a discretionary authority under their duty to lay down general rules for the good of the polity. In effect, they were declaring their determination that juries of twelve often delivered sounder judgments than juries of six, and that it was a good idea, accordingly, to use full size juries in cases in which the monetary stakes were high. Consequently, they were "empowering" justices of the peace, "hereafter," to call juries of twelve in such seizure cases.

Read in light of surrounding circumstances, the text strongly implied that these amendments to the earlier laws had not been based on a legislative judgment that the constitution "legally" required the use of juries of twelve in such cases. The legislature drove home this point by "empowering" rather than "requiring" Justices of the Peace to call juries of twelve. In every other statute, from the colonial small causes acts through the 1778 smuggling acts, and again in the later 1780 smuggling act that would amend this one, the laws "required" justices of the peace to call juries of the specified size, whenever either party demanded them. The omission of the word "required" is strong evidence of the legislature's intention to give justices the option to call a jury of six or twelve depending upon the circumstances in a case, including, one supposes, whether goods of "considerable value" were in dispute.

That the legislature made juries of twelve optional was a way of declaring that they were treating the question of juries as a "political" (a matter of good policy) rather than as a "legal" question, and that the constitution, as they interpreted it, did not require such juries. If this legislative judgment prevailed, there would be no question that the earlier proceedings under the original acts had been legally valid. Hence, there would be no need explicitly to address the issue of the earlier trials, and it would be sufficient to empower the justices to call full juries only "hereafter."

In December 1779, of course, when the legislature enacted this statute, the court was still more than nine months away from announcing its decision in *Holmes v. Walton*. But even at this point, the view seems to have been widely held that the court was likely to find that the use of six men juries conflicted with the constitution, at least in causes of great value. By passing this statute, the legislature seems to have been attempting to "revise" the law to address the problem pointed out with six men juries in the November hearing at the court, while resisting the idea that the problem amounted to a violation of the constitution that might call into question the validity of earlier proceedings.

To the extent the legislature was listening in and responding to problems with the smuggling acts that had been pointed out in the court, the judges in turn seem to have been paying careful attention to the developments in the legislature. They must have recognized that the recently passed amendments would eliminate, as a practical matter, the constitutional problem going forward, so long as justices of the peace took the hint and availed themselves of the option to seat juries of twelve in cases of considerable value. But they must simultaneously have realized that the statute had done nothing to address one of the critical problems Governor Livingston had identified in his letter. What would become of claims brought under the 1778 acts if the court declared the proceedings held pursuant to them legally invalid? The judges seem to have found themselves facing the kind of dilemma Governor Livingston also described in his letter, not wanting to see a Tory triumph at this dangerous moment in the Revolution, but determined to make certain that proceedings in smuggling seizure cases conformed to the constitution as the court understood it, despite the consequences.

In order to extricate itself from this difficulty, the court took on itself to assist the legislature in devising a strategy to address the anticipated problem of preserving claims brought under the original statutes. The court in effect undertook to participate expressly in the "revisionary" process that traditional constitutionalists would have said was the only constitutionally proper one for courts.

At the Supreme Court's next term, on April 7, 1780, the court again stated that it was not "ready to give judgment" in the case, needing more time to consider the arguments presented to it. It again entered a *Curia advisare vult* until its next term in September.[59] In the meantime, the judges drafted and sent a letter to the General Assembly advising that body how it should proceed in light of the fact, which all parties seemed to take for granted, that the court would probably invalidate the proceedings conducted under the original smuggling statutes. On May 13, 1780, a

> letter from the Justices of the Supreme Court to the Speaker [of the Assembly] was presented and read, recommending that on Reversal of Judgment for Error in Cases of Seizures of Goods, supposed to have been brought from within the Enemy's Lines, the Defendant in Error, on Payment of Costs, may be allowed a Trial *de Novo* in the Court below upon the Merits of the Cause.[60]

[59] "Minutes of the Supreme Court," April 7, 1780, http://njlegallib.rutgers.edu/hw/Minutes.html

[60] *Votes and Proceedings of the General Assembly of the State of New Jersey At a Session Begun in October, 1779* (Printed by Isaac Collins, Printer to the State, 1780) (May 13, 1780), 187, http://njlegallib.rutgers.edu/hw/vp.html#1780_05_13

On the advice of the court, the Assembly ordered a committee to be formed "to revise the Laws" and referred the letter to that committee.[61] On May 31 the committee reported out the draft of a bill for that purpose. It was entitled "An Act declaring the Effect of the Reversal of Judgments of Justices of the Peace in Prosecutions [under the smuggling acts], for Error in the Proceedings, and to enable the Supreme Court to award new Trials in such causes."[62] On June 16, the bill was read again and engrossed, and on the 17th was passed by the Assembly and sent to the Council for their concurrence.[63] The Council passed the bill without amendment the same day and it became law.[64] The statute itself carried out the court's advice.

> WHEREAS *Causes to a very considerable Value* are now frequently brought to trial before, and determined by, *a single Justice of the Peace in a summary Manner,* by Virtue of the [smuggling Acts]: AND WHEREAS *some of the Justices* before whom such Trials are had, *commit Errors in the Determination of them in Matters of Form,* whereby the Judgment is reversed on *Certiorari*, and the Cause lost without any Default of the Party, *although the Merits* are in his Favour; For Remedy whereof,
>
> BE IT ENACTED *by the Council and General Assembly of this State, and it is hereby Enacted by the Authority of the same,* That in all such Causes where the Judgment of the Justice shall be reversed in the Supreme Court on *Certiorari for Informality of Proceedings, or any other Cause not essential to the Merits of the Suit,* such Judgment of Reversal shall only affect the Parties with respect to the Costs of Suit: and *it shall and may be lawful for the Supreme Court* on such Reversal *to award a new Trial on the Merits in the Court below* where the Cause was originally determined; any Law, Usage or Custom to the Contrary nothwithstanding.[65] (emphasis added)

The statute empowered the Supreme Court to order new trials in smuggling cases should they reverse a lower court judgment for "errors" in the procedures justices of the peace had utilized (juries of six), but not for flaws that went to the merits of the case. But as elsewhere in the New Jersey record, this statute made no mention that the fault in the proceedings below was attributable to an unconstitutional statute. Instead, the problem in the proceedings below was framed as errors in matters of form that the justices of the peace had committed. The implication of the court's

[61] Ibid., 187. http://njlegallib.rutgers.edu/hw/vp.html#1780_05_13

[62] Ibid., 212 (May 31, 1780). [63] Ibid., 241, 243 (June 16, 17, 1780).

[64] Ibid., 246 (June 17, 1780).

[65] *Acts of the General Assembly of the State of New Jersey, at a Session Begun in October, 1779* (Printed by Isaac Collins, Printer to the State, 1780), Chap. LIII (June 17, 1780), 121.

advice and the statute that followed from it was that the substantive offences created by the original smuggling statutes posed no constitutional problem and remained valid. All that had to be corrected was the process justices of the peace afforded in such cases, and the recently passed December 1779 "Supplement" to the smuggling statutes addressed that problem by "empowering" justices to call juries of twelve. Since this was a procedural revision, and did not create a new offence, there should be no question of it being an unjust ex post facto law.

The Supreme Court, having suggested the idea in the first place, seemed completely comfortable ordering retrials (using juries of twelve) otherwise under the terms of the original statutes. And even though the legislature had now only "authorized" rather than "required" such juries, the focus of the litigation in *Holmes v. Walton* and of the Supreme Court itself seems to have been on the unconstitutional "use" of juries of six, rather than on the statutes themselves. It seems that so long as a justice of the peace actually called a jury of twelve to rehear a case, it did not matter to the court that the revised statute only "authorized" such juries. Working together, the legislature and the court corrected the smuggling laws going forward, and limited the damage that would result when the court actually proceeded to invalidate the earlier proceedings.

The court could now feel free to vindicate constitutional principle, knowing full well it's action would not inflict great harm on Patriots, and so at its next term in September 1780, the court proceeded to announce its decision in the case, reversing the judgment of the justice of the peace and ordering that the defendants below "be restored to all Things &c."[66]

Although the judges' opinions do not survive, in light of what is known, it seems highly probable that the judges reversed the judgment below on the ground that the justice of the peace had used an unconstitutional jury of six. It is not known what, if anything, they said about the statutes that had authorized justices to use such juries. But even if they did not explicitly mention the statutes in their opinions, the clear implication of their judgment of reversal on those grounds would have been that the legislature did not possess the power to "legalize" such juries. Whatever the court may have said, by giving legal effect to the requirements in the constitution (as the court interpreted them), the judges were treating that instrument as a form of fully "legal" superior law that governed the

[66] "Entries in the Minutes of the New Jersey Supreme Court" (September 7, 1780), http://njlegallib.rutgers.edu/hw/Minutes.html

case, presumably superseding, at the very least, the provisions in the statutes. In this sense, this was an act of judicial review. Merely ignoring the jury provisions in the statutes, however, as though they did not enjoy the force of law fell somewhat short of forthrightly declaring that the court judged them to be null and void and without effect. To be full throated judicial review, the court would have had expressly to declare their opinion that those parts of the statutes were not law because they conflicted with the constitution, and to provide a reasoned justification for their authority to do so. This cannot be conclusively shown to have happened, leaving the court's constitutional claim about the power it was exercising entirely unelaborated.

It seems altogether odd, moreover, that the constitution (or constitutional violations) were not mentioned, not once, in any of the surviving "Supreme Court Minutes" or other official case files (except in a few of Willcocks's arguments). Nor was the constitution (or constitutional violations) mentioned in any of the legislative debates, or the remedial statutes the legislature enacted to address the issue of small juries. The entire absence of any mention of the constitution in the official records that survive (save for a few of Willcocks's arguments) leaves a large question mark over the entire episode.

Two contemporaneous sources, however, took for granted that the court had in fact engaged in an act of judicial review. In December 1780, a few months after the judgment of reversal, some inhabitants of Monmouth County petitioned the legislature for redress, stating their belief that the Supreme Court had "set aside some of the Laws as unconstitutional, and made void the Proceedings of the Magistrates, though strictly agreeable to the said Laws, to the Encouragement of the disaffected, and great Loss of the loyal Citizens of the State . . . ."[67] And in later arguments before the court, Willcocks suggested that their decision had nullified the original smuggling acts: "as trial by six men is unconstitutional there is no law existing by which this cause could be tried."[68] But that is all.

On the same day the Court ordered the reversal of the justice of the peace's judgment, they also ordered the defendants below to "shew Cause

[67] *Votes and Proceedings of the General Assembly of the State of New Jersey, At a Session begun in October, 1780* (Isaac Collins Printer, Printer to the State, 1780) (December 8, 1780), 52, http://njlegallib.rutgers.edu/hw/vp.html

[68] "Certiorari with State of facts affidavits &c., Reason," No. 2 (September 1781), NJSA, New Jersey Supreme Court, Case File No. 44928, http://njlegallib.rutgers.edu/hw/State_of_Facts.html

by next Term why a new Trial in this Cause should not be order'd."[69] And at its next term, on November 16, 1780, the court did in fact order "a new Trial be had on this Cause in the Court below, agreeable to [the] Act of Assembly ... "[70] That trial was held in July 1781 conducted by the same justice of the peace who had handled the original proceedings, only on this occasion, seating a jury of twelve who delivered the verdict. The outcome of the new trial was identical to the first, verdict and judgment in favor of Walton against Holmes and Ketcham.[71] Defendants again sought and were granted a certiorari, but in the end the Supreme Court, rejected their arguments, and upheld the results of the second trial.[72] Not only did Walton prevail in his seizure claim in the end, but by upholding the results, the Supreme Court implicitly reaffirmed the validity of the strategy they and the legislature had worked out to preserve the claims brought under the original smuggling acts, simple retrial using juries of twelve.

There is a final twist in this story which bears noting. The Supreme Court ordered a new trial in the *Holmes* v. *Walton* case on November 16, 1780. Less than a week later, on November 21, 1780, and very much like the year before, a bill was introduced in the Council proposing to revise the smuggling acts again. After many days of discussion and debate, and after many amendments, the Council and Assembly passed the bill into law on December 22, 1780.[73] The most significant aspect of the new law, for our purposes, is that it "required" juries of twelve in seizure cases, rather than merely authorizing them.[74] It may be that after the Supreme Court had announced its decision in September 1780 reversing the justice of the peace's judgment, and after a new legislature had been elected in October, the legislature had revised its judgment, and determined that the constitution did actually "require" juries of twelve in such cases, or perhaps the legislature was merely responding strategically to the

69 "Entries in the Minutes of the New Jersey Supreme Court" (September 7, 1780, http://njlegallib.rutgers.edu/hw/Minutes.html

70 Ibid. (November 16, 1780), http://njlegallib.rutgers.edu/hw/Minutes.html

71 http://njlegallib.rutgers.edu/hw/Certiorari_and_Return.html

72 "Entries in Minutes of the New Jersey Supreme Court" (April 4, 5, 1783), http://njlegallib.rutgers.edu/hw/Minutes.html#1781_09

73 *Journal of the Proceedings of the Legislative Council of the State of New Jersey, 1780* (Trenton, Printed by Isaac Collins, Printer to the State, 1781), 18, 24, 25,26, 27, 46, 48, 50, 51; *Votes and Proceedings of the General Assembly of the State of New Jersey, 1780* (Trenton, Printed by Isaac Collins, Printer to the State, 1780), 50, 60, 73, 74, 76, 80, 82, 83.

74 *Acts of the Fifth General Assembly of the State of New Jersey, At a Session Begun in October, 1780* (Trenton, Printed by Isaac Collins, Printer to the State, 1781), Chap. V, Section 13, pp. 11, 17.

Supreme Court's order for a new trial (on November 16), by attempting to guarantee that the court would find the proceedings at any retrial beyond reproach.

What is to be made of the Holmes v. Walton litigation in the larger history of the emergence of judicial review? It seems in every respect to have been a transitional case, combining elements of traditional constitutionalism, in which the legislature (particularly the Council) took the lead in initiating a "revisal" of the laws to bring them into conformity with the constitution (as the legislature interpreted it), advised by the court along the way, to which was added a rudimentary act of judicial review– after the law had already been changed and the negative consequences of the judicial act had been, through the cooperation of the legislature and the court, reduced to a minimum.

The judges' action did provoke a group of citizens to complain to the legislature that the judges had "set aside some laws," but, so far as the evidence reveals, it did not elicit either intense opposition from the legislature, or a wider discussion about whether courts legitimately possessed the authority to declare duly enacted statutes not to have the force of law. This should hardly seem surprising given that their judgment was announced after the law had already been changed, and perhaps without an explicit declaration that the jury provisions in the statutes were void. The court's action, moreover, may have been seen as acceptable in this case in so far as the constitution itself contained a very specific clause governing the right to trial by jury that could be straightforwardly read to prohibit the legislature's action, and by its explicit terms, deprive any attempt to alter that right of the force of law. But as the court seems to have merely disregarded parts of the statutes at issue without comment, the case does not advance our understanding of the ideas that underlay the view that courts in general possessed the legitimate power to strip duly enacted statutes of the force of law. The available evidence from New Jersey suggests that at this stage in its development, judicial review was a practice based on a few simple ideas, still in search of a fully worked out constitutional rationale.[75]

The case was transitional in a deeper sense as well. Though there seem to have been minor disagreements between the legislature and the court as the case developed, the two were largely in accord about the larger issue,

[75] See Mary S. Bilder, "Idea or Practice? A Brief Historiography of Judicial Review" (2008) 20 *Journal of Policy History*, 6–26.

arraying themselves against New Jersey Patriots who were agitating to subject Loyalists to extralegal forms of revolutionary justice.

Some months before the court reversed the justice of the peace's judgment, certain residents of Monmouth County, including Walton himself and the justice of the peace in the case, John Anderson, together with congressman Nathaniel Scudder, formed an association "for the Purpose of Retaliation on the Persons and Property of the notoriously disaffected yet residing among us, for all Damages, Depredations, Burnings, Kidnapings &c."[76] Just a few weeks after the court delivered its judgment reversing the results of the first trial, the group

> presented [to the Assembly] a Memorial from a Number of Inhabitants of the County of Monmouth, setting forth the daily Depredations committed on the loyal Subjects residing in said County, to the great Danger of their Liberties, Lives and Property; and praying that a Law may be passed to authorize the well- affected Inhabitants to retaliate upon the Property of the disaffected of said County . . . .[77]

The group had included in its memorial "a Copy of [the Retaliators] Association." The Assembly referred the memorial to a committee, which reported six days later, denouncing the group in the strongest terms.

> That the Association for Retaliation, referred to in the said Memorial, is an illegal and dangerous Combination, utterly subversive of the Law, highly dangerous to Government, immediately tending to create Disunion among the Inhabitants, directly leading to Anarchy and Confusion, and tending to the Dissolution of the Constitution and Government.[78]

On October 2, 1780, the Assembly as a whole voted to adopt the language in the committee's report.[79]

In *Holmes v. Walton*, the New Jersey Supreme Court was not yet playing a role as an indispensable constitutional check, defending individual rights against legislatures that had been swept away by popular enthusiasm. Over the course of this case, the court and legislature worked together, by and large, to uphold traditional Anglo/American standards of justice in the face of invasion and civil war. It is hard to frame this case in

[76] Letter from Nathaniel Scudder to Henry Laurens (June 17, 1780), Pennsylvania Historical Society, Philadelphia, Dreer Collection, Members of Old Congress, Vol. 8:2, p. 111, quoted in Hamburger, Law and Judicial Duty, 421 fn. 60.

[77] *Votes and Proceedings of the General Assembly of the State of New Jersey, at a Session Begun in October, 1779 and continued by Adjournment* (Trenton, Printed by Isaac Collins, Printer to the State, 1780), September 23, 1780, 270; see also Hamburger, Law and Judicial Duty, 421, and 421 fns. 60, 61 and 62.

[78] *Votes and Proceedings of the General Assembly, 1779–1780* (September, 29, 1780), 275.

[79] Ibid., Votes and Proceedings, etc. (October 2, 1780), 280–81.

terms of the binary court vs. legislature in another sense as well; part of the legislature was itself the highest court in the state. This court/legislative body, the Council, in fact took the lead in moving the rest of the legislature toward a resolution of the constitutional issue, playing a role that was not completely different from the one the other court in the case, the Supreme Court, played in advising the Assembly as to how it should go about preserving prior claims. A more historically sensitive understanding of this case would depict it as an example of complicated, transitional late eighteenth-century constitutionalism involving an ordinary judicial court-a superior legislative court-and a legislature.

Despite the large degree of cooperation between the legislature and Supreme Court, and the rudimentary nature of the judges' act, the New Jersey case soon came to be seen as a revolutionary precedent for the emerging practice of judicial review. In 1785, Gouverneur Morris, by then a fervent supporter of the new practice, wrote an address to the Pennsylvania legislature warning them against repealing the charter of the Bank of North America, which they had granted just a few years earlier, lest they provoke the Pennsylvania courts into taking the (impliedly unprecedented) step of declaring their act void, following in the footsteps of a New Jersey court that had exercised this dangerous (but necessary) power. Morris wrote,

> wise representatives of free citizens .... know that the boasted omnipotence of legislative authority is but a jingle of words. In the literal meaning it is impious .... A law was once passed in New Jersey, which the judges pronounced to be unconstitutional, and therefore void. Surely no good citizen can wish to see this point decided in the tribunals of Pennsylvania. Such power in judges is dangerous; but unless it somewhere exists, the time employed in framing a bill of rights and form of government was merely thrown away.[80]

If it is not possible to learn a great deal about the thinking behind the early development of judicial review from the *Holmes* v. *Walton* case, the same certainly cannot be said of a case that arose in Virginia less than two years later, where the issue of the legitimacy of the new practice was debated thoroughly and at great length.

80 Jared Sparks (ed.), *The Life and Times of Gouverneur Morris, With Selections from his Correspondence and Miscellaneous Papers* (Boston, Mass., Gray & Bowen, 1832), III, 438.

5

The Debate over Judicial Review in the Virginia Court of Appeals: *The Case of the Prisoners*, 1782

Commonwealth v. *Caton* (*The Case of the Prisoners*) also emerged from the turmoil of the Revolutionary war. During the spring and summer of 1781, the British army, which had operated in Virginia earlier in the war, invaded the state again. General William Phillips landed his troops, and marched to Petersburg, conducting raids as far west as Amelia. Benedict Arnold, having deserted the Patriot cause and now serving as a British general, moved his troops up the James River, leaving a trail of destruction. General Cornwallis marched his large army into Virginia from the Carolinas, and dispatched Lieutenant Colonel Banastre Tarleton to try to capture Virginia's legislature along with its governor, and they chased the governor and members of the General Assembly across the mountains, capturing seven. Thomas Jefferson, then serving his last months as Virginia's governor narrowly escaped by fleeing from Monticello to his plantation at Poplar Forest in southwest Virginia.[1]

In a number of Virginia counties, a significant population of Loyalists had been present throughout the war, and now these local inhabitants not only cooperated with the British as they conducted military operations, but also mounted their own raids on Patriots, at times in reprisal for earlier Patriot attacks. But the fortunes of the British army and of the local Loyalists who assisted them were about to change. In the fall of 1781, the British general Cornwallis and his entire army found themselves trapped in Yorktown, Virginia with their backs to the sea, and in October 1781 were

[1] This paragraph and the next are based in large part on the account offered by David John Mays, *Edmund Pendleton, 1721–1803: A Biography* (Cambridge, Mass., Harvard University Press, 1952), II, 187–88.

forced to surrender to the American army, bringing to an end further large-scale military operations in Virginia, and in the rest of the nation. With the larger war effectively over, and in an effort to restore order in several of the counties that had experienced the worst Loyalist violence, the government of Virginia began in the spring of 1782 to bring treason prosecutions. It was out of these events that the well-known Virginia *Case of the Prisoners* arose.

Three men, John Caton, Joshua Hopkins, and James Lamb, all inhabitants of Princess Anne County, were arrested and tried, apparently for several different incidents,[2] and on June 15, 1782, convicted of treason and sentenced to death by the Virginia General Court.[3] At the end of its session the court recommended that a pardon be granted to one of the men, James Lamb, but not to the others.

> The power to pardon for treason [now] lay in the legislature, and Governor Benjamin Harrison [in a letter dated June 17, 1782] therefore sent the judges' recommendations concerning the three men to the Speaker of the House [of Delegates]. Lamb simultaneously petitioned the House that he was between sixty and seventy years old and had been "forced into the service of the enemy" for a nighttime raid by "a party of Men styled Refugees." The next day, Patrick Henry moved in the House "to pardon Lamb & [the] others." The House passed this resolution and sent it up to the Senate, but the upper house returned the pardon resolution later that day, "refusing to have anything to do with it" [according to a later newspaper account].[4]

"On the day appointed for the[ir] Execution" apparently sometime in the middle of July, 1782,[5] the men produced for the sheriff the pardon resolution passed by the House of Delegates, without notifying him that the Senate had refused to concur, and demanded to be freed.[6] Not quite sure how to proceed, the sheriff put off the execution, but kept the prisoners confined until the case could be heard by the General Court at

[2] Ibid., 384–85 note 2.

[3] Ibid., 189; Philip Hamburger, *Law and Judicial Duty* (Cambridge, Mass., Harvard University Press, 2008), 487. See also William Michael Treanor, "The Case of the Prisoners and the Origins of Judicial Review" (1994) 143 *University of Pennsylvania Law Review* 491, 500–2.

[4] Hamburger, Law and Judicial Duty, 487–88, and associated footnotes.

[5] See "A True Whig," *Virginia Gazette* (July 27, 1782), as quoted in Hamburger, Law and Judicial Duty, 489 fn. 26.

[6] Pendleton's "Notes on the Case of the Prisoners" have been printed in David John Mays (ed.), *The Letters and Papers of Edmund Pendleton, 1734–1803* (Charlottesville, Va., The University Press of Virginia, 1967), II, 416–27, the reference above is to pages 416–17.

its next session in October. At the October session of the General Court, Attorney General Edmund Randolph

> moved that the Prisoners might be brought up, and a new Rule made for their Execution: [The defense] pleaded the Resolution of the House of Delegates ... as a Pardon [now disclosing to the court that the resolution had been sent up to the Senate which had refused to concur], and prayed to be discharged. The Attorney General replied that the paper produced was Invalid, and could not operate as a Pardon.[7]

In their mid-July confrontation with the sheriff, it appears that those who were representing the three men were already framing the matter as a question of the constitutionality of Virginia's Treason Act, which appeared to conflict with Virginia's constitution, as the Act required the concurrence of both houses of the legislature for the grant of a pardon, while the constitution itself appeared to require only a vote of the House of Delegates.[8] In a letter dated July 18, 1782, Randolph reported to James Madison that a "late incident will probably try the fortitude of our judiciary, by calling upon them to say, whether a law, contrary to the constitution is obligatory."[9]

The constitution had been adopted in June 1776, and just a few months later, in October 1776, the members of the convention, now reconvened as the House of Delegates, passed (together with the newly elected Senate),[10] "An act declaring what shall be Treason."[11] Section III of the statute deprived the governor of the power to pardon those convicted of treason, as the pardon clause in the constitution permitted them to do. But the law then went on to add that the entire legislature, the General Assembly, rather than the House of Delegates alone, should, in that case, have the power to pardon for treason. On its face, the pardon

7 Pendleton's "Notes on the Case of the Prisoners," in Mays (ed.), Letters and Papers, II, 417.

8 Both Randolph and Chancellor Pendleton referred at times to the Virginia Constitution of 1776 as "the act of government" or "the act for the constitution of government," see Pendleton "Notes on the Case of the Prisoners," in Mays (ed.), Letters and Papers, II, 417.

9 William T. Hutchinson and William M. E. Rachal (eds.), *The Papers of James Madison* (Chicago, ILL., University of Chicago Press, 1965), IV, 424 (letter from Edmund Randolph to James Madison, July 18, 1782); see also the manuscript of Randolph's argument to the Virginia Court of Appeals made at the November 1782 hearing of the case where he observed: "On these circumstances the genius of mercy has fixed her hold, and for a moment chained the hand of the Executioner. She terrified him with this suffocated fetus of a pardon, [baring?] at the same time what she called the sword of the constitution, and requiring the liberation of the culprits," 2.

10 The Senate, newly created by the constitution, was chosen in a separate election.

11 William Waller Hening (ed.), *Laws of Virginia* (Richmond, Va., Printed for the Editor, 1821), IX, 168.

provision in the Treason Act appeared to support the prisoners claim that its terms conflicted with the clause in the constitution, which stated that where the law deprived the governor of the power to pardon "in such cases, no reprieve or Pardon shall be granted, but by resolve of the House of Delegates."[12]

At the October 1782 session of the General Court, the lawyers for the prisoners opposed Randolph's motion to set a new execution date, arguing that the pardon they had received from the House of Delegates was valid under the clause of the constitution, and that to the extent the Treason Statute required such pardons to be issued by both houses of the legislature, the court should declare it void as contrary to the constitution. After hearing these arguments, the judges on the General Court apparently disagreed among themselves both on the question whether the pardon was valid and on the larger issue whether a court had the power to declare an act of the legislature void. Two of the General Court's justices, James Mercer and Peter Lyons, seem to have taken opposing positions on the two questions. Justice Lyons seems to have declared "[a]gainst the Power of the Court to declare an Act of the Legislature void, because it was against the Constitution" but to have been of the opinion that the treason statute was not in fact in conflict with the constitution and therefore that under that statute the pardon issued by a single house was not valid.[13] On the other hand, Justice James Mercer appears to have taken the positions that "[t]he Court must declare the Constitution Superior to the Act" and consequently that the pardon issued by the House of Delegates alone was "good" under the constitution.[14] On October 26, following the hearing in the General Court, Randolph reported to Madison that "[t]he great constitutional question which I mentioned to you two or three months ago has been agitated in the general court. But its immense magnitude caused it to be adjourned into the court of appeals," although Randolph believed that if the General Court had come to a decision they would "have pronounced the nullity of the law as being against the constitution."[15]

[12] Virginia Constitution of 1776, in Francis Thorpe (ed.), *The Federal and State Constitutions, Colonial Charters, and Other Organic Laws of the States, Territories and Colonies* (Washington, D.C., Government Printing Office, 1909, Reprint Buffalo, N.Y., William S. Hein, 1993), VII, 3817.

[13] This is an inference based on Pendleton's brief description of the opinions later delivered by these judges in the Court of Appeals, Pendleton's "Notes on the Case of the Prisoners," in Mays (ed.), Letters and Papers, II, 426.

[14] Ibid.

[15] Randolph letter to Madison, October 26, 1782, in Hutchinson and Rachal (eds.), Papers of James Madison, V, 217–18.

During the previous summer, the question whether courts could legitimately wield the power to nullify a law had already begun to generate public debate. Citing an article published in July 1782 in the Virginia Gazette, Philip Hamburger notes that "[t]he case was already a matter of controversy when the sheriff in the summer delayed execution, and commentators soon encouraged local lawyers to 'exercise their talents in defence of [their] principles.'"[16] According to Chancellor Pendleton, it was the newspapers that began to characterize the issue of the court's power as the "great Constitutional question,"[17] and the resulting controversy, he wrote a few weeks later, had made "such noise."[18] By the time the General Court heard the case in October a number of members of the legislature seem to have become concerned enough about the way the controversy was unfolding that they suggested an alternative method for resolving the constitutional dispute.

In his October 26 letter, Randolph reported to Madison that "[i]t is proposed by some of the members of the assembly, to convene a committee from the legislative, and judiciary departments who shal[l] enter into a discussion of the subject, and defin[e] the powers of each." Randolph appears to have been amenable to this idea because of his own doubts about judicial review (discussed below), and his own convictions that where a law and the constitution were in conflict, the people should ordinarily be the ones to resolve the controversy in the traditional way through constitutional politics triggered by their right of "opposition," as he was to put it. "At first sight," he wrote, "the [proposed] measure appears eligible, as without an accommodation fou[n]ded upon a reasonable construction of the constitution the appeal must be made to the people."[19]

The group of legislators who approached Randolph proposed "as part of the scheme, that a council of revisi[on] shall be established, to keep the legislature in future[e] cases within its just limits,"[20] apparently hoping that it might serve as an alternative to judicial resolution of such disputes. At any rate, the evidence points squarely to the fact that many Virginians considered the question whether courts legitimately possessed the power

[16] Hamburger, Law and Judicial Duty, 490.

[17] Pendleton letter to James Madison, November 8, 1782, in Mays (ed.), Letters and Papers of Edmund Pendleton, II, 428.

[18] Pendleton letter to Madison, December 9, 1782, in Hutchinson and Rachal (eds.), Papers of James Madison, V, 382.

[19] Randolph letter to Madison, October 26, 1782, in ibid., V, 218.

[20] Ibid.

to nullify laws they judged to be unconstitutional as yet unresolved and of "immense magnitude."[21]

The following May (1783), "discussions with [a group of Virginia legislators led Thomas Jefferson] to the conclusion that a convention to revise the Virginia Constitution was imminent."[22] In anticipation, he drew up a proposed draft of a new constitution for Virginia, which, among other matters, added a Council of Revision modeled on New York's.[23] Jefferson's proposal appears to have been subsequently picked up by Madison, who went on to argue for the establishment of such a Council at the Federal Convention. It seems probable that Madison's interest in Councils of Revision originated with the early controversy over the constitutional powers of courts that grew out of the *Case of the Prisoners.*

Not able or willing to decide "the great constitutional question" at its October session, the General Court "Ordered the Case to be adjourned, for Novelty and difficulty into" the Court of Appeals,[24] Virginia's highest court, which consisted of the judges of the Chancellor's court, the Admiralty court, and the General court sitting together as the court of final appeal in the state. As senior member, Chancellor Edmund Pendleton presided over this court, which opened its October 1782 session on the 29th, when Pendleton took the opportunity to state the facts of the case and to ask for the assistance of "Gentlemen of the Bar," who were "not engaged as Counsel" to offer their opinions as amici on the weighty constitutional questions he thought the case posed.[25]

In addition to the question whether the Court of Appeals had jurisdiction to hear the case in the first place,[26] Pendleton thought the facts presented two major questions: was the pardon provision of the Treason Act actually "contrary to the clause in the Constitution?" but more

[21] Ibid.

[22] "Editorial Note: Jefferson's Proposed Revision of the Virginia Constitution," 1, in Founders Online, National Archives, Source: Julian P. Boyd (ed.), *The Papers of Thomas Jefferson, 21 May 1781–1 March, 1784* (Princeton, N.J., Princeton, Princeton University Press, 1952), VI, 278–84.

[23] "III. Jefferson's Draft of a Constitution for Virginia, [May–June 1783]," 4, Founders Online, National Archives; Source: Boyd (ed.), The Papers of Thomas Jefferson, VI, 294–308.

[24] Pendleton's "Notes on the Case of the Prisoners," in Mays (ed.), Letters and Papers, II, 417.

[25] Ibid.

[26] The arguments presented on this question, and the judges' opinions, will not be discussed here, because they are not directly relevant to the larger inquiry.

importantly, if it was, could "a Court of Law ... declare an Act of the Legislature void because it was repugnant to the Act for the Constitution of Government?"[27] Pendleton adjourned the court until October 31 when "the Questions were fully and learnedly discussed" by Attorney General Randolph "on one side and Mr. [Andrew] Ronald, Counsel for the Prisoners, on the other, and by Mr. John Mercer, Mr. Wm. Nelson and Mr. St. George Tucker Voluntiers, at large and differing amongst themselves in several points, particularly as to the Power of the Court to declare an Act of Assembly void in any case."[28] If it seems pretty clear that several judges disagreed among themselves about whether courts possessed the power to nullify an act of the legislature, it seems equally clear that real disagreements on this fundamental issue also existed among the lawyers. The surviving evidence indicates that among the lawyers Attorney General Randolph and the amicus John Francis Mercer, working from a set of traditional constitutional understandings, rejected the idea that courts possessed a legitimate authority to nullify acts of the legislature, while the amicus St. George Tucker formulated, for what appears to be the first time, a strikingly innovative, transformative argument, based on a series of widely accepted assumptions about constitutions, legislatures, and courts, demonstrating that they did.[29]

At the time the *Case of the Prisoners* was heard, Virginia, like most states did not have a system of published law reports.[30] A report of the case did not appear until 1827 when Daniel Call published an account based on "the notes and memoranda of the judges and lawyers, who attended the courts" and on his "diligent examination of the records."[31]

27 Pendleton's "Notes on the Case of the Prisoners," in Mays (ed.), Letters and Papers, II, 417.

28 Ibid., 417–18.

29 Randolph's and St. George Tucker's arguments in the case are discussed in detail below. John Francis Mercer's opinion on the matter is inferred from the position he later took at the Federal Constitutional Convention opposing judicial review, see Max Farrand (ed.), *Records of the Federal Convention of 1787* (New Haven, Ct., Yale University Press, c. 1966), II, 298 (Mr. Mercer "disapproved of the Doctrine that Judges as expositors of the Constitution should have authority to declare a law void. He thought laws ought to be well and cautiously made, and then to be uncontroulable"). According to Pendleton's "Notes on the Case of the Prisoners" Mercer's older brother, James Mercer, sitting on the Court of Appeals as a justice of the General Court took the opposite position when the *Case of the Prisoners* was heard, in Mays (ed.), Letters and Papers, II, 426.

30 J. M. Sosin, *The Aristocracy of the Long Robe: The Origins of Judicial Review in America* (Westport, Ct., Greenwood Press, 1989), 203–4.

31 Daniel Call, *Reports of Cases Argued and Decided in the Court of Appeals of Virginia*, "The Reporter's Preface to the Fourth Volume" (Richmond, Va., Robert I. Smith, 1833).

But a number of historians have raised questions about the accuracy of some aspects of Call's report, published decades after the case was heard. Fortunately for historians, manuscripts of the argument made in the case by Attorney General Randolph and the amicus St. George Tucker have survived along with presiding judge Edmund Pendleton's contemporaneous notes, which include a description of the opinion he delivered in the case, and briefer accounts of the opinions pronounced by the other judges.[32] No one has done more to highlight the importance of this manuscript evidence than William Treanor who was the first scholar fully to utilize the manuscripts produced by Randolph and Tucker.[33]

These sources reveal that the case yielded a comprehensive, searching, mainly disinterested inquiry, into the question of whether American courts possessed the legitimate authority to nullify laws passed by legislatures. And precisely because this inquiry returned a mixed verdict, it serves to illuminate the complicated contours of an American constitutional landscape on the verge of great changes. These sources make it possible to recover a distinct sense of how people like Randolph, reared in an earlier American constitutional tradition, could possibly imagine that judicial review might be improper, by exposing to view the different deep logic of this earlier constitutional system. This tradition, sustained by a set of everyday assumptions about the proper relationships between constitutions, legislatures, courts, and the people, began to lose its salience as everyday common sense almost as soon as the apparently unassailable reasoning justifying judicial review began to be presented. By the time the court and the lawyers got round to addressing the issue in the Virginia Court of Appeals, it seems apparent that the possibility that courts might have the power to declare unconstitutional laws void was already in the air; the lawyers for the prisoners certainly hadn't hesitated to try to make that argument on behalf of their clients. The sources that have survived from the case make it possible to watch St. George Tucker as he assembled, in this climate, out of a series of

[32] Edmund Randolph's manuscript argument in the case is preserved in the James Madison papers held at the Library of Congress, 91 James Madison Papers, Manuscript Division, Library of Congress, Washington, D.C. and online at www.loc.gov/item/mjm021836/; St. George Tucker's argument has been printed in Charles F. Hobson (ed.), *St. George Tucker's Law Reports and Selected Paper, 1782–1825* (Chapel Hill, N.C., University of North Carolina Press, 2013), III, 1741–48; and Chancellor Pendleton's notes on the case in Mays (ed.), Letters and Papers of Edmund Pendleton, II, 416–27.

[33] See William Michael Treanor, "The Case of the Prisoners and the Origins of Judicial Review" (1994) 143 *University of Pennsylvania Law Review* 491.

relatively uncontroversial propositions about constitutions and the function of judges, a powerful argument for judicial review, perhaps for the first time, one that stood on its head the underlying logic of the traditional constitutional system.

The argument, once developed, seemed obvious, almost self-evident and quickly transformed the constitutional landscape. Constructed out of a few simple, widely accepted assumptions, moreover, it was an argument that several other distinguished lawyers in other states, operating in similar environments, seem also to have worked out within a few years, and apparently mainly independently of one another.

In some ways, the *Case of the Prisoners* was not a straightforward test of judicial review. There were at least two different constitutional issues at stake and those tugged in opposite directions. On the one hand, there was the question whether the Treason Statute was in conflict with the constitution, and if it was, whether the court had the authority to do anything about it. But on the other hand, there was the equally significant question whether one house of the legislature, especially the lower house, could ever have the constitutional authority to perform binding acts without the participation and agreement of the other house. This was a particular anxiety in the Anglo/American constitutional tradition, dating back to the seventeenth-century English Civil War, when the Commons during the Long Parliament, having usurped the authority of the King and House of Lords, ruled alone for more than a decade.

According to Call's report, it was this aspect of the case that agitated Chancellor Wythe most deeply. This constitutional value, of course, pushed strongly in the direction of finding the Treason Statute to be consistent with the constitution, as the statute required both houses of the legislature to agree on pardons. And to believe, consequently, that the legislature had acted properly by exercising its traditional constitutional powers to improve (modify) the badly drafted constitution by subsequently passing the Treason Statute. To the extent the other judges shared Wythe's concerns, it would have inclined them toward finding the statute to be consistent with the constitution, as a majority of them did, obviating the need to make a determination about the court's power to nullify unconstitutional statutes. And this is indeed what happened. It was precisely because of this posture, however, that the case presented a perfect opportunity safely to undertake an exhaustive examination of the question whether courts did legitimately possess the authority to nullify statutes they judged to be unconstitutional. The results of that inquiry reveal a good deal about the American constitutional system at the moment a formal doctrine of judicial review began to be introduced and fleshed out.

5.1 ATTORNEY GENERAL RANDOLPH'S TRADITIONALIST ARGUMENT OPPOSING JUDICIAL REVIEW

Randolph divided his argument to the court into two parts. In the first, he would examine whether the Treason Statute was in fact in conflict with the constitution. In the second, he would consider whether, if it was in conflict with the constitution, a court of judicature "can pronounce its nullity."[34]

He began by summarizing his conclusion as to the first question: "the association of the senate in the function of pardoning treason is justified by the constitution."[35] He then undertook a discussion of how he had arrived at this conclusion. According to Call's Report of the case, the lawyers for the prisoners had been arguing "[t]hat the words of the constitution, and not conjectures drawn from the supposed meaning of the framers of it, should give the rule. That the act of assembly was contrary to the plain declaration of the constitution; and therefore void."[36] And on their face, the words of the constitution certainly did seem to support the prisoners' case. But drawing on what was apparently the more common approach to construing the terms of constitutions, Randolph argued that a constitution had to be interpreted according to its "spirit,"[37] and in this respect differently from the way one went about explicating a statute.

Randolph proceeded to determine what the "spirit" of the constitution required in a noteworthy way. "Pursuing this principle of liberality," he wrote, "it is fit to ask upon what ground of *political wisdom*, the senate ought to [be] excluded from a participation of the power of pardoning... ?"[38] (emphasis added).

The thrust of Randolph's argument was that in determining the "spirit" of the constitution, it was "political wisdom" that had to be interrogated. If there were no sound "political" rationale for excluding

[34] Randolph manuscript argument in *Case of the Prisoners*, in James Madison Papers, Manuscript
Division, Library of Congress, Washington, D.C., XCI, 2. [35] Ibid.

[36] *Commonwealth* v. *Caton et al.*, 4 Call 5 (Va., 1782), at 7.

[37] See discussion in Chapter 2 of the use of the terms "spirit of" and "principles of" the constitution, used in constitutions themselves, to describe how their terms should be explicated.

[38] Randolph manuscript argument, 4.

the Senate, then it should not be supposed that the "spirit" of the constitution required that body to be barred. He traced the peculiarity of the pardon clause in the Virginia constitution to British tradition. And argued that while that tradition made good political sense in the British context, where an all-powerful monarch and a hereditary aristocracy sitting in an upper house wielded enormous power, it made little sense to exclude the Senate under the very different political conditions in Virginia, where the Senate was elected, and where no pardon could occur without the assent of the House of Delegates.[39]

Randolph summed up by saying that "[i]n the eyes of *political wisdom* . . . the delegates have nothing to fear from the improper intrusion of a pardon in their impeachments. Still less is to be apprehended from [the Senate's] interference in other cases. Where is the crime in which the danger is to be found? Is it in treason?"[40] (emphasis added). And proceeded to show that Senators would have the same interest in punishing treason as any other citizen.

Randolph's reference to "political wisdom" seems to have been setting up a contrast between the kind of narrow "legal" explication of statutes carried out by judges under a set of rigid rules, with a more flexible, open ended analysis that was required for determining the "spirit" of a constitution (where its words were ambiguous). Unlike the "legal" explication carried out by judges, "political" judgment had long been understood to involve the exercise of broad discretion, constrained by the duty to promote the good of the whole. Just a few months earlier, in an opinion letter to Governor Benjamin Harrison, Randolph had invoked a similar distinction. He wrote to the governor that he was of the opinion that the Treason Act did not deprive the governor of the power to pardon before conviction, hence such pardons continued to be a matter for sound gubernatorial discretion. "The matter being thus reduced to the question of *expediency* [the fitness, or suitability of the pardon for promoting the public good], and this being a *political* rather than a *legal* inquiry I shall trouble your excellency no farther . . . ."[41] The conclusion that Randolph drew from his "political" analysis was that the "spirit [of the constitution

[39] Ibid., 5. [40] Ibid., 5–6.

[41] Letter from Edmund Randolph to Governor Benjamin Harrison (June 15, 1782), in Benjamin Harrison Papers, quoted in Hamburger, Law and Judicial Duty, 488–89 fn. 25. In *Marbury* v. *Madison*, John Marshall, another Virginian, set up a similar distinction between "legal" and "political" based on whether an official was entitled to exercise "discretion" or was constrained to act under a set of fixed "legal" rules, *Marbury* v. *Madison*, 5 U.S. 137 (1803), 170–71.

not only did not require but actually] opposes the exclusion of the senate." Randolph apparently was of the view that the good of the commonwealth was better served by including both houses of the legislature in decisions about whether a pardon for treason should be granted. And since "political wisdom" yielded this conclusion, the "words [of the constitution] must be free from ambiguity and decided, or cannot have the Supremacy."[42]

In the subsequent section of his argument, he proceeded to show that the words of the constitution were susceptible to several different interpretations, hence could not be dispositive in themselves of the question of the compatibility of constitution and statute. The object of this exercise was "to open the way for reconciling by construction the law with the constitution."[43] The interpretation he himself thought best construed the problematic words in the constitution to mean that the constitution required the House of Delegates to be included in any decision to grant a pardon, no pardon that excluded the Delegates was constitutionally permissible. According to Randolph's construction, then, the constitution required the participation of the House of Delegates in the pardon power, but it did not require that they exercise the pardon power exclusively. In a sense, Randolph's interpretation turned the apparent meaning of the clause on its head. The words of the constitution that mentioned only the Delegates in the pardon power did not mean the Senate was excluded from the pardon power, they only meant that the constitution required the inclusion of the Delegates. And since the Treason Act certainly included the Delegates in the pardon power, it was not in conflict with the constitution.

At the General Court, recall, Randolph had argued in favor of setting a new execution date, and against the validity of the pardon passed only by the lower house. And he seemed to fear that the General Court might be disposed to find the Treason Statute unconstitutional. Evidently, he like Wythe, believed that the greater constitutional danger was posed by one house of the legislature (the lower) exercising the pardon power alone.

Randolph understood that his interpretation had a certain counterintuitive quality as he confessed to James Madison a few days later. "But I doubt not, that to any but lawyers the construction, by which the two were reconcile[d,] would appear unintelligible.[44] It is not surprising,

[42] Randolph, manuscript argument in Case of Prisoners, 5–6. [43] Ibid., 6.

[44] Letter of Edmund Randolph to James Madison 8 November 1782, in Hutchinson and Rachal (eds.), Papers of James Madison, V, 262.

therefore, that Randolph did not take for granted that the court would adopt this interpretation, or otherwise find the statute to be compatible with the constitution. And so, he proceeded to the second part of his argument, in which he addressed "the great constitutional question."

If the statute was found to be in conflict with the constitution did a court have the power to pronounce its nullity? In his account of the case Call reported that Randolph argued against the power of judicial review, quoting him as saying that even if the statute was in conflict with the constitution "the court were not authorized to declare it void."[45] But in recent years several distinguished scholars have rejected Call's account, arguing that though there are some ambiguities and changes of direction in his argument, at the end of the day, Randolph's manuscript reveals that he came out in favor of judicial review.[46] Having reexamined Randolph's words closely and taken care to understand precisely how he structured his argument, this book is of the view that Call's account of Randolph's position is more accurate. Indeed, it shows that what appear to modern eyes to be inconsistencies in his argument, were not in fact inconsistencies in Randolph's world. When properly understood, these apparent contradictions help to shed light on the character of the very different constitutional logic with which Randolph was working.

As noted earlier, when Randolph introduced his argument to the court, he made clear that it was divided into two parts, the second devoted to whether the court possessed the authority to nullify a statute that was against the constitution. Just as he did with the first question, he announced here, at the outset, his position on this question: "that, howsoever adverse the law which vests this power in the general assembly may be to the constitution, no court of judicature can pronounce its nullity."[47] Randolph's statement resonates eerily with Chief Justice Michie's earlier pronouncement in a case challenging the constitutional validity of a South Carolina provincial act in 1760. "[W]hatever dissonance," Michie wrote, [the provincial act at issue in the case] "may have to the laws and customs of England, or how repugnant soever it may be to them, it is apprehended that this court can give no relief."[48] When Randolph returned to this part of his argument after showing that the statute could be reconciled with the

45 *Commonwealth* v. *Caton, et al.*, 4 Call 5 (Va., 1782), at 7.

46 See Treanor, "The Case of the Prisoners," 507; and Hamburger, Law and Judicial Duty, 491–92.

47 Randolph manuscript argument, 2.

48 See Chapter 1, and Joseph H. Smith, *Appeals to the Privy Council from the American Plantations* (New York, Columbia University Press, 1950), 591.

constitution, he began crucially by subdividing his inquiry into two further questions.

1. Is the treason law to be declared void, so far as it is repugnant to the constitution?
2. If it can be declared void, can any court of judicature pronounce its nullity?[49]

Modern readers will be tempted to collapse these two inquiries: if a law is repugnant to the constitution and hence void, then it should follow as a matter of simple logic that a court can pronounce its nullity. But note that in the first question Randolph employs a passive construction suggesting that the issue of whether a law can be declared void i.e., unconstitutional, is separate from the question of who may have a power to nullify it. And he follows this structure when he answers these two questions in the following paragraphs. It is true that he answers the two questions in an odd way, by posing them as questions about his own courage to take the positions he does. Perhaps this format indicates he felt a degree of diffidence about his answers. But the questions he frames are about his courage, not about whether he has taken these positions unconditionally. He does not say, would I be afraid "if" I took such a position, he says rather: "Do I tremble at the decision of my own mind, that a law against the constitution may be declared void?" A law against the constitution, he says, *may be declared void*. But then he returns to the second question "can any court of judicature pronounce its nullity?" and here he answers in the negative, and not conditionally: "or do I dread the resentment of the court *when* I bear testimony *against their competency* to pronounce the invalidity of the law?" (emphasis added). And goes on to say why he feels empowered to take these positions. "No! the revolution has given me a coat of mail for my defense, while I adhere to its principles." He continues by adding that the judges raised in the same tradition will in any case not claim an authority that the constitution has not conferred on them. "That bench too is reared on the revolution, and will arrogate no undue power."[50]

He concludes this section of his argument by repeating the answer he has given to the *first* question: "I hold then, that every law against the constitution *may be declared void*." But he never returns to the second question: does a court have "the competency to pronounce" its nullity. The only answers he has given to this question are in the negative. And

[49] Randolph, manuscript argument, 8. [50] Ibid., 9.

nowhere in the remainder of his argument does he readdress the issue to try to reverse his position.

What he does do in the remainder of his argument is to discuss "the precise idea of a constitution in general."[51] In the final two pages of his argument, as it has been preserved,[52] he extols the virtues of the mixed constitution, which combine elements of monarchical, aristocratic and democratic government to create a balanced set of institutions. The constitution itself is crucial for maintaining this balance. "[H]ow could laws, whose object is public happiness, be enacted subservient to this end, without a touchstone, by which to ascertain the degree of restraint or countenance, which may be given to each of the simple forms of government_"[53]

> Hence I deduce this definition of a constitution: a compact, in which the people themselves are the sole parties and which they alone can abrogate, delineating the degree, to which they have parted with legislative, executive and judiciary power, as well as prescribing how far each of the simple forms of government is to be pursued in acts of the legislature.[54]

Certainly, if the legislature exceeds the power conferred on it by the people under the constitution, its act, as Randolph has already said, may be declared void. But if the judiciary does not possess the authority to pronounce its nullity, does anyone? In another sentence in the same section, he hints at the answer. "Without [the constitution] it cannot be decided *how far the people*, the fountain of power, have chosen to deposit it in the hands of their legislative servants *nor determine, when the right of resistance commences_*"[55] The constitution provides a touchstone against which legislative acts are to be measured. If a legislative act goes beyond the power the people conferred in their constitution, it triggers the people's right of resistance.

[51] Ibid.

[52] Randolph's manuscript preserved in the James Madison Papers, Manuscript Division, at the Library of Congress consists of 11 pages of text and a 12th docketing page. It appears to be incomplete in that it ends abruptly as he is about to address a new issue. On March 7, 1783, Randolph wrote to James Madison that he was enclosing "a part of my notes on the question before the court of appeals. Inaccurate as they are (for they were the first rude sketch & the second is lost) you must content yourself with them. The remainder which is equally interesting [?] shall be sent to you by the next post, if I can transcribe in time," in Hutchinson and Rachal (eds.) Papers of James Madison, VI, 319. William Treanor has written of the manuscript preserved in the Madison papers that "it appears that he never sent the remainder of his notes to Madison," Treanor, "The Case of the Prisoners," 506.

[53] Randolph, manuscript argument, 11. [54] Ibid. [55] Ibid.

Randolph seems to have changed his mind about one important issue as he developed his argument. In the first pages of his manuscript, he has lined through the words: "the constitution delegates to the legislature every power of the people except that of opposition . . . ."[56] By the latter part of his argument, he has begun to say that in their constitution the people define the extent (degree) of the power they've delegated to the legislature. But the remedy has not changed; it remains the "power of opposition." By adopting the definition of a constitution as a delegation to legislatures from the people of circumscribed powers, however, he has brought to the surface a deep tension in traditional constitutionalism between conception and institutional remedy, one that will leave the traditional position vulnerable to arguments for judicial review. Can a law that the legislature has no "power" to enact really be a law that courts must enforce?

Randolph's answer grows out of the deep assumptions of traditional constitutionalism; these make the people directly responsible for enforcing "a compact, in which the people themselves are the sole parties and which they alone can abrogate."[57] The best evidence that Randolph's answer was a serious one, growing out of mainstream constitutional tradition, comes ironically from James Iredell, one of the distinguished early proponents of judicial review. In a remarkable document addressed "To the Public," itself penned in reaction to a North Carolina case that was testing the idea of judicial review just a few years later,[58] Iredell laid out a powerful argument for judicial review that resembled in many ways, the one St. George Tucker makes in the *Case of the Prisoners*, to be discussed shortly. In presenting his justification for judicial review, Iredell evidently felt the need to discredit the traditional response to unconstitutional acts, and as he did, succeeded in making the traditional position seem somewhat ridiculous.

> I have therefore no doubt, but that the power of the Assembly is limited and defined by the constitution . . .. These are consequences that seem so natural, and indeed so irresistible, that I do not observe they have been much contested. The great argument is, that though the Assembly have not a *right* to violate the constitution, yet if they *in fact* do so, the only remedy is, either by a humble petition that the law may be repealed, or a universal resistance of the people. But that in the meantime, their act, whatever it is, is to be obeyed as a law; for the

[56] Randolph, manuscript argument, 3. [57] Ibid., 11.
[58] *Bayard* v. *Singleton* (N.C., 1787).

judicial power is not to presume to question the power of an act of Assembly.[59] (Italics in original)

Iredell was being slightly disingenuous here, failing to mention the central role frequent elections played in "popular resistance" under traditional constitutionalism, an omission he would later address in correspondence with his friend Richard Spaight.[60] Even some twenty odd years later, John Marshall seems to have found it expedient to attack the traditional constitutional position on this question in his opinion in *Marbury*.

> If an act of the legislature, repugnant to the constitution is void, does it, notwithstanding its invalidity, bind the courts, and oblige them to give it effect? Or, in other words, though it be not law, does it constitute a rule as operative as if it was a law? This would be to overthrow in fact what was established in theory and would seem, at first view, an absurdity too gross to be insisted on. It shall, however, receive a more attentive consideration.[61]

Marshall then proceeded to demonstrate that judges did have the authority to declare such laws null and void, using arguments closely resembling those St. George Tucker and Iredell made in the 1780s.

By 1803, when Marbury was decided and thanks to the compelling constitutional logic justifying judicial review that had been developed in the 1780s, the traditional position had come to seem increasingly, as Marshall put it, "an absurdity too gross to be insisted on." The taken-for-granted assumptions that underlay the argument for judicial review made the logic of the earlier system seem increasingly incomprehensible. Today it remains a challenge to resurrect even an imperfect sense of how people like Randolph could seriously have held, at the same time, the beliefs that while laws in conflict with the constitution "may be declared void," the judiciary did not have "the competency" to "nullify" them.

For Randolph, operating under that earlier constitutional logic, the answer begins with an understanding of the perceived character of constitutions themselves. The constitutional historian, Larry Kramer, building on the work of the political scientist, Sylvia Snowiss, has presented a vivid description of this earlier view.

59 "To the Public," in Griffith J. McRee (ed.), *Life and Correspondence of James Iredell* (1857, repr. New York, Peter Smith, 1949), II, 146–47.

60 Letter to Richard Spaight, August 26th, 1787, in McRee (ed.), Iredell, II, 172–76.

61 *Marbury* v. *Madison*, 5 U.S. 137 (1803), at 177.

> [T]he people's restrictions on which laws could be enacted were directed to the lawmaking branch, and not to the other branches. It was the legislature's delegated responsibility to decide whether a proposed law was constitutionally authorized, subject to oversight by the people. Courts simply had nothing to do with it, and they were acting as interlopers if they tried to second-guess the legislature's decision.[62]

That judges had no legitimate role to play in the enforcement of constitutions followed from the fact that fundamental (constitutional) law differed qualitatively from ordinary law, from the statute and common law in effect under any government. Fundamental law stood above and over governments, it was the law under which the government itself was organized; it was a form of law, which ordinary courts created under that government simply had no jurisdiction to consider in their decisions.

> [Unlike ordinary law, [f]undamental law, consequently, was to be enforced by electoral or other political action. If these were insufficient, revolution or threat of revolution was the only recourse.[63]

When a law was declared to be void as unconstitutional in the traditional sense, it did not mean that the act lost the force of law under the government that had enacted it. Rather it meant that the legitimacy of the law had been called into question and a right of resistance had been triggered, entailing attacks on and mobilization against the law and perhaps refusal to obey it. This right of resistance was somewhat akin to civil disobedience and was full of many of the same tensions and ambiguities. On the one hand, those who engaged in resistance against a law often believed not only that it should not be law, but in fact that in some abstract sense it was not binding law at all. Yet, it would not be "disobedience" if their declarations and actions had actually deprived the act of its status as enforceable law under that government. The right of resistance was part of a (political) process aimed at pressuring or persuading existing legislators (or electing new ones) to reconsider their original decision. But unless and until the legislature did repeal the law, and even though it might be actively contested, it continued to be the law of the land. It was in this sense that during the run up to the Revolution, Americans denounced the Stamp Act, for example, as unconstitutional and void, triggering a right of resistance perhaps even in colonial judges. Here is Kramer again.

[62] Larry Kramer, *The People Themselves: Popular Constitutionalism and Judicial Review* (Oxford, Oxford University Press, 2004), 58–59, 71.

[63] Sylvia Snowiss, *Judicial Review and the Law of the Constitution* (Yale University Press, New Haven, 1990), 5.

> [J]udges *no less* than anyone else, should resist unconstitutional laws. This obligation did not arise from any special competence the judges possessed as judges, and it certainly was not based on the notion that constitutional law was ordinary law subject to judicial control. It was, rather, simply another instance of the right of every citizen to refuse to recognize the validity of unconstitutional laws – a "political legal" duty and responsibility rather than a strictly legal one.[64]

But this is not the sense in which the "great constitutional question" was posed in the *Case of the Prisoners*. The inquiry there was not about whether the judges, along with other citizens, could exercise a right of resistance to unconstitutional laws, whether they could, in effect, engage in civil disobedience by refusing to enforce an act that continued to be the law of the land, it was the subtly but significantly different question of whether the judges acting in their capacity as government officials charged with the duty to decide cases according to the law of the land, possessed the legitimate authority acting in their official role to rule that a duly enacted statute did not possess the force of law and would not be recognized among the laws of the land they would apply in arriving at their formal decisions. It was, in other words, the question whether the judges possessed the authority to engage in judicial review in something approximating the modern sense.

That the question in the *Case of the Prisoners* was the importantly different one of the official power of judges may reasonably be inferred from Randolph's argument itself, which recognized the traditional right of resistance but denied that this right conferred on judges the "competency" to pronounce the nullity of a law. That the framing of the issue in the case involved whether judges possessed the legitimate constitutional power to nullify statutes rather than their right to engage in a form of civil disobedience may also help to explain a seeming contradiction in Chancellor Pendleton's behavior.

In his opinion in the *Case of the Prisoners*, Pendleton held back from deciding that the judges have the authority to pronounce statutes void, suggesting that there might be a serious constitutional obstacle to the exercise of such a power. But sixteen years earlier in 1766, sitting as a justice of the peace and magistrate of the Caroline County Court, Pendleton had no problem pronouncing on the constitutionality of the Stamp Act. In the revolutionary situation provoked by Parliament's passage of the Stamp Act, patriotic judges were confronted with the unpleasant choice between closing their courts in resistance to the Act, as some

64 Kramer, The People Themselves, 38–39.

Virginia courts decided to do, or continuing to perform their judicial duties without stamped paper, possibly subjecting themselves to penalties for violating the Act. Pendleton chose the latter course, pretty clearly understanding it to be an act of civil disobedience potentially exposing him to penalties, and the parties who came before him, to having his acts invalidated. In a letter to James Madison, Sr., Pendleton wrote

> [a]s a majestrate, I thought it my duty to sit, and we have constantly opened court, and I shall not hesitate to determine what people will desire me *and run the risque of themselves*, and having taken an oath to determine according to law, shall never *consider* that act as such for want of *power (I mean constitutional authority)* in the Parliament to pass it.
>
> Were I applied to for an attachment, or any other thing within my office out of court, I would grant it *at the party's risque as to the validity of it*, for *I am not afraid of the penalty*, at least so much as of breaking my Oath.[65] (emphasis added)

But in 1782, in the *Case of the Prisoners*, Pendleton faced a different situation and confronted a different question. Did judges, serving loyally in a government chosen by the people, and not facing revolutionary conditions, possess the formal constitutional authority as part of their office to pronounce duly enacted laws void as a matter of course, legitimately depriving such acts of the force of law in their courts, and perhaps more widely. Since Pendleton, like Randolph, had been reared in an older constitutional tradition, his answer to this question, discussed in greater detail below, was considerably more hesitant. A certain unresolvable ambiguity remains, of course, because, after all, the judicial act involved in both kinds of situations is similar, a simple refusal to apply a duly enacted statute. And there is undeniably a certain cultural continuity that connects the two situations. That the question of judicial review was on the table at all certainly owes something to the tradition of denouncing unconstitutional acts as void. What is different about this situation is the meanings placed on the term void, the characterization of the judges' acts of refusal, and the ways those acts are justified. In the *Case of the Prisoners*, the question being asked and the framing of answers are all directed toward assessing whether judges have a formal authority to nullify a law they judge to be unconstitutional, rather than whether they, along with other citizens, have a right to resist such a law by

[65] Letter from Edmund Pendleton to James Madison, Sr. (February 15, 1766) in Mays (ed.), Letters and Papers of Edmund Pendleton, I, 23. See also Hamburger, Law and Judicial Duty, 276–78, 493–94.

disobeying it. And to this question, the answer of traditional constitutionalism, as Randolph's argument makes clear, is that they do not.

5.2 ST. GEORGE TUCKER OFFERS A DEFINITIVE RATIONALE FOR JUDICIAL REVIEW

That these were the perceived stakes in this case seems even clearer when the argument for judicial review presented to the court by St. George Tucker is considered. Tucker, arguing as an amicus, disagreed with Randolph about both major issues in the case. Unlike Randolph, Tucker believed that the Treason Statute was in fact in conflict with the Virginia constitution, and also unlike Randolph, believed that courts possessed the authority to nullify such statutes. Tucker's argument has been preserved in manuscript, but has also been printed in a multi-volume edition of his law reports and papers.[66] In it, he first takes up the question "[w]hether the Judges have a right to decide on the validity or nullity of a positive Act of Assembly passed with all the Formalities used in framing or enacting Laws?"[67]

His argument begins with a conventional account of the powers of the judiciary. "I hold it to be incontrovertible that the power properly belonging to the Judiciary Department, is, to explain the Laws of the Land as they apply to particular Cases . . .," [68] then he proceeds to take this argument a step further. Since the Virginia Constitution's separation of powers clause guarantees that "[t]he Legislative, executive and Judiciary Departments shall be separate and distinct, so *that neither exercise the powers properly belonging to the other*"[69] (italics in original), it must be that where particular cases arise, "the Interpretation of the Laws of the Land is in the *Judiciary alone*–"[70] (italics in original). "T]he Spirit of our Constitution ... will not permit the Legislative to expound or interpret a Law as applying to *particular* Persons or Cases, altho' they have undoubtedly the right to explain their *General Policy*"[71] (italics in original). In other words, the legislature is entitled to correct judicial misinterpretations of its own laws by passing supplementary general legislation to make their meaning clearer. "Yet," as Tucker put it, "if the Legislative shall find that Mischiefs have, or may arise from such [judicial] Interpretations it is undoubtedly their province to explain their own Acts, so that no further Doubts may occur in the future Construction of

[66] Hobson (ed.), St. George Tucker's Law Reports and Selected Papers, III, 1741–48.
[67] Ibid., 1741. [68] Ibid., 1742. [69] Ibid., 1741. [70] Ibid., 1742. [71] Ibid.

them in such particular Cases as shall be brought before the Judiciary for their Explanation or Interpretation."[72] This kind of legislative clarification being an elaboration of general and uniform rules, does not violate the separation of powers "[f]or every Interpretation of a Law by the G.A. (General Assembly) in reality amounts to enacting a new Law which is their undoubted province."[73] He sums up by saying that "it is the undoubted province of the Judiciary to interpret *all* Laws whatsoever: altho' the Legislative may by a future Act explain any point not sufficiently clear in a former Act"[74] (emphasis added).

There is an important constitutional reason the power to interpret "all" laws (as applied to particular cases) is in the judiciary alone. Citing Montesquieu, Tucker writes that if the legislature possessed a power of interpretation, it would open the way for tyrannical government in which the legislature could first make tyrannical laws and "then tyrannically execute[] or interpret[]" them. The checks and balances in a system of strict separation of powers make the emergence of tyranny less likely.

> For if the Legislative have a right to determine or explain the Laws judicially, that is to decide in *particular* Cases the Judiciary, who are by the Constitution appointed as a counterpoise to it, is entirely annulled, & one of the Pillars on which our Government is established is totally destroyed. [¶] But as this right of Interpretation does not exist in the Legislative, nor yet in the Executive, it is consequently vested in the judiciary alone, for neither according to the constitution *shall exercise the powers properly belonging to the other*."[75] (italics in original)

At this time, of course, legislative bodies in a number of states still sat as courts of final resort, and in more states still settled disputes between individuals by enacting private bills.[76] But if Tucker's description was not an altogether accurate account of institutional realities, it was an accurate account of the aspirational project of many judges during this period to strip legislatures of the other-than-general lawmaking functions they had long possessed, under the guise of strictly adhering to separation of powers principles. His account did nevertheless also draw upon an old, well-established tradition in common law thought that sharply contrasted

[72] Ibid. [73] Ibid. [74] Ibid. [75] Ibid.

[76] See, for example, Zephaniah Swift's account of the judicial powers the Connecticut legislature wielded during this period, in *A System of the Laws of the State of Connecticut: in Six Books* (Windham, Ct., 1795, repr. Arno Press, 1972), I, 59, 73–82; see also the discussion of the judicial and quasi-judicial roles the New Hampshire and Rhode Island legislatures played during this period, in Chapters 7 and 8 below.

legislative and judicial functions. Legislatures, this tradition held, make law, the general rules that govern society (*Jus dare* or *Legem facere*) while judges expound or say what the law is (*Jus dicere* or *Legem dicere*) in deciding particular cases.[77] Because the constitution mandates a strict separation of powers, Tucker contended, legislatures do not have a general constitutional power to interpret or expound the laws; the judges alone have this power. There is a limited exception to this distribution of constitutional authority in that legislatures may legitimately explain, in general terms, their own statutes.

One implication of this power of exposition in the common law tradition is that it authorizes judges to declare what the law is in any particular case. Judges, for example, commonly confront situations in which two irreconcilably conflicting laws apply to the same set of facts. The power to expound the laws as part of the duty to decide cases means that judges have no choice but to determine which of the conflicting statutes should have the force of law in this situation, and which should be treated as a nullity. Referring to Blackstone's Commentaries, with which many American lawyers were familiar, Tucker notes that "[i]n Britain I have generally understood that it is a rule in the Construction of Statutes to consider a later Statute, which contradicts a former (so essentially as that they can not be construed so as to stand together) as repealing the former Statute. The same Rule may with equal propriety I presume be adopted in construing all acts of the General A[ssembly]: of this Commonwealth."[78] Blackstone had laid it down as one of "the rules to be observed with regard to the construction of statutes . . . .[79] [that] "where the common law and a statute differ, the common law gives place to the statute; and an old statute gives place to a new one."[80]

Tucker draws this broader conclusion about the interpretive authority of judges when faced with conflicting laws: as "the power of interpreting all the Laws of this Commonwealth in particular Cases, is vested in the Judiciary alone, it follows that *they alone* (if any of the Departments of Government can do it) *can decide what is or is not Law*, and consequently

77 Hamburger, Law and Judicial Duty, 218–34, includes an excellent discussion of this common law tradition.

78 Tucker, Argument in the *Case of the Prisoners*, in Hobson (ed.), St. George Tucker's Law Reports and Selected Papers, III, 1742.

79 William Blackstone, *Commentaries on the Laws of England* (1765) (Facsimile edition, University of Chicago Press, 1979), I, 87, 89.

80 Ibid.

(I should presume) *on the validity or nullity of different Laws contradicting each other*"[81] (emphasis added).

As he has been addressing the question whether a court possesses the power to pronounce the nullity of a statute that is in conflict with the constitution, it is now possible to understand where this remarkable argument is heading. The power of judges to pronounce the nullity of a statute, far from being extraordinary, simply grows out of the routine authority they "incontrovertibly" possess to expound the law in situations in which two laws are in conflict, in order to decide cases. Furthermore, under the separation of powers clause of the constitution, the judges alone possess this power of exposition; the legislature possesses the distinct power of making the laws. The implications of this argument, which is based on a few simple, widely accepted propositions about the office of judges pulled from common law culture, are far-reaching. Not only does the argument provide a compelling justification for the power of judges to pronounce the nullity of a statute as a matter of course; it begins to turn the traditional constitutional priority of legislatures over the judiciary on its head. In Tucker's account, who has the better, more "natural" claim to the power to interpret "all" laws?

But two important problems that traditional constitutionalism continued to pose for judicial review remained to be addressed. The first was whether the constitution was the kind of law of which ordinary judges could legitimately take notice. The second was in some ways even more fundamental. Even if the constitution was "law," did the legislature have the power to change or explain it by enacting a new statute, as it would in the case of its own statutes, and as Parliament had certainly done repeatedly in the case of the British constitution?

Tucker does not have much to say about the first question, apparently believing that his brief answer would suffice. He has already repeated multiple times that the power of the judiciary is to interpret "all laws whatsoever." He says this about the constitution as law. "For altho' it be true that the Judges are sworn to decide in all matters brought before them agreeably to the Laws of the Land, yet is the Constitution the first Law by which they are bound, and any Decision contrary thereto is absolutely subversive of that Government of which it is undoubtedly the Basis & Foundation."[82] It seems plausible to think that the experience of electing

[81] Tucker, Argument in the *Case of the Prisoners*, in Hobson (ed.), St. George Tucker's Law Reports and Selected Papers, III, 1742.

[82] Ibid., 1744.

representative bodies to adopt written constitutions during the 1770s, in a process resembling the ordinary lawmaking process, had begun subtly to alter the tacit understandings many had of constitutions.

The Virginia constitution of 1776 was itself adopted by a convention that also passed numerous ordinary ordinances. And it was first printed as part of a volume entitled "Ordinances passed at a General Convention of Delegates and Representatives … ."[83] In his "Notes on the State of Virginia" originally drafted in late 1781 and early 1782 shortly before the *Case of the Prisoners* arose, Jefferson pressed an argument that the Virginia constitution was no more than an ordinary law that subsequent legislatures were free to change. Because, Jefferson contended, the people had not authorized the convention to form a permanent new government, the convention had no authority to do so.

> So far, and no farther authorized, they organized the government by the ordinance entitled a constitution or form of government. It pretends to no higher authority than the other ordinances of the same session; it does not say, that it shall be perpetual; that it shall be unalterable by other legislatures; that it shall be transcendent above the powers of those, who they knew would have equal power with themselves. Not only the silence of the instrument is a proof they thought it would be alterable, but their own practice also: for this very convention, meeting as a house of delegates in general assembly with the senate in the autumn of that year, passed acts of assembly in contradiction to their ordinance of government: and every assembly from that time to this has done the same.[84]

To make the constitution fixed and unalterable by the legislature, Jefferson believed, Virginia would have to follow the example of other states.

> The other states in the union have been of opinion, that to render a form of government unalterable by ordinary acts of assembly, the people must delegate persons with special powers. They have accordingly chosen special conventions to form and fix their governments.[85]

Jefferson's position on the alterability of the Virginia constitution was certainly controversial, and he seems to have been in a distinct minority among Virginians on the issue. But his argument reveals a good deal about one of his most important unspoken assumptions. He took completely for granted that the law of the constitution was enough like ordinary law so

83 Thorpe (ed.), Constitutions, VII, 3812 fn.

84 Thomas Jefferson, *Notes on the State of Virginia* (Boston, Lilly and Wait, 1832), 126.

85 Ibid., 129.

that it could be embodied in an ordinance and that passage of a subsequent statute could change it. The written texts of constitutions like the written texts of statutes were given force by the representative bodies that adopted (enacted) them. Under these circumstances, the law of the constitution began to seem more like a form of "ordinary" law, except that it might, if properly produced, be unalterable by the legislature.

Ultimately, it would be the lawyers and judges, who, for the purpose of making an argument for judicial review, would distill out of the cultural ether this new sense of the character of constitutions as superior ordinary law. More than a century ago, Edward Corwin had this to say about the process. The new constitutions

> were acts of revolution, social compacts .... The power of *enacting* laws ... was a function of *government*. How then, could constitutions, bills of rights, frames of government, the work of the people themselves, be regarded as laws in the strict sense of the term? Their moral supremacy none doubted, nor yet that a breach of them by government destroyed its right to be, but until the *people* should be regarded as having an *enacting power*, exercisable directly and without the intervention of their legislative representatives the *supremacy* of constitutions was a real barrier to their *legality*.[86]

The new procedures for adopting constitutions and the ideas upon which they rested made plausible the view that the people were exercising just such an enacting power when constitutions were adopted in these ways. But as Corwin also pointed out, it was the conduct of the judges, finally, that transformed constitutions from a kind of fundamental, political/legal, higher law into a form of law directly analogous to statute law (but superior), when ordinary courts began to consider these documents in their decisions. "The fact of the matter is," Corwin wrote, "that the establishment of judicial review gave ... constitution[s] the character of law .... "[87]

There is no evidence that the participants in the argument in the *Case of the Prisoners* had seen Jefferson's "Notes on the State of Virginia" at the time they addressed the court,[88] but one of the lawyers or judges involved

[86] Edward S. Corwin, "Marbury v. Madison and the Doctrine of Judicial Review" (1914) 12 *Michigan Law Review* 538, 555.

[87] Edward S. Corwin, "The Establishment of Judicial Review I" (1910) 9 *Michigan Law Review* 102, 110.

[88] A version of Jefferson's original draft had apparently reached James Madison's hands by the summer of 1782, but Edmund Randolph did not receive a copy until the beginning of 1783. See "Notes on Jefferson's Memorandum for Barbe-Marbois," in Hutchinson and Rachal (eds.), Papers of James Madison, V, 7–11; and letters from Edmund Randolph to

in the case evidently made a similar argument (that the legislature possessed the power to explain or modify the constitution by enacting a subsequent statute) based on British constitutional precedent. This argument had the potential to overturn the entire framing of the case. If this argument were conceded, the Treason Act might well be understood as an explanatory modification (improvement) of the constitution completely within the legislature's traditional province, as it likely had originally been understood to be when enacted by the legislature during the autumn of 1776 immediately following the adoption of the constitution. At any rate, the other participants in the case seem to have taken the argument seriously enough to want to address it at length, in the process propounding doctrine that would begin to separate irrevocably the American and British constitutional traditions.

Edmund Randolph's manuscript broke off at just the point he began to address the issue, but St. George Tucker and Chancellor Pendleton devoted considerable efforts to contesting the notion that following British constitutional precedent, the Virginia legislature had the power legitimately to explain or modify the constitution by enacting new laws.

It is worth quoting Tucker's argument on the issue in full. "But it may be urged," he began,

> Magna Charta the Habeas Corpus Act, & the British Bill of Rights tho' constitutional Acts, may, nay, have been altered by the British Parliament, more than once.
>
> To this I reply that no parallel can possibly be drawn between the Constitution of G. B. & this Country. The Act above referred to are by some of the ablest Politicians of that nation considered only as Acts explanatory of that Constitution, which has existed to use their own phrase from time beyond memory of Man .... Therefore the Constitution of G. B. partakes of the nature of their common Law, which can only be collected from immemorial Usages, or such Statutes as have from time to time been made to explain it; or amend it.
>
> Now the Parliament of G. B. having power not only to explain the Common Law, but also the Constitution, it follows that they may by a subsequent Act explain certain points of the Constitution differently from what they were explained in a former Act, which different explanation while it amounts to a repeal of a former Act, is only considered as placing what really was the Constitution in it's [sic] proper light.

James Madison, November 16, 1782, and from Madison to Randolph, November 26, 1782, in the same volume at 282 and 331; see also the letter from Randolph to Madison, March 7, 1783, in ibid., VI, 319.

Thus by this Fiction in Law (for it seems to deserve that name), the British Constitution may be modeled agreeably to the Will of Parliament, whose omnipotence in this Instance seems generally admitted.

But the Case is otherwise with our Constitution – the British is constructive – Ours is express – the British is traditional; and different points of it have been explained at different Times & by different Parliamts. and in different Modes. Ours on the contrary was framed with all the solemnity of an original Compact between Citizens about to establish a Government most agreeable to themselves. That it might not be liable to be infringed it is founded on a Bill of Rights which is declared to form the Basis & Foundation of Government; and that it might not be misinterpreted it was committed to writing and made public to all the Citizens who became parties thereto.[89]

This "express" written constitution was unalterable by the legislature for several basic reasons, the first being that any alteration would destroy the "Basis and Foundation of Government" and presumably the legislature's powers with it.[90] But there was an even more fundamental logic to unalterability. The ordinary legislature was no longer considered by many to be the author of constitutions in the way it was the author of statutes. Representative bodies that adopted constitutions were increasingly viewed as fundamentally different from ordinary legislatures, somehow representing the people differently. Constitutions, although penned by a body of their representatives, were increasingly considered the people's own act, "an original Compact between the Citizens of the Commonwealth," as Tucker put it.

It was perhaps more difficult to maintain this position in Virginia than in almost any other state, because as Jefferson pointed out, the Virginia convention had not been elected with an explicit mandate to establish a permanent new government, and the same body of men who wrote and adopted the constitution also passed ordinary ordinances and subsequently reconvened themselves as the lower house of the ordinary legislature. In other states, conventions had been elected with an explicit mandate to write a new constitution. In Massachusetts, a single purpose convention had been elected to write the constitution of 1780, submit it to the people afterward for ratification, and then go out existence. This represented a clear institutional repudiation of the idea that a single representative body could fully embody the people and that its acts were acts of the people whether it was sitting as a convention to adopt a constitution, or as a legislature to enact a statute that explained or modified it. By the early 1780s, a spreading

[89] Tucker, Argument in the *Case of the Prisoners*, in Hobson (ed.), St. George Tucker's Law Reports and Selected Papers, III, 1744–45.

[90] Ibid., 1744.

distrust of legislatures had eroded faith in this older idea.[91] Increasingly, it came to be thought that for republican governments to be properly established it was necessary for the people to be represented by two different bodies, one to write their constitutions in order to establish the fundamental ground rules for their governments, then to have the people ratify that work, the other to make their laws. The two bodies would express the will of the people in fundamentally different ways. Conventions (and ratification by the people) would operate in effect as a direct act of the people themselves, expressing their permanent, superior will and embodying it in a fixed constitution. Legislatures would merely represent the people's transient, changeable, inferior wills. Legislatures would be the authors of statutes, but the people themselves through their conventions (and through ratification) would be the authors of and parties to their original compact.[92] And as legislatures were not the authors of constitutions, they could have no power to alter them.

Unlike Jefferson, Tucker was not deterred by the procedures that had been used to adopt the Virginia constitution under an older set of ideas about the relationship of representative bodies to constitutions. Arguing that the body of men who comprised the Virginia convention had sat in two fundamentally different capacities, Tucker relied on what appears to be an ad hoc distinction formulated specifically for the purpose of demonstrating that no ordinary legislative body had authored the Virginia constitution.

[91] See in general Gordon Wood, *The Creation of the American Republic, 1776–1787* (Chapel Hill, N.C., University of North Carolina Press, 1969).

[92] For critiques of the fiction that constitutional conventions represented the people differently, more genuinely than legislatures, see Noah Webster, "Government," *American Magazine*, I (1787–88) quoted in Gordon Wood, Creation of the American Republic, 379 ("Why a body of men chosen by the people in the manner they choose the members of the Legislature, and commonly composed of the same men, but at any rate they are neither wiser nor better. The sense of the people is no better known in a convention, than in a Legislature." "A convention can therefore have no more power and differs no more from an ordinary Legislature, than one Legislature does from another."); see also James Madison, #49 Federalist, in Clinton Rossiter (ed.), *The Federalist Papers* (New York, Mentor Books, 1999), 284, arguing against holding a second Federal Constitutional Convention. ("But the legislative party would not only be able to plead their cause most successfully with the people. They would probably be constituted themselves the judges. The same influence which had gained them an election in the legislature would gain them a seat in the convention .... The convention, in short, would be composed chiefly of men who had been, who actually were or who expected to be, members of the department whose conduct was arraigned.")

> For the Constitution being the Act of the *political Legislature*, and in nature of an original Compact between the Citizens of the Commonwealth, the *civil Legislature* ... being an *inferior subordinate Institution* can not have power to annul or avoid any part of the Constitution so established.
>
> But if every Act of the General Assembly, tho diametrically opposed to the Constitution, be valid as a Law, it follows that the G: A: may at any time alter, repeal, or annul any part or the whole Body of the Constitution ....
>
> Consequently, all Laws repugnant thereto are ab Initio void. For if they are not void the Assembly have a right of altering repealing, or annulling the Constitution. Now this Right being by universal concurrence of Opinion in the Citizens of the Commonwealth denied to exist in Any General Assembly convened *for the purposes of civil Legislation only*, it follows that any Attempt to exercise such a Right is subversive of the Basis and Foundation of Government, & consequently is, & ought to be deemed absolutely void.[93] (emphasis added)

This appears to be a purely definitional affair. A representative body that drafts and adopts a constitution must by definition be sitting as a "political legislature." The ordinary "civil" legislature has no power to alter the constitution, not only because by definition it is "inferior and subordinate" but also because it has not been the constitution's author in the first place. Only the people, presumably acting through a new "political legislature," have the power to change the law of the constitution. Consequently, a statute enacted by the ordinary ("civil") legislature that contradicts the constitution must be completely void as an ultra vires attempt by the ordinary legislature to modify the constitution.

It is now possible to grasp what Tucker has accomplished with his argument. Ordinary judges have the formal authority to pronounce the nullity of a statute as a result of the power their office confers to interpret (expound) the law, including the law of the constitution, in particular cases. In the ordinary course, when judges are confronted with an irreconcilable conflict between two laws, the authority to "expound" the law means that they must declare what the law is, relying on some well-founded rule of construction to determine which of the conflicting laws governs the outcome of the case and which must be treated as a nullity, in order to fulfill their duty to decide the case. In the situation where a statute conflicts irreconcilably with the constitution that well-founded rule of construction is that the legislature has no power to enact such a statute, and the statute consequently cannot have the force of law. In this situation, the court must, as part of its duty to decide cases according to the

[93] Tucker, Argument in the *Case of the Prisoners*, in Hobson (ed.), St. George Tucker's Law Reports and Selected Papers, III, 1745.

law of the land, give effect to the law of the constitution and declare the statute to be void and of no effect.

Tucker's argument provides a compelling justification for the legitimacy of the judges' power to pronounce the nullity of a statute, the immediate question he was addressing, but it goes much further, in many ways turning the existing constitutional system upside down. Constitutions had been widely understood to be a kind of political law directed at legislatures. Evaluations of constitutionality had been tied up intimately with the lawmaking power and reserved primarily to legislative bodies. In the process of making laws, legislatures were to consider whether the proposed statute was compatible with the constitution, and if they determined it was, were empowered to enact it into law, their judgment on the matter being final, except in so far as the people might later contest it.

The logic of Tucker's argument makes the judiciary constitutionally superior to the legislature in a number of fundamental ways. Under it, not only would judges have the power to reconsider the legislature's judgments about constitutionality, but in a deeper, more profound sense they would have a claim to be the constitution's final interpreters (within government). According to Tucker, judges alone possess the power to interpret, explain, expound the laws, legislatures have no such power, except in so far as they may explain their own statutes. But since ordinary "civil" legislatures are not the authors of the law of the constitution, it follows that they have no (or at least a considerably weaker) claim to a power to interpret that law. Legislatures, of course, have no choice but to undertake the interpretive task as they go about enacting statutes, but this duty now appears in a somewhat different light, as slightly anomalous, beyond their normal constitutional capacity to make and not to interpret law.

The judges' authority to "expound" the law of the constitution placed them, by comparison to the legislature, in a special relationship to the people. These by and large unelected officials are by the logic of Tucker's argument placed in the position of being oracles of the people. They represent and serve the people in a different sense than do legislators. The people, through their constitution, have conferred on judges the duty to expound "all the laws," making them responsible for explaining and enforcing the people's permanent, fundamental will. By comparison, any claim the legislature may have to act as an interpreter of the constitution must be based, not on a formal grant of authority from the people, but on what they have learned of the people's transient sentiments from a recent election, or from public opinion, a form of knowledge distinctly inferior to that to be gained by expounding the solemn, permanent writing the people have formally adopted. This is perhaps the basis of Tucker's claim that in the constitution "are explained those Fundamental Principles of our Government which the Judiciary Department is constituted the Guardian."[94] Above all, it is the authority and duty to expound the law, in the process of deciding cases, that places judges in a position different from every other governmental official and citizen, arguably entitling them to deprive a duly enacted statute of the force of law.

There is one final implication of Tucker's argument that may be even more profound for the future of American republics. Tucker has shown that the legislature may correct judicial misinterpretations of its own statutes by passing subsequent legislation to clarify or explain their meaning. But as the people are the authors of the written law of the constitution, only they can act to correct judicial misinterpretations of this law, presumably by adopting clarifying amendments to the "legal" constitution (as legislatures do in the case of statutes) using the same solemn procedures they employed to adopt it in the first place. But until the people act formally to amend or clarify their fundamental written law, the judicial interpretation of it would seem to bind even the people themselves, in the sense that however much they might come to desire their legislature to enact a particular statute, a judicial interpretation of the constitution might foreclose the possibility that the courts would recognize the statute as possessing the force of law.

The genius of this argument is that it is constructed as a simple, logical deduction from a few straightforward, relatively uncontroversial premises. Accept these commonplace premises, and the conclusion seems to follow inexorably. (1) The office of judges is to expound the law (2) in particular cases in which judges confront conflicting laws, their authority to expound the law means that they must declare what the law is (3) the constitution is a law like other laws, except that it is the "first law by which [the judges] are bound" (4) legislatures have no power to enact statutes that would change the constitution (5) in deciding a case in which a statute and the constitution are in conflict, the power to expound the law means that the judges, applying the well-founded rule that legislatures have no power to change the law of the constitution, can legitimately hold the statute to be void for want of power in the legislature. Accepting these few premises, it is difficult to argue with the conclusion.

[94] Ibid.

The character of the argument helps to explain a good deal about the subsequent history of the doctrine of judicial review. Very similar arguments appeared in a number of states over the next few years, apparently developed independently of one another. In North Carolina, James Iredell made an argument (discussed in detail in a later chapter) justifying judicial review that was remarkably similar to Tucker's argument. In New York, Alexander Hamilton was developing his own argument for judicial review (also discussed in a later chapter), which came to resemble Iredell's and Tucker's in critical respects. There is no evidence of an active correspondence between these men but it is not uncommon in history for the state of the times to produce similar innovations by several people independently of one another. Iredell and Hamilton had both been deeply preoccupied with the problem of the (perceived) excesses of their respective state legislatures, and with the absence of any appropriate check on legislative power. Perhaps it should come as no surprise that these sophisticated lawyers, working from a few commonplace premises (the constitution is higher ordinary law, legislatures have no power to alter this law, the duty of judges is to expound the law and to decide cases according to it) would be capable of working out similar arguments for judicial review.

Although there were a number of different strands in the arguments made in support of judicial review during this period, the one that Tucker worked out (and later variants on it) would principally shape the emerging constitutional doctrine on the subject. Its seemingly irresistible logic helps to explain the speed with which many lawyers and judges came to accept the legitimacy of the practice, even as it remained deeply controversial. Defenders of traditional constitutionalism were hard pressed to come up with arguments nearly as compelling as those presented by the lawyer proponents of judicial review.

The Traditionalist case against judicial review tended to take a different form, focusing on the negative political and constitutional consequences that would follow from depriving the legislature of, and giving to the judges, the final word in lawmaking. But because the argument in favor of judicial review was carried on mainly in the form of a logical demonstration from unexceptional premises, the more complicated, less clear-cut arguments that depended upon contested political assessments about whether the constitution was in fact the kind of law that ordinary judges should be entitled to take notice of, whether legislatures had a better claim, based on their elective relationship to the people, to continue to be the constitution's final interpreters, whether the people themselves should be removed from the central role they traditionally played in interpreting and enforcing constitutions, and whether in general the political dangers judicial review might pose to republics outweighed its benefits as a check on legislatures, tended to receive considerably less attention.

Perhaps as important to the success of the arguments for judicial review was the widespread feeling among political and legal elites that something simply had to be done to place limits on the power of state legislatures to make law. This sense left many Americans receptive to ideas that under different circumstances might not have gained support so quickly. After all, judicial review represented a radical constitutional innovation based not on explicit constitutional grants of power, but on a judicial interpretation in which the judges themselves decided that their own powers included the constitutional authority to set aside duly enacted laws. Over the next few years, the doctrine of judicial review would gain acceptance among a substantial number of lawyers and judges, but in 1782, the Virginia Court of Appeals was not prepared to accept Tucker's argument, deciding not to decide whether courts possessed the authority to pronounce the nullity of an unconstitutional statute.

5.3 CHANCELLOR PENDLETON'S PRUDENCE

According to Pendleton's notes, only one judge (Mr. Justice Mercer) agreed with St. George Tucker that the Treason Act was in conflict with the constitution. Given that a clear majority of the court found the act not to be "against" the constitution, there was less urgency about deciding the question whether if it had been, the court could pronounce its nullity. As a result, Pendleton reports five members of the court took no position on this question. He writes that "Mr. Chan[cello]r Blair ... waved the question upon the power of the Court to declare an anti-constitutional Act of Assembly void ..., " as did Mr. Justice Dandridge who "declined the question upon the Power of the Court to declare an Act void ... ." Chancellor Pendleton himself joined the others in reserving the question for the future.[95] Three members of the court did take positions on the

[95] Pendleton's Notes are quite clear that 5 of the judges took no position on the question of their power to pronounce the nullity of an unconstitutional act, Mays (ed.), The Letters and Papers of Edmund Pendleton, II, 426. But in his later report of the case Call writes that "Chancellor Blair and the rest of the judges, were of opinion, that the court had power to declare any resolution or act of the legislature, or of either branch of it, to be unconstitutional and void ... ." 4 Call 5 (Va., 1782), at 20. Under the circumstances, it is likely that Pendleton's contemporaneous notes contain a more accurate description of the judges' positions.

"great constitutional question," but they disagreed among themselves on the answer. Two (Chancellor Wythe and Mr. Justice Mercer) held in favor of the court's power to pronounce the nullity of an unconstitutional statute, but one, Mr. Justice Lyons "Against the Power of the Court to declare an Act of the Legislature void."[96] All and all it looks as though at this transitional moment the court, hearing the Attorney General's opposition to the power, being internally divided, and seeing no immediate need to decide the question, "prudently" decided to leave it unanswered, as Randolph wrote in a letter to James Madison a few days later.[97]

Pendleton himself appears to have been influenced by both Randolph and Tucker but in complicated cross cutting ways. On the question whether the Treason Act was in conflict with the constitution, Pendleton discussed a number of interpretations of the controversial clause that had been proposed to the court, but settled on the one Randolph also considered the best: the clause merely prohibited the exclusion of the House of Delegates from the pardon power and as the Treason Act did not exclude the Delegates, it was not in conflict with the constitution.[98]

As to the second principal question, the court's power to pronounce unconstitutional statutes void, like Tucker, Pendleton rejected the idea that the court could find an answer by consulting the constitutional history of other countries, including Great Britain.

> In discussing this great Constitutional Question, as it has been announced to the Public, very little light has been thrown upon the Subject, by researches into the history of other Countreys .... Even in Britain, where we might most expect to get some Rule to assist Us, We find the same author Lord Coke asserting at one time the omnipotence of Parliament, who may even change the Consti[tu]tion, and another

[96] Pendleton's "Notes on the Case of the Prisoners," in Mays (ed.), The Letters and Papers of Edmund Pendleton, II, all quotes from 426. Call's report of the case contains a long opinion by Chancellor Wythe, which has not been discussed in detail here because its accuracy cannot be confirmed from contemporary sources. This chapter relies instead on the shorter description of Wythe's opinion contained in Pendleton's Notes. According to Pendleton's contemporaneous account in his Notes of the case, Wythe "urged several strong and sensible reasons of the nature of those used by Lord Abblington, to prove that an Anti-constitutional Act of the Legislature would be void; and if so, that this Court must in Judgment declare it so, or not decide according to the Law of the Land," II, 426. From this brief description, it looks as though Wythe agreed with the main points in Tucker's argument about the power of the court.

[97] Letter from Edmund Randolph to James Madison, November 8, 1782, in Hutchinson and Rachal (eds.), The Papers of James Madison, V, 262.

[98] Mays (ed.), The Letters and Papers of Edmund Pendleton, II, 425; see also Pendleton's letter to James Madison, November 8, 1782, reiterating his adoption of this interpretation, II, 428.

exalting the Judiciary above them, giving Courts power of declaring Acts of Parliament void because they are impertinent or contrary to right and Reason, both of which are mere speculative opinions and neither of them worthy of adoption by the Legislature or Judiciary.[99]

Like Tucker, Pendleton began to argue that the American and British constitutional systems were fundamentally different from one another and that British precedent could carry no weight in deciding upon the powers of American courts. But he also seems to have been drawing on Randolph's description of constitutions.

We however have happily in our hands the certain record of our Constitution containing the Original Social Compact, wherein the People have made their Government to consist of three great branches, the Legislative, Executive and Judiciary, allotting to each, its proper powers, and declaring that they shall be kept separate and distinct, neither exercising those which belong to another. Like all other declared Powers each has its limits, the Legislative as well as the others, which if they Pass, it would seem their Act would be void, as well as that of an Attorney would be, which was not Warranted by his appointment.[100]

That Pendleton took constitutions to be analogous to Powers of Attorney set up the argument for judicial review beautifully. Duncan Kennedy has this to say about the use of similar analogies.

The argument was that the people were a legal principal ... who had created an agency or trust and an agent or trustee. No one could doubt the fully legal character of what a common law judge did in enforcing the limits on the scope of an agency or the terms of a trust.

The use of the common law analogy gave both structure and legitimacy to the judicial role. Since the constitutions generally said nothing at all about the theory and practice of review, it was necessary to go somewhere else for suggestions about the basic organization of the process. Take the question of whether the court should enjoin the enforcement of an unconstitutional statute the day it was enacted into law. The analogy to common law suggested that the role of the courts was the passive one of responding to concrete complaints by particular parties aggrieved ....

But the common law agency or trust analogy served also to legitimate review by affirming its wholly legal, apolitical, everyday character .... Through the appeal to the Constitution as "law like any other law" and to the common law of agency and trusts, judicial review achieved full legality ...[101]

[99] Ibid., II, 422. [100] Ibid.
[101] Duncan Kennedy, *The Rise and Fall of Classical Legal Thought* (1975) II, 61–63

But then Pendleton did something unexpected; he hesitated, declining to decide the question. What he has to say about the reason for his doubts is especially illuminating. He has said that the act of any branch that goes beyond the powers delegated to it by the people would seem to be void. But then goes on, as Randolph had, to consider the separate question whether the court has the power to pronounce a statute's nullity.

> But how far this Court in which it has been properly said the Judiciary Powers of the State are concentrated, can go in declaring an Act of the Legislature void, because it is repugnant to the Constitution, *without exercising the Power of Legislation, from which they are restrained by the same Constitution*? Is a deep, important, and, I will add, an awful question; from which, however, I will not shrink, if ever it shall become my duty to decide it: at present I am happy in having no occasion to make the decision; and still more happy in a Sanguine hope that the wisdom and prudence of the Legislature, in making the Principles of the Constitution direct the Spirit of their Laws, will render it unnecessary ever to determine it.[102] (emphasis added)

With these few words, Pendleton rejected the main premises of Tucker's argument for judicial review, reasserting traditional understandings about the proper relationship of legislatures to constitutions. Traditionally, judgments of constitutionality were mainly considered to be an aspect of the lawmaking process, a legislative function. Pendleton's point seems to have been that a decision to unmake, repeal or nullify a statute based on a determination of constitutionality might be as much a legislative act as the decision to pass the law in the first place. He then went one step further showing that Tucker's separation of powers reasoning could be turned on its head, into an argument against judicial review. If in performing judicial review, courts turned out to be exercising legislative authority, that would be in violation of the Virginia constitution's separation of powers clause, presumably making the practice of judicial review unconstitutional.

Several modern commentators have had difficulty taking Pendleton at his word, suggesting that he could not possibly have been serious in saying what he did, or that he only wrote the things he did out of an excess of political caution. It is true that there had been an agitation by some members of the Assembly just before the decision was to take place, apparently attempting to preempt the possibility that the court would engage in judicial nullification by proposing that a joint committee of judges and legislators be convened to resolve the issue, and further

[102] Mays (ed.), The Letters and Papers of Edmund Pendleton, II, 422.

suggesting that a Council of Revision might be added to the form of government.[103] According to the historian David Mays, on the days the case was being heard and when the decision was delivered, the courtroom was "packed to the windows." Mays speculates that among the audience were a considerable number of legislators who were in town awaiting the start of the legislative session.[104] Pendleton himself wrote that "[a] very numerous and respectable audience attended the Argument and delivering the Judgment."[105]

That there was considerable political interest in the case seems clear, but less clear, based on the scattered evidence, is in how many different directions the political pressures emanating from the legislature (and public) ran. For shortly after the judgment was declared, the House of Delegates weighed into the controversy by attempting, in essence, to exercise *its* traditional legislative authority. It announced its own judgment that in so far as the Treason Act gave the pardon power to both houses, it was in fact *unconstitutional.*[106] They subsequently passed a bill to implement that judgment by moving to repeal the parts of the statute that had conferred the pardon power on the entire General Assembly.[107] The Senate, naturally enough, refused to concur, as the bill would effectively have stripped the upper house of the right to participate in granting Treason pardons.

In one sense, the House of Delegates was moving to challenge the finality of the court's interpretation of the constitution, attempting to vindicate the traditional legislative prerogative to render the final judgment (in government) on constitutionality in the making and repealing of laws. But in another sense, the behavior of the Delegates was certainly odd. Legislative bodies do not normally object when a court finds a statute

103 See letter from Edmund Randolph to James Madison, October 26, 1782, in Hutchinson and Rachal (eds.) James Madison Papers, V, 218.

104 Mays, Edmund Pendleton, a Biography, 191, and 385 fn. 28.

105 Mays (ed.), Letters and Papers of Edmund Pendleton, II, 427.

106 *Journal of the House of Delegates of the commonwealth of Virginia: begun and held in the town of Richmond, in the county of Henrico,* November 1782, 24 (Richmond, Va., 1782). Notice that the Delegates did not consider an unconstitutional act to be void in itself; the remedy rather for unconstitutional legislation was amendment or repeal. As the Court of Appeals had found the prisoners' pardons to be invalid, on November 15, 1782, they again petitioned the House of Delegates to pardon them for their crime, ibid., 18–19. The House agreed to do so and on December 11, 1782, the Senate joined in, ibid., 60, and the men were conditionally pardoned.

107 Ibid., 33.

to be constitutional. Yet here, the Delegates did just that, declaring the Treason Act to be *unconstitutional* and moving to repeal it.

From another perspective, however, the conduct of the Delegates is perfectly understandable in that they seem to have believed that they alone were entitled to exercise the pardon power under the text of the constitution. But these circumstances certainly muddy the waters when it comes to the question whether members of this house of the legislature had indeed been agitating against the court's power to engage in judicial review or had, on the contrary, been encouraging the judges to declare the Treason Act unconstitutional and void.[108] These circumstances seem to confirm Chancellor Wythe's opinion that the most immediate and dangerous constitutional issue facing the commonwealth in this case involved whether the lower house of the legislature was entitled under the constitution to assume the power to act alone without the participation of the upper house on the critical issue of granting pardons to Loyalists convicted of treason. By contrast, the issue of whether the Treason Act was in conflict with the constitution arose secondarily in so far as it bore on this more pressing constitutional matter.

This case had not been framed as one in which an irresponsible legislature had enacted a piece of destructive legislation, making the need for judicial review seem obvious. On the contrary, when the Treason Act was passed in the autumn of 1776, not only had Thomas Jefferson been a member of the House of Delegates, Chancellor Pendleton himself had presided over the House of Delegates as its Speaker. The previous spring Pendleton had presided over the convention that adopted the first Virginia constitution. Edmund Randolph had also participated in that convention. And according to Pendleton, at the time the Treason Act was passed, the House of Delegates had debated the question of its constitutionality, in line with its traditional duty to deliberate upon the question of constitutionality before enacting a bill into law. The House had concluded on that occasion that the proposed act was *not* in conflict with the spirit of the constitution. During those legislative debates, Chancellor Pendleton had formed the same opinion. Pendleton put it this way in his notes.

108 In a letter to Madison, Randolph wrote that he believed that if the General Court had decided the case, they would have "pronounced the nullity of the law as being against the constitution," letter of Randolph to Madison, October 26, 1782, Hutchinson and Rachal (eds.), Papers of James Madison, V, 218. Might this court's apparent sympathy for nullifying the act reflect in some measure pressures coming from the lower house of the legislature?

Upon this point therefore I am of opinion that the Treason Act is not contrary to the constitution, but a proper exercise of the Power reserved to the Legislature . . . ; an opinion not taken up on this occasion, but formed at the time the law passed, when the Question whether it was anti-constitutional, was Warmly agitated: Being honoured with the chair at that time, I took no part in the debate, but deliberately settled my opinion on the Negative side of the Question, which I have found no reason to alter.[109]

From the perspective of eminent men such as Pendleton and Randolph, the real problem in this case was not so much the Treason Act or the legislature that had enacted it as "the Inaccurate words of the Constitution" as Pendleton put it in a letter to James Madison just a few days after the case had been decided,[110] and the current behavior of the lower house. Not only did the court's determination that the Treason Act was not in conflict with the constitution, remove the immediate necessity for deciding whether it possessed the power to pronounce the nullity of an unconstitutional statute, but so also did the larger context. The legislature that had debated the constitutionality of the Treason Act before passing it into law was composed of distinguished men, at least one of whom now sat on the court that was being asked to re-decide the question of that act's constitutionality.

The very thorough debate over judicial review mounted in the *Case of the Prisoners* took place more as a lawyerly exercise than as an effort to address an immediate, pressing, systemic constitutional problem. And as there seemed to be no urgent need at that moment to abandon the traditional constitutional system by embracing a judicial negative on legislation, men like Randolph and Pendleton showed themselves reluctant to do so. At the same time, it is quite clear that the issue of judicial review was already squarely on the table, and that the argument for its legitimacy was already well developed.

[109] Mays (ed.), Letters and Papers of Edmund Pendleton, II, 425–26. [110] Ibid., 428.

11

THE EMERGENCE OF AMERICAN JUDICIAL REVIEW, 1784–1787: DEVELOPING JUDICIAL REVIEW AS A CHECK ON LEGISLATURES AND ON THE PEOPLE

Following the cessation of hostilities and the signing of the Treaty of Peace in 1783,[1] the nature of the cases traditionally listed as the sources of American judicial review down to 1787 changed subtly. The principal cases that arose following the war, *Rutgers* v. *Waddington* (N.Y., 1784), Trevett v. *Weeden* (R.I., 1786), the New Hampshire Ten Pound Act Cases (1786), and *Bayard* v. *Singleton* (N.C., 1787)[2] all featured challenges to statutes enacted by legislatures in response to popular pressures for action in two areas: (1) laws to hold Loyalists responsible for their role in supporting the British during the war and (2) laws to ease the economic burden of those (often small farmers) who were being ruined by a sharp post-war economic downturn, and by the hard currency tax policies adopted by a number of states following the war. These cases now starkly pitted legislatures, and the populist measures they enacted, against lawyers and judges who sought to use the courts to protect political and economic minorities by limiting the power of the people to confer (through their legislatures) the force of law on just any measure they might believe advanced their interests or promoted their political views.

The first of these cases, *Rutgers* v. *Waddington*, it is sometimes argued, should not be included among the early sources of judicial review but should be understood as an example of common law equitable interpretation.[3] In

[1] *The Provisional Articles of Peace* had been signed on November 30, 1782, and ratified on April 15, 1783; the *Definitive Treaty of Peace*, which incorporated in its essentials the terms of the Provisional Articles, was signed on September 3, 1783, but not finally ratified until January 1784.

[2] The *Symsbury Case* (Ct., 1785) is sometimes listed among these cases, but its import seems sufficiently obscure to be passed over here.

[3] See the discussion in Hamburger, *Law and Judicial Duty* (Cambridge, Mass., Harvard University Press, 2008), 346–48.

a literal sense, this might be true, as the opinion in the case expressly claimed to be grounded on an "equitable" interpretation of the statute. There are nevertheless good reasons to include the case among the early sources of American judicial review. One of Alexander Hamilton's arguments in the case, for example, asserted that the Trespass Act had to be interpreted to avoid conflicts with the laws of the "superior" Confederation government (i.e., the Articles of Confederation and the Treaty of Peace). If, however, the laws were irreconcilably in conflict, he continued, New York judges would have to act as judges of the "superior" Confederation government and strike down the non-conforming law of the "subordinate" state jurisdiction.[4] But other reasons include that quite a few New Yorkers at the time considered the court's equitable interpretation rationale for "disregarding" the statute to be purely pretextual. They believed it provided the judges with a patina of Blackstonian legitimacy for doing what they in fact had no authority to do, set aside a "known law of the state" based on their judgment that it was improper or unreasonable. Beyond that, there are elements of the court's reasoning that resonate deeply with the emerging doctrine of judicial review. In particular, that the judges' authority to "disregard" statutes flows from their duty to "expound the law," in order to decide a case in situations where two applicable laws conflict. A more detailed discussion of these issues follows.

[4] See Hamilton's briefs in *Rutgers v. Waddington*, reproduced in Julius Goebel (ed.), *The Law Practice of Alexander Hamilton* (New York, Columbia University Press, 1964) I, 352, 377, 378, 380, 382; Hamburger takes especial issue with Goebel's statement (made at I, 282) that the case "stands out, a marker on the long road that led to the ultimate formulation of the American doctrine of judicial review," see Hamburger, Law and Judicial Duty, 347 fn. 38.

6

The Reappearance of "Vertical" Judicial Review in the Case of *Rutgers v. Waddington*, New York, 1784

Like the two earlier cases, *Rutgers* v. *Waddington* grew directly out of the events of the Revolutionary war. After being driven out of Boston in the spring of 1776, the British army adapted its strategy in America, determining to invade and occupy New York City, preparing the groundwork for an attempt to drive a military wedge between the New England colonies, parts of New York and the remainder of the country. Following a series of American defeats in the late summer and early fall of 1776, the British Army took possession of New York City and its immediate surroundings, where it remained for the next seven years, only departing in November, 1783 after the Definitive Treaty of Peace had been signed. Great numbers of Patriots fled the British occupation, abandoning the properties they owned in the city. In turn, many Loyalists left upstate homes to seek refuge in New York City under the protection of the British army. The occupying British, of course, did not hesitate to make use of the homes and business properties Patriots had left behind.

Mrs. Rutgers, a widow, was one of those displaced Patriots, whose brewery in lower Manhattan was commandeered by the British Commissary General and occupied by Royal forces until 1778,[5] when the Commissary General licensed it to two British merchants, Benjamin Waddington and Evelyn Pierrepont. Their agent Joshua Waddington, who had remained in the city after the British evacuation, managed it on

[5] *The Case of Elizabeth Rutgers versus Joshua Waddington … With an Historical Introduction by Henry B. Dawson* (Morrisania, N.Y., 1866), xii; and Julius Goebel (ed.), *The Law Practice of Alexander Hamilton* (New York, Columbia University Press, 1964), I, 289 and fn. 19

their behalf.[6] Benjamin Waddington contended, in his statement in the Rutgers suit, that the brewery had been "stripped of everything of value" by the time they took possession, and that they had had to invest £700 in repairs before they could begin brewing operations again.[7] They ran the brewery (under license from the Commissary General) without paying rent until May 1780 "when all those occupying abandoned Patriot premises were ordered by the British Commander-in Chief to pay rent to British agent John Smythe for the Vestry for the Poor .... .. For the next three years, Waddington and Pierrepont paid £150 per year rent [under license from the British Commander-in-Chief] ... until on June 10, 1783, in anticipation of the British evacuation of New York, they were ordered by ... the British Commandant of the City, to commence payment of rent to the owner's agent, Anthony Rutgers [Mrs. Rutgers' son]."[8] But the negotiations between Waddington and Rutgers over the appropriate rent broke down and no rent was subsequently paid.[9]

> On November 23, 1783, two days before the British evacuated the city, a fire broke out that reduced the brewery "to ashes" and caused the merchants [Benjamin Waddington's statement contended] a loss computed at "upwards of £4000." The following month, Waddington and Pierrepont turned over to Rutgers the keys ... expressing their desire to settle with him. He, however, "appeared disinclined." In February 1784, [Mrs. Rutgers brought] an action for [trespass against the firm's agent Joshua Waddington seeking back rent or damages of £8000] ... in the Mayor's Court of the City of New York.[10]

Mrs. Rutgers' suit was based in part on a trespass statute the New York legislature had enacted nearly a year earlier on March 17, 1783, in anticipation of the end of the war. The Provisional Articles of Peace had been signed a few months before, on November 30, 1782; and copies had reached Philadelphia by March 12, 1783, but did not arrive in New York until after the legislature had already passed "An Act for granting a more effectual relief in cases of certain trespasses."[11] The Provisional Treaty was ratified a month later, on April 15, 1783, opening the way for the final version of the treaty to be signed on September 3, 1783. Although the legislature had not seen the Provisional Treaty before enacting the statute,

[6] Goebel, Law Practice of Alexander Hamilton, I, 289. [7] Ibid., I, 290. [8] Ibid.

[9] Ibid. [10] Ibid., I, 291.

[11] Ibid., I, 288; ironically, James Duane was sitting as a member of the New York Senate the day the Trespass Act was passed. It is not known what his view of the bill was as the debates and vote were not recorded, see Edward Alexander, *A Revolutionary Conservative: James Duane of New York* (Columbia University Press, New York, 1938), 161.

it seems pretty clear that they expected New York City refugees to return to reclaim their properties immediately upon the restoration of peace, and passed the Trespass Act to permit them to recover for the damages they had suffered as a result of being forced to vacate those properties. The Council of Revision, which had vetoed, and would go on to veto, a number of other anti-Loyalist bills, did *not* find the Trespass Act to be "improper ... [and was of the opinion that it] should ... become [a] law[] of this State."[12]

The act gave a statutory trespass remedy to patriots who had abandoned their property during the war "against any person or persons who may have occupied, injured, or destroyed his, her or their estate, either real or personal within the power of the enemy ...."[13] But the main controversy about the law arose over the short second paragraph, which denied to defendants the right to plead, in justification of these trespasses, "any military order or command whatever of the enemy for such occupancy, [etc.] nor to give the same in evidence ... ."[14] Such a justification for trespass was not known at common law,[15] but a number of classic treatises on the subject declared that such a justification was available under the customary Law of Nations, in situations in which an invading army had occupied a foreign territory. Several of the most respected treatises held that under the Law of War (part of the Law of Nations) occupation by conquest transferred to the conqueror during the period of the conquest all rights of usufruct, the right to the rents and profits of houses and lands. It seems pretty clear that in anticipation of the refugees' return, the New York legislature was seeking definitively to settle in the negative the question whether that justification for trespass would be legally available in New York State. The text of the statute could hardly have been clearer on this point, but it failed expressly to mention that by adopting this measure the legislature intended to "repeal" or "alter" the Law of Nations. This should come as little surprise in that it was far from certain that the customary Law of Nations even constituted part of the law of New York.

The Mayor's Court of New York City met for the first time since the British occupation on February 10, 1784.[16] Only a few days earlier, on

12 *Votes and Proceedings of the Assembly of the State of New York; At the second meeting of the sixth session* (Poughkeepsie, N.Y., Printed by John Holt, 1783), 161 (March 17, 1783).

13 "AN ACT for granting a more effectual relief in cases of certain trespasses," *Laws of the State of New York Passed in The Second Meeting of the Sixth Session of the Legislature*, CHAP. 31, 552 (March 17, 1783).

14 Ibid. 15 Goebel, Law Practice of Alexander Hamilton, I, 295–96. 16 Ibid., I, 217.

February 5, 1784, the New York Council of Appointment had made the prominent New York political figure, lawyer, and land speculator, James Duane, mayor.[17] As mayor, Duane presided over the court, which was composed of himself, the City Recorder, Richard Varick, and the Aldermen. Although Duane would go on to serve as mayor for the next half decade, under the New York constitution he held his office at the pleasure of the Council of Appointment.[18] *Rutgers* v. *Waddington* was already being mentioned in court papers on February 24, 1784, the first day of actual court business.[19]

Alexander Hamilton, who had been retained to defend Waddington, filed his plea in the case on April 21, 1784.[20] "The business of the Mayor's Court at this time was 'quadruple that of the supreme court'"[21]; and a significant number of these suits were being brought under the Trespass Act.[22] Over the years, Hamilton would participate in forty-four additional Trespass Act cases.[23] Arguments in *Rutgers* were heard on June 29, but the court did not deliver its decision until August. In the months between January and June 1784, however, litigation was far from being the only business that occupied Hamilton.

During the war, the New York legislature had passed a series of anti-Loyalist laws that provided for the confiscation of Tory estates and for the imposition of contractual disabilities on Loyalists, among other matters. Two of the best known of these wartime measures were the 1779 Confiscation Act and the 1782 Citation Act, which restricted the rights of "persons within the enemies' lines" to collect preexisting debts from Patriots.[24] The Council of Revision had vetoed a number of these anti-Loyalist bills, and in several instances the legislature had failed to override

[17] Alexander, James Duane Revolutionary Conservative, 159; the State Council of Appointment was established by Article XXIII of the New York Constitution of 1777, see Francis Thorpe (ed.), *The Federal and State Constitutions, Colonial Charters, and Other Organic Laws of the States, Territories and Colonies* (Washington, D.C., Government Printing Office, 1909, Reprint Buffalo, N.Y., William S. Hein, 1993), V, 2633–34.

[18] See Article XXVIII of the New York Constitution of 1777 in ibid., V, 2634.

[19] Goebel, Law Practice of Alexander Hamilton, I, 315. [20] Ibid., I, 320.

[21] Ibid., I, 217–18.

[22] Ibid., I, 218, and fns. 95 and 96. Indeed, several of the City Aldermen, who sat on the Mayor's Court, and a number of people on the committee formed to oppose the decision in Rutgers were plaintiffs in other cases brought under the Trespass Act, see below for details.

[23] Ibid., I, 202, 419.

[24] Ron Chernow, *Alexander Hamilton* (New York, Penguin Books, 2004), 195; and Goebel, Law Practice of Alexander Hamilton, I, 199.

these vetoes.[25] But while the war was being waged, there were sound justifications for these measures. Confiscation of Tory estates served simultaneously to deprive the enemy of resources, and to enhance the Patriot capacity to carry on the conflict. Similar reasons justified Patriot debt relief. In fact, early in the war, the Continental Congress had supported the idea of confiscating Tory estates as a means to buttress the war effort.[26]

But now that the treaty had been signed, it was more difficult to justify the anti-Loyalist legislation the New York legislature continued to pass. One historian has described this stream of legislation as being driven by a complicated amalgam of "[r]evenge, greed, resentment, envy, patriotism ... an inflammatory mix."[27] It should perhaps come as no surprise that after a long occupation by a foreign power, Patriots would seek retribution against "collaborators." But that perhaps universal human impulse surfaced in a particular historical context, one in which a risky, novel experiment in republican government was being launched at a time when many among the educated and wealthy continued to harbor ancient doubts about the capacity of the common people actually to govern themselves.[28] In this context, anti-Loyalist legislation was often seen as flowing from popular mob like resentments and violence. Many in the elite came to believe, during these critical years, that significant constitutional reforms to correct basic defects in republican government were urgently needed. Hamilton himself wrote during the months he was litigating *Rutgers* that "the effects of the popular phrenzy" in New York would damage the city for decades to come.[29] The political situation in New York only served to exacerbate traditional fears, in that the legislature was now full of men who had *not* been drawn from the upper reaches of society. Decades ago, Jackson Turner Main published a classic analysis of these developments.

[25] See, for example, the Council's veto of an early version of the 1779 Confiscation Act, which the legislature failed to override, in Alfred B. Street, *The Council of Revision of the State of New York, and Its Vetoes* (Albany, William Gould Publisher, 1859), 219–26.

[26] Allan Nevins, *The American States During and After the Revolution, 1775–1789* (New York, Augustus M. Kelley, 1969), 268.

[27] Chernow, Hamilton, 195.

[28] For a more detailed discussion of this issue, see Chapter 2 above.

[29] Letter of Hamilton to Robert R. Livingston, August 13, 1783, in Harold C. Syrett (ed.), *The Papers of Alexander Hamilton, 1782–1786* (New York, Columbia University Press, 1962), III, 431, quoted by Goebel, Law Practice of Alexander Hamilton, I, 216.

The wealthy upper class of southern New York, which had controlled both houses of the legislature during the colonial period, was shattered by the Revolution. Although many of its members furnished leaders for the new government, collectively they now played inferior roles. Power was seized by men who were new to the political scene, or who had previously held only lesser offices, and who derived their strength primarily from the support of upstate farmers. Their leader, George Clinton, was governor continuously after 1776 ....

After 1776, the influence of th[e] old elite was sharply reduced. The new constitution transferred power to the areas in which yeoman farmers were dominant; for the counties west of the Hudson and north of Westchester now chose a majority of both houses. As a result of these developments, the balance of power shifted northward from New York City and downward both socially and economically. After 1776, not over 40 percent of the senators and only one-sixth of the representatives were wealthy. Three out of four councilors had been merchants, but now only one in four senators and one in seven assemblymen were in commerce. Farmers, almost excluded from the colonial legislature, now comprised one-third of the senators and actually outnumbered men of the upper class in the Assembly.[30]

On January 15, 1784, the Council of Revision vetoed two of the most recently passed post-war pieces of anti-Loyalist legislation.[31] The first, "An act declaratory of the alienism of the persons therein described," sought to do just what its title suggested, declare those who had remained with the enemy to be aliens, in essence, forfeiting their citizenship and the legal privileges and rights that came with it. The second bill sought to amend the Citation Act, which had restricted the legal rights of Loyalists to collect debts from Patriots, by now authorizing debtors to pay off their Loyalist creditors with "State securities."[32] The legislature was not able to muster the votes to override either veto, however, and neither of these bills became law.[33]

But while the Alienism bill was still pending before the legislature, Hamilton published, in January 1784, an open letter to the citizens of New York under the name Phocion, attacking the proposed law.[34] He argued that it would conflict with the Treaty of Peace,[35] which, he suggested, was paramount to state law.

[30] Jackson Turner Main, *The Upper House in Revolutionary America: 1763–1788* (Madison, Wisc., University of Wisconsin Press, 1967), 133–35.

[31] Street, Council of Revision Vetoes, 246, 248. [32] Ibid., 248. [33] Ibid., 247, 249.

[34] The legislature did not take up the Alienism bill again until February 11, 1784, see "A Letter from Phocion to the Considerate Citizens of New York" (January 1784), in Syrett (ed.), Papers of Alexander Hamilton, III, 483–97, and editorial note 1 following the text of the letter.

[35] Article Six of the Treaty in particular, which Hamilton quoted, prohibited "prosecutions commenced against any person or persons, for, or by reason of the part which he or they

Does not the act of confederation place the exclusive right of war and peace in the United States in Congress? Have they not the sole power of making treaties with foreign nations? Are not these among the first rights of sovereignty, and does not the delegation of them to the general confederacy, so far abridge the sovereignty of each particular state? .... It follows that ... these states are bound by [the treaty], and ought religiously to observe it.[36]

As important, he argued that the Alienism bill might also violate the 13th article of the New York Constitution in that it sought to "disfranchise or punish whole classes of citizens by general descriptions, without trial and conviction of offences known by laws previously established ... ." The 13th article, Hamilton urged, required that classes of persons not be deprived "of the rights or privileges sacred to the subjects of this state" without "*due process of law, that is by indictment or presentment of good and lawful men*,-and trial and conviction in consequence."[37] In his "Second Letter from Phocion," Hamilton carried this point further, contending "that the constitution we have formed makes the trial by jury the only proper mode of ascertaining the delinquencies of individuals- that legislative discriminations, to supersede the necessity of inquiry and proof, would be *an usurpation on the judiciary powers of the government* ... "[38] (emphasis added). Hamilton's argument on this point was part of a wider movement of ideas and sentiments during the period to deny to legislatures the exercise of certain of their traditional adjudicative powers, and to insist that these instead were the peculiar province of the judiciary.

Hamilton's pamphlet was itself attacked in a well-known reply, published under the name Mentor, probably during February or March, 1784.[39] In April, Hamilton published his "Second Letter From Phocion" as a reply to Mentor, and as an attempt to persuade the legislature not to enact a new anti-Loyalist bill they were considering.[40] The new

may have taken in the present war, and no person shall, on that account suffer any future loss or damage, either in his person, liberty, or property."

36 "A Letter from Phocion" (January 1784).

37 Ibid. "It is true, that in *England*, on extraordinary occasions, attainders for high treason, by act of parliament have been practiced, but many of the ablest advocates for civil liberty have condemned this practice, and it has commonly been exercised with great caution upon individuals only by name, never against *general descriptions* of men .... If there had been no treaty in the way, the legislature might, by *name*, have attainted particular persons of high treason for crimes committed during the war, but independent of the treaty it could not, and cannot, without tyranny, disfranchise or punish whole classes of citizens by general description, without trial and conviction ...."

38 "Second Letter from Phocion" (April 1784), in Syrett (ed.), The Papers of Alexander Hamilton, III, 530–58.

39 See editorial note 1 following "Second Letter from Phocion," in ibid.

40 Ibid.

bill, "An Act to Preserve the Freedom and Independence of this State, and for other Purposes therein mentioned," aimed to prohibit those who had remained with the enemy from voting or holding public office. This bill reflected in part the anxiety that Loyalists, who had continued to pledge their allegiance to a monarchical government throughout the war, might now want to vote and seek office in order to subvert the young republic. On May 12, 1784, the Council of Revision vetoed this bill as well, but in this case, "Notwithstanding the objections, the Legislature passed the bill into a law."[41]

By the time Hamilton published his "Second Letter from Phocion" in April (the same month he filed his pleadings in the Rutgers case), he had become more agitated by the seemingly endless stream of anti-Loyalist bills and had thought more deeply about the wider political and constitutional implications of these events. For Hamilton now, the very fate of republican government, and with it the idea that ordinary people possessed the capacity to govern themselves, seemed to hang in the balance.[42] "The world," he wrote,

> has its eye upon America. The noble struggle we have made in the cause of liberty, has occasioned a kind of revolution in human sentiment. The influence of our example has penetrated the gloomy regions of despotism, and has pointed the way to inquiries, which may shake it to its deepest foundations. Men begin to ask every where, who is this tyrant, that dares to build his greatness on our misery and degradation? What commission has he to sacrifice millions to the wanton appetites of himself and the few minions that surround his throne? To ripen inquiry into action, it remains to us to justify the revolution by its fruits.
>
> If the consequences prove, that we really have asserted the cause of human happiness, what may not be expected from so illustrious an example? In a greater or less degree, the world will bless and imitate!
>
> But if experience, in this instance, *verifies the lesson long taught by the enemies of liberty; that the bulk of mankind are not fit to govern themselves, that they must have a master*, and were only made for the rein and the spur: We shall then see the final triumph of despotism over liberty.[43] (emphasis added)

41 Street, Council of Revision Vetoes, 254–55.

42 For a discussion of "the People" as problem, see Gordon Wood, *The Creation of the American Republic, 1776–1787* (Chapel Hill, N.C., University of North Carolina Press, 1969), 400–13.

43 "Second Letter from Phocion," in Syrett (ed.), The Papers of Alexander Hamilton, III, 530–58. Hamilton was far from alone in harboring this sentiment. In reaction to Shay's Rebellion a few years later, for example, George Washington wrote to the Virginian Henry Lee (in nearly identical words) that the violent unrest in Massachusetts "exhibit a melancholy proof of what our transatlantic foe has predicted … – that mankind left to

Hamilton urged the legislature to "pause for a moment, and contemplate with an eye of reverence, the vast trust committed to them" and to act wisely and with restraint.[44]

Ironically, Hamilton himself shared many of these traditional doubts about the capacity of the actual people to govern themselves, as his well-known remarks at the Federal Convention and elsewhere testify.[45] Now, the political climate in New York, incited him to launch, in his second Phocion letter, a frontal assault on the foundational premises of traditional constitutionalism; most especially the idea that legislatures were the appropriate interpreters of constitutions within government, as they proceeded to determine what laws ought to be enacted for the good of the polity, subject only to correction by the people's sense of what their own constitutions required, conveyed to the legislature at frequent elections (or by other means). Hamilton had by now concluded that if republican governments were to survive, real limitations had to be imposed, not only on legislatures, but more problematically, on the sovereign people themselves, in so far as it was apparent that much of the detested legislation passed in New York (and elsewhere) had been enacted, not in opposition to the will of the people, but pursuant to it.[46]

Hamilton recognized that an essential step in this process would be to offer a comprehensive reconceptualization of the constitutional system, one that would turn traditional constitutional understandings on their head. As the people had proved a weak vessel with which to entrust the task of holding legislatures within constitutional bounds, Hamilton now declared that contrary to a great deal of conventional wisdom, the people themselves were actually bound by their own constitutions. He argued that it was simply not true that the people's interpretation of what their

themselves are unfit for their own government;" quoted in Michael J. Klarman, *The Framer's Coup: The Making of the United States Constitution* (Oxford, Oxford University Press, 2016), 73 (from a Washington letter written to Henry Lee October 31, 1786). See also Gordon Wood, Creation of the American Republic, 409–13 ("Yet there were some Americans who perceived that the problems of the 1780s' were not due to the drifting and unrepresentative character of the legislatures, but were rather due to the legislatures very representativeness. The distresses of the period, in other words, did not arise because the people-at-large had been forsaken by their legislatures, 'but because their transient and indigested sentiments have been too implicitly adopted.'"), 409–10

44 "Second Letter from Phocion," in Syrett (ed.), Papers of Alexander Hamilton, III, 530–58.

45 Max Farrand (ed.), *Records of the Federal Convention of 1787* (New Haven, Ct., Yale University Press, c. 1966), II, 299. For more details on Hamilton's views, see Chapter 2 above.

46 See in general, Wood, Creation of the American Republic, 400–13.

constitutions required could "sanctify" the acts of the legislature. In this open letter to the public, however, Hamilton did not go so far as to indicate how, institutionally, the task of binding the sovereign people to their constitutions might be accomplished, but his arguments in Rutgers, framed during these same months, suggest that he was certainly considering the courts to be one real possibility. Among other matters, his description of the constitutional system fundamentally recast the relationship of the people to their legislatures. His brilliant attack on traditional constitutionalism, and vivid depiction of what, at this point, was an aspirational constitutionalism, is worth quoting in full.

> Among the extravagancies with which these prolific times abound, we hear it often said that the constitution being the creature of the people, their sense with respect to any measure, if it even stand in opposition to the constitution, will sanctify and make it right.
>
> Happily, for us, in this country, the position is not to be controverted; that the constitution is the creature of the people; but it does not follow that they are not bound by it, while they suffer it to continue in force; nor does it follow, that the legislature, which is, on the other hand, a creature of the constitution, can depart from it, on any presumption of the contrary sense of the people.
>
> The constitution is the compact made between the society at large and each individual. The society therefore, cannot without breach of faith and injustice, refuse to any individual, a single advantage which he derives under that compact, no more than one man can refuse to perform his agreement with another. If the community have good reasons for abrogating the old compact, and establishing a new one, it undoubtedly has a right to do it; but until the compact is dissolved with the same solemnity and certainty with which it was made, the society, as well as individuals, are bound by it.
>
> All the authority of the legislature is delegated to them under the constitution; their rights and powers are there defined; if they exceed them, tis a treasonable usurpation upon the power and majesty of the people; and by the same rule that they may take away from a single individual the rights he claims under the constitution, they may erect themselves into perpetual dictators. The sense of the people, if urged in justification of the measure, must be considered as a mere pretext; for that sense cannot appear to them in a form so explicit and authoritative, as the constitution under which they act; and if it could appear with equal authority, it could only bind, when it had been preceded by a declared change in the form of government.[47]

Hamilton had begun to assert that constitutions were, in effect, a kind of (legally) binding contract of all with all, which the legislature could not alter even at the behest of a majority of the people. The people were bound by

[47] "Second Letter from Phocion" (April 1784), in Syrett (ed.), Papers of Alexander Hamilton, III, 530–58.

their constitutions as much as their legislatures were, unless and until they first acted to "dissolve [the constitution] with the same solemnity and certainty with which it was made" and changed the "form of government," a very high hurdle. In an inspired twist, Hamilton declared that if the legislature passed an unconstitutional act "tis a treasonable usurpation upon the power and majesty of the people," even if it was perfectly clear that the legislature had done so in order to carry out what a majority of the people actually wanted. Evidently, the people had two entirely different kinds of wills, one a superior, permanent, fixed will embodied in their constitutions; the other a changeable, inferior, temporary will, carried by their legislatures. The changing views and sentiments of the people could not authorize legislatures to go beyond the bounds of the constitution. The question that Hamilton's reconceptualization inevitably raised was, who would have the interpretive authority to determine whether legislatures (and the people) had gone too far? In a quite real sense, the ultimate power over the laws would rest with them, rather than with legislatures or the people themselves.

This would be a constitutional system, Hamilton thought, that would address a number of the most serious problems republican governments now faced, including perhaps the knottiest: the propensity of the sovereign people themselves to be swept away by dangerous, momentary passions, and in these situations to "seldom judge or determine right"[48]– by explicitly binding the people to the limitations on legislation contained in their own constitutions.

The *Rutgers* case, as already mentioned, was filed in February, 1784, Hamilton presented his plea to the court in April, but in May the legislature passed a bill "to extend the remedy" of the Trespass Act, to cover defendants who had withdrawn themselves from the state.[49] After the British army evacuated New York City, the legislature began to hold its sessions there. In the small municipality that the city was at the time,[50] members of the legislature would almost certainly have been aware of the growing controversy over *Rutgers*.[51] If so, they nevertheless proceeded to

[48] From Hamilton's remarks at the Federal Convention, in Farrand (ed.), Records of the Federal Convention, II, 299.

[49] See *Laws of the State of New York, passed at the First Meeting of the Seventh Session of the Legislature,* Chap. 54, 700–2 (May 4, 1784).

[50] In 1776 the population of New York City was approximately 25,000 inhabitants, growing by 1790 to approximately 33,000.

[51] Goebel, Law Practice of Alexander Hamilton, I, 292–94 ("The already incendiary Whig-Tory nature of *Rutgers* was enlivened when the Attorney General of New York, Egbert Benson, with John Lawrence, took the plaintiffs case. *Rutgers* to the man in the street became a melodrama the plot of which involved an aged Patriot widow who was done out

re-affirm their original decision to enact the Trespass Act by extending the act's reach, even after the pleadings in that case had been filed. In itself, the legislature's decision did not appear to provoke a wider controversy. In January, the Council of Revision had vetoed two bills on the ground (among others) that they conflicted with the Law of Nations and/or the Provisional Treaty of Peace,[52] but nearly a year earlier, the Council had approved the original Trespass Act, and now they also found that the new remedial extension of the act "does not appear improper to the Council ... [and] should ... become [a] Law[] of this State."[53] Unlike the earlier situation in the New Jersey case of *Holmes* v. *Walton*, where the legislature moved quickly to attempt to remedy a constitutional problem that had been pointed out by arguments presented in a case pending before the courts, in New York, despite the growing controversy over *Rutgers*, both the legislature and the Council of Revision were apparently of the opinion, even upon second reflection, that the Trespass Act posed no serious difficulties. Alexander Hamilton was definitely not of the same view.

6.1 HAMILTON'S LEGAL ARGUMENTS: VISIONARY AND TRADITIONAL

Hamilton's argument that Waddington should not be "answerable" for occupying the Rutgers property during the war consisted of a number of intricately interwoven strands. The first involved a complicated argument about the Law of Nations. Although the treatise writers disagreed among themselves about the rule, Hamilton argued that "the best Writers will tell us – The Fruits [of real property] *during the possession* belong to the Conqueror."[54] Hence, occupiers who had held under license from the

of her property by two prosperous British merchants .... Public interest in the case became even more intense when, along with Brockholst Livingston and Morgan Lewis, Alexander Hamilton was retained as defense counsel. The political air was still brisk with the stinging arraignment published only a month before by Hamilton ... in his 'Letter from Phocion' ....")

[52] Ibid., I, 288, 292; and Street, Council of Revision Vetoes, 247, 248.

[53] *Journal of the Assembly of the State of New York, At their first Meeting of the Seventh Session, begun and holden at the City Hall in the City of New York, on Tuesday the sixth Day of January*, 1784 (New York: Printed by E. Holt, Printer to the State, 1784), May 5, 1784, 159–60.

[54] Hamilton's arguments are laid out in six surviving briefs from his papers, which are reprinted in Goebel, Law Practice, I, 338–91, but are also summarized in Duane's opinion in the case, which is also reprinted in ibid., I, 392–419. None of the briefs are dated and on pages 331–38 Goebel presents a convincing analysis of why he has arranged them in the order he has. In addition, only the first brief is specifically labelled *Rutgers*

invaders should not be liable to returning Patriots for rent, as rents from these properties properly belonged to the conquerors during their occupation. But this argument immediately encountered a problem. Whatever the correct rule under the Law of Nations might be, was it conceivable that that customary rule enjoyed the force of law in New York State? To answer this problem, Hamilton contended that the Law of Nations was part of the common law, and that as Article XXXV of the New York Constitution of 1777 had adopted the common law, the Law of Nations became in that way part of the law of the land in New York.[55] But this argument raised another problem. Article XXXV of the New York Constitution of 1777 explicitly subjected all these laws "to such alterations ... as the legislature of the state shall, from time to time, make concerning the same."[56] It would seem that the same Article of the New York Constitution that had made the Law of Nations part of New York law had also granted the legislature power to alter it, in precisely the ways the Trespass Act arguably had. As a result, Hamilton was forced to add one more epicycle to his already complex argument in an attempt to show that while the Law of Nations was indeed part of the law of the state, the New York legislature lacked the power to alter it. This is where his argument began to tip into the visionary.

The New York Constitution recited the text of the Declaration of Independence in its preamble and concluded by declaring that the [New York] convention "approve[d] the same and ... join[ed] with the other colonies in supporting it."[57] Hamilton contended that this pronouncement had brought the State of New York into existence as part of the union. Under the Declaration of Independence "which [,Hamilton avowed,] is the fundamental constitution of every state, the UNITED STATES assert their power to levy war conclude peace and contract alliances all which is acceded to by the NEW YORK CONVENTION."[58] Only Congress has "full power to levy war, conclude peace, contract alliances ... [and] to do all other acts and things which

v. Waddington, and here too Goebel demonstrates pretty convincingly that they were all prepared by Hamilton at various times to be used in the Rutgers case. The quote is drawn from Brief No. 6, which may only have been prepared for the appeal, but makes the point that Hamilton has made in earlier briefs, ibid., 369.

55 Thorpe, Constitutions, V, 2635 (Article XXXV of the 1777 New York Constitution), and Hamilton briefs in Goebel, Law Practice, I, 346, 347–48, 353, 368.

56 Thorpe, Constitutions, V, 2635.

57 Ibid., 2625–28 (Quoted from the Preamble to New York Constitution of 1777).

58 Quoted from Hamilton Brief No. 6 in Goebel, Law Practice, I, 374.

independent States may of right do."[59] From the beginning, Hamilton maintained, New York and the other states existed, in their external relations, only through the union. His case notes put the matter this way.

> Our sovereignty began by a Foederal act– Externally exists only in the Union
> Declar of Ind: which is FUND constitution of each state asserts the Power of Congress to *levy war conclude peace contract alliances*
> New York Convention approves
> Congress then had in fact complete Sovereignty–[60]

Hamilton argued that in theory no individual nation enjoyed power to alter the Law of Nations, but "If such a power does exist in our Government tis in Congress,"[61] as the Law of Nations came under Congress' exclusive jurisdiction over the external relations of the country. Individual states simply had no power to alter the Law of Nations. Consequently, if a state legislature enacted a law with the express intention and for the purpose of altering the Law of Nations the act would be void.[62] But an analysis of what precisely were the duties of a state court when confronting such a statute in the course of adjudication, he left for another part of his argument, discussed later.

The second prong of Hamilton's argument was devoted to the Treaty of Peace. Making the defendant "answerable" for the trespass charged would, Hamilton maintained, not only violate the Law of Nations, it would also violate the Treaty of Peace. But this argument as well immediately encountered a difficulty. The Treaty of Peace did not have any provision that expressly covered the situation in *Rutgers*. The closest was the amnesty agreed to by Article 6.

> That there shall be no future confiscations made nor any prosecutions commenced against any person or persons for, or by reason of, the part which he or they may have taken in the present war, and that no person shall on that account suffer any future loss or damage, either in his person, liberty, or property . . . .[63]

[59] Quoted from Declaration of Independence.
[60] Quoted from Brief No. 3, Goebel, Law Practice, I, 349; in brief No. 6 (ibid., at I, 374) Hamilton elaborates on all these points.
[61] Quoted from Brief No. 3, ibid., I, 351, 356; see also Brief No. 6, ibid., I, 378–79 ("for Congress have the exclusive direction of our foreign affairs & of all matters relating to the Laws of Nations . . . . No single state has any legal jurisdiction to alter them.")
[62] Brief No. 3, in ibid., I, 352; and Brief No. 6, ibid., I, 382.
[63] Quoted from Article 6 of "The Definitive Treaty of Peace of 1783" (The Paris Peace Treaty), in http://avalon.law.yale.edu/18th_century/paris.asp

Article 6 only prohibited prosecutions of persons "for, or by reason of, the part which he or they may have taken in the present war." Under a strict reading of this language, running a private brewery during the war would hardly seem to qualify. Here again, Hamilton had to supplement his case, arguing that under the Law of Nations peace treaties always implied a general amnesty for acts related to the war, and in this case the act relating to the war was the occupation of New York itself, and the defendant's holding property by virtue of that occupation.

But larger questions loomed. Even if the Trespass Act conflicted with the Treaty of Peace, was the Treaty actually a law, and even if it was a law of the Confederation, was it a law that bound New York State? The duty of state courts was to enforce state law. At this point, Hamilton conjured into existence a federal system that did not yet exist.

> Congress have the exclusive right of war & peace
> Congress have made a Treaty of peace pursuant to their power
> A breach of the treaty is a violation of their constitution[al]
> authority & a breach of the Confederation

But perhaps more significantly, the Treaty, according to Hamilton, was actually law, and not only law but a superior law that bound the state.

> The power of Congress in making Treaties is of a Legislative kind
> Their proclamation enjoining the observance of it is a law.
> And a law Paramount to that of any particular state .... [as] Each
> State has delegated all power of this kind to Congress.[64]

But given all this, what was the duty and authority of a state court? And here, crucially, Hamilton's argument simultaneously looked backward to a British constitutional tradition in which judges possessed the power to declare laws of subordinate jurisdictions void if they did not conform to the laws of the superior government, but also forward to the Supremacy Clause of the Federal Constitution of 1787, which did not yet exist.

If the Mayor's Court found the Trespass Act to be irreconcilably in conflict with the Law of Nations or the Treaty of Peace, Hamilton argued, the judges would enjoy the power and have the duty to declare that act void, because, as unlikely as this might seem, they should operate as judges of the United States, enforcing that jurisdiction's "paramount" law

[64] Brief No. 6 in Goebel, Law Practice, I, 377–78.

against subordinate state law.[65] The judicial review, Hamilton was contending for here, was primarily of the traditional "vertical" variety. His case notes in *Rutgers* indicate that in justifying judicial review in this 1784 case, he mainly relied on these traditional constitutional assumptions.

> We might as well say a particular County has a right to alter the Laws of the state as a particular state the laws of the Confederation–[66]
> While the Confederation exists a law of a particular state derogating from its constitutional authority is *no law*
> But how are the judges to decide – They are servants of the state?
>
> Answer. The CONFEDERATION vesting no judicial powers in Congress . . . .
> The judges of each state must of necessity be judges of the United States–
> And they must take notice of the law of Congress as a part of the law of the land – [67]

Hamilton also cited Coke's report of Bonham's case, in his notes, but as "a Rule of Construction of Statutes,"[68] noting that Coke gave "several strong examples in which statutes have been adjudged void."[69] In Brief No. 6, he cited Bonham's case again. The point he was contending for here and in the earlier brief, however, was that the court must interpret the Trespass Act to be consistent with rather than in conflict with the Law of Nations and Treaty of Peace, because if it could not, "[i]f [it found these violations were] intended [by the legislature] the *act is void* – " [citing Bonham's case].[70] The word "void" used in Coke's report of Bonham's case,

[65] Recall that the Articles of Confederation did not establish either an executive or judicial branch. Recall also the language of the Supremacy Clause (Art. VI) of the as yet to be written 1787 Federal Constitution, which replaced the Articles of Confederation. "[A]ll treaties made, or which shall be made, under the Authority of the United States, shall be the supreme Law of the Land; and the judges in every State shall be bound thereby, any Thing in the Constitution or Laws of any State to the Contrary notwithstanding."

[66] Brief No. 6 in Goebel, Law Practice, I, 378; see also same point made in Brief No. 3, ibid., I, 350. This line of thought evokes a statement Madison made several years later at the Federal Convention. ("The states never possessed the essential rights of sovereignty. These were always vested in congress . . . . The states, at present, are only great corporations, having the power of making by-laws, and these are effectual only if they are not contradictory to the general confederation.") in Farrand (ed.), Records of the Federal Convention, I, 471 (Yates Report, June 29, 1787).

[67] Brief No. 6, in Goebel, Law Practice, I, 380, and in Brief No. 3, ibid., I, 351.

[68] Brief No. 3, ibid., I, 357. [69] Ibid., I, 358. [70] Brief No. 6, ibid., I, 382.

was not, however, an argument for holding statutes void, but rather for equitable interpretation. As has been seen, judges used arguments about what was void in conscience or against natural equity to establish the moral foundation for their equitable interpretation of statutes, and this is what Coke did in *Bonham's Case*.[71]

And this is also the way Hamilton appears to have used Bonham's case in his notes. He cited Bonham's case in connection with his argument that the court had a duty to interpret the Trespass Act so that it was consistent with the Law of Nations and Treaty of Peace, but did not invoke Bonham's case as a basis for authorizing the court to deny the force of law to the Trespass Act. Modern historians largely agree that after the publication of Blackstone's Commentaries, most Americans understood the rule in Bonham's case to be a rule of equitable interpretation.[72] Hamilton made no attempt, his notes indicate, to use Bonham's case to build a wider argument for judicial review, beyond the traditional "vertical" review argument he had already made. In this respect, Hamilton's lines of reasoning on these points appear to have been almost completely traditional, relying on long established British constitutional assumptions, and on the prevailing understanding of the rule in Bonham's case.

It may be that the *Rutgers* case did not lend itself to a broad theory of judicial review based on constitutional violations, but (for whatever reason) Hamilton's notes contain no evidence that he had developed such a broader, non-traditional argument for judicial review by 1784. This may seem a little surprising in that the legitimacy of "horizontal" judicial review had been and would continue to be one of the principal issues raised in other state cases during the 1780s, and would be a doctrine and practice crucial for implementing Hamilton's vision of a constitutional system that bound the people themselves. But it serves to drive home the point that such a doctrine and practice were significant innovations only in the early stages of their development. By contrast, in Federalist #78, written just 4 years later, Hamilton demonstrated command of a fully developed set of arguments for the broad ("horizontal" and "vertical") power of judges to deny the force of law to unconstitutional acts, which became, indeed, one of the classic justifications for American judicial review.

71 Hamburger, Law and Judicial Duty, 274, and fn. 45.

72 Ibid., 278; and Goebel, Law Practice, I, 284; Larry Kramer, *The People Themselves: Popular Constitutionalism and Judicial Review* (Oxford, Oxford University Press, 2004), 19–23.

At the time *Rutgers* was being heard, Hamilton must have felt uncertain enough about the chances the judges on the lowly Mayor's Court would take it upon themselves to declare and treat a state statute as not law, that he did not press hard for them to do so. Instead, he used Bonham's case in the traditional way to establish the moral basis for the argument he urged on the court that it had the duty to interpret the Trespass Act so that it was consistent with the Law of Nations and the Treaty of Peace. He made the transition to this equitable interpretation section of his brief in the following way.

> We have seen that to make the Defendant liable would be
> TO VIOLATE the laws of nations & forfeit character
> To violate a solemn treaty of peace & revive state of hostility
> To infringe Confedered & endanger peace of the Union
> Can we suppose all this to have been intended by the Legislature–
> The LAW cannot suppose it
> And if it was intended the act is void![73]
> Many of these Argument[s] suppose Trespass act repugnant to the law of nations-
> It may however receive a construction consistent with all
> And to give it this Construction is the duty of the Court[74]

Hamilton proceeded to demonstrate how that might be done. The language of the Trespass Act was very general, and might be read to impose liability in cases the legislature unquestionably had not intended. The legislature, for example, could not possibly have meant to make American prisoners of war held in New York City liable to pay damages for occupying premises in which the British had confined them. But the bare language of the Trespass Act was broad enough to cover their case. Consequently, the legislature must have intended that there would be exceptions to the act, even where the bare language appeared to cover a case.[75] And where might the court find a rule for identifying those exceptions? The answer seemed clear to Hamilton.

> And if these exceptions must be made where shall we stop, but where the Laws of Nations direct us to stop – short of everything that is a contravention of them?[76]

[73] Brief No. 3 in Goebel, Law Practice, I, 352.

[74] Ibid., these 3 lines actually precede the earlier ones in Hamilton's notes. I have rearranged them in order to present the argument in a more orderly way. Hamilton repeats these points in Brief No. 6, in ibid., I, 381–82.

[75] Brief No. 3, in Goebel, Law Practice, I, 358, and Brief No. 6, ibid., I, 387.

[76] Brief No. 6, ibid., I, 387–88, same points made in Brief No. 3, ibid., I, 358.

It was the duty of the court, Hamilton argued, to construe the legislature's intention so that conflicts between the Trespass Act and the Law of Nations or Treaty of Peace would be avoided, and the way to do that was to hold that the Trespass Act stated a general rule, but that exceptions to that rule were defined by the Law of Nations and the Treaty of Peace.

6.2 DUANE'S OPINION AND BLACKSTONE'S COMMENTARIES

Arguments in the case were heard on June 29. Upon their conclusion, the court adjourned to take time to deliberate on the issues, entering a *Curia Advisare vult*. It delivered its judgment a month and a half later on August 17, and its full opinion, written by Duane, ten days after that on August 27.[77] As is well known, Duane seems to have split the difference, holding defendant liable for rent during the period Waddington occupied the brewery under license from the Commissary General (who had no authority under the Law of Nations to issue such a license, Duane held, and during which no rent was paid), but accepting defendant's legal justification for the period Waddington paid rent for the brewery under a direct license from the British military Commander (who did have, according to Duane, the authority under the Law of Nations to issue such a license). Significantly, Duane found the defendant's plea under the Treaty of Peace to be legally insufficient, refusing to endorse Hamilton's even more deeply controversial claim that the Treaty of Peace was not only law, but law that was paramount, and that bound the state of New York.[78]

The Trespass Act, of course, specifically prohibited the pleading of "any military order or command whatever of the enemy [to justify] such occupancy … nor [permitted defendants] to give the same in evidence … ."[79] In accepting defendant's plea under the Law of Nations for the period the Rutgers property had been occupied under license from the British military Commander, Duane would

[77] Ibid., I, 306; Goebel transcribed Duane's opinion from a pamphlet that had been printed in 1784, see "Arguments and Judgment of the Mayor's Court of the City of New-York, in a Cause between Elizabeth Rutgers and Joshua Waddington" (New York, Printed by Samuel Loudon, 1784), https://quod.lib.umich.edu/e/evans/N14804.0001.001/1:3?rgn=div1;view=fulltext

[78] Goebel, Law Practice, I, 306.

[79] "Trespass Act," March, 1783, "AN ACT for granting a more effectual relief in cases of certain trespasses," *Laws of the State of New York Passed in The Second Meeting of the Sixth Session of the Legislature*, CHAP. 31, 552 (March 17, 1783).

seem to have "disregarded" a clear statutory rule enacted by the legislature. His action pointedly raised the question whether a court had authority to "disregard" a "known" law of the state in reaching its judgment, and if so on what grounds might it do so. It is important to see that despite taking this step, Duane felt it essential to bring his opinion clearly within the bounds of the still dominant, traditional understanding of the proper relation of courts to legislatures. As Blackstone put it, judges were "sworn to determine, not according to [their] own private judgment, but according to the known laws and customs of the land; *not delegated to pronounce a new law*, but to maintain and expound the old one"[80] (emphasis added). Judges had the duty to maintain and interpret the known laws of the land, not to make or repeal laws. Those powers lay exclusively in the legislature. Formally adhering to this understanding, Duane implicitly rejected Hamilton's arguments that the court possessed the power to declare the Trespass Act not to be law – on any ground. As Hamilton probably anticipated, however, Duane was favorably impressed by his equitable interpretation argument.

Following Hamilton's lead, Duane found that the New York Constitution, by adopting the common law, had made the Law of Nations part of New York law. He also accepted Hamilton's reading of the Law of Nations: that it provided a legal justification for trespasses licensed by the military commander of a conquering foreign army. Arguably, however, the Trespass Act had altered this rule of the Law of Nations, and Hamilton's response to that issue had been to say that the legislature simply had no power to do so. But in order to keep his opinion within the parameters of the dominant constitutional understanding that legislatures possessed plenary authority to enact, alter, or repeal laws of the state, Duane had to reject, if only implicitly, Hamilton's position. He held, instead, that there was no express evidence that the legislature had intended to alter or repeal this rule under the Law of Nations when it enacted the Trespass Act, implying that had they clearly so intended, they would certainly have had the power to do so.[81] Duane concluded this section of his opinion by holding that both the Law of Nations and the Trespass Act continued to enjoy the force of law in New York.

80 William Blackstone, *Commentaries on the Laws of England* (1765) (Facsimile edition, Chicago, University of Chicago Press, 1979), I, 69.

81 "Opinion of the Mayor's Court," reprinted in Goebel, Law Practice, I, 417.

This determination also gave Duane the opening he needed. The only legitimate authority judges exercised over statutes, under traditional understandings, was that based on their power to expound the law in connection with deciding a case. In cases like the one before him, in which two laws conflicted, the power to expound the law might authorize a judge to choose to enforce one, and to disregard the other, in order to reach a determination. Blackstone had said as much.

But Hamilton had also pointed out an alternative method for dealing with the problem of two apparently conflicting legal rules. Use the judge's interpretive authority to declare one to be the general rule, and the other to be an exception to that rule, giving effect, in a fashion, to both. And to begin with Duane seemed to deploy his interpretive authority in this way.

> [I]t seems to be agreed, on both sides, that the provision in the [Trespass] statute, being general, cannot extend to all *cases:* and must therefore receive a *reasonable interpretation* according to the *intention*; and not according to the *latitude of expression* of the legislature: It follows as a necessary consequence, that the interpretation is the province of the court, and, however difficult the task, that we are bound to perform it.[82] (italics in original)

Duane went on to hold that

> [w]hoever then is *clearly exempted* from the operation of this statute [the Trespass Act] by the law of nations, this Court must take it for granted, could never have been *intended* to be comprehended within it by the Legislature.[83] (italics in original)

Evidently, Duane seems to have felt that even when framed this way, the court's act of refusing to enforce the Trespass Act was likely to be greeted, under prevailing constitutional assumptions, as an illegitimate exercise of judicial power, and a challenge to the legislature's supreme authority to make and repeal law. He went out of his way to emphasize and reemphasize that the court's opinion was based squarely on its traditional authority to expound the law, and was sanctioned even by such an ardent supporter of legislative supremacy as Blackstone himself. Drawing directly on Blackstone's tenth Rule of Construction,[84] Duane wrote,

[82] "Opinion of the Mayor's Court," reprinted ibid., I, 414.
[83] "Opinion of the Mayor's Court," reprinted ibid., I, 418.
[84] Blackstone, Commentaries, I, 91.

[t]he supremacy of the Legislature need not be called into question; if they think fit *positively* to enact a law, there is no power which can controul them. When the main object of such a law is clearly expressed, and the intention manifest, the Judges are not at liberty, altho' it appears to them to be *unreasonable,* to reject it: for this were to set the *judicial* above the legislative, which would be subversive of all government.

But when a law is expressed in *general words,* and some *collateral matter,* which happens to arise from those general words is *unreasonable,* there the Judges are in decency to conclude, that the consequences were not foreseen by the Legislature; and therefore they are at liberty to expound the statute by *equity,* and only *quoad hoc* to *disregard* it.

When the judicial make these distinctions, they do not controul the Legislature; they endeavor to give their *intention* it's [sic] proper effect.[85] (italics in original)

But in attempting to place his opinion on firmer (traditional) constitutional grounds, Duane, it seems, went too far. Rather than relying exclusively on a rules and exceptions formulation, he now, perhaps inadvertently, acknowledged that the court had, in effect, found the Trespass Act to be "unreasonable" when applied to the facts, and as a result, had "disregarded" it.[86]

In general, Duane was highly sympathetic to Hamilton's views about the Trespass Act, but presumably also felt that it was crucial for his opinion formally to adhere to conventional constitutional norms about the proper relationship of courts to legislatures. In a sense, he wanted to have it both ways, to expand the power of judges to offer a remedy when they confronted "unreasonable" statutes, while denying that he was seeking to do so. He must have hoped, in vain as it turned out, that resting his opinion on Blackstone's rule of construction would insulate his effort from criticism. He may have forgotten that Blackstone had also said of judges' interpretive powers that

[t]he liberty of considering all cases in an equitable light must not be indulged too far, lest thereby we destroy all law, and leave the decision of every question entirely in the breast of the judge. And law, without equity, tho' hard and disagreeable is

[85] "Opinion of the Mayor's Court," reprinted in Goebel, Law Practice, I, 415. It is noteworthy that Hamilton cited Blackstone's *Commentaries* on several occasions in his briefs, including two of Blackstone's "Rules of Construction," but he studiously avoided all mention of Blackstone's legislative supremacy Rule 10, upon which Duane rested his opinion. See Hamilton's Brief No. 2 in Goebel, Law Practice, I, 340, Brief No. 3, 353, 355, and Brief No. 6, 363, 368, 384, 386.

[86] Duane also devoted nearly a full page of his opinion to justifying the court's view of the Trespass Act as "unreasonable," given that the Council of Revision had found the Act "does not appear improper to the Council." See "Opinion of the Mayor's Court," reprinted in Goebel, Law Practice, I, 416.

much more desirable for the public good, than equity without law; which would make every judge a legislator, and introduce infinite confusion ....[87]

Duane's critics, however, had not forgotten. The central thrust of Blackstone's *Commentaries* had always been to vindicate the claim that legislatures possessed the plenary power to make and unmake the laws, and to deny that judges possessed any authority to act as legislators by doing the same.

As important as Hamilton's arguments and the Court's opinion may be for our understanding of the significance of the *Rutgers* case, the reaction to Duane's Opinion in the city and in the legislature are perhaps even more important. They reveal just how controversial and at odds with the terms of the existing constitutional system Duane's opinion was commonly understood to be, and how it was viewed as posing a direct threat to the constitutional relationships of governance that had prevailed in American republics until then.

6.3 DEFENDING THE TRADITIONAL CONSTITUTION AGAINST A JUDICIARY TESTING THE LIMITS OF ITS LEGITIMATE POWERS

Pursuant to the judgment and opinion of the Mayor's Court a jury was convened on September 2, 1784, "at Simmon's tavern, near the City Hall, to ascertain the sum due from Mr. Waddington, for the occupation of the estate belonging to the Rutger's [sic] family in Maiden-lane, when the inquest gave a verdict of seven hundred and ninety-one pounds thirteen shillings and four pence, to be paid by Mr. Waddington,"[88] a small fraction of the eight thousand pounds for which Mrs. Rutgers had sued.[89] On September 7, within days of the announcement of damages, "a meeting of a number of the Citizens of New York" took place at "Mrs. Vandewater's" to consider what steps should be taken in reaction to "the late decision of the Mayor's Court," which the meeting resolved was "a matter pregnant with the most mischievous consequences."[90] A second meeting at Mrs. Vandewater's appears to have taken place two days later on Thursday, September 9.[91] At that meeting, if not at the first,

[87] Blackstone, Commentaries, I, 62.

[88] See *The New York Packet and the American Advertiser* (Monday, September 6, 1784).

[89] Goebel, Law Practice, I, 218.

[90] See *The Independent Journal Or, The General Advertiser* (New York, Saturday, September 11, 1784).

[91] See *Columbian Herald* (S.C., November 23, 1784) reprinting several September articles from New York newspapers.

a committee of three persons seems to have been appointed, consisting of Mrs. Rutgers' son Anthony and two others, Peter Ricker and Jonathan Lawrence.[92] The meeting(s) resolved that this committee should "prepare and cause to be printed, advertisements, earnestly requesting a (general) meeting of (our fellow) citizens ... to deliberate and determine on the measures necessary to be pursued in this case" to be held the following Monday evening, September 13, at the same location.[93]

The revolutionary spirit that had produced mass meetings to deliberate on events, and extra-legal committees to administer the functions of government prior to the British invasion, reawakened in the city in some measure following the British evacuation. "At a huge meeting on the Common called by the revivified Sons of Liberty in March, [1784]," for example, "speakers urged the massive crowd to expel all Tories by May 1 . . . ."[94] The meetings at Mrs. Vandewater's seem to have been called in the same spirit.

The committee of three published an advertisement for the September 13 meeting in the *Independent Journal* a few days later.[95] In it, they sought to "state more fully the reasons" that made such a meeting necessary, and offered a sophisticated indictment of the Mayor's Court opinion. They began by saying that if the *legislature* had "abrogated" the Trespass Act in deference to "the general usage of nations," they might have disagreed with the decision on policy grounds, but could not have questioned "their right" to do so. On the other hand, "an enlightened, jealous, and free people will surely never consent to a Bench's assuming such a power." For a court to "abrogate" a statute violated separation of powers principles fundamentally, eroding "a clear and insuperable line of distinction between the legislative and

[92] See *Columbian Herald* (S.C., November 23, 1784); and *The Independent Journal Or, The General Advertiser* (New York, Saturday, September 11, 1784).

[93] See *The Independent Journal Or, The General Advertiser* (New York, Saturday, September 11, 1784).

[94] See Chernow, Alexander Hamilton, 197.

[95] This sophisticated critique of the Rutgers opinion, which made a number of the key points that were also made in the better known, more elaborate, critique published later on November 4, 1784, was signed only by the three original committee members, Peter Ricker, Jonathan Lawrence and Anthony Rutgers. Melancton Smith, to whom the November appeal is often attributed, was only added to the committee after this advertisement had been published, See *The Independent Journal Or, The General Advertiser* (New York, Saturday, September 11, 1784); and the *Columbian Herald* (S.C., November 23, 1784).

judicial branches of government . . . ." And the committee worried that the judicial claim to this power might be just plausible enough to undermine, over time, the existing constitutional system. Significantly, they characterized this judicial effort as an "illegal" usurpation of legislative power.

> In what other way can a perversion of the principles of our Constitution be attempted with so much plausibility; consequently with so fair a chance of success as by the judicial bodies gradually exceeding their legal limits, assuming legislative powers . . . .[96]

The committee continued by pointing out that the Trespass Act was "clearly and strongly expressed," and that it had just recently been "reviewed, enlarged and confirmed by the very last Session of the Legislature." If a citizen could not reliably "proceed upon" such a law, "then it may be fruitless to take such methods as our laws direct in any other respects for the security or recovery of our property." Such an "unnatural conjunction" of powers as the judges now sought would undermine our "boasted privilege of making our own laws, the operation of which we are incapable of foreseeing, because we do not know how conformable they may be to *indeterminate laws of nations,* or to other laws and opinions by which the judge may chuse to interpret them" (italics in original).

The committee had put together, in a few days, a sophisticated, comprehensive indictment of the Mayor's Court Opinion, founded squarely on prevailing constitutional norms. By "abrogating" a law of the state, the court had "illegally" gone beyond the accepted boundaries of its authority, exercising a legislative power to which it was not entitled, and by doing so had rendered property rights insecure, in so far as no citizen could reliably depend, any longer, on existing law to vindicate those rights. In this way, the court's opinion had placed the very rule of law itself in jeopardy. Beyond all this, the Opinion of the Mayor's Court represented an attack on the settled terms of republican governance, threatening to deprive the people of their plenary power, acting through their legislatures, to make the laws by which they were to be governed.

The traditional view then was that courts must administer the law of the land as it was written, they did not possess the authority to question

96 All quotations are from the advertisement for "The Meeting at Vandewater's" published in *The Independent Journal* (New York, Saturday, September 11, 1784), and reprinted in the *Columbian Herald* (S.C.) in the November 23, 1784 issue.

the basis of legislative enactments, let alone the power to "disregard," "dispense with," or otherwise "nullify" them. The British still lived under such a constitutional system in the nineteenth century, and it is worth quoting a high court opinion from that period, in order to bring more fully to life, the way many New Yorkers in the 1780s seem to have seen the behavior of the Mayor's Court, which, on one ground or another, failed or refused to execute a clearly expressed law of the state.

Here is what Lord Justice Willes had to say about the proper relationship of courts to the legislature in *Lee* v. *Bude and Torrington Junction Railway Company*, in 1871.

> [A]s to these Acts of Parliament ... they are the law of the land; and we do not sit here as a court of appeal from Parliament .... If an Act of Parliament has been obtained improperly, it is for the legislature to correct it by repealing it: but, so long as it exists as a law, the courts are bound to obey it. The proceedings here are judicial, not autocratic, which they would be if we could make laws instead of administering them.[97]

The committee formed at Mrs. Vandewater's concluded by urging citizens to attend the meeting on the 13th "to lend their aid in concerting the proper measures to be adopted on an occasion which we conceive may affect their most valuable privileges."[98]

The committee of three was soon expanded to a committee of nine, and now included Melancton Smith, and others whose names are well known to historians from the newspaper appeal "To the People of the State of New York" published in the November 4, 1784 issue of the *The New York Packet and the American Advertiser*.[99] Remarkably, of the nine committee members, three, Anthony Rutgers, Thomas Tucker, and Daniel Shaw, were personally interested in the outcome of the *Rutgers* case; all were plaintiffs (or the child of a plaintiff), in Trespass Act litigation.[100] But Trespass Act prosecutions were even more common than that at this moment in the life of the city. Several Aldermen, who

[97] L.R. 6 C. P. 576 ff (1871), quoted in J. W. Gough, *Fundamental Law in English Constitutional History* (Oxford, Oxford at the Clarendon Press, 1971), 205–6.

[98] Quoted from the advertisement for "The Meeting at Vandewater's" published in *The Independent Journal* (New York, Saturday, September 11, 1784), and reprinted in the *Columbian Herald* (S.C.) (November 23, 1784).

[99] See, for example, Goebel, Law Practice, I, 313 fn. 85, among numerous other cites to that appeal. For the expansion of the committee to nine members see, the *Columbian Herald* (S.C.) (November 23, 1784).

[100] Goebel, Law Practice, I, 313.

themselves sat as judges on the Mayor's Court (by virtue of their office), were also plaintiffs in other Trespass Act cases.[101]

Three days before he issued the Court's judgment in the case, Duane had made a desultory effort to consult with the Aldermen. He had already devoted, he wrote to them, a number of days to "considering the Authorities & Arguments offered by the Counsel on both Sides" and hoped to deliver an opinion the following Tuesday, just three days later. In the meantime, since it had not been "practicable for all the Members of the Court to sit down together to read & consider the Briefs & Authorities," he now made these available in his office "for the Inspection of any of the other Members of the Court who may wish to give them an attentive Perusal & Consideration ... [i]f any of You Gentlemen have Leizure and Inclination and will take the Trouble ... ."[102] Three days later, Duane delivered the judgment of the court, although he did not produce an accompanying opinion until ten days after that. It was unclear how much input into the court's decision the Aldermen had had.

At the September 13 meeting at Mrs. Vandewater's tavern, the committee submitted a surprising report to the chairman of the meeting, in which they stated that they had met with the Aldermen to quiz them about their participation in the court's deliberations, and their opinions about the resulting decision.

> [T]he subscribers waited on the Aldermen of this city ... and desired an answer to the following question, viz. "Had or had not the Mayor your consent that the subject should be deprived of any part of the remedy which the Trespass Law gives, by its literal construction?"[103]

And six Aldermen responded. Alderman Broome had not attended the trial, the committee reported, recusing himself because "he had a case depending on the Trespass Law, and did not chuse to judge of it." It being "a great law question," Alderman Neilson was reported to have said, he did "not conceive himself adequate to judge of the matter" and left it "wholly to the Mayor and Recorder, as the law officers of the Corporation." But three Aldermen, unequivocally, and one, more

[101] For Alderman Broome see the *Columbian Herald* (S.C.) (November 23, 1784); for Alderman Ivers see Goebel, Law Practice, I, 301.

[102] Letter from James Duane to the Aldermen of the City of New York, Aug 14, 1784, ALS, Duane Paper (Ms. LC), as reprinted in Goebel, Law Practice, I, 306.

[103] See *Columbian Herald* (S.C.) (November 23, 1784); and Hamburger, Law and Judicial Duty, 348–49 and fn. 42.

ambiguously, reported that they were in favor of awarding plaintiff full damages, under a literal construction of the Trespass Act. Alderman Lott did not attend the entire trial, he was reported to have said, "but was asked his opinion by the Mayor or Recorder, his answer to them was, that the plaintiff should have the full benefits of the law, agreeable to its literal construction." Aldermen Blag and Ivers answered that "the plaintiffs ... should have full remedy agreeable to the literal construction of the Trespass Act, and were much surprised to find that any distinction of time was held up in favor of the defendant." Unlike Alderman Broome, who had recused himself, Alderman Ivers, who also had a Trespass Act case pending, participated in the proceedings. More ambiguously, Alderman Gilbert was reported to have said that "Rutgers was a proper plaintiff and was entitled to damages from the defendant." Consequently, three, and possibly as many as four, of the seven members of the Mayor's Court who took part in hearing the case would have held fully in favor of plaintiff. Yet, there is not the slightest hint in Duane's opinion that any division of opinion had arisen on the court.[104]

The meeting at Mrs. Vandewater's tavern adopted several resolutions, at least two of which bear mentioning here. In the revolutionary spirit in which the meeting had been called, the committee was charged with writing "circular letters to the different counties." The committee was also authorized to "draught a memorial to the next Legislature," which may have been the reason the Assembly began to take up the question of the propriety of the Mayor's Court's opinion the following month, on October 27.[105]

Not everyone in the city supported these kinds of out of doors actions, however. On the very day the meeting at Mrs. Vandewater's was to take place, September 13, an anonymous appeal "To the Citizens of New York was published in *The New York Packet and the American Advertiser*. It began by saying that "before you accept this invitation, let me request you to reflect on the impropriety and danger of meddling in this business ...."[106] It continued:

> Because a few interested and heated people, are pleased to think the decision, in this case, was contrary to law, and in the face of an act of the Legislature. There are

[104] All quotations in this paragraph are drawn from the report in the *Columbian Herald* (S.C.) (November 23, 1784).

[105] Evans, Early American Imprints, First Series; no. 18649, *Votes and Proceedings of the Assembly of the State of New York* (October–November 1784), 22 (October 27, 1784).

[106] "To the Citizens of New York" published in *The New York Packet and the American Advertiser* (September 13, 1784).

many others, full as good patriots, and of at least as much discernment as they, who think the decision will do honour to the state, and that a contrary one would have fixed upon it the imputation of barbarism.[107]

The anonymous letter then turned to the question of what should be done going forward, even if one believed the *Rutgers* decision to be against law. The remedy, the letter writer said, should not be sought in the streets, or by attempting to pressure the judges, that would be to undermine the critically important independence of the judiciary. The constitutionally correct way to proceed would be to appeal the decision to higher courts, and to have those courts correct any legal errors the Mayor's Court may have committed. This remedy, of course, while preserving the independence of judges, would leave up to the judges themselves the decision about what precisely were the constitutionally legitimate powers of courts. Under this framing of the issue, when courts (appeared to) exceed the bounds of their rightful authority, judges would be the ultimate arbiters of their own powers; judges, as it were, in their own case. This would prove to be a fateful way of conceptualizing the issue of judicial overreach for the future of traditional constitutionalism, placing in immediate jeopardy the idea that legislatures enjoyed the plenary authority to make laws, subject only to supervision by the people themselves. Here is what the anonymous "appeal to the citizens" had to say.

But let it be admitted, that those who think the determination of the Court wrong, are in the right; does it follow that the citizens are to be called together to rectify it? Is not the Mayor's Court an inferior court of limited jurisdiction? And if that Court has erred in a point of law, is there not a natural and easy remedy – an appeal to the Supreme Court by writ of error? If that Court should not reverse but confirm the sentence of the Mayor's Court, is there not still left a further and higher mode of legal and constitutional redress– an appeal to the Court ordained by the thirty second article of the constitution, for the trial of impeachments and the correction of errors? A Court which will consist of one branch of the Legislature, to wit, the Senate, together with the Chancellor, and Judges of the Supreme Court?[108] Can we believe that all these Courts would be in a combination against the laws of the state, and that those who have right on their side could not obtain it in a regular legal channel? What then must we think of the attempt by meetings of the citizens to overawe the decisions of Courts of Justice? . . .. Can we believe [those who instigated these meetings] are not actuated by other motives

[107] Ibid.

[108] The Court for The Correction of Errors had been authorized in the constitution of 1777, but the legislature had not yet passed a bill to institute it. That omission would be corrected a month later when the legislature passed such a bill, following its debate over the *Rutgers* case. Further discussion of these developments follows below.

than a desire to preserve the Judicial authority from infringing on the Legislative?– Can we doubt *what their motives are,* when we see men *deeply interested,* appointed members of the committee .... [If these men succeed] it would destroy the independence of Courts of Justice, which once effected, they would cease to be Courts of Justice.[109] (italics in original)

There are only two constitutionally proper ways to proceed, the anonymous appeal concluded,

[i]f the Judges of the Mayor's Court have acted erroneously, let their error be rectified by an appeal to a higher tribunal; if they have acted corruptly, let them be impeached. This last is the proper business of the Legislature, and let us leave the Legislature to do their own business.[110]

A dispute over whether the Mayor's Court had illegally usurped the constitutional authority of the legislature had been (re)characterized as a question of judicial error. So long as the judges had not acted corruptly, the only constitutionally proper remedy for correcting this sort of "judicial error" was by appeal to a higher court.

The New York Constitution of 1777 was one of only a few early state constitutions to grant the high court judges, and "the first judge of the county court in every county," tenure during good behavior, without also providing for their removal upon address of the legislature.[111] Under the constitution, these judges could only be removed from office by impeachment for "mal and corrupt conduct."[112] The anonymous letter writer seems to have extended this standard even to judges who held their offices "during the pleasure of the council of appointment," as Duane and Varick did.[113] By 1784, the Constitution's treatment of the state's top judges had evidently had a broader influence, contributing to the establishment of a political culture in which the norm of judicial independence appears to have been widely respected, as the unfolding drama in the *Rutgers* case makes clear.

The legislature, however, still operating in a constitutional tradition that left the ultimate decisions about the laws to them (or to the people) was not prepared at this moment completely to defer to the judiciary to

109 "To the Citizens of New York" published in *The New York Packet and the American Advertiser* (September 13, 1784).

110 Ibid.

111 "New York Constitution of 1777," Article XXIV, in Thorpe, Constitutions, V, 2634; see Chapter 2 above for a more detailed discussion of judicial independence under the first state constitutions.

112 "New York Constitution of 1777," Article XXXIII, ibid., V, 2635.

113 Article XXVIII, ibid., V, 2635.

resolve these fundamental constitutional issues. On October 27, 1784, William Harper of Montgomery County made a motion in the Assembly characterizing the Mayor's Court Opinion as saying that a portion of the Trespass Act "was incompatible with the law of nations; and that the plaintiff ought not to recover" for the period defendant occupied the property under order of the British commander.[114] And introduced a resolution in two parts to address the problem.

> *Resolved,* That the adjudication aforesaid, is in its tendency, subversive of all law and good order, and leads directly to anarchy and confusion, because if a court instituted for the benefit and government of a Corporation, may take upon them to dispense with, and act in a direct violation of a plain and known law of the State, all other courts, either superior or inferior, may do the like; and therewith will end all our dear bought rights and privileges, and Legislatures become useless.[115]

Simply put, courts have no authority to "dispense with, and act in direct violation of a plain and known law of the State" and when they do, they undermine the rule of law and open the door to anarchy and confusion.

What remedy for this act of judicial overreach did Harper's resolution propose? As the Mayor (and the Recorder) served at the pleasure of the Council of Appointment, he thought that they should simply be removed from office.[116]

> *Therefore resolved,* That it be recommended to the Honorable the Council of Appointment, at their next appointments, to appoint such persons to be Mayor and Recorder of the City of New York, *as will govern themselves by the known laws of the land.*[117] (emphasis added)

[114] Evans, Early American Imprints, First Series; no. 18649, *Votes and Proceedings of the Assembly of the State of New York, First Meeting of the Eighth Session of the Legislature, Assembly-Chamber, In the City of New York, beginning October 12th, 1784*, 22 (October 27, 1784).

[115] Ibid.

[116] The New York Council of Appointment was composed of 4 senators (one from each "great district") nominated and appointed annually by the Assembly. The governor was to be president of the Council but was only to have a "casting voice" (i.e., a vote only to break a tie). Though the language in the constitutional clause establishing the Council was somewhat ambiguous, by custom the governor nominated all officers ("other than those who, by this constitution are directed to be otherwise appointed"), and the Council voted either to appoint them to office or reject them, see Thorpe, Constitutions, V, 2633–34 (Section XXIII of the New York Constitution of 1777).

[117] Evans, Early American Imprints, First Series; no. 18649, *Votes and Proceedings of the Assembly of the State of New York" (First Meeting of the Eighth Session of the Legislature, Assembly-Chamber, In the City of New York, beginning October 12th, 1784*, 22 (October 27, 1784).

After extended debates, further consideration of Harper's motion was put over to another day. Harper's proposal that Duane and Varick be removed from office for a judicial act performed without corruption would prove to be considerably more controversial among legislators than the general statement of Blackstonian constitutional principle, contained in the first part of his resolution. The question of Harper's motion and resolution was raised again two days later on October 29, and after some discussions, the Assembly found it best to proceed by ascertaining precisely what the Mayor's Court had actually done in the case. As the legislature was sitting in the City at the time, the Assembly ordered the Clerk of the Mayor's Court to appear before it three days later "with the records of the trial."[118]

On November 2, after the records in the case, and Harper's motion and resolutions had been read to the Assembly, a motion was made to amend the words of Harper's original motion to delete the statement that the court had found certain portions of the Trespass Act to be "incompatible with the law of nations" and to add a less inflammatory, more lawyerly, statement of what the court had done. The amended motion simply said that despite the clear language of the statute prohibiting the pleading of military orders in justification of such trespasses, the court had accepted defendant's plea to that effect, and had given judgment accordingly. Following the passage of that amendment, the full text of the first part of Harper's resolution, containing the statement that "the adjudication ... is in its tendency subversive of all law and good order, and leads directly to anarchy and confusion" was read and put to a vote, passing the Assembly easily 25 to 15.[119]

But immediately afterward, the remedy aspect of his resolution, which called for Duane's and Varick's removal from office, failed decisively by a vote of 31 to 9.[120] Evidently, the Assembly was prepared to stand up forthrightly for the traditional constitutional principle that legislatures possessed plenary power to make law, and that judges enjoyed no legitimate authority to "dispense" with such laws, but was not prepared to undermine the independence of the judiciary by removing from office judges who violated that principle, even those who only held their offices at pleasure.

[118] Ibid., 29–30 (October 29, 1784). [119] Ibid., 33 (November 2, 1784).
[120] Ibid., 34 (November 2, 1784).

The Assembly instead leaned toward a more judicious remedy for the problem, one closer to the moderate views propounded by the anonymous letter writer in September, who had come out against the meetings at Mrs. Vandewater's. On the afternoon of the day the Assembly voted upon Assemblyman Harper's resolutions, Assemblyman D'Witt, who had voted against both parts of the resolution, made a motion "that a Committee be appointed to bring in a bill for the institution of a court for the trial of impeachments and correction of errors."[121] The Assembly passed the motion without controversy and ordered "That agreeable to the 32nd and 33rd articles of the constitution a bill be prepared and brought in to institute a court for the trial of impeachments and correction of errors ... " and appointed a committee "to prepare and bring in the same."[122]

The 1777 Constitution had authorized such a court, but the legislature had never passed a statute to implement the constitutional provision. By the terms of the constitution, this court of final resort in the state was to consist of the popularly elected Senate, sitting together with the state's appointed high court judges. In its composition, the court resembled traditional courts of final resort that had operated in many American colonies, and which, were themselves modeled on the British House of Lords.[123] The very make-up of the court should serve as a reminder that New Yorkers were still operating in a constitutional universe whose unspoken ground rules were quite different from modern American ones.

The anonymous September letter writer had obviously been familiar with this highest New York court, accurately describing its composition even before the legislature had actually acted to bring it into being.[124] Since a majority of the court of final appeal in the state would consist of one branch of the popularly elected legislature, that branch, acting in its judicial capacity, would be in an unassailable position to defend the legislature's traditional prerogatives, by reversing as legal error any contrary judicial doctrine. Here was an elegant resolution for the legislature's dilemma as to how to proceed against judges who overreached, without calling judicial independence into question. And it obviously attracted wide support in the legislature, even among some of the less radical

121 Ibid. 122 Ibid.

123 For a fuller discussion of these traditional courts of final resort, see Chapter 3.

124 This court served both as a court for the correction of errors, and as a court for the trial of impeachments. As such, it provided an ultimate remedy for judicial overreach, whether erroneous or corrupt.

Assemblymen like D'Witt, who had voted against Harper's resolutions. All that remained to be done was for the legislature to institute such a court, and the Assembly lost no time in doing so. The same neat resolution, however, would not be available to legislatures in states in which legislative bodies no longer sat on courts of final resort.

On November 13, 1784, the committee appointed for the purpose "brought in a bill, entitled, *An act for instituting a Court for the trial of impeachments and the correction of errors*"[125] (italics in original). After the bill was amended and further debated, it passed both houses of the legislature, and was approved by the Council of Revision on November 24.[126]

A little less than a month after the Assembly had first intervened in the controversy over the decision in the *Rutgers* case, the state had a new court of final resort, itself a feature of traditional constitutionalism, which would leave the New York legislature in a commanding position to defend its traditional powers against attempts by the judiciary to infringe upon them, at least for some decades to come.

On November 2, 1784, the Assembly passed a portion of Harper's resolution, and initiated the legislative process to establish the Court for the Correction of Errors. Two days later, on November 4, the expanded committee appointed at Mrs. Vandewater's in September, moved the controversy beyond the confines of the legislature's chambers, publishing an open appeal "To the PEOPLE of the State of New-York."[127]

Two significant features of the pamphlet length appeal stand out. First, the committee presented a greatly elaborated, comprehensive indictment of the Mayor's Court opinion, together with a sophisticated defense of traditional constitutionalism. But second, the committee's proposals for addressing the problem raised by judicial overreach were now self-consciously confined to the moderate proposals that had been taken up by the legislature, i.e., appeals to higher courts. The committee, did, however, emphasize just how crucial the Court for the Correction of Errors was likely to be for maintaining the integrity of the constitutional system "against judicial tyranny," and how vital, as a result, it would be

[125] *First Meeting of the Eighth Session of the Legislature, Assembly-Chamber, In the City of New York, beginning October 12th, 1784*, 50 (November 13, 1784).

[126] Ibid., 54 (November 16, 1784), 59 (November 17, 1784), 60 (November 18, 1784), 67 (November 22, 1784), 70 (November 24, 1784).

[127] See *The New York Packet and the American Advertiser* (November 4, 1784). This document is entirely familiar to historians of the *Rutgers* case.

for citizens to be certain they were electing the right kind of Senators. The Committee's appeal is worth quoting at length.

The committee rejected, as purely pretextual, the court's claim that it was not "disregarding a known law of the state," but was merely giving effect to the legislature's intention.

> With regard to the meaning and intention of the Legislature, it may be inferred from the very enacting of the law; for in doing that they suppose that as laws before stood, actions could not lie in cases of this nature; to remedy this, they make it lawful for persons described in the act, to bring actions of trespass against, &c. and declare no military authority whatsoever of the enemy shall be plead, or evidenced in justification of the trespass.
>
> No point of controversy can arise on the case but must turn upon the propriety or impropriety of the law itself; not upon its construction .... We can hardly conceive it possible for the legislature to have chosen words that would make the intention of their law more clear.[128]

Consequently, there could be no question that the Court had "assumed and exercised a power to [judge and] set aside an act of the state .... an assumption of power in that Court, which is inconsistent with the nature and genius of our government, and threatening to the liberties of the people."[129] Later in the pamphlet, the committee elaborated on this indictment. Courts do not have authority "whereby they might controul the supreme legislative power .... Such power in the courts would be destructive of liberty and remove all security of property .... [E]very citizen knows what the remedy the laws give him, for every injury. But this cannot be the case, where Courts, if they deem a law to be unreasonable may set it aside."[130] And weaving in another familiar theme, lectured that "[t]he design of courts of justice in our government, from the very nature of their institution, is to declare laws, *not to alter them*. Whenever

128 The quotes and pagination in this and the following paragraphs are drawn from the pamphlet subsequently published by the committee, "An Address from the Committee Appointed at Mrs. Vandewater's on the 13th Day of September, 1784. To the PEOPLE of the STATE of NEW-YORK." (New York, Printed by Shepard Kollock, Opposite the Coffee-House, 1784), Evans, Early American Imprints, 7.

129 Ibid., 6.

130 Although the debate over the *Rutgers* decision was specifically addressed to the question of whether a court had power to disregard a statute it found to be "unreasonable," and did not explicitly address the question whether a determination of unconstitutionality would pose a different case, the expansive political terms in which the critics attacked the court's decision were certainly broad enough to encompass judicial review based on constitutionality, if that question had been more directly posed by the decision in the case.

they depart from this design of their institution, *they confound legislative and judicial powers*"[131] (emphasis added).

The committee continued by describing other evils "which would result from the exercise of such a power in our courts .... [above all] that it would render[] abortive the first and great privilege of freemen, the privilege of making their own laws by their representatives. For if the power of abrogating or altering them be assumed by our courts, and submitted to by the people, then as far as liberty and the security of property are concerned, [the laws duly enacted by the representatives of the people] become ... useless ...."[132]

As for the delicate question of judicial independence, the committee had this to say.

> We do not wish to lessen their independency;– for while they are content to move in their proper sphere, while they speak the plain and obvious meaning of the law, and do not presume to alter it, or explain it to mean any thing or nothing. While in the duties of their real province they cannot be too independent: nor ought they be liable to a removal but for misbehavior. But if they are to be invested with a power to over-rule a plain law, tho' expressed in *general words*, as all general laws are and must be. When they may judge the law unreasonable .... We say, if they are to assume and exercise such a power, the probable consequence of their independence will be, the most deplorable and wretched dependency of the people.
>
> [For the power to make laws "absolute" (i.e., final)] "is not lost in the controversy, but transferred to judges who are independent of the people.[133]

These were all criticisms that contained much truth about the constitutional consequences that would flow from a judicial power to reject duly enacted laws. And the committee saw, correctly, that the establishment of such a power would itself amount to a constitutional revolution. "[We] earnestly ... intreat [all citizens] to join us in a watchfulness against every attempt that may be used, either violently and suddenly, or gently and imperceptibly, to effect a revolution in the spirit and genius of our government ...."[134]

131 Ibid., 10. 132 Ibid., 11.

133 Ibid., 12; this was the second mention of the fact that the assumption of this kind of power by the judges would "transfer" the final word on the laws from legislatures to judges. In a remark that resonates with one James Madison would later make, the committee wrote that "the reasoning of the Court and the reasoning of the legislature may lead them to very different conclusions [about the meaning and coverage of the law], and as the Court reason last upon the case, it is utterly impossible for any man to guess when he brings suit, however exactly it may apply to the law, until ... he obtains the opinion of the Court whether he shall recover or not," at 11.

134 Ibid., 15–16.

But when the committee turned to discuss practical remedies for the problem, it grew a little defensive about the question of the people out of doors, and self-consciously confined proposed remedies to the moderate ones to which the legislature had already turned. "[W]e do not advise our fellow-citizens to measures which are unconstitutional . . . .[135] The mode of redress which our excellent constitution points out is, First, by an appeal to the supreme court, where this cause will be carried by Writ of Error. We feel a confidence from the characters of the gentlemen who preside in that court, the law will have its operation restored in its plain and obvious meaning,"[136] But if that hope "should be disappointed,"

> [t]he next mode pointed out by the constitution, is an appeal to the court of Errors, one part of which the Senate constitute. Preparatory to such an event, we exhort you to be cautious in your future choice of members, that none be elected but those on whom, from long and certain experience you can rely, as men attached to the liberties of America, and firm friends to our law and constitution. Men who will spurn at any proposition that has a tendency to curtail the privileges of the people . . . .[137]

This would be a delicate task for Senators, the committee thought, as they would have to strike the right balance between curtailing judicial overreach, on one hand, and preserving the independence of the courts, on the other. The independence of courts meant that in coming to their decisions, judges should not have to fear either dismissal from office by the legislature, or violence from the people acting out of doors. Citizens would have to choose Senators

> who at the same time, that they protect us against judicial tyranny have wisdom to see the propriety of supporting that necessary independency in courts of justice, both of the legislature and people, without which the fear of dismission from office on the one hand, and of personal violence on the other, might steal their decisions, and render them interested and corrupt.[138]

Defenders of the traditional constitution in New York were placing their ultimate faith in appeals to the Court for the Correction of Errors, which would presumably have the lawful constitutional authority to correct fallacious judicial doctrine about the legitimate scope of the powers judges were entitled to exercise, while preserving the independence of the courts. Sitting on a traditional legislative court of final resort

135 In another paragraph they reinforced this point. "Having confined ourselves to constitutional measures, and now solemnly declaring our disapprobation of all others . . . we feel a freedom in sounding the alarm to our fellow citizens," Ibid., 15.

136 Ibid., 13–14. 137 Ibid., 14. 138 Ibid., 14–15.

made that task relatively straightforward.[139] In states in which old fashioned courts of final appeal no longer existed, however, or in which a legislature's long-standing claim that it could act as such a court had been called into question by developing separation of powers doctrine, that option was not available. And in such situations, increasingly, even where legislatures arguably possessed the constitutional authority to remove judges for acting upon the emerging, revolutionary doctrine of judicial review,[140] a developing American consensus that robust judicial independence was crucial for the impartial delivery of justice, operated in practice to leave legislatures divided, making it considerably less likely that they would, on a consistent basis, be able to muster the votes to take aggressive action against judges, even as many legislators continued to

[139] In a few years, courts of final resort on which one chamber of the legislature sat, became a subject of controversy among other reasons because, as the events surrounding the *Rutgers* case demonstrate, they were likely to undermine the effectiveness of judicial review as a check on legislatures. Defenders of the traditional constitution attacked the newly proposed Federal Constitution in the ratification debates in New York on a number of grounds, one of which was that it did not include a court of final resort constituted in the way New York's was. One of *Brutus'* primary objections to the Federal Constitution was that by failing to include such a court, no constitutional power existed to "correct" the errors of the judges of the new U.S. Supreme Court. Echoing the controversy over judicial independence in New York a few years earlier in connection with the *Rutgers* case, *Brutus* went on to say that the framers "have made the judges *independent*, in the fullest sense of the word. There is no power above them, to control any of their decisions. There is no authority that can remove them, and they cannot be controlled by the laws of the legislature. In short, they are independent of the people, of the legislature, and of every power under heaven. Men placed in this situation will generally soon feel themselves independent of heaven itself," *Brutus*, XV, 20 March 1788, in Ralph Ketcham (ed.), *The Anti-Federalist Papers and the Constitutional Convention Debates* (New York, Signet Classics, 2003, c. 1986), 305. Advocates for the new constitution and for judicial review, like Hamilton, responded to *Brutus'* charges, arguing that such courts might not only violate separation of powers principles, but were a bad idea for other reasons as well, acknowledging, at the same time, that "one of the branches of the legislature," constituted the court of final resort, "in the government of Great Britain and in that of this State," #81 Federalist, Clinton Rossiter (ed.), *The Federalist Papers* (New York, Mentor Books, 1999, c. 1961), 451. At least from the time of *Rutgers*, both traditional constitutionalists and advocates of judicial review realized that the effectiveness of the emerging judicial practice might well hinge, to some degree, on whether legislators continued to serve on courts of final resort.

[140] In the *Rutgers* case, for example, Mayor Duane and Recorder Varick formally held their offices at the pleasure of the Council of Appointment. In other states, even judges who held their offices during good behavior were subject to removal by the legislature "upon address," or by impeachment, not only for "mal and corrupt conduct," but for "mal-administration." This subject is addressed at greater length in later chapters.

believe (as in New York) that, in principle, those judges had illegitimately usurped the authority of the legislature.

By the time the committee appointed at Mrs. Vandewater's had published its open letter on November 4, the plaintiff in the *Rutgers* case (as well possibly as the defendant) had already sued out a Writ of Error to the (New York) Supreme Court.[141] Before the Supreme Court could issue a decision, however, the case was apparently settled for an undisclosed sum; a new lawyer for the defendant noting that "the [case's] Determination [is] by no means certain."[142] Goebel wrote that "[a]s is evident from the calendar of cases, what happened in other Trespass Act suits is uncertain. [On one hand] [s]urely *Rutgers* was a precedent for cases in the Mayor's Court .... [But on the other] [p]resumably, after *Rutgers*, more cases were brought in the Supreme Court than in the Mayor's Court .... because the precedent made victory through the Mayor's Court uncertain"[143] (italics in original).

6.4 LEGISLATIVE REPEAL OF THE CONTROVERSIAL PROVISIONS OF THE TRESPASS ACT

The *Rutgers* case, however, did have a definitive final chapter. After rejecting an earlier attempt to run him for the New York Assembly, Hamilton finally agreed to stand for office in 1786, and was elected in April to a one-year Assembly term.[144] "Hamilton told [Robert] Troup he had stood for election because he planned to 'render the next session' of the Assembly 'subservient to the change he meditated.'"[145] And he was good to his word.

The editors of the Hamilton papers write that "[i]n May, 1786, John Jay, Secretary for Foreign Affairs, wrote to Governor George Clinton requesting information on the compliance of New York with a congressional resolution of January 14, 1784, which called on the several states to repeal all laws inconsistent with the [newly ratified] treaty of peace between the United States and Great Britain."[146] Clinton replied by sending Jay entries from the Assembly and Senate Journals of March 30 and 31, 1784, which essentially rebuffed Congress's request.[147]

[141] Goebel, Law Practice, I, 310–11 (October 10, 1784). [142] Ibid., 311.

[143] Ibid., 523.

[144] Chernow, Alexander Hamilton, 219, 221. In the 1780s, annual elections for the Assembly were held during the last days of April, and sessions of the legislature often ran through April of the following year.

[145] Ibid., 221–22.

[146] Syrett (ed.), Papers of Alexander Hamilton, IV, 22, editor's note 2.

[147] Ibid. Duane's reluctance to adopt Hamilton's Treaty arguments in his decision in *Rutgers* delivered in August 1784, a few months after the New York legislature had

The following January, 1787, the New York Assembly, with Hamilton now seated, adopted a resolution recommending the appointment of a committee "to consider and report on" the letter Jay had sent to Governor Clinton, and on two statutes, the Citation Act of 1782, and the Trespass Act passed in March, 1783. The Assembly proceeded to appoint Hamilton, and a number of other members, to a newly formed committee "to consider and report on" those matters.[148] On March 10, "Mr. Hamilton from the Committee . . . reported, that it is the opinion of the said committee, that so much of the [Trespass] Act . . . as declares that no military order shall be pleaded or given in evidence in justification of the defendant, ought to be repealed . . . " and that the committee had drawn up a bill for that purpose. The Assembly agreed to the committee report, and allowed Hamilton to bring in his bill.[149]

On March 21, Hamilton addressed the Assembly, attempting to convince that body to pass the Trespass Act repeal bill. His most persuasive argument must certainly have been that passing the bill might help persuade the British to abandon the posts they still maintained on New York's frontiers in retaliation for what they perceived to be continuing violations of the treaty by the United States. But he also dusted off his arguments in the Rutgers case to make the point that the sections of the Trespass Act he sought to repeal placed New York judges in an impossible position.

> Col. Hamilton said that this amendment to the trespass law, was only to repeal that part which was in violation of the public treaty. The courts of justice were at present in a delicate dilemma, obliged either *to explain away* a positive law of the state or openly violate the national faith by counteracting the very words and spirit of the treaties now in existence . . . .[150] (emphasis added)

It is striking that Hamilton chose to characterize his equitable interpretation argument in the *Rutgers* case, and Duane's exposition of the

made its resistance to Congress' resolution clear, may have reflected his prudent desire to avoid a direct confrontation with the legislature on that subject.

148 *Journal of the Assembly of the State of New York, at their TENTH SESSION, begun and holden in the City of New York, the Twelfth Day of January, 1787* (New York, Printed by Samuel and John Loudon, Printers to the State, 1787), 20 (January 23, 1787); see also, Syrett (ed.), Papers of Alexander Hamilton, IV, 21.

149 *Journal of the Assembly of the State of New York, at their TENTH SESSION, begun and holden in the City of New York, the Twelfth Day of January, 1787* (New York, Printed by Samuel and John Loudon, Printers to the State, 1787), 91 (March 10, 1787); see also, Syrett (ed.), Papers of Alexander Hamilton, IV, 112.

150 Hamilton, "New York Assembly. Remarks on an Act for Repealing Part of the Trespass Act," delivered March 21, 1787, reported in *The [New York] Daily Advertiser*, March 23, 1787, reprinted in Syrett (ed.), Papers of Alexander Hamilton, IV, 121.

Trespass Act itself, not simply as *explaining*, but as "*explaining away* a positive law of the state," an evaluation with which Duane's critics would probably have agreed. On April 4, the legislature did pass the bill into law,[151] and Hamilton must have felt a sense of vindication that his arguments in the *Rutgers* case had finally played a role in rendering the despised section of the Trespass Act "not law." But this outcome also represented a kind of defeat. To achieve his goal, Hamilton had had to play by the rules of the traditional constitution; the Trespass Act had continued to operate as the law of the land, despite the treaty, until, as the traditional constitutional script required, the legislature was persuaded to repeal it.

And when later in the same month, Hamilton attempted to push further, the legislature rebuffed his efforts. On March 21, 1787, the Confederation Congress had again called on the states to "repeal all acts repugnant to the treaty of peace." In response, on April 13 a bill was introduced in the Assembly calling for the repeal of all state laws inconsistent with the treaty.[152] Among other disputes, disagreements arose about how this might be accomplished. One Assemblyman thought that "the laws [that were actually being repealed] should be mentioned particularly."[153] Hamilton reassured the Assembly that he believed "there was no law in direct opposition to the treaty, [and hence] no difficulty could arise from passing the bill."[154] But just in case, he thought it should be left up to the judges to make the decisions about which specific statutes, or parts of statutes, actually violated the treaty, and had, consequently, been repealed by the legislature under the general terms of the bill. And he argued that the legislature should not fear turning over this kind of power to the courts, as the judges already performed the task of expounding the laws in a wide variety of situations, as a normal part of their duty to decide cases according to the laws of the land.[155]

The proposed law would do two things, according to Hamilton. It would formally make the Treaty of Peace the law of New York, and

[151] "An ACT to repeal Part of an Act, entitled, An Act for granting a more effectual Relief, in Cases of certain Trespasses," Ch. LXXI, passed April 4, 1787, in *Laws of the State of New York Passed by the Legislature at their Tenth Session*, 496.

[152] Hamilton, "New York Assembly. Remarks on an Act Repealing Laws Inconsistent with the Treaty of Peace" (April 17, 1787), reported in *The [New York] Daily Advertiser*, April 23, 1787, reprinted in Syrett (ed.), Papers of Alexander Hamilton, IV, 150–52, see also editors' note 1, at 152–53.

[153] Ibid., 153 editors' note 3. [154] Ibid., 150, Hamilton repeated the point on 151.

[155] Ibid., 152.

would, in addition, declare it to be paramount to other New York laws. Any state law in conflict with the treaty was declared repealed. But it would be left up to the judges to decide which statutes actually to "do away" with, as Hamilton put it.[156] Recall that in *Rutgers*, Hamilton had argued that the treaty was the law of the land and paramount to other laws, and consequently that the court could declare conflicting portions of the Trespass Act "not law." But Duane had refused to adopt this part of Hamilton's argument. Now, the legislature stood on the verge of formally enacting Hamilton's position into law, and by doing so would strengthen immeasurably the New York judges' claim that they legitimately possessed the power to declare statutes they determined to be in conflict with the treaty, not law, in this case by giving effect to the legislature's expressed intention to repeal them.

In this bill, the New York Legislature would have brought into being a form of judicial review that bore a notable resemblance to the one that was actually brought into being under the Supremacy Clause of the Federal Constitution, just a year later. Hamilton had argued in support of the New York bill that "as all treaties were known by the constitution as the laws of the land, so must the judges act on the same, any law to the contrary notwithstanding."[157]

The Supremacy Clause presumed to settle the still controversial question of whether constitutions were actually a form of ordinary, though paramount, law cognizable by judges, or whether they were instead a form of fundamental law, for violations of which only the people were entitled to seek redress, by expressly declaring the Federal Constitution to be the "Law of the Land." Many state constitutions did not explicitly say this, nor did most of them expressly declare duly enacted statutes that conflicted with their terms to be void. Did statutes that conflicted with such constitutions remain the law of the land until legislatures reconsidered their judgments of constitutionality, and repealed them? The Supremacy Clause explicitly stated not only that the Federal Constitution was the Law of the Land, but that it was the "supreme Law of the Land," and that state judges were bound to obey it, anything in their constitutions or laws to the contrary notwithstanding.[158] State judges would now have a considerably stronger claim that when they engaged in judicial review, under the Federal Constitution, they were not exercising legislative powers but merely executing their duty to

[156] Ibid. [157] Ibid., 151–52.

[158] The Constitution of the United States of America, Article VI, paragraph 2.

expound the laws to decide cases, by determining whether an inferior law was in conflict with a superior law, and hence void. The adoption of the Federal Constitution, with its Supremacy Clause, and with its Article III definition of the judicial power as extending to cases arising under the constitution, almost certainly had a broader impact on American constitutional culture. It bolstered the claim that whether constitutions explicitly said so or not, they were indeed "the supreme Law of the Land," and in doing so placed the case for judicial review on considerably firmer foundations.

But on the evidence of the events surrounding the *Rutgers* case, traditional constitutionalism was still well entrenched in New York political culture, and for this reason, as well as for a number of others, the New York legislature refused to go along with Hamilton's proposal; the repeal bill passed the Assembly, but failed to secure the necessary votes in the Senate.[159] New York judges would not be deciding whether to "do away" with duly enacted New York statutes on the ground they conflicted with the treaty of peace anytime soon. The legislature, which had expressly repealed the controversial section of the Trespass Act shortly before, refused to cede to the judges its plenary power to determine which were the binding laws of the state in other cases. The following month Hamilton headed off to the Federal Convention.

[159] Hamilton, "New York Assembly. Remarks on an Act Repealing Laws Inconsistent with the Treaty of Peace" (April 17, 1787), reported in *The [New York] Daily Advertiser*, April 23, 1787, reprinted in Syrett (ed.), Papers of Alexander Hamilton, IV, 153 fn. 3.

7

The Successful Battle to Establish Judicial Review in New Hampshire: The Ten Pound Act Cases, 1786–1787, and Their Aftermath

In the years immediately following the end of the Revolutionary War, the united states experienced a severe economic downturn, brought on by a variety of causes, that included British commercial retaliation, a collapse in domestic demand following the end of fighting, the flight of hard currency abroad, and a large increase in state taxes to pay off the war debt.[1] "Per capita gross national product plummeted nearly 50 percent in the fifteen years after Americans declared independence."[2] In response to these hard economic times, a number of states enacted debtor relief legislation of various kinds, which became, along with anti-Loyalist laws, the second major impetus for the further development of judicial review.

The New Hampshire legislature was reasonably judicious in its response to the crisis; like Massachusetts, it refused to adopt paper money to facilitate the repayment of debts. In the fall of 1785, however, the New Hampshire legislature did enact two relatively modest reforms in an attempt to address the grim economic situation. On November 8, it passed "An Act To prevent the Bodies of Debtors from being taken on execution" when they could tender real or personal property in kind to satisfy the debt.[3] The act's preamble declared that given "the present

[1] For an excellent summary of the causes, see Michael J. Klarman, *The Framer's Coup: The Making of the United States Constitution* (Oxford, Oxford University Press, 2016), 75–76.

[2] Ibid., 75.

[3] "An Act To prevent the Bodies of Debtors from being taken on execution, when real or personal estate can be found, or is tendered, to satisfy the demand," *New Hampshire Session Laws* (November 8, 1785).

scarcity of cash, it is extremely difficult for debtors to discharge the demands against them, in silver and gold," and it would consequently "be very injurious" to continue to allow creditors to "commit[] persons to prison" where they can find or the debtor can tender real or personal property to discharge the debt.[4]

The second statute, passed the following day, November 9, 1785, made it simpler and less expensive to bring actions to recover debts. Rather than forcing creditors and debtors to travel to a county Inferior Court of Common Pleas, where their claims would be adjudicated following common law formalities, which often required a lawyer, and included the expense of seating a jury, the new act authorized local justices of the peace, "in the town where [they] reside[]," to adjudicate summarily (without a jury) "all actions of debt and trespass, where the title of land is not concerned" up to the value of ten pounds.[5] Until then, New Hampshire had strictly adhered to the traditional English rule that justices of the peace were only authorized to hear cases summarily up to the value of two pounds (forty shillings).[6]

Although the act has sometimes been characterized as one of those pro-debtor laws that states passed during this period, it is far from clear that it should be understood that way. The act did provide relief for debtors in so far as it lowered the costs of defending suits, but it also made it easier and less expensive for creditors to bring such cases. In fact, it was debtors, rather than creditors, who initiated most of the first constitutional challenges to the Ten Pound Act.

In addressing the upsurge in debt collection cases, brought on by the economic crisis, the legislature appears to have been interested in reducing for all parties what legislators seem to have considered the unnecessary legal costs that ordinarily attended the process of collecting "small debts." If the measure was "radical," it was not in so far as it provided blanket relief to debtors, but because it paid too little regard to legal formality, reflecting a widespread antipathy toward lawyers and their fees that was then common in New Hampshire.[7] To many in the state, simple republican justice seemed superior to the elaborate legal refinements and

[4] Ibid.

[5] "An Act For the recovery of small Debts, in an expeditious way and manner," *New Hampshire Session Laws* (November 9, 1785).

[6] This subject has been discussed at length in connection with the New Jersey case of *Holmes* v. *Walton* in Chapter 4.

[7] See John Phillip Reid, *Legislating the Courts: Judicial Dependence in Early National New Hampshire* (DeKalb, Ill., Northern Illinois University Press, 2009), 123–31.

accompanying expenses that characterized common law adjudication. At the same time, many prominent New Hampshire lawyers and judges felt just as strongly that legal formality was essential for the preservation of property and liberty rights in a small republic. "At one end," John Phillip Reid writes, "were those who wanted a government of law defined and administered by men educated in the common-law jurisprudence of England, making rulings and applying principles without regard for the politics of day. Against them, at the other extreme, were people who mistrusted the law of professional lawyers and wanted all law to originate from republican institutions . . . ."[8]

It is important to understand another aspect of the New Hampshire Ten Pound Act. The act did authorize parties who had lost a case before a justice of the peace, to appeal that judgment to the Inferior Court of Common Pleas for the county, where they would be entitled to have the suit re-tried and re-decided de novo by a jury. Under the act, however, parties could not bring cases to the Court of Common Pleas *in the first instance*, if the amount in controversy was less than 5 pounds. In those cases, they could only have them tried, to begin with, by a justice of the peace, acting without a jury. For amounts between 5 and 10 pounds, plaintiffs could choose between initiating their actions before a justice of the peace, or before the common pleas court of the county. Before the Ten Pound Act had been passed, the people of New Hampshire had had a legal right to have their debt cases tried by a jury in a common pleas court initially in any situation in which the amount in controversy was greater than 2 pounds. In the interests of making the collection of "small debts" less expensive, the legislature had unquestionably curtailed the scope of the right to a jury trial somewhat–at least at the first stage of adjudication.

Almost immediately, it became obvious that this change in the scope of the legal right to trial by jury in New Hampshire appeared to conflict with language in the new state constitution, which had been adopted just a year earlier in 1784. Article XX of the Bill of Rights of the New Hampshire constitution declared: "In all controversies concerning property, and in all suits between two or more persons, *except in cases in which it has been heretofore otherwise used and practiced, the parties have a right to a trial by jury*; and this method of procedure shall be held sacred"[9] (emphasis added). The constitutional provision evidently aimed to freeze the scope of

[8] Ibid., 4.

[9] Article XX, Bill of Rights, Constitution of New Hampshire, 1784, in Francis Thorpe (ed.), *The Federal and State Constitutions, Colonial Charters, and Other Organic Laws of the*

the right to jury trials as it had been at the time the constitution was adopted: any party in a case that involved more than 2 pounds should have a right to have their case decided by a jury. The day the Ten Pound Act was enacted, however, only one legislator, William Plumer, entered an objection to its passage, recalling, many years later, that he had done so "principally on the ground that it was unconstitutional."[10]

After the Ten Pound Act took effect, creditors regularly brought debt cases involving more than 2 pounds to local justices of the peace, where they were adjudicated summarily. Historians have reconstructed a number of these cases in exquisite detail.[11] In *Wallace* v. *Tarlton*, initially brought in January 1786, the lawyer Samuel Sherburne who represented the defendant debtor, appealed the award of nine pounds in damages by a justice of the peace to the next sitting of the Inferior Court of Common Pleas of Rockingham County, seeking a de novo jury trial. When that new trial again resulted in a damages award against his client, this time for slightly in excess of 2 pounds, Sherburne tried a new approach, probably for the first time, moving the Court of Common Pleas to arrest the judgment, on the ground that the action had been initiated in violation of the constitution.[12] The court reported him as saying that

> at the Time of Forming the present Constitution for this State it was & for a Long time before even beyond the Memory of man it had been the Law & Custom of this State for Inferior Courts to Try all Matters of more than forty shillings Value & for Justices of the peace to Try only Civil Matters under that value & by the Same Constitution it is Declared that all Trials of Property should be as had before that time been used & Accustomed & this Action being brought Against the Express Letter & Spirit of [the] constitution & Against the Law of the Land .... Judgment ought to be arrested.[13]

States, Territories and Colonies (Washington, D.C., Government Printing Office, 1909, Reprint Buffalo, N.Y., William S. Hein, 1993), IV, 2456.

[10] Albert Stillman Batchellor (ed.), *Early State Papers of New Hampshire, including the Constitution of 1784, Journals of the Senate and House of Representatives, etc.* (Manchester, N.H, J. B. Clark, Public Printer, 1891), XX, 450 (Journal of the House of Representatives, November 9, 1785); and William Plumer, Jr., *Life of William Plumer* (Boston, 1859, repr. Da Capo Press, New York, 1969), 59; see also Philip Hamburger, *Law and Judicial Duty* (Cambridge, Mass., Harvard University Press, 2008), 424 and fn. 70.

[11] See Richard M. Lambert, "The 'Ten Pound Act' Cases and the Origins of Judicial Review in NH," 43 *New Hampshire Bar Journal*, 37 (2002); and Hamburger, Law and Judicial Duty, 422–35.

[12] Hamburger, Law and Judicial Duty, 425–26; and Lambert, "Ten Pound Act Cases," 41.

[13] NHSA, Rockingham County Inferior Court, Minute Book, New Entries, February term 1786, Case No. 13, quoted in Hamburger, Law and Judicial Duty, 426.

Sherburne's plea did not expressly mention the Ten Pound Act, arguing only that the action had been brought in violation of the constitution, but the implication that the statute could not have conferred the necessary authority on the justice because it conflicted with the language of the constitution, must have been clear enough. The Rockingham Court of Common Pleas took Sherburne's motion under advisement and waited until its May term to deliver a decision, when it ruled, agreeing with Sherburne, that the judgment "ought to be Arrested."[14]

In a second case, tried by a justice of the peace beginning a month later in March, and continuing into April 1786, *Macgregore* v. *Furber*, the plaintiff sued the defendant to recover ten pounds. At the trial before the justice of the peace, the lawyer for the defendant, John Sullivan, who was also a prominent state political figure,[15] pleaded, in an argument resembling the one Sherburne had made just the month before, that the justice of the peace

> "ought not to take cognizance of this Action" because the plaintiff's claim was for more than forty shillings, and the Bill of Rights had "guaranteed a continuance of Tryal by Jury in all Cases where Tryals by Jury had been practiced."[16]

But on this occasion, plaintiff's lawyer answered by asserting that the statute itself, as the existing law of the land, conferred legal authority on the justice to hear cases up to ten pounds, and that rightly interpreted, the statute did not conflict with the constitution. The justice of the peace, plaintiff Macgregore's lawyer argued, "'has a right and ought to take cognizance of the said Writ and declaration,' first because of the 'late Law of this State' and, second ... because the Constitution did not "say that in Causes triable of more than forty shillings value, that the party shall have right to trial by Jury *in the first instance*'" (emphasis added). The defendant remained free to appeal his case to the Inferior Court of Common Pleas, where he would be fully entitled to a jury trial de novo. By defending the constitutionality of the statute, plaintiff's lawyer had placed the issue of its validity squarely before the justice of the peace, who proceeded to reject the defendant's challenge to his jurisdiction, and to hold a trial, where he awarded plaintiff Macgregore the ten pounds he had demanded.[17]

[14] Ibid.

[15] Speaker of the House, and President elect of the state at the time, see Lambert, "Ten Pound Act," 41 (*Macgregore* v. *Furber*).

[16] Hamburger, Law and Judicial Duty, 427, quoting from Certified Record of Judgment, NHSA, Rockingham County Superior Court Record No. 9320

[17] Ibid.; and Lambert, "Ten Pound Act," 42–43.

The defendant debtor's lawyer, John Sullivan, immediately appealed the decision to the Rockingham County Inferior Court of Common Pleas, where at its May term the court proceeded to reverse the justice's decision, on the ground that plaintiff's action could not be maintained, because the Ten Pound Act "empowering" the justice to hear it was ineffective to confer that authority, as it conflicted with the terms of the constitution.

> [I]t Appearing to the Court that the Act of the Legislature impowering a Justice to hear & Determine Civil Actions of More than Forty Shillings is Manifestly Contrary to the Constitution of this State & this Action being originally Commenced before a Justice for more than forty Shillings ... Plt James McGregore [should] take nothing by his Writ.[18]

During its May term the Rockingham Inferior Court of Common Pleas made rulings similar to this one in at least 5 different cases, holding, explicitly or implicitly, that the Ten Pound Act was (legally) ineffective to confer jurisdiction on justices of the peace, when the amount in controversy exceeded forty shillings, because the statute conflicted with the scope of the right to jury trials conferred by the constitution.[19]

These were primitive statements of judicial review, which did not clearly specify the constitutional premises on which they rested. In general, it was far from settled at the time[20] that constitutions (legally) limited the power of legislatures to confer the force of law on their enactments, or to the extent they were thought in some abstract sense to limit their power, that legislatures nevertheless had the final interpretive authority to say definitively what those limitations were, subject only to review by the people themselves. Nor was it clear why judges, unlike anyone else, could ignore a duly enacted law of the state, simply because they had formed an opinion that it conflicted with the constitution.

But in another case brought in Rockingham County during these spring months of 1786, *Treferrin* v. *Cate*, the lawyer Samuel Sherburne,[21] who

[18] NHSA, Rockingham County Inferior Court, Minute Book, New Entries, May term 1786, Case No. 51, quoted in Hamburger, Law and Judicial Duty, 427–28.

[19] *Wallace* v. *Tarlton*, *Bartlet* v. *French*, *Macgregore* v. *Furber*, *Treferrin* v. *Cate*, *Furber* v. *Mason*, see Lambert, "Ten Pound Act Cases," 40–44; Hamburger, Law and Judicial Duty, 425–29.

[20] See in particular, the discussions in Chapters 2 and 3.

[21] After changing his name to John Samuel Sherburne to avoid being confused with a different Samuel Sherburne, he went on to become a prominent figure in New Hampshire, a Congressman, U.S. District Attorney, and Federal District Court Judge, see Hamburger, Law and Judicial Duty, 425 fn. 75; and Reid, Legislating the Courts, 62, 93–98, 101, 102, 103–4.

was representing yet another defendant debtor in a Ten Pound Act case, went on to elaborate, in considerably greater detail, the constitutional premises underlying his claim that the Ten Pound Act did not possess the force of law. Sherburne argued to the justice of the peace,

> 1st that the Constitution of this State is the source from whence all Legislative Power flows –
>
> 2d. That the Legislative of course cannot exercise a Power which is not deriv'd from the constitution –
>
> 3d. that every attempt of the Legislature to exercise a Power not deriv'd from the Constitution is A Tyranical usurpation of an Authority never delegated to them and an infringement of the Peoples Liberty. A treasonable conspiracy against the Constitution and no Law –
>
> 4th. That the Constitution has not vested the Legislature with Power to enable Justices to try causes of more than forty shillings Value[;] consequently the aforesaid Statute is an Arbitrary & unwarranted usurpation and cannot have the force of Law –
>
> 5th. because the first buddings of Tyranny ought to be carefully *watched by the Judicial Courts of this State which are the constitutional Barriers between the Power of the Legislature and the liberty of the People* and ought early to be blasted before they increase to A size that may involve the People in the dark shades of slavery – (emphasis added)

The justice of the peace rejected Sherburne's argument, finding in favor of the plaintiff creditor, and his judgment, like the others discussed earlier, was appealed to the Rockingham County Court of Common Pleas, where it too was reversed. Once again, the court held that "the Act of the Legislature impowering a Justice to hear and Determine Civil Actions of more than Forty Shillings is Manifestly contrary to the Constitution of this State,"[22] and consequently that plaintiff could not maintain his action under it.

7.1 SHERBURNE'S ARGUMENT AND THE NEW HAMPSHIRE CONSTITUTION OF 1784

By the time the new "Bill of Rights" and "Form of Government" had been adopted in New Hampshire in 1784, prevailing constitutional ideas and usages had evolved significantly in parts of New England, weakening the conceptual foundations upon which traditional constitutionalism rested,

22 NHSA, Rockingham County Inferior Court, Minute Book, New Entries, May term 1786, Case No. 113, quoted in Hamburger, Law and Judicial Duty, 428–29; and in Lambert, "Ten Pound Act Cases," 44-5.

and making Sherburne's argument seem considerably more plausible, less controversial, and more solidly grounded in "commonsense," than it might have been even a few years earlier.

In 1776, after the royal governor had fled New Hampshire, the people elected a representative body, a congress, to establish a new form of government. Declaring themselves to be "*WE, the members of the congress of New Hampshire*, [and] chosen and appointed by the free suffrages of the people ... and authorized and empowered by them ... to establish some form of government ... ." proceeded to do just that[23] (emphasis added). They drafted a new constitution and put it into effect without first submitting it to the people for their approval. As *THE* representatives of the people, this body then transformed itself into a legislature, "RESOLV[ING] that this Congress assume the name, power and authority of a house of Representatives or Assembly for the *Colony of New-Hampshire.*"[24] At the time, many would not have considered these actions to be a usurpation of the rights of the people, because it was commonly taken for granted that there was little distance between the people and their elected representatives. Their elected representatives, it was often supposed, carried on as an embodiment of the people themselves. As such, it mattered little whether they exercised their powers as a congress, convention, or legislature. As a result, constitutions were often considered to be a product of the people acting through their representatives, just as legislation was.

By contrast, the language in the constitution of 1784 reflected a significantly different set of attitudes. It declared that it was the work of the people themselves, rather than of their representatives. "The people inhabiting ... New-Hampshire, do hereby solemnly and mutually agree with each other, to form themselves into a free, sovereign, and independent Body-politic, or State, by the name of the State of New Hampshire."[25] The distance between these two formulations marked the profound changes that had taken place in constitutional culture, institutions, and text in New Hampshire (and elsewhere in New England) between 1776 and 1784.

Gordon Wood, who has done so much to explain these changes, wrote that "[i]t was in two ... New England states ... Massachusetts and New Hampshire, that the modern conception of the people's creating and

[23] Constitution of New Hampshire 1776, in Thorpe (ed.), Constitutions, IV, 2451, and fn. a.
[24] Ibid., IV, 2452. [25] Ibid., IV, 2458.

amending their constitution through special institutional representation and through personal ratification was most fully developed."[26]

In the fall of 1776 three-fourths of the Massachusetts towns that responded to an appeal by the House of Representatives favored granting authority to the General Court [the legislature] to form a new constitution for the state. For some dissidents, however, the idea that the General Court could by itself "enact" a constitution which was supposed to be its controller was intolerable.[27]

These dissidents pressed for two critical innovations. First, to have a new constitution drafted by an entirely separate representative body, a convention, that would be elected by the widest possible suffrage, and have as its only purpose the writing of a constitution before it would cease to exist. But second, once that had been done, to present the draft of that constitution directly to the people, seeking their approval before it could be put into effect.[28]

The Massachusetts House of Representatives rejected the call to have the new constitution written by a separate convention, but did implement the idea that any draft it developed would have to be ratified by a vote of at least two thirds of those who were free and twenty-one.[29]

By 1778 such personal ratification was no longer sufficient and the Constitution enacted by the [Massachusetts] General Court in 1778 was rejected by a five to one majority of towns, partly because it had not been drafted by a separate body. Boston was now convinced that the legislature had no business at all in making a constitution. "A Convention for *this* and *this alone*, whose existence is known no longer than the Constitution is forming, can have no prepossessions in their own favour."[30]

Pauline Maier has written of these developments that

[t]he alternative, embraced by several towns throughout Massachusetts, was for the people to elect delegates to a special convention whose only purpose would be to draft a constitution, which would then be ratified directly by the people of the towns. In that way the constitution would draw its authority clearly and unequivocally from the sovereign people, which would make it superior to the ordinary laws enacted by legislatures .... A constitution created and ratified in the Massachusetts way was literally a direct act of

[26] Gordon Wood, *The Creation of the American Republic, 1776–1787* (Chapel Hill, N.C., University of North Carolina Press, 1969), 339.
[27] Ibid., 340.
[28] Pauline Maier, *Ratification: The People Debate the Constitution, 1787–88* (New York, Simon & Schuster, 2010), 138–40.
[29] Wood, *Creation of the American Republic*, 340–41. [30] Ibid., 341.

legislation by the people, a fundamental law distinct from the ordinary laws passed by a legislature.[31]

In New Hampshire in 1776, when the provisional Congress put the constitution it had drafted into effect, and turned itself into a legislature, the negative reaction it provoked was nearly as deep as in Massachusetts.[32] "The same intense mistrust of the existing legislature that was leading other Americans to the convocation of separate bodies eventually compelled the New Hampshire Assembly in February 1778 to call for a special convention to form a permanent constitution, which was to be approved by three-fourths of the inhabitants in their town meetings."[33] Thereafter, the people of New Hampshire, in their town meetings, deliberated upon, and argued over several proposed constitutions.

> [After rejecting one proposed constitution in 1779, a] new Constitution, was framed by another convention in 1781 and submitted to the people for a necessary two-thirds approval. The people in their town meetings rejected this 1781 Constitution, and another in 1782, before the Convention, empowered to continue in session until an acceptable constitution was framed, devised a form of government in 1783 that was finally ratified by the requisite majority of the people.[34]

A number of the most important of the new ideas found their way into the text of New Hampshire's 1784 Constitution. Article VIII of the Bill of Rights declared: "All power residing originally in, and being derived from the people, all the magistrates and officers of government, are their substitutes and agents, and at all times accountable to them."[35] As for the legislature, the constitution affirmed that the people had granted them very broad powers to make law, "as they may judge for the benefit and welfare of this state," but had also imposed a fundamental limitation, found expressly only in two earlier constitutions.[36] "[F]ull power and authority are hereby given and granted to the said [legislature] . . . to make, ordain and establish, all manner of wholesome and reasonable orders, laws, statutes, ordinances, directions and instructions . . . ; *so as the same*

[31] Maier, Ratification, 139–40. [32] Wood, Creation of the American Republic, 341.
[33] Ibid., 341–42. [34] Ibid., 342.
[35] New Hampshire Constitution of 1784, Bill of Rights, Art. VIII, in Thorpe (ed.), Constitutions, IV, 2454.
[36] The Georgia Constitution of 1777, and the Massachusetts Constitution of 1780, from the latter of which New Hampshire's 1784 constitution borrowed heavily; see Chapter 2 for an extended discussion of the word "repugnancy" in the first constitutions.

be not repugnant, or contrary to this constitution"[37] (emphasis added). The constitution made explicit that legislative power was exercised as a direct grant from the people, but that the people were also imposing a specific limitation on that power; the laws should not be "repugnant or contrary to this constitution." Finally, the constitution expressly stated that it was to "be a part of the laws of the land,"[38] arguably moving it from the realm of fundamental "political law"[39] (appropriate only for the people themselves to enforce against their governments) into the realm of judicially cognizable "ordinary" law, except in this case, "law" promulgated directly by the people themselves, and consequently superior to any laws the legislature might enact. In one respect, however, the 1784 constitution had not advanced beyond earlier ones. It provided no institutional mechanism to enforce its terms, beyond directing that a new constitutional convention be called after seven years in order "[t]o preserve an effectual adherence to the *principles* of the constitution, and to correct any violation thereof, as well as to make such alterations therein, as from experience may be found necessary" (emphasis added).[40]

In a sense, the argument Sherburne made filled an obvious gap, offering an institutional mechanism to enforce these explicit constitutional limitations. The first four parts of his plea followed the text of the constitution itself closely. The constitution is an act of the people themselves that has been promulgated as a law of the land. All governmental power originates in and is derived from the people. The people granted their legislature broad power to enact laws, withholding from them, however, the authority to make laws that conflict with the constitution itself. Hence, having been delegated no power to enact a statute that contradicts the constitution, such a statute cannot possess the force of law.

This much is straightforward. In the fifth part of his plea, however, Sherburne attempted to complete his argument for judicial review, by demonstrating that courts were the body that possessed the legitimate authority to enforce the constitutional limits the people had imposed on

[37] New Hampshire Constitution of 1784, "The General Court" section of "The Form of Government," in Thorpe (ed.), Constitutions, IV, 2458.

[38] New Hampshire Constitution of 1784, "The Form of Government," in ibid., IV, 2470; the constitution also stated that "no alteration shall be made in this constitution before the same shall be laid before [the people]."

[39] On the characteristics of "political law," see Larry Kramer, *The People Themselves: Popular Constitutionalism and Judicial Review* (Oxford, Oxford University Press, 2004), 24.

[40] New Hampshire Constitution of 1784 (final paragraph), in Thorpe (ed.), Constitutions, IV, 2470.

their legislature. He asserted that the "Judicial Courts . . . are the constitutional Barriers between the Power of the Legislature and the liberty of the People," but did not describe the constitutional bases for this claim, which many, at the time, would not have found to be self-evident.

To begin with, the judges were not elected by the people; how could they possibly represent them more faithfully than their own annually elected legislators. Besides, the people's representatives had already determined (presumably) that the statute they were enacting complied with the *principles* of the constitution. In the case of the Ten Pound Act, the House of Representatives would pass a resolution explicitly saying so just a month later.[41] And one lawyer had already mounted a pretty good argument that the statute and constitution, when rightly interpreted, were not in conflict with one another. Presumably there were other possible interpretations as well. The act, for example, it might be argued, represented a trivial reduction in the scope of the right to a trial by jury, and consequently did not violate the *principles* of the constitution in so far as it was justified by the benefits it brought to the polity as a whole in the midst of a crisis. Recall that in the Virginia *Case of the Prisoners*, the lawyers had produced a variety of plausible interpretations showing that the statute either was or was not in conflict with the constitution, and the court had seriously considered these before deploying its interpretive authority to find that the statue was not in conflict with the constitution.[42]

Sherburne himself admitted in the fifth part of his plea that the statute represented only a minor infringement of the constitution, and a number of the act's opponents seem to have agreed. They nevertheless insisted that it was crucial to stop even such minor violations of the constitution lest they inevitably lead to tyranny. A September 1786 newspaper appeal "To the Inhabitants of the State of New Hampshire," for example, observed that the "encroachment" "was a trifling one," but went on to say that "the designing make that a precedent for a much greater . . . . If the legislative body have power to destroy one Trial by Jury, I aver, they have the same power to declare one of their members king . . . ."[43] In his plea, Sherburne made a similarly over heated slippery slope argument. "[T]he first buddings of Tyranny ought to be carefully watched . . . [and] ought early to be

[41] "Journal of the House of Representatives" (June 16, 1786) in Batchellor (ed.), Early State Papers of New Hampshire, XX, 653.

[42] See discussion of the *Case of the Prisoners* in Chapter 5.

[43] *The New Hampshire Mercury* (September 6, 1786).

blasted before they increase to A size that may involve the People in the dark shades of slavery."[44]

But a clear majority in the House of Representatives, and at least one lawyer doubted whether the statute violated the constitution.[45] In light of these interpretive disagreements, what was to be found in the constitution to justify Sherburne's claim that the judges' interpretive authority on the matter could displace the legislature's, entitling them to declare, in their official capacity, that a duly enacted law of the land was in conflict with the constitution, and did not consequently possess the force of law, or bind either the judges or the parties who had come before them. But Sherburne did not flesh out this part of his argument, did not explain why, under the constitution, judges might possess this kind of authority. Nor did he specify what in the constitution supported his claim that the "judicial courts" "are the constitutional Barriers between the Power of the Legislature and the liberty of the People."

By this time, however, there was a powerful common-sense logic to his position, a logic that had been brought into being by the developments in constitutional culture, practices, and text that had occurred in New Hampshire (and elsewhere) over the previous few years. The constitution of 1784 had explicitly said that it was being promulgated by the people themselves and was a law of the land. The laws of the legislature and the law of the people were now clearly separate and distinct. Legislatures simply had no role in making, or changing the law of the constitution. And the people had expressly withheld from them the power to make a law that was repugnant to it.

As for the role of the courts under the new constitution, the Bill of Rights declared that: "In the government of this state, the three essential powers thereof, to wit, the legislative, executive and judicial, ought to be kept as separate from and independent of each other, as the nature of a free government will admit . . . ."[46] Drawing on well-established common law conceptions, the convention that drafted the constitution had explained what each of these three separate and essential powers of

44 5th section of Sherburne's Plea, Record of Trial before Justice of the Peace Joseph Parsons (May 20, 1786), certified by Parsons to Rockingham County Inferior Court, NHSA, Rockingham County Superior Court Record No. 9347, quoted in Hamburger, Law and Judicial Duty, 428; also quoted in Lambert, "Ten Pound Act Cases," 44.

45 "Journal of the House of Representatives" (June 16, 1786), in Batchellor (ed.), Early State Papers of New Hampshire, XX, 653.

46 Article XXXVII of The Bill of Rights of the New Hampshire Constitution of 1784, in Thorpe (ed.), Constitutions, IV, 2457.

government consisted in: "The Legislative, or power of making laws,– The Judicial, or power of expounding and applying them to each particular case – And the Executive, to carry them into effect ...."[47] The address of the Constitutional Convention went on to add that "[i]f the Legislative and Judicial power should be united, the maker of the law would be the interpreter thereof, and might make it speak what language best pleased him, to the total abolition of justice .... These several powers should ... be independent; in order to which they are formed with a mutual check upon each other."[48]

The constitutional duty of the judiciary was to expound and apply the law to individual cases. It involved no great leap, at this point, to say that this duty extended to expounding the law of the constitution. When, in expounding the laws, the judges found the law of the legislature to be in conflict with the law of the constitution, it was their duty to apply the superior law of the people, and to declare void laws which the legislature had no power to make. In this way, it could reasonably be said, as Sherburne did, and as improbable as it sounded to some, that the judicial courts served as a constitutional barrier between the people and their own legislature.

Of the legislature itself, it was said that their principal constitutional duty was to make law; and arguably, under the separation of powers clause, not to interpret it, which was a judicial function. Of course, as a practical matter, separation of powers could never be total since the legislature certainly would have an interpretive say in the meaning of their own statutes. The legislature also had to have some authority to interpret the constitution if only for the purpose of initially determining whether a proposed law infringed upon it. But under this constitutional scheme, the legislature's authority to interpret law was clearly ancillary to their primary constitutional role of making law, while the primary constitutional role of the judges was to expound law, including the law of the constitution. Moreover, as the judicial power "should [also] be independent," judges should be entitled to maintain their independent opinions

[47] "An Address of the Convention For Framing A New Constitution of Government, For the State of New Hampshire, To The Inhabitants of Said State" (1781), in Nathaniel Bouton (ed.), *Town Papers: Documents and Records Relating to Towns in New Hampshire, With An Appendix Embracing the Constitutional Conventions of 1778–1779; and of 1781–1783; and the State Constitution of 1784* (Concord, N.H., 1875), IX, 847; a "Second Address of the Convention" sent out in 1782 contained identical language, IX, 879.

[48] Ibid., 847.

about the constitutionality of a statute, in the face of the legislature's contrary views.

Indeed, there were at least two senses in which the judges' independent opinions about the validity of a statute were likely, even at this point, to prevail over the contrary judgments of the legislature. For one, the judges' constitutional responsibility (and presumably their expertise) lay in interpreting law; legal interpretation was not the legislature's function or strength. Consequently, the courts could draw on an inchoate sense that their interpretations of law were more legitimately rendered than those of the legislature. But second, as a practical matter, judges were in a position to put their opinions into effect, and to thwart the legislature's efforts to definitively confer the force of law on one of their acts. If the legislature resolved that a statute was constitutional, but the judges uniformly decided it was not, and refused to enforce it in their courts, the law became a dead letter in effect. The judges' opinions would, as a practical matter, have deprived a statute of the force of law. This was the sense in which, as James Madison put it just a few years later, the opinion of the courts was likely to prevail over the opinion of a legislature, and make the courts paramount. "[T]he Courts," he wrote, "are generally the last in making their decision, it results to them, by refusing or not refusing to execute a law, to stamp it with its final character. This makes the Judiciary Dept paramount in fact to the Legislature, which was never intended, and can never be proper."[49] And if the legislature were not prepared to take further steps against the judges, or to adopt other measures, they might well find it futile to continue to insist on their view of the constitutionality of a statute.

Sherburne's argument, however, also rested on an increasingly powerful political logic. The economic crisis had brought out deep divisions in New Hampshire society, often pitting poorer small farmers and mechanics against their wealthier, and more educated neighbors. People on both sides of the resulting clashes felt increasingly alienated from the legislature. On one side, many felt that their legislature had failed to do enough to relieve their distress, and began to engage in mass mobilization to persuade or pressure legislators to adopt more radical measures. On the other side, there were those who feared that if legislatures succumbed to these popular pressures, their own property and other fundamental rights

[49] "Observations on the 'Draught of a Constitution for Virginia'," in Robert A. Rutland and Charles F. Hobson (eds.), *The Papers of James Madison* (Charlottesville, Va., University Press of Virginia, 1977), XI, 281–95.

might be placed at risk. These men tended to see the courts as a refuge, less directly accountable to the people, and more reliant upon a well-established system of common law rules that offered protection for property and liberty rights. Increasingly, many among the educated and propertied, were coming to see the courts as a practical barrier they hoped might protect them in some measure from a legislature they feared might surrender to popular pressures to invade those rights.

In November, 1785, the New Hampshire legislature had adopted several modest reform measures to address the economic crisis, including the Ten Pound Act. But they had not passed a paper money measure, and by May 1786 even the Ten Pound Act had been declared unconstitutional by the Rockingham County Court of Common Pleas. In the fall of 1786, shortly after Shay's Rebellion had broken out in western Massachusetts, a minor uprising also took place in New Hampshire. Throughout the summer of 1786, according to William Plumer,

> [t]own and county conventions were held in various places, to petition the Legislature for a redress of grievances, and delegations from some of these conventions were sent to Concord, in June of this year, to present these petitions ... [These] requested the Legislature, among other things, to abolish the Court of Common Pleas, to establish town courts, to restrict the number of lawyers to two in a county, and to provide for the issue of state notes to the amount of three millions of dollars, the same to be a legal tender in payment of all debts.[50]

Not satisfied with the legislature's response to their petitions, the Rockingham convention sent

> a body of armed men to enforce their claims. On the 20th [of September 1786] about two hundred men ... some armed with muskets, and others with clubs, marched into Exeter [where the legislature was meeting] and sent in their petition to the General Court, for a redress of grievances, declaring their intention, if it was not granted to do themselves justice. They surrounded the house in which the Legislature was in session, and, placing sentinels at the doors and windows, demanded an immediate answer to the petition .... [T]he Senate, refused to act on the subject, while they were thus besieged by the mob ....[51]

Unlike in Massachusetts, this incipient uprising was quickly put down,[52] and although the New Hampshire legislature had refused to submit to popular pressure on this occasion, in light of the constant turnover in its membership at annual elections, there could be no great

[50] William Plumer, Jr., Life of William Plumer, 73. [51] Ibid., 75–76.
[52] Plumer, Life of William Plumer, 76–78.

certainty that it would remain steadfast on another. These circumstances help to explain why many on the bench and in the bar felt it to be essential to seek the protection of the courts by challenging even the legislature's trivial infringement of the constitution in its modest Ten Pound Act reform– lest it become a precedent for much worse.

Sherburne's argument resonated deeply with men like William Plumer and other lawyers, who saw in the courts, the state's best hope to fend off the distinct possibility that the legislature would become considerably more responsive to popular pressures.[53] On May 31, 1786, shortly after the Court of Common Pleas had declared the Ten Pound Act unconstitutional, Plumer described the situation in New Hampshire this way.

> The aspect of public actions in this State are gloomy. Money scarce, business dull and our Feeble government unhinged. [But] our courts of law are firm, and in these degenerate days dare to be honest. The Inferior Court of Common Pleas have resolved that the Law authorizing justices to try actions under £10 is unconstitutional .... I am glad the Court have had firmness to act their own opinion. If our elected government is long supported, it will owe its existence to the Judiciary. That is the only body of men who will have an effective check on a numerous Assembly."[54]

7.2 THE SUPREMACY OF THE LEGISLATURE UNDER THE NEW HAMPSHIRE CONSTITUTION OF 1784

But this is only half the story, for if the 1784 constitution incorporated many innovations that strengthened substantially the argument for judicial review, it remained a document that also preserved a great deal of the New England republican tradition of legislative supremacy. The contrast between the legislative and the judicial, one makes law, the other expounds it, that was well established in common law discourse, fell far short of accurately capturing the complicated institutional reality of the time. In New Hampshire, and in other New England states, an important aspect of the legislature's supremacy was that it assumed the authority to act as a "legal tribunal," and often behaved as though it were the court of final resort in the state. The New Hampshire Constitution itself recognized this tradition, styling the legislature "THE GENERAL COURT OF

[53] For a similar analysis in a different political key, see Hamburger, Law and Judicial Duty, 324.

[54] Letter from William Plumer to William Coleman (May 31, 1786), quoted by Hamburger, Law and Judicial Duty, 324 and fn. 99; and by Lambert, "Ten Pound Act Cases," 47.

NEW HAMPSHIRE."[55] (caps in original) The term "General Court" reflected the reality that the House and Senate not only operated as a legislature, but also adjudicated private disputes, and in response to petitions from individuals, often reversed judgments delivered by ordinary courts. "General Court" was a term indicating that the legislature possessed legislative, quasi-judicial, and purely judicial capacities, and in these capacities was supreme. By contrast ordinary courts, which possessed only one type of authority, were referred to as "judicial" courts.

There were a number of other provisions in the constitution that supported this tradition. The constitution mandated that the General Court was the source from which all judicial authority flowed. The constitution itself did not establish any courts. "The general court shall forever have full power and authority to erect and constitute judicatories and courts of record, or other courts, to be holden in the name of the state . . . ."[56] And it made judges removable upon "the address of both houses of the legislature,"[57] and impeachable not only for "misconduct" but also for "mal-administration," presumably neglect of office or incompetence.[58] The constitution also granted the legislature authority "to impose fines, mulcts, imprisonments, and other punishments . . . ."[59] The Bill of Rights, moreover, declared that the people have the right "to request of the legislative body, by way of petition or remonstrance, redress of the wrongs done them and of the grievances they suffer."[60] Petitions by individuals to the legislature were common, and often asked that body to settle private disputes. Frequently, the result was a legislative adjudication, that yielded a special legislative act to settle the controversy. But commonly, this right was also exercised in a somewhat different way, to petition the legislature for relief from a decision by a "judicial" court. In these kinds of cases, the legislature acted, in effect, as an appellate court of

[55] The New Hampshire Constitution of 1784, "The General Court" in Thorpe (ed.), Constitutions, IV, 2458. In Massachusetts and Connecticut as well, the state legislature was also called the General Court, see Massachusetts Constitution of 1780 in Thorpe (ed.), Constitutions, III, 1893, and for Connecticut see Zephaniah Swift, *A System of the Laws of the State of Connecticut* (Windham, Ct., Printed by John Byrns, 1795, repr. Arno Press, 1972), I, 59, 72.

[56] "The General Court" the New Hampshire Constitution of 1784, in Thorpe (ed.), Constitutions, IV, 2458.

[57] "Judiciary Power," the New Hampshire Constitution of 1784, in ibid., IV, 2466.

[58] Ibid., IV, 2461. [59] Ibid., IV, 2458

[60] "Bill of Rights," Article XXXII of the New Hampshire Constitution of 1784, in ibid., IV, 2457.

final resort. "[T]he laws of New Hampshire for the years 1784–1792," Edward Corwin wrote,

> [a]re replete with entries showing that throughout this period the state legislature freely vacated judicial proceedings, suspended judicial actions, annulled or modified judgments, cancelled executions, reopened controversies, authorized appeals, granted exemptions from the standing law, expounded the law for pending cases, and even determined the merits of disputes.[61]

A good example of these practices is to be found as Chapter 5 of the *Laws of New Hampshire* passed November 2, 1785, the result of a petition from one Thomas Pinkham. The law that was passed as a result of the petition was entitled "An Act to Annul & Make Void Two Judgments of Court Obtained by Margaret Frost Against Thomas Pinkham . . . ." The final paragraph of the act recited: "Be it enacted by the Senate and House of Representatives in *general court convened* that the said two judgments obtained by the said Margaret against the said Thomas . . . be and hereby are reversed annulled & made void" (emphasis added).[62]

Zephaniah Swift's 1795 account of the similar constitutional arrangements in Connecticut, helps to make this tradition more intelligible. In one place, he described the steps the general assembly followed in "proceeding in private matters," as they, in effect, conducted legislative adjudications, sitting as what Swift called "a legal tribunal."[63] The process bears a striking resemblance to that of adjudication in ordinary judicial courts, except that it led to the passage of a special legislative act, which governed only the particular parties.

> The mode of bringing private controversies before the assembly, is by preferring *a petition* or memorial, stating the nature of the dispute, and signed by the party; to which must be annexed a citation to the opposite party to appear, signed by proper authority, . . . which must be legally served on the opposite party, by leaving a copy

[61] Edward S. Corwin, "The Progress of Constitutional Theory Between the Declaration of Independence and the Meeting of the Philadelphia Convention" (1925), 30 *The American Historical Review* 514; see also, John Phillip Reid, Legislating the Courts, 9–10, 28.

[62] Henry Harbison Metcalf (ed.), *Laws of New Hampshire, Including Public and Private Acts, Resolves, Votes, Etc.* (Concord, N.H., Rumford Press, 1915), V (First Constitutional Period, 1784–92), Chap. 5, 89; see also Chap. 6 at 90, "An Act to Establish a Certain Judgment of the Quarter Sessions of the Peace for the County of Hillsborough in Favor of John Smith Against the Selectmen of Peterborough," the legislature also reciting there that they were "in general court convened."

[63] Swift, A System of the Laws of Connecticut, I, 76.

with him, at least twelve days before the first Tuesday after the commencement of the session of the assembly; on which Tuesday, the party must be notified to appear. The petitioner must appear the next Wednesday after the commencement of the session ....

The mode of trial of adversary matters is as follows – The respondent may plead in abatement to the petition ... or that the matters contained in it, do not warrant the interposition of the legislature, in the nature of a general demurrer. If there be no plea in abatement, it is usual to go to trial on the merits without pleading. The governor calls both houses together, when the proceedings are public. Witnesses are introduced, and examined and the counsel argue the causes. When the public hearing is finished the houses separate and take the cases into consideration and debate the matter if they please. Both houses must concur in any grant .... If a grant be made, a bill in form is drawn pursuant to the grant, and passed into a resolve, which is in the nature of a decree. If on trial, it appear that either party has given the other unjust trouble, the party wronged, shall recover his just cost, and damages.[64]

But according to Swift, the Connecticut legislature not only functioned as a "legal tribunal" acting upon petitions, it also functioned formally as a court of law hearing *suits* in equity. "The general assembly," he wrote,

reserved to themselves original jurisdiction, in all suits for relief in equity, where the value of the matter, or thing in demand, exceeds the sum of sixteen hundred pounds. At first the assembly reserved all the power of a court of equity in their hands; but experience teaching the inconvenience of the practice, induced them *to delegate all their power* in all matters under sixteen hundred pounds, *to the superior and county courts*. Why the whole power was not delegated, and why the superior court is not as able to decide all controversies in equity, exceeding sixteen hundred pounds, as they are in law, no reason can be given.[65] (emphasis added)

All judicial authority in Connecticut was understood to be exercised as a delegation from the legislature, as it was in New Hampshire under the constitution of 1784. Depending upon how the matter had reached them procedurally, the legislature might sit either formally as a court of law, or alternatively, as a legislative body acting as a "legal tribunal." The latter practice, in particular, provoked Swift's ire. "It ought to be deemed an inviolable maxim," he wrote, "that when proper courts of law are instituted, the legislature are divested of all judicial authority."[66] "It must however be acknowledged," he conceded,

that the legislature have paid no regard to these principles .... I have known repeated instances where they have sustained applications that manifestly and

[64] Ibid., I, 81–82. [65] Ibid., I, 74 [66] Ibid., I, 74.

expressly were excluded from relief by the general laws. I have known *petitions* preferred to obtain relief in cases against decisions of courts and juries, and the assembly have gone over the head of such decisions and granted relief.[67]

Swift, generally a supporter of legislative supremacy,[68] and an opponent of judicial review,[69] nevertheless took issue, by 1795, with the idea that the legislature should be acting as a "legal tribunal," arguing that it violated both separation of powers principles and constitutional restrictions on the making of retroactive laws.

> The constitutional power of the legislature is to make laws, of a court of judicature to expound them; but where shall we stop if the legislature, in private disputes, may make a law, which shall relieve against the operation of a prior law of their own making .... We shall have one grade of tribunals to act by established, uniform, and general rules, and another to reverse their decrees without regard to rules.[70]
>
> [Such interference] not only destroys the certainty, and uniformity of laws, but is of itself, an ex post facto law, which no legislature can constitutionally pass.[71]

On the other hand, Swift seems not to have been bothered by the Connecticut practice of formally establishing the legislature as a whole, before 1784, and thereafter, its upper house, as the court of "last resort" for the state, exercising formal judicial (rather than legislative or quasi-judicial) authority.[72] "The Supreme Court of Errors," he wrote, "consists of the governor, lieutenant-governor, and council [upper house of the legislature] .... This is [now] the highest court of law in the state, and is the dernier resort in all matters of law and equity, brought by way of writ of error, or complaint from the judgment, or decree of the superior court, wherein the rules of law, or principles of equity, appear ... to have been mistakenly adjudged, and determined."[73] Recall that members of the upper house of the legislature also sat on the courts of final resort in New York, and New Jersey. In New York, as in New Hampshire and Connecticut, however, the entire legislature would also sometimes sit as a "legal tribunal" (rather than as a formal court of law), to adjudicate certain kinds of private disputes.[74]

67 Ibid., I, 76. 68 Ibid., I, 59–60 69 Ibid., I, 51–53. 70 Ibid., I, 77.
71 Ibid., I, 76. 72 Ibid., I, 93, 63. 73 Ibid., I, 93.
74 Christine Desan, "The Constitutional Commitment to Legislative Adjudication in the Early American Tradition" (1998) 111 *Harvard Law Review* 1381–1503.

Swift offered no criticism of the legislature's undisputed power to supervise the judiciary, and to control the scope of the courts' jurisdiction. The general assembly, he observed,

> may call any court or magistrate, or any other officer or person whatever, to account for any misdemeanor, or mal-administration, and for just cause may fine, displace, or otherwise punish them, as the nature of the case requires.[75] [Moreover, [t]hey can enlarge, diminish and countroul the jurisdiction and authority of the other powers . . . and can do all the acts of a sovereign independent state.[76]

For the modern reader, these practices leave the sense of an unfathomable tangle between the purely legislative, the purely judicial, and the mixed "legal tribunal" capacities of New England (and other) legislatures in this period. And it seems that even some lawyers like Swift, who were otherwise ardent supporters of legislative supremacy, had come to feel, by this historical juncture, that certain fundamental constitutional values demanded a significant narrowing, at the very least, of the legislature's customary operation as a "legal tribunal." In particular, many in the legal community had come to feel that where a legislative body had not been formally instituted as a court of law, its "legislative" practices should conform more closely to the simple common law paradigm: legislatures make general, uniform laws, courts expound them. This shift in attitudes also played an important role in supporting the new practice of judicial review.

In May 1786, the judges of the Rockingham Court of Common Pleas, delivering their opinions in several different cases, declared the Ten Pound Act, in effect, to be unconstitutional. The next month the legislature opened its June session. By the time the legislative session began, a small group in the House of Representatives was calling for the outright repeal of the Ten Pound Act. At this stage, however, only a relatively few House members supported them, and a motion to repeal the act, made on June 15, was overwhelmingly defeated, 64 to 16.[77] But if the House showed little enthusiasm for complete repeal, there seems to have been widespread support among members for fixing the act's perceived problems. The very next day, June 16, a joint committee of both houses was appointed to re-examine the Ten Pound Act, and to "report such alterations as they may judge necessary."[78]

[75] Swift, A System of the Laws of Connecticut, I, 72. [76] Ibid., I, 60.

[77] "Journal of the House of Representatives" (June 15, 1786), in Batchellor (ed.), Early State Papers of New Hampshire, XX, 634–35.

[78] "Journal of the House of Representatives" (June 16, 1786), in ibid., XX, 638–39, and "Journal of the Senate," XX, 592.

The following week, on June 22, the committee did report, proposing two significant changes to the Act. The first might well have resolved the constitutional difficulty altogether – if the legislature had adopted it. It called for empowering justices of the peace to call a jury, "at the request of either party," in any case in which the amount in controversy exceeded forty shillings.[79] The lower house voted to adopt this proposal. Although this amendment might well have removed one difficulty, it would not have addressed another controversial feature of the act. For those in the community who believed that courts in republican governments needed more rather than less legal formality, leaving controversies involving up to ten pounds to be resolved by informal, local courts, overseen by ignorant justices, seemed in itself to represent "a wanton sacrifice of Liberty."[80]

The committee's second proposal, to allow appeals from justices of the peace to go either to the Inferior or Superior Courts, was also adopted by the full House, after it had been amended to cut the Inferior Courts completely out of the process; appeals from the justices' courts were to go only to the Superior Court.[81] It is not known precisely why the Senate failed to take action on these proposed amendments, but its behavior undoubtedly reflected deep disagreements between the two houses, about both the Ten Pound Act itself, and the legislature's proper role in addressing the constitutional controversy that had developed as a result of its passage.

Until this moment, the House had been acting in a purely legislative capacity, deliberating upon whether to repeal or amend a previously enacted law of the state. But following these deliberations, the House silently shifted modes, convening, in effect, as a "legal tribunal." On June 22, it took up a petition submitted by James Macgregore, a plaintiff in one of the Ten Pound Act cases, who had had a judgment in his favor reversed by the Rockingham County Inferior Court, when the

[79] "Journal of the House of Representatives" (June 22, 1786), in ibid., XX, 652.

[80] In an article condemning the possibility that the legislature might "raise the Jurisdiction of the Justices to hear and determine Actions of all kinds, and to any amount," one writer, for example observed that "[t]o give the Justices [such great] power, indiscriminately, to determine causes ... when the Justice at the same time, is ignorant of the nature of the cause he takes cognizance of, who cannot even tell you, why an action of debt differs from an action on the case: I say, to submit your property to the judgment of this *ignoramus*, is ... a wanton sacrifice of Liberty ...." *Junius*, "To the Inhabitants of the State of New Hampshire," *New Hampshire Mercury* (Portsmouth, September 6, 1786).

[81] "Journal of the House of Representatives" (June 22, 1786), in Batchellor (ed.), Early State Papers of New Hampshire, XX, 652.

court found the law unconstitutional.[82] Following the well-established custom, Macgregore petitioned the legislature for redress, asking them, in effect, to review the court's judgment, and to set it aside. He complained to the House that the Inferior Court of Common Pleas had reversed the justice's judgment, which had awarded him damages, on the ground that "a justice of the peace ought not to take cognizance of any action, wherein the damage alleged, exceeds the sum of forty shillings ... [and the court did so, he continued] *notwithstanding a late act of this state* [the Ten Pound Act] ... whereby the said Macgregore conceived himself to be greatly injured, and prayed for direction and redress in the premises"[83] (emphasis added).

Now sitting in a quasi-judicial posture, the House set the stage for its subsequent order by, in effect, delivering its judgment about the constitutionality of the Ten Pound Act. It "*Resolved*, That [the Ten Pound Act] *is a constitutional law of this state, and ought to be observed as such*" (emphasis added). The House's opinion directly contradicted the Inferior Court's. Obviously believing that they possessed the power to overrule the judgment (and opinion) of the Common Pleas, the House "*Resolved*, That the judgment of the Inferior Court ... be and hereby is rendered null and void ... ." They proceeded to reinstate Macgregore's suit, empowering him "to enter his said action [anew] at the Superior Court," notwithstanding the judgment of the Inferior Court.[84]

The House acted in a way that the General Court had on numerous previous occasions, setting aside, upon the petition of an individual, the judgment of a lower court, and reinstating a suit. So long as New Hampshire judges believed that the legislature was supreme, and that it possessed the authority to overturn their judgments, judicial review could not possibly have become an effective constitutional check, even where a court initially ventured to engage in it.[85] Here, the New Hampshire House sought to address the emerging problem of judicial review it now faced in the simplest, most direct way possible, simply by overturning the lower court's decision. If the legislature actually possessed the authority to

[82] See *Macgregore* v. *Furber* discussed above, and in Lambert, "Ten Pound Act Cases," 41–43, 47–48; see also Hamburger, Law and Judicial Duty, 427–28.

[83] "Journal of the House of Representatives" (June 22, 1786), in Batchellor (ed.), Early State Papers of New Hampshire, XX, 653.

[84] Ibid.

[85] On this point, see Timothy A. Lawrie, "Interpretation and Authority: Separation of Powers and the Judiciary's Battle for Independence in New Hampshire, 1786–1818" (1995) 39 *American Journal of Legal History* 310, at 311.

overrule a lower court decision, that might well have put an end to a nascent judicial review. In this respect, the New Hampshire situation was not unlike New York's, where those who were outraged by Mayor Duane's decision in *Rutgers* v. *Waddington* settled on the simple expedient, if it became necessary, of appealing his judgment to the court of final resort in the state, where it would be reviewed by the upper house of the legislature. But unlike in New York where the court of final resort had been formally instituted under the constitution, in New Hampshire the legislature had merely assumed its (quasi-judicial) role as a matter of custom. Over the next few years, the New Hampshire courts would themselves call into question the constitutional legitimacy of the legislature's (quasi-judicial) authority, placing in doubt one of the legislature's best expedients for neutralizing judicial review. But on this occasion, the question of the New Hampshire legislature's (quasi-judicial) power was not directly tested, as the Senate failed to act on the House's resolution, which, as a result, failed to be enacted into law by the General Court.

These events, however, did not conclude the legislature's June 1786 dealings with the Ten Pound Act. A few days later, on June 27, the House took up a second petition, this time submitted by Thomas Bartlet, a lawyer acting on behalf of Joseph Hall Bartlet (no relation). Joseph Hall Bartlet had had his favorable judgment as plaintiff in a justice of the peace's court in *Bartlet* v *French* also reversed by the Inferior Court of Common Pleas, on the ground that the Ten Pound Act was unconstitutional.[86] The lawyer Thomas Bartlet, acting as a justice of the peace in another case, *Wallace* v *Tarlton*, had had his own judgment overturned by the Inferior Court of Common Pleas on similar grounds. He now took up the gauntlet on behalf of Joseph Hall Bartlet, writing to the legislature that "[y]our petitioner having full faith to the Laws of the State of New Hampshire ... in order for to Recover his money brought an action agreeable to the Laws of the Said state before a Justice of the Peace ... and Recovered Judgment against Said French." But that judgment, he continued, was overturned on appeal to the Inferior Court of Common Pleas. "[T]o [my] great surprise the Justices of *Said Court by the assistance of the Bar were in there* [sic] *own opinion wiser than the whole Legislature* & would not Sustaine Said action but Dismised the Same ... Contrary to Law"[87] (emphasis added). Bartlet was

[86] See *Bartlet* v. *French* discussed above and in Lambert, "Ten Pound Act Cases," 44–45; see also Hamburger, Law and Judicial Duty, 430–31.

[87] Petition of Joseph Hall Bartlet (June 12, 1786), NHSA Petitions to the General Court, quoted by Lambert, "Ten Pound Act Cases," 48.

asserting a commonplace of traditional constitutionalism. The legislature would not have enacted a law until it had first arrived at the judgment that it did not conflict with the constitution. It was absurd to think that the opinions of the judges and lawyers in the Inferior Court of Common Pleas were "wiser than the whole Legislature," and could replace that judgment with their own view that the statute conflicted with the constitution, and was therefore not law, despite the legislature's formal enactment.

The crux of the matter was relatively straightforward: whose opinion should prevail at the end of the day; did a particular statute (continue to) possess the force of law, or not. Zephaniah Swift captured the essence of this dispute perfectly in his 1795 treatise on the laws of Connecticut, and took a strong stand on what he believed was the right answer.

> Previously to their passing any act, [the legislature] must consider and determine whether it be compatible with the constitution. Being the supreme power, and bound to judge with respect to the question, in the first instance, their decision must be final and conclusive. It involves the most manifest absurdity, and is degrading to the legislature, to admit the idea, that the judiciary may rejudge the same question which they have decided; and if they are of a different opinion, reverse the law, and pronounce it to be a nullity. It is an elevation of the judiciary over the heads of the legislature; it vests them with supreme power, and enables them to repeal all the laws . . . .[88]

Concluding his petition, Bartlet asked the House to "impeach said Justices for Male Conduct," and if it should be determined "that they have acted Contrary to Laws that they may be Dismissed from there Said office and others may be appointed in there stead, that will make the Laws there Rule of Conduct . . . .[89] But the House took no steps to initiate impeachment proceedings against the judges, perhaps believing that there was no need to do so, given that they possessed the authority simply to overturn the judges' decisions. After reading and considering Bartlet's petition, the House simply "Voted" that "there [should] be no further process" in the Inferior Court in cases in which the court had reversed a justice's judgment on the ground that the Ten Pound Act was unconstitutional, "until further order of the General Court."[90]

88 Swift, System of the Laws of Connecticut, I, 52.

89 Petition of Joseph Hall Bartlet (June 12, 1786), NHSA Petitions to the General Court, quoted by Lambert, "Ten Pound Act Cases," 48.

90 Ibid., and "Journal of the House of Representatives" (June 27, 1786), in Batchellor (ed.), Early State Papers of New Hampshire, XX, 668.

The House obviously believed that they possessed the authority to act as a higher court of appeal, staying further proceedings in the Inferior Court, including, presumably, the execution of judgments.[91] But when they sought the concurrence of the Senate, that body again not only refused to agree, but seemed to call into question the constitutional legitimacy of the House's action. "The Senate are of the opinion that the Vote of the honble. House, on the within Petition does not constitutionally come before them for their consideration."[92] It is not possible to say with complete certainty, but it seems as though the Senate may have been taking the position that the House had no constitutional authority to intervene in the proceedings of ordinary courts, presumably because that would be a judicial act, prohibited by the separation of powers provision in the constitution. If this is so, it would be a noteworthy constitutional development.

7.3 THE MULTI-DIMENSIONAL JUDICIAL ASSAULT ON LEGISLATIVE SUPREMACY

Over the next few years, assumptions about the practical application of separation of powers principles appear to have evolved enough throughout New England to provide judges with a powerful rationale for rejecting the legislature's further attempts to exercise a traditional quasi-judicial authority. The Massachusetts General Court, like the General Courts in Connecticut, New Hampshire, and Rhode Island, had also frequently "restored petitioners to their Law," by annulling the judgments of lower courts. When defendants in one such Massachusetts case, moved to enforce the legislature's Resolve a few years later in February 1789 in the Suffolk County Supreme Judicial Court, plaintiff's lawyer demurred to any further proceedings in the court, arguing that

> by the thirtieth article of the declaration of rights [of the Massachusetts Constitution of 1780], it is declared, "That in the Government of this Commonwealth, the legislative department shall never exercise the executive and *Judicial* power, or either of them." That the Legislature of this

[91] See Hamburger, Law and Judicial Duty, 431.

[92] Ibid., 431 and fn. 94, "Petition of Joseph Hall Bartlet (June 12, 1786), NHSA Petitions to the General Court, with the vote of the Senate endorsed on the verso (June 27, 1786)." In December 1786, the Senate followed up by proposing a bill that "'all petitions for any ... persons to be restored to their law' should be heard by the court in which the cause was 'last pending' and that such court should decide 'in as ample a manner as the General Court have usually done'" whether to rehear the cause. The House predictably refused to concur, Hamburger, Law and Judicial Duty, 530, and 530 fn. 54.

Commonwealth cannot by act or resolve nullify and revoke a Judgment of Court, and the consequent proceedings thereon, without exercising the Judicial powers.[93]

The court, after hearing plaintiff's argument, rejected the defendants' plea, refusing to act on the legislature's resolution.[94]

In the years following that decision, the continued legitimacy of the Massachusetts legislature's interference in court proceedings began to be discussed more widely. On April 15, 1790, one Solon in a letter published in the *Massachusetts Spy*, wrote: "No judgment of a Court of law, be it ever so small, inconsiderable, or erroneous, should by the legislature be declared *null and void*. Because it is a direct exercise of the judicial power, and an express determination that the judgment, thus reversed, is wrong and erroneous; Which the Constitution plainly and clearly asserts, they shall not use or exercise."[95]

The debate in Massachusetts may well have spilled over into New Hampshire. A little more than six months later, on December 11, 1790, someone also calling himself "Solon" published a new letter in the *New Hampshire Gazette* elaborating on the earlier argument. In this case, "Solon" argued that the New Hampshire constitution prohibited the legislature from intervening in the proceedings of judicial courts, and that if they continued to do so, the courts would be fully justified in "pay[ing] no regard to such legislative Acts." As in the case of the Massachusetts letter, Solon began by referring to the similar text in the New Hampshire constitution.

It seems agreed, that the three great powers in government, Legislative, judicial and Executive should be kept as distinct and separate from each other as possible. – And that the blending these power together, or uniting them in . . . one body of men, and keeping them distinct, makes the *essential* difference between a free and *despotic Government*. Our constitution wisely provides, that the Legislative shall never exercise the Judicial or Executive powers, or either of them . . . .

But may it not be asked, have our legislative bodies strictly adhered to this part of the Constitution? Are they not every session usurping the Judicial powers in a variety of instances? If this is not the case, how comes it to pass, that the determinations of our *judicial* Courts in this State, are frequently set aside: Insomuch that a suitor has no certainty, that after obtaining a *final* judgment his cause will not undergo a revision in the General Court. Can this be any thing less than the General-Court's erecting themselves into a Court superior to the Superior Court? . . ..

I lay it down as a proposition uncontrovertible – that reversing, setting aside, nullifying, or abrogating the judgment of a court of law, for any cause whatever, is

93 Quoted in Hamburger, ibid., 527–28. 94 Ibid., 528.

95 Solon, Letter to Mr. Thomas (April 2, 1790), *Massachusetts Spy* (April 15, 1790), quoted in Hamburger, ibid., 528 fn. 50.

an exercise of the judicial authority. That a new trial originating otherwise than by Appeal, Writ of Review, or Writ of Error, according to the standing laws of the state is an appendage of the judicial authority.

And whenever the General Court of this state, by act or resolve, interfere in such matters, they are acting directly counter to the letter and spirit of the Constitution. And *the judges would be fully justified* by the Constitution (which I hold to be a fixed law of the state, by which the legislature are *bound*, and which *they*, the legislature, have no power, or authority to infringe, alter or amend) and their oaths, *to pay no regard to such legislative Acts, Orders or Resolutions.*[96] (emphasis added)

At the very time Solon published this letter in the *New Hampshire Gazette*, Elizabeth McClary had a petition pending in the legislature, asking that body to set aside a Superior Court judgment against her.[97] In, January 1791, finally acting on her petition, the legislature passed a special act, "restoring her to her law,"[98] which authorized her to reenter her case at the Superior Court, in effect reversing the earlier judgment of the Superior Court against her. That judgment had been won by Nathaniel Gilman, who was represented by none other than William Plumer. At the Superior Court's term in September 1791, McClary sought to enforce the legislature's special act. Plumer, arguing for Gilman, urged the court simply to disregard the legislature's act on the ground that the law was unconstitutional and void. One can only wonder whether Solon's letter, published the previous December, had had an influence on Plumer's thinking. According to his son, Plumer argued to the court

that the law [under which McClary was now seeking to reenter her case] was unconstitutional, and therefore void, on the ground, that, if it reversed the former judgment, it was repugnant to the bill of rights, and the constitution of the state; and that, if it did not reverse it, the court could not render another judgment in the same case, while the first remained in force.[99]

The court, "[a]fter a full hearing of the parties by their counsel learned in the law and fully deliberating upon the constitution of the State and nature and operation of the act," adopted Plumer's argument completely. "[I]t appears to the Court that if the act virtually or really reverses the [earlier] judgment of this Court it is repugnant to the bill of rights and constitution of

[96] Solon, "From the GAZETTEER," *New Hampshire Gazette* (December 11, 1790).

[97] For an account of the case, see Reid, Legislating the Courts, 63–64; and Lawrie, "Interpretation and Authority," 322–23.

[98] "Journal of the House of Representatives" (June 14, 1790, and January 14 and 21, 1791), "Senate Journal" (June 16, 1790, and January 14 and 25, 1791), in Batchellor (ed.), Early State Papers of New Hampshire, XXII, 22, 104, 113, 67, 156, 168.

[99] William Plumer, Jr., The Life of William Plumer, 170–71. It is also possible that Plumer himself had written the Solon letter.

this state ... . It is therefore considered by the Court that the said Act is ineffectual and inadmissible and that the said action be dismissed."[100] The Superior Court, in other words, held the legislature's special act to be unconstitutional and void, presumably on the ground that it was a judicial act, which violated the Bill of Rights' separation of powers article, and less certainly, the Bill of Rights' prohibition on the making of retrospective laws.[101]

This was a striking development. Not only had the judges again claimed a right to engage in judicial review, to declare an act of the legislature "ineffectual and inadmissible" in their court because they judged it to be unconstitutional; they had done so in a case that would simultaneously deprive the legislature of the power directly and easily to counter the court's assertion of their new found authority. The court was now in effect claiming the authority not only to judge the legitimate scope of the legislature's powers to make law but through that power of review also to judge more broadly the legitimate scope of the legislature's other powers. Where previously the legislature was not only understood to be the final judge of their authority to legislate but also of the legitimate scope of the

[100] Manuscript record, Superior Court for the County of Rockingham, September 1791, quoted in Walter F. Dodd, "Gilman v. McClary: A New Hampshire Case of 1791" (1907), 12 *American Historical Review* 349–50.

[101] New Hampshire Bill of Rights of 1784, in Thorpe (ed.), Constitutions, IV, Article XXIII (2456), and Article XXVII (2457); the Article XXIII prohibition on the making of retrospective laws was not limited to criminal statutes, but applied expressly both to laws "for the decision of civil causes, or the punishment of offences." As legislative adjudications did not provide for jury trials, it is also possible, as John Phillip Reid has argued, that Plumer's reference to the Bill of Rights may also have included Article XX of the Bill of Rights, guaranteeing jury trials "[i]n all controversies concerning property, and in all suits between two or more persons ... ." at 2456., see Reid, Legislating the Courts, 64. In 1786, the Vermont Council of Censors argued that similar legislative practices in that state violated both the constitution's separation of powers principles and guarantees of trial by jury, see Hamburger, Law and Judicial Duty, 530 fn. 54. By 1795, the assault on the legislative exercise of judicial authority generally, and on legislative adjudication in particular, had been taken up by a justice of the U.S. Supreme Court. In *Van Horne's Lessee*, 2 Dall. 304 (1795), Justice Paterson ruled that a special act the Pennsylvania legislature had passed in order legally to resolve an old and highly significant land dispute in the state, was unconstitutional. It (like legislative adjudications generally) had not provided the landowners with a jury trial as the Pennsylvania constitution required. Paterson would not even condescend to recognize what the legislature had done as an "adjudication" (however flawed), labelling it instead a naked, unconstitutional taking of property without just compensation. This characterization represented a significant step on the road not only to rendering legislative adjudications completely illegitimate, but to making the very idea of such "adjudications" practically unimaginable. Judges and courts adjudicated disputes, legislatures passed general acts.

judges' powers, now it would be the opposite way round. The question that remained was whose opinion in these fundamental matters would prevail.

The traditionalist side of the New Hampshire constitution gave the legislature formidable powers to combat the judges' overreach. For one, they could simply seek a judge's removal by voting an address to the President of the state.[102] The standards for removal upon address in New Hampshire were unsettled at this time, but it would become clear, over the next few decades, that removal of a judge "by address . . . could be made for any cause, or for no cause, and no reasons needed to be assigned."[103]

The legislature also possessed the authority to impeach judges for "misconduct or mal-administration in their offices."[104] And as one petitioner had already argued in June, 1786, a judge who willfully decided a case "contrary to the laws" would arguably have breached a fundamental duty of his office and committed impeachable misconduct. But according to John Phillip Reid, "in all of New Hampshire's history, [the legislature] did not oust a single judge by impeachment."[105] And although, over the following decades, the legislature did "address out" judges on several occasions, they never did so in order to oust a judge who had engaged in judicial review.[106]

Following the McClary decision, William Plumer reported, "[s]ome clamor was indeed made against the judges, as putting themselves above the Legislature,"[107] but the legislature itself took no action against the judges. Thereafter, the Superior Court refused, from time to time, to enforce special legislative acts of this kind, on the ground that they were an unconstitutional invasion of the judicial power, and these judgments culminated in the well-known 1818 *Merrill* v. *Sherburne* decision.[108] No action was taken by the legislature against the judges in any of these cases. The McClary decision, moreover, seems to have

[102] New Hampshire Constitution of 1784, "Judiciary Power," in Thorpe (ed.), Constitutions, IV, 2466 ("the president with the consent of [the executive] council, may remove [the judges] upon the address of both houses of the legislature").

[103] Reid, Legislating the Courts, 59.

[104] New Hampshire Constitution of 1784, "Senate," in Thorpe (ed.), Constitutions, IV, 2461.

[105] Reid, Legislating the Courts, 11.

[106] Ibid., 119, 144–46, 159–60. During the second decade of the nineteenth century, the New Hampshire legislature also "legislated" judges out of office on several occasions, by repealing the statute that had created the courts on which they sat, 158–61. Given the range of measures the legislature could constitutionally deploy against judges, it is remarkable that they never did remove a judge specifically for engaging in judicial review.

[107] Plumer, Life of William Plumer, 171.

[108] *Merrill* v. *Sherburne*, 1 N.H. 199 (1818), the opinion in the Merrill case reported these earlier instances as "*Gilman vs. M'Clary. Rock. Sept. 1791, Chickering vs. Clark [1808], Hills., Butterfield vs. Morgan. Ches. May 1797. Jenness & al. Exrs. vs. Seavey, Rock.*

had a significant impact on the legislature's conduct. According to one legal historian, after that decision was handed down, the legislature passed many fewer of these kinds of special acts.[109] And so, it seems that as early as 1791, the New Hampshire judges had largely prevailed against the legislature on these issues, successfully expanding the scope of their own traditional authority, while restricting the legislature's. Through their resolute acts, the judges had established judicial review as an integral feature of a new constitutional order.

The likelihood of this outcome was already apparent in 1786, when the controversy over the Ten Pound Act and judicial review were being played out in the legislature and courts. At its June 1786 session, the House had attempted to take several actions to support the Ten Pound Act, but these efforts had been thwarted by the Senate's refusal to concur. Not surprisingly, at their August 1786 term, the judges of the Rockingham Inferior Court picked up where they had left off in May, continuing to quash the judgments of justices of the peace who had adjudicated cases involving more than 2 pounds.[110]

All during the summer of 1786, as mentioned earlier, "[t]own and county conventions were held in various places, to petition the Legislature for redress of [economic] grievances, and delegations from some of these conventions [were dispatched] to present these petitions ... "[111] When the legislature met in September, a joint committee of both houses was again appointed to consider "such alterations and amendments [to the Ten Pound Act], as they may judge necessary.[112] Perhaps, as a result of the popular pressures that were being brought to bear against the legislature at this moment, the committee, on the very next day, reported that "the said act stands in need of no alterations or amendments."[113] In November, the Rockingham County Inferior Court of Common Pleas continued its assault on the Ten

Feb. 1799," at 216–17 of the Merrill decision; see also, Lawrie, "Interpretation and Authority," 324–25; and Reid, Legislating the Courts, 64.

109 Lawrie, "Interpretation and Authority," 323, and Appendices I & II; Hamburger argues that the change in the legislature's behavior may have been the result of a similar decision in another case, Law and Judicial Duty, 532–33.

110 Hamburger, Law and Judicial Duty, 431–32; and Lambert, "Ten Pound Act Cases," 45.

111 Plumer, Life of William Plumer, 72.

112 "Journal of the House of Representatives" (September 15, 1786), in Batchellor (ed.), Early State Papers of New Hampshire, XX, 698.

113 Ibid. (September 16, 1786), XX, 704; the following week an armed crowd would descend on the legislature, demanding that it enact, among other matters, a paper money bill.

Pound Act, quashing the judgment of a justice of the peace in a case involving more than 2 pounds again on the ground "that the sum Demanded Exceeds the Jurisdiction of the said Justice, and that no Justice of the Peace can take cognizance thereof according to the Constitution of this State."[114]

On December 25, 1786, perhaps in reaction to the Inferior Court's November decision, the House of Representatives reiterated its earlier judgment that the Ten Pound Act was constitutional. The House voted overwhelmingly (44 yes, 14 no) to reaffirm that it was the House's opinion that the act was constitutional.[115] Two days later on December 27, perhaps to lay the groundwork for an investigation into the judges' conduct, the House voted "That the Clerk of this House [should] write to the Clerk of the Inferior Court of Common Pleas, for the county of Rockingham, and request of him, a copy of the proceedings of said Court in each action brought before them by appeals from Justices of the Peace, in cases which exceed forty shillings."[116] But the House did not send its resolutions over to the Senate for their concurrence, and nothing seems to have come of this proposed documents request.[117]

Despite the clear opinion expressed by the House in December that in their judgment the Ten Pound Act was constitutional, the courts continued to adhere to their contrary view. Indeed, the judicial insurgency spread. At its February 1787 term, the Strafford County Inferior Court of Common Pleas joined the Rockingham County Court in holding the Ten Pound Act to be unconstitutional; it dismissed two "Ten Pound Act cases on the ground that 'the Justice could not by the Constitution of this State hold cognizance of the Original Plea.'"[118] In June, the Strafford court did so again in another case.[119]

While the judges of the Rockingham and Strafford county inferior courts, steadfastly adhered to their views, opinions in the legislature were divided. From the outset of the controversy, the House and Senate

[114] Rockingham County Inferior Court, Minute Book, November term, 1786, New Entries, Case No. 9, NHSA, quoted in Hamburger, Law and Judicial Duty, 432 and fn. 96.

[115] "Journal of the House of Representatives" (December 25, 1786), in Batchellor (ed.), Early State Papers of New Hampshire, XX, 759.

[116] Ibid. (December, 27, 1786), XX, 762.

[117] Hamburger, Law and Judicial Duty, 434, and fns. 101–3.

[118] Ibid., 432; and Lambert, "Ten Pound Act cases," 46–47. Rockingham and Strafford counties were the two coastal counties in New Hampshire with significant concentrations of merchants, lawyers, and others with nonfarm occupations. Other counties were less commercial, having larger proportions of small farmers.

[119] Ibid.

appear to have fundamentally disagreed about the legitimacy of the judges' conduct, and perhaps about the constitutionality of the act and the legislature's own authority to reverse judicial decisions.[120] At new annual elections held in the spring of 1787, the party of legal formality appears to have picked up a significant number of seats. Turnover in the legislature was high,[121] and with the change in membership, the weight of sentiment in the House shifted decisively. This sort of turnover occurred frequently in the legislatures of the period, when annual elections, conducted in the absence of an organized party system and at a time of deep political divisions, often produced wild swings in membership and sentiment, and an accompanying instability and fluctuation in the laws from year to year.

For legislatures that might want to defend their traditional constitutional privileges against the judges' steadfast assertion of their own newfound powers, these swings in opinion put legislatures at a decisive structural disadvantage. And this was not the legislature's only practical disadvantage. By virtue of the judges' position in the administration of the laws, they were situated at a natural veto point. Contemporaries well understood this fact, repeatedly saying that judicial review would give judges' the de facto final word on the laws, placing them above the legislature.[122]

Even if the entire New Hampshire legislature had been able to unite behind resolutions judging the Ten Pound Act to be constitutional, to the extent the judges in Rockingham and Strafford counties held firmly to

[120] "Whereas the Senate consisted mostly of merchants, lawyers and others with nonfarm occupations, the House had a substantial majority of men engaged solely in agriculture. Indeed, most of them were small farmers .... The senators lived in towns; the representatives in rural villages. Most of the senators were at least well-to-do; most of the representatives were of moderate property .... The only issue of any real consequence [on which the senate and house generally disagreed] was economic: the Senate consistently followed a pro-creditor monetary policy. The House tried to maintain artificially the value of the various state and federal certificates and to accept them for taxes at a higher rate than their actual worth ... The Senate ... tried to repeal an act that had protected debtors from being imprisoned when they offered real or personal property in settlement," *Jackson Turner Main, The Upper House in Revolutionary American, 1763–1788* (Madison, Wisc., University of Wisconsin Press, 1967), 178–79.

[121] Compare list of legislators voting in June 1786, in Batchellor (ed.), Early State Papers of New Hampshire, XX, 634, 759, with those voting in June 1787, ibid., XXI: 73,79, 83.

[122] Blackstone, of course, made the same point several decades earlier, see William Blackstone, *Commentaries on the Laws of England* (1765) (Facsimile edition, Chicago, University of Chicago Press, 1979), I, 91; see also James Madison's statement in "Observations on the 'Draught of a Constitution for Virginia'," in Rutland and Hobson (eds.), The Papers of James Madison, XI, 281–95.

their opposing view, and persisted in refusing to enforce the law, the Ten Pound Act would not, in any meaningful sense, have continued to be the law of the land in those counties.[123] The judge's opinions, not only about the constitutionality of the particular statute, but about the legitimacy of their own authority to nullify it, would inevitably, in this way, prevail over the legislature's – unless the legislature was prepared to take further steps, by, for example, ousting any judge who engaged in the practice, and replacing them with others "that will make the Laws there Rule of Conduct … .[124] The same was true of the special acts the legislature would pass in pursuance of its quasi-judicial authority after 1791. In those cases, the courts simply declared the acts to be "ineffectual," and ignored them. Short of removing from office judges who engaged in the practice, bare declarations of constitutionality or reversals of judgments, would almost certainly prove futile. And the divided and fluctuating opinions in legislatures, together with the growing support for the "independence" of the judiciary, only made this structural disadvantage worse.

The New Hampshire legislature opened its new session in June 1787. James Macgregore, one of the original plaintiffs in a Ten Pound Act case, who had had his judgment reversed by the Rockingham County Inferior Court the previous year, and whose June 1786 petition to the legislature has already been discussed, now brought a new petition to the legislature.[125]

In his new petition, Macgregore asked the legislature to "restore him to his law." A joint committee of the House and Senate agreed to redress one of Macgregore's grievances, but completely ignored his plea that the legislature should once again take up its role as a high court, by "restoring him to his law."[126]

The issue of the judges' conduct, however, was certainly under active discussion. On June 16, one House member moved to read some papers "purporting to be an impeachment of the Honbl Justices of the Inferior

[123] Of course, whether the law would be a dead letter throughout these counties also depended upon what position the Superior Court might take.

[124] Petition of Joseph Hall Bartlet (June 12, 1786), NHSA Petitions to the General Court, quoted by Lambert, "Ten Pound Act Cases," 48.

[125] Macgregore actually submitted three petitions to the legislature about his Ten Pound Act case, the first at the June 1786 session, the second in September 1786, and the final one here in June 1787, see Lambert, "Ten Pound Act Cases," 47–49.

[126] Ibid., 49.

Court of Common pleas for the County of Rockingham."[127] A motion to proceed with the initial reading of the papers passed the House by a fairly close vote of 31 to 25, but further consideration of the matter was put over until the following day.[128] On June 27 a committee of 13 was appointed "to take [the impeachment papers] under consideration." One outside commentator agreed with the members of the House who had initiated impeachment proceedings. "[A]lthough the [General] court solemnly determined after a full hearing and debating," he wrote, "that a said act of the legislature was NOT UNCONSTITUTIONAL," the judges "firmly refused to admit it as a law." "What then ought to have been the consequence but an immediate impeachment and dismission, if the judges would not conform [to the law and constitution]?"[129] (caps in original) For those who adhered to traditional constitutionalism, this was an unexceptional position, and was frequently repeated. But the committee saw matters differently, and wasted little time in delivering their report, informing the House the same afternoon that it was "their opinion that the said Justices are not impeachable for Mal-administration *as their conduct is justified by the constitution of this State*"[130] (emphasis added). The entire House then voted to adopt the committee's report,[131] by a vote of 35–21, a significant minority apparently favoring impeachment.

The majority was now rejecting several earlier House resolutions that had judged the Ten Pound act to be constitutional, seemingly agreeing with the court's contrary opinion. The committee's murky statement, however, fell somewhat short of expressly saying that they now found the Ten Pound Act to be unconstitutional. Their statement might well have meant that. But it might also have conveyed the broader message that the House was of the view that the constitution justified the judges' in engaging in judicial review itself, regardless of whether they had judged rightly or wrongly in this particular instance, and under the constitution were not impeachable for that type of conduct. If the latter correctly reflects how the House's statement was generally understood at the time, it would mean that the House was taken to have endorsed the idea that judges were fully justified by the constitution in maintaining their

[127] "Journal of the House of Representatives" (June 26, 1787), in Batchellor (ed.), Early State Papers of New Hampshire, XXI, 72–3.

[128] Ibid., XXI, 73.

[129] "Watchman," *New Hampshire Spy* (Portsmouth, June 30, 1787).

[130] Batchellor (ed.), Early State Papers, XXI, 78–79. [131] Ibid.

own independent opinions about statutes, even where the legislature had definitively judged to the contrary. If that is how this declaration was generally understood, it may help to explain why, thereafter, the legislature never attempted to remove any New Hampshire judge who had struck down a piece of legislation, and why no serious dispute about the practice of judicial review seems subsequently to have arisen in the state.

But the House vote also indicates that there was still substantial support in that body for the doctrines of traditional constitutionalism. This state of affairs reflected the deep tensions within New Hampshire's constitution itself (and in the constitutional culture), between a rapidly emerging regime of constitutional legality, and a traditional one of (republican) legislative supremacy. The "popularity" tended to support the older tradition, while the newer one received more focused backing from an influential group of politically prominent lawyers, judges, and others. The final act in the story of the New Hampshire Ten Pound law seems to reflect these tensions, and to leave the impression that judicial review may have triumphed in New Hampshire as much as a result of acquiescence, as by positive approval.

Following the vote to accept the committee's report, the House appointed a committee to draft a bill to repeal the Ten Pound Act. But before it enacted a repeal law, the legislature first passed a bill to create a new procedure for "the more speedy recovery of small debts, and to save the cost usually attending the recovery thereof."[132] The new act's main aim was to preserve the benefits of the Ten Pound Act, while removing its constitutional difficulties. It set up a new process for collecting small debts that was to be administered by justices of the peace, and again extended to controversies involving up to ten pounds. And it proclaimed that it was passing this act, for the same reasons it had originally passed the Ten Pound Act, because "the common and ordinary method of recovering small debts, proves very burthensome to poor debtors . . . ."[133]

With the new process in place, the legislature proceeded the same day to repeal the Ten Pound Act. But several aspects of the repeal act also seem noteworthy. In it the legislature declared that it was repealing the Ten Pound act because it "is not thought necessary to be longer continued in force," presumably since a replacement had already been put into place.

132 New Hampshire Sessions Laws (June 28, 1787), 448, the repeal bill appears two pages later on 450 in the Sessions Laws. On the order of passage, see also "Journal of the Senate" (June 28, 1787), 30–31.

133 Ibid.

The preamble studiously avoided saying that the legislature was repealing the Ten Pound Act because they judged it to be unconstitutional.[134] The final Proviso of the repeal act raises a further question along the same lines. "*[I]t is hereby further enacted*, That the repeal of the before recited act, shall not in any way or manner, hurt, alter or make void any proceedings or doings of any Justice of the peace done under the authority of said Act."[135] The legislature went out of its way to make explicit that repeal was prospective only; and that this repeal should not be understood to have rendered the act invalid earlier. As far as the legislature was concerned, the proviso seemed to indicate, the act possessed the force of law until the moment the legislature repealed it.

The proviso inevitably raises a number of questions whose answers remain unclear. If the Ten Pound Act continued to possess the force of law until it was repealed, shouldn't the judges have been impeachable for violating their duty to decide cases according to the law of the land, as traditionalists argued? Or did the proviso mean that two opposite opinions about whether the act possessed the force of law could be maintained at the same time. Were judges entitled to maintain and act upon their independent opinion that the act was "ineffectual," while the legislature was entitled to hold its contrary opinion, leaving the statute as the law of the land in some counties of the state, but not in others? an infrequently discussed consequence of judicial review with which we live to this day.

No votes were recorded during the passage of these acts, suggesting that the bills were enacted without a great deal of controversy. Might a kind of compromise have been worked out by legislators to secure broad support for passage. Conceding neither that the Ten Pound Act was being replaced because it was unconstitutional, nor that it had lost the force of law before being repealed, might the minority of legislators who supported impeachment, have joined with the others (after that attempt failed), throwing up their hands, in a sense, and agreeing to devise a work around for the Ten Pound Act, rather than continue a futile struggle with the intractable judges (and with their own colleagues) over the constitutionality of the act. If this is so, perhaps this episode in the constitutional history of judicial review should be understood as one in which the judges' managed to prevail in their constitutional views by dint of their natural veto, their stubborn persistence, and the continuing divisions in the legislature. But at the time, legislative acquiescence (failing to remove the judges for their conduct, then repealing the act) would have

[134] Ibid. (June 28, 1787), 450. [135] Ibid.

been sufficient in themselves to confer a degree of constitutional legitimacy on the judges' actions, and that seems to have been the conclusion a fair number of contemporaries drew. In the following weeks several newspapers printed and re-printed one letter writer's view that "[t]he General Court, during their last session, repealed the Ten Pound act, and thereby justified the conduct of the justices of the inferior court, who have uniformly opposed it as unconstitutional and unjust."[136]

[136] "Correspondence," *New Hampshire Spy* (July 3, 1787), reprinted under "American Intelligence, Portsmouth, July 3," in *The Independent Gazetteer* (Philadelphia) (July 18, 1787), while the Federal Convention was meeting there.

8

Judicial Review and Legislative Supremacy in Rhode Island: The Case of *Trevett* v. *Weeden*, 1786, and Its Aftermath

The economic crisis that crippled New Hampshire in 1786 also beset other New England states. Throughout the region during the summer and fall of 1786, the economic hard times led to political and constitutional turmoil that took partially different forms in each state. In Massachusetts, a legislature that was almost completely unresponsive to popular petitions for relief, contributed to setting off a sizeable armed (Shay's) rebellion in western counties beginning in the late summer. In New Hampshire, where the legislature had been somewhat more responsive to popular outcries for relief, a smaller armed uprising was quickly put down, and a bridgehead against unconstrained majoritarian politics was established in the courts. In Rhode Island, as in other states, small farmers, who commonly needed to borrow to plant new crops, felt the burden of increased taxation to pay off the war debt especially acutely. But what in other states had only been a fear on one side and an aspiration on the other became a reality in Rhode Island. At the Spring 1786 annual elections, the "Country Party" won enough seats to take control of the legislature. Thereafter, they pursued an aggressive policy of debt relief.

At its May 1786 session, the legislature passed "An ACT for emitting *one hundred Thousand Pounds*" in paper money.[1] The preamble to the statute recited that "WHEREAS from a Variety of Causes . . . the Currency of this State, now in circulation, has become altogether insufficient in

[1] *At the General Assembly of the Governor and Company of the State of Rhode Island and Providence Plantations, begun and holden at Newport . . . on the first Wednesday in May, in the Year of our Lord One Thousand Seven Hundred and Eighty-six . . . .* (Providence, Printed by John Carter), 13–17.

Point of Quantity for the Purposes of Trade and Commerce, and for paying the just Debts of the Inhabitants" the legislature was establishing "a circulating Medium ... for facilitating that Interchange of Property so essential to a commercial State ... ."[2] The statute made the paper money "lawful Tender, for the complete Payment and final Discharge of all Debts ... ." in the state.[3] And it established a procedure through which a debtor could indirectly force a creditor to accept the paper in discharge of a debt, by lodging repayment with a Justice of the Superior Court or of the Court of Common Pleas for the county where the debtor lived. Every issue of the leading Rhode Island newspapers in this period contained public notices placed by Justices advising creditors that they were holding money for them, which discharged the debtor's legal obligation, and which the creditors would forfeit altogether unless they timely appeared to collect it.[4]

The purpose of the act was undoubtedly to inject greater liquidity into the economy and to facilitate the repayment of debts. But many recognized that the paper money was likely to depreciate against hard currency, as it subsequently did, which had the practical effect of empowering debtors to repay loans at a discount to their original value. Resistance to the new paper was quick to arise among creditors and merchants, and at the adjourned session held the next month in June, the legislature attempted to buttress the original act by passing a forcing act.

The June statute was passed not only in an effort to compel merchants to accept the paper money as legal tender for the purchase of any goods they were offering for sale but also in an attempt to prevent further depreciation in the currency's value. The act made it a criminal offence subject to the substantial fine of 100 pounds for

> any Person or Persons, [hereafter to] refuse to [accept the paper money] for any Article or Articles, which he, she or they, may have for and expose to Sale, agreeable to and for the Value mentioned on the Face of the said Bills, or shall, by making two Prices for his, her or their Goods, a Silver-Money less than a Paper Money Price, or shall make any Difference in bartering or exchanging his, her or, their Goods, in affixing a Value to his, her or their Goods, between the Paper Bills ... and the Goods so to be exchanged, or shall ... by any Ways, Means or Manner, whatsoever, or howsoever, tend to depreciate [the paper money].[5]

[2] Ibid., 13–14. [3] Ibid., 16.

[4] Ibid., 16–17; the four-page September 30, 1786 issue of *The Providence Gazette*, for example, contained nearly 20 such notices. Roughly the same number of notices were published in the four-page October 2, 1786 issue of *The Newport Mercury*.

[5] "An ACT in Addition to and Amendment of an Act, made and passed by the General Assembly of this State, at their last May Session at Newport, for emitting the sum of One

The act was to be enforced by a "Person who shall inform of and appear to prosecute" an offender, by bringing a *qui tam* action (on their own behalf and on behalf of the state), which would entitle the prosecuting "informer" to half the resulting fine, with the other half going to the state.[6]

By all accounts the economic situation grew worse following passage of these acts. A number of shopkeepers closed their doors, in order to avoid being forced to accept depreciated currency for their wares, and food shortages became common.[7]

Evidently, the state of affairs had deteriorated so far that the governor felt the need to call the legislature back into special session in August. Rather than completely relent, however, in August the legislature amended the June act by reducing the fine for a first offence to no less than six pounds but no more than thirty pounds.[8] At the same time, however, they created a speedy summary process for handling violations of the act. More than anything else, it was the legislature's creation of this summary process that triggered the ensuing constitutional controversy.

Under the new act, an "informer" was to "lodge his certain information" with a judge of the Superior or Inferior courts, who was then to convene a special court "in Three Days" to hear and determine the case and was "hereby authorized so to do, *without any Jury, by a Majority of the Judges present*, according to the Laws of the Land[9] (emphasis added). The judgment of the court, moreover, was to be "final and conclusive, and from which there shall be no Appeal . . . ."[10] As before, the prosecuting

Hundred Thousand Pounds," *At the General Assembly of the Governor and Company of the State of Rhode Island and Providence Plantations, begun and holden, by Adjournment, at Newport ... on the Fourth Monday in June, in the Year of our Lord One Thousand Seven Hundred and Eighty-six* . . . . (Providence, Printed by John Carter), 8–9.

[6] Ibid., 9.

[7] See the description of the doleful situation in Philip Hamburger, *Law and Judicial Duty* (Cambridge, Mass., Harvard University Press, 2008), 438 (based on contemporary diaries and letters).

[8] "An ACT, in Addition to and Amendment of an Act, entitled, 'An Act, in Addition to and Amendment of an Act, made and passed by this Assembly of this State, at their Session holden at Newport, in May last, for emitting the sum of One Hundred Thousand Pounds . . .,' " *At the General Assembly of the Governor and Company of the State of Rhode Island and Providence Plantations, begun and held (in Consequence of Warrants issued by his Excellency the Governor) at Newport ... on Tuesday the Twenty-second Day of August, in the Year of our Lord One Thousand Seven Hundred and Eighty-six* . . . . (Providence, Printed by Bennett Wheeler), 5–7, at 7.

[9] Ibid., 5–7. [10] Ibid., 7.

"informer" and the state were to share in any fine the court assessed. The legislature explained that it was establishing this summary process because "the usual and stated Methods and Times of holding Courts within this State are impracticable, inexpedient, and inapplicable ... and altogether insufficient to carry into Effect the good Purposes of this Legislature ... ."[11] But one historian has speculated that the Assembly adopted this measure because juries had proved to be reluctant to enforce the earlier June statute.[12]

The very next month, on September 13, John Trevett, a poor Newport cabinetmaker, filed a complaint in Superior Court against an almost equally poor Newport butcher, John Weeden, for refusing to accept paper money in payment for some beef. The complaint was subsequently rewritten as a formal "information," initiating Trevett's *qui tam* action against Weeden. The Chief Justice of the Superior Court, Paul Mumford, proceeded to call a "Special Superior Court" in accordance with the August act, but when the Superior Court convened for its regular September term, the judges adjourned the "Special Court" "over into the [regular] Superior Court," where the case subsequently went forward.[13] On Monday, September 25, the court heard the arguments in the case. It was on this occasion that James Varnum, the defendant Weeden's lawyer, made his well known, highly elaborate argument that the August act was unconstitutional and void, principally on the ground that it deprived the defendant of the right to a jury trial,[14] and that the court consequently should refuse to take cognizance of the case. The court

[11] Ibid., 5. [12] Hamburger, Law and Judicial Duty, 439.

[13] For these and additional details, see Hamburger, ibid., 440–41. Trevett apparently also brought a similar case against at least one other butcher, but it was the Weeden case that the court heard first, ibid., 440–41. According to another historian, a few other cases against butchers were also pending at this time, see Irwin H. Polishook, *Rhode Island and the Union, 1774–1795* (Evanston, Ill., Northwestern University Press, 1969), 134.

[14] Varnum made several other arguments as well, see the pamphlet Varnum subsequently published recalling his arguments in the case, James M. Varnum, *THE CASE, TREVETT against WEEDEN: On INFORMATION and COMPLAINT, for refusing Paper Bills in Payment for Butcher's Meat, in Market, at Par with Specie. Tried before the Honourable SUPERIOR COURT, in the County of Newport, September Term, 1786. ALSO, The Case of the Judges of said Court, Before the Honourable GENERAL ASSEMBLY, at Providence, October Session, 1786, on Citation, for dismissing said Complaint ... .* (Providence: Printed by John Carter, 1787). At the time, Varnum not only practiced law, but was a Major-General in the Rhode Island militia, and one of its delegates to Congress. Varnum's co-counsel, Henry Marchant, was a prominent lawyer, and also a member of Rhode Island's lower House of Deputies from Newport, see John Russell Bartlett (ed.), *Records of the State of Rhode Island and Providence Plantations in New England* (Providence, 1865), X (1784–92), 191, 239.

adjourned overnight to consider the arguments until the next morning, Tuesday, September 26, when the judges presented their opinions orally from the bench, agreeing in the main with Varnum, and delivered the court's judgment, in which they formally refused to take cognizance of Trevett's action.[15] Before discussing Varnum's argument and the judges' opinions at greater length, however, it is important to say something about the larger constitutional context in which the case arose, and against which Varnum's arguments were directed.

8.1 DID RHODE ISLAND HAVE A CONSTITUTION?

Rhode Island, along with Connecticut, were the only two states that did not write new constitutions in 1776, or over the following few years. One critical purpose of the new constitutions was to establish frames of government that would be suitable for the newly formed republics. In all the other colonies, it was necessary to make significant modifications to their frames of government in order to make them proper republics. In all the colonies, except Rhode Island and Connecticut, the governors and the upper houses of the legislature[16] had been appointed by the king or proprietor, rather than popularly elected. And in all them, governors had wielded an absolute veto over legislation. By contrast, in Rhode Island and Connecticut (under their Restoration charters) both governors and the upper house of the legislature had been annually elected by the freemen. Not only were governors popularly elected in these two colonies, no power resembling a veto over legislation had been conferred on them.[17] Once the king had been eliminated, the governments of Rhode Island and Connecticut required no alterations to their frames of

[15] The dates of the hearing, and the judges' opinions in the case are reported in a number of newspaper accounts from the period, see *Providence Gazette* issues of Saturday, September 30, 1786, at 2, and Saturday, October 7, 1786, at 2–3; *Newport Mercury*, Monday, October 2, 1786, at 2–3; *United States Chronicle*, Providence, R.I., Thursday, October 5, 1786, at 2; *Independent Chronicle*, Boston, Mass., Thursday, October 5, 1786, at 3; and *The Massachusetts Gazette*, Boston, Mass., Tuesday, October 3, 1786, at 3.

[16] Except in colonies with unicameral legislatures, and in Massachusetts where the upper house was chosen by the lower house and by outgoing members of the upper house, subject to the governor's veto, Jackson Turner Main, *The Upper House in Revolutionary America: 1763–1788* (Madison, Wisc., University of Wisconsin Press, 1967), 68.

[17] In Connecticut, the governor sat as a member of the upper house with a single vote, like other members, and an additional vote when it was necessary to break a tie, see Zephaniah Swift, *A System of the Laws of the State of Connecticut* (Windham, Ct., Printed by John Byrns, 1795, repr. Arno Press, 1972), I, 63.

government to make them properly republican. And even in the midst of revolution, the people of these two colonies appeared to show little interest in changing the form of their long-established governments.

As a consequence, the concrete experience of revolution was significantly different in these two colonies. In the other colonies, Independence entailed changing the officers of government. Royal and proprietary governors fled, and appointed members of upper houses could simply not continue on the old terms. In the absence of governors and upper houses, the representative bodies that began to administer the governments in these colonies could not properly claim the status of legislatures. They were called congresses or conventions, which Americans then commonly viewed as "legally imperfect legislatures."[18] After the New Hampshire and Virginia representative congresses wrote new constitutions, for example, and established new governments that included governors and upper houses, these representative congresses, having "perfected" themselves, simply reconvened as part of the legislature. None of this was necessary in Rhode Island and Connecticut, where the sitting governors, and the sitting legislatures simply continued to administer their governments as before. As the representative bodies in these two states continued to function as normal legislatures, there was no need for the extralegal representative bodies called congresses or conventions. But it is important to understand that in 1776, the constitutional authority of these legislatures was not yet sharply distinguished from that of the representative congresses and conventions that wrote constitutions in other states, and then reconvened as legislatures. Both were understood to be an embodiment of the people, possessing similar constitutional authority.

Hence, when in October, 1776, the Connecticut legislature "Resolved ... That they approve of the Declaration of Independence ... and that this Colony is, and of Right ought to be, a Free and Independent State, and the Inhabitants thereof are absolved from all Allegiance to the British Crown, and all political Connections between them and the King of Great-Britain is, and ought to be totally desolved," they continued by reenacting into law, the "Form of Government" they had long enjoyed.[19]

[18] Gordon Wood, *The Creation of the American Republic, 1776–1787* (Chapel Hill, N.C., University of North Carolina Press, 1969), 307.

[19] Connecticut Session Laws, *Acts and Laws Made and passed by the General Court or Assembly of the State of Connecticut, in New-England, in America; holden at New-Haven, in said State, on the second Thursday of October, Anno Domini, 1776*, "Independence established," 431.

And be it Enacted by the *Governor, Council, and Representatives, in General Court assembled, and by the Authority of the same*, That the Form of Civil Government in this State shall continue to be as established by Charter received from CHARLES the Second, King of *England* so far as an Adherence to the same will be consistent with an absolute Independence of this State ... ; and that all Officers, Civil and Military, heretofore appointed by this State, continue in the Execution of their several Offices, and the Laws of this State shall continue in Force until otherwise ordered ....[20]

In taking this step, the Connecticut legislature was doing something not all that different from what was being done in other states where representative congresses were writing constitutions that established new frames of government, as *the* representatives of the people. The Connecticut legislature, as *the* representatives of the people of Connecticut, was formally enacting into law, the foundational constitutional document of Connecticut to serve as the frame of government for the newly independent state.

In Rhode Island, however, the legislature did not even do this much. At its May 1776 session it stripped all mention of the king out of the colony's name, and out of its official processes.[21] Two months later, after publication of the Declaration of Independence, it voted to "approve the [Declaration]; and [to] most solemnly engage, that we will support the said General Congress with our Lives and Fortunes." But then it simply enacted a law changing the name of the government to "the State of

[20] Ibid., "Form of Government," 431–32, only later, in the 1784 statutory revision, did the legislature combine the 1776 "Form of Government" act with several older statutes that had declared a variety of fundamental rights, enacting that compilation into law as what amounted to a frame of government together with a brief bill of rights, see the editor's annotations to "An act containing an abstract and declaration of the rights and privileges of the people of this State, and securing the same" in *The Public Statute Laws of the State of Connecticut*, Book I (Published by Authority of the General Assembly, Hartford, Printed by Hudson and Goodwin, 1808), 23–24. Beginning with the 1784 statutory revision, the text of Charles the Second's Charter was printed at the beginning of the volume along with the text of the Articles of Confederation (in later editions, the United States Constitution).

[21] "AN ACT repealing an Act, intitled, 'An Act for the more effectually securing to his Majesty the Allegiance of his Subjects, in this his Colony and Dominion of Rhode-Island and Providence Plantations;' and altering the Forms of Commissions, of all Writs and Processes in the Courts, and of the Oaths prescribed by Law," *At the General Assembly of the Governor and Company of the English Colony of Rhode-Island and Providence Plantations, in New-England, in America, begun and holden at Newport, within and for the said Colony, on the First Wednesday in May, in the Year of our Lord, One Thousand, Seven Hundred and Seventy-six*, 22–26. The legislature changed the colony's name to "The Governor and Company of the English Colony of Rhode-Island, and Providence Plantations."

Rhode-Island and Providence Plantations," and that was all.[22] But in as much as the form of government, established by the Restoration charter, continued to operate, uninterrupted, exactly as before, it would not have been completely out of the question to view the charter as the constitution of Rhode Island, to which the people had assented simply by acquiescing in its continuation.

In the years following 1776, constitutional ideas and practices evolved rapidly,[23] and by the early 1780s these changes had raised serious questions about whether Connecticut and Rhode Island actually possessed constitutions at all.[24] Especially in New England, the ideas that constitutions must be drafted by stand-alone conventions and ratified by the people, if they were to be binding on legislatures, had become commonplace. A constitution "enacted" by the legislature itself could hardly be called a constitution. From the perspective of these new ideas, however, the constitutional situation in Virginia did not seem so different from the one in Connecticut, and Rhode Island, and by implication New Hampshire, none of whom had followed the procedures that were now beginning to seem necessary to adopt a fixed and unalterable constitution that would be superior to the legislature. Under the sway of these new ideas, Thomas Jefferson began in fact to argue in the early 1780s that Virginia itself did not possess a genuine constitution, precisely because of the faulty procedures that had been used to adopt that document in 1776.[25] At the time legislatures in Connecticut and (more ambiguously) Rhode Island first re-enacted their charters, it seems fairly clear, they were not behaving as the constitutional outliers they would subsequently be taken to be, but in general accord with the conventional constitutional understandings of that time, which also governed the conduct of constitution makers in other states.

In disputing assertions that Connecticut had no constitution, Zephaniah Swift, writing as late as 1795, made an acquiescence argument similar to the one critics of Jefferson's position had made in Virginia.[26] Even if the Connecticut legislature had not possessed the legitimate

[22] "Independence declared," *At the General Assembly of the Governor and Company of the English Colony of Rhode-Island and Providence Plantations, in New-England, in America, begun and holden in Consequence of Warrants issued by his Honor the Governor, at Newport, within and for the said State, on Thursday the Eighteenth Day of July, in the Year of our Lord, One Thousand, Seven Hundred and Seventy-six*, 127–28.

[23] See the discussion of these developments in Chapter 7.

[24] Wood, Creation of the American Republic, 276–77.

[25] See Thomas Jefferson, *Notes on the State of Virginia, 1781–82* (1787, reprinted Boston, Lilly and Wait, 1832), 126, 129; for a more detailed discussion see Chapter 5 above.

[26] See Jefferson, "Notes on the State of Virginia," 128.

authority to adopt the royal charter as the state's constitution in the first place, Swift wrote,

> yet the subsequent conduct of the people, in assenting to, approving of, and acquiescing in the acts of the legislature, have established, and rendered them valid, and binding and given them all the force, and authority of an express contract. For there is no particular mode pointed out, by which the assent of the people to any particular form of government, is to be obtained. It may be expressed by delegates chosen for that purpose, to meet in convention, or it may be implied by a tacit acquiescence, and approbation.[27]

The same, of course, might be argued of the constitution of Rhode Island, where the people indicated by their conduct that they had "acquiesced" in the continued functioning of the form of government established by the royal charter, long after independence.

Swift was more than a little evasive on the question whether he believed the Connecticut constitution to be merely customary, as was Britain's, or whether the people's "tacit acquiescence" had established the written royal charter as "an express contract." He seems to have argued the issue both ways over several pages, without ever offering a clear resolution.[28] James Varnum's argument in *Trevett* v. *Weeden*, discussed below, suffered from similar obscurities about the kind of constitution Rhode Island possessed. It is possible that neither man considered the distinction to be of great constitutional significance.

Even though Swift, unlike Varnum, completely rejected judicial review, he felt no doubt that while the Connecticut constitution (whether customary or written) allowed the legislature great leeway to make alterations, there were some fundamental lines beyond which it could not go without destroying the government.[29]

When James Varnum made his argument that the Rhode Island forcing act of August 1786 was contrary to the state's constitution and void, it is important to see that he was drawing on a body of living constitutional understandings to support his case not only that Rhode Island possessed a constitution, that might even be written, but that in either case, there were some fundamental lines under that constitution beyond which the legislature could not go. At the same time, there were now those in Rhode Island who simply refused to accept the idea that the state possessed a bill of rights and constitution at all.[30]

[27] Swift, A System of the Laws of Connecticut, I, 58. [28] Ibid., 55–59. [29] Ibid., 62.

[30] See, for example, "The American Whig, No. IV," in *The Providence Gazette* (April 24, 1779), 1, discussing arguments on both sides. For a similar debate at the time that *Trevett*

8.2 RHODE ISLAND'S TRADITIONAL CONSTITUTION OF LEGISLATIVE SUPREMACY

Before examining Varnum's argument in the case more closely, however, it is important to say something about the long-established practice of legislative supremacy in Rhode Island, which had been bequeathed to the state by the 1663 charter. As mentioned earlier, under the charter, the governor and both houses of the legislature were elected annually by the freemen. And the governor, who sat as a member of the upper house, did not possess a veto over the laws. "The charter did not create judicial tribunals, but [as in New Hampshire] empowered the general assembly to create them ... "[31] Under the charter, the only check on the power of the legislature to make law, or otherwise, was that wielded by the king in council, upon legislative or judicial review. But after Independence, with the elimination of the king from the government, no established institutional check on the power of the legislature remained.

A little more has to be said about the history of the "judicial" powers the governor and legislature long exercised in Rhode Island. "[A]t its first session under the charter," the historian Thomas Durfee writes, the General Assembly "provided that either the governor or the deputy governor, with at least six assistants, [i.e., members of the upper house of the legislature] should hold the general court of trials at Newport every year in May and October."[32] At the same time, the Assembly established special courts for Providence and Warwick for the trial of matters under ten pounds. These courts were "to be held by three assistants every six months ... "[33] In 1729, the legislature revised the court system substantially, establishing civil and criminal courts in each county. County justices of the peace were to hold the criminal general sessions, and "four judicious and skillful persons," selected by the legislature, were to sit on the civil courts.[34] The original general court of trials was now renamed "The Superior Court of Judicature, Court of Assize, and General Gaol Delivery," but its authority was modified to make it a mainly appellate

was being agitated, see letter "To the Freemen of the State of Rhode Island and Providence Plantations," by "A Farmer" (September 7, 1786), and reply letter "To the Inhabitants of the State of Rhode Island," by "Tacitus" (September 16, 1786), reprinted in *The United States Chronicle* (Providence, October 5, 1786), 1–2. "Tacitus" quotes "A Farmer" as "declaring" in a speech in the House of Deputies "that we had neither *bill of rights or constitution*," at 2.

[31] Thomas Durfee, *Gleanings from the Judicial History of Rhode Island* (Providence, S.S. Rider, Rhode Island Historical Tracts, 1st Ser., No. 18, 1883), 11.

[32] Durfee, Judicial History of Rhode Island, 11. [33] Ibid. [34] Ibid., 14–15.

court. As before, however, this highest court in the colony continued to be held by the Governor, or Deputy governor, and the Assistants, who were all, as one historian has put it somewhat anachronistically, "political officers."[35] The staffing of the Superior Court did not change until 1747, when the legislature passed an act replacing "the governor or deputy governor and the ten assistants," with "five judges, a chief and four associates ... who were to be chosen annually by the general assembly ... ."[36] And this was the form the Superior Court still took when the case of *Trevett* v. *Weeden* was brought to that court in 1786.

But this was only part of the story of judicial authority in Rhode Island. The General Assembly itself had a long tradition of acting as what has been described in Chapter 7 as a "legal tribunal."[37] One historian of Rhode Island's judicial system, Thomas Durfee, has written,

> the general assembly seems to have considered itself a court as well as a legislature, and in its proceedings it often denominated itself a court. As a court, however, its action, though in some sense judicial, was not so purely so as that of ordinary tribunals, but was often tempered by some admixture of legislation. In fact, the assembly was very frequently petitioned (not to enforce but) to modify the law in [a] particular case, or make it specifically for the case .... It thus sat as a court to dispense justice not according to law but according to equity and according to equity in the popular as distinguished from the juridical meaning of the word. The records are full of illustrations of the jurisdiction.[38]

The General Assembly's jurisdiction, Durfee explains, also had other dimensions.

> Another phase of the jurisdiction is exemplified in the matter of appeals and petitions for new trial. The right of appeal was granted in 1680 in favor of any party to any "actional case" aggrieved by any judgment rendered in the higher [later Superior] court. The appeal seems to have taken the case up for re-trial on all ... issues [of fact and law]. At the conclusion of the hearing the judgment of the court below was either confirmed or modified ... or entirely reversed. In 1712 [as a result of several earlier interventions by the Board of Trade and Queen in Council], appeals to the assembly, technically so called, were abolished, though under another form, namely by way of petition, the jurisdiction continued [uninterrupted.][39]

35 Ibid., 17. 36 Ibid., 20–21.

37 For a detailed discussion of the legislature as "legal tribunal," see Chapter 7.

38 Durfee, Judicial History of Rhode Island, 34–35.

39 Ibid., 36–37, and 59–60, another historian of the Rhode Island judiciary has made the same point, see Edward Stiness, "The Struggle for Judicial Supremacy," in Edward Field (ed.), *State of Rhode Island and Providence Plantations at the End of the Century*, III, (Boston, 1902), III, 91–169, at 101.

Another historian of Rhode Island's judicial system has described the procedures the General Assembly followed upon receiving private petitions. They closely resembled those to which the Connecticut legislature adhered when it received similar petitions.[40]

> We have seen that despite the denial by Great Britain of the right of the Assembly to act as a court of appeal, that that body had continued, almost by subterfuge in reality, to act by way of petition, exercising practically the same authority. Indeed, the procedure of this body when hearing petitions differed in hardly any respect from that of a court. A body of rules was adopted by an act of the Assembly which prescribed the manner in which appeals should be brought before them. Any person who petitioned the Assembly praying that any judgment or determination of the courts of the Colony might be set aside, or that execution might be stayed on a judgment rendered against him, was required, at least three weeks prior to the next session of the Assembly to file his petition with the secretary of state and at the same time give a bond to pay the costs of the proceedings. Thereupon the secretary issued a *citation which was served by the sheriff upon the adverse party*, requiring him to appear and show cause why the prayer of the petition should not be granted. At the beginning of the session a time was assigned for hearing these petitions. The clerk of the lower house of the Assembly kept a docket, and at the time assigned the cases were called in their order. If the petitioner did not appear, the petition was dismissed, practically a non-suit. If the respondent in turn did not put in an appearance, the petition was granted; practically a default.[41] (emphasis added)

"The assembly," Thomas Durfee writes, "also exercised a jurisdiction, neither appellate nor revisory, which was exceedingly heterogeneous, [covering a variety of other miscellaneous "judicial" matters].[42] He summarizes the General Assembly's jurisdiction this way. "So the assembly corrected judicial mistakes ... arrested legal proceedings, or issued its mandates to the courts directing or prohibiting their action."[43] "After the Revolution," he concludes, "there was no power to dispute the jurisdiction, and the assembly continued to exercise it without question."[44] The historian Edward Stiness reaches a similar conclusion. "The Assembly down to the adoption of the constitution of 1843 exercised their power both as a court of original jurisdiction in some cases and as a court of review in others without serious question."[45]

[40] See discussion in Chapter 7.

[41] Stiness, "The Struggle for Judicial Supremacy," 111. Compare the description of the Connecticut legislature's process in such cases, see Swift, A System of the Laws of Connecticut, I, 81–82.

[42] Durfee, Judicial History of Rhode Island, 44–45. [43] Ibid., 46. [44] Ibid., 61.

[45] Stiness, The Struggle for Judicial Supremacy, 112.

8.3 VARNUM'S ARGUMENT TO THE SUPERIOR COURT

Now that something has been said about the broader constitutional context, it is possible to understand just how radically Varnum's argument to the Superior Court broke with Rhode Island's long settled practice of legislative supremacy. It was long winded, rambling, ambiguously worded, composed of multiple loosely connected parts that did not always follow one another in a discernible order, and is therefore difficult to summarize. But it does contain a number of threads that can be recounted. Varnum began by saying that

> we must necessarily call in question the validity of the legislative act upon which the information [in the case] is grounded. We shall attempt most clearly to evince, that it is contrary to the fundamental laws of the State, and therefore, as the civilians express it, a mere nullity, and void, *ab initio* . . . .[46]

By page eleven, Varnum has gotten to the main point: "That the trial by jury is a fundamental right, a part of our *legal* constitution: That the Legislature cannot deprive the citizens of this right: And that your Honours can, and we trust will, so determine."[47] He proceeded to devote pages to showing how trial by jury has been a fundamental right of British and American subjects for centuries. In Rhode Island that fundamental right had been enshrined by a statute the Assembly passed immediately after receiving the royal charter in 1663. That legislative act "declar[ed] the rights and privileges of his Majesty's subjects within this Colony," prominent among them being the right to trial by jury.[48]

But the linchpin of Varnum's argument, was his discussion of the Rhode Island constitution, which he only began on page twenty-one, and which leaves the reader in some doubt about whether he considers the Rhode Island constitution to be customary or written. "THE powers of our Legislature," he wrote, "are so clearly defined in the Charter, which is conclusive evidence of the compact of the people, as well as of the royal intention, that a recurrence to them will greatly assist us in the present question."[49]

The charter is evidently a writing that is not itself the compact of the people but confirms, in some fashion, that there was a prior (unwritten, implied) compact. The charter is a writing that derives, from a petition to the king, as the result of an earlier (implied) original compact of the people, and to the extent it faithfully reflects the terms of that original

[46] Varnum, THE CASE, TREVETT against WEEDEN, 4. [47] Ibid., 11. [48] Ibid., 15.
[49] Ibid., 21–22.

compact, and puts them into writing, has made those, in some sense, express terms imposed by the people themselves? Crucial for this argument is that the written royal charter "clearly defined . . . the powers of our Legislature," and expressly limited them. Ironically, those express limitations were contained in the familiar repugnance clause imposed by the king on colonial governments. The charter, Varnum wrote, granted broad powers to the Rhode Island legislature to make laws "so [long] as such laws, ordinances and constitutions, so made, be not contrary and repugnant unto, but, as near as may be, agreeable to the laws of this our realm of England, considering the nature and constitutions of the place and people there."[50]

And here is his hard to pin down conclusion about all this.

> THIS grant [from the king], which was obtained in consequence of an association of all the people for that purpose, expressly limits the legislative powers; and by invariable custom and usage they are still so confined, that they cannot make any laws repugnant to the general system of laws which governed the realm of England at the time of the grant. The revolution hath made no change in this respect, so as to abridge the people of the means of securing their lives, liberty and property: To preserve which they have ever considered the trial by jury the most effectual.[51]

These "express" constitutional limitations on legislative power, "obtained in consequence of an [implied] association of all the people for that purpose," and carried forward by "invariable custom and usage" after the Revolution had eliminated the entire apparatus of imperial government, left the whole matter of constitutional limitations an ill-defined mixture of express written and implied customary constitutional conditions. This mixture most clearly resembles that of the customary British constitution itself, composed, as it was, of both written and unwritten elements. But if this is the case, the Rhode Island Assembly, like Parliament (under prevailing British constitutional understandings), should have the power to modify, i.e., "to explain," the constitution by statute.[52]

[50] Ibid., 22. [51] Ibid., 23.

[52] Hamburger, Law and Judicial Duty, 436; Varnum's response to the contention that Rhode Island had no constitution at all was to argue from first principles, rather than to point to any concrete historical instrument of government. "If we have not a constitution, by what authority doth our General Assembly convene to make laws, and levy taxes? Their appointment by the freemen of the towns, excluding the idea of a pre-existing social compact, cannot separately give them power to make laws compulsory upon the other towns . . . . When met, they make laws and levy taxes, and their constituents obey those laws, and pay their taxes," Varnum, THE CASE, TREVETT against WEEDEN, 25.

Varnum's response to this problem, was to draw on emerging American ideas about constitutions and legislatures to flip the traditional (British) presumption. There was no indication, Varnum argued, that the people of Rhode Island had ever expressly granted to their legislature the power to modify the constitution, and in the absence of such an express grant, it cannot be taken for granted that they did.

> Have the citizens of this State ever entrusted their legislators with the power of altering their constitution? – If they have, when and where was the solemn meeting of all the people for that purpose? – By what public instrument have they declared it, or in what part of their conduct have they betrayed such extravagance and folly? – For what have they contended through a long, painful and bloody war, but to secure inviolate, and transmit unsullied to posterity, the inestimable privileges they received from their forefathers?[53]

Varnum draws on emerging American constitutional understandings, which found little purchase in the actual structure and practice of Rhode Island government, to conjure into existence a constitutional system which more nearly resembled those in other states where separation of powers clauses, repugnance, and law of the land clauses had been expressly adopted as part of the constitution.

But Varnum's argument did resonate deeply with American experience during the recent Revolution in which the American people made war in order to hold the king and parliament to the terms of the British constitution, as they interpreted it. That, however, had been an example of the people enforcing a customary constitution "politically." Of course, in doing so, it was true that many Americans had also considered the "unconstitutional" laws enacted by parliament not to be valid, and binding upon them. The line between disobedience to duly enacted laws, on the ground they are unconstitutional and void, and actually rendering such acts not law, can be blurry, and come down to whether the party repudiating them possesses the (legitimate) authority to deprive them of the force of law, if, in their judgment, they violate the constitution.

The question remained, nevertheless, did anyone other than the people themselves have the formal authority to judge the acts of the legislature to be unconstitutional? Varnum's answer was yes, under certain circumstances, the courts have the formal authority to judge the constitutionality

[53] Varnum, *Trevett* v. *Weeden*, 24–25; it is difficult to see how the people could possibly have made such an express, public declaration, given that, in Varnum's telling, there was no definite, concrete historical moment when the people of Rhode Island are recorded as having gathered together explicitly to form a constitution, and might have done so.

of legislative enactments, as a kind of substitute, it seems, for the people themselves, and in order to avoid revolution, which was understood to be the principal traditional remedy for serious violations of the constitution.

> But as the Legislative is the supreme power in government, who is to judge whether they have violated the constitutional rights of the people? …. [T]he people themselves will judge, as the only resort in the last stages of oppression. But when they proceed no farther than merely to enact what they may call laws, and refer those to the Judiciary Courts for determination, then, (in discharge of the great trust reposed in them, and to prevent the horrors of a civil war, as in the present case) the Judges can, and we trust your Honours will, decide upon them."[54]

If part of the reason the judges should possess such authority is so that they can stand in for the people (who would otherwise have the exclusive right to interpret and enforce constitutional limitations), in order to avoid civil war, a natural question arises. In Rhode Island, the people enjoyed the constitutional right to elect (and replace) their legislators annually. Why did this right to change their government peacefully every year, not suffice to secure every other constitutional right, without the need to overturn the government, or to empower the judges to nullify statutes? Varnum does provide an answer for this question later in his argument. It will turn out that the current system of government lacks, in his view, what the charter and system of colonial government previously included, an enforceable check on the people themselves, lost at the Revolution; a check which the judges can restore, in some measure. Annual elections are useless as a remedy for the problem of the people's rash conduct; indeed, annual elections are themselves a significant source of that very problem.

There is a good deal more, however, underlying his claim that the judges' must possess such power. To a crucial extent, his contention is based on a particular version of separation of powers principles, which has, by this time, become well established in American constitutional culture. And even though he cannot point to any Rhode Island practice or instrument of government that actually enshrines those principles, it does not stop him from invoking the oft repeated idea that where the three distinct powers of government, the legislative, judicial and executive, fall into the same hands, the inevitable result is tyranny.[55] Hence, the judges

[54] Ibid., 26.

[55] "There are, in all free governments," Varnum says at the outset of his argument, "three distinct sources of power, the legislative, the judiciary, and executive," ibid., 7.

must exercise their constitutional powers completely independent of the legislature, if free government is to be sustained.

> [I am not] capable of distinguishing between an established tyranny, and that government where the Legislative makes the law, and dictates to the Judges their adjudication. For in that case, were they to enact tyrannical laws, they would be sure to have them executed in a tyrannical manner ... and the people must be enslaved, or fly to arms.[56]

But what is the distinct constitutional power of the judges that permits them to render such judgments? Varnum's answer, like so much else in his argument, does not spell out the logic of his position as clearly as one might like, but it may be approximately construed.

> Have the Judges a power to repeal, to amend, to alter laws, or to make new laws? – God forbid! – In that case they would become Legislators. – Have the Legislators power to direct the Judges how they shall determine upon the laws already made? – God forbid! – In that case they would become Judges.– The true distinction lies in this, that the Legislative have the incontroullable [sic] power of making laws not repugnant to the constitution:– The Judiciary have the sole power of judging of those laws, and are bound to execute them; but cannot admit any of the Legislative as law, which is against the constitution.[57]

For Varnum, it seems, the judges have the duty, by virtue of the interpretive authority inherent in their office, formally to decide whether the terms of a particular statute conflict with the supposed "express" Rhode Island "constitutional" prohibition against making laws repugnant to the laws of England. Functionally, he is proposing that the judges act as a substitute for the Privy Council. If the judges determine that a statute is repugnant, they have the duty to declare it to be beyond the powers of the legislature to make, and consequently not law.[58]

Varnum's account leaves many steps out of this argument, outlines others only in the most fragmentary form, and does not attempt to wrestle, in any serious way, with a range of difficult questions about the current legal and constitutional status of the charter, of the precise nature of the prohibitions it supposedly imposes, about the legal status of an implied constitution, and much else. It is an audacious, inventive, free-wheeling

[56] Ibid., 26–27. [57] Ibid., 27.

[58] Varnum concluded his long argument with these words: "That this Court hath power to judge and determine what acts of the General Assembly are agreeable to the constitution; and, on the contrary, that this Court is under the most solemn obligations to execute the laws of the land, and therefore cannot, will not, consider this act as a law of the land," ibid., 35.

argument that has just enough plausibility, given the American experience with the British constitution leading up to the Revolution, to persuade more than a few Americans– under the right political circumstances.

If Varnum's argument lacked the rigor of similar arguments made by St. George Tucker, Alexander Hamilton, and James Iredell, which were based on express written constitutions, some actually containing separation of powers clauses, law of the land clauses, and clauses expressly restricting the legislative power to make conflicting laws, it should nevertheless be understood as a member of the same family. It was during these years that bold, imaginative, mainly elite lawyers began to invent and disseminate their much more rigorous and compelling arguments for judicial review. These other lawyers, of course, had greatly superior materials with which to work.

Varnum's argument may have lacked the compelling legal/constitutional logic of the others, but it shared with them a powerful political appeal that certain groups of Americans found extremely persuasive. The palpable attraction of separation of powers principles at this historical moment was that they offered the possibility that the judiciary might serve as a refuge from majoritarian politics. The economic situation in Rhode Island was close to disastrous, and the legislature's actions had arguably made things worse. Legislators seemed prepared to sacrifice property and contract rights along with the sacred right to trial by jury, in order to advance the controversial effort to assist the farmer and debtor portions of the population. Even Varnum's reference(s) to civil war were not so far-fetched. As these events were unfolding in Rhode Island, Shay's rebellion was playing out next door in Massachusetts, and in New Hampshire a small armed uprising had taken place only a few weeks earlier. Under these circumstances, many felt great anxiety, and great vulnerability, that there might not be any limits to how far a popularly elected legislature might be prepared, and had the power, to go. Varnum's argument drew upon these fears.

> The life, liberty and property of the citizens are secured by the general law of the State. We will then suppose ... that the General Assembly should pass an act directing that no citizen should leave his house, nor suffer any of his family to move out of the same, for the space of six months, upon the pain of death .... Suppose they should enact that every parent should destroy his first-born child .... upon the common principles, the Court would be as much bound to execute these acts as any others. For if they can determine upon any act, that it is not law, and so reject it, they must necessarily have the power of determining *what* acts are laws, and so on the contrary. There is no middle line. The Legislative hath power to go

all lengths, or not to overleap the bounds of its appointment at all. So it is with the Judiciary; it must reject all acts of the Legislative that are contrary to the trust reposed in them by the people, or it must adopt all.[59]

But for Varnum, the root of the problem lay in the structure of the government itself, which failed to provide the kind of check on the people that the charter (ironically) had provided in the provincial government. His general diagnosis would not have surprised James Madison or Alexander Hamilton.

The Legislative of one House being composed of new members, or members newly elected twice in the year, *feels and carries into effect the sentiments of the people founded upon the extremes of liberty.* The electors in the respective towns have generally some point to obtain; or, which more unfriendly to public liberty, they are divided by parties, and so the members elected become the advocates of local, interested measures, without comparing them with the more extensive objects of the community. The sessions seldom exceed the limits of a week: New laws are proposed, acted upon and adopted, according to the first or the preconcerted impressions of passion, without time for deliberation or reflection. The Upper House, it is true, hath a negative upon the House of Deputies, but they never persist in exercising it without endangering their next election. The appointment of the Judges, Justices of the Peace, and other officers of government, being made by the members of both Houses in a Grand Committee, is very often the result of political arrangements: ... *so the people feel no great restraint from this quarter.*

What is there then, in the nature of our government, to prevent anarchy and confusion on the one hand, or tyranny and oppression on the other? – *Before the revolution, the king, as Supreme Executive, formed the balance*; but since, the Executive Power hath become blended with the Legislative, and we have not, like the other States in the union, adopted any substitute for this defect.[60] (emphasis added)

[59] Ibid., 29.

[60] Ibid., 33–34, on the problem of untethered majorities, see also a letter "To the Inhabitants of the State of Rhode Island," by "Tacitus" (September 16, 1786), reprinted in *The United States Chronicle* (Providence, R.I., October 5, 1786), at 2 ("Therefore because they are the majority ["A Farmer," to whose letter Tacitus is replying, believes] they need none of the[] [public] virtues.") In his own letter "To the Freemen of the State of Rhode-Island and Providence Plantations" (September 7, 1786), reprinted in the same issue of the *United States Chronicle*, "A Farmer" argued that far from being an unconstitutional deprivation of trial by jury, the Rhode Island statute at issue in the *Trevett* case differed little from a range of other matters that had traditionally been handled through summary justice proceedings, and had long been accepted as "consistent with the law." ("Notwithstanding the aforegoing [general] principles of trial by jury have for time immemorial remained uncontested, how often has a single justice of the peace, even consistent with the law, an opportunity of determining against a man, his character and

He concluded this final section of his argument by expressing a hope.

> If the Legislature are blindly guided by the general impulse. Or should these attachments be more strongly fixed to the interests of a few designing men than to the public wish, tyranny would spring out of anarchy. *In either case, the interposition of the Judiciary may save the constitution, at least for a time*; and, by averting the immediate evil, will give scope for reflection, and so prevent a dissolution of the government.[61] (emphasis added)

The state's newspapers were primarily published in the coastal commercial towns of Providence and Newport, and the great majority of reports printed in them heaped praise on Varnum's argument. The account printed in the October 7, 1786 *Providence Gazette*, for example, devoted nearly two full columns to a detailed description of Varnum's approximately three hour argument.[62] According to the reporter, Varnum "displayed the oratorical strength of a Demosthenes, and the eloquence of a Cicero."[63] By contrast, Henry Goodwin, the attorney arguing on the other side of the question on behalf of Trevett, was reported as having "said but little."[64] Another paper reported that "Mr. Goodwin (Attorney for the Plaintiff) spoke as well on the subject as could be expected."[65] Only one report actually included a brief account of the argument Goodwin made, and it may have been as brief as it was because Goodwin did not believe that defendants had any legal ground to stand on, as Rhode Island did not actually have a constitution that expressly protected individual rights. "Mr. Goodwin (Attorney for the Complainant) spoke in favour of the [Forcing] Act, and said we had no Bill of Rights . . . ."[66]

The court adjourned over night to consider the arguments of the attorneys and came back the next morning with their decision. According to the reports in the *Newport Mercury* and *Providence Gazette*, the judges were apparently as unbothered by the weaknesses and omissions in Varnum's constitutional argument as the press was. Four of the five judges declared that their judgment was that the court should not take cognizance of the case, two judges, Howell and Devol, on the ground that the

his property, without the intervention of his peers; and how much oftener have three justices the same power"), at 1.

61 Ibid., 34. 62 "Newport, October 2," *Providence Gazette* (October 7, 1786), 2–3.

63 Ibid., 3. 64 Ibid., 3.

65 "Providence, October 5," *The United States Chronicle* (Providence, R.I., October 5, 1786), at 2.

66 "Providence, Sept. 30," *Providence Gazette* (September 30, 1786), 2.

forcing act was unconstitutional; a third, judge Hazard, adopting one of Varnum's other more antiquated constitutional arguments, gave as his opinion that the words of the act contradicted one another, and hence were impossible to perform.[67] It will turn out to be significant that the fifth judge, Chief Justice Mumford, did not take part in the decision, and "did not declare his sentiments."[68] He merely reported the majority's determination not to take cognizance of the information. The *Gazette* reported that

> Judge Howell, in a firm, sensible and judicious speech, assigned the reasons which induced him to be of the opinion, that the information was not cognizable by the Court – declared himself independent as a Judge – the penal law to be repugnant and unconstitutional, and therefore gave it as his opinion that the Court could not take cognizance of the information– Judge Devol was of the same opinion – Judge Tillinghast took notice of the striking repugnancy in the expressions of the act, "*Without trial by jury, according to the laws of the land*" – and on that ground gave his Judgment the same way – Judge Hazard voted against taking cognizance– The Chief Judge [Mumford] declared the judgment of the Court, without giving his own opinion.[69]

The papers also reported that the crowd in the courtroom were elated by the decision and opinions.

> The emotions of joy expressed by the audience on this occasion, strongly manifested how deeply interested they were in the preservation of a *constitutional Birthright*; which, till then, had never been arraigned at the tribunal of our own Courts.[70]

But the overwhelmingly favorable reception that Varnum's argument and the judges' decision enjoyed (as reported in the press) may not accurately reflect the broader state of opinion in Rhode Island. The actions of the legislature over the next six months perhaps speak more loudly about the (silent) majority's unswerving determination in the legislature to preserve the traditional constitution of legislative supremacy.

[67] See Varnum's argument in *Trevett* v. *Weeden*, 30–31.

[68] "Providence, Sept. 30," *Providence Gazette* (September 30, 1786), 2.

[69] "Newport, Oct. 2," in *Providence Gazette* (October 7, 1786), 3, see also *The Newport Mercury* (October 2, 1786), 2–3; other reports of the decision appear in the *Providence Gazette* (September 30, 1786), 2, *The United States Chronicle* (Providence, R.I., October 5, 1786), 2, *The Massachusetts Gazette* (Boston, October 3, 1786), 3, and *The Independent Chronicle* (Boston, October 5, 1786), 3.

[70] "Newport, Oct. 2," in *The Newport Mercury* (October 2, 1786), at 3; see also *Providence Gazette* (October 7, 1786), 3.

8.4 THE CASE OF THE JUDGES

At this moment in Rhode Island's constitutional history, the General Assembly was still operating as the supreme power in the state, exercising both final legislative and judicial authority. In his long and complicated argument in *Trevett* v. *Weeden*, James Varnum argued both that Rhode Island actually possessed a constitution that imposed "legal" limitations on the power of the legislature to make law, and that the judges were entitled to maintain their independent interpretation of the law, even in the face of a contrary interpretation by the legislature. Varnum's argument amounted to an all-out assault on Rhode Island's traditional constitution of legislative supremacy. Four of the five judges on the Superior Court appeared to adopt his argument, in whole or in part, with at least two judges declaring in open court that the statute was unconstitutional. The General Assembly reacted as one might expect the supreme (legislative and judicial) power in the state to react.

It is not clear why the governor decided to call a special legislative session for October 2, barely a week after the Court had rendered its decision in *Trevett*, but he may have been prompted to do so by the constitutional crisis the decision precipitated, which had only inflamed the already grave situation the state faced as a result of the ongoing economic depression.[71] At any rate, early in the session, the legislature took notice of the judges' opinions. The text of the legislature's resolution, passed in reaction, says a good deal about the General Assembly's constitutional position.

> Whereas, it appears that the Honourable the Justices of the Superior Court of Judicature ... at the last September Term of the said Court ... have by Judgement [sic] of the said Court declared and adjudged an Act of the *Supreme Legislature* of this State to be unconstitutional, and so absolutely Void: And whereas it is suggested that the aforesaid Judgment is *unprecedented* in this State, and may tend directly to abolish the Legislative Authority thereof: *It is therefore*, [etc.] ... .[72] (emphasis added)

[71] The legislative session was held in Newport where the Superior Court sat rather than in Providence; Session Laws, *At the General Assembly of the Governor and Company of the State of Rhode-Island and Providence Plantations, begun and held (in Consequence of Warrants issued by his Excellency the Governor) at Newport, within and for the State aforesaid, on Monday, the Second Day of October, in the Year of our Lord One Thousand Seven Hundred and Eighty-six, and in the Eleventh Year of Independence.* Varnum, however, reported that after the judges handed down their decision, economic conditions improved markedly, Varnum, *Trevett* v. *Weeden*, 37.

[72] Session Laws for the special session called for Monday, the Second Day of October, at 3.

The legislature seems to have been advancing the familiar idea that by engaging in the entirely "unprecedented" act of nullifying a duly enacted statute of the state, the court was in effect "abolishing" the legislature's authority, by asserting its own power to unmake any law the legislature had previously made, if they judged it to be unconstitutional. In this part of its resolution, the legislature framed the court's decision as an attack on its supreme legislative authority. But the text of the resolution continued as though it was being delivered by a high court, calling the judges to account for their usurpation of the legislature's legitimate constitutional authority. The resolution ordered the sheriffs of the respective counties to issue summons' to the judges to appear immediately before the bar of the Assembly to explain their reasons. It also ordered that the record in the case be brought to the Assembly.

> *It is therefore Voted and Resolved,* That all the Justices of the Said Court be forthwith cited by the Sheriffs of the respective Counties in which they live or may be found, to give their immediate Attendance on this Assembly, *to assign the Reasons and Grounds of the aforesaid Judgment*: And that, the Clerk of the said Court be directed to attend this Assembly at the same Time, with the Records of the said Court which relate to the said Judgment.[73] (emphasis added)

Shortly afterward, the legislature passed another resolution, which may have been aimed at prohibiting Henry Marchant, Varnum's co-counsel in *Trevett*, and a sitting member of the House, from participating in the argument of the judges' case when it came before the Assembly. The language of the resolution itself makes clear that the Assembly saw itself as a high court.

> *It is Voted and Resolved*, That no sworn Attorneys, as such, while a Member of this Assembly, shall be admitted to Speak or Plead out of his Seat and at the Bar of this Assembly, on *any private Petition, when on Trial before this Assembly.*[74] (emphasis added)

Several days later, two of the Superior Court justices let the Assembly know, presumably in response to sheriffs' citations, that they were

[73] Ibid., 3; according to Philip Hamburger, some words were stripped out of an earlier draft of this resolution as a result of pressure from the upper house. The deleted words said that once the legislature had heard the judges' reasons and grounds for their decision, they would be in a position to "adopt such measures as may establish the Supremacy of the legislative authority," Law and Judicial Duty, 444. This may have represented an incipient revolt by the upper house against the idea that the Assembly possessed supreme judicial, along with its supreme legislative authority, but the evidence seems too fragmentary to arrive at a firm conclusion.

[74] Session Laws for special session called for October the Second, at 4.

indisposed and unable to attend. The Assembly voted to cite them to appear at its next, regular legislative session, which was to begin several weeks later on the last Monday in October.[75] When three of the five judges finally did appear at the next session of the legislature, they not only testified on their own behalf but also had James Varnum, now their lawyer, argue in their defense on the floor of the legislature. In his well-known pamphlet about the *Trevett* case, Varnum himself characterized these events as: "The Case of the Judges of [the Superior] Court, Before the Honourable GENERAL ASSEMBLY, at Providence, October Session, 1786, on Citation for dismissing [the] Complaint [in *Trevett* v. *Weeden*]."[76]

The Assembly had had the sheriffs issue summons requiring the judges to appear before them to present "the Reasons and Grounds of their Judgment." Presumably, the General Assembly planned to review those reasons to determine whether they actually justified the judges' "unprecedented" conduct in nullifying a duly enacted law of the state. If the legislature judged that the proffered reasons were inadequate to vindicate the judges, and consequently that their conduct exceeded the legitimate limits of judicial authority, illicitly invading the constitutional powers properly belonging to the legislature, the judges would be subject to removal from office for something like mal-practice or abuse of office. The Assembly then planned to fill those posts with new judges who would presumably administer the laws of the state as written. Varnum reported that "candidates were upon the spot ready to fill the seats thus to be made vacant ... "[77]

It is not exactly clear what the nature and basis of this disciplinary proceeding was, however, as Rhode Island did not have a written constitution (or statute) that explicitly conferred on the General Assembly the power to remove judges "by address," or "for cause," or by "impeachment." Likely, the General Assembly claimed this supervisory power as an attribute of its "supremacy," but no clear criteria seem to have been previously worked out for its exercise. As a result, the subsequent hearings before the legislature served not only to adjudicate whether the judges

[75] Ibid., 7; and Session Laws, *At the General Assembly of the Governor and Company of the State of Rhode-Island and Providence Plantations, begun and holden at Providence, within and for the State aforesaid, on the last Monday in October, in the Year of our Lord One Thousand Seven Hundred and Eighty-six, and in the Eleventh Year of Independence.*

[76] See the title page of James M. Varnum's pamphlet, The Case, Trevett against Weeden.

[77] Varnum, *Trevett* v. *Weeden*, 44.

were to be removed from office but also to define, probably for the first time, precisely what such proceedings required for removal. As the case had not come before the legislature as the result of a petition submitted by one of the original parties to the Superior Court action, however, the General Assembly did not appear to be sitting as a "legal tribunal," reviewing the judges' reasoning in order to reverse, affirm or modify their judgment.

On one level, the argument of the judges was clear enough. They contended that they could not be removed from office for their judicial opinions, even if these were erroneous, so long as they had been rendered without corruption or criminality. The reasons upon which they had based their judgment, they argued, could not constitute grounds for disciplinary proceedings against them, even if their reasoning should turn out to be incorrect. This argument is familiar enough from similar ones made in other states at this time. But the judges here went further. They contended that since their judicial opinions were completely irrelevant for purposes of resolving the disciplinary question, the judges did not have to explain themselves to the legislature at all. The legislature simply had no authority to require the judges to describe the grounds of their decision. They were asserting, in effect, that the legislature had jurisdiction only to consider whether the judges had been motivated by corruption or criminality. Their judicial opinions, rendered in the course of adjudicating the great constitutional question, could not, they insisted, be treated any differently, for purposes of disciplinary proceedings, than any other opinion they rendered in any ordinary case which did not involve a question of the basic distribution of constitutional power in the government.

The direct implication of this argument was that the legislature entirely lacked the authority to judge the question of the legitimate scope of judicial power– only the judges could make that determination. If the judges' reasoning led them to conclude that they possessed the power to strike down statutes, so long as that decision had not been rendered for corrupt or criminal motives, the legislature lacked the authority to re-examine and judge that logic.

The judges' argument operated to reframe an act many in the legislature clearly considered to be an illicit constitutional usurpation of legislative authority, into, at most, simple judicial error, unreviewable (and unpunishable) by the legislature. If this argument prevailed, it would not only leave the judges, henceforward, as the sole judges of the scope of their own powers but, as a practical matter, would leave them free to strike down statutes in the future without fear that they would be subject to removal from office for doing so. But in Rhode Island, the judges' arguments had even more far-reaching implications. If the legislature did not possess the authority to demand that the judges present "the reasons and grounds of their judgment," it would lose its ability to function as an appellate court of final resort.

According to Varnum, the first judge to testify before the legislature, Judge Howell, seemed to take this maximalist position at the very opening of his six-hour speech. Howell

> observed, that the order by which the Judges were before the House might be considered as calling upon them to assist in matters of legislation, or to render the reasons of their judicial determination, as being accountable to the Legislature for their judgment.
>
> That in the former point of view, the Court was ever ready, as constituting the legal counsellors of the State, to render every kind of assistance to the Legislative, in framing new, or repealing former laws: But that for the reasons of their judgment upon any question judicially before them, they were accountable only to God, and their own consciences.[78] (emphasis supplied)

Howell continued by "demonstrat[ing], by a variety of arguments, that [the statute at issue] was unconstitutional, had not the force of a law, and could not be executed."[79] He also went on to reiterate his earlier point.

> It would be out of the power, therefore, of the General Assembly to determine upon the propriety of the Court's judgment, without a particular explanation. If this could be required in one instance, it might in all: and so the Legislative would become the Supreme Judiciary. A perversion of power totally subversive of civil liberty![80] (emphasis supplied)

Howell proceeded to cite Montesquieu, among others, for the proposition that public liberty required a clear separation of powers, and that it had long been established that judges could not be punished "for a mere error of judgment," so long as they have not been "partially, maliciously or corruptly influenced in the exercise of" that judgment.[81] Judge Tillinghast testified next, followed by Judge Hazard. At the conclusion of their statements,

78 Varnum, "The Case of the Judges," in Trevett v. Weeden, 38. 79 Ibid., 38.
80 Ibid., 39, the Superior Court, at the time, was the highest *judicial* court in Rhode Island.
81 Ibid., 40–42.

a very serious and interesting debate [took place] among the members [of the General Assembly], wherein many arguments and observations were adduced on both sides. At length a question was taken, "whether the Assembly was satisfied with the reasons given by the Judges in support of their judgment?" – It was determined in the negative.[82]

But the members apparently could not agree upon what precisely to do about their dissatisfaction with the position the judges had taken. "Some were for displacing the Judges at all events; some were for saving appearances by drawing out a concession on the part of the Court, and others were determined fully to justify them" when the judges intervened by presenting a memorial that changed, according to Varnum, the entire tone and tenor of the debate.[83] This document elaborated the foundations of the judges' case, and argued that the General Assembly did not possess the power to dismiss them from office summarily before the end of their terms, "upon a mere suggestion of a mere error of judgment." And it requested that the legislature give them an opportunity to answer any "certain and specific charges" which that body might subsequently bring before "some proper and legal tribunal."[84]

The judges' memorial

concluded, by utterly denying the power of the Legislature to call upon them – For the particular reasons of their judgment in that, or any other case; and declining to render the same – alledging [sic] and maintaining, by arguments and authorities of law, that for the same they are "accountable only to God (under the solemnities of their oath of office) and to their own consciences!"[85]

The memorial went on to advance a claim that departed radically from long established Rhode Island practice but reflected newer separation of powers principles that, however, had no basis in any Rhode Island constitutional document: "they [the judges] conceive that the *entire power* of *construing and judging* of the [laws], *in the last resort*, is vested *solely* in the Supreme Judiciary of the State"[86] (emphasis added). It would be difficult to imagine a more direct challenge to legislative supremacy in Rhode Island.

Varnum then took the floor of the General Assembly to support the judges' memorial by asserting that they enjoyed a kind of property in their offices during the fixed term of one year for which they had been elected, and could not be divested of their office unless they had neglected, misused or abused their trust.[87] And in ascertaining whether they had, the judges

[82] Ibid., 44. [83] Ibid., 44. [84] Ibid., 46. [85] Ibid., 45. [86] Ibid., 45. [87] Ibid., 48.

were entitled to due process of law. "[H]ow can such [a determination] take place until the facts or charges are particularly stated, and the party accused have an opportunity of making defence, [sic] in such way as he shall deem most beneficial to himself?"[88] But "[s]hould no such accusation be made, what remains but that the Judges be immediately discharged from any farther attendance upon this Assembly?"[89] Varnum went on to complicate matters further by arguing that the legislature could not be the proper forum for any subsequent trial because, as the complaining party, they suffered from a fatal conflict of interest.[90]

These arguments apparently worked to slow the momentum of the removal party even further.

> The claim and demand of the Judges, as stated in their memorial, and enforced by their counsel, were followed by a concise, but rational debate, in which the fury of passion, excepting in one or two instances, surrendered to cool reflection, and prepared the way for vindicating the honour of the law, and the dignity of the State.[91]

The General Assembly then adopted a motion to seek the advice of the Attorney General, William Channing, and other "professional gentlemen" that were present, on the question "whether constitutionally, and agreeably to law, the General Assembly can suspend, or remove from office, the Judges of the Supreme Judiciary Court, without a previous charge and statement of criminality, due process, trial, and conviction thereon?"[92]

Channing himself had attended the Trevett trial in the Superior Court, and had been reported as voicing his opinion about the constitutionality of the forcing act.

> The Attorney-General, Mr. Channing, was full in opinion against the legality of the act, and refused to plead for the informer ....[93]

And so it must not have come as much of a surprise when Channing rose to voice "his private opinion, [that the judges'] determination was conformable to the principles of constitutional law. – But be their judgment agreeably to law or not, confident he was, that there would be a fatal interruption, if not annihilation to government, if they could be suspended, or removed from office, for a mere matter of opinion, without a charge of criminality."[94] The following May, Channing's opposition to

[88] Ibid., 48. [89] Ibid., 49. [90] Ibid., 49–50. [91] Ibid., 51. [92] Ibid., 51.

[93] "Extract of a letter from a gentleman at Newport, dated Sept. 28, 1786," in *The Massachusetts Gazette* (October 3, 1786), at 3.

[94] Varnum, "The Case of the Judges," in Trevett v. Weeden, 51.

the Forcing Act, and favorable view of the judges' power to nullify statutes, would come back to haunt him.

Henry Goodwin, who was also present in the General Assembly, added his opinion. As the prosecuting attorney in *Trevett*, Goodwin had taken positions directly contrary to those Channing had. He had argued that the Forcing Act was good law, because Rhode Island had never adopted a bill of rights. Presumably, he believed that the judges had no power to nullify a statute for violating a right to trial by jury, when that right had not been expressly declared in a state constitution. The legislature would later reward him for these positions. But now he agreed with all the other "professional gentlemen" that the judges could not be summarily removed from their offices. Goodwin said "that no sentence could be passed against the Judges, but by regular process, in which a specification of the charges is essentially requisite."[95]

The Speaker of the House, William Bradford, announced that before these proceedings,

> he never doubted but the General Assembly were vested with constitutional authority to try and remove any officer by them appointed, for any mal-practice in his office, but that from the observations that had been made, he very much doubted the propriety of his former opinion:– That one point, however, was clear and certain, that as the Judges were commissioned and sworn for the term of a year, they could not be deprived of their powers during that term, but by regular impeachment, in which the charges against them must be particularly stated; trial, in which they would have an undoubted right for time to prepare their defence, [sic] and to be heard by counsel; and condemnation, upon full proofs of the charges:– That in the proceedings now before the House there was not a charge, or the appearance of one, against the Court, to which they could, in any manner, be held to answer . . .[96]

As there seemed to be total agreement among the legal experts, on all sides, that the judges could not be punished for their judicial opinions alone, and were entitled to due process before they could be removed from office, when the question was put to the General Assembly "whether the Judges should be discharged from any further attendance upon the General Assembly, as no accusation appeared against them?" the Assembly "*decided by a very great majority*" that the judges should be "discharged from any further attendance upon this Assembly, on that account"[97] (emphasis added).

[95] Ibid., 53. [96] Ibid., 52. [97] Ibid., 53.

The attempt by some in the legislature to remove judges from office for engaging in the constitutionally transformative practice of judicial review failed in Rhode Island, as it had in New York and New Hampshire. That advocates for judicial review prevailed almost everywhere in their contention that a judicial opinion, which radically altered the distribution of powers in the constitutional system, should be treated in the same way as any other judicial opinion, represented a decisive step on the road to securing the future of this unprecedented judicial practice. If striking down a state statute was not to be treated as an illicit invasion or usurpation of the legislature's constitutional authority but as a simple judicial opinion, which might or might not be erroneous, the legislature's recourse against judges for engaging in the radically new practice would be substantially narrowed.

The *Trevett* case added one more to the string of precedents that limited legislative options for checking the spread of the new practice. And the course of events over the next month also followed a pattern familiar from other states. After the judges struck down a statute, and the legislature failed to remove them from office for doing so, the statute, often became, in effect, a dead letter, and the legislature saw fit to repeal it, further legitimizing the judges' actions. Rhode Island followed this pattern. At the next (adjourned) session of the General Assembly held in December, the legislature repealed, without comment, the penal forcing acts.[98] Of course, there may well have been other reasons the legislature decided upon this step. They may well have come to the conclusion that the acts themselves had not only exacerbated the dismal economic situation but ironically had led to wider opposition to paper money. According to Varnum, as soon as the judges handed down their decision,

> [t]he shops and stores were generally opened, and business assumed a chearful [sic] aspect . . . . The paper currency obtained a more extensive circulation, as every one found himself at liberty to receive or refuse it. The markets, which had been illy [sic] supplied, were now amply furnished, and the spirit of industry was generally diffused.[99]

[98] Session Laws, *At the General Assembly of the Governor and Company of the State of Rhode-Island and Providence Plantations, begun and holden by Adjournment, at East-Greenwich, within and for the State aforesaid, on the Fourth Monday in December, in the Year of our Lord One Thousand Seven Hundred and Eighty-six, and in the Eleventh Year of Independence,* at 23.

[99] Varnum, "The Case of the Judges," in Trevett v. Weeden, 37.

Far from abandoning its paper money policy, however, the Rhode Island legislature did what other legislatures also did when faced with similar situations; they attempted to shore up the existing policy by creating a work around. In Rhode Island, the General Assembly expanded the remedy debtors already possessed for lodging repayments in paper money with judges in order to legally acquit themselves of a debt. In a new act the legislature passed during the same December session, it announced that the existing remedy "has been found ineffectual, as the Judges in some of the Counties where Debtors live or are resident, refuse or neglect to receive the Money tendered for the Payment of Debts." And so the legislature authorized debtors to lodge repayments either with Justices of the Superior Court, or with Justices of any Inferior Court of Common Pleas *anywhere in the state*, "whether residing in the County where the Debtor lives, or out of the same. And such Justice is required to receive the same and notify the Creditor agreeably to the said Act . . . ."[100]

In addition to perhaps not having a constitution, Rhode Island was different from other states in one additional, crucial respect. Many early state constitutions had thought it a good idea to make judges accountable to the legislature (and the people), by leaving them to be removed "upon address," and/or by having them serve during a fixed, relatively short term, rather than during good behavior.[101] This view of judges (and all other officers of government) was built squarely into the foundations of Rhode Island's constitutional system. In Rhode Island, all members of both houses of the legislature, as well as the governor, were elected by the freemen every spring. When a new legislature met in May, it, in turn, appointed the other officers of government, who also only served from election to election: Justices of the Superior as well as Inferior Courts, the Judge of the Court of Admiralty, Justices of the Peace in the several Towns, but also the Attorney General, Delegates to Congress, Sheriffs, Collectors of Impost, etc.[102]

[100] "An ACT in Addition to an Act for emitting the Sum of *One Hundred Thousand Pounds*, Lawful Money, in Bills of Credit, passed at *May* Session last," Session Laws, *At the General Assembly of the Governor and Company of the State of Rhode-Island and Providence Plantations, begun and holden by Adjournment, at East-Greenwich, within and for the State aforesaid, on the Fourth Monday in December, in the Year of our Lord One Thousand Seven Hundred and Eighty-six, and in the Eleventh Year of Independence*, 6.

[101] See discussion in Chapter 2 of the widespread lack of provision for judicial independence in the first state constitutions.

[102] Session Laws, *At the General Assembly of the Governor and Company of the State of Rhode-Island and Providence Plantations, begun and holden at Newport, within and for the State aforesaid, on the First Wednesday in May, in the Year of our Lord One*

Unlike the press and certain other observers who had celebrated the judges' decision, the actions of the new legislature at its May 1787 session indicate that a majority in that body had quite the opposite view of the affair. A letter to the governor from the most outspoken of the judges in the case, Justice Howell, in April 1787 indicates that he also believed that the views of the legislature actually reflected "the wishes of the bulk of the people relating to the penal law & the late ... paper money."[103] In their deliberations during the May session, the General Assembly would seem to have adopted a strict litmus test not only in their selections of Justices for the Superior Court but also in their selection of an Attorney General. The Judges who had come out against the constitutionality of the Forcing Act in *Trevett*, and in favor of nullification, were not selected for reappointment to office. But the Chief Justice, Mumford, who had remained silent, tacitly refusing to concur with the majority, was returned to office.[104]

There was no question that the General Assembly possessed the constitutional authority to select whoever they wished to fill these offices, and they carried out their program systematically. The sitting Attorney General, William Channing, who had also spoken out against the validity of the Forcing Act at the trial, and in favor of the power of the judges to strike it down, was also not reelected. Instead, the legislature chose to replace him with none other than the lawyer Henry Goodwin, who had served as the prosecutor in the *Trevett* case, and who had argued in favor of the validity of the act, and against the power of the judges to nullify it.[105]

Thousand Seven Hundred and Eighty-Seven, and in the Eleventh Year of Independence, 3–7 ("This being the anniversary Election of all Officers, both Civil and Military, in and throughout the State, for the ensuing Year, the Gentlemen whose Names are set down in the subsequent List were chosen to the Offices ascribed to their Names respectively, to wit:") followed by complete list of names, see Attorney General Henry Goodwin, at 3, and Justices of the Superior Court including Chief Justice Mumford, at 7.

103 "Letter from David Howell to Governor John Collins" (April 30, 1787), Newport Historical Society, King Papers, Vault A, Box 134, Folder 3, quoted in Hamburger, Law and Judicial Duty, 446 fn. 141.

104 Session Laws, *At the General Assembly held on the First Wednesday in May 1787*, 7. Philip Hamburger has uncovered documents indicating that the most vocal of the Justices of the Superior Court in the *Trevett* case, Judge Howell, had written the governor to withdraw his name from further consideration before the May elections, Law and Judicial Duty, 446 and fn. 141. Interestingly, Hamburger also notes that one of the judges the legislature selected in May 1787 to replace the previous judges may have been an Inferior Court judge who had acted as one of Trevett's witnesses at the trial, 446 fn. 142.

105 Session Laws, *At the General Assembly held on the First Wednesday in May 1787*, 3.

The Rhode Island Assembly, it seems, remained determined to prevent the establishment of judicial review in the state, and because they had the constitutional power to appoint judges annually, they could fill the bench with individuals, who like their English brethren, considered it their duty to execute the laws the legislature had enacted as written. As a result, the Rhode Island Assembly was able to maintain a position of constitutional supremacy, operating not only as a legislature but as a high court, almost to the middle of the nineteenth century. "Never again under the charter of 1663 did the courts in Rhode Island openly challenge the validity of the Assembly's laws."[106] The *Trevett* case itself makes clear that the critical factor in preserving the constitution of legislative supremacy in Rhode Island, and halting the further development of judicial review, was not that Rhode Island lacked a conventional written constitution (that had not stopped the judges from engaging in the practice in the first place) but that the Assembly possessed the lawful constitutional power annually to appoint (and reappoint) to the bench only judges who did not subscribe to (or act upon) the new ideas.

As a result, for many more decades, Rhode Island maintained a constitutional system like the ones the majority of states had initially adopted following Independence. Those frames of government had intentionally eliminated all checks on the legislature, other than those the people themselves exercised at frequent elections. These constitutional systems placed great faith in the virtue of the people. But the emergence of a fractious majoritarian politics in Rhode Island and in other states in the 1780s, raised the fundamental question whether a check on the people themselves was necessary, in order to preserve the new republics. In Rhode Island that question was in effect debated in the *Trevett* case, and a resolution arrived at through the contingent play of constitutional politics and law, a result, however, that because of Rhode Island's distinctive constitutional traditions was unlike the one the play of constitutional politics and law produced in other states. In the 1780s, Rhode Island steadfastly refused to permit a judicial check to be placed on the will of the people acting through their legislatures.

[106] Irwin H. Polishook, *Rhode Island and the Union, 1774–1795* (Evanston, Ill., Northwestern University Press, 1969), 141.

9

The Struggle Between Traditional Constitutionalism and the Constitution of Judicial Review in North Carolina: The Case of *Bayard* v. *Singleton*, 1786–1787, and Its Aftermath

The years 1786–87 marked a decisive turning point in the history of judicial review. Of the half dozen legal disputes that historians normally place on the list of early judicial review precedents down to the Federal Convention, fully half arose during the years 1786–1787.[1] During these two years, in a variety of cases in three different states, lawyers argued on behalf of their clients that a court must declare a state statute not to be law, and in every case, the judges obliged. The North Carolina case of *Bayard* v. *Singleton* was one of these.

Two great causes gave rise to all the post-war cases. The first involved efforts by state legislatures to respond to popular pressures to ease economic distress by modifying traditional common law property, contract, and process rights. The second involved efforts by state legislatures, often also in response to popular pressures, to punish, in a variety of ways, those who had remained loyal to Great Britain, or to finalize the confiscation of their often considerable property, or to force them to compensate Patriots for damage to or use of Patriot property during the war.

Although the rationales offered in these cases to support the judges' authority to declare statutes void were certainly broad enough to encompass any type of constitutional violation, the post-war cases themselves primarily challenged legislative attempts to restrict or eliminate one kind of right, trial by jury. It has sometimes been suggested that the judges felt especially emboldened to strike down such statutes because they involved court procedures, which they viewed as coming uniquely under their

[1] See Chapter 7 discussing The New Hampshire Ten Pound Act Cases (N.H., 1786–87), and Chapter 8 discussing *Trevett* v. *Weeden* (R.I., 1786).

jurisdiction. But since the proffered rationales for judicial review were much wider, perhaps an equally good explanation is that the conservative lawyers who mainly brought these cases were especially provoked to take action by legislatures' efforts to expand summary (revolutionary) justice, or to claim finality for legislative adjudication, which they viewed as an especially grievous form of political tyranny, subjecting the people to loss of liberty or property without the benefit of the full array of common law procedural protections, especially trial by a jury of one's peers, in which one's fate would be decided by a body that included no government official.

In these cases, lawyers were not only striving to defend their clients, they were working to modify the basic constitutional settlement that had been reached during the first state congresses and constitutional conventions, by introducing a check on legislatures, which almost every one of the first state constitutions had intentionally omitted. Many of the same causes that impelled prominent lawyers to seek to revise the original constitutional settlement in these years, also led to broader efforts formally to refashion the constitutional system. The constitutional question raised in *Bayard* v. *Singleton* was finally decided by the Superior Court in May 1787. The same month, the Federal Convention convened in Philadelphia, with the aim of producing a comprehensive plan for addressing the ills facing republican governments.

The introduction of judicial review in a few states during these years altered fundamentally the character of those republics. In a very real sense, it gave judges a kind of veto over legislation, a veto that many recognized could also be used to rein in the power of the sovereign people to act through their legislatures. In a very real sense, it stripped legislatures of the final word on the laws, transferring that authority to the judges. These fundamental changes were introduced by lawyers and judges acting on their own initiative, creating a refuge from majoritarian politics. The effort to modify the character of state republics by introducing judicial review came together, at the Federal Convention, with broader efforts comprehensively to refashion the American constitutional system. Battles for judicial review and this wider movement operated to reinforce one another. The constitutional settlement that emerged from the Federal Convention guaranteed that judicial review would become a normal, if still controversial, feature of the new constitutional system that the Convention brought into being.

North Carolina could serve as a paradigm for the kinds of problems judicial review (and the Federal Convention) sought to address. In coastal counties, mainly in the northeast, merchants and professionals (lawyers) tended to dominate politics. But further west and south, the population was composed predominantly of small farmers, and smaller or larger planters, and it was from these areas that popular pressures to pass laws to ameliorate economic distress and to punish Loyalists mainly emanated.[2] North Carolina had a history of popular mob action, the regulator movement of 1769–70 being the best-known example.

When the prominent North Carolina lawyer and political leader, Samuel Johnston, having been denounced as a Tory, was defeated at an October 1776 election to choose members for a congress to write the state constitution, the people out of doors celebrated by burning him in effigy. His brother-in-law, James Iredell, erupted, penning a bitter screed. Iredell, and many of the lawyers with whom he made common cause during these years, saw society in traditional eighteenth-century terms. The common people and "gentlemen" were fundamentally different species of humanity, occupying separate, higher and lower, stations in life. These men often viewed the mass of the people as uneducated, ignorant, unruly, violent, prone to cupidity, unthinking in their passions, and by implication, not fit to assume the reins of government. The sarcastic "Creed of a Rioter," which Iredell wrote in reaction to the election disturbances, was expressed in this traditional language and fully reflected those views.

1. I am a sworn enemy of all gentlemen. I believe none in that station of life can possibly possess either honor or virtue.
2. I believe the best way to have a good understanding is never to cultivate the mental powers, and that the most ignorant in appearance, are in fact the most knowing.
3. I impute to *gentlemen* all our present difficulties . . . .
6. I believe I have a right to take another man's property, if it will be useful to me . . . .
10. I think that man alone a whig, who has sagacity enough to mind his own interest, resolution enough to plunder his neighbors . . . and discovers his principles by getting honestly drunk and abusing *gentlemen*.
11. I believe it honorable and proper to persecute poor distressed individuals, when we have them *in our power*, provided we want

[2] Jackson Turner Main, *Political Parties Before the Constitution* (New York, W. W. Norton & Co., 1973), 311–17.

courage to prove, in any other manner, the alacrity of our zeal against those we suppose enemies of our country.

Lastly, I am of opinion that our affairs would prosper much better, if gentlemen who read and consider too deeply for us, were totally banished from all public business, and if those who neither read nor think at all ... were intrusted with the management of our present arduous concerns.[3]

Iredell's views had not changed significantly by the 1780s. In 1784 he wrote to Pierce Butler of South Carolina that "I have long learnt to despise that sort of popularity which is to be gained by flattering the passions of the multitude ...."[4]

Popular pressures often prevailed in the North Carolina legislature in these years. Responding to the post war economic downturn, the legislature passed paper money and legal tender laws, an act temporarily to stay debt collections, and laws to increase the jurisdictional amount for justices to hear small claims, first up to ten pounds, later to twenty pounds.[5] In other states these kinds of statutes gave rise to constitutional challenges. But in North Carolina, as in New York, it was the other great cause that did so, the legislative effort to punish Loyalists in a variety of ways, and to

[3] Griffith McRee (ed.), *Life and Correspondence of James Iredell* (1857, repr. New York, Peter Smith, 1949, I, 335–36 (1776).

[4] McRee (ed.), Iredell, II, 93 (Iredell to Pierce Butler, March 14, 1784).

[5] See "An act for emitting one hundred thousand pounds in paper currency ...." passed *At a General Assembly, begun and held at Hillsborough, on the Eighteenth Day of April, in the Year of our Lord One Thousand Seven Hundred and Eighty-three ... Being the First Session of this Assembly*, Chap. I, 320; "An act for emitting one hundred thousand pounds paper currency" .... passed *At a General Assembly, begun and held at Newbern, on the Nineteenth Day of November, in the Year of our Lord One Thousand Seven Hundred and Eighty-five* .... Chap. V, 393; for the paper money emissions and the stay law see McRee (ed.), Iredell, II, 63–64 (Items 2 and 3 in the Instructions to the Representatives from Chowan County and the Town of Edenton, August 1783); on the debtor relief stay law, see "An Act to Suspend the operation of executions, for a time therein mentioned," *At a General Assembly begun and held at Hillsborough, on the eighteenth day of April, in the year of our Lord, one thousand seven hundred and eighty three .... Being the first Session of This Assembly*, Chap. VII, 490–91; see also Willis P. Whichard, *Justice James Iredell* (Durham, N.C., Carolina Academic Press, 2000), 5; for the laws increasing the jurisdictional amount to hear small claims up to ten, later twenty, pounds, see Philip Hamburger, *Law and Judicial Duty* (Cambridge, Mass., Harvard University Press, 2008), 471–72 fn. 14; see also Donna Kelly and Lang Baradell (eds.), *The Papers of James Iredell, 1784–1789* (Raleigh, N.C., Office of Archives and History, North Carolina Dept. of Cultural Resources, 2003), III, 17 notes 3 and 4, 180–81, 180 note 3, 182 note 2; Jackson Turner Main, *The Upper House in Revolutionary America, 1763–1788* (Madison, Wisc., University of Wisconsin Press, 1967), 159–60; and Main, Political Parties Before the Constitution, 317.

finalize the confiscation of their property. The passage of these various acts, however, reinforced for many the view that in accommodating popular pressures, state legislatures had been led to enact a series of laws that were unwise, unjust, and quite often unconstitutional.

9.1 BAYARD V. SINGLETON, AND THE NORTH CAROLINA CONFISCATION STATUTES

North Carolina's Superior Court first took up the case of *Bayard* v. *Singleton* at its May 1786 term. Elizabeth Bayard (with her husband) had brought a common law ejectment action against Spyers Singleton, seeking to regain title to certain lands[6] that Bayard's father, Samuel Cornell, had transferred into her name in 1777, in an effort to prevent it from being confiscated. That initial effort had failed; in 1779 a court, following a jury trial, adjudged the property to be forfeit to the state. A few years later, Commissioners of Forfeited Estates sold the property to Spyers Singleton. Like numbers of other returnees, Elizabeth Bayard filed her new suit in an effort to reclaim title to the land. At the Superior Court's first hearing, Singleton's attorney argued that the case should be dismissed without further hearing, citing a recently passed (Dec., 1785) North Carolina statute. Plaintiff's attorney responded by arguing that the statute itself was unconstitutional and void.[7] As the facts suggest, the case had its beginnings many years earlier in the late 1770s; recounting its long genesis offers a window onto the broader circumstances under which judicial review emerged in North Carolina.

9.2 THE BACKGROUND

On November 27, 1777, the Continental Congress passed a resolution recommending to the states that "as soon as may be," the states should "confiscate and make sale of all the real & personal estate therein of such of their inhabitants and other persons who have forfeited the same, and the right to the protection of their respective states . . . ."[8] Confiscation (and sales), it was hoped, would not only provide the states with a source of revenue to carry on the war, but would simultaneously deprive the enemy of the same resources, and punish those who remained loyal to Britain. Not a month later, in December 1777, the North Carolina

[6] *Bayard* v. *Singleton*, 1 N.C. (Martin's Reports, 1787), 42–43. [7] Ibid.
[8] *Journals of the Continental Congress, 1774–1789* (Washington, D.C., Govt. Printing Office, 1907), IX (1777), 971.

General Assembly responding to the congressional recommendation, appointed a committee chaired by Archibald Maclaine to consider the possibility of confiscation. At this moment, support for confiscation among Patriots of all classes seems to have been widespread, as Maclaine, who would later become one of its staunchest opponents, reported favorably on Congress' recommendation.

> Mr. Maclaine from the Committee appointed to take into consideration sundry resolves, &c., from Congress and to prepare and bring in a Bill for confiscating the property of persons who have forfeited the protection of this State, reported as follows: . . . .
>
> That it is expedient to pass a law for confiscating the estates [of those who have withdrawn from the state and who do not return timely to swear allegiance to the same].[9]

The bill itself became law on December 23, 1777. By its terms it not only confiscated the property of any person who had "attached himself to, or aided or abetted the enemies of the United States" but also of *all persons who had absented themselves from the state* (and the country) before or during the war, and not returned.[10] The law not only imposed on property owners, a negative duty prohibiting them from supporting or adhering to the British cause, but a broader positive duty to return to the state at this perilous moment in its young history, and by their presence to lend support to the (Patriot) cause– or have their property confiscated. "[I]t is expedient and just that every person for whom Property is protected in any State should be and appear within the same or join in Defence thereof whenever the same is threatened or invaded."[11]

Under the North Carolina act, however, all initial confiscations were to be conditional, allowing persons a period of time to return to the state in order to pledge their allegiance, and reclaim their property. The statute decreed that the property of all persons described in the act "are hereby declared to be confiscated to the Use of this State; unless such person shall,

[9] Walter Clark (ed.), *The State Records of North Carolina* (Winston, M. I. & J. C. Stewart, Printers to the State, 1895), XII (1777–78), 228–29; Maclaine went on to vote in favor of the bill, at 252, see also 222–23, 402, 410–12, 424–25.

[10] "An Act, for confiscating the Property of all such Persons as are inimical to the United States . . . ." passed *At a General Assembly begun and held at New Bern on the Fifteenth Day of November, in the Year of our Lord One Thousand Seven Hundred and Seventy-Seven* . . . . Chap. XVII, 123–24 (December 23, 1777).

[11] Laws of North Carolina, 1777, Chap. XVII; this sentiment appears to have been widespread in the states, see T. H. Breen, *The Will of the People: The Revolutionary Birth of America* (Cambridge, Mass., Harvard University Press, 2019), 95, 104, 134, 138, 140.

at the next General Assembly ... [which was to begin the first of October 1778, 10 months later] appear, and be by the said Assembly admitted to the Privilege of a Citizen of this State, and restored to the Possessions and Property which to him once belonged within the [state]."[12] Note that the statute specified that returning owners must appear before the legislature itself by the deadline, and that the Assembly would determine whether to admit the person to citizenship, and to restore their property.

Samuel Cornell, Elizabeth Bayard's father, had withdrawn to Britain in August 1775 after armed hostilities had broken out in the colonies. Cornell was a Newbern merchant, who had served as a member of North Carolina's upper house, the Council, before the Revolution. Sometime in 1777, he arrived back in New York City, which was then occupied by the British army, and proceeded by ship to North Carolina in early December 1777, a few weeks before the legislature passed the first confiscation act. He reached the harbor at Newbern on December 4, 1777, informing North Carolina's governor, Richard Caswell, that he (Cornell) had "arrived in this port, from New York, in the Brigantine Edwards, in consequence of a Flag of Truce, obtained [from the British commanders] in order to settle our private affairs in this State, and we wait your Excellency's permission to come on shore."[13]

Through several notes, back and forth, he negotiated with Governor Caswell for permission to come ashore, which Caswell granted "in order to give Mr. Cornell an opportunity of making an Inventory of the several articles of his house Furniture, the names of his family and also the names of his servants, which he also propose conveying with him .... but ... Mr. Cornell [is not] to proceed further, into the Town, than [his own] dwelling House ... [and his] Inventory [is] to be laid before me in Council, Friday morning next at ten O'clock .... ."[14] On December 20, Caswell wrote to give Cornell permission "to return to the State of New York in the Brigantine Edwards with [his] family, [including Elizabeth and a married daughter] Mrs. Edwards and her Daughters. Mr. Cornell has leave to take with him the servants and articles mentioned in his Inventory ...."[15]

[12] "An Act, for confiscating the Property of all such Persons as are inimical to the United States ...." Chap. XVII, Section II, 124 (December 23, 1777).

[13] Letter from Samuel Cornell and John London to Gov. Caswell, December 4, 1777, Clark (ed.), The State Records of North Carolina, XI, 690.

[14] See Letter from Gov. Caswell to Cornell & London (December 5, 1777), Clark (ed.), State Records of North Carolina, XI, 691–92.

[15] Ibid., 698.

While waiting on board the Brigantine Edwards, Cornell had obtained a copy of the bill to confiscate Loyalist property, then under consideration in the legislature. Apparently, he had no intention of pledging his allegiance to North Carolina, and so, on December 19, 1777, in an obvious effort to transfer the land out of his own name before the confiscation bill passed the General Assembly, Cornell executed deeds transferring various parcels of his land to his daughters, including Elizabeth. Elizabeth's deed was back dated to December 11 in an apparent attempt to make the transaction appear to have been completed, at least several weeks before the confiscation legislation passed.[16] Since his wife and children were to accompany Cornell back to New York, he also arranged, a day later on December 20, to have his daughter Elizabeth execute a lease of the parcels he had just transferred to her, to Spyers Singleton, for a period of three years at the considerable rent of £1200.[17] Just a few days after that, on December 23, the legislature passed the confiscation act into law. Sometime after Christmas, Cornell, along with his wife, daughters, and servants, sailed for New York, where they remained, and where Cornell "lived and died a British subject, under the British government."[18]

In January 1779, toward the end of the next session of the legislature, which the first confiscation act had established as the deadline for returnees to pledge their allegiance and recover their property, the legislature took note of the failure of many absentees to return timely, and passed a new confiscation act "to carry into Effect" the original act by making confiscations absolute.[19]

[16] See "Law case, tried and determined, at a Supreme court of law and equity, for the district of Newbern, North Carolina, on the 30th of November, 1787," in *American Museum; or Repository of Ancient and Modern Fugitive* Pieces (April 1788), 371–72, cited in Hamburger, Law and Judicial Duty, 451.

[17] John Charles Waldrup, "James Iredell and the Practice of Law in Revolutionary Era North Carolina" (Ph.D. Diss., University of North Carolina at Chapel Hill, 1985), 260, and 290 notes 15 and 18.

[18] See Letter from Samuel Cornell to Gov. Caswell (December 26, 1777), in Clark (ed.), State Records of North Carolina, XI, 700; and "Law case, tried and determined, at a Supreme court of law and equity, for the district of Newbern, North Carolina, on the 30th of November, 1787," 372.

[19] "An Act to Carry Into Effect [the original confiscation act]" passed at the January 1779 session, *At a General Assembly begun and held at New Bern, on the Fourteenth day of April, in the Year of Our Lord One thousand Seven Hundred and Seventy Eight, and from thence continued by Adjournments and Prorogations to the Nineteenth day of January at Halifax, in the Year of Our Lord One Thousand Seven Hundred and Seventy Nine. Being the third Session of this Assembly,* Chap. V, 209–14.

And whereas, many Persons who come within the Descriptions of the [first confiscation act] ... have failed or neglected to appear before the General Assembly during the present session, and submit to the State whether they shall be admitted as Citizens thereof, and restored to their possessions ... whereby all such Persons have clearly incurred, and are become liable to the Penalties of the aforesaid Act:

II. Be it therefore enacted [that all their property] shall be, and are hereby declared to be forfeited to the State, and shall be vested in the same, for the uses and Purposes hereafter mentioned ....[20]

The January 1779 act established a procedure by which the County Courts would appoint Commissioners of Forfeited Estates, who were then to conduct investigations to determine which property was subject to confiscation, and to take possession of it.[21] "Commissioners shall enter in a Book, to be kept for the Purpose, all [personal and real property] forfeited by this Act, which shall come to their Knowledge or Possession ... together with the names of the former Owners, and also whether the same, or any Part thereof, be claimed by any Subject of this State, or of any of the United States ....[22] The act gave the County Courts authority to order Commissioners to rent out confiscated lands for up to one year. But apparently, there was as yet little appetite to create an irrevocable situation by selling the land off.[23]

Perhaps most significantly, the act established a procedure to challenge confiscations.

VII. Provided, that if it shall appear to any County Court that any Person, *being a subject of this State, or of any of the United States*, has or pretends to have any Right or Title in Law, to any [property] declared forfeited by this Act, such [county] court shall send up a true and exact State of such Claim to the Superior Court of the District, which Superior Court shall proceed to inquire into and determine the Legal Right and Title of the Person so claiming *by Jury, in the same Manner as in Suits at Common Law*, and such Determination ... *shall be final* ....[24] (emphasis added)

In June 1779, just a few months after this confiscation act went into effect, Spyers Singleton and another person, joined together to avail themselves of its dispute procedures. The two petitioned the County Court, challenging the confiscation of all parcels of land that Samuel

[20] Ibid., 210. [21] Ibid., Chap. V, Sections III–IV, 210–11.

[22] Ibid., Chap. V, Section VI, 211.

[23] Ibid. Chap. V, Section VI, 211. Personal property, however, was to be sold. ("[T]he said courts shall order all Negroes, or other Personal Property forfeited by this Act, to be sold at Public Auctions ....")

[24] Ibid., Chap. V, Section VII, 212. The Act also provided a procedure to claim compensation if the property had already been sold, see Section VIII, 212.

Cornell had transferred to his daughters a year and a half earlier. They hired several lawyers to represent their cause including Abner Nash, a prominent political figure in the state, who would also represent Singleton in the later, better known *Bayard* v. *Singleton* litigation in 1784–87. The lawyers argued to the County Court that the property at issue actually belonged to Cornell's daughters, who had acquired ownership of the parcels before the first confiscation law went into effect; and since the daughters had neither attached themselves to the enemy, nor absented themselves from the United States, their property should not be subject to confiscation. The judges of the County Court rejected this petition, however, finding that the daughters were not citizens of North Carolina, and did not have ownership rights in the property.

But Singleton quickly filed a second petition, focusing on his own situation. He was currently, he told the court, in possession of Elizabeth Cornell's parcels under a three-year lease executed by her on December 20, 1777, and had already paid a considerable portion of the £1200 rent, and given a bond for the balance. In attempting to defend the Cornell title, Singleton was simultaneously attempting to protect his possessory interest in the land. He asked the County Court to stay all further proceedings against the property until the Superior Court could consider the case. The court saw enough merit in his petition to send the case up to the Superior Court for final determination by a jury, as the act mandated. In the meantime, the County Court upheld the confiscation of the other daughters' property, ordering that the real property be leased out for a year, and the personal property be sold at auction, as the act specified.[25]

Singleton's case came on for hearing at the next term of the Superior Court in November, 1779. By then James Iredell had become Attorney General of the State, and in that role prosecuted the case for confiscation against Singleton. Like Maclaine, Iredell would, over the next few years, become an intractable enemy of confiscation. But now he argued that the confiscation of Elizabeth's parcels had been proper, and that Singleton's claim should be denied.[26]

[25] The account in this paragraph is derived from Waldrup, "James Iredell and the Practice of Law ... ," 259–61, and notes 12–16 and is based on documents in "The Samuel Cornell" folder in the Craven County Estates Records, SANC, and on the June 1779 Minute Docket, Craven County Court Minutes, 1779–84, SANC.

[26] Waldrup, "James Iredell and the Practice of Law," 261–62, and 290–91 note 18; for Iredell's prosecution of treason and disloyalty cases, see Whichard, Justice James Iredell, 21–22.

In a special verdict, the jury found the following facts:

> that Cornell was the owner of the property on July 4, 1776; that he had attached himself to the British cause; that he continued to own the property until December 11, 1777 when, visiting New Bern in a ship under a flag of truce, he signed a deed of gift of the property to his 15 year old daughter, Elizabeth; and that Cornell had complied with all the formalities in executing and recording this deed. [It also found] that the legislature which had enacted the confiscation law had already begun its session in the town of New Bern before the transfer of the property; that Cornell then left for New York, taking Elizabeth with him, where both still remained; and that on December 20, 1777 Singleton had leased the property and that the lease had not yet expired.[27]

It may have been decisive that the jury found that the legislature had begun its session before Cornell deeded the property to his daughter. The common law rule was that a statute possessed the force of law from the first day of the legislative session in which it was ultimately enacted. The jury's finding of fact that the legislative session had begun earlier would have established that in law the land had been confiscated before Cornell had the chance to transfer it to his daughter Elizabeth. There could be no question that Cornell himself came squarely within the description of persons whose property was to be confiscated. Hence, because Cornell no longer held title to the property, Elizabeth could not have acquired any interest in it through his deed to her. Since the new confiscation act, however, only called for the leasing of forfeited real property, it seems that Singleton may have continued to remain in possession thereafter.

At almost the same time the Singleton case was being prosecuted in the Superior Court, the General Assembly, meeting in Halifax, had apparently become convinced that it had not dealt decisively enough with the Loyalists in the act it had passed 10 months earlier in January 1779. It now passed a new act "to carry into effect" the original confiscation law, repealing the act of the previous January.[28] The new act, passed at the October 1779 session, expressed the legislature's exasperation. It had been nearly two years since the Assembly had established a deadline for returnees and nearly a year since that deadline had passed. "And whereas,

[27] Waldrup, "James Iredell and the Practice of Law," 290 note 18, from the "*State* v. *Spyers Singleton*" folder, New Bern Superior Court Miscellaneous Records, SANC.

[28] "An Act to carry into Effect [the original confiscation act] passed at New Bern in November, [1777] … ." *At General Assembly, begun and held at Halifax on the eighteenth day of October, in the year of our Lord one thousand seven hundred and seventy-nine … . Being the second session of this Assembly,* Chap. II, Section XVI, 267–68.

divers persons, who come within the description [of the original act] have failed or neglected to appear before the said General Assembly ... or at any General Assembly since, and submit to the State whether they shall be admitted as citizens thereof, and restored to their possessions which to them once belonged .... " the legislature decided to leave no further ambiguity. It named 67 persons whose property it was specifically confiscating for their failure to return and to appear before them. Samuel Cornell was one of these. The properties of these 67 "shall be and are, hereby declared to be confiscated, fully and absolutely forfeited to this State, and shall be vested in the hands of commissioners [of forfeiture]."[29] And the legislature also decided that there should be no turning back in this enterprise, ordering the confiscated real estate to be sold off at auction, rather than temporarily leased out as it had previously.[30] Over the next few months into the early part of 1780, some of the forfeited property was sold off,[31] but apparently not the property Singleton seems to have been occupying.[32] The new harsher act, however, did retain the procedures to challenge confiscations (including a trial by jury) that the previous law had included.[33]

In May 1780, a British army invaded and took possession of Charleston, South Carolina. Thereafter, the British sent their military forces through the south, including across parts of North Carolina. In September 1780, in consequence, the North Carolina legislature temporarily suspended sales of confiscated estates, observing that they had "not answered the purposes intended thereby, and the army of the enemy now in the State of South Carolina, would occasion the said property to sell greatly under it intrinsic value, ... whereas the [confiscated lands] would, if reserved, establish a valuable and permanent fund [for the war effort]."[34] At its January 1781 session, the legislature continued the May suspension "in force until the General Assembly shall otherwise direct."[35] But in the fall of 1781, the war turned decisively against the

[29] Ibid., "An Act to Carry into Effect ...." (October 1779), Chap. II, Sections I and II, 263–64.

[30] Ibid., "An Act to Carry into Effect ...." (October 1779), Chap. II, Section VII, 265.

[31] See Waldrup, "James Iredell and the Practice of Law ...," 291–92 notes 20 and 21.

[32] Ibid., 261–62.

[33] "An Act to Carry into Effect ...." (October 1779), Chap. II, Sections VIII and IX, 266.

[34] "An Act for Suspending the operations of an Act, for carrying into effect an Act, commonly called the Confiscation Act," *At a General Assembly, begun and held at Hillsborough on the fifth day of September, in the year of our Lord one thousand seven hundred and eighty .... Being the second session of this Assembly*, Chap. VI, Sec. I, 352.

[35] "An Additional Act to an Act ... for continuing an Act, intituled An Act for suspending the operation of an Act, etc ...." *At a General Assembly begun and held at Halifax on the*

British with General Cornwallis's defeat and surrender at the battle of Yorktown in Virginia.

From that point on, North Carolinians looked forward to the end of the war,[36] sorting themselves into increasingly strident factions on the issue of confiscation, and on the question of further sales of land that had already been confiscated. The feeling among opponents of confiscation was complicated. Partly they believed that the confiscation laws had unjustly swept up many innocent people; partly they believed that an abiding reconciliation must follow the end of the war, if the polity was to function harmoniously thereafter. Partly they thought that reconciliation would cast the new country in the best possible light with the rest of the world. And partly, their affinities were a matter of class. Many Loyalists had come from the same ranks as their Patriot defenders, substantial landowners, merchants, lawyers, and the view was widespread among opponents that the anti-Loyalist confiscation rage was driven more than anything else by crude desires for vengeance, and a thirst for illicit gain by the common people, although the facts were certainly more complicated, as *Bayard* v. *Singleton* itself makes clear.

On March 27, 1782, in the spring following Cornwallis's defeat, Archibald Maclaine, now an opponent of confiscation, expressed his hopes that further sales of confiscated lands could be delayed. It is possible he believed that if sales were postponed long enough a treaty of peace might intervene to require states to restore confiscated properties to their original owners. Maclaine wrote that "I confess I am no friend to absolute confiscations in our circumstances. At all events, I would postpone all sales except of perishable articles . . . ."[37]

The following month, the legislature did what Maclaine had feared it would. The danger from the British having passed, in April 1782, the Assembly ended the suspension of sales. In a new confiscation act, it again

Eighteenth Day of January, in the Year of Our Lord One Thousand Seven Hundred Eighty-one . . . . Being the Third Session of this Assembly, Chap. IV, Section VIII, 377.

36 See, for example, Iredell's letter to his wife Hannah, July 3, 1782, in McRee (ed.), Iredell, II, 17 ("We have very great news from the southward. 'That a change in the ministry had certainly taken place; that a vote had been passed, declaring any man shall be deemed an enemy who advises a further prosecution of the American War; that Dr. Franklin had been sent for, and was actually in London, and that General Leslie had received advice of a truce having been agreed upon to the northward.' These accounts . . . have been brought from General Greene's camp [where an aide of General Leslie] said he was convinced a peace would very soon take place . . . .")

37 Letter of Archibald Maclaine to Gov. Thos. Burke (March 27, 1782), in Clark (ed.), State Papers of North Carolina, XVI, 246, at 247–48.

listed the names of the 67 persons whose property had been previously forfeited to the state, including Samuel Cornell's, and now rushed to have all the confiscated properties sold no later than the first day of the following January 1783.[38] In December 1782, just weeks shy of the statutory deadline, the Commissioners of Forfeiture sold Spyers Singleton the parcels of land Samuel Cornell had conveyed to his daughter Elizabeth,[39] and which Singleton may have been in possession of all along.

A few months later, in March 1783, the Provisional Treaty of Peace arrived in Philadelphia from England and was sent out to the states. The American negotiators had resisted British demands that the treaty include a mandatory return of confiscated Tory estates. Writing to Governor Martin from Philadelphia on March 24, 1783, North Carolina's congressional representatives Hugh Williamson and William Blount described the struggle over confiscation during the peace process. "The British Minister contended long for ... a full act of oblivion and restitution of [Loyalist] property; he alleged that the King's honor made this Article necessary. Our Ministers had a natural reply, the King's passions, cherished by the falsehoods and frauds of Tories had continued the War and might prevent a Peace, but we should not accept Peace on the humiliating Terms of cherishing the Plunderers of our Property and murderers of our friends .... At present nothing is given them but the promise of a recommendation. Light food; however, the reward is equal to the Service."[40]

And the Americans prevailed on this point. In Article 5 of the Provisional Treaty, the United States only "agreed that the Congress *shall earnestly recommend* it to the Legislatures of the respective States, to provide for the restitution of all estates, rights and properties, which have been confiscated, belonging to real British subjects ... [and to] persons resident in districts, in the possession of his Majesty's arms, and

38 "An Act directing the sale of Confiscated Property," *At a General Assembly, begun and held at Hillsborough, on the Thirteenth day of April, in the year of our Lord One Thousand Seven Hundred and Eighty Two .... Being the First Session of this Assembly*, Chap. VI, Sections II & XI, 424–25, 427.

39 See Waldrup, "James Iredell," 262, and 291 note 19, citing Singleton's affidavit in the "*Bayard* v. *Singleton*" folder, New Bern Superior Court, Miscellaneous Records. SANC.

40 Letter from Hugh Williamson and William Blount to Governor Martin (March 24, 1783), in Clark (ed.), State Records of North Carolina, XVI, 753, at 758; see also "Extract of a Letter from Doctor Franklin to Mr. Oswald [the British Peace Commissioner] respecting Tories and forfeited property" in which Franklin vigorously resisted the British demand that confiscated estates be restored to their owners, ibid., at 914–15.

who have not borne arms against the said United States"[41] (emphasis added). By contrast, Article 6 flatly prohibited "future confiscations ... and [also] any prosecutions commenced against any person or persons, for, or by reason of the part which he or they may have taken in the present war ... ."[42] Article 5, however, did arguably contain one mandatory provision. The final paragraph stated that "it is agreed, that all persons, who have any interest in confiscated lands ... shall meet with no lawful impediment in the prosecution of their just rights."[43]

A month later, in April 1783, the North Carolina General Assembly passed "An Act of Pardon and Oblivion," seemingly in an effort to conform to the treaty terms, especially Article 6. But the legislature was careful to exclude from the coverage of this act all persons who "are named in any of the laws commonly called confiscation laws ... ."[44] Congress, in any case, had not yet even issued the recommendation that Article 5 called for, as the treaty had not yet been finalized.[45]

By the spring of 1783, however, James Iredell had become convinced that the General Assembly would never restore confiscated estates that had already been sold off, holding out only slightly greater hope that confiscated estates that had not yet been sold, might ultimately be restored to their original owners. Writing to his English cousin, Henry Eustace McCulloh, from whom the state had confiscated almost 50,000 acres of land,[46] Iredell observed that

> I am satisfied any claim on your behalf never can be preferred with the least prospect of success but upon this footing – that the execution of the

[41] Article 5 of the "Provisional Treaty of Peace," in Clark (ed.), State Records of North Carolina, XVI, 748, at 751.

[42] Article 6, ibid., at 752. [43] Article 5, ibid., at 751.

[44] "An Act of Pardon and Oblivion," passed *At a General Assembly begun and held at Hillsborough, on the eighteenth cay of April, in the year of our Lord, one thousand seven hundred and eighty three .... Being the first Session of this Assembly*, Ch. VI, 489, and 490 Section III.

[45] See letter from Robert R. Livingston to Sir Guy Carlton, April 12, 1783, in Clark (ed.), State Records of North Carolina, XVI, 870 ("It cannot be doubted Sir, as you justly observe, that Congress will embrace the earliest opportunity to perform the stipulations contained in the 5th as well as every other of the provisional articles, immediately after the same shall have been ratified. In the meanwhile it must be obvious to your Excellency that a recommendation to restore to the Loyalists the estates they have forfeited, will come with less weight before Legislatures composed of men whose property is still withheld from them by the continuance of his Britannic Majesty's Fleets and armies in this Country, than it will do when Peace and the full enjoyment of their rights shall have worn down those asperities which have grown out of eight years [of] War.")

[46] Whichard, Justice James Iredell, 8.

Confiscation Act shall proceed no farther, and that you shall have restored what is yet in the hands of the public. For I find it to be the sentiment of the most moderate men, that those who have purchased under faith of Acts of the Assembly, cannot rightfully have their estates taken from them . . . .[47]

The Definitive Treaty of Peace, which changed little that had been agreed upon in the Provisional Treaty, was signed several months later on September 3, 1783, and ratified by Congress on January 14, 1784. On October 5, Archibald Maclaine wrote to Iredell.

The latest accounts give us every reason to expect that the Definitive Treaty is signed; and my ardent wish is, that it may be laid officially before the Assembly. Without it, I despair of doing any thing of immediate consequence. Should it be laid before us it will then be seen whether we will suffer anger and resentment so far to get the better of reason and sound policy, as to render us infamous over all Europe.[48]

Shortly after Congress ratified the treaty of peace in January 1784, it went on to pass a resolution complying with the treaty's terms; the resolution "*earnestly recommended* to the Legislatures of the respective States to provide for the restitution of all estates, rights and properties which have been confiscated"[49] (emphasis added). But if there was a group of people in the state, like Iredell and Maclaine and others, who hoped that the congressional recommendation might move the Assembly to return at least the unsold estates, there was another group that seemed satisfied with the confiscation process as it had unfolded, and pleased that the treaty had required no such thing.

Richard Dobbs Spaight came from a prominent family. His father had been a crown official in the colonial government, and he was the grand-nephew of Arthur Dobbs, one of the colony's royal governors, but he had early joined the Patriot cause. In the spring of 1784, he was serving as a North Carolina delegate to Congress. In March, he wrote to Governor Martin (and the General Assembly) from Annapolis, eager to let them know that Congress' recommendation was intended as nothing more than a pro forma compliance with the terms of the treaty.

As I make no doubt but that the attention of the General Assembly has been called to the restoration of the property of refugees, in consequence of the 5th article of

[47] James Iredell to Henry Eustace McCulloh (May 1, 1783), Don Higginbotham (ed.), *The Papers of James Iredell, 1778–1783* (Raleigh, N.C., Division of Archives and History, Dept. of Cultural Resources, 1976), II, 395–96; and McRee (ed.), Iredell, II, 53.

[48] Maclaine to Iredell (October 5, 1783), McRee (ed.), Iredell, II, 70.

[49] "By the United States in Congress Assembled, January 14th, 1784," in Clark (ed.), State Records of North Carolina, XVII, 3.

the definitive Treaty; I think it my duty to transmit to your Excellency Copies of two Letters which passed between our Commissioners & the British Commissioner previous to the signing of the provisional articles: It plainly appears from these that the restoration of the property of the refugees, or compensation for the same was never intended to be made by our Commissioners nor expected by the British.[50]

That spring a struggle over Congress' resolution developed in the General Assembly. Only a small minority, however, supported complying with the congressional recommendation as it bore on Article 5 of the Treaty. Samuel Johnston, Iredell's brother-in-law, and a prominent political figure in the state, wrote to Iredell of the failure of efforts in the Assembly to persuade a majority to adopt Congress' recommendation.

The fifth Article of the Treaty has been under the consideration of both Houses, where it has met with the most illiberal reception. They have paid no regard to the recommendations of Congress; and there appears a settled resolution against the restoration of any part of the confiscated property.[51]

Abner Nash, who had been the second governor of North Carolina, and had served as Spyers Singleton's attorney in the 1779 judicial proceedings that challenged the confiscation of the Cornell daughter lands, now sat in the General Assembly. He "was at the head of the large majority who opposed any compliance with the Recommendatory Article … ."[52] On May 29, 1784, the Assembly defeated, by an overwhelming vote of 62 against, 18 in favor, a bill that would have "restored to and vested" in their original owners all confiscated properties that remained unsold.[53]

Having suffered these decisive defeats in the Assembly, it was at this moment that several well-connected lawyers began to turn their focus to the courts, which they held out some hope might just serve as a refuge from undiluted majoritarian politics. Archibald Maclaine, along with Samuel Johnston, began to mull over the possibility of litigation. "[S]uits brought for British debts, & by persons who during the war lay under disabilities,

50 "Hon. Richard D. Spaight Delegate in Congress to Gov. Martin" (Annapolis, March 12, 1784), in Clark (ed.), State Records of North Carolina, XVII, 21.

51 Samuel Johnston to Iredell (May 1, 1784), in McRee (ed.), Iredell, II, 99; see also letter from William Hooper to Iredell, May 1, 1784, in ibid., II, 99–100 ("The vote was called, and not ten in favor of the clause of the report which applies to the recommendatory article of the treaty.")

52 Iredell to Henry Eustance McCulloh (June 15, 1784), in McRee (ed.), Iredell, II, 103.

53 "Bill to amend and reduce to system the Confiscation Laws now in force in this State," in Clark (ed.), State Records of North Carolina, XIX, 671–73.

[he agreed with Johnston], may now be maintained."[54] Maclaine, however, also offered a pessimistic assessment of the likely outcome.[55]

At its October 1784 session the legislature effectively eliminated any hope that it might be persuaded to restore unsold confiscated estates. At that session, it passed into law "An Act Directing the Sale of Confiscated Property,"[56] which noted that the state had confiscated "considerable quantities of lands [and other property]," which "yet remain unsold; and it being just and necessary that the same should be sold for the use and benefit of the State" ordered the commissioners of forfeited estates to sell it all.[57]

It was at roughly this time that Samuel Johnston began to act on a plan to turn to litigation in an effort to restore at least some of the confiscated estates. The November, 1784 "New Action Docket" of the New Bern Superior Court lists eleven separate common law actions of ejectment that Johnston brought on behalf of one or another of the Cornell sisters, including Elizabeth.[58] These were filed against a variety of defendants, who had purchased the several parcels of land from Commissioners of Forfeited estates; the suits sought their recovery. The defendants in these actions were themselves substantial members of the community, merchants and justices. Among the suits was an ejectment action that Elizabeth Cornell brought, with her husband under her married name Bayard, against Spyers Singleton, seeking the return of the properties her father had transferred to her in 1777, and which she in turn had leased to Singleton. This filing initiated the case of *Bayard* v. *Singleton.* Singleton himself was a significant figure in the community, a New Bern merchant, who served in the Assembly in 1784–85, and over the longer term, as a justice of the peace in Craven County. In all but one of these cases, the

54 See letter of Archibald Maclaine to George Hooper (June 25, 1784), in Clark (ed.), State Records of North Carolina, XVII, 148, at 150.

55 Ibid.

56 "An Act Directing the Sale of Confiscated Property," *At a General Assembly begun and held at New Bern on the Twenty Second of October in the Year of our Lord One Thousand Seven Hundred and Eighty-Four … . Being the First Session of this Assembly*, Chap. VI, 661–64.

57 Ibid.

58 For a detailed description of the various actions, see Waldrup, "James Iredell," 262–64, and 291–92 note 21; and the November 1784 New Action Docket, in New Bern Superior Court Law and Equity Dockets, 1780–86, part 2; the narratives and affidavits in the "Samuel Cornell" folder, New Bern Superior Court Estates Records; the "*Bayard* v. *Singleton*" folder, and the "*Chads* v. *Singleton*" folder, both in New Bern Superior Court Miscellaneous Records, SANC.

lawyer and prominent political figure, Abner Nash, served as counsel for the assorted defendants.[59]

Samuel Johnston continued his litigation campaign at the court's next term in May 1785. He joined with the lawyer William Davie, to file "sixteen suits in trover or detinue" seeking the return of one or another of the Cornell sisters' confiscated personal property, most often slaves. In one of these suits, Elizabeth Bayard and her husband, sued Singleton for "the return of Jack," a slave they valued at £300.[60] At the next term of the court in November, 1785, Johnston and Davie filed "five more trover and detinue actions for the return of additional slaves."[61]

Under the circumstances, it is not surprising that the legislature reacted to Johnston's mass filing of lawsuits. On December 29, 1785, it passed into law "An Act to Secure and Quiet in Their Possessions all Such Persons . . . who Have Purchased, or May Hereafter Purchase [confiscated properties] Which Have been Sold, or May Hereafter Be Sold by Commissioners of Forfeited Estates . . . ."[62] The act sought to protect the title of persons who had purchased a confiscated estate from a Commissioner of Forfeiture. It declared that such persons "shall be *deemed not liable to answer any suit or suits in law or equity*, which hath been, or may be commenced by any person or person [described as inimical to the State in any confiscation act], *or by any person or persons whatsoever, claiming by, from, or under them*"[63] (emphasis added). The statute went on to "require" courts "in all such cases upon the motion or affidavit of the defendant ... and by his deeds and other documents, making it appear that he holds and derives his title to the [property] under and by the sale of a commissioner ... of forfeited estates ... *to dismiss* all such suitors, suits, action or actions"[64] (emphasis added). The statute's stated objective was to protect good faith purchasers of confiscated estates "from expensive and vexatious law-suits which have been or may be commenced against them ... by obnoxious and disqualified persons ... specified in [the] Confiscation Acts, *or by any person ... whatsoever, claiming by, from or under them ... by any Act, deed, gift, will or other conveyance whatsoever*, unless the same were actually made [before July 4, 1776]"[65] (emphasis added).

[59] Waldrup, "James Iredell," 292 note 21. [60] Ibid., 293 note 23. [61] Ibid., 263.

[62] Session Laws passed *At a General Assembly, begun and held at New Bern on the nineteenth day of November, in the year of our Lord one thousand seven hundred and eighty-five, ... it being the first session of this Assembly*, Ch. VII, 730–31.

[63] Ibid., Ch. VII, Section I, 730 [64] Ibid., 730–31. [65] Ibid., 730.

While the statute required ordinary courts to dismiss such suits, it did provide a procedure by which those whose land had been confiscated and sold could "receive all such sums of money or monies which such [property] did sell for, [plus six percent interest on the sum]," if they were able to establish that they were not "meant to be included in the penalties of the said confiscation laws . . . ."[66] But the statute did not leave this determination to a judicial court; the General Assembly itself was to "adjudicate" these cases. Claimants had to demonstrate "such favorable circumstances . . . to the satisfaction of the General Assembly . . . ."[67]

In both aspects of the statute, the Assembly was implicitly claiming a kind of supreme judicial power. On one hand, the statute included a general "legislative" decree requiring ordinary courts to dismiss pending confiscation cases, on the other, it reserved to itself the residual authority to judge and determine the individual cases of remaining claimants.

Abner Nash, who was representing most of the defendants in the recently launched Cornell family suits, also sat in the Assembly at this time, and, whether out of personal interest or principle or both, had spoken up strongly in favor of passing the new act, when it was being debated in the legislature.[68] Recall, however, that the previous year, Nash had stood with a large majority in the Assembly who had opposed the return of confiscated estates to their original owners, and had done so months before he began to serve as a lawyer for the defendants in the Cornell family suits. Recall too, that Elizabeth Bayard's claim had already been adjudicated and rejected by a jury in a trial held in the Superior Court six years earlier, in 1779.

It was the December 1785 statute that became the focus of the constitutional controversy in *Bayard* v. *Singleton*. From its passage, men like Maclaine and Iredell believed that the act was unconstitutional, and (in some sense) void. What seems to have infuriated them was that the Assembly had substituted legislative adjudication in confiscation cases for traditional common law judicial proceedings.

Maclaine, joined by eight others, entered a long protest against the new law in the Assembly's journals. In it, he began by arguing that the act "is an *ex post facto* Law . . . and therefore contrary to the Constitution."[69]

66 Ibid. 67 Ibid.

68 See letter from Archibald Maclaine to Samuel Johnston (New Bern, December 24, 1785), in Kelly and Baradell (eds.), The Papers of James Iredell, 1784–1789, III, 181; see also Waldrup, "James Iredell," 294 note 27.

69 Maclaine protest (December 28, 1785), in Clark (ed.), State Records of North Carolina, XVII, 419.

Section XXIV of the 1776 constitution's Declaration of Rights stated "[t]hat retrospective laws, punishing facts committed before the existence of such laws, and by them only declared criminal, are oppressive, unjust, and incompatible with liberty; wherefore no *ex post facto* law ought to be made."[70]

The new statute was certainly a retrospective law in that the legislature had in effect retroactively eliminated causes of action that were legally available to the Cornell plaintiffs at the time they filed their suits. But whether it amounted to an *ex post facto* law in the precise sense the constitution seems to have intended is considerably more doubtful. What the new act clearly amounted to, however, was a legislative decree in the form of a general law that decided a large number of suits against a certain class of plaintiffs, leaving others to be adjudicated through some unspecified legislative process.

And this was the burden of much of the rest of Maclaine's dissent. Some of the early confiscation laws, he observed, had permitted Loyalists to dispose of their property before they left the state. The new blanket law, he implied, would not allow for adequate assessment of facts of this kind. The land of others, citizens of the state, he continued, would not have been subject to confiscation, until the date they committed treasonable acts. The new law, he again implied, did not provide adequate means to determine whether these persons had sold their land before committing such acts.[71]

In his closing paragraph, he summed up what he believed to be the act's overriding constitutional difficulty. His language is somewhat opaque, but its thrust, translated into later terms, was that the statute was a special (not general and uniform) law that was directed against a certain group of people, and deprived that minority of the ordinary protections for their property that common law procedures provided for everyone.

> Because the Laws of this State and the rules of their construction must apply to all ranks of Citizens, nor do we conceive it possible under the present bill to preclude any subject from the benefit of Law by a denial of the known and established rules of Justice, which protect the property of all Citizens equally, nor to place any of them under the adjudication of the General Assembly, whose desire to redress the grievance may be fluctuating, uncertain and ineffectual.[72]

[70] Section XXIV of the 1776 North Carolina Declaration of Rights, in Francis Thorpe (ed.), *The Federal and State Constitutions, Colonial Charters, and Other Organic Laws of the States, Territories and Colonies* (Washington, D.C., Government Printing Office, 1909, Reprint Buffalo, N.Y., William S. Hein, 1993), V, 2788.

[71] Maclaine protest, in Clark (ed.), State Records of North Carolina XVII, 420.

[72] Ibid., 421.

It seems significant that except for his (problematic) argument that the new act violated the *ex post facto* clause of the 1776 constitution, he did not make more of an effort to base his constitutional objections squarely on constitutional text. His arguments sound very much like they are being drawn from an older, looser, more "political," constitutional tradition of disputation.

Maclaine's sentiments about the new law were of course shared by others. James Hogg wrote to Iredell that he had sent Samuel Johnston a "copy of the wonderful [new] law by which the Assembly have arrogated to themselves the judicial power in all suits regarding confiscated property."[73] Iredell himself denounced it as an "infamous law" that he would absolutely refuse to cooperate in carrying into effect.[74] He was already thinking about the courts as a possible source of redress, but had concluded that they offered "very little prospect of relief."[75]

In fact, a few months later, in March, Maclaine wrote Iredell to point out that the courts had actually been cooperating with the legislature's policy.

> The Assembly and the Judges have indeed found an easy way to evade the treaty. The former refuse to point out any method to ascertain what is confiscated, (for they know they cannot,) and the Judges refuse to let any person, whose property may be taken by a rapacious Commissioner, maintain a suit; so that we seem to be at the mercy of a set of needy adventurers, whose interest it is to pillage us; and that no loophole may be left unguarded, an act was passed last session, intended to give a sanction to every thing that has been done, and may be done for the future.[76]

Maclaine's complaints, however, ran wider and deeper.

> How it happened I know not, but notwithstanding the intentions of so many of the gentlemen to get into the Assembly last year, they almost all failed .... [P]ossibly to this we owe a fresh influx of paper money. To this it is owing that we have so many wicked, and scandalous acts last session; and it is certainly owing to this, that the bills which I introduced, and were recommended by Mr. Johnston and you, fell to the ground in the Senate. Want of principle, and want of knowledge have occasioned these evils .... There is no dealing with fools and knaves, unless they are powerfully opposed. There will be no living in the country without a reform, and in truth it will be a disgrace to live in it. If there are no hopes of having a better legislature, I shall bid adieu to public business for ever.[77]

But Maclaine did hold out some slight hope "if the Judges are beset by the principal gentlemen of the bar [like Iredell] in a proper manner ...."[78]

[73] Letter of James Hogg to James Iredell (January 19, 1786), in McRee (ed.), Iredell, II, 132.
[74] Ibid., II, 133–34. [75] Ibid., II, 134.
[76] Letter of Archibald Maclaine to James Iredell (March 6, 1786), in ibid., II, 137.
[77] Ibid., II, 138. [78] Ibid., II, 138.

At its May 1786 session, the Superior Court heard arguments in *Bayard* v. *Singleton.* Singleton produced an affidavit attesting that he held "the disputed property under a sale from a commissioner of forfeited estates ... "[79] His lawyer, Nash, then moved to dismiss the suit, citing the recent "act to secure and quiet in their possession all such persons [who have purchased confiscated estates from commissioners of forfeiture]."[80] "This brought on long arguments from the counsel on each side, on constitutional points."[81] Before examining these arguments in greater detail, it seems important to say something about the North Carolina Constitution of 1776, on which they were mainly based.

9.3 THE NORTH CAROLINA CONSTITUTION OF 1776

The North Carolina Constitution was among the first generation of written constitutions adopted in the months following publication of the Declaration of Independence. As such, it lacked a number of features that later constitutions would often include. It was framed by a "Congress" that had been specially elected for the purpose but was not submitted to the people for ratification, although some groups had argued for popular ratification.[82] And it failed to state that the constitution itself was a direct act of the people. Instead, it stated that "*we, the Representatives of the freemen of North Carolina*, chosen and assembled in Congress, for the express purpose of framing a Constitution, *under the authority of the people* ... do declare that a government shall be established, in manner and form following"[83] (emphasis added). The Congress, moreover, was not yet the stand-alone constitutional convention of later development. The constitution itself conferred on the Congress the authority to act as a legislature temporarily until a General Assembly had been formed.[84] Moreover, the constitution had been adopted in a procedure that bore some resemblance to the one used in enacting ordinary laws, i.e., by being "read the third time, and ratified in open Congress."[85] On the other hand,

79 *Bayard* v. *Singleton*, 1 Martin's 42 (N.C., 1787), at 43. 80 Ibid. 81 Ibid.

82 1776 North Carolina Declaration of Rights and Constitution, Thorpe (ed.), Constitutions, V, 2787 footnote (not submitted to the people); for calls to hold such a vote, see "Instructions to the Delegates from Mecklenburg to the Provincial Congress at Halifax in November, 1776," William Saunders (ed.), *Colonial Records of North Carolina, 1775–1776* (Raleigh, N.C., Josephus Daniels, Printer to the State, 1890), X, 870d note 22; and "Instructions to the Delegates from Orange in the Halifax Congress to be held in November, 1776," in ibid., X, 870g note7.

83 North Carolina Constitution of 1776 in Thorpe (ed.), Constitutions, V, 2789–90.

84 Ibid., V, 2794. 85 Ibid.

this adoption process could also make the constitution seem more like ordinary "law."

Unlike New Hampshire's constitution of 1784, however, the North Carolina constitution did not expressly make the document part of the "law of the land." Nor did it include a clause, also like one in New Hampshire's, expressly depriving the legislature of power to make laws repugnant or contrary to the constitution. But it did have a number of provisions that could serve as support for the case for judicial review. The Declaration of Rights, a separate part of the constitution, contained a provision that declared, in more abstract traditional language, that that part of the constitution (and only that part?) "ought never to be violated on any pretence whatsoever."[86] Some in the state clearly understood this provision to impose a constitutional constraint on the legislature. "Instructions to the [Congress'] Delegates from Mecklenburg," County for example, directed representatives to "endeavor" to include a bill of rights in the constitution "which shall never be infringed in any future time by the law-making power . . . ." and to further endeavor to see that "[t]he law making power shall be restrained in all future time from making any alteration in the form of Government."[87]

On the other hand, the Declaration of Rights also contained a traditional English anti-suspension clause that could be read as unhelpful to the case for judicial review. "That all powers of suspending laws, or the execution of laws, by any authority, without consent of the Representatives of the people, is injurious to their rights, and ought not to be exercised"[88] Structurally, moreover, the constitution left the legislature completely unchecked by other branches of the government, in effect, institutionally supreme. The governor was to be elected annually by the legislature itself, and had not been granted a veto over the laws.

But there were other features of the constitution that could be drawn upon to sustain the case for judicial review. The Declaration of Rights made clear at the outset that "all political power is vested in and derived from the people only" and "[t]hat the people of this State ought to have

[86] Ibid.

[87] "Instructions to the Delegates from Mecklenburg to the Provincial Congress at Halifax in November, 1776," Saunders (ed.), Colonial Records of North Carolina, 1775–1776, X, 870a note 4, 870b note 9.

[88] North Carolina Constitution of 1776, in Thorpe (ed.), Constitutions, V, 2787 (Declaration of Rights, Section V). Traditionally, of course, these clauses had been aimed at the executive, but the language in them was broad enough so that under the right circumstances they could be read as encompassing judicial suspensions as well.

the sole and exclusive right of regulating the internal government and police thereof."[89] In effect, these sections declared that all governmental power was held as a delegation from the people. And there was certainly sentiment in the state for the view that the people had delegated that power on certain conditions and with certain limitations that were laid out in the Declaration of Rights, and the Form of Government, even though the traditional language often used in the text seemed more precatory than mandatory. The Mecklenburg county "Instructions to the [Congress'] Delegates," for example, stated that "The principal supreme power is possessed by the people at large, the derived and inferior power by the servants which they employ [and that] [w]hatever is constituted and ordained by the principal supreme power can not be altered, suspended or abrogated by any other power, but the same power that ordained may alter, suspend and abrogate its own ordinances. [Moreover] [t]he rules whereby the inferior power is to be exercised are to be constituted by the principal supreme power, and can be altered, suspended and abrogated by the same and no other."[90] The Orange county "Instructions to the Delegates" went somewhat further. "That the power of making laws shall have authority to provide remedies for any evils which may arise in the community, subject to the limitations and restraints provided by the principal supreme power."[91]

And Section IV of the Constitution's Declaration of Rights called for a separation of powers. "That the legislative, executive, and supreme judicial powers of government, ought to be forever separate and distinct from each other."[92] This seemed to be an especially important provision as both Mecklenburg and Orange counties instructed their delegates to include separation of powers provisions in the constitution.[93] In addition, Section XIV of the Declaration of Rights called for the safeguarding of trial by jury in property disputes, albeit in traditional precatory language.

[89] Ibid., Declaration of Rights, Sections I and II.

[90] "Instructions to the Delegates from Mecklenburg to the Provincial Congress at Halifax in November, 1776," Saunders (ed.), Colonial Records of North Carolina, 1775–1776, X, 870b notes 2nd, 4th, 5th.

[91] "Instructions to the Delegates from Orange in the Halifax Congress to be held in November, 1776," Saunders (ed.), Colonial Records of North Carolina, X, 870h ("Fifthly").

[92] North Carolina Constitution of 1776, Thorpe (ed.), Constitutions, V, 2787 (Declaration of Rights, Section IV).

[93] "Instructions to the Delegates from Mecklenburg to the Provincial Congress at Halifax in November, 1776," Saunders (ed.), Colonial Records of North Carolina, X, 870b note 6, "Instruction to Delegates from Orange," X, 870g ("Fourthly").

"That in all controversies at law, respecting property, the ancient mode of trial, by jury, is one of the securities of the rights of the people, and ought to remain sacred and inviolable."[94] The Declaration's *ex post facto* clause has already been mentioned.[95]

Although there was some sentiment in the state that judges should be "appointed by the General Assembly and hold their offices during one year,"[96] the Halifax Congress of November, 1776, which wrote the constitution, decided, after debate, that judges should instead enjoy their offices during good behavior, and "have adequate salaries during their continuance in office."[97] There was no mention in the constitution, moreover, of removal upon address. This was one of the relatively few early state constitutions to confer such an independent tenure on judges. The Orange county "Instructions to Delegates" made clear that many in the state saw judicial independence as an important constitutional value. "That the judging power shall be entirely *distinct from and independent of* the law making and executive powers"[98] (emphasis added). Judges could only be removed from office by being impeached by the General Assembly, for "maladministration, or corruption."[99]

The Mecklenburg and Orange county instructions, moreover, made clear that many viewed the role of judges in adjudicating individual cases as especially crucial to the scheme of separation of powers. One instruction provided that by "such [constitutional] limitations and restraints," the lawmaking power "shall be prevented" from "depriving any individual of his civil or natural rights unless by way of punishment for some declared offence clearly and plainly adjudged against him by the judging power."[100] Another "[t]hat the law making power shall have full and ample authority for the good of the people to provide legal remedies for all

[94] North Carolina Constitution of 1776, Thorpe (ed.), Constitutions, V, 2787 (Declaration of Rights, Section XIV).

[95] Ibid., 2787 (Declaration of Rights, Section XXIV).

[96] "Instructions to the Delegates from Mecklenburg to the Provincial Congress at Halifax in November, 1776," Saunders (ed.), Colonial Records of North Carolina, X, 870d.

[97] Sections XIII and XXI of the North Carolina Constitution of 1776, in Thorpe (ed.), Constitutions, V, 2791 and 2792.

[98] "Instructions to the Delegates of Orange," in Saunders (ed.), Colonial Records of North Carolina, X, 870h ("Eighthly").

[99] Section XXIII of the North Carolina Constitution of 1776, in Thorpe (ed.), Constitutions, V, 2792.

[100] "Instructions to the Delegates of Orange," in Saunders (ed.), Colonial Records of North Carolina, X, 870h ("Sixthly").

evils and abuses that may arise in the State, the executive power shall have authority to apply the legal remedies when the judging power shall have ascertained where and upon what individuals the remedies ought to be applied."[101] Understood this way, separation of powers left little room for legislative adjudication, which, from that perspective, began to seem increasingly anomalous.

With these sentiments and the constitutional text in hand, a strong case could be made that the people had delegated to the legislature the power to make laws, but only on the condition and under the limitation that these laws not violate any of the prohibitions contained, at the very least, in the Declaration of Rights. Arguably, the people had granted no power to the legislature to confer the force of law on a bill that violated these terms.

Even so, a crucial element was missing from the case for judicial review. There was not the slightest shred of evidence, either in the constitution or in other sources, that anyone had ever even considered the possibility that judges should possess the power to enforce the constitutional limitations the people had imposed. The constitution itself had deliberately omitted any institutional mechanism that might operate as a check on the legislature, aside from the annual popular elections it required.[102] And these were meant to make, as the very first section of the constitution stated, the "two distinct branches [of the legislature] both dependent on the people ... "[103] As elsewhere, it was taken for granted that the people themselves would enforce, primarily through elections (but also through petitions, pamphletting, and actions out of doors) the limitations they had imposed on their legislatures. The constitution had put into place an institutional design that itself made out a compelling case for legislative supremacy, subject only to supervision by the people.

The litigation in *Bayard* v. *Singleton*, brought to the surface and pitted against one another, these two, opposed views about the kind of system the constitution had created, and at a deeper level, about the character of the republican government it meant to establish.

101 "Instructions to the Delegates of Mecklenburg," in Saunders (ed.), Colonial Records of North Carolina, X, 870b note 7.

102 Sections II and III, North Carolina Constitution of 1776, in Thorpe (ed.), Constitutions, V, 2790.

103 Section I in ibid.

9.4 THE MAY 1786 HEARING AT THE SUPERIOR COURT, AND ITS AFTERMATH

While the official report of the case, which was published some years later in 1796,[104] only mentioned that counsel engaged in "long arguments" on "constitutional points" at the May hearing, contemporaneous newspaper reports describe those arguments in greater detail. They show that plaintiffs and defendants lawyers engaged in a fundamental debate about the constitution and the nature of republican government in North Carolina.

After Singleton's lawyer Nash had moved to dismiss the case on the authority of the recently passed statute "which debars from the benefit of instituting any suit such persons as have been inimical to the United States," Bayard's lawyers, Samuel Johnston and William Davie, argued that the court should find the statute to be unconstitutional, and not binding law.[105] At this point, they were still arguing that the statute was void because it was a retrospective law that violated the *ex post facto* article in the Declaration of Rights. In enacting this statute, they contended,

> the Assembly had clearly exceeded the limits of the power which the people, in whom all political power is vested, and from whom, solely, it derives, had delegated to their representatives met in general assembly, and that an act so illegally passed, was *not to be looked upon* as a law, nor were the people, said they, *obliged to obey an act*, so diametrically opposite to the established form of government.[106] (emphasis added)

Singleton's lawyers responded by saying "that all acts of Assembly were laws, and [perhaps invoking the anti-suspension article in the constitution] their execution could not be prevented."[107] In their view, legislatures were the final arbiters of what was and was not law in the state, what was and was not consistent with the constitution, subject only to a right of resistance, electoral or otherwise, in the people at large, who might seek to persuade, pressure or replace the legislature in an effort to have them repeal the offending act. Until that had happened, however, the act continued to possess the force of law.

On the other side, Bayard's lawyers were doing what Edmund Randolph had refused to do in his argument in the *Case of the*

[104] J. M. Sosin, *The Aristocracy of the Long Robe: The Origins of Judicial Review in America* (Greenwood Press, Westport, Ct. and London, 1989), 218.

[105] "Newbern, (N.C.) June 7," in *The Pennsylvania Packet, and Daily Advertiser* (Philadelphia, Pa., July 1, 1786), 2.

[106] Ibid. [107] Ibid.

Prisoners. They were eliding the distinction between a law that might be "void" in some "political" sense, because the impression of a certain group of people was that it contradicted the constitution (which could give rise to a right of popular resistance), with the question whether a court possessed the legitimate interpretive authority to make that determination, in the face of the legislature's contrary conclusion, so as to formally empower the judges to treat the statute as not possessing the force of law. According to the newspaper account, Bayard's lawyers said nothing about the legitimate scope of judicial power, simply assuming the power of judicial review, without expressly arguing this final, crucial point.

It is important to understand, how deeply held, at this time, was the assumption that legislative enactment alone gave statutes the unquestionable force of law, and what a large and controversial step it represented to move from a general statement that a law was unconstitutional and void (in a "political" sense), to a position energetically urging judges, in open court, flatly to disobey a duly enacted law of the state. One of Bayard's lawyers, William Davie, was apparently so zealous in agitating for this course of action that immediately after the hearing Singleton and others brought his conduct to the attention of the sitting grand jury. Singleton, Abner Nash, and Richard Dobbs Spaight, among others, testified about what Davie had "said in open court, all the judges and attorney general being present," after which the grand jury proceeded to present the lawyer for his criminal conduct.[108] The grand jury charged that

> William R. Davie Esquire ... in the Course of his Pleadings did in open Court ... Assert and say the Act of Assembly was in every respect unjust and expressly against the Constitution, that the said Act was the arbitrary edict of a leading party or faction of the Assembly, that altho it was passed by the Assembly, the said Act was Null and Void; and was not Law; and ought not to be Obeyed by the People; or words fully to those purposes ....[109]

They concluded that "his free investigation of the Assembly's conduct [was] a criminal step, in its nature injurious to, destructive of, and against the peace and dignity of the State ... "[110] The Superior Court judges, however, "either more indulgent, or better acquainted with the rights of

[108] "Newbern (N.C.) June 1," in *The Pennsylvania Packet and Daily Advertiser* (Philadelphia, PA., August 23, 1786), 3; see also "Newbern (N.C.) June 7," in ibid., July 1, 1786, 2; and Hamburger, Law and Judicial Duty, 456–57 and fn. 163.

[109] Quoted in Hamburger, Law and Judicial Duty, 456 fn. 163.

[110] "Newbern (N.C.) June 7," in *The Pennsylvania Packet* (July 1, 1786), 2.

a lawyer defending his client, or an unprejudiced citizen the liberty of his country, discharged him," quashing the grand jury presentment.[111] This was one of those small but consequential victories for lawyers and judges that contributed to establishing the ground rules under which the struggle between courts and legislatures over their respective constitutional powers would be conducted.

One of the judges, Samuel Ashe, recollected, six months later,[112] that he had made a statement at the May hearing about the importance of separation of powers in the constitution. This statement would later find its way into the official report of the case published some years later. He recalled that he had said that the

> system or those fundamental principles comprised in the Constitution, divid[ed] the powers of Government into separate and distinct branches, to wit: the Legislative, the Judicial and the Executive and assign[ed] to each several and distinct powers, and prescribe[ed] their several limits and boundaries.[113]

But "[t]his I said," he continued, "without disclosing a single sentiment upon the cause, or the proceeding, or the law introduced in support of it."[114] It is not possible to say with certainty what his ambiguous statement indicated about his constitutional concerns at that moment, but it is tempting to think that he was mulling over the question whether in enacting the statute, the legislature had invaded the judicial power, by settling so many outstanding individual cases, and relegating the rest to legislative adjudication, and/or perhaps whether the judges actually possessed the "separate and distinct" power under the constitution, to declare as much.

Although a number of lawyers, and perhaps several of the judges, thought the statute to be unconstitutional, it seems as though they had also begun to feel a need to point to specific violations of constitutional language to support their claims but were still in the process of figuring out precisely what provisions of the constitution the statute might have violated.

Bayard's claim was novel and controversial enough so that the court, in May 1786, decided not to issue a decision, while it further considered the

[111] Ibid.; and Hamburger, Law and Judicial Duty, 456 fn. 163.

[112] See Ashe's letter to the General Assembly, December 14, 1786, submitted in the course of a legislative investigation into the judges' conduct, in Clark (ed.), State Records of North Carolina, 1786, XVIII, 137–42, at 138.

[113] Ibid., see also *Bayard* v. *Singleton*, 1 Martin's Reports 42 (N.C., 1787), at 43.

[114] Ibid.

arguments counsel had made.[115] In his December 1786 letter to the Assembly, Judge Ashe asserted that he, at least, had been motivated to leave the matter undecided out of deference to the legislature's traditional authority. In his statement, he implied that it should be up to the legislature to decide whether and how to "revise" a statute, after questions about its constitutionality had been raised. Ashe wrote that he "had reason to believe the next Assembly meant to revise the law, and in respect to them wished to decline an opinion . . . ."[116] A newspaper account of the hearing reported that "[t]he judges, unwilling to approve of a law which seems unconstitutional, or of disapproving an act of the legislature without the most mature consideration, have declined giving an immediate decision."[117]

9.5 IREDELL'S AUGUST 1786 LETTER "TO THE PUBLIC"

It is not known for certain whether James Iredell participated in the May hearing. His name does not appear on any of the original court dockets in the case, although it was added to the official report of the case published years later.[118] His precise role is not clear, because immediately after Samuel Johnston began to file the Cornell suits late in 1784, and before passage of the statute that raised the principal constitutional issue in the case in December, 1785, Singleton had taken the precaution of retaining Iredell, Maclaine, and William Hooper, in order, as Maclaine put it in a letter informing Iredell of the maneuver, to "silence[] you, Mr. Hooper, and myself."[119] But it is possible that Iredell nevertheless participated in the litigation as an amicus.[120]

[115] Ibid., at 44.

[116] Ashe's letter to the General Assembly, December 14, 1786, submitted in the course of a legislative investigation into the judges' conduct, in Clark (ed.), State Records of North Carolina, 1786, XVIII, 137–42, at 139.

[117] "New Bern," (N.C.) June 7, [1786], in *The Pennsylvania Packet, and Daily Advertiser* (July 1, 1786), 2.

[118] Waldrup, "James Iredell and the Practice of Law," 268; and Whichard, Justice James Iredell, 11.

[119] Letter from Archibald Maclaine to James Iredell (March 7, 1785), in McRee (ed.), Iredell, II, 119–20; see also Whichard, Justice James Iredell, 11; and Waldrup, "James Iredell and the Practice of Law," 267–68.

[120] Letter from Archibald Maclaine to James Iredell (March 7, 1785), in McRee (ed.), Iredell, II, 119 ("At present my own opinion is, that delicacy should prevent us from taking fees on the other side; but I do no see any reason why we should be altogether silent. If we at the trial should declare we are volunteers, and give the reasons for our conduct, I think I may venture to rely upon the facts for my justification . . . . I suppose

At any rate, Iredell was not silenced for long. In August, he published an anonymous appeal "To the Public," under the name of "An Elector." In an obvious effort to persuade the judges that they did in fact possess the power to take the step they had failed to in May, Iredell presented a fully worked out theory of judicial review that has become a classic early statement of the doctrine. In particular, he filled in a crucial gap that Johnston's and Davie's arguments had left. He presented a powerful logic for the claim that judges possessed the legitimate authority to enforce the constitutional limitations the people had imposed on their legislature. But his open letter to the public did considerably more. As it went about presenting a comprehensive case for judicial review, it simultaneously mounted a systematic attack on the constitutional doctrine of legislative supremacy. It seems that Iredell had been thinking about these matters for some years, having announced in a set of instructions to legislators from the town of Edenton which he had drafted in August 1783 that "in a Republic ... the Law is superior to any or all the individuals, and the Constitution superior even to the Legislature, and of which the Judges are the guardians and protectors."[121]

In his letter "To the Public," he began by going over familiar ground. He declared that in the constitution, the people had delegated power to their legislature, but only on certain conditions and limitations. And as the legislature was entirely a creature of the constitution itself, they possessed no power to alter or modify it. And then in a rhetorically powerful move, he identified this view of the legislature's constitutionally limited powers with the American Revolution itself, and the competing view that legislatures were supreme (within government), with the constitutional traditions of the British enemy.

> We had not only been sickened and disgusted for years with the high and almost impious language from Great Britain, of the omnipotent power of the British Parliament, but had severely smarted under its effects. We felt in all its rigor the mischiefs of an absolute and unbounded authority ... and [we] should have been guilty of the basest breach of trust, as well as the grossest folly, if in the same moment when we spurned at the *insolent despotism* of Great Britain, we had established a *despotic* power among ourselves.[122] (italics in original)

Mr. Johnston will laugh that we have been so damnably taken in."); see also Whichard, Justice James Iredell, 11; and Waldrup, "Iredell and the Practice of Law," 268.

[121] McRee (ed.), Iredell, II, 60–66, at 64.

[122] "To the Public" (August 1786), in McRee (ed.), Iredell, II, 145–49, at 146.

He continued by setting the colonists' very concrete experience of the evils of living under a supreme legislature against the "speculative" (Blackstonian) theory that legislative supremacy was a necessary aspect of sovereignty.

Theories were nothing to us, opposed to our own severe experience. We were not ignorant of the theory *of the necessity of the legislature being absolute in all cases*, because it was the great ground of the British pretensions. But this was a mere speculative principle, which men at ease and leisure thought proper to assume. When we were at liberty to form a government as we thought best, without regard to that or any theoretical principle we did not approve of, we decisively gave our sentiments against it.[123] (italics in original)

It is clear, moreover, that Iredell believed that the British principle of legislative supremacy had been rejected in order that individuals (and minorities) might be protected not only against the arbitrary acts of legislatures but also against the unfettered power of the people themselves.

We provided, or meant to provide (God grant our purpose may not be defeated), for the security of every individual, as well as the fluctuating majority of the people. We knew the value of liberty too well, to suffer it to depend on the capricious voice of popular favor, easily led astray by designing men, and courted for insidious purposes.[124]

He concluded this section of his letter by saying that "I have therefore no doubt, but that the power of the Assembly is limited and defined by the constitution. It is a *creature* of the constitution," and then in an obvious reference to the May effort to prosecute the lawyer William Davie, Iredell added in a sardonic parenthetical "(I hope this is an expression not prosecutable.)"[125] Iredell, did however, clearly recognize that although the abstract proposition was widely held that the constitution imposed limitations on the legislature, and, he contended, has not "been much contested ... [t]he great argument is, that though the Assembly have not a *right* to violate the constitution, yet if they *in fact* do so, the only remedy is, either by a humble petition that the law may be repealed, or a universal resistance of the people. But that in the meantime, their act, whatever it is, is to be obeyed as a law; for the judicial power is not to presume to question the power of an act of Assembly"[126] (italics in original). And this was the crucial juncture where he decisively parted company with the

[123] Ibid. [124] Ibid. [125] Ibid. [126] Ibid., at 147.

position Edmund Randolph had adopted in the *Case of the Prisoners*, and with others who supported the constitution of legislative supremacy.

Iredell continued his argument by showing how deeply flawed and ineffective were the two traditional "remedies" he had mentioned for constitutional violations. Some years earlier, he himself had suffered a humiliating experience "humbly" presenting a petition to the General Assembly on behalf of his cousin Henry Eustace McCulloh, who was then facing confiscation of his lands. On that occasion, he had written to his wife Hannah that "I have not yet had the courage to present my memorial. I have been two or three times on the eve of doing it, but unexpected and threatening circumstances have deterred me. I have some faint hopes of the suspension of the evil day by a general law, but hold myself prepared for a different event."[127] It is not surprising that in his open letter to the public he mocked petitions as a remedy for constitutional violations.

> [T]he remedy by petition implies a supposition, that the electors hold their right by the *favor of their representatives* .... [And resorting to a familiar hypothetical, asked] [w]hat if the Assembly say, we shall elect only once in two years, instead of electing annually, are we to petition them to repeal this law? To request that they will be graciously pleased not to be our tyrants ...[128] (italics in original)

Iredell, of course, was being somewhat disingenuous in specifying only two traditional remedies for constitutional violations; he omitted mention of perhaps the most important one, annual elections, although that was the "remedy" he seemed most anxious that the legislature not alter the terms of. In this August 1786 open letter to the public, Iredell may have been tempering somewhat his remarks about the problem of popular majorities. But in his later private correspondence with Richard Spaight, he made it perfectly clear that he viewed elections less as a remedy for constitutional violations, than as part of the problem that republican governments faced. "I conceive the remedy by a new election to be of very little consequence," he wrote to Spaight, "because this would only secure the views of a majority; whereas every citizen in my opinion should have a surer pledge for his constitutional rights than the wisdom and activity of any occasional majority of his fellow citizens .... ."[129] As a remedy for the problem of popular majorities pressuring legislatures

[127] Letter of Iredell to Hannah (January 26, 1779), in McRee (ed.), Iredell, I, 415; the Assembly later refused to act on the petition.

[128] "To the Public" (August 1786), in McRee (ed.), Iredell, II, 145–49, at 147.

[129] Letter of Iredell to Richard Spaight (August 26, 1787), in McRee (ed.), Iredell, II, 172–76, at 175.

into passing laws that invaded fundamental rights, elections were of absolutely no use. Like all the other leading, early advocates for judicial review, Alexander Hamilton in New York, James Varnum in Rhode Island and William Plumer in New Hampshire, Iredell made it abundantly clear that he viewed judicial review as a necessary check, not only on legislatures, but more crucially, on the power of the people themselves to enact, through their legislatures, just any piece of legislation they desired.

The difficulty with elections as a remedy for constitutional violations, however, ran even deeper for men like Iredell and Hamilton. They were an integral aspect of a system that understood constitutions as declaring a set of abstract rights and principles that were subject to a number of possibly conflicting, equally legitimate interpretations when applied to concrete situations; viewed as stating foundational "political" norms, rather than as defining a set of determinate "legal" rules. The deeper problem was that this view of constitutions made the people the direct, final interpreters of constitutions. As a consequence, their changing "sense" of a constitution, expressed at elections or in popular opinion, could sanctify revisions to traditional common law rights that a legislature might undertake. By challenging the primacy of popular elections as a method for enforcing constitutions, Iredell, and men like him, were simultaneously challenging the view of constitutions as fluid and "political," in their effort to transform these documents into a disabling "legal" restraint on the otherwise absolute power of legislatures to confer the force of law on their enactments.[130] As much as anything else, Iredell, Hamilton, Varnum and other lawyers with similar views, sought to make the courts into a refuge from overheated majorities of the people, by bringing the new practice of judicial review into being.

Having argued that traditional remedies for constitutional violations were completely inadequate, Iredell proceeded to offer a compelling logic demonstrating that judges must of necessity have the power to nullify laws, when they construe them to be in conflict with the constitution. He began with the proposition that the constitution was a "law" like other laws, only superior. This was a critical move in that if the constitution was "law" like other laws, that brought its interpretation under the

[130] Judicial decisions about constitutionality are said to have been either rightly or wrongly decided, implying that there is a correct answer under a set of fixed rules, rather than a range of choices under a more complicated calculus about the good of the polity and the preservation of basic constitutional principles.

jurisdiction of the judges. From there, it was a relatively straightforward matter to show that judges, to whom the people had assigned the duty of deciding cases, "according to the law of the land," possessed the authority, in the course of doing so, to declare that in so far as a statute conflicted with the constitution, the legislature could not have had the power to make it part of the "law of the land," and they were duty bound not to enforce it, as they went about making their decisions.

"These two [traditional] remedies," for constitutional violations, Iredell observed,

> then being rejected, it remains to be inquired whether the judicial power hath any authority to interfere in such a case. The duty of that power, I conceive, in all cases, is to decide according to the *laws of the State*. It will not be denied, I suppose, that the constitution is a *law of the State*, as well as an act of Assembly, with this difference only, that it is the *fundamental* law, and unalterable by the legislature, which derives all its power from it. One act of Assembly may repeal another act of Assembly. For this reason, the latter act is to be obeyed, and not the former. An act of Assembly cannot repeal the constitution, or any part of it. For that reason, an act of Assembly, inconsistent with [that tries in effect to change] the constitution, is *void*, and cannot be obeyed, without disobeying the superior law to which we were previously and irrevocably bound. The judges, therefore, must take care at their peril, that every act of Assembly they presume to enforce is warranted by the constitution, since if it is not they act without lawful authority. This is not a usurped or a discretionary power, but one inevitably resulting from the constitution of their office ....[131] (emphasis added)

The unquestionable authority and duty of judges was to interpret the law as they went about deciding individual disputes. As they did so, they often identified conflicts between laws, which it was their duty to resolve in order to apply a clear legal rule to decide a case. Where judges identified an unresolvable conflict between a statute and the constitution, the resolution was straightforward; they must apply the superior law and refuse to enforce the inferior act (which legislatures in any case had no power to enact) as they went about deciding disputes according to the law of the land.

The final section of Iredell's argument is devoted to reassuring "the public" that the judges' power of review did not pose the kind of dangers to republican government some people appeared to believe it did. "[T]he danger," he wrote, "about which there is so much alarm, attending the exercise of this power is, in my opinion, the least that can be imagined to

[131] "To the Public" (August 1786), in McRee (ed.), Iredell, II, 145–49, at 148.

attend the exercise of any important power whatever."[132] But on this question, he was considerably less convincing. Although the judges did hold their offices during good behavior under the constitution, Iredell pointed out, their salaries were dependent on the legislature and "precarious." He was "persuaded" that this form of "dependence" "will in general be found ... effectual, at least to prevent a wanton abuse of power ... ."[133] Aside from that, Iredell assured his readers, that in a republican government judges would have a natural tendency to want to seek "popular favor," which would serve to make it less likely that they would stray far from their duty. Besides, Iredell added, if judges might be prone to abuse their power by "willfully misconstruing" the constitution, they might be equally prone to willfully misconstrue statutes, and there could be no question that they possessed the authority to engage in that form of interpretation. What he failed to say in this regard, however, was that while legislatures had the power to correct judicial misinterpretations of their statutes, they would possess no similar power to correct judicial misinterpretations of constitutions. He concluded by contending that all courts, even the lowest, possessed the power to engage in constitutional interpretation. But, according to Iredell, because judges alone possessed the authority to interpret the laws, they alone could refuse to obey, indeed declare null and void, standing laws of the state. Other ministerial officials, like sheriffs, lacking this power of judgment, did not share their unique privilege but were sworn to execute the laws as the legislature had enacted them.[134]

All of this provided thin reassurance about the unprecedented power Iredell was arguing that judges possessed. A year later, in his correspondence with Richard Spaight, he was somewhat more candid, acknowledging how great this power would actually be, and sought to add the idea that a "Court of Appeal" was perhaps necessary to provide some check on the judges' authority to decide in the last resort what the law of the land was to be. Iredell conceded in his letter to Spaight that

> [t]he power of the judges, take it altogether, is indeed alarming, as there is no appeal from their jurisdiction, and I don't think any country can be safe without

[132] Ibid., II, 148; compare Hamilton's description of the least dangerous branch in #78 Federalist.

[133] Iredell, "To the Public," at 148; some years earlier, Iredell had sought to eliminate the very safeguard he was now extolling. He had argued that judges' salaries should be made "permanent with their commissions," see "Instructions from the Town of Edenton to their representatives" (No. 5) (August 1783), in McRee (ed.), Iredell, II, 64.

[134] "To the Public" (August 1786), in McRee (ed.), Iredell, II, 145–49, at 148.

some Court of Appeal that has no original jurisdiction at all, since men are commonly careful enough to correct the errors of others, though seldom sufficiently watchful of their own, especially if they have no check upon them.[135]

It could not have escaped Iredell's notice that this "remedy" for unchecked judicial power would nevertheless leave the judiciary with the final word, not only about their own powers, but also about the legitimate constitutional scope of the legislature's. In one stroke, Iredell's argument turned legislative supremacy on its head.

9.6 THE DECEMBER, 1786 LEGISLATIVE INVESTIGATION OF THE CONDUCT OF THE JUDGES

At its November term, the court once again failed to decide the motion to dismiss that Singleton's lawyer had made in May. Under the constitution, the General Assembly possessed the authority to impeach governmental officials for "offending against the State, by violating any part of this Constitution, mal-administration, or corruption . . . ."[136] In December 1786, the legislature launched an "enquiry into the present state of the administration of justice in the Superior Courts . . . ." and summoned the judges to appear before them.[137] The failure of the judges to decide the motion to dismiss in *Bayard* v. *Singleton*, when the statute, by its express terms, "required" dismissal, became one of the charges brought against the judges in the Assembly "[a]t the instigation of John Hay and Archibald Maclaine."[138] On December 14, Alfred Moore wrote to inform Iredell that the Superior Court term was over "and the Judges have notice of charges against them before the Assembly; that they may attend if they *please* . . . . Judge Spencer showed me to-day an abstract from a letter of Mr. Hay, containing the charges . . . "

> "High fines, and a shameful appropriation of them.
> "Admitting new, and illegal prosecutions . . . .
> "The banishment of Brice and McNeil.
> "*Dispensing with laws (the Newbern case).*
> "Negligence of their duty, and delay of business.
> "Ill behavior to Mr. Hay at Wilmington.[139]
>
> (emphasis added)

[135] Letter of Iredell to Spaight (August 26, 1787), in McRee (ed.), Iredell, II, 172–76, at 176.

[136] North Carolina Constitution of 1776, Article XXIII, in Thorpe (ed.), Constitutions, V, 2792.

[137] Clark (ed.), State Records of North Carolina, XVIII, 42.

[138] Kelly and Baradell (eds.), The Papers of James Iredell, 1784–1789, III, 246 fn. 1.

[139] Letter of Alfred Moore to Iredell (December 14, 1786), in McRee (ed.), Iredell, II, 153–54.

In a letter to the Assembly, Judge Ashe declined to attend the legislative hearings. "I am at a loss to know what purpose my being present would answer. I presume the Houses do not mean to go into a formal exercise of Judicial power; to hear 'finding and proving' and to pass final decision ...."[140] It was not clear what precisely the Assembly intended by charging the judges, but some members certainly must have hoped that it would lead to their removal from office for mal-administration or corruption. The other two Superior Court judges did appear before the Assembly, testifying on their own behalf.[141]

The charges were essentially of two types. The first set of charges involved a combination of neglect of duty, mal-administration, minor corruption, and mistreatment of the lawyers who appeared before them. The second set are more relevant to the concerns of this book. Those involved claims that the judges had overreached in the exercise of their power.[142] They had, for example, ordered the banishment of two Loyalists, Brice and McNeil, when there was no state law authorizing that punishment. In that instance, the judges were reported to have said "that no Sovereign State or Government was without a power to prevent its receiving injury; that the return of [Brice and McNeill] was a misdemeanor ... & that a Law *should have* been made against the return of such characters to the State"[143] (emphasis added). In a dissent from the House of Commons' vote to exonerate the judges of all charges, Maclaine wrote of the Brice and McNeill affair that by acting without clear legal authority, the judges had "[a]rrogat[ed] to themselves the Authorities vested by the Constitution in the Legislative and Executive departments of the State, and the more easily to accomplish their purposes of grasping all powers to themselves ... "[144]

Richard Spaight certainly agreed with Maclaine that the judges had overreached in the case of Brice and McNeill, but he was equally certain that they had overreached in the case of *Bayard v. Singleton*, by failing to dismiss the plaintiff's case when the statute expressly "required" them to

140 Clark (ed.), State Records of North Carolina, 1786, XVIII, 137–42 (Ashe's letter of December 14, 1786), at 137.

141 Ibid., XVIII, 137–42 (Ashe's letter of December 14, 1786); (Judges Spencer and Williams attendance at the Assembly), at 194.

142 See a more detailed description of the charges against the judges in Clark (ed.), State Records of North Carolina, XVIII, 213–17.

143 Ibid., 214–15.

144 Maclaine's dissent from "the resolution of the House of Commons declaring that the Judges ought not to be accused of any Misdemeanors in office," in ibid., XVIII, 479.

do so, thus "Dispensing with laws." But in so far as they had also refused to decide the question of the statute's constitutionality, out of deference to the legislature, Spaight believed they had certainly done the right thing. Judges had no legitimate interpretive authority to pronounce a law null and void. If they had doubts about a statute's constitutionality, it was their duty, under the traditional constitution, to refer the matter to the legislature, which possessed the final authority to determine whether or not the act was constitutional, and whether and how it should be revised.

Maclaine was equally certain that the judges had committed an offence by failing to decide the motion in *Bayard* v. *Singleton*, but for precisely the opposite reason. They should have proceeded to rule on the constitutional validity of the statute, rather than refusing to do so "out of respect to the General Assembly."[145] The judges, Maclaine seemed to have no doubt, not only possessed the legitimate power to render a judgment about constitutionality but were duty bound to do so "if they were decided and uniform in their opinions."[146] Only if they were not uniformly agreed, only if the judges "doubted," as Maclaine put it, were they "to state such doubts to the Legislature."[147] Maclaine's formulation of this rule has something of an ad hoc quality to it, representing a nod in the direction of traditional usage, as part of a rule that would radically transform it.

In this way, the struggle between judicial review and the constitution of tradition was carried into the North Carolina legislature. In the same legislative session, Richard Spaight attempted to have the traditional norm codified into law, by enacting a legislative provision that would have prohibited judges from "presuming" to exercise any authority to dispense with a duly enacted statute.

In a "Bill Declaratory of the Powers of Courts and the Rights of Juries," Spaight and another member, included the following provision:

> to prevent . . . usurpation[s] in Judges of Law of powers which are unknown to the Constitution and Laws of this State . . . . [W]hen Matters Occur wherein the Operation of the Constitution and any particular Act of the legislature may interfere, [the judges] are not to presume a dispensing or suspending power with the said Act but to Relate their opinion or doubt thereon to the next General

[145] Ibid., 482. [146] Ibid., 482.

[147] Ibid.; compare Iredell's formulation of a "doubtful case" rule, see Iredell letter to Spaight (August 26, 1787), in McRee (ed.), Iredell, II, 175 ("In all doubtful cases, to be sure, the Act ought to be supported: it should be unconstitutional beyond dispute before it is pronounced such.")

Assembly that whatever doubts Arising between the construction of law and Constitution may be fully Resolved by the said Assembly.[148] (emphasis added)

Maclaine quickly moved to counter Spaight's proposal, offering an amendment to this section of Spaight's bill, which attempted to change the language to recognize a duty in the judges to decide the question of constitutionality. Maclaine moved to "expunge" the words "to relate their opinion or doubt thereon to the next General Assembly that whatever doubt arising between the construction of Law and the Constitution" and to replace them with "but shall decide according to the true spirit and meaning of the Constitution and General Laws of the Land."[149] Maclaine's amendment, however, was soundly defeated by a vote of 58–24, Spaight, not surprisingly, joining with the majority, and for a moment it looked like Spaight might succeed in his efforts.[150]

"[B]ut [his] proposal was soon altered and shelved."[151] An effort was made shortly afterward, however, to revive it in a modified form, preserving the essential idea that the legislature should possess the final word on the constitutionality of the laws, but permitting the judges to exercise, in effect, a qualified, rather than a final, veto over the laws, similar to the one judges possessed in New York's Council of Revision. Under the proposal, if the judges had doubts about the constitutionality of a statute, its operation would be suspended until the legislature had time to reconsider its decision to enact it. If there was a broad consensus among legislators (2/3) that the law was indeed constitutional, that would end the matter; the statute would thereafter enjoy the full force of law, despite any constitutional objections the judges had raised. The amendment provided that:

when Matters Occur wherein the Operation of the Constitution and any particular Act of the legislature may interfere, [the judges] are not to presume a dispensing or suspending power with the said Act but to Relate their opinion or doubt thereon to the next General Assembly [that] the Act so objected to shall not have the force and

[148] The language in Spaight's original "Bill Declaratory of the Power of Courts" had found its way into "A Bill to Amend and Alter the Court System," 18, NCSA, General Assembly, Session Records 1786–87, Box % Folder House (December 16, 1786), quoted in Hamburger, Law and Judicial Duty, 467.

[149] Clark (ed.), State Records of North Carolina, XVIII, 361; and Hamburger, Law and Judicial Duty, 467 and fn. 7.

[150] Clark (ed.), State Records of North Carolina, XVIII, 361.

[151] Hamburger, Law and Judicial Duty, 467.

operation of law unless two thirds of the members of the General Assembly … shall be of opinion that the said Act is constitutional.[152]

This language was incorporated into the bill, which, however, was laid over until the following legislative session, and ultimately died. Spaight's further efforts to pass his original bill into law were also defeated in the Senate.[153]

Opinion was apparently too divided for the legislature to take a definitive position on the question of the legitimacy of judicial review, either to affirm it or to (attempt) to prohibit it. This failure would leave the judges in a strong position to define their own constitutional powers.

And like other state legislatures in this period, North Carolina's also ultimately refused to take direct action against the judges for the conduct with which they had been charged, including "dispensing with laws."

In his letter to the Assembly, Ashe had defended his actions in a way that judges, and lawyers arguing on behalf of judges, had also done in other states, where judges had been accused of constitutional overreach for refusing or failing to enforce a law of the state. Like them, Ashe argued that he might have been guilty of errors in judgment, but that simple judicial error, not accompanied by corruption, could not legitimately constitute grounds for dismissal from office.

> [F]ar be it from me to say I have committed no errors, it would be a presumption I am incapable of, for I do not pretend to infallibility; but my errors have been those of the head unattended with any corruption or turpitude. The wisest men daily fall into such; look into the law books where may be seen a Judge giving an opinion one day and retracting it as error at another; where may be seen the Judge of one Court reversing for error the opinion of a Judge of another Court and where may be seen the House of Lords reversing the opinion (as erroneous) of a whole Bench of Judges, and yet these errors have never yet been considered criminal, nor the Judges put to answer for them.[154]

This was a successful argument elsewhere, and seems to have contributed to a favorable outcome for the judges in North Carolina as well. It served to transform the claim that the judiciary was engaged in a wrongful usurpation of constitutional authority, into a claim that their conduct represented, at most, judicial error, correctable upon appeal to a higher

[152] "A Bill to Amend and Alter the Court System," 18b (rider number 22), NCSA, General Assembly, Session Records 1786–87, Box 5, Folder House (December 16, 1786), quoted in ibid., 468 and fn. 9.

[153] Ibid., 468 and fns. 9 and 10.

[154] Clark (ed.), State Records of North Carolina, XVIII (Ashe's Letter), 140–41.

court, and did not subject the judges to legislative discipline for maladministration, or other misdemeanors.

The Assembly ultimately voted by a substantial majority to exonerate the judges of all charges, 49 in favor, 22 opposed.[155] Both Spaight and Maclaine voted against acquitting the judges, for their quite different reasons. Once again, as in other states, the judges left these hearings with the independence of their offices (implicitly) reaffirmed, the threat of legislative removal for failing or refusing to enforce the law of the state now significantly reduced.

But as in some other states, where legislatures also failed to discipline judges for engaging in judicial review, the North Carolina legislature also attempted to maintain its traditional constitutional authority by giving its own definitive answer to the question whether the 1785 act was, or was not, constitutional. It proceeded to consider whether the statute, whose constitutionality had been called into question, should undergo a "revision." A "Bill to repeal" the offending 1785 act was taken up in the same session of the legislature and met some early success.[156] But by the end of the session in January, the Assembly had instead passed into law a bill "to amend" rather than repeal the 1785 act.[157]

The new (revised) law stated that it was addressing the "doubts [that] have arisen whether the citizens of this state, claiming property by any title whatsoever, which had been seized and sold by the commissioners [of forfeited estates] were enabled to claim, or commence and prosecute a suit or suits in any of the courts of law in this State for the aforesaid property ...." And the answer the statute gave was yes, certainly, citizens of the state have such a right, EXCEPT for those citizens who "*hold or derive their titles, by, from or under any person or persons named or described by some one of the laws commonly called the Confiscation Laws*"[158] (emphasis added). After reconsidering the matter, in other words, the legislature sought to lay to rest all doubts that had been raised about whether such citizens could or could not maintain suits to recover their property, by reaffirming their original answer, that no they could not. Rather than requiring courts to dismiss such actions, as the 1785 act

[155] Ibid., 428–29. [156] Ibid., 188, 399, 419.

[157] Ibid., 453, 466; and "An Act to Amend an Act, Entitled, 'An Act to Secure and Quiet in Their Possessions, etc.'" *At a General Assembly, begun and held at Fayetteville on the eighteenth day of November, in the year of our Lord one Thousand Seven Hundred and Eighty-Six, ... being the first session of the said Assembly*, Ch. VI (January 6, 1787), in State Records of North Carolina, XXIV, 794–95.

[158] Ibid.

did, however, the new statute apparently sought to avoid the need to rely on the courts for such a decision by simply stripping such citizens of the right "to claim, or commence and prosecute" such suits altogether. The legislature evidently did not believe the original statute had offended against the (true spirit and meaning of the) constitution, and were now, in effect, reinforcing their earlier answer, and hoping, presumably, to lay to rest all further doubts about the statute's constitutionality.

9.7 THE MAY 1787 SUPERIOR COURT DECISION, AND ITS AFTERMATH

But despite these legislative maneuvers, at the end of the day, the court, rather than the legislature, would turn out to have the final say, not only about the fate of the Bayard (and similar) lawsuits, but also about the legislature's confiscation policy. At its term in May 1787, the court made a sustained effort to persuade the parties to settle, but when this failed, and the judges were forced to render a decision, they "with much apparent reluctance, but with great deliberation and firmness," forged ahead, ruling against the motion to dismiss, by holding the statute on which the motion was based, to be unconstitutional and void.[159]

As much as they expressed their wish to avoid "a disagreeable difference between the Legislature and the Judicial powers of the State," they may have been emboldened to take their unprecedented step not only by the legislature's vote, several months earlier, to absolve them of all wrongdoing in the case,[160] but by Iredell's argument "To the Public" the previous August, which had laid out a compelling logic for their position. Indeed, some of what they said in their opinion resonated with several of Iredell's points. The judges observed that the legislature could by no means "repeal or alter the constitution, because if they could do this, they would at the same instant of time, destroy their own existence as a Legislature .... Consequently, the constitution (which [and this point was crucial] *the judicial power was bound to take notice of as much as of any other law whatever*), standing in full force as the fundamental law of the land, [the act, which was in conflict with the constitution,] must of course ... stand as abrogated and without any effect."[161]

[159] *Bayard* v. *Singleton*, 1 Martin's Reports 42 (N.C., 1787), at 45.
[160] See Hamburger's evaluation in Law and Judicial Duty, 460 and fn. 171.
[161] *Bayard* v. *Singleton*, at 45.

Rather than base their decision on a finding that the 1785 statute was unconstitutional as an *ex post facto* law, or as an illegitimate legislative invasion of judicial powers, which violated the separation of powers clause, however, both of which had been mooted earlier, the judges now settled on the rationale that the act deprived citizens of the "right to a decision of [their] property by a trial by jury," which "by the constitution every citizen had undoubtedly a right to."[162] Although the relevant jury trial clause in the Declaration of Rights had been cast in traditional precatory language, it did provide a clear textual basis for their determination.[163] The motion to dismiss had relied on the 1785 statute, and having disposed of that motion, the opinion said nothing about the "revised" 1787 statute, one way or the other, although the court's constitutional logic would certainly have extended to the latter act.

In one respect, the court's May decision did little more than restore the procedural protections the legislature had originally included in several pre-1785 confiscation statutes. Those earlier statutes had contained provisions giving individuals rights to challenge confiscation in a jury trial in the Superior Court. And under these provisions, the Bayards' case had already been unsuccessfully tried to a jury in 1779.

Now, having ruled against the motion to dismiss, the court proceeded to announce that the matter would be tried to a jury at the court's next term in November, 1787. This trial would turn out exactly the same way the 1779 trial had. At the hearing in November, the judges instructed the jury as to the law, and set out the facts as they knew them, pretty much assuring that the outcome would favor the defendant Singleton. The judges described Samuel Cornell as always having been "a British subject, and having always lived under the British government," owing his allegiance to the king, "and consequently was never a citizen of this, or any other of the United States ...."[164] The judges instructed the jury that if Samuel Cornell were shown to be an "alien," i.e., not a citizen, then "by the civil, as well as by the common law of England, *aliens* are incapacitated to hold lands" (italics in original).

162 Ibid.

163 Art. XIV of the 1776 Declaration of Rights provided "That in all controversies at law, respecting property, the ancient mode of trial, by jury, is one of the best securities of the rights of the people, and ought to remain sacred and inviolable," in Thorpe (ed.), Constitutions, V, 2788. Traditionally, of course, juries played no role in legislative adjudication, and this kind of ruling would have had the consequence of limiting the legislature's power to engage in adjudication.

164 *Bayard* v. *Singleton*, at 46–47.

That the premises in question upon these invariable principles of law, could not from the time our government commenced, have been held by Mr. Cornell; because that in consequence of his owing no allegiance to the State, he had no capacity to hold them, and according to the letter of the law of the land, they have consequently been forfeited to the sovereignty of the State. That the act of confiscation, in which Mr. Cornell was expressly named, and more particularly the act which especially directed the sale of the very premises in question, must have been at least as effectual in vesting them in the State, as any *office found*, according to the practice in England can be, for vesting any forfeited property in the King.[165]

Not surprisingly, the jury found a verdict for the defendant, and the judges, having announced these principles in the course of the trial, "twenty-seven other[] [cases] depending in the same Court, and subsisting upon similar or less substantial grounds, were all swept off the docket, by nonsuits voluntarily suffered."[166] In the end, ironically, the legislature's policy, both substantive and procedural, had prevailed– through the good offices of the court. While basing its jury instructions primarily on the common (and civil) law of alienage, the court had also relied on North Carolina's confiscation statutes in its statement of the applicable law. And given that the remaining cases on the docket were all concluded without the benefit of a jury trial, legislative policy, even in this regard, would seem to have won out– despite the court's May decision.

Thus ended Samuel Johnston's effort to reverse the legislature's policy by appealing to the courts. Given these outcomes, it is perhaps not a surprise that the legislature took no further action against the judges. From one perspective, any practical effect the May declaration of nullity might have had, was entirely swamped by the outcome of the November proceedings.

But from another perspective, the May decision was highly consequential– in several respects. For one, it represented a significant constitutional moment; judges in yet another state, had wielded, for the first time, an extraordinary power they asserted they possessed, to strike down a law, and again did so with apparent impunity. To the extent these decisions were successfully maintained, even in the face of legislative attempts to quash them, each one established another judicial precedent for the unprecedented practice. During the course of the litigation in each case, moreover, the arguments for judicial review were refined and elaborated. In North Carolina, the controversy over the Bayard case led James Iredell to publish a fully worked out justification for the new practice; and similar reasoning in several states, rapidly became part

[165] Ibid., 47. [166] Ibid., 48.

(if a contested part) of the conventional legal wisdom in those states, as more lawyers and judges embraced its logic.

The May decision, however, also had a subtler but equally significant effect on the distribution of constitutional authority in the state. No longer, could the North Carolina legislature take its legislative supremacy for granted. In the Bayard case, the legislature's policy had prevailed in the end, but only after the judges had, in effect, signed off on (most of) it. The Bayard case subtly changed the distribution of constitutional authority in another way, as well. The May decision meant that all forms of legislative adjudication (being conducted without a jury) would thereafter be liable to constitutional challenge. In a sense, this decision contributed to depriving the legislature of an important aspect of its traditional constitutional authority. Arguably, now only courts could engage in certain acts, like deciding an entire class of cases (through a set of jury instructions).

At the same time, it is clear that the doctrine of legislative supremacy was alive and well in North Carolina. But given that no final authority existed in government to definitively resolve the dispute, the conflict between these two constitutional visions was likely only to be settled piecemeal, by an ongoing struggle between the branches– unless some "superior" authority should intervene to impose its views.[167]

9.8 THE SPAIGHT/IREDELL CORRESPONDENCE

At bottom, the controversy over judicial review represented an argument about the character of the republican governments Americans were to have, and in particular over precisely what role the sovereign people would play in these governments. This argument was, for the most part, under-theorized, but there were a number of occasions when the fundamental issues at stake were openly debated. One such occurred in the well-known correspondence between Richard Spaight and James Iredell, following the North Carolina Superior Court's May 1787 decision. Spaight and Iredell had both waged struggles on behalf of their respective positions during the Bayard litigation, Spaight working assiduously to

[167] The people themselves were handicapped in acting as the final authority in this dispute as the North Carolina constitution had no amendment procedure. At a deeper level, one of the issues underlying the dispute over judicial review was whether "The people themselves" should have a direct voice in constitutional interpretation through their elected legislatures, or only an ultimate, twice removed one.

reinforce legislative supremacy, and Iredell to establish judicial review as a viable doctrine and practice.

Spaight's position is especially noteworthy because he was far from being an unconditional defender of the legislature's conduct. Like many other conservative Whigs, he was particularly critical, for example, of the tender laws, and of the acts that had raised the jurisdictional amount for summary justice. He thought these laws were even more objectionable "than the one which the judges, *by their own authority*, thought proper to set aside and declare void."[168] But he was also no fan of the 1785 Confiscation Act. His was an entirely principled objection to the introduction of judicial review, and together with the positions that Abner Nash and Singleton took (more interestedly) during the case and in the legislature, may indicate that elite opinion on the question of the radical new judicial practice was as divided in North Carolina, as it seemed to have been in Virginia several years earlier.

In his letter to Iredell, Spaight pointed out that the judges had simply presumed to exercise this extraordinary authority. The 1776 constitution contained not the slightest suggestion that the people had intended to confer such a power on the judges. And if the people, from whom all governmental power derived, had not expressly (or even impliedly) delegated that authority to the judges, how could they legitimately claim it. Nor could the practice be defended by reference to previous usage, it was completely unprecedented. Its unilateral introduction by the judges, moreover, threatened to alter fundamentally the character of republican governments, and expose them to serious new political dangers. They would be transformed from republican polities in which the people (through their elected representatives) made the laws by which they would govern themselves, into polities that would be governed, in the last resort, by a few men, who were not accountable to the people, and whose decisions would not be subject to correction. The practice would leave the safeguarding of property and liberty to the "disposal" of these men, the very definition of despotism.

Spaight was in Philadelphia attending the Federal Convention as a delegate from North Carolina, when he learned of the judges' decision. He wrote Iredell to denounce it. "I do not pretend to vindicate the law, which has been the subject of controversy," Spaight wrote, "it is immaterial what law they have declared void." They have no basis for claiming this

168 Letter from Spaight to Iredell (August 12, 1787), in McRee (ed.), Iredell, II, 168–70, at 169.

power apart from the constitution of North Carolina, and that document most certainly does not grant them that authority either expressly or impliedly.

> [I]t is their usurpation of the authority to do it, that I complain of, as I do most positively deny that they have any such power, nor can they find any thing in the Constitution, either directly or impliedly that will support them, or give them any color of right to exercise the authority.[169]

Such a practice is unprecedented in all the world, and for very good reason. It would create a judicial despotism. Like many others in the period, Spaight viewed judicial review as an exercise of legislative authority (undoing an existing law), and as such, he condemned it as a dangerous violation of separation of powers.[170] Judicial review would allow the judicial branch to combine judicial power with a newly assumed legislative power, and leave that enormous power totally unchecked. As others in the period had observed, moreover, the practice would effectively confer on the judges an absolute veto over the laws.

> [I]t would have been absurd, and contrary to the practice of all the world, had the Constitution vested such powers in them, as they would have operated as an absolute negative on the proceedings of the Legislature, which no judiciary ought ever to possess; and the State, instead of being governed by the representatives in general Assembly, would be subject to the will of three individuals who united in their own persons the legislative and judiciary powers, which no monarch in Europe enjoys .... If they possessed the power what check or control would there be to their proceedings? Or who is there to take the same liberty with them, that they have taken with the Legislature, and declare their opinions to be erroneous? None that I know of .... [T]hey might at pleasure set aside every law, however just or consistent with the Constitution, to answer their designs; and the persons and property of every individual would be completely at their disposal.[171] (emphasis added)

Spaight did concede "that our Constitution unfortunately has not provided a sufficient check to prevent the intemperate and unjust proceedings of our Legislature, though such a check would be very beneficial, and, I think, absolutely necessary to our well-being ... " It is not clear why he failed to mention the possibility of establishing a Council of Revision, but he proceeded to say, following the conventional wisdom, that "the only [check] that I know of, is the annual election which, by leaving out such

[169] Ibid.

[170] Edmund Pendleton had made a similar point in his opinion in *The Case of the Prisoners*, see Chapter 5.

[171] Letter from Spaight to Iredell (August 12, 1787), in McRee (ed.), Iredell, II, 169

members as have supported improper measures, will in some degree remedy, though it cannot prevent, such evils as may arise."[172] But the clear implication of this observation was that however flawed the current check on the legislature might be, it was certainly better than a system in which a few men exercised ultimate power over the laws, without any check at all. For Spaight, leaving the supreme power over the laws in the hands of a few judges, rather than in a large body elected by and regularly accountable to the people, was un-republican, and however imperfect the present republican government might be, the alternative of allowing a small number of individuals to exercise that kind of ultimate power in a republican government was much worse.

That is certainly not how Iredell saw the matter. For Iredell, the people themselves posed greater dangers to republican government than the presumably impartial judges did. For him, the essential core of republican government involved the protection of individual rights, often from popular majorities that might seek to infringe them. Beneath it all, Iredell had little faith that the people themselves could be relied upon to respect the rights of individuals, particularly if such individuals were in a minority. This being the case, elections could not possibly serve as an effective remedy for these kinds of constitutional violations. Final authority over the laws had to be lodged somewhere, and a difficult choice about which authority should exercise this ultimate power, he thought, was inevitable. "[W] must choose between evils of some sort or other: the imperfection of man can never keep entirely clear of all."[173] It seemed obvious to Iredell that judicial review represented the lesser evil.

> In a republican Government ... *individual liberty* is a matter of the utmost moment, as, if there be no check upon the public passions, it is in the greatest danger. The Majority having the rule in their own hands, may take care of themselves, but in what condition are the minority, if the power of the other is without limit? These considerations, I suppose, or similar ones, occasioned such express provisions for the personal liberty of each citizen, which the citizens, when they formed the Constitution, chose to reserve as an unalienated right, and not to leave at the mercy of any Assembly whatever .... The Constitution, therefore, *being a fundamental law*, and a law *in writing* ... the judicial power, in the exercise of their authority, must take notice of it as the groundwork of that [authority] as well as of all other authority; and as no article of the Constitution can be repealed by a Legislature, which derives its whole power from it, it follows either that the *fundamental unrepealable* law must be obeyed, by the rejection of an act

[172] Ibid., 169–70.

[173] Letter from Iredell to Spaight (August 26, 1787), in McRee (ed.), Iredell, II, at 173.

unwarranted by and inconsistent with it, or you must obey an act founded on an authority not given by the people, and to which, therefore, the people owe no obedience.[174] (italics in original)

The stakes for republican government were high. Where judges both held their offices during "good behavior," and enjoyed suitable and permanent salaries (for which both Iredell and Hamilton argued), they would be "rendered absolutely independent," not only of the legislature, but of the people themselves. By assuming the authority to wield a kind of absolute veto over legislation, the judges (and lawyers) would have succeeded in establishing the kind of check on popular government for which some had been (unsuccessfully) contending at various state constitutional conventions, at least since 1777 – without the need to seek the approval of any popularly elected body.

9.9 AFTERMATH, STATE V. ––– (N.C., SUPERIOR COURT), 1794[175]

Over the next seven years, outright opposition to judicial review seems to have become substantially less common among North Carolina lawyers and judges.

In 1793, the North Carolina legislature passed an act "authorising the Attorney General to take judgment against the receivers of public moneys, by motion, and that their delinquencies should be sufficient notice to them ... "[176] When the Attorney General moved for judgment against several collectors of public monies (at the April 1794 Term of the Superior Court), without having given them notice of the proceeding, as the act authorized, Judge Williams "stopped him, saying he could not permit judgments to be taken in that manner. That he conceived the act to be unconstitutional, it was to condemn a man unheard."[177] By 1794, this judge was confidently and forcefully asserting the legitimacy of his authority to engage in judicial nullification.

I think the act unconstitutional, and I can not ... give my assent to its being carried into effect– the Judges of the land are a branch of the Government, and are to administer the constitutional laws, not such as are repugnant to the constitution; it is their duty to resist an unconstitutional act. In fact, such an act made by the General Assembly, who are deputed only to make laws in conformity to the constitution, and within the limits it prescribes, is not any law at all. Whenever

[174] Iredell to Spaight (August 26, 1787), ibid., at 173–74.
[175] *State* v. –, 2 N.C. Rep. 50 (1794). [176] Ibid., 50. [177] Ibid., 51.

the Assembly exceeds the limits of the constitution, they act without authority, and then their acts are no more binding than the acts of any other assembled body.[178]

Despite the judge's statement, the next day the Attorney General returned to renew his motion for a judgment in the state's favor. And he made a long and complicated argument to the court in support of this motion. He did not, however, directly question the court's authority to engage in judicial review, as Richard Spaight had done seven years earlier. Instead, he did something more subtle, harnessing a series of arguments, drawn primarily from traditional constitutionalism, which sought to depict the legislature's constitutional position in a more favorable (traditional) light, but only for the purpose of creating doubts in the judges' minds about whether, given the legislature's contrary judgment, the judges could be absolutely certain that the law was unconstitutional. He began by arguing that provisions in the North Carolina constitution which might be read as limitations on the power of the legislature to make law, were actually an effort to prohibit any foreign or usurped power from enacting laws that would be binding on the people.

[t]he clauses of the constitution that are objected to the validity of this act, are declarations the people thought proper to make of their rights; not against a power they supposed their own representatives might usurp, but against oppression and usurpation in general. The second clause for instance, could not be intended as a restraint upon the Legislature; it could not be supposed the Legislature would ever attempt to oppose the right of the people to regulate their internal government; it was intended to assert the right of the people against the power of the British King and Parliament, and against all other foreign powers, who hereafter might claim a right under any pretence whatsoever ....[179]

And he repeated variations on this contention several times later in his argument.[180] The Attorney General then referred to the traditional anti-suspension clause in the constitution, perhaps slyly cautioning the judges that they themselves might be exceeding their legitimate constitutional authority by refusing to execute a duly enacted law of the state, and should have no doubts about their judgment that it was not law before proceeding to do so.[181]

The Attorney General was confident that in adopting the law of the land clause in the constitution the framers could not have intended to deprive the legislature of the power to make necessary changes to common

[178] Ibid., 51–52. [179] Ibid., 52. [180] Ibid., 55 and 56–57.

[181] Ibid., 53. Recall that "dispensing with laws" was one of the accusations made against the judges in the legislative investigation of their conduct carried out in December 1786.

law procedures as the novel needs of their newly fashioned republican government became apparent.

> There is no part of this Constitution that directs the process by which a suit shall be instituted, or carried on, and the Legislature are therefore free to direct what mode of proceeding in Courts they think proper; and accordingly in a great variety of instances, both in England ... and in this country, since the Constitution, judgments have been rendered against defendants without their having had any previous actual notice, [their delinquency alone should serve as sufficient notice,] and the Judges have never intimated a doubt of the constitutionality of these proceedings.[182]

The Attorney General then launched into a history of the notice provision in the act, showing that over the years, the people's representatives had repeatedly included similar provisions in revenue acts, because of its obvious public utility.

In a 1784 act "for the better security of the revenue," the legislature, for the first time, "directed judgments to be taken against delinquents [without the need for actual notice] and declared that such judgments should be as valid as if the usual processes of law had been observed; the same in effect is repeated in [the] 1787 [act]," and in the current 1793 act.[183]

And over this period, the Attorney General went on, the legislature had undoubtedly made the judgment that the notice provisions were not repugnant to the constitution. The repeated judgments of this large body of men, elected by the people, and acting in the public good, was entitled to considerable weight.

> Since the year 1784, there have been nine Assemblies of this State, the most of them have approved, some have amended this part of the revenue laws, and none have ever thought proper to repeal it. Would so many Assemblies, each of whom has done something upon the revenue business, have suffered those clauses to have remained unrepealed, had they believed them to be unconstitutional? Are these legislative bodies, charged and entrusted by their countrymen with their most important concerns, to be all regarded as men who either could not discover the unconstitutionality of a law, or were willing to countenance it? What interest have they in the continuance of an unconstitutional act more than the rest of their fellow citizens? Had the clauses been repugnant to the Constitution, they would undoubtedly have repealed them. The Legislature, though frequently blamed, are undoubtedly in general entitled to this commendation, that they seek the good of their country; with men elected as they are, and for such a period, it can hardly be otherwise.[184]

[182] Ibid., 56–57. [183] Ibid., 59. [184] Ibid., 60.

All of this suggests, at the very least, the Attorney General submitted, that the answer to the question whether the statute is or is not constitutional is far from clear and obvious. Men of good faith, all serving the people, clearly disagree about the question. "In doubtful cases," the Attorney General continued, the fact that the law clearly promoted the public good was entitled to considerable weight in arriving at a final determination of whether it was constitutional.[185]

The cost to the state of giving notice to receivers of public monies and other public debtors, the Attorney General then showed, was at least one thousand pounds annually, and knowing that process servers were on the road after the first day of October each year, delinquents would frequently conceal themselves or "go out of the neighborhood." The public treasury, moreover, was nearly empty; and if the act were struck down the legislature would be powerless to improve the state's dire budgetary situation.

> *[I]f the Court should adhere to its opinion of yesterday ... the Legislature will be utterly deprived of every power competent to its remedy.* It will be in vain for them to pass any act similar to the present, or to adopt any other mode but that of the old time .... At this time there are but a few hundred pounds in the Treasury ....[186] (emphasis added)

After hearing the Attorney General's arguments, Judge Williams "still adhered to his opinion" that the act was unconstitutional and void, but a few days later the entire court reconvened with judges Ashe and Macay in attendance, and the Attorney General renewed his motion. After hearing the Attorney General's arguments, the court took a few days to consider the question. According to the official report of the case, Judge Macay "was very clear in his opinion that the judgments might be taken, and had given such strong reasons, that ... (Judge Ashe's) objections were vanquished, and therefore that the Attorney General might proceed– but that yet he [Ashe] did not very well like it. So the judgments were taken."[187]

It is difficult to say with any degree of certainty why the court decided not to declare the act void. It is possible that the Attorney General's traditionalist arguments that the legislature's judgment about the constitutionality of the act should be accorded substantial weight, convinced at least one of the judges, Macay. His opinion does not seem so surprising given that the financial health of the entire state government seemed to depend on the act. And Ashe may have decided to join Macay in granting

[185] Ibid., 60. [186] Ibid., 61. [187] Ibid., 63.

the Attorney General's motion, despite his own misgivings, for the same reason, and/or under some version of a doubtful case rule, given that the judges were not "decided and uniform" in their views about the constitutionality of the act.

What stands out simultaneously, however, is that the Attorney General seemed to have had no doubt that if the court struck down the act, that would end the matter; it would leave the legislature entirely powerless to remedy the state's desperate budgetary situation. The Attorney General, at least, seemed to believe that the court unquestionably possessed the final word on the laws of the state. His traditionalist arguments about the nature of constitutional limitations, and of the weight to which the legislature's judgments about constitutionality were entitled, now have the feel of being deployed in a rearguard action. Where not so many years earlier, the legislature might well have claimed a plenary authority, as the people's representatives, to make final judgments about the laws of the land, now the Attorney General appears to have been invoking these traditional understandings only as one view of the matter, sufficient to raise doubts in the judges' minds about the constitutionality of the act, but not enough, in themselves, to determine the question. That final determination, he quite clearly seems to have believed, now lay in the hands of the judges.

In both the Bayard case and in the present case, the court did ultimately go along with the legislature's judgments, but as they did, they simultaneously helped to build an understanding that in the end, the legislature possessed the power to give its acts the force of law only when the court agreed with its judgments, or was otherwise willing to stay its hand. This assumption fundamentally altered the distribution of constitutional authority in the state and makes clear that in North Carolina traditional legislative supremacy was essentially a thing of the past by 1794.

PART THREE

JUDICIAL REVIEW AT THE FEDERAL CONVENTION

10

Judicial Review and the Fate of Traditional Constitutionalism at the Federal Convention

10.1 JUDICIAL REVIEW IN THE STATES ON THE EVE OF THE CONSTITUTIONAL CONVENTION

By the eve of the Federal Convention, judicial review had laid down solid foundations in New Jersey, New Hampshire, and North Carolina. And even though further development of the practice was thwarted for several decades in New York, and for more than half a century in Rhode Island, the case of *Trevett* v. *Weeden* was nevertheless being cited as a precedent for judicial review beyond Rhode Island's borders. It was mentioned with approval, for example, at the Federal Convention, where the Rhode Island legislature was condemned for "displacing" the judges who had engaged in it.[1]

In every one of these states, the primary driving force behind the development of judicial review came from the lawyers, at a time when leading members of the bar and bench in each state were also often prominent political figures. Lawyers initiated and defended the cases, produced the reasoning to justify the courts' authority, and persuaded judges actually to "dispense with laws." The ideas they developed took root in and were carried by the legal community in each state.[2] Not every

[1] Max Farrand (ed.), *Records of the Federal Convention of 1787* (New Haven, Ct., Yale University Press, 1966), II, 28.

[2] "Undoubtedly," Richard Lambert writes in his definitive article on the N.H. Ten Pound Act cases, "the argument against the Ten Pound Act was quickly circulated among New Hampshire's small fraternity of lawyers, which in 1786 numbered fewer than thirty. For, soon after Sherburne's plea in late February before the Rockingham County Inferior Court, the argument would surface in at least four other cases and no less of a figure than Speaker of the House and state President-elect John Sullivan would make the argument in a case tried before a justice of the peace in Londonderry," Richard Lambert, "The Ten Pound Act Cases" (2002) 43 *The New Hampshire Bar Association Journal* 37–55, at 41.

leading lawyer, of course, became a supporter of judicial review. In North Carolina, Abner Nash, for example, remained an opponent. But James Iredell probably characterized the situation accurately, not only in North Carolina, but in other states as well, when he wrote to Richard Spaight, who was an unyielding opponent of the new practice, that "I believe many think as you do upon this subject, though I have not heard much said about it .... [But m]ost of the lawyers, I believe, are of my opinion."[3]

Within states, it is hard to imagine that the innovative arguments lawyers produced in the course of presenting their high-profile cases would not have been the subject of lively conversations among members of the relatively small fraternity of bar and bench in each state, many of whom had personal or professional ties to one another. Alexander Hamilton, to take one example, knew or worked with two of the lawyers, Elias Boudinot and William Willcocks, who had participated in the first successful challenge to a state law next door in New Jersey in 1780.[4]

In every one of the four states in which post-war constitutional cases arose, accounts of the proceedings were reported in local newspapers.[5] In New York, the arguments in *Rutgers* v. *Waddington*, together with James Duane's opinion, were re-printed as a stand-alone pamphlet the same year the case was litigated.[6] In Rhode Island, James Varnum published a detailed account of the proceedings in *Trevett* v. *Weeden*, together with its legislative aftermath, shortly after the events there took place.[7] Multiple reports

[3] Letter of James Iredell to Richard Spaight (August 26, 1787), in Griffith McRee (ed.), *Life and Correspondence of James Iredell* (1857, repr. New York, Peter Smith, 1949), II, 175–76.

[4] Elias Boudinot, who was one among several lawyers in the *Holmes* v. *Walton* litigation, had become Hamilton's patron following the young man's immigration to New Jersey in the early 1770s, and remained Hamilton's lifelong friend, see Ron Chernow, *Alexander Hamilton* (New York, Penguin Books, 2004), 43–47, 72, 113–14, 181, 334, 387; William Willcocks was a New York lawyer who moved to New Jersey during the British occupation of the city and took part in *Holmes* v. *Walton*, but returned to New York City after the peace and served as one of plaintiff's lawyers opposing Hamilton in the *Rutgers* v. *Waddington* litigation, see *Arguments and Judgment of the Mayor's Court of the City of New York in a Cause Between Elizabeth Rutgers and Joshua Waddington* (Printed by Samuel Loudon, New York, 1784), at 4, reprinted in *The Case of Elizabeth Rutgers versus Joshua Waddington Determined in the Mayor's Court in the City of New York With an Historical Introduction by Henry B. Dawson* (Morrisania, N.Y., 1866) (plaintiff's counsel at xvii).

[5] See footnotes accompanying the discussion of each case in Chapters 6, 7, 8 and 9.

[6] *Arguments and judgment of the Mayor's Court of the City of New York, in a cause between Elizabeth Rutgers and Joshua Waddington* (New York, Printed by Samuel Loudon, 1784).

[7] James M. Varnum, Esq., Major-General of the State of Rhode Island, &c. Counsellor at Law, and Member of Congress for said State, *The Case, Trevett against Weeden: on Information and Complaint, for refusing Paper Bills in payment for Butcher's Meat, in Market, at Par with Specie. Tried before the Honourable Superior Court, in the County of*

about the *Trevett* case appeared in Rhode Island and Boston newspapers. But accounts of these cases were also regularly reported by out of state papers. A long account of the litigation in *Rutgers* v. *Waddington* was (re) printed in a South Carolina newspaper the same month the case was being debated in the New York legislature.[8] A report about the New Hampshire Ten Pound Act cases appeared in a Philadelphia paper at the time the Federal Convention was meeting.[9] Accounts of the North Carolina litigation in *Bayard* v. *Singleton* appeared in newspapers and in a journal in Pennsylvania and Virginia.[10] This is not to speak of the raw notoriety the cases gained simply as a result of being passionately debated by legislatures in each state.

It is possible, moreover, that the meetings of the Confederation Congress, which brought together leading lawyers from across the states, might have provided an additional setting for the dissemination of the new ideas. It is worth noting, for example, that James Duane and James Varnum were both delegates to Congress in 1781 and worked with each other, alongside James Madison, to produce the draft of a committee report that was to serve as a preamble for a proposed amendment to the Articles of Confederation. The report included the statement that it was "consonant to the spirit of a free Constitution that . . . all exercise of power should be explicitly and precisely warranted."[11]

Based on the remarks delivered by delegates to the Federal Convention from half a dozen states, well placed men from around the country, many of them lawyers, appear by 1787 to have taken the legitimacy of judicial review largely for granted. At the same time, a smaller number of lawyer delegates continued to oppose the new practice.[12] Most of those who

Newport, September Term, 1786. Also, The Case of the Judges of said Court, Before the Honourable General Assembly, at Providence, October Session, 1786, on Citation, for dismissing said Complaint. Wherein the Rights of the People to Trial by Jury, &c. are stated and maintained, and the Legislative, Judiciary and Executive Powers of Government examined and defined (Providence, Printed by John Carter, 1787).

8 *Columbian Herald* (Charleston, S.C.) (November 23, 1784).

9 *The Independent Gazetteer* (Philadelphia, Pa.), July 18, 1787.

10 *Pennsylvania Packet* (July 1 and August 23, 1786); *Virginia Independent Chronicle* (July 4, 1787); *American Museum or Repository of Ancient and modern Fugitive Pieces* (April 1788) (Philadelphia, Printed by Mathew Carey, 1788).

11 Jonathan Gienapp, *The Second Creation: Fixing the American Constitution in the Founding Era* (Cambridge, Mass., Harvard University Press, 2018), 48, citing *Journals of the Continental Congress, 1774–1789* (Govt. Printing Office, 1904–37), XX, 470.

12 See favorable remarks by Elbridge Gerry (Mass.) and Rufus King (Mass.) (lawyer), June 4, 1787, in Farrand, Records of the Federal Convention, I, 97–98, and 109; by Gouverneur Morris (Pa.) and Roger Sherman (Ct.) (both lawyers), July 17, 1787, in ibid.,

spoke in favor of judicial review seem to have believed that the authority of judges to declare laws void flowed naturally from their duty to "expound" the laws, a by now familiar feature of the early doctrine.[13] The judges' "exposition of the laws ..., " Elbridge Gerry observed for example, "involved a power of deciding on their Constitutionality."[14] Between the powerful new ideas the lawyers had developed, the stubborn doggedness of the judges in adhering to their views, and the resulting inability (or unwillingness) of legislatures to put a stop to the practice in several states, judicial review seems to have emerged from its encounters with state legislatures, having achieved, by 1787, a certain significant degree of constitutional legitimacy among a sizeable number of members of the bench and bar throughout the country.

Lawyers and judges constituted the vanguard in the fight for judicial review, but, in a larger sense, it was the general climate that moved them to initiate (and develop) this transformative constitutional practice and doctrine. With the end of the war, many Patriots had come to feel that the time had arrived to settle scores with Loyalists, and the New York and North Carolina legislatures (among others) responded favorably to the resulting popular pressures. And when hard economic times descended on the country shortly afterward, a large number of Americans began to appeal to their legislatures for relief from high taxes and unyielding debts. And again, a number of popularly elected assemblies saw fit to take action on their behalf. Other Americans, of course, believed just as fervently that a good deal of the resulting legislation infringed on fundamental common law property, contract, and process rights. Many of them were also of the opinion that none of this was surprising in light of the faulty design of early republican governments.

On a practical level, the lawyers who began to argue these early constitutional cases were often simply attempting to protect their clients

II, 27–28; by James Wilson (Pa.) (lawyer), July 21, 1787, in ibid., II, 73; by Luther Martin (Md.) (lawyer), July 21, 1787, in ibid., II, 76; by George Mason (Va.), July 21, 1787, in ibid., II, 78, and by James Madison (Va.) (studied law), July 23, 1787, in ibid., II, 93. New Jersey delegates (and lawyers) William Paterson and David Brearley, and New York delegate (and lawyer) Alexander Hamilton certainly also supported the new practice. Add to these, the substantial support for judicial review that has been shown to exist in New Jersey, New Hampshire, Rhode Island, North Carolina, and, to a lesser extent New York. Voicing disapproval of the practice were John Francis Mercer (Md.), John Dickinson (Del.), August 15, 1787, in ibid., II, 298–99, and Gunning Bedford (Del.) June 4, 1787, in ibid., I, 100–1 (all lawyers). We can also be certain that the North Carolina delegate Richard Spaight was an avowed opponent.

[13] Ibid. [14] Comments of Elbridge Gerry, in ibid., I, 97.

from the outcomes of majoritarian politics by seeking refuge in the courts. But many of the prominent lawyers who undertook these cases also had a larger goal – to bring into being a durable check on legislatures and, in that way, to place enforceable limits on the power of the sovereign people to enact through their representatives just any law they might desire.

In developing this innovation, the lawyers found themselves working with increasingly favorable constitutional materials. When Americans undertook their struggles with Britain, they repeatedly claimed that such and such an act of Parliament was unconstitutional and void, and did not bind Americans. In the context of the traditional Anglo/American constitutionalism of the time, these statements did not mean what they would later come to mean. The British constitution was understood to be a foundational "political" agreement, customary to a significant extent, not primarily a "legal" contract. It enshrined a set of fundamental norms and principles, not a set of "legal" rules in the modern sense. It was perhaps best understood, Larry Kramer has argued, as a distinctive early modern type of fundamental law, captured best by the term "political-legal," a form of higher law that most believed did not fall within the purview of ordinary courts.[15] When revolutionary era Americans asserted that a British statute was unconstitutional and void, they were contending that Parliament had violated basic constitutional norms and principles, and were advancing a primarily "political" claim that triggered a right in the people to resist the unconstitutional law. Disobeying or refusing to abide by such an unconstitutional law was usually understood as an act of political defiance. To put it somewhat simplistically, what American lawyers succeeded in doing over the following decade was to transform this traditional constitutional claim into what amounted to a primarily "legal" claim, cognizable by ordinary courts.

They were assisted in effectuating this transformation by a series of rapidly developing constitutional ideas, which found broad support among Americans. When the states first adopted written constitutions, these were mainly understood in the traditional British way to establish norms and principles to which legislatures ought to adhere, as they pursued the good of the polity through legislation. And the new frames of government placed Americans in a strong position to enforce these basic principles "politically." The new legislatures' constitutional obligations were understood to run directly to the people, and if the people agreed

[15] Larry Kramer, *The People Themselves, Popular Constitutionalism and Judicial Review* (Oxford, Oxford University Press, 2004), 24.

with their interpretations of the constitution, that would be an end of it. If they did not agree, they could simply vote their representatives out of office at the next annual election. No permanent early state constitution, other than New York's and Pennsylvania's, created any institutional mechanism (other than elections, or in a few cases official oaths and impeachment) to enforce a constitution. And even the New York and Pennsylvania constitutions, at the end of the day, left their legislatures with the final word as to whether a statute conflicted with the constitution, subject only to review by the people.

But even at this early date Americans rejected particular aspects of the British constitutional tradition, or perhaps gravitated toward certain of that tradition's subordinate currents. Several early state constitutions contained provisions explicitly denying to legislatures the power to modify or repeal any part of the document. But even in the case of these constitutions, the idea that the legislature lacked the power to alter the instrument remained a largely "political" restriction, in that they failed to create an institutional mechanism (other than elections) to enforce that or any other limitation.

The deep distrust many Americans felt about the exercise of all governmental power, however, even when wielded by their own representatives, led, in a few years to the development of several uniquely American constitutional institutions, most importantly the stand-alone constitutional convention, and popular ratification of the resulting drafts. These innovations embodied the idea that constitutions were the direct "legal" enactments of the people, not the products of legislatures. As a result, the new institutions helped to reinforce the idea that legislatures could not possibly possess power to alter constitutions. And though few constitutions of the period had actually been put into place using the new procedures, these ideas quickly came to define the archetypal process for making constitutions.

Several second-generation constitutions, like those of Massachusetts (1780), and New Hampshire (1784), were actually drafted and adopted using the new procedures. And these constitutions also included several new kinds of clauses that reflected the emerging constitutional reality. One clause expressly withheld from the legislature the power to pass any law that was repugnant to that constitution. Another clause explicitly declared that the constitution was part of the "laws of the land." Some earlier constitutions had included separation of powers provisions, but in these two second-generation constitutions, separation of powers clauses appeared in tandem with these other newer clauses, providing a more substantial textual foundation for constructing the argument for judicial review. As the ideas underlying the new constitutional provisions spread, moreover, the essence of these clauses came simply to be read into the more numerous constitutions that did not actually contain them. Nevertheless, underneath it all, these were still "political" restrictions, in that none of the constitutions created an institution to enforce their terms, other than frequent elections. The Massachusetts constitution did confer a conditional veto on the governor, but in the traditional way, as part of the lawmaking process.

A distinctive view of constitutions had begun to emerge among Americans, and the lawyers were quick to grasp its deep logic, as they sought protection from legislative acts in the courts. Initial excursions into the possibilities of this new constitutional reasoning were explored early on in New Jersey and Virginia. But once the war had been settled, and legislatures began to take up the passionate concerns of the people, the pace of development accelerated. The four cases which arose following the war were all adjudicated in the three years between 1784 and 1787.

If constitutions were law, like other law, except that having been directly enacted by the sovereign people, they were higher law, the lawyers argued, then the courts would have a solid basis to claim the authority to "expound" them in the same way they "expounded" other laws, and to give effect to their interpretations by enforcing the superior law of the constitution (as they interpreted it) over the inferior law of legislatures. Moreover, if constitutions were "law" directly enacted by the people, an analogy to statutory law suggested that judicial interpretations of them bound even the people themselves, at least until they moved formally to amend the constitution, in the same way that judicial interpretations of statutes bound legislatures until those bodies formally moved to amend the law.

At the same time, because separation of powers had become an increasingly important constitutional value, thought necessary to avoid tyrannical concentrations of governmental power, courts were now in an especially strong position to claim that as the branch of government responsible for "expounding" the laws, it was uniquely their job, not the legislature's, to interpret the law of the constitution. Legislatures were responsible for making laws, the courts' primary duty was to interpret the laws, and as legislatures were not the authors of constitutions, their interpretations of those documents should naturally be subordinate to the courts, whose primary duty and expertise lay precisely in performing this interpretive task. The leading lawyers who pressed for judicial review were quick to understand this point. In mid-1788, a few months after the Federal Convention ended, Alexander Hamilton wrote in #78 Federalist that

> [t]he interpretation of the laws is the proper and *peculiar* province of the courts. A constitution is, in fact, and must be regarded by the judges as, a fundamental law. It therefore belongs to them to ascertain its meaning as well as the meaning of any particular act proceeding from the legislative body.[16] (emphasis added)

These developments had far reaching consequences. Courts could now begin to claim the authority to deliver definitive interpretations not only of their own powers under constitutions but also of the powers of legislatures. Emboldened by their new constitutional position, judges began to intervene to "dispense with laws," but they also began to pare down certain of the powers legislatures had traditionally exercised in some states, especially their authority to act as legal tribunals, or as customary courts of final resort, on the ground (among others) that these amounted to unconstitutional invasions of the judicial power.[17]

A foundational "political-legal" document was being transformed into a (predominantly) "legal" one, although it would never be possible to completely suppress the fundamental "political" choices frequently at stake in its interpretation. As the traditional British and American understandings of constitutions began to be challenged, it was natural for the lawyers who were cultivating ("horizontal") judicial review in the states to begin to distance themselves from the British constitutional tradition, as St. George Tucker in his argument in the Virginia *Case of the Prisoners*, Edmund Pendleton in his opinion in that case, and James Iredell, in his writings in connection with the North Carolina *Bayard* case, all decisively did.[18]

The new constitutional logic suited the "political" interests of those who saw an urgent need to reshape early republican governments to establish a check, not only on legislatures, but on the power of an often turbulent, volatile, sovereign people. The leading lawyers who agitated for

[16] #78 Federalist, in Clinton Rossiter (ed.), *The Federalist Papers* (New York, Mentor, c. 1961, 1999), 435.

[17] So long as a constitution did not formally institute them as a court of final resort, as the New York Constitution of 1777 had.

[18] See Chapter 5 for detailed descriptions of Tucker's and Pendleton's positions. Iredell's views are described in detail in Chapter 9. By contrast those who promoted "vertical" judicial review of state laws, as Hamilton did in the *Rutgers* case, tended initially to base their arguments on more traditional British constitutional assumptions; see the discussion of "horizontal" and "vertical" judicial review later in this chapter.

judicial review in the early period, Alexander Hamilton (N.Y.), William Plumer (N.H.), James Varnum (R.I.), and James Iredell (N.C.), all openly acknowledged that part of the rationale for judicial review was to bind the people to the terms of their own constitutions (as the courts interpreted those).[19]

The view of constitutions as open ended, fluid, foundational political-legal documents that laid down fundamental norms and principles, and whose proper interpreters were the people's chosen representatives, overseen by the people themselves, however, still carried a good deal of weight. And a struggle between this primarily "political" view of constitutions, and the emerging, primarily "legal" view, took place just below the surface at the Federal Convention, in the debates over the kinds of restraints on legislatures that the new government should have. James Madison agreed with most of the delegates that checks on legislatures and on the people were essential in republican governments, but his proposals for establishing such checks, a Council of Revision exercising a qualified veto over Congressional acts, and a national legislative negative on state laws, reflected an older understanding of constitutions as largely "political-legal" documents. In the end, however, the Federal Convention voted to reject Madison's proposals and instead (1) to adopt a judicial check on the states, (2) to expressly make the constitution the supreme "law" of the land, and (3) to formally extend the judicial power to cases arising under it, adopting, in effect, the view of constitutions as superior conventional "law," whose natural interpreters were the judges, with all that entailed for the character of republican government, and for the future of judicial review.

10.2 MADISON'S PROPOSAL FOR A COUNCIL OF REVISION: THE BACKGROUND

Just before the Virginia Court of Appeals took up the *Case of the Prisoners* in 1782, members of the Assembly approached Edmund Randolph with the idea of forming a committee of legislators and judges to try to come to an agreement that would "define the powers of each" and suggested as one possible method "to keep the legislature in future[e] cases within its

[19] For Hamilton's views, see Chapter 6, for Plumer's, Chapter 7, for Varnum's, Chapter 8, and for Iredell's, Chapter 9.

just limits" that a Council of Revision, presumably based on New York's, be added to the Virginia frame of government.[20]

Thomas Jefferson appears to have picked up the idea for a Council of Revision the following May 1783, when he traveled to Richmond to meet with members of the Assembly to discuss the possibility of calling a constitutional convention to amend Virginia's constitution.[21] After the meetings, Jefferson hastened back to Monticello to draft a constitution so that he would be prepared with a concrete plan if a convention were actually called. By late May or June, he had a fairly complete proposal for a revised Virginia constitution.[22]

Jefferson's draft stated that the "General assembly shall not have power to infringe this constitution,"[23] and presumably to enforce this provision, he proposed the addition of a Council of Revision.[24] Jefferson's proposed council differed from New York's not only in the personnel that were to sit on it but also in one other significant respect. He did not explicitly charge his council with the duty to consider the constitutionality of proposed laws, an omission, which must not have been accidental given that Jefferson possessed the text of the New York Constitution. But it makes his precise views about the role the council was to play in constitutional review a little unclear.

Jefferson's proposed constitution did not mention judicial review, one way or the other, but this should not be surprising as the Virginia high court had not yet endorsed the doctrine. Over the next several years, however, the question would arise whether a Council of Revision should be adopted instead of judicial review in evaluating the constitutionality of

[20] See letter from Edmund Randolph to James Madison, October 26, 1782, in William T. Hutchinson and William M. E. Rachal (eds.), *The Papers of James Madison* (Chicago, ILL., University of Chicago Press, 1967), V, 218.

[21] Letter from Thomas Jefferson to James Madison, May 7, 1783, in Julian Boyd (ed.), *The Papers of Thomas Jefferson* (Princeton, N.J., Princeton University Press, 1952), VI, 265; see also Jefferson's letter to Madison of June 17, 1783, at 277 ("A Convention for the amendment of our Constitution having been much the topic of conversation for some time, I have turned my thoughts to the amendments necessary.") The "agitation" for a new convention apparently continued from 1783 through 1785, but Patrick Henry, who opposed calling a convention succeeded in thwarting the movement's momentum, see "Editorial Note: Jefferson's Proposed Revision of the Virginia Constitution," in Boyd (ed.), Papers of Thomas Jefferson, VI, 278–84.

[22] Jefferson "Draft of A Constitution for Virginia," [May–June 1783], in Boyd (ed.), Papers of Thomas Jefferson, VI, 294.

[23] Ibid., under the section devoted to the General Assembly.

[24] "Editorial Note: Jefferson's Proposed Revision of the Virginia Constitution," in Boyd (ed.), The Papers of Thomas Jefferson, VI, 278–84.

legislative acts, preserving the core values of traditional constitutionalism, or as a supplement to it, considerations of the constitutionality of laws being consigned primarily to judicial review while the Council of Revision would operate as a broad conditional "political" veto, similar to modern gubernatorial and presidential vetoes. In one respect, however, Jefferson's proposal did seem clearly traditional in that he referred to the council's vetoes as "advice" to the legislature, which he also seemed to understand to be the body that would exercise the authority to determine in the final resort whether a bill was to become law.

Only a year later, the ambiguity in Jefferson's proposal became more apparent. In a letter to Edmund Pendleton, he repeated his proposal for a Council of Revision, but seems also to have wanted unconstitutional acts to be "adjudged null."[25] Jefferson's opinion about judicial review and Councils of Revision, as with so many of his other views, would fluctuate over time and remain unclear.[26] By the mid-1780s, he seemed quite sympathetic to the idea of judicial review. In his 1786 "Answers to Demeunier's First Queries," he treated the practice as though it were uncontroversial, writing that "I have not heard that in the other states they have ever infringed their constitutions; and I suppose they have not done it: as the judges would consider any law as void, which was contrary to the constitution."[27] In 1789, he urged Madison to go forward with a bill of rights, which would put a "legal check ... into the hands of the judiciary."[28] During and after his presidency and confrontations with John Marshall, he would become more hostile to judicial review, but in the 1780s he does not seem to have been firmly committed to the idea of a Council of Revision as an alternative to the new practice.

The same cannot be said of James Madison who, despite some inconsistencies in his statements over time, more often gravitated toward a Council of Revision as the more legitimate means for placing a constitutional check on legislatures, in part because it preserved key features of the traditional constitution, which Madison seemed to believe were more consistent with the basic premises of republican government.

So far as it is possible to tell, Madison's interest in a Council of Revision originated with Jefferson's proposal for a new Virginia constitution,

[25] Thomas Jefferson to Edmund Pendleton (May 25, 1784), in ibid., VII, 292–93.

[26] Wallace Mendelson, "Jefferson on Judicial Review. Consistency Through Change" (1961–62) 29 *University of Chicago Law Review* 327–37.

[27] Boyd (ed.), Papers of Thomas Jefferson, X, 18.

[28] Ibid., XIV, 659 (March 5, 1789 letter to James Madison).

which in turn seems to have grown out of the litigation in *The Case of the Prisoners*.[29] In July 1783 Madison wrote to Jefferson acknowledging receipt of Jefferson's draft of a new Virginia constitution.[30] The next year in "Notes of Speech on Proposed Amendment to the Constitution of Virginia," Madison adopted much of Jefferson's critique of the Virginia Constitution, noting among other matters that it established "no mode of expounding constitution & of course no check to Gen. Assembly."[31] By August 1785 when Madison wrote to Caleb Wallace offering advice about how a Kentucky constitution should be framed, he seems not to have developed his ideas about a Council of Revision much further. In his letter, he suggested that a constitution might specify exceptions to legislative power as a means of restraining it, and went on to add that

> [a]s a further security against fluctuating & Indegested laws the constitution of New York has provided a Council of Revision. I approve much of such an institution & believe it is considered by the most intelligent citizens of that state as a valuable safeguard both to public interests & to private rights.[32]

He did not explicitly discuss either constitutional violations or judicial review in the letter, but his references to private rights and limitations on legislative power suggest that he may have been thinking about the council as a remedy for constitutional violations.

Madison's views on the subject of a Council of Revision crystallized to a considerably greater extent a few years later during the time he was developing ideas for a federal government, and during the subsequent debates over those ideas at the Convention itself. He showed himself inclined at this moment to rely on express mechanisms written into constitutions to check legislatures, leaving judicial review unmentioned in his proposals. He advocated checks that would be wielded by a Council

[29] It is also possible that Madison became interested in the idea as a direct outgrowth of *The Case of the Prisoners*, when Edmund Randolph wrote to him to say that legislators were proposing one in response to the litigation in that case, see letter from Edmund Randolph to James Madison, October 26, 1782, in William T. Hutchinson and William M. E. Rachal (eds.), *The Papers of James Madison* (Chicago, ILL., University of Chicago Press, 1967), V, 218.

[30] Letter from Madison to Jefferson, July 17, 1783, in ibid., Papers of James Madison, VII, 229.

[31] Gaillard Hunt (ed.), *The Writings of James Madison: His Public Papers and His Private Correspondence* (New York, G. P. Putnam's Sons, 1901), II, 54 fn. 1 (June 1784).

[32] Letter from James Madison to Caleb Wallace, August 23, 1785, in Robert A. Rutland and William M. E. Rachal (eds.), *The Papers of James Madison* (Chicago, ILL., University of Chicago Press, 1973), VIII, 350–51.

of Revision over the federal legislature, and by the national legislature over the states, both acting as part of the lawmaking process.

To be certain, Madison's proposals at the Convention called for thoroughgoing reform of the traditional constitution. But at the same time, they retained a number of its core principles, most importantly, that determinations of constitutionality were primarily a legislative function, and that the (federal) legislature ought to enjoy the final word on what the laws of the land were to be. After long debates, described in more detail below, the Convention voted against Madison's proposals. Instead, simply put, the Convention agreed to rely on judicial review as the primary method for enforcing the Constitution against state legislatures, and, if the remarks of other delegates are to be credited, against legislatures generally, including by implication, Congress itself. These decisions at the Convention virtually guaranteed a role thereafter for judicial review in the American constitutional system.

10.3 THE FATE OF MADISON'S PROPOSAL FOR A COUNCIL OF REVISION AT THE FEDERAL CONVENTION

If, as some historians have sought to argue, Alexander Hamilton and James Iredell were outliers before 1787, in believing that the people themselves were an important source of danger in republican governments, this was certainly no longer the case by the time the Federal Convention convened. Edmund Randolph, Virginia's governor, opened the Convention by describing the defects of the Confederation government and by introducing as a remedy the Virginia plan, which James Madison had been primarily responsible for drafting. But he quickly turned his attention to one of the deeper problems the delegates had come together to address. "Our chief danger," he said, "arises from the democratic parts of our constitutions. It is a maxim which I hold incontrovertible, that the powers of government exercised by the people swallows up the other branches. None of the constitutions have provided sufficient checks against the democracy."[33] He was not alone in his thinking.[34]

In the course of the Convention's deliberations, Madison offered the delegates a more sophisticated analysis of the basic problem they faced,

[33] Farrand, Records of the Federal Convention, I, 26–27 (McHenry's report of Randolph's speech).

[34] See remarks of Sherman, Gerry and Mason, ibid., I, 48–49.

a diagnosis he would largely repeat in #10 Federalist. "All civilized Societies," he told the delegates, "would be divided into different Sects, Factions, & interests, as they happened to consist of rich & poor, debtors & creditors, the landed the manufacturing, the commercial interests, the inhabitants of this district, or that district, the followers of this political leader or that political leader, the disciples of this religious sect or that religious sect."[35] Offering an analysis broadly similar to the ones Hamilton, Iredell and Varnum had also produced, Madison concluded that "[i]n all cases where a majority are united by a common interest or passion, the rights of the minority are in danger."[36] He proposed to address the problem of "the inconveniences of democracy consistent with the democratic form of Govt."[37] "In a Republican Govt.," he told the delegates, "the Majority if united have always an opportunity [to make the rights of the minor party insecure]. The only remedy is to enlarge the sphere [of the government]."[38]

He recognized, however, that even after enlarging the new government's sphere, there would remain the need to impose an independent check on the Federal legislature.[39] And to serve this purpose, the Virginia plan proposed that a Council of Revision be established "to examine every act of the National Legislature before it shall operate, & every act of a particular Legislature before a [Federal legislative] Negative thereon shall be final . . . ."[40] As in New York, the Council was to be composed of the chief executive of the state, and members of the judiciary. And as in New York, "the dissent of the said Council shall amount to a rejection, unless the Act of the National Legislature be again passed, or that of a particular Legislature be again negatived by" some unspecified (super majority) vote of the National Legislature.[41] As in New York, the proposal left the final decision about the laws in the hands of the legislature, even if at times only following a super-majority vote.

Over the following weeks, three main controversies arose concerning the proposed Council of Revision: (1) should their veto be absolute or should it be conditional (whether wielded by the Executive alone or a Council).[42] There were those like James Wilson, Gouverneur Morris,

[35] Ibid, I, 135. [36] Ibid. [37] Ibid. [38] Ibid., I, 136.

[39] See the comments of Madison on June 4, in ibid., I, 108 (King's Notes), and Mary Bilder's very helpful discussion of Madison's "interests" analysis as it applied to his proposal for a Federal Council of Revision in *Madison's Hand: Revising the Constitutional Convention* (Cambridge, Mass., Harvard University Press, 2015), 71–74.

[40] Farrand, Records of the Federal Convention, I, 21. [41] Ibid.

[42] Ibid., I, 94, 103, 104, II, 200 (absolute or conditional).

and Alexander Hamilton who wished to see the Convention adopt an absolute veto, and argued on several occasions in its favor.[43] But Madison, and others, opposed such a veto, and on every vote to which it was put, the absolute veto lost.[44] But (2) if the veto was to be conditional, what percentage of votes should be required to override it. At first, the Convention voted to adopt a two-thirds requirement, as in New York and Massachusetts.[45] At the urging of some of the same delegates who had wanted to establish an absolute veto, however, the Convention voted to increase the necessary percentage to three-quarters, moving the veto in the direction of the absolute veto they had initially wanted.[46] Later on, having thought better of the matter, the Convention voted to reverse itself again, and to re-adopt the original two-thirds requirement, which is retained to this day.[47]

The controversy most central to the concerns of this book, however, involved (3), whether members of the judiciary should sit on a Council of Revision at all, or whether the veto should be wielded by the Executive alone. It was clear to all that a Council veto could be based, just as it was in New York, on a range of objections to proposed laws; a bill could be vetoed if it was "unjust," or "unwise," was bad policy, or otherwise conflicted with the "public good," but also if the Council found it to be "unconstitutional."[48] Under traditional British and American constitutional understandings, "unconstitutionality" was primarily understood to be a form of "political" objection to a bill, and this seems to have been the way Madison mostly treated the matter in this period. The constitutionality of a bill, along with other kinds of considerations about the good of the "polity," were for legislatures finally to judge in the process of law making, even if only after a super-majority consensus had been reached in that body.

Almost from the beginning, however, a number of delegates opposed the idea that judges should participate in exercising such a veto and proposed that the Executive alone should wield it. On June 4, Elbridge Gerry of Massachusetts spoke up to object to the Council of Revision proposal.

43 Ibid., I, 98, 103, 105, 107, II, 299 (Wilson, Hamilton and G. Morris press for absolute veto and fail).

44 Ibid., I, 100, 103, 106, 107 (Madison opposes absolute veto).

45 Ibid., I, 94, 104, II, 181 (2/3 to override).

46 Ibid., II, 294–302 (3/4 to override).

47 Ibid., II, 582, 585–87 (2/3 to override).

48 See, for example, remarks of James Wilson, in ibid., II, 73 (July 21).

Mr. Gerry doubts whether the Judiciary ought to form a part of it, as they will have a sufficient check agst. Encroachments on their own department by their exposition of the laws, which involved a power of deciding on their Constitutionality. In some States the Judges had (actually) set aside laws as being agst. the Constitution. This was done too with general approbation. It was quite foreign from the nature of ye. Office to make them judges of the policy of public measures.[49]

Rufus King, also from Massachusetts, agreed with Gerry on the ground that if the judges participated in the formation of laws, it might bias their decisions in performing their principal duty of expounding the laws.[50] John Dickinson thought "the Judges must interpret the Laws they ought not to be legislators."[51] The same day, the delegates voted 8–2 to confer the veto on the Executive alone.[52] Two days later, Madison, joined by James Wilson, attempted unsuccessfully to have the judges added back in.[53] On July 21, Madison (and Wilson) tried once again, and once again failed.[54] On August 15, Madison made a final unsuccessful attempt to have the judiciary included in a modified version of the revisory veto he now put forward.[55]

Those who opposed the judiciary's participation in the veto seem to have based their objections primarily upon the version of separation of powers doctrine that had become increasingly popular over the prior decade. It called for a strict functional separation of the powers of the branches: legislatures make the laws, judiciaries expound the laws, executives execute the laws. From the perspective of this thinking, permitting any branch to exercise more than one kind of power, as had long been typical in Anglo/American governments, was increasingly frowned upon (in principle), as unduly concentrating governmental powers, and risking the creation of a tyranny.

This rendering of separation of powers was part of an evolution in the thinking about the branches of government. The expertise of judges lay ("peculiarly") in the realm of the "legal," in the specialized, technical

[49] Ibid., I, 97–98. [50] Ibid., I, 98.

[51] Ibid., I, 108 (King's Notes); on June 6 according to Yates' Notes, Dickinson is also reported as saying that including the judiciary in the Council of Revision "involved an improper mixture of powers," ibid., I, 140.

[52] Ibid., I, 104, 108. [53] Ibid., I, 131, 140 [54] Ibid., II, 73, 80.

[55] Ibid., II, 298. By this time, Madison had altered the proposal considerably, moving it in the direction of an absolute veto, in an effort, presumably, to build greater support for it. He now suggested that bills be submitted separately "to the Executive and Supreme Judiciary Departments, that if either of these should object [there should be a 2/3 vote requirement to override but] if both should object, ¾ of each House, should be necessary to overrule the objections and give the act the force of law," ibid., II, 298.

common law reasoning they deployed to expound the laws. They had no particular proficiency in assessing the advisability of particular "policies" that lawmaking required. Nor was it seen as appropriate for impartial, independent judges to be taking part in the partisan politics that were increasingly viewed as inseparable from the lawmaking process itself.

Elbridge Gerry made several of these points in his criticism of Madison's proposal on June 4. On July 21 when the question of the judges was raised again, Mr. Ghorum opposed their inclusion, observing that "[a]s Judges they are not to be presumed to possess any peculiar knowledge of the mere policy of public measures."[56] Mr. Strong added "that the power of making ought to be kept distinct from that of expounding the laws."[57] Luther Martin reinforced this point. "A knowledge of mankind, and of Legislative affairs cannot be presumed to belong in a higher degree to the Judges than to the Legislature."[58] But then he went on to make the crucial point that it was precisely because of their expertise in the realm of the "legal" that they possessed a veto over statutes in one particular kind of situation, when their exposition of the laws in the course of deciding cases led them to judge a statute to be in conflict with the law of the constitution, and to be void and without effect. He concluded that if judges were also given a veto over legislation sitting on a Council of Revision, they would enjoy "a double negative" on the laws, implying that that would certainly be improper.[59]

When the question whether the judges should sit on a Council of Revision came up for the final time in August, "Mr. Pinkney opposed the interference of the Judges in the Legislative business: it will involve them in parties, and give a previous tincture to their opinions."[60]

From the perspective of these views, the objection to legislation on the ground it was unconstitutional was seen as an entirely different type of objection. Unconstitutionality was, at its core, a "legal" objection, "peculiarly" appropriate for the judges to assess by virtue of their authority and expertise in "expounding" the laws. Other possible kinds of objections to proposed legislation were viewed, from this perspective, as matters of "policy," often involving partisan politics, and proper for legislatures (but certainly not for judges) to decide upon as they went about making the laws.

Where did this logic leave understandings about legislative determinations of constitutionality, which inevitably, if often only implicitly, had to play some role in lawmaking? Legislative determinations of

[56] Ibid., II, 73. [57] Ibid., II, 75. [58] Ibid., II, 76. [59] Ibid. [60] Ibid., II, 298.

constitutionality remained what they had long been, a particular kind of determination about the good of the "polity" that legislatures arrived at in the course of lawmaking. But now those kinds of determinations began to take on a different coloration as they were starkly contrasted, implicitly or explicitly, with the "legal" judgments about constitutionality the judges were understood to deliver. Legislative determinations of constitutionality began to appear by contrast, softer, less authoritative, "policy" or "political" assessments of the question, in contrast to the judges' more rigorous (non-partisan) "legal" ones.

Madison's disagreements with the delegates who objected to including judges in the legislative veto were certainly based in part on his pragmatic assessment of the situation. He repeatedly argued that adding judges to the Council of Revision was critical if the veto was to stand a realistic hope of becoming an effective counterweight to the enormous power of the legislature.

But his arguments also reflected a more profound difference of opinion with the others.[61] Much of the time at the Convention, Madison seemed to embrace an older, more traditional view of separation of powers, derived more or less explicitly from the British constitutional tradition. Since the seventeenth century, it had certainly been a maxim of the common law that legislatures made the laws and judges interpreted them. Even Blackstone had pointed out how important separation of powers was for the preservation of "public liberty."[62] But the stark functional binary between the legislative and the judicial that this maxim conjured up did not begin to reflect the institutional realities of Anglo/American governments, in which the branches frequently exercised a mixture of powers. The king wielded not only executive but also legislative and judicial authority. Parliament not only possessed legislative powers but also exercised judicial authority.

And a similar mixture of powers was characteristic of a number of early American governments. The New York Constitution of 1777 stood as the perfect example of how traditional mixing of powers could be used to create an effective system of checks and balances, which also maintained the integrity of the separate branches. The New York Constitution

61 By contrast, James Wilson, Alexander Hamilton, and Gouverneur Morris all seem to have been committed to a "legalistic" view of the constitution, even while they supported Madison's Council of Revision. Their support seems to have been based less on principle than upon a pragmatic judgment that the more robust the veto over the legislature the better.

62 William Blackstone, *Commentaries on the Laws of England* (Chicago, ILL., University of Chicago Press, 1979, reprint of 1765 ed.), Book I, Ch. 2, 142.

conferred legislative power on the judges and governor sitting on the Council of Revision, in order to establish a check on the legislature. It conferred judicial power on the upper house of the legislature, the Senate, sitting on the Court for the Correction of Errors, so that they in turn could serve as a check on the judges. And it conferred executive power on a group of Senators sitting on the Council of Appointment, in order to create a check on the executive's exercise of the appointment power.[63]

With all this in mind Madison argued that placing judges on the Council of Revision would not in fact be inconsistent with separation of powers principles, if those were properly understood in the traditional way. And he added that traditional mixing of powers would actually create a more robust system of checks and balances than the emerging functional system of separation of powers. He pointed to British tradition contending that

> [t]here wd. in truth ... be no improper mixture of these distinct powers [on a Council of Revision]. In England, whence the [separation of powers] maxim itself had been drawn, the Executive had an absolute negative on the laws; and the supreme tribunal of Justice (the House of Lords) formed one of the other branches of the Legislature. In short, whether the object of the revisionary power was to restrain the Legislature from encroaching on the other co-ordinate Departments, or on the rights of the people at large; or from passing laws unwise in their principle, or incorrect in their form, the utility of annexing the wisdom and weight of the Judiciary to the Executive seemed incontestable.[64]

And he made practically the same points about the proper understanding of separation of powers based on British practice again in July.[65] But now he also elaborated on one of the other points he had made in passing in June. The traditional version of separation of powers, implemented through a Council of Revision, he urged, would actually improve the quality of the decisions both the executive and the legislature were likely to make. For one, including the judges on a Council of Revision would serve as a check on the executive in his exercise of legislative power.[66] But simultaneously, their presence would

> be useful to the Executive, by inspiring additional confidence & firmness in exerting the revisionary power: [And i]t would be useful to the Legislature by

[63] See Articles III, XXXII, XXIII of the New York Constitution of 1777, in Francis Thorpe (ed.), *The Federal and State Constitutions, Colonial Charters, and Other Organic Laws of the States, Territories and Colonies* (Washington, D.C., Government Printing Office, 1909, Reprint Buffalo, N.Y., William S. Hein, 1993), V, 2628, 2635, 2633.

[64] Farrand, Records of the Federal Convention, I, 139 (June 6, 1787).

[65] Ibid., II, 77 (July 21, 1787). [66] Ibid., I, 138 (June 6, 1787).

the valuable assistance it would give in preserving a consistency, conciseness, perspicuity & technical propriety in the laws, qualities peculiarly necessary; & yet shamefully wanting in our republican Codes.[67]

Madison added, perhaps thinking about the arrangements in New York, that the mixing of powers actually helped to sustain separation of powers, as each branch could more readily defend itself against the others. "Instead therefore of contenting ourselves with laying down the Theory in the Constitution that each department ought to be separate & distinct, it was proposed to add a defensive power to each which should maintain the Theory in practice. In so doing we did not blend the departments together. We erected effectual barriers for keeping them separate."[68]

But he also pointed out that the delegates were being deeply inconsistent in using functional separation of powers to justify the elimination of judges from a Council, when they continued to support the idea that the executive should enjoy a veto over legislation. Wouldn't conferring legislative power on the executive in such a veto violate functional separation of powers just as much as conferring legislative power on the judges would? Madison argued that "[i]f such a union [of the judiciary and executive branches on a Council of Revision] was an improper mixture of powers, or such a Judiciary check on the laws was inconsistent with the Theory of a free Constitution, it was equally so to admit the Executive to any participation in the making of laws; and the revisionary plan ought to be discarded altogether."[69]

This was a sly and deep objection that served implicitly to support Madison's main point: to create effective checks on one branch, it was imperative to confer some of its powers on the other branches. Indeed, his criticism showed in effect that that was precisely what the delegates who were calling for the exclusion of judges from a Council of Revision, were proposing to do by retaining an executive veto. It may be added that later on the Framers did not shy away from conferring executive power on the Senate in the appointments process. Many, moreover, would have said at the time that when judges engaged in judicial review itself, they were not actually exercising a "separate" judicial power but were assuming legislative authority. It seems pretty clear from all this that the functional

67 Ibid., II, 74 (July 21, 1787); he had also made this point more briefly in June, ibid., I, 139 (June 6, 1787)

68 Ibid., II, 77 (July 21, 1787).

69 Ibid., II, 77 (July 21, 1787); see also ibid., I, 138–39 (June 6, 1787).

separation of powers arguments employed at the Convention in the Council of Revision debates, served more than anything else to promote the deep constitutional logic underlying the judges' claim to an entirely separate power of judicial review.[70]

What also seems apparent from Madison's comments made over the weeks the Council of Revision was being debated, is that he believed (in the traditional way) that it was proper and desirable for both legislators and judges (and the executive) to enjoy the authority to examine the full range of possible objections to a bill during the lawmaking process, questions about whether it was "unwise in principle," or "incorrect in form," as well as whether it "encroached on the rights of the people." Implicit in Madison's view was not only that legislatures possessed the capacity to "expound" constitutions, on the one hand, but that judges possessed important technical expertise that could benefit lawmaking, on the other. Each branch could add its particular wisdom, and weight of judgment to the question of determining whether the bill should be enacted into law. It was proper to address these different kinds of objections together in the lawmaking process because all of them, at bottom, were merely different dimensions of the larger question whether a proposed law promoted the good of the polity. At this moment in his political development, Madison seems to have been of the view that the question of constitutionality should not be cabined off in a separate category as a "peculiarly" legal-judicial determination, to be handled primarily by the judges, but should remain a determination about the preservation of the principles of the constitution that the representatives of the people should continue to make in the final resort in the course of lawmaking, if now enriched by advice and pressure from the other branches, and at times only pursuant to a super-majority vote.

It quickly became apparent in the course of the debates, however, that the Convention was not about to agree to a Council of Revision, purporting to base that decision largely on separation of powers grounds. In voting to adopt the (conditional) executive veto instead, the Convention was simultaneously voting to endorse the view that the proper role for judges in the constitutional system was not to participate in the "political" process of lawmaking but to determine the question of the constitutionality of laws entirely separately, as part of judicial proceedings. Judges

70 It is worth noting in this regard that the delegates discussed the subject of judicial review more often in connection with the Council of Revision than with practically any other matter they deliberated upon.

would render decisions about constitutionality in the course of deciding cases, by "expounding" the laws. The "legalistic view of the constitution" was embedded in this decision.[71]

By October 1788, slightly more than a year after the Convention ended, and partly no doubt as a result of its debates and decisions, Madison had worked out his thinking about Councils of Revision and judicial review more fully. Reacting to the defeat of his proposal at the Convention, Madison produced a memo in which he strongly reasserted the position that a (modified form of) a Council of Revision would be superior to any other possible option for establishing a check on popularly elected legislatures in republican governments. And in this document, he was completely clear that the conditional veto of the judicial and executive departments should operate not as a supplement to the absolute veto of judicial review but as a complete substitute for it. Under Madison's proposal, the (modified) Council of Revision veto would entirely replace judicial review.[72]

What seems most significant about this proposal was that even at this stage in the development of judicial review, Madison, was proposing an alternative that was based largely on a still vital, traditional view of the nature of constitutions, and of determinations of the constitutionality of legislation that was inconsistent with the premises upon which judicial review rested. From the perspective of Madison's proposal, constitutions were foundational "political-legal" documents, and determinations of constitutionality primarily involved a particular form of assessment of the good of the "polity," undertaken in the course of lawmaking.

Madison produced his memo in response to a letter from John Brown, requesting advice about the features a future Kentucky constitution ought to contain. Madison proposed that a such a constitution should include something akin to a Council of Revision and explained that

[71] The term is Edward Corwin's, see Corwin, "Marbury v. Madison and the Doctrine of Judicial Review" (1914) 12 *Michigan Law Review* 538, at 565.

[72] Another alternative to a regime of pure judicial review was suggested by the frames of government in certain states where upper houses of the legislature sat on courts of final resort; New York and Connecticut were two such states. Legal commentators there who were skeptical of judicial review, stressed that review of legislation by ordinary courts might be acceptable, but only if a branch of the legislature sat on the court of final resort to correct the judges' errors; for New York, see *Brutus* XV (March 20, 1788) in Ralph Ketcham (ed.), *The Anti-Federalist Papers, and the Constitutional Convention Debates* (New York, Signet Classics, c. 1986, 2003), 304–9; for Connecticut see Zephaniah Swift, *A System of the Laws of the State of Connecticut* (Windham, Ct., 1795, repr. Arno Press, 1972), I, 53.

[a] revisionary power is meant as a check to precipitate, to unjust, and to unconstitutional laws. These important ends would it is conceived be more effectually secured, *without disarming the Legislature of its requisite authority*, by requiring bills to be separately communicated to the Exec: & Judicy. Depts.. If either of these object, let 2/3 if both ¾ of each House be necessary to overrule the objection; and if either or both protest agst. a bill as violating the Constitution, let it moreover be suspended, notwithstanding the overruling proportion of the Assembly, until there shall have been a subsequent election of the H. of Ds and a repassage of the bill by 2/3 or ¾ of both Houses, as the case may be. *It sd. not be allowed the Judges or the Ex[ecutive] to pronounce a law thus enacted, unconstitul. & invalid.* (emphasis added)

In the State Constitutions & indeed in the Fedl. one also, no provision is made for the case of a disagreement in expounding them; and as the Courts are generally the last in making their decision, it results to them, by refusing or not refusing to execute a law, to stamp it with its final character. *This makes the Judiciary Dept paramount in fact to the Legislature, which was never intended, and can never be proper.*[73] (emphasis added)

This was a plan to establish a mechanism for determining the constitutionality of the laws that could be finely calibrated "politically," by adjusting precisely how large the legislative consensus must be in order to overturn a veto by the other branches, and that would, in addition, require a new election before a bill (against which constitutional objections had been raised) could become law, even with a supermajority vote. In effect, this proposal authorized the legislature to alter the constitution by a supermajority vote, after the people had conferred the authority to do so at a new election; it resembled similar arrangements found in several early state constitutions, and was based on similar constitutional assumptions. At bottom, Madison proposed to settle explicitly a fundamental question about the terms upon which republican governments were to operate: were "the people" to express their sovereign will about the laws through their elected legislative representatives, in the final resort, or through the judges? Madison's proposal left intact the legislature's and the people's traditional authority to decide questions of the constitutionality of the laws directly and finally.

But by this time Madison was certainly aware that judicial review had become an important fact of constitutional life. It should come as no

[73] "Observations on the 'Draught of a Constitution for Virginia'," in Robert A. Rutland and Charles F. Hobson (eds.), *The Papers of James Madison* (Charlottesville, Va., University Press of Virginia, 1977), XI, 281–95.

surprise that there are numerous references to it in his writings and speeches,[74] and given the failure of his own preferred proposals to gain acceptance, that some of these would be favorable to the practice, as he certainly understood the critical need for a check on legislatures of one kind or another.[75] In a speech Madison gave in the new House of Representatives the following June, 1789, he recognized the potency of the argument for judicial review while continuing to contend, now seemingly as a fall-back position, that the legislature also possessed the power to expound constitutions in determining "the powers of the several departments." His view harked back to an older understanding that legislatures did not merely exercise "will" but also forms of "judgment," apparent not only in the "judicial" and quasi-judicial powers they sometimes wielded but also in the determinations they made about the good of the polity and the preservation of constitutional principles in the course of lawmaking.[76]

> I acknowledge in the ordinary course of Government that the exposition of the laws and Constitution devolves upon the Judiciary, but I beg to know upon what principle can it be contended, that any one department draws from the Constitution greater powers than another, in marking out the limits of the powers of the several departments? … I cannot imagine it will be less safe, that the exposition should issue from the Legislative authority than any other …."[77]

Even decades later, Madison had not let go of the idea that there had been a lost opportunity, an alternative to judicial review in the form of something akin to a Council of Revision that would have provided a superior solution to the problem of legislative excesses, a solution more firmly in line with the fundamental principles of republican government. In December 1817, Madison wrote to James Monroe to discuss the question of the constitutionality of the Internal Improvements act. Referring back to arguments he had made at the Convention, Madison wrote that "[t]hese Considerations,"

> remind me of the attempts in the Convention to vest in the Judiciary Dept. a qualified negative on Legislative bills. Such a control restricted to constitutional

[74] See Ralph L. Ketcham, "James Madison and Judicial Review" (1956–57) 8 *Syracuse Law Review* 158–65.

[75] For several of Madison's favorable comments about judicial review, see Bilder, Madison's Hand, 118, 200.

[76] Of course, it also looked forward to the emerging "departmental" theory of judicial review.

[77] Speech in the House of Representatives, June 17, 1789, in Hunt (ed.), The Writings of James Madison, V, 403.

points, besides giving greater stability and system to the rules of expounding the Instrument, would have precluded the question of a Judiciary annulment of Legislative Acts.[78]

Still later in his career, Madison may have changed his mind again, lauding judicial review on several occasions,[79] but that did not change the fact that during the 1780s he saw the possibility of and promoted a different kind of constitutional check on legislatures, one that was express rather than implied, and that would have given legislative "expositions" of constitutions (with the "advice" of the judiciary and the executive, and the support of the people) the incontestable finality they had enjoyed not so many years before.

10.4 REJECTION OF A LEGISLATIVE NEGATIVE AND ADOPTION OF A JUDICIAL CHECK ON THE STATES

Over the course of many weeks of deliberation, the Convention decided not only to reject a Council of Revision as part of the new constitution but another of Madison's key proposals as well, his national legislative veto of state laws. The Convention's decision to discard the Council of Revision was a decision, implicitly, to rely on the judges to decide questions of constitutionality, presumably even in the case of acts of Congress. In its decision to reject a Federal legislative veto, the Convention voted explicitly to rely on a judicial check on laws emanating from state legislatures. These decisions at the Convention played a critical role in transforming judicial review from an emergent practice in a few states into an institution that would henceforth be a permanent, central feature of the American constitutional system. Why the Convention decided to adopt a judicial check to enforce the new Federal Constitution against the states is a critical part of the history of early American judicial review.

If enlarging the sphere of government was Madison's principal strategy for reducing republican vices in the proposed new Federal government, that solution was not available for addressing the problem of popular majorities in the states. The Convention simply did not enjoy the authority to enlarge the spheres of state governments. For this problem the Virginia

[78] Letter from James Madison to James Monroe, December 27, 1817, in Farrand, Records of the Federal Convention, III, 424; and in David B. Mattern, J. C. A. Stagg, Mary Parke Johnson and Anne Mandeville Colony (eds.), *The Papers of James Madison, Retirement Series* (Charlottesville, Va., University of Virginia Press, 2009), I, 190–92.

[79] Ketcham, "James Madison and Judicial Review," 162.

plan relied on an entirely different approach. It proposed to give the new Federal legislature a power "to negative all laws passed by the several States, contravening in the opinion of the National Legislature the articles of Union,"[80] and initially, the Convention voted in favor of this idea.[81] It is important to understand that Madison's national legislative veto was rooted in a larger constitutional vision. Madison himself spoke several times at the Convention of the deeper model he was drawing upon. "Some contend," he said,

> that [the] states are sovereign, when in fact they are only political societies. There is a gradation of power in all societies, from the lowest corporation to the highest sovereign. The states never possessed the essential rights of sovereignty. These were always vested in congress .... The states, at present, are only great corporations, having the power of making by-laws, and these are effectual only if they are not contradictory to the general confederation. The states ought to be placed under the control of the general government – at least as much so as they formerly were under the king and British parliament.[82]

Later on, defending the national legislative veto in a fruitless effort to retain it as part of the proposed new constitution, Madison made himself even clearer about the origins of the proposal.

> A power of negativing the improper laws of the States is at once the most mild & certain means of preserving the harmony of the system. Its utility is sufficiently displayed in the British System. Nothing could maintain the harmony & subordination of the various parts of the empire, but the prerogative by which the Crown, stifles in the birth every Act of every part tending to discord or encroachment. It is true the prerogative is sometimes misapplied thro' ignorance or a partiality to one particular part of ye. Empire: but we have not the same reason to fear such misapplications in our System. As to the sending all laws up to the Natl. Legisl: that might be rendered unnecessary ... so far at least, as to give a temporary effect to laws of immediate necessity.[83]

Madison's plan aimed, in effect, to create a domestic version of the British Empire. The national legislature would assume the role the Privy Council had formerly played. Madison imagined that bills passed by the

[80] Farrand, Records of the Federal Convention, I, 21. To begin with, Madison had wanted a broader version of this veto, one that would have allowed the national legislature to veto state laws "in all cases whatsoever." For a thorough examination of Madison's veto proposal and its background, see Alison LaCroix, *Ideological Origins of American Federalism* (Cambridge, Mass., Harvard University Press, 2010), chapter 5; see also Bilder, Madison's Hand, 78.

[81] Farrand, Records of the Federal Convention, I, 54.

[82] Ibid., I, 471; see also LaCroix, Ideological Origins, chapter 5.

[83] Farrand, Records of the Federal Convention, II, 28.

states would be transmitted to the national legislature for review, as they had formerly been to the Board of Trade and Privy Council.

Madison appears to have believed at this moment that the states were subordinate polities, constitutionally analogous to dependent domestic jurisdictions. This was a plan to erect a United States on traditional British constitutional principles. The national legislature would exercise its power to veto state laws by virtue of its "vertical" superiority, the states merely being great corporations, with only the power to enact "by-laws." Review by the national legislature would be political/legislative in nature, just as it had primarily been in the empire. Hence, Madison's proposal could be viewed as implicitly casting the constitution in traditional terms as a political-legal compact.

Madison was not alone at this moment in thinking that American government could benefit from adoption of core features of the British system, domestic and imperial, which Americans had spurned earlier.[84] Madison's Virginia plan incorporated one critical feature of the British imperial constitution, but on June 18 Alexander Hamilton delivered a speech to the Convention in which he laid out a plan that drew comprehensively on it.

Hamilton told the Convention that he believed "the British Govt. was the best in the world: and he doubted much whether any thing short of it would do in America."[85] But modifications would be necessary because while he was prepared to stretch republican principles as far as they could be made to go, he thought "that it would be unwise to propose [a government] of any other form."[86] He is reported to have said "[t]hat we ought to go as far in order to attain stability and permanency, as republican principles will admit."[87] Britain's upper house was, of course, hereditary, as was its Executive. Hamilton proposed that in the new federal government both the chief executive, called the "Governour" in his plan, and the members of the upper house, be elected for life, "or at least during good behaviour."[88] "But is this a Republican Govt. it will be asked? Yes," Hamilton declared, "if all the Magistrates are appointed, and vacancies are filled, by the people, or a process of election originating in the people."[89] Like the British monarch the "Governour" of the United States was "to have a negative on all laws about to be passed, and the

[84] Gordon Wood, *The Creation of the American Republic, 1776–1787* (Chapel Hill, N.C., University of North Carolina Press, 1969), 430–31.

[85] Farrand, Records of the Federal Convention, I, 288. [86] Ibid. [87] Ibid., I, 289.

[88] Ibid., I, 289, 291, 292. [89] Ibid., I, 290.

execution of all laws passed ... ."[90] But that was not all. Under Hamilton's plan, the states were to be reduced to their former status as limited dependent jurisdictions more completely than under Madison's plan. Like the royal governors formerly appointed by the king, under Hamilton's plan the general government would appoint the governors of each state, and like royal governors these governors would also "have a negative upon the laws about to be passed in the State ... ."[91]

Hamilton's scheme was certainly more extreme than Madison's. It may even have been offered as a provocation designed to make Madison's proposal appear moderate by comparison. But both Hamilton's and Madison's diagnosis of the problems facing the country had led them to conclude that an absolute veto over state legislation was essential if republican government was to be preserved. In both plans, these vetoes were based on traditional British constitutional principles. Review was to be carried out as part of the lawmaking process by the national legislature or a governor. Both plans rested on the traditional idea that it was the superiority of one jurisdiction over another that constituted the basis of the power to review and veto.

Hamilton's proposal gained no traction with the delegates. But Madison's national legislative veto, and a broader version of that veto that Charles Pinckney proposed and Madison supported, were the subjects of repeated debates. In June, the delegates voted to reject Pinckney's expansive version of the national legislative veto.[92] More than a month later they voted to reverse their earlier decision and to reject Madison's original national legislative veto.[93] Neither the absolute vetoes that Hamilton proposed nor those proposed by Pinckney and Madison or any other delegate managed in the end to win the approval of the Convention. In voting to reject all absolute veto proposals, the members of the Federal Convention were following a well-worn path. No state constitutional convention, which had considered a proposal for an absolute veto over legislation, had voted in the end to adopt it.[94]

After Pinckney's version of a national legislative veto had been voted down, but while Madison's still remained part of the draft constitution, William Paterson, governor of New Jersey, introduced, on June 15, what

[90] Ibid., I, 292.

[91] Ibid., I, 293; see also Yates' report of Hamilton's plan, in ibid., I, 299–301.

[92] Ibid., I, 168, 171. [93] Ibid., II, 28.

[94] See discussions of the New York Constitutional Convention of 1777, and the Massachusetts Constitutional Convention of 1780 in chapter 2.

would become known as the New Jersey Plan.[95] The plan had been cobbled together by delegates from several states who, for a variety of reasons, wished to see a less robust national government, one that merely added some new powers to the Confederation government.[96] One critical concern of the group was that under the Virginia Plan, the large states would dominate the small ones. Apparently, delegates from Connecticut (Roger Sherman), New York, Delaware and Luther Martin from Maryland joined with Paterson and David Brearley from New Jersey to draft an alternative plan, which Paterson presented to the Convention.[97] The New Jersey Plan proposed a judicial remedy for the problem of the states, at least as the first line of defense. This would be a remedy carried out not by a national legislature or a national executive but by state judges.[98] It would rely on state judges to enforce, in the proposal's initial iterations, the *laws* passed by congress and the treaties into which the national government had entered. Paterson's 6th resolution stated that "all Acts of the U. States in Congs. made ... and all Treaties made & ratified under the authority of the U. States shall be the supreme law of the respective States ... and ... the Judiciary of the several States shall be bound thereby in their decisions, any thing in the respective laws of the Individual States to the contrary notwithstanding ....[99] This was an early version of what would become the Supremacy Clause in the new Federal Constitution.[100] Recall that American colonial legislatures had operated under the imperial constitutional restriction that their acts not be "repugnant to the *laws* of England." It seems striking that this early formulation of the Supremacy Clause limited itself to Federal laws (and treaties) in the same way, suggesting that the delegates may initially have been seeking merely to substitute state judges for the national legislature, while otherwise relying on the same traditional British understandings of "vertical" review that also underlay Madison's proposal.

But it is also possible to speculate, along with Austin Scott,[101] that Paterson embraced a state judicial remedy in the Convention in part

95 Farrand, Records of the Federal Convention, I, 242–45. 96 Ibid., I, 242 Note.

97 Several different versions of the New Jersey Plan survive, see Farrand, Records of the Federal Convention, III, Appendix E.

98 Roger Sherman's version of the plan also required state executive officers to carry national law into effect, ibid., III, 616.

99 Ibid., I, 245.

100 On the origins of the Supremacy Clause, see also Kramer, The People Themselves, 73–76.

101 Austin Scott, "Holmes vs. Walton: The New Jersey Precedent" (1899) 4 *The American Historical Review* 456, at 467–68.

because his experience in New Jersey had shown that the judges could operate as an effective, albeit softer, check on legislatures. David Brearley, his fellow New Jersey delegate, had long been and continued at this time to serve as Chief Justice of the state. He "was the one man in the Convention who as a judge had pronounced a law unconstitutional [in *Holmes vs. Walton*]. [And] William Paterson had been at the time of the suit of Holmes against Walton the attorney-general of the state."[102] In this way, the New Jersey case of *Holmes* v. *Walton* may have served as one of the sources of inspiration for the Supremacy Clause. At the same time, the proposed clause also fulfilled Alexander Hamilton's great aspiration, expressed in his arguments in *Rutgers* v. *Waddington* and in the New York legislature, to see the treaty of peace with Britain declared to be the law of the land, which state judges would be required to enforce over inconsistent, subordinate state laws.[103]

The day following Paterson's speech, a debate arose among the delegates in which the New Jersey Plan was compared in detail to the Virginia Plan.[104] John Lansing, a delegate from New York who had participated in drafting the New Jersey Plan,[105] commented on Madison's national legislative veto that "[t]he States will never feel a sufficient confidence in a general Government to give it a negative on their laws."[106] During the debates that led to the vote rejecting Pinckney's proposal for a broad national legislative veto a week earlier, Elbridge Gerry had made a similar point. "The Natl. Legislature with such a power may enslave the States. Such an idea as this will never be acceded to. It has never been suggested or conceived among the people."[107]

On July 17, the Convention re-considered Madison's national legislative veto. In the debate that led up to the vote, the lines were drawn between Madison and those who argued against his veto, and in favor

[102] Ibid.

[103] Edward Corwin made out a strong case that the Supremacy Clause could be traced back most directly "to the Circular Letter of Congress of the previous April, provid[ing] that 'all acts of the United States in Congress made by virtue of and in pursuance of the powers hereby ... vested in them and all treaties made or ratified under the authority of the United States shall be the supreme law of the respective states, ... and the judiciary of the several States shall be bound thereby in their decisions, anything in the respective laws of the individual states to the contrary notwithstanding,'" in Corwin, "The Establishment of Judicial Review, I" (1910) 9 *Michigan Law Review* 102, at 121.

[104] Farrand, Records of the Federal Convention, I, 249–80. [105] Ibid., III, 613.

[106] Ibid., I, 250.

[107] Ibid., I, 165; see also the similar remarks of John Rutledge of South Carolina, ibid., II, 391 ("If nothing else, [a national legislative veto] would damn and ought to damn the Constitution.")

of a judicial remedy that relied, one way or another, on state judges. Roger Sherman, one of the delegates who had helped draft the New Jersey Plan "thought [Madison's national legislative veto] unnecessary, as the Courts of the States would not consider as valid any law contravening the Authority of the Union . . . ."[108] He added that [Madison's proposal] involves a wrong principle, to wit, that a law of a State contrary to the articles of the Union, would if not negatived, be valid & operative."[109] Luther Martin, another one of the delegates who had contributed to the New Jersey Plan, said that he "considered the power [Madison was proposing to give the national legislature] as improper & inadmissible."[110] Gouverneur Morris added that "[t]he proposal of it would disgust all the States. A law that ought to be negatived will be set aside in the Judiciary departmt . . . ."[111]

Madison defended the national legislative veto by arguing that state courts were unreliable and their judges too weak to operate as an effective remedy for state violations of the articles of union. He observed that "[c]onfidence can (not) be put in the State Tribunals as guardians of the National authority and interests." "In all the States these are more or less dependt. on the Legislatures. In Georgia they are appointed annually by the Legislature. In R. Island the Judges who refused to execute an unconstitutional law were displaced, and others substituted, by the Legislature . . . ."[112]

In the vote that followed, the Convention rejected Madison's national legislative negative seven states to three.[113] Luther Martin quickly moved to substitute the New Jersey Plan's alternative. He proposed a resolution that would make national laws and treaties "the supreme law of the respective states" and would bind the judiciaries in the states to enforce these national laws "any thing in the respective laws of the individual states to the contrary notwithstanding."[114] And the Convention adopted his proposal.

A month later, perhaps having thought more deeply about the implications of their July decision, the Convention began to amend the Supremacy Clause, hybridizing the original proposal, which appeared

[108] Ibid., II, 27. [109] Ibid., II, 28. [110] Ibid., II, 27. [111] Ibid., II, 28. [112] Ibid.

[113] Ibid.

[114] Ibid., II, 28–29; compare Paterson's earlier 6th Resolution in the New Jersey Plan above. For a similar account of the origins of the Supremacy Clause, see Kramer, The People Themselves, 73–75; see also LaCroix, Ideological Origins, 162–64. Thomas Jefferson also seems to have preferred a judicial remedy to the national legislative veto being proposed by Madison, see LaCroix, Ideological Origins, 159, 161–62.

initially to be based primarily on traditional British conceptions of "vertical" review, by adding in several of the fundamental new constitutional ideas that had emerged in the country over the preceding decade: particularly the views that constitutions were a species of conventional law, and as such that they were cognizable by ordinary courts. And the Convention moved to write this "legalistic view of the Constitution" expressly into its text, making the principal premises upon which the case for judicial review rested unambiguously part of the document. The earlier version of the Supremacy Clause had made only national laws and treaties "supreme." On August 23, adopting a motion of John Rutledge of South Carolina, the Convention now amended the Supremacy Clause in two significant ways. First, they added the words "this constitution" to the kinds of "laws" that were expressly made supreme, and second, state constitutions were added to the kinds of "laws" that state judges were expressly required to ignore, or refuse to enforce, or to hold invalid, when they conflicted with the Federal Constitution, or national laws, or treaties.[115] A few days later on August 27, the Convention amended the article defining the judicial power of the United States to leave no question that the jurisdiction of Federal judges would extend not only to national laws and treaties but, and now listed first, to "all cases" "arising under this Constitution."[116]

It was probably part of the larger strategy that during these same August days, the delegates added a number of specific prohibitions on the power of states to enact laws, which would ultimately find their way into Article I, Section 10 of the Constitution. On August 28, the Convention added to an earlier version of that section the following words: "'nor emit bills of credit' after the word 'money;'" and "nor make any thing but gold and silver coin a tender in payments of debts;" and "nor pass any bill of attainder or ex post facto laws."[117] Now that an open-ended Federal legislative veto had

[115] Farrand, Records of the Federal Convention, II, 381–82, 389.

[116] Ibid. II, 423; Alison LaCroix, drawing on Lawrence Sager's work, observes that "on August 27 – four days after the delegates had agreed on the final language of the Supremacy Clause – they revisited and retooled the description of the Supreme Court's power in what would become Article III of the Constitution. The jurisdictional language of the judiciary article was edited to conform to the language of the Supremacy Clause. For example, the delegates added the phrase 'under this Constitution' to expand the Supreme Court's jurisdiction to include cases that were based on constitutional claims. In this way, the judiciary article was 'tailored to facilitate Supreme Court enforcement' of the Supremacy Clause. The Supremacy Clause, therefore, defined the final language of Article III," Ideological Origins, 163–64.

[117] Farrand, Records of the Federal Convention, II, 435 and 444; see also, Corwin, "The Establishment of Judicial Review, I," at 122.

been ruled out, these specific prohibitions would give judges a bounded but significant number of concrete "legal" prohibitions they could enforce to nullify state laws, on subjects about which the delegates felt state legislatures had been particularly abusive.

These decisions at the Convention represented the pivotal moment when American judicial review was transformed into an indispensable institution in the new constitutional design. By adopting the Supremacy and Judicial Power Clauses, the Convention was embracing the emerging practice of judicial review as a linchpin of the new constitutional system, the principal mechanism, under ordinary circumstances, by which the Constitution (and Federal laws) were to be enforced against the states. And while no similar clause expressly conferred on judges the power to evaluate the constitutionality of laws passed by Congress, the rejection of the proposal that judges should participate in a Council of Revision served to reinforce the idea, widely accepted by the delegates, that questions of constitutionality were to be committed to the judiciary separately as part of their general duty to expound the laws. Presumably, this power would also extend to review of Congressional statutes. And the necessary premises to make that argument had now been expressly written into the Constitution.

But there were certainly disadvantages to leaving the question of judicial review of Congressional statutes in this condition; it made the practice more vulnerable to attack. In this respect, however, it perhaps left such review at no greater risk than "horizontal" judicial review generally, which had emerged in the states without express constitutional authorization.

And omitting this step may have brought certain advantages. The propositions that the Constitution was the "Supreme Law," and cognizable by the judiciary, were likely to have been considerably less controversial than a broad declaration that judges enjoyed the authority to "dispense with laws" in all situations. Perhaps it seemed prudent to leave the practice generally founded, in the end, on acts of judicial interpretation. In that way, its legitimacy could be made to appear a matter of pure logical deduction from the nature of limited (written) constitutions, together with the "peculiar" authority of judges to expound the laws, as Alexander Hamilton would shortly argue in #78 Federalist. Whenever delegates discussed judicial review at the Convention, they referred to it as a practice in which the judges simply engaged as part of their normal duties.[118] As such, it could continue to

[118] See the remarks of Roger Sherman, in Farrand, Records of the Federal Convention, II, 27; and Luther Martin, ibid., II, 76; and even those of John Mercer and John Dickinson (who disapproved of the practice), ibid., II, 298, 99.

be viewed as an intrinsic attribute of the judicial office in a system of written constitutions, rather than as a political choice; one that might be reversed at any time as the result of fluctuating sentiments at popularly elected constitutional conventions.

Perhaps something else also helps to explain the differential treatment these two forms of judicial review received in the Constitution. "Vertical" review, in which the laws of an "inferior" government had to give way to the laws of a "superior" government whenever the two conflicted, was based upon long established British constitutional practices and ideas. It was the theory of judicial review that Hamilton seems most clearly to have relied upon in the *Rutgers* case, and that the Confederation Congress attempted to apply to the states even before the Constitution had been adopted. The theory of ("horizontal") judicial review was one that lawyers and judges in the states had developed independently during the 1780s, and was founded upon significantly different premises.[119] It was not the "laws of a superior" government that mattered but rather the stand alone "superior" law of the people embodied in their constitution, the very precondition for government itself, that mattered. It looks as though, in the minds of the delegates, these two theories may not yet have been completely amalgamated into a broader, more general theory.

If so, just months after the Convention ended, Alexander Hamilton, who had spoken hardly a word about judicial review during the Convention debates, and who had shown surprisingly little interest in "horizontal" review until then,[120] proceeded to publish #78 Federalist. In it he presented a general theory of judicial review, which made no distinction between the two kinds of cases. In both situations, judges would be enforcing the superior will of the people embodied in a constitution against the inferior will of a legislature. In #78 Federalist, Hamilton, as part of the campaign to ratify the new Constitution, and facing *Brutus*'

[119] On this point, see also Keith Whittington, *Repugnant Laws: Judicial Review of Acts of Congress from the Founding to the Present* (Lawrence, Kans., University Press of Kansas, 2019), 44–45.

[120] In the *Rutgers* case (1784), Hamilton had relied primarily on a traditional "vertical" argument for judicial review. His culminating contention in *Rutgers* was that the Mayor's Court was obligated to serve as a court of the Confederation government, and to apply the superior treaty law of the Confederation in deciding the case, "dispensing with" the conflicting, inferior New York statute. At that stage in the development of his thinking, there is surprisingly little evidence that he had as yet seriously devoted himself to a "horizontal" account of the practice. The kinds of arguments he made at the Convention suggest that even by that time, he favored more traditional approaches to placing checks on legislatures.

weighty criticisms of its judicial arrangements,[121] took the strands of the constitutional logic that had been developing in the states and circulating at the Convention, and shaped them into a comprehensive, unified theory of judicial review. Hamilton's argument for judicial review was quickly and widely disseminated by a New York newspaper, but more importantly in volumes of "The Federalist" essays that were published and republished over the following years.[122] Beginning with the very first Congress, the ideas contained in these essays were regularly cited in debates about the Constitution.[123]

Despite Hamilton's broad and general theory, however, the distinction between "vertical" and "horizontal" judicial review persisted, possibly because the Federal-State relationship was, in significant ways, different from the relationship of judges to their own legislatures. For one, it was concretely a case in which the constitution *and laws* of a "superior government" in fact trumped the laws and constitutions of "inferior jurisdictions." But on a more practical level, it was also true that Federal judges had little to fear from state legislatures as they engaged in acts of "vertical" judicial review, while the same could not be said of their "horizontal" relationship to Congress. Perhaps, it is not surprising, therefore, that over the decade following the Convention, the newly created Federal courts engaged in "vertical" review more often than "horizontal" review, striking down more state laws than Federal laws,[124] as the framers had no doubt intended.[125]

121 *Brutus* attacked two main weaknesses in these arrangements. Under the proposed constitution, he argued, judges would be entirely unaccountable for their decisions. First, they would not, as in England, be subject to removal upon address, but second, their opinions would also not be subject to correction by a higher court consisting of a branch of the legislature, as in England, and we may add, New York, see especially, *Brutus* XV (March 20, 1788), in Ketcham (ed.), The Anti-Federalist Papers, 304–9.

122 The first 77 Federalist Papers were published in New York newspapers as they were written, but Nos. 1–37 were also collected into a separate volume published by J & A McLean of New York in March 1788. McLean thereafter published the remaining numbers in a second volume soon thereafter in May 1788. #78 Federalist appeared in the second McLean volume even before it appeared in a New York newspaper. "The Federalist" seems never to have been out of print thereafter. New editions were published in 1792 (McLean's French edition), 1799, 1802, 1810, 1817, 1818, see "The Federalist" in the Hollis Online Catalogue, Harvard University.

123 On citations to the Federalist Papers in the first Congresses, see Gienapp, The Second Creation, 154–55 (1789), and 236–37 (1791).

124 See William Michael Treanor, "Judicial Review Before Marbury" (2005) 58 *Stanford Law Review* 455, especially 517; for a detailed account of these decisions, see 517–33.

125 Recent scholarship, however, has shown that from the beginning the Supreme Court reviewed Congressional legislation much more often than had previously been thought,

In addition, the first Congress passed the Judiciary Act of 1789, which strengthened the hand of the Federal government in "vertical" judicial review. Section 25 of the act empowered the Supreme Court to act as the final judicial arbiter of matters involving conflicts between state and Federal law. The section gave the Federal high court appellate jurisdiction to review and overturn the decisions made by the judges of the highest court in every state, whenever they ruled against Federal authority in a conflict with state law.[126]

Ultimately, the Federal Convention's decisions to rely on judicial review, explicitly in the case of "vertical" review of state legislation, and by implication in the case of "horizontal" review of Congressional statutes, rather than on a national legislative veto and a Council of Revision, were also votes to adopt "the legalistic view of the Constitution," which the Convention then proceeded to write into the Supremacy and Judicial Power clauses.

That the centrality of judicial review in our constitutional system might rest in some measure on the political choices the delegates made at the Federal Convention, may strike some as odd. But that is precisely how both Hamilton and Madison saw the matter. In #80 Federalist, Hamilton wrote:

> [T]here ought always to be a constitutional method of giving efficacy to constitutional provisions .... No man of sense will believe that such prohibitions would be scrupulously regarded without some effectual power in the government to restrain or correct the infractions of them. This power must either be a direct negative on the State laws, or an authority in the federal courts to overrule such as might be in manifest contravention of the articles of Union. There is no third course that I can imagine. The latter appears to have been thought by the convention preferable to the former, and I presume will be most agreeable to the States.[127]

see especially Keith Whittington, Repugnant Laws, chapter 3; and Whittington "Judicial Review of Congress Before the Civil War" (2009) 97 *Georgetown Law Journal* 1257; see also Mark A. Graber, "Naked Land Transfers" (2000) 53 *Vanderbilt Law Review* 73.

126 Judiciary Act of 1789 (First Congress, Sess. I., Ch. 20, 1789), Sec. 25.

127 #80 Federalist, in Rossiter (ed.), The Federalist Papers, 443–44; decades later Madison was even more explicit in describing the decision as one between alternative forms of a veto over state laws, see Farrand, Records of the Federal Convention, III, 516 (Madison letter to N. P. Trist, December 1831) ("The obvious necessity of a controul on the laws of the States, so far as they might violate the Constn. & laws of the U.S. left no option but as to the mode. The modes presenting themselves, were 1. A Veto on the passage of the State laws. 2. A Congressional repeal of them, 3 a Judicial annulment of them. The first tho extensively favord, at the outset, was found on discussion, liable to insuperable objections, arising from the extent of Country, and the multiplicity of State

Down to the date of the Convention, roughly half a dozen constitutional cases had been brought in the states. Following the Convention, however, judicial review blossomed. In the sixteen years between the Convention and the decision in *Marbury* v. *Madison* (1803), there were at least 31 cases in which a court struck down a statute as unconstitutional, and 7 more in which at least one judge on a court ruled in favor of doing so.[128] Over the following few decades, lawyers persuaded judges in an ever-expanding list of states to adopt the doctrine and practice.[129]

There can be little question, however, that early judicial review fell far short of judicial supremacy broadly speaking. It would be a long time before the other branches were prepared to defer to courts as final interpreters of constitutions in every respect. But in one significant dimension, decisions about which laws judges would permit legislatures to put into effect, judicial review, almost from the beginning, gave courts a significant if circumscribed form of judicial supremacy. As a practical matter they would determine what the laws of the land were to be, wielding a power that extended as far as judges were able to enforce their decisions by successfully refusing to put into operation laws they had found to be unconstitutional.

At the same time, it is beyond dispute that over the next few decades judicial review continued to face serious challenges. Its acceptance as a fundamental feature of the constitutional system continued to be deeply controversial. One of the most important attacks on the institution took place following Jefferson's election to the presidency.[130] And significant opposition to judicial review also arose intermittently in the states.[131] Its continuing vulnerability was a product in part of its origins as a judicial

laws. The second was not free from such as gave a preference to the *third* as now provided by the Constitution").

128 Treanor, "Judicial Review Before Marbury," 457–58.

129 On the spread of judicial review in the states, see the footnotes in Edward S. Corwin, "The Basic Doctrine of American Constitutional Law" (1914) 12 *Michigan Law Review* 247–76.

130 See Richard E. Ellis, *The Jeffersonian Crisis: Courts and Politics in the Young Republic* (Oxford, Oxford University Press, 1971); and James M. O'Fallon, "Marbury" (1992) 44 *Stanford Law Review* 219, at 224–30.

131 Donald F. Melhorn, Jr., *"Lest We Be "Marshall'd": Judicial Powers and Politics in Ohio, 1806–1812* (Akron, Ohio, University of Akron Press, 2003); Theodore W. Ruger, "'A Question Which Convulses a Nation': The Early Republic's Greatest Debate About the Judicial Review Power" (2004) 117 *Harvard Law Review* 826 (Kentucky); Beverly B. Bates, "Two Courts for the Price of One: The Superior Courts of Georgia and the Convention of the Judges, 1797–1845" (1993) 2 *Georgia Journal of Southern Legal History* 219.

practice that had not, with one significant exception, been expressly authorized by written constitutions, and which permitted judges to play an inescapably "political" role as re-evaluators of the propriety of legislation.

But having propagated a durable constitutional logic among members of the bench and bar, and political leaders throughout the country, a logic that had been incorporated into the Federal system itself thanks in great part to decisions at the Convention, judicial review was able to survive every serious assault on its existence. Its ideological and institutional roots were now set deeply and firmly enough to withstand every effort to extirpate it. And every additional judicial precedent in which courts successfully claimed the power left it more securely established. Judicial review would operate not only as a fundamental constraint on legislatures but as important from the perspective of those who had labored hardest to bring it into being, on the sovereign people themselves.

Perhaps there is no better short description of the role judges have played in the American constitutional system from that time than one produced by a foreigner in the mid-1830s. "The judicial organization of the United States," Alexis de Tocqueville wrote in *Democracy in America*,

> is the institution which a stranger has the greatest difficulty in understanding. He hears the authority of a judge invoked in the political occurrences of every day, and he naturally concludes that in the United States the judges are important political functionaries; nevertheless, when he examines the nature of the tribunals, they offer at the first glance nothing that is contrary to the usual habits and privileges of those bodies; and the magistrates seem to him to interfere in public affairs only by chance, but by a chance that recurs every day.[132]

[132] Alexis de Tocqueville (Henry Reeve, transl.), *Democracy in America* (New York, D. Appleton & Co., 1899), I, Chap. VI, 90 (originally published in 1835).

Index

CPSIA information can be obtained
at www.ICGtesting.com
Printed in the USA
LVHW090353220921
698426LV00001B/41

9 781108 839235